PAUL and the HOPE of GLORY

PAUL and the HOPE of GLORY

An Exegetical and Theological Study

CONSTANTINE R. CAMPBELL

ZONDERVAN ACADEMIC

Paul and the Hope of Glory
Copyright © 2020 by Constantine R. Campbell

Requests for information should be addressed to:
Zondervan, *3900 Sparks Dr. SE, Grand Rapids, Michigan 49546*

Zondervan titles may be purchased in bulk for educational, business, fundraising, or sales promotional use. For information, please email SpecialMarkets@Zondervan.com.

ISBN 978-0-310-52120-4 (softcover)

ISBN 978-0-310-52122-8 (ebook)

Material adapted from Constantine R. Campbell, "With Christ over the Powers," in *Christ's Victory over Evil: Biblical Theology and Pastoral Ministry*, ed. Peter G. Bolt (Nottingham: Apollos, 2009), 150–65, used with permission.

Chapter 16 uses content from Constantine R. Campbell, "Judgment of Evil as the Renewal of Creation," in *Evil and Creation: Historical and Constructive Essays in Christian Dogmatics*, ed. David J. Luy, Matthew Levering, and George Kalantzis (Bellingham, WA: Lexham, 2020), used with permission.

All Scripture quotations, unless otherwise indicated, are taken from the Christian Standard Bible®, Copyright © 2017 by Holman Bible Publishers. Used by permission. Christian Standard Bible®, and CSB®, are federally registered trademarks of Holman Bible Publishers.

Any internet addresses (websites, blogs, etc.) and telephone numbers in this book are offered as a resource. They are not intended in any way to be or imply an endorsement by Zondervan, nor does Zondervan vouch for the content of these sites and numbers for the life of this book.

All rights reserved. No part of this publication may be reproduced, stored in a retrieval system, or transmitted in any form or by any means—electronic, mechanical, photocopy, recording, or any other—except for brief quotations in printed reviews, without the prior permission of the publisher.

Cover design: Studio Gearbox
Cover image: © Shutterstock and Ultimate Symbol
Interior design: Kait Lamphere

For Dimitra
A rock, an angel

Contents

Detailed Table of Contents xi
Acknowledgments xix
Preface xxi
Abbreviations xxiii

Part 1: Introductory Matters
1. Introduction and Methodology 3
2. A Recent History of Pauline Eschatology 9

Part 2: Exegetical Study
3. Two Ages and Two Realms 65
4. The Parousia 103
5. The Last Day 123
6. Judgment 133
7. Resurrection 167
8. Eternal Life 204
9. Inheritance 214
10. New Creation 234
11. Israel 242
12. Glory 254
13. Hope 287

Part 3: Theological Study
14. Christocentric Eschatology 325
15. Apocalyptic Eschatology 356
16. The Age to Come 382
17. This Present Age 423
18. Conclusions 452

Bibliography 465
Scripture Index 477
Subject Index 488
Author Index 501

Detailed Table of Contents

Acknowledgments xix
Preface xxi
Abbreviations xxiii

Part 1: Introductory Matters

1. Introduction and Methodology 3
   - 1.1. . . . . . . Paul and the Hope of Glory 3
   - 1.2. . . . . . . What Do We Mean by "Eschatology"? 4
   - 1.3. . . . . . . An Exegetical-Theological Approach 6
   - 1.4. . . . . . . Determining the Exegetical Data 6
   - 1.5. . . . . . . The Pauline Canon. 7
   - 1.6. . . . . . . The Shape of the Study. 8
   - 1.7. . . . . . . The Major Conclusions of the Study 8

2. A Recent History of Pauline Eschatology 9
   - 2.1. . . . . . . Introduction 9
   - 2.2. . . . . . . Albert Schweitzer (1930) 9
   - 2.3. . . . . . . Geerhardus Vos (1930) 13
   - 2.4. . . . . . . Rudolf Bultmann (1948–53). 16
   - 2.5. . . . . . . Karl Barth (1932–68) 19
   - 2.6. . . . . . . Oscar Cullmann (1962) 22
   - 2.7. . . . . . . Ernst Käsemann (1965) 25
   - 2.8. . . . . . . George Eldon Ladd (1974) 28
   - 2.9. . . . . . . E. P. Sanders (1977) 30
   - 2.10. . . . . . J. Christiaan Beker (1980, 1982). 31
   - 2.11. . . . . . Andrew Lincoln (1981) 35
   - 2.12. . . . . . Martinus C. de Boer (1988) 40
   - 2.13. . . . . . Ben Witherington (1992) 42
   - 2.14. . . . . . Jürgen Moltmann (1996) 45
   - 2.15. . . . . . J. Louis Martyn (1997). 48
   - 2.16. . . . . . Douglas Campbell (2009) 50

2.17	N. T. Wright (2013)	52
2.18	Synthesis	55
2.18.1	Jewish Antecedents	55
2.18.2	Apocalypticism	56
2.18.3	Two Ages and Two Realms	57
2.18.4	Inaugurated Eschatology	58
2.18.5	The Importance of Eschatology	58
2.18.6	The Eschatological Character of the Death and Resurrection of Christ	59
2.18.7	Judgment, Annihilationism, and Universalism	60
2.18.8	Hope, New Creation, and Glory	61
2.18.9	Time and Eternity	61
2.19	Moving Forward	62

Part 2: Exegetical Study

3. Two Ages and Two Realms ... 65
   - 3.1. Introduction ... 65
   - 3.2. Two Ages/Realms Texts ... 66
   - 3.3. Summary ... 101

4. The Parousia ... 103
   - 4.1. Introduction ... 103
   - 4.2. Parousia Texts ... 103
   - 4.3. Summary ... 121

5. The Last Day ... 123
   - 5.1. Introduction ... 123
   - 5.2. Last-Day Texts ... 123
   - 5.3. Summary ... 131

6. Judgment ... 133
   - 6.1. Introduction ... 133
   - 6.2. Judgment Texts ... 133
   - 6.3. Summary ... 165

7. Resurrection ... 167
   - 7.1. Introduction ... 167
   - 7.2. Resurrection Texts ... 167
   - 7.3. Summary ... 202

8. Eternal Life	204
8.1. Introduction	204
8.2. Eternal-Life Texts	204
8.3. Summary	213

9. Inheritance	214
9.1. Introduction	214
9.2. Inheritance Texts	214
9.3. Summary	233

10. New Creation	234
10.1. Introduction	234
10.2. New-Creation Texts	234
10.3. Summary	241

11. Israel	242
11.1. Introduction	242
11.2. Israel Texts	242
11.3. Summary	252

12. Glory	254
12.1. Introduction	254
12.2. Glory Texts	254
12.3. Summary	285

13. Hope	287
13.1. Introduction	287
13.2. Hope Texts	287
13.3. Summary	320

PART 3: THEOLOGICAL STUDY

14. Christocentric Eschatology	325
14.1. Introduction	325
14.2. Christ as Lord of the New Realm	325
14.3. Christ and His Parousia	326
14.4. Christ at the Eschaton	327
14.5. Christ the Judge	327
14.6. The Resurrection of Christ and Believers	327
14.7. Christ and Eternal Life	328

14.8	Christ and Inheritance	328
14.9	Christ and the New Creation	329
14.10	Christ and Israel	329
14.11	Christ and Glory	330
14.12	Christ and Hope	330
14.13	Synthesis	331
14.14	The Death, Resurrection, and Ascension of Christ as Eschatological Events	332
14.14.1	The Resurrection of Christ as Eschatological Event	332
14.14.1.1	The Firstfruits of the Resurrection	333
14.14.1.2	Resurrection as Eschatological Vindication	335
14.14.1.2.1	Romans 4:25b	336
14.14.2	The Death of Christ as Eschatological Event	339
14.14.2.1	1 Corinthians 15:56	340
14.14.2.2	Overpowering the Powers	341
14.14.3	The Ascension of Christ as Eschatological Event	342
14.14.3.1	1 Corinthians 15:23–28	343
14.14.4	Participation in the Death, Resurrection, and Ascension of Christ	345
14.14.4.1	Participation in the Eschatological Death of Christ	346
14.14.4.2	Participation in the Eschatological Resurrection of Christ	347
14.14.4.3	Participation in the Eschatological Ascension of Christ	348
14.14.5	Conclusion	349
14.15	The Roles of Christ in the Eschaton	350
14.15.1	The Parousia of Christ	351
14.15.2	Executing Judgment	352
14.15.3	Resurrecting the Dead	352
14.15.4	Eternal Life with Christ	353
14.15.5	Sharing the Promised Inheritance	353
14.15.6	Conclusion	354
14.16	Chapter Conclusion	355
15. Apocalyptic Eschatology		356
15.1	Introduction	356
15.2	Paul's Apocalypticism and Pauline Studies	356
15.3	Paul's Apocalypticism and Jewish Apocalyptic Studies	362
15.4	Evaluation of Paul's Apocalypticism from the Perspective of Jewish Apocalyptic Studies	364
15.4.1	Mystery Language	365

15.4.2	The Imminent Coming of the Son of Man	367
15.4.3	Urging to be Watchful and Alert	371
15.4.4	Two-Age Eschatology	373
15.4.5	Epistemology of Revealed Knowledge	374
15.4.6	Soteriology of Victory	376
15.4.7	Conclusion	378
15.5	Evaluation of Paul's Apocalypticism from the Perspective of Pauline Studies	378
15.5.1	Conclusion	380
15.6	Chapter Conclusion	380

16. The Age to Come 382

16.1	Introduction	382
16.2	The Two Realms and the Age to Come	382
16.3	The Parousia and the Age to Come	383
16.4	The Last Day and the Age to Come	383
16.5	Judgment and the Age to Come	384
16.6	Resurrection in the Age to Come	384
16.7	Eternal Life in the Age to Come	385
16.8	Inheritance in the Age to Come	385
16.9	New Creation in the Age to Come	385
16.10	Israel in the Age to Come	386
16.11	Glory in the Age to Come	386
16.12	Hope and the Age to Come	386
16.13	Synthesis	387
16.14	Resurrection	388
16.14.1	Resurrection and Cosmic Renewal	389
16.14.2	The Nature of Resurrection Life	389
16.14.3	A General Resurrection from the Dead?	390
16.15	Judgment and Justification	393
16.15.1	Resurrection before Judgment?	395
16.16	Wrath, Condemnation, Destruction ... and Hell?	397
16.16.1	Annihilationism?	399
16.16.2	Universalism?	401
16.17	Renewal and Re-creation	405
16.17.1	New-Creation Language	406
16.17.1.1	"Cosmic" New Creation	408
16.17.2	Genesis 2–3	410
16.17.3	Isaiah 65–66	411
16.17.4	2 Peter 3	413

16.17.5	Revelation 19–22	415
16.17.6	Conclusion	417
16.17.6.1	Renewal, Not Replacement	418
16.17.6.2	Judgment of Evil as the Renewal of Creation	419
16.18	Glory	419
16.18.1	What Is Glory?	419
16.18.2	The Glory of God, in Christ, for Believers	420
16.19	Conclusion	421

17. This Present Age 423

17.1	Introduction	423
17.2	The Two Realms and This Present Age	423
17.3	The Parousia and This Present Age	424
17.4	The Last Day and This Present Age	424
17.5	Judgment and This Present Age	424
17.6	Resurrection in This Present Age	425
17.7	Eternal Life and This Present Age	425
17.8	Inheritance and This Present Age	425
17.9	New Creation and This Present Age	426
17.10	Israel in This Present Age	426
17.11	Glory and This Present Age	426
17.12	Hope in This Present Age	427
17.13	Synthesis	427
17.14	Living in the Now and the Not Yet	428
17.15	Living by the Spirit	431
17.16	Church	433
17.17	Mission	436
17.18	Work	439
17.19	Ecology	442
17.20	Death	443
17.20.1	An Intermediate State?	444
17.20.1.1	Philippians 1:23–24	445
17.20.1.2	2 Corinthians 5:1–10	446
17.20.2	Praying for the Dead	448
17.21	Hope	449
17.22	Conclusion	450

18. Conclusions 452

| 18.1 | Introduction | 452 |
| 18.2 | Apocalypticism | 453 |

18.3	Two Ages and Two Realms	454
18.4	Christocentric Eschatology	455
18.5	The Parousia and the Last Day	457
18.6	Death and Judgment	457
18.7	Inheritance and Eternal Life	458
18.8	New Creation	459
18.9	Hope and Glory	460
18.10	Life Today . . . in Light of Tomorrow	461

Bibliography 465
Scripture Index 477
Subject Index 488
Author Index 501

Acknowledgments

I am grateful to Zondervan Academic for the publication of this volume, and special thanks are offered to Chris Beetham for his excellent copyediting, and to Katya Covrett for her editorial oversight of the project and her ongoing friendship and encouragement over several years.

I also wish to thank the faculty and administration of Trinity Evangelical Divinity School. Most of this book was written while I served on the faculty of TEDS, including a productive sabbatical during the spring semester of 2017. It was a privilege to teach alongside such esteemed colleagues and to be inspired by them and scores of wonderful students. Thanks also go to my research assistant, Jonathan Wright, who tracked down dozens of journal articles for this project.

The final year of writing, 2019, was the most difficult of my life. But through its many challenges I was enormously helped by the love and support of my youngest sister, Dimitra. She was steadfast as a rock and was a messenger from God, reminding me that this, too, shall one day pass. I dedicate this book to her. Thanks, sis. I love you.

Preface

One of the major interests arising out of my book *Paul and Union with Christ: An Exegetical and Theological Study*, published by Zondervan at the end of 2012, was the theme of Paul's eschatology. Like just about everything Paul wrote, the two themes of union with Christ and eschatology are intertwined, and the study of one necessarily invites study of the other. When I first wrote *Paul and Union with Christ*, it was intended to exist as a stand-alone volume. But about a year after its publication, Zondervan's Katya Covrett and I hashed a plan to create a long-range series to follow it. The volume you are now reading is the second in the series. The intention is that each volume should focus on a major theme of Paul's writings—and I'm especially interested in the ones that are very important but are not widely appreciated—employing the same methodology developed in *Paul and Union with Christ*. Though it took eight years for the second volume to appear, I hope that subsequent iterations of the series will arrive in a timelier fashion.

The methodology developed in *Paul and Union with Christ* was, I believe, the most effective way to achieve my goals, though it necessarily has some shortcomings and in certain ways bucks against current trends in New Testament scholarship. The methodology involves bringing together every Pauline text that impinges on the chosen theme. Each text is exegeted in turn, then a synthesis of the texts is offered, showing how the pieces of the puzzle fit together. That synthesis is then related back into Paul's overall theology to demonstrate how the theme functions within his wider thought.

One potential weakness of this approach is that texts are lifted out of their immediate contexts and are read together. We all know that everything Paul wrote must be understood against the historical context of each occasional letter, but my approach necessarily downplays the significance of that fact. I take it for granted that Paul's writings must be understood historically, along with due respect shown for literary genre, theme, structure, purpose, and so forth. So I have been careful to approach each text with such issues in mind, though the nature of the book does not allow me to address those issues directly. Commentaries and other monographs do that work well. The intention here, however, is to achieve something that commentaries and other monographs may not do as well, which is to relate thematic elements together across the Pauline corpus. Since that is my major goal, the methodology is best suited to that end, even though it may leave other important elements to one side.

Another potential weakness of this methodology is that it sidesteps complex (and sometimes important) discussions about various texts, unless those discussions directly impinge on the theme of the book. Since priority is given to the assessment of every relevant text, some texts are not able to be engaged with the depth they invite and with which they have been treated in the scholarly literature. As one reviewer commented about *Paul and Union with Christ*, the strength of that work is that it attempts a comprehensive, inductive study of "union with Christ" in the Pauline letters. The weakness of the work is that it attempts a comprehensive, inductive study of "union with Christ" in the Pauline letters. Some of the discussions are necessarily brief. No doubt a similar critique could be offered of this new book. But, as the same reviewer commented, the book is already lengthy enough.

The book's original, contracted title was *Paul and the Age to Come*. Borrowing a phrase from Ephesians 1:21, there would have been no doubt that the book was about eschatology. But as I worked on the manuscript, I was struck by how central the themes of hope and glory were for Paul's eschatological expectation. I began to wonder whether *Paul and the Hope of Glory* would be a better title, borrowing a phrase from Colossians 1:27. I ran the idea by Katya Covrett, who liked it. I ran it by some of my TEDS classes, who also liked it. But the clincher was Michael Gorman. During a conversation at the 2017 Symposium on the Theological Reading of Scripture at North Park Seminary (addressing the theme of union with Christ), I asked Mike for his opinion about the two potential book titles. He said, "If you had asked me that question twenty years ago, I would have said 'Paul and the Age to Come.' But now, I would definitely choose 'Paul and the Hope of Glory.'" That was the push I needed to change the title of the book. While the new title might not be as explicit as the original, it much better captures the heart of Paul's eschatology.

The study of Paul's eschatology has been a major undertaking, which partly accounts for the eight-year gap between this book and *Paul and Union with Christ*. (Writing other books in between was also a factor.) I have kept an eye open for what other major themes most naturally arise out of this volume, and my mind is now mulling over the concept for the next one. But you, dear reader, will have to wait and see.

ABBREVIATIONS

AB	Anchor Bible
ABCS	Africa Bible Commentary Series
AYB	Anchor Yale Bible
BDAG	Danker, Frederick W., Walter Bauer, William F. Arndt, and F. Wilbur Gingrich. *Greek-English Lexicon of the New Testament and Other Early Christian Literature*. 3rd ed. Chicago: University of Chicago Press, 2000
BECNT	Baker Exegetical Commentary on the New Testament
BCE	Before the Common Era
BHGNT	Baylor Handbook on the Greek New Testament
BNTC	Black's New Testament Commentaries
BST	Bible Speaks Today
BTCP	Biblical Theology for Christian Proclamation
ca.	circa
CE	Common Era
CTQ	*Concordia Theological Quarterly*
ECL	Early Christianity and Its Literature
EGGNT	Exegetical Guide to the Greek New Testament
ExAud	*Ex Auditu*
ExpTim	*Expository Times*
FBC	Focus on the Bible
ICC	International Critical Commentary
Int	*Interpretation*
IVPNTC	IVP New Testament Commentary
JETS	Journal of the Evangelical Theological Society
JSJSup	Supplements to the Journal for the Study of Judaism
JSNT	*Journal for the Study of the New Testament*
JSNTSup	Journal for the Study of the New Testament Supplement Series
JTS	*Journal of Theological Studies*
HBT	Horizons in Biblical Theology
LNTS	The Library of New Testament Studies
NCBC	New Cambridge Bible Commentary
NCCS	New Covenant Commentary Series

NICNT	New International Commentary on the New Testament
NIDNTTE	*New International Dictionary of New Testament Theology and Exegesis*. Edited by Moisés Silva. 2nd ed. 5 vols. Grand Rapids: Zondervan, 2014.
NovTSup	Supplements to Novum Testamentum
NSBT	New Studies in Biblical Theology
NT	New Testament
NTS	*New Testament Studies*
PNTC	Pillar New Testament Commentary
PRSt	*Perspectives in Religious Studies*
SBG	Studies in Biblical Greek
SBLDS	Society of Biblical Literature Dissertation Series
SGBC	Story of God Bible Commentary
SJT	*Scottish Journal of Theology*
SNTSMS	Society for New Testament Studies Monograph Series
TDNT	*Theological Dictionary of the New Testament*. Edited by Gerhard Kittel and Gerhard Friedrich. Translated by Geoffrey W. Bromiley. 10 vols. Grand Rapids: Eerdmans, 1964–1976
THNTC	Two Horizons New Testament Commentary
TNTC	Tyndale New Testament Commentaries
TynBul	Tyndale Bulletin
NovT	*Novum Testamentum*
WBC	Word Biblical Commentary
WUNT	Wissenschaftliche Untersuchungen zum Neuen Testament
ZECNT	Zondervan Exegetical Commentary on the New Testament

Part 1

Introductory Matters

Part 1

Introductory Matters

CHAPTER 1

INTRODUCTION AND METHODOLOGY

1.1 Paul and the Hope of Glory

All's well that ends well.

It will all be worth it in the end.

He who laughs last laughs loudest.

It ain't over till the fat lady sings.

We live with the often unspoken understanding that the *end* gives the final shape to all things. For all the drama of a good sporting match, the game is ultimately shaped by the end and who comes out on top. Nothing could be truer if we are to understand Paul's eschatology—what happens in the end shapes everything that has come before.

The theme of eschatology in the writings of the apostle Paul is vast, rich, and immensely profound. His entire theological outlook was shaped by it, as was his life.[1] While it has a genuine simplicity about it, Paul's eschatology is also complex once we explore the details. This is amply demonstrated in the scholarly literature, which evinces relatively little uncertainty about the big picture of Paul's eschatological thought, but also wages sophisticated debates concerning particular issues. Indeed, from a wider perspective, "eschatology has always been one of the most disputed fields within New Testament exegesis."[2]

---

1. James D. G. Dunn, *The Theology of Paul the Apostle* (Grand Rapids: Eerdmans, 1998), 180–81.
2. Jörg Frey, "New Testament Eschatology—an Introduction: Classical Issues, Disputed Themes, and Current Perspectives," in *Eschatology of the New Testament and Some Related Documents*, ed. Jan G. van der Watt; WUNT 2/315 (Tübingen: Mohr Siebeck, 2011), 3.

And, as explored below, this even includes what is meant by the term *eschatology*, which will require careful articulation.

Not only must *eschatology* be defined, but what we mean by *Paul's* eschatology must likewise be handled with care. As will become evident, once we understand Paul's beliefs about the "end," the term *eschatology* itself necessarily undergoes redefinition. After all, if the "end" has already come, then *eschatology* cannot refer just to the end of all things anymore. In fact, we will see that eschatology for Paul includes the full sweep of the end, the present, and the past, with each informing and shaping the others.

Such an insight, and others like it, arise from engaging Paul's writings through detailed exegesis. And yet, if our definition of *eschatology* is already fluid, it may not be immediately obvious to know what to look for in exegesis as we attempt to unpack Paul's eschatological vision. Building on the advances of previous scholarship, this book represents a fresh investigation of the Pauline material, examining the minutiae and moving through to the wide spheres of Paul's thought. The work is therefore self-consciously exegetical and theological, allowing exegesis to shape theology and vice versa.

1.2 What Do We Mean by "Eschatology"?

According to Jörg Frey, the term *eschatology* was first coined in the seventeenth century, in the title of the fifth part of the work of theological dogmatics by Philipp Heinrich Friedlieb, published in 1644.[3] The etymology of the term involves the Greek word *eschatos* (ἔσχατος), which means "last,"[4] so that *eschatology* is the study of "last things"—the end of human history as a whole or the end of human life.

While the term *eschatology* seems simple enough when considered from an etymological perspective, that's where the simplicity ends. During the twentieth century it saw a broadening of meaning, largely due to the influence of theologians such as Karl Barth and Rudolf Bultmann, who used it differently from its traditional reference to the "last things." Instead, "these theologians used the term to express timeless realities or the ultimate perspective on human existence in the present."[5] Since then, the rudimentary task of agreeing on what should or should not be included when discussing the eschatology of the New Testament has proven a challenge, leading to intense debates.[6]

---

3. Frey, "New Testament Eschatology," 6.
4. BDAG 397–98.
5. Frey, "New Testament Eschatology," 7. According to Höhne, "the key theological question changed from 'What happens when the world ends and when will that be?' to 'What effect should the world's approaching end have on our everyday existence?' How should life in the Middle be affected by, from or for *The End*?" (David A. Höhne, *The Last Things*, Contours of Christian Theology [London: Inter-Varsity Press, 2019], 4).
6. Jan G. van der Watt, ed., *Eschatology of the New Testament and Some Related Documents*, WUNT

The most obvious blurring of meaning is at the level of temporality. Instead of referring strictly to "last things," *eschatology* is now regularly used to refer to the so-called "overlap of the ages," the "already-not yet,"—otherwise known as inaugurated eschatology.⁷ Inaugurated eschatology is a widely accepted feature of the New Testament in general, and of Paul in particular. As explored below in chapter 3, Paul perceives that the age to come at the eschaton has broken into the present through the resurrection of Christ. This means that the old age and the new age now coexist in an overlapping fashion. Hence Paul's eschatology can no longer be restricted to "last things" since the "end" has already dawned in the "middle" of time, as it were.⁸ His eschatology must therefore include certain elements of contemporary existence. Indeed, Paul's eschatology cannot even be restricted to the present and the future, but also includes the past, as Wolter states:

> The specific distinction of Paul's eschatology can be recognized in how he interrelates firstly the *past*, with Christ's death and resurrection, the proclamation of the Gospel, and the conversion of the believers; secondly, the *present* situation of the Christian communities; and thirdly, the *future*, with the aforementioned expectations as parts of one single eschatological narrative."⁹

Once the dualism of ages is acknowledged as a key feature of Paul's eschatology, it immediately introduces a further element of blurring, this time at the spatial level. A key characteristic of the old age is its reign of sin and death—cosmic overlords who control and shape the age over which they rule. But the new age is ruled by Christ by the power of the Spirit. The two overlapping and competing ages therefore introduce the notion of overlapping and competing *realms*, or *dominions*. Such realms are spatial in nature since they mark out the "territory" over which their rulers exercise influence and power, controlling those who belong to them. Thus, eschatology is now not only a temporal concept but is inevitably spatial as well. The two-age structure of Paul's eschatology therefore necessarily includes a cosmological element.¹⁰

2/315 (Tübingen: Mohr Siebeck, 2011), v. Some have simply given up on the term: "I eschew 'eschatology' altogether because of its vagueness and its tendency to divert thought from consideration of the *novissima*" (Paul J. Griffiths, *Decreation: The Last Things of All Creatures* [Waco: Baylor University Press, 2014], 9).

7. Dunn, *Theology of Paul the Apostle*, 466.

8. "Messiah the end point of history had become also Christ the midpoint of history" (Dunn, *Theology of Paul the Apostle*, 463).

9. Michael Wolter, "The Distinctiveness of Paul's Eschatology," in van der Watt, *Eschatology of the New Testament*, 416.

10. "This is understandable since cosmology and eschatology so clearly impinge upon each other in early Jewish apocalyptic texts" (Joel White, "Paul's Cosmology: The Witness of Romans, 1 and 2 Corinthians, and

1.3 An Exegetical-Theological Approach

For all the emphasis on Paul's writings as occasional, missional documents, there can be little doubt that Paul was a theologian. Of course, he was not a systematic theologian in the technical sense, but this does not mean he was "a jumbled, rambling sort of thinker, who would grab odd ideas out of the assortment of junk in his mental cupboard." Rather, as Wright adds, "the more time we spend in the careful reading of Paul, and in the study of his worldview, his theology and his aims and intentions, the more he emerges as a deeply *coherent* thinker."[11] More boldly, Dunn claims that "Paul was the first and greatest Christian theologian."[12] This means that a proper approach to Paul must be theological as well as exegetical. In fact, the ideal way to approach a theological writer such as Paul is to hold exegesis and theology hand in hand.

This explains the macrostructure of this book (detailed below), which moves from an exegetical pole to a theological one. We begin by giving attention to the details of particular texts,[13] studied in context, before moving to wider theological discussions as the results of the exegetical analyses are interpreted with respect to Paul's broader thought. This study, then, is exegetical-theological, belonging to the discipline of New Testament theology. This differs from traditional systematic theology in that it begins with textual minutiae and develops through to the conceptual big picture. Rather than starting with the whole, it progresses from one pole to the other.

1.4 Determining the Exegetical Data

To begin at the "exegetical pole" of the topic, it is necessary to address the essential task of determining which data this will include. We are concerned to ask which texts within the Pauline canon are relevant to the wider task at hand. For the theme of eschatology, there are several subtopics that are self-evidently relevant, such as the parousia, judgment, resurrection, and eternal life. Some other subtopics are less immediately obvious, but after some consideration are clearly related to eschatology too, such as Israel, glory, and hope.

Some of these subtopics are indicated by specific vocabulary items, such as *parousia*, the *last day*, *inheritance*, and *hope*. But it would be a mistake to approach this exploration through a series of word studies. In some cases, multiple concepts

---

Galatians," in *Cosmology and New Testament Theology*, ed. Jonathan T. Pennington and Sean M. McDonough, LNTS 355 [London: T&T Clark, 2008], 92).

11. N. T. Wright, *Paul and the Faithfulness of God* (Minneapolis: Fortress, 2013), 568.
12. Dunn, *Theology of Paul the Apostle*, 2.
13. Attention will be given to the relevant contribution of selected texts rather than offering full commentary on said texts. There will be several exegetical questions, fault lines, and controversies raised by various texts that simply must be ignored in order to retain our focus of investigation.

must be included, so that the subtopic of the parousia should also include the revelation of Christ, his appearing, and his descending from heaven. These are different expressions with the same referent—namely, the future event of the arrival of Christ. In other cases, there is no set vocabulary at all, and the subtopic is discerned through variable means of expression, such as Paul's concept of *realm*. His realm theology may be found through references to concepts such as the kingdom, elemental forces, spiritual warfare, visible and invisible forces, and authorities, powers, and dominions. All this means that the exegetical part of the book is populated with texts that are included because of relevant subthemes that are evident through certain concepts and vocabulary.

1.5 THE PAULINE CANON

As with my earlier book, *Paul and Union with Christ*,[14] this study treats the entire Pauline corpus rather than a truncated canon that excludes the Pastoral Epistles, and often Ephesians and/or Colossians. While this approach may stand in tension with the current climate of New Testament scholarship, it is in keeping with the arguments advanced by Brevard Childs. The goal of his "canonical hermeneutic" is "to reflect on the theology expressed in various forms within the Pauline corpus."[15] Acknowledging an apparent distinction between the "historical Paul" and the Paul reflected in the Pauline corpus, Childs rejects "any permanent separating of a reconstructed 'historical Paul' from the witness of the 'canonical Paul.'"[16] The chief weakness of current scholarly approaches to Paul lies in "the assumption that one could recover Paul's theology apart from its ecclesial reception.'"[17]

Childs does not assume direct Pauline authorship of all the letters bearing his name, but nevertheless acknowledges "their status within a traditional apostolic collection."[18] The author(s) of each letter that bears his name will be addressed as Paul, regardless of which part of the canon is in view. While some readers may prefer to understand the author as "Paul (so-called)," depending on the letter in question, no such distinction will be made in this study.

The study of Pauline theology is not ultimately for the purpose of reconstructing a purified "theology of Paul" but rather to operate within the larger

---

14. Constantine R. Campbell, *Paul and Union with Christ: An Exegetical and Theological Study* (Grand Rapids: Zondervan, 2012). Section 1.5 in the current work is a rearticulation of the argument offered in that previous work (pp. 27–28).
15. Brevard S. Childs, *The Church's Guide for Reading Paul: The Canonical Shaping of the Pauline Corpus* (Grand Rapids: Eerdmans, 2008), 77.
16. Childs, *Reading Paul*, 77.
17. Childs, *Reading Paul*, 77. After all, "the historical Paul of the first century has been transmitted by Christian tradents who have received and shaped their testimony into the form of a canonical Paul" (256).
18. Childs, *Reading Paul*, 79.

context of the Bible, in order "to understand the full range of the message of the Pauline corpus whose witness continues to instruct, admonish, and sustain the apostolic faith of the church."[19] Ultimately, treatment of the entire Pauline canon is necessary here because this book is for the academy *and* the church.

1.6 The Shape of the Study

The book consists of three parts. Part 1 raises introductory matters in this chapter, and the following chapter provides a selective survey of major academic developments through the twentieth century to the present time. Part 2 addresses the exegesis of relevant texts. Chapters 3–13 deal with the subthemes of the two ages and realms, the parousia, the last day, judgment, resurrection, eternal life, inheritance, new creation, Israel, glory, and hope. Part 3 draws on the results of the exegetical studies conducted in part 2 and seeks to integrate them into the broad spheres of Paul's thought. Chapters 14–17 address Christocentric eschatology, apocalyptic eschatology, the age to come, and this present age, respectively. Chapter 18 draws together the fruit of the entire study in order to articulate a comprehensive description of Paul's eschatology.

1.7 The Major Conclusions of the Study

The major conclusions of this study are established in chapter 18, but it is worth outlining them from the outset. Paul's eschatology is shaped by two overlapping ages, with the new age breaking into the present day, thus creating two competing realms of authority and dominion. The gift of the Spirit connects believers to the new realm and shapes life now in preparation for a glorious future. Paul expects the parousia of Christ to usher in the resurrection of the righteous dead and judgment of all humanity. He believed that the entire created order would be renewed with the glory of God in Christ permanently radiating through it. He looked forward to Christ sharing his eternal glory with his people, who will enjoy perfected resurrected bodies made fit for eternal life with God in Christ. And at the very heart of it all is the death, resurrection, and ascension of Christ—past events from which Paul's Christocentric eschatological outlook unfurls.

Paul was an apocalyptic theologian but did not necessarily expect Christ to come in his lifetime. He probably believed in a temporary, disembodied, intermediate state between death and bodily resurrection. He endorsed heavenly rewards based on deeds. Paul does not talk about hell in the classical sense, and could possibly fit an annihilationist position, but it is unlikely that he was a universalist. Paul did not envisage the end of the current physical universe but rather its renewal.

---

19. Childs, *Reading Paul*, 112.

CHAPTER 2

A Recent History of Pauline Eschatology

2.1 Introduction

Before engaging Paul's writings directly, it is necessary to survey the scholarly conversation that will most affect our study, and the field to which this study will most directly contribute. While Christian eschatology in general has of course been a topic of enquiry since the birth of the New Testament, it is not possible to survey its entire history. Rather, because of the nature of this current study as a work of New Testament exegesis and theology—with exclusive interest in the Pauline canon—we will limit our scholarly survey to the past century. While most of the scholarly contributions surveyed here are concerned with Paul specifically, some are broader in scope, such as those of Barth and Moltmann. These systematic theologians are included because their work offers insights that are helpful for studying Paul and because their contributions have helped to shape Pauline eschatological studies and are thus relevant for understanding the unfolding discussion.

Beginning with Schweitzer in 1930 and moving through to the present day, we will note the contours of discussion and debate in order to set the stage for the study that will unfold through the remainder of the book. We will refrain from evaluating these voices at this stage, acknowledging that we will only be in a position to do so once we have conducted our own study of the Pauline material. At the end of this study, however, we will be able to assess some of the issues of debate raised in this chapter and, it is hoped, to contribute to the discussion.

2.2 Albert Schweitzer (1930)

While Albert Schweitzer's *The Mysticism of Paul the Apostle* became a landmark study on the topic of its central theme—Paul's "mysticism," or his theology of union with Christ—it also made an indelible impression on the study of Paul's eschatology. Indeed, the two themes go hand in hand for Schweitzer, since his chief argument is that Paul's mysticism can only be understood eschatologically—"his mysticism of the Dying and Rising again with Christ is centered in an ardent eschatological expectation."[1] Eschatology provides the theological structure over which Paul's theme of Christ-mysticism is set, as Schweitzer evocatively described:

> As the spider's net is an admirably simple construction so long as it remains stretched between the threads which hold it in position, but becomes a hopeless tangle as soon as it is loosed from them; so the Pauline Mysticism is an admirably simple thing, so long as it is set in the framework of eschatology, but becomes a hopeless tangle as soon as it is cut loose from this.[2]

Schweitzer argued that Paul's eschatological conception was derived from late-Jewish eschatology—apocalyptic theology in particular—drawing on earlier and later Hebrew Prophets as well as the Book of Enoch, the Psalms of Solomon, and the Apocalypses of Baruch and of Ezra.[3] Paul's Jewish theological contemporaries—whom Schweitzer called "the Scribes"—held an eschatology that was represented by the Apocalypses of Baruch and Ezra in particular and that embraced the expectations expressed in the Hebrew Prophets, including Daniel, seeking to bring these into harmony.[4] Schweitzer regarded all of Paul's conceptions and thoughts as rooted in Jewish eschatology, claiming that those who attempt to explain him on the basis of Hellenism "are like a man who should bring water from a long distance in leaky watering-cans in order to water a garden lying beside a stream."[5]

Paul was forced to reckon with the significance of the death and resurrection of Jesus as cosmic events. He saw that the resurrection of Jesus was the beginning of the resurrection of the dead in general, and as such "the traditional eschatology could not maintain itself unchanged: the Messiah having already appeared in the flesh, having died, having risen again, the eschatological expectation had to recast itself to those facts."[6] According to Schweitzer, Paul's understanding of redemption was that "Jesus Christ has made an end of the natural world and is bringing in the Messianic Kingdom. It is thus cosmologically conceived."[7]

---

1. Albert Schweitzer, *The Mysticism of Paul the Apostle*, trans. William Montgomery (New York: Seabury, 1968), 36.
2. Schweitzer, *Mysticism*, 140.
3. Schweitzer, *Mysticism*, 54.
4. Schweitzer, *Mysticism*, 88–89.
5. Schweitzer, *Mysticism*, 140.
6. Schweitzer, *Mysticism*, 100.
7. Schweitzer, *Mysticism*, 54.

Redemption transfers believers from the perishable world to the imperishable and is not a mere transaction between the individual and God and Christ but a sharing in a world-event.[8] This world-event is nothing less than the coming messianic kingdom, which will dawn with the return of Christ.

The coming of the messianic kingdom with Jesus's return is the fulfillment of all that Christ has achieved for redemption, so the fact that Jesus has not yet returned raises a series of eschatological tensions and problems. By his death and resurrection, Jesus has been exalted above all angelic beings and spiritual powers, but "he is only to enter fully into this authority on the day of the beginning of the Messianic Kingdom."[9] It is no surprise, then, that "from his first letter to his last Paul's thought is always uniformly dominated by the expectation of the immediate return of Jesus, of the Judgment, and the Messianic glory."[10]

Paul exhibits a two-age eschatology, in keeping with his contemporaries, but alters the prevailing perception of it. The fact that the Messiah had appeared before the messianic age, and died and rose again, raised an eschatological problem for Paul concerning the period between the resurrection of Jesus and his return.[11] The Messiah had come, but he had evidently not ushered in the messianic age, as expected. Schweitzer argued that the period between the resurrection of Jesus and his return outwardly appeared as the natural world-age, but it is in fact a period in which powers of the supernatural world were, through the resurrection, already at work within the created world.[12] "With the Resurrection of Jesus the supernatural world had already begun, though it had not as yet become manifest."[13] With the resurrection of Jesus, the messianic period had actually already begun, and the resurrection of the dead in general was in progress.[14] And because of the death of Jesus, believers are no longer subject to the angels and spiritual powers, since the coming redemption has already come into operation.[15]

If Jesus has risen, it is now already the supernatural age. Paul "cannot regard the resurrection of Jesus as an isolated event, but must regard it as the initial event of the rising of the dead in general."[16] In order to share in the coming messianic kingdom, believers must possess the resurrection mode of existence "since the future Messiah Himself lived, died, rose again before the coming of

---

8. Schweitzer, *Mysticism*, 54.
9. Schweitzer, *Mysticism*, 63–64.
10. Schweitzer, *Mysticism*, 52.
11. Schweitzer, *Mysticism*, 98.
12. Schweitzer, *Mysticism*, 98.
13. Schweitzer, *Mysticism*, 99.
14. Schweitzer, *Mysticism*, 100.
15. Schweitzer, *Mysticism*, 64.
16. Schweitzer, *Mysticism*, 98.

the Kingdom."[17] Those believers who died before Jesus's return would be raised in order to share in his kingdom when it comes. But what of those still alive when Jesus comes? Will they need to die in order to be resurrected in order to share in the resurrection mode of existence? Schweitzer argued yes and no. They die and rise again through their union with Christ, and in this way they "are swept away out of their ordinary mode of existence, and form a special category of humanity."[18] Those who are living when Christ returns are not natural people, but "have in some way passed through death and resurrection along with Christ, and are thus capable of becoming partakers of the resurrection mode of existence,"[19] while others pass under the dominion of death.

Bringing these threads together, Schweitzer found that Paul's Christ-mysticism enables him to solve three major eschatological problems:

(1) that those who have died in Christ have not by dying missed the Messianic Kingdom, but, as being already risen with Christ, participate in it by means of a special pre-dated resurrection; (2) that at the Return of Christ those who are alive do not need first to die in order to enter on the resurrection state of existence, but, as having already died and risen again with Christ, can enter on it by a simple transformation, that is by sloughing off the natural existence which clings to them as a sort of outer covering; (3) that with the Resurrection of Jesus the resurrection of the dead in general—and therewith the supernatural world—has already begun, though the substitution of mortality by immortality is, to begin with, only operative in the corporeity of those who are elect to the Messianic Kingdom, and even in their case, without becoming outwardly manifest.[20]

Finally, Schweitzer pointed to Paul's conception of the Spirit of Christ as an eschatological character, who is the life-principle of Jesus's messianic personality. Sharing in the Spirit of Christ is nothing less than sharing in the glory of the Messiah.[21] The Spirit is the manifestation of the powers of the resurrection, giving to believers the assurance of sharing in the resurrection of Christ.[22] Possession of the Spirit also confirms that believers have already been "removed out of the natural state of existence and transferred into the

---

17. Schweitzer, *Mysticism*, 95.
18. Schweitzer, *Mysticism*, 96–97.
19. Schweitzer, *Mysticism*, 96–97.
20. Schweitzer, *Mysticism*, 111.
21. Schweitzer, *Mysticism*, 165.
22. Schweitzer, *Mysticism*, 166.

supernatural."[23] To be in the eschatological Spirit means no longer to be in the flesh and is a manifestation of being-in-Christ.[24]

2.3 GEERHARDUS VOS (1930)

Published in the same year as the original German edition of Schweitzer's *The Mysticism of Paul the Apostle*, Geerhardus Vos's *The Pauline Eschatology* presented a balanced exposition of the eschatological nature of Paul's thought. While Schweitzer's treatment became far more influential, Vos's treatment is more easily accepted today, with less material that has been rejected, disproved, or superseded than Schweitzer's.

The chief advance of Vos's treatment, in concord with Schweitzer, was to demonstrate the inextricably eschatological nature of Paul's theology; indeed, "to unfold the Apostle's eschatology means to set forth his theology as a whole."[25] For Paul, eschatology becomes "philosophico-theological," and rather than constituting one item within his teaching, "draws within its circle as correlated and eschatologically-complexioned parts practically all of the fundamental tenets of Pauline Christianity."[26] Vos expounded Paul's conception of two ages or worlds, the Jewish shape of his thought-world, the connection between eschatology and soteriology, the parousia of Christ, Paul's theology of resurrection, the Spirit, the millennium, judgment, and the eternal state.

Paul's eschatological worldview is structured around two *ages* or *worlds*. While the contrast between the two ages is only explicitly drawn in Ephesians 1:21, it is implied in several other passages in which "this age" appears, presupposing its opposing partner (Rom 12:2; 1 Cor 1:10; 2:6, 8; 3:18; 2 Cor 4:4; Gal 1:4; Eph 2:2; 1 Tim 6:17; Titus 2:12).[27] Vos argues that the notion of *age* or *aion*, which is temporally defined, effectively takes on the shape of a "world" because the temporal period is so defined by a certain set of characteristics that it appears "a coherent totality of specific character"—"the age constituted, as it were, a world when regarded as to its complexion."[28] The structure of Paul's eschatology is built on the antithesis "between a world (age) that *is* and a world (age) that *is to come*."[29] In this regard, Paul stands in line with the teaching of Jesus, Jewish theology in general, and apocalyptic literature such as 4 Ezra and the Apocalypse of Baruch.[30]

---

23. Schweitzer, *Mysticism*, 167.
24. Schweitzer, *Mysticism*, 167.
25. Geerhardus Vos, *The Pauline Eschatology* (Phillipsburg, NJ: P&R, 1994), 11.
26. Vos, *Pauline Eschatology*, 10–11.
27. Vos, *Pauline Eschatology*, 12.
28. Vos, *Pauline Eschatology*, 17.
29. Vos, *Pauline Eschatology*, 36.
30. Vos, *Pauline Eschatology*, 14, 26.

Vos articulated the integral connection between Paul's eschatology and soteriology by first recognizing the eschatological nature of the death and resurrection of Christ. Concerning the death of Christ, Vos saw it as cutting through the bond that had tied Christ to the cosmos. He writes, "It threw Him out from the world, and He departed from it to enter another world, which was his real home."[31] As for the resurrection, Vos regarded its eschatological nature to be self-evident, as is its position at the beginning of the general epoch of resurrection life.[32] Paul also incorporated the resurrection of Christ into his forensic scheme since it is "a declarative, vindicatory, justifying act."[33] By raising Christ from the dead, God "declared that the ultimate, the supreme consequence of sin had reached its termination. In other words, resurrection had annulled the sentence of condemnation."[34]

Though he explored it to a lesser extent than Schweitzer, Vos also acknowledged the eschatological nature of Paul's mysticism. To be raised in or with Christ means "to have through a radical change of life one of the two fundamental acts of eschatology applied to one's self."[35] In other words, the eschatological resurrection of Christ is applied directly to the eschatological status of the believer. The "resurrection-force" stored up in Christ produces an anticipative eschatological effect upon those "who are still abiding in the present world."[36]

Vos regarded the eschatological nature of the Spirit as reaching back far into the Old Testament, where the Spirit's supernatural manifestations heralded the approach of the future world.[37] The Spirit's association with the Messiah also included an eschatological projection,[38] and is cast as "the source of the future new life of Israel."[39] Paul's view of the Spirit included a twofold eschatological function. First, the Spirit is the resurrection-source; second, he is the "the substratum of the resurrection-life" in which "the life of the coming aeon shall be lived."[40] The Spirit properly belongs to the future aeon and projects himself into the present, becoming "a prophecy of Himself in his eschatological operations."[41]

---

31. Vos, *Pauline Eschatology*, 48–49.
32. Vos, *Pauline Eschatology*, 44–45.
33. Vos, *Pauline Eschatology*, 152.
34. Vos, *Pauline Eschatology*, 151.
35. Vos, *Pauline Eschatology*, 45.
36. Vos, *Pauline Eschatology*, 45.
37. Vos, *Pauline Eschatology*, 160.
38. Vos, *Pauline Eschatology*, 161.
39. Vos, *Pauline Eschatology*, 161.
40. Vos, *Pauline Eschatology*, 163.
41. Vos, *Pauline Eschatology*, 165.

Vos critiqued the language of the "return" of Christ, pointing out that "parousia signifies 'becoming present' and 'being present.'. . . The noun means 'arrival,' not 'return.'"[42] The parousia of Christ should not, therefore, be known as his *second coming*.[43] Alongside *parousia*, Paul uses the language of *revelation* (ἀποκάλυψις) to refer to the eschatological coming of Christ. The latter term chiefly concerns believers—with Jesus's previously hidden glory now revealed to them—while the former term primarily concerns the enemies of God's people as vengeance is exacted upon them.[44]

With respect to the resurrection of the dead subsequent to the coming of Christ, Vos explored the question of the extent of the resurrection—did Paul believe that all the dead would be raised at the end, or only a limited section of the dead?[45] Since Vos had already demonstrated that for Paul resurrection was a *pneumatic* event—powered by the Spirit—how could it apply to the non-Christian who does not share in the Spirit?[46] Since Paul does not mention the resurrection of the wicked in his letters (but note Acts 24:15),[47] we are left to ask whether it should be assumed, given his Jewish theological heritage. Vos regarded it far from certain that an all-inclusive resurrection was firmly established within Judaism in Paul's time—notwithstanding the Pharisees and Josephus's belief in a general resurrection of the dead. Rather, "in various quarters, in various forms, the range of the resurrection was limited."[48] While Paul supposes unbelievers to be present at the judgment following resurrection, it is possible that judgment would be passed on disembodied souls rather than fully resurrected and restored human beings—a notion that does occur in some Jewish sources. Vos concludes that we must "reckon with the possibility that both the resurrection and the judgment will deal with the wicked in an incorporeal state."[49]

Vos addressed the question of chiliasm (millennialism) in Paul, acknowledging contemporary efforts to read him in line with some Jewish sources, such as 4 Ezra and the Apocalypse of Baruch.[50] But Vos found that the apostle's teaching as a whole did not favor chiliasm, especially since his concatenation of eschatological events—such as the conjoined nature of the parousia, resurrection, and judgment—excludes any intermediate state. Moreover, Vos suggested that Paul's

---

42. Vos, *Pauline Eschatology*, 75.
43. Vos, *Pauline Eschatology*, 75.
44. Vos, *Pauline Eschatology*, 78–79.
45. Vos, *Pauline Eschatology*, 215.
46. Vos, *Pauline Eschatology*, 216.
47. Vos, *Pauline Eschatology*, 223.
48. Vos, *Pauline Eschatology*, 219.
49. Vos, *Pauline Eschatology*, 224.
50. Vos, *Pauline Eschatology*, 234.

conception of the present Christian state "lived on so high a plane that nothing less nor lower than the absolute state of the eternal consummate Kingdom appears worthy to be its sequel."[51] After considering the four texts from which chiliasm has been argued (1 Cor 15:23–28; 1 Thess 4:13–18; 2 Thess 1:5–12; Phil 3:10–14), Vos concluded that in none of them could it be defended.[52]

According to Vos, resurrection and judgment are two correlated acts of the final consummation of things, with the pronouncement of vindication already wrapped up in resurrection.[53] But the Christian nevertheless has further interest in the judgment to come, since Paul clearly envisions "discrimination as to the future rank and enjoyment in the life to come between individual Christians," though the entirety of this range sits within the realm of salvation.[54] The eternal state following resurrection and judgment will be free of sorrow, death, sin, and sin-born evils; "such things as dishonor and weakness are incompatible with the life-state in heaven."[55] Death and everything in its wake will be swallowed up in victory, and the body will be delivered from all that causes its bearer to groan.[56]

2.4 Rudolf Bultmann (1948–53)

Rudolf Bultmann's *Theology of the New Testament* recognized the eschatological shape of Paul's major themes of thought, such as the "kosmos," righteousness, Christ's death and resurrection, hope, and the present life of believers. Regarding the *kosmos*, or world, Bultmann claimed it was for Paul "much more a time-concept than a space-concept; or, more exactly it is an *eschatological concept*."[57] As a time-concept, according to Bultmann, Paul regarded the world of human activity as temporally conditioned, "hastening toward its end (1 Cor. 7:31)."[58] But as such, it was "the sphere of anti-godly power under whose sway the individual who is surrounded by it has fallen."[59] It is the sphere of the rulers of this age, the god of this age.

Paul's eschatological-historical understanding of the *kosmos* entails humanity's enslavement to spiritual powers, for which humanity is itself responsible. Paul offers *mythological statements* about such spirit powers and Satan because

---

51. Vos, *Pauline Eschatology*, 235.
52. Vos, *Pauline Eschatology*, 236–59.
53. Vos, *Pauline Eschatology*, 261.
54. Vos, *Pauline Eschatology*, 269–70.
55. Vos, *Pauline Eschatology*, 308.
56. Vos, *Pauline Eschatology*, 309.
57. Rudolf Bultmann, *Theology of the New Testament: Volume I*, trans. Kendrick Grobel (London: SCM, 1952), 256.
58. Bultmann, *Theology*, 256.
59. Bultmann, *Theology*, 256.

of their roles within this eschatological *kosmos*, not in order to engage in "cosmological speculation," nor "to explain terrifying or gruesome phenomena or to relieve men of responsibility and guilt."[60] In other words, Bultmann did not believe that Paul's statements about the spiritual powers could be mined for cosmological information, since his statements were mythological rather than cosmological in nature. Nor could human failure be excused by appeal to the powers, though humanity remained enslaved to them.

Bultmann regarded the eschatological nature of justification to be self-evident, since Paul speaks of "a future verdict of righteousness to come in the eschatological judgment" in texts such as Romans 2:13 and Galatians 5:5.[61] Paul's conception of righteousness is parallel to those found within contemporary Judaism, except that for Judaism righteousness "is a *matter of hope*," while for Paul it is "a *present reality*—or, better, is also a present reality."[62] That is, Paul's distinct eschatological vision is what sets his conception of righteousness apart from those found within contemporary Judaism.

Paul understood the death and resurrection of Christ as cosmic events, "not incidents that took place once upon a time in the past."[63] These cosmic events have stripped the old aeon of its power. Christ's death was more than a sacrificial guilt-offering—it was also "*the means of release from the powers of this age: Law, Sin, and Death.*"[64] Bultmann questioned how Christ's death could have such an effect, and concluded that "*Paul describes Christ's death in analogy with the death of a divinity of mystery religions.*"[65] In such religions, the mystery-divinity grants the initiate participation in both the dying and reviving of the divinity, leading the initiate into death, then delivering him from death.[66]

But, according to Bultmann, Paul does not only interpret the death of Christ in light of the mystery religions; he also interprets it "*in the categories of the Gnostic myth*, regarding his death as unified with his incarnation and resurrection or exaltation."[67] The gnostic myth speaks of the Redeemer's coming and going as humiliation and exaltation, but not implying that his departure from the earth is caused by a violent death.[68] Thus, Christ's death may be seen as a combination of the mystery-divinity's death and revivification and the gnostic myth's humiliation and exaltation of the Redeemer.

---

60. Bultmann, *Theology*, 257–58.
61. Bultmann, *Theology*, 273.
62. Bultmann, *Theology*, 278–79 (italics original).
63. Bultmann, *Theology*, 299.
64. Bultmann, *Theology*, 297–98 (italics original).
65. Bultmann, *Theology*, 298 (italics original).
66. Bultmann, *Theology*, 298.
67. Bultmann, *Theology*, 298 (italics original).
68. Bultmann, *Theology*, 298.

The death and resurrection of Christ constitute what Bultmann called the "salvation-occurrence," which is inherently eschatological and puts the old aeon to an end. While the end of the old world is still to come with the parousia of Christ, that cosmic event will simply constitute the completion and confirmation of the eschatological occurrence that has already begun.[69] This cosmic drama that will bring the redemption of the body has already begun with the resurrection of Christ, with its consummation coming near.[70] Paul holds fast to an apocalyptic expectation of final judgment and of "the cosmic drama which will end the old world and introduce the new world of Christ."[71] That day of the Lord will see the end of Christ's reign as he hands the kingdom over to his Father, so that God will be all in all.[72] But the time between Christ's resurrection and parousia constitutes the Messiah's reign "as the Now in which the proclamation is sounding forth (1 Cor. 15:23–28)."[73]

As for the Christian life, Bultmann drew attention to its future-oriented nature. The hope of the believer is freedom for the future and an openness toward it which "the man of faith has because he has turned over his anxiety about himself and his future to God in obedience."[74] The unbeliever, in contrast, relies on his own resources and resorts therefore to anxiety about his future, falsely believing he has some control over it. Faith is a response to the proclaimed word and is itself part of the eschatological salvation-occurrence.[75] Indeed, the believer's entire existence is eschatological, as it is an existence in joy, which is ultimately forward pointing.[76]

Yet life is also a present reality in one's openness for the future and in being determined by the future. The old person has been crucified with Christ, so the "world" no longer exists for him; he is a new creation.[77] Christ's resurrection is not just the first case of rising from the dead, but is the origin of the resurrection life of all believers, "which necessarily proceeds from it and hence can be regarded as already present in its origin."[78] Having now freedom from death, "*freedom from the world and its powers* are also given" to the believer.[79]

---

69. Bultmann, *Theology*, 306.
70. Bultmann, *Theology*, 347.
71. Bultmann, *Theology*, 346.
72. Bultmann, *Theology*, 346.
73. Bultmann, *Theology*, 307.
74. Bultmann, *Theology*, 320.
75. Bultmann, *Theology*, 329.
76. Bultmann, *Theology*, 339.
77. Bultmann, *Theology*, 348.
78. Bultmann, *Theology*, 347–48.
79. Bultmann, *Theology*, 351 (italics original).

2.5 Karl Barth (1932–68)

Karl Barth's planned fifth volume of his *Church Dogmatics* was to be dedicated to eschatology, but he died before writing it. The *Church Dogmatics* are nevertheless woven through with eschatological insights, and four major sections address eschatological matters directly: "Ending Time" (CD III/2 §47.5); "The Promise of the Spirit" (CD IV/3.1 §69.4); "The Condemnation of Man" (CD IV/3.1 §70.3); "The Subject of Hope and Hope" (CD IV/3.2 §73.1). While Barth was not, of course, limited to Paul's writings, his contributions to eschatology have nevertheless helped to shape subsequent readings of Paul.

In "Ending Time" (CD III/2 §47.5), Barth addressed the topic of death. Death stands under the sign of divine judgment but also "the sign of the setting aside of this judgment and therefore the defeat of death."[80] But before exploring its defeat, Barth pressed into the bleakness of human death. It is a tyrannical onslaught to human life,[81] not a harmless, neutral negation of it.[82] Death is not a tyrant in its own right, however, but rules only because "God is in the right against His creature and His creature is in the wrong against Him."[83] The destructive work of death reveals our nothingness before God and brings upon humanity an intolerable evil such that our fear of death is actually grounded in the inevitable fear of God.[84]

Death as humanity's last enemy is not free to do whatever it likes. God has appointed it to its office and can also dismiss it. "He has armed it, but He can also disarm it."[85] For Barth, this means that in death we are not subject to death alone, or under the rule of a second god. On the contrary, in death the Lord of death is also present.[86] The terror of death is actually due to the fact that "in death we shall finally fall into the hands of the living God."[87] And as such, we will be convicted of secret sin and guilt and "we shall look quite foolish, stripped of all our glory, and standing helpless and naked before Him."[88]

But the God who is the Lord of death is the gracious God. He is for man and "speaks to us in His eternal Word incarnate in Jesus Christ and crucified and put to death for us."[89] Indeed, God's curse of death upon humanity falls

---

80. Karl Barth, *Church Dogmatics*, III/2: *The Doctrine of Creation*, ed. G. W. Bromiley and T. F. Torrance; trans. G. W. Bromiley (Edinburgh: T&T Clark, 1960), §47.5, 593.
81. Barth, *Church Dogmatics*, III/2 §47.5, 593.
82. Barth, *Church Dogmatics*, III/2 §47.5, 608.
83. Barth, *Church Dogmatics*, III/2 §47.5, 608.
84. Barth, *Church Dogmatics*, III/2 §47.5, 608.
85. Barth, *Church Dogmatics*, III/2 §47.5, 608.
86. Barth, *Church Dogmatics*, III/2 §47.5, 609.
87. Barth, *Church Dogmatics*, III/2 §47.5, 609.
88. Barth, *Church Dogmatics*, III/2 §47.5, 610.
89. Barth, *Church Dogmatics*, III/2 §47.5, 609.

hard on us because it is surrounded by "the rainbow of His covenant."[90] It is the dark side of his blessing on humanity.[91] This means that even in death, "He will be our gracious God, the God who is for us," and he will necessarily work in it for our good.[92]

For Barth, participation in Christ means that believers in Jesus can no longer consider death as ahead of them. Rather, it is behind them since they belong to him who has already suffered for them, abolished death, and made it irrelevant along with their sin and guilt.[93] From an eschatological perspective, the work of Christ in redemption, reconciliation, and the destruction of death marks "the end of time, the last day, or to be more precise, the midnight hour of the last night when the last day has dawned for each individual and all humanity."[94]

Barth summarized these insights into three points, acknowledging first the relationship between the crucifixion of Jesus, the abolition of death, and the fulfillment of time; second, the relationship between the resurrection of Jesus as the inauguration of the last time and his return in glory as its conclusion; and third, the relationship between the resurrection of Jesus and the new birth of believers who, through his resurrection, are born again to a life in God that is now concealed but will be revealed when Jesus returns in glory.[95]

In "The Promise of the Spirit" (CD IV/3.1 §69.4), Barth explored the concept of Christ's parousia, arguing that it must be understood to include the Easter event, not just the future coming of Christ. And indeed, the gift of the Spirit is regarded as the coming of Christ in between these two, so that his parousia is properly understood as "one continuous event" in which nothing different takes place in its three stages. Whether in the Easter event, the impartation of the Spirit, or the final return of Christ, "always and in all three forms it is a matter of the fresh coming of the One who came before."[96] Having said that, however, Barth posits that the Easter event provides the basic pattern for the other two modes of the coming of Christ, so that he is tempted to describe the whole event "simply as one long fulfillment of the resurrection of Jesus Christ."[97] Working backwards from the third stage of Christ's parousia (his return at the end of this age), which is obviously eschatological, Barth likewise assigns eschatological significance to the second stage (this current age of the Spirit)

---

90. Barth, *Church Dogmatics*, III/2 §47.5, 610.
91. Barth, *Church Dogmatics*, III/2 §47.5, 610.
92. Barth, *Church Dogmatics*, III/2 §47.5, 610.
93. Barth, *Church Dogmatics*, III/2 §47.5, 621.
94. Barth, *Church Dogmatics*, III/2 §47.5, 622.
95. Barth, *Church Dogmatics*, III/2 §47.5, 623.
96. Karl Barth, *Church Dogmatics* IV/3.1: *The Doctrine of Reconciliation*, ed. G. W. Bromiley and T. F. Torrance; trans. G. W. Bromiley (Edinburgh: T&T Clark, 1961), §69.4, 292–93.
97. Barth, *Church Dogmatics*, IV/3.1 §69.4, 293.

and therefore also to the original Easter event, since in the death of Christ "the character and stamp of the last time is given to all the time which remains."[98] Indeed, Barth went so far as to say that the new creation has already taken place in the resurrection of Christ.[99]

Regarding the eschatological notion of the "now and not yet," Barth supposed that the "not yet" is grounded in that fact that "it is the good will of Jesus Christ Himself to be not yet at the goal but still on the way, so that the rest of creation has no option but to participate in and adapt itself to His situation."[100] This period between the Easter event and the final appearing of Christ is a dynamic one that is still in process, not yet completed, in which the reconciled but not yet redeemed creature has freedom to move from and to the revelation of its reconciliation. The creature is given time and place and opportunity for such "by this distance between the occurrence of the coming again of Jesus Christ in its two forms"—this being "the good and kind and gracious reason for this distance."[101]

In "The Condemnation of Man" (CD IV/3.1 §70.3), Barth opened the question of God's "withdrawal of that final threat" leading to "the super-abundant promise of the final deliverance of all men."[102] In other words, Barth asks if the grace of God points in the direction of eternal divine patience and deliverance, resulting in universal reconciliation. Barth regards it appropriate to hope and pray—notwithstanding all that proclaims the opposite—that God's compassion should not fail but result in ultimate mercy.[103]

In "The Subject of Hope and Hope" (CD IV/3.2 §73.1), Barth returned to the issues of the now-and-not-yet and the single continuous parousia of Christ. He admits the clear contradiction between the christological already and not yet, but this is "no flat contradiction."[104] Instead, the already and the not yet are equally forms of the one parousia. The commencement, continuation, and consummation of Christ's prophetic activity are equal elements, since they are performed by "the same person who was yesterday, is to-day, and will come to-morrow and for ever."[105] In other words, Barth's solution to the contradiction between the already and not yet is entirely christological. The "then" of Christ's

---

98. Barth, *Church Dogmatics*, IV/3.1 §69.4, 295–96.
99. Barth, *Church Dogmatics*, IV/3.1 §69.4, 300.
100. Barth, *Church Dogmatics*, IV/3.1 §69.4, 329.
101. Barth, *Church Dogmatics*, IV/3.1 §69.4, 334.
102. Barth, *Church Dogmatics*, IV/3.1 §70.3, 477.
103. Barth, *Church Dogmatics*, IV/3.1 §70.3, 478.
104. Karl Barth, *Church Dogmatics* IV/3.2: *The Doctrine of Reconciliation*, ed. G. W. Bromiley and T. F. Torrance; trans. G. W. Bromiley (Edinburgh: T&T Clark, 1961), §73.1, 910.
105. Barth, *Church Dogmatics*, IV/3.2 §73.1, 910.

resurrection included the "now" of Pentecost, which in turn includes the "one day" of his future coming.[106] All moments are one in the one coming of Christ.

Turning to the notion of Christian hope, Barth likened it to Christian faith and love. One's faith is not what justifies, but the One in whom faith is placed; love does not sanctify, but the One loved sanctifies. Likewise, a believer's hope is directed toward the One who has accomplished reconciliation with God on the basis of the "then" of his resurrection and therefore the "now" in his presence in the Holy Spirit.[107] Nevertheless, Christian hope, even for all its participation in the One hoped for, cannot be more than hope. While it is clear and certain in the power of Christ, it has yet to be confirmed as an absolutely positive expectation of the future; "what is true in itself has yet to become true."[108] That is, the reality of Christian existence given in hope has yet to be worked out as salvation in the time ahead.[109] Nevertheless, the believer will rejoice in the end to come because in the final parting of death he expected his Lord and expects to be with him. The believer cannot really look or move to his end except in hope.[110]

2.6 Oscar Cullmann (1962)

The original 1946 German publication of Cullmann's *Christ and Time* was significantly revised in 1962 (1964 in English) in response to criticisms from Barth and Bultmann in particular. Cullmann addressed the redemptive-historical essence of New Testament eschatology, observing the tension between the present "(the already accomplished)" and the future "(the not yet fulfilled)."[111] Cullmann employed the now-famous analogy of D-Day and V-Day to illustrate this tension.[112] Just as D-Day represented the decisive turning point toward Allied victory in World War II, so did the death and resurrection of Christ for his victory over the powers. And just as V-Day was the final victorious conclusion of the war, so the future coming of Christ will see his final and conclusive victory:

> *The decisive battle in a war may already have occurred in a relatively early stage of the war, and yet the war still continues.* Although the decisive effect of that battle is perhaps not recognized by all, it nevertheless already means

---

106. Barth, *Church Dogmatics*, IV/3.2 §73.1, 910.
107. Barth, *Church Dogmatics*, IV/3.2 §73.1, 914–15.
108. Barth, *Church Dogmatics*, IV/3.2 §73.1, 917.
109. Barth, *Church Dogmatics*, IV/3.2 §73.1, 917.
110. Barth, *Church Dogmatics*, IV/3.2 §73.1, 928.
111. Oscar Cullmann, *Christ and Time: The Primitive Christian Conception of Time and History*, rev. ed.; trans. Floyd V. Filson (Philadelphia: Westminster, 1964), 3.
112. Cullmann, *Christ and Time*, 3.

victory. But the war must still be carried on for an undefined time, until "Victory Day." Precisely this is the situation of which the New Testament is conscious, as a result of the recognition of the new division of time; the revelation consists precisely in the fact of the proclamation that *that event on the cross, together with the resurrection which followed, was the already concluded decisive battle.*[113]

Cullmann refuted Bultmann's claim that the present-future tension of New Testament eschatology was merely a solution developed by the early church to explain the embarrassing failure of the parousia to eventuate. Rather, Cullmann insisted that the redemptive-historical eschatology of the New Testament was not a secondary element but was part of the core character of its message.[114] Agreeing with Schweitzer, Cullmann argued that any treatment of Paul (or Jesus for that matter) that interprets him without eschatology at the center of his thought simply does violence to the historical truth.[115] Indeed, Cullmann pointed to the central significance of the Christ-event for world history, not just for the eschatology of the New Testament. Our system of accounting time does not progress as a continuous forward-moving series but proceeds from a *center*, namely, the birth of Jesus Christ of Nazareth: "Thence proceeds in opposite directions two enumerations, one forward, the other backward: 'after Christ,' 'before Christ.'"[116]

Cullmann's study began with the relevant terminology for time found in the Greek New Testament—demonstrating its notably theological character—that provides the temporal framework in which redemptive history unfolds.[117] According to Cullmann, "God chooses these moments or periods of time for the realization of his plan of salvation and does so in a way that the joining of them in the light of this plan forms a meaningful time line."[118] He argues that eternity is not "outside time" or contrasts to time; rather, eternity is time without limit—eternity is unlimited time.[119] Thus time is the "means of which God makes use in order to reveal his gracious working."[120]

In contrast to Greek thinking about time as circular, so that it enslaves humans as a curse, the Bible presents a linear understanding of time, conceiving

---

113. Cullmann, *Christ and Time*, 84 (italics original).
114. Cullmann, *Christ and Time*, 3–4.
115. Cullmann, *Christ and Time*, 29.
116. Cullmann, *Christ and Time*, 17, 118.
117. Cullmann, *Christ and Time*, 38–39.
118. Cullmann, *Christ and Time*, 44.
119. Cullmann, *Christ and Time*, 46, 62–63.
120. Cullmann, *Christ and Time*, 51.

it as a process. This means that the coming kingdom of God is not "always standing in the situation of decision."[121] The progressing nature of time makes it possible for something to be "fulfilled" and for a divine plan to move forward to execution.[122] The goal at the end of the line gives the entire process "the impulse to strive thither," just as the decisive midpoint of the Christ-event "serves as guidepost for all the process that lies behind and for all that lies ahead."[123] The entire structure of biblical eschatology is characterized "not as timeless but rather as occurring in time."[124]

Cullmann argued against the Platonic notion of timeless eternity by pointing out that the coming age is *"not a mere return to the primitive beginning."*[125] Rather the New Testament exhibits three ages: first, the age before the creation; second, the present age between the creation and the end; and third, the coming age in which the eschatological drama falls.[126] The first and third ages obviously cannot coincide; but nor can first and second since in the first age the creation is not yet present but only being prepared. In the third age, the first creation is replaced by the new creation. Cullman's point was that "all this can take place only in the time framework that continuously moves straight forward; it cannot occur in the framework of a dualism between time and timeless eternity."[127]

Cullmann found his eschatological schema adequate to solve the two particularly Pauline problems of the delayed parousia and the intermediate state. He argued that viewing the decisive center of time as the Christ-event meant that Paul's hope suffered no loss by the apparent delay of the parousia, since its starting point had been the past fact of Christ's work rather than any future event. As such, his hope is *"an assured fact which cannot be touched by the delay in the Parousia."*[128] Regarding the intermediate state, Cullmann acknowledged Paul's strong distaste for the idea of being "stripped of the body" should believers die before the return of Christ. The "nakedness" brought on by death is an imperfect condition, overcome on the basis that believers have already received the Spirit as a guarantee. By this guarantee the resurrection of the body at the last day is secured.[129] All resurrection hope in the New Testament is founded upon a fact of the past—"The mid-point of the redemptive line to which the

---

121. Cullmann, *Christ and Time*, 52–53.
122. Cullmann, *Christ and Time*, 53.
123. Cullmann, *Christ and Time*, 53–54.
124. Cullmann, *Christ and Time*, 66.
125. Cullmann, *Christ and Time*, 67 (italics original).
126. Cullmann, *Christ and Time*, 67.
127. Cullmann, *Christ and Time*, 67.
128. Cullmann, *Christ and Time*, 88 (italics original).
129. Cullmann, *Christ and Time*, 239.

apostles bear witness: that Christ is risen."[130] In addition, such hope is built on a further fact founded on the former: that the resurrection power of the Holy Spirit is already at work in those who believe in the Risen One. In the end time, that same Spirit who raised up Christ from the dead will also raise believers' mortal bodies (Rom 8:11).[131]

The implications of this for the believer are that he or she must live precisely in the present (not the past nor the future), but by faith share in the saving gifts of the entire timeline, even those of the future. The work of the Spirit invades the present time, occasionally bringing redemptive action that only comes to its full expression in the future.[132] The believer therefore does not share in God's lordship over time, somehow competent to leap over periods of time; she must remain in the present. But her "participation in specific future gifts of grace is always provisional; the such who are healed and the dead who are raised, in The Acts as well as in the Gospels, must indeed all die again, in order to be finally raised only at the end."[133]

2.7 Ernst Käsemann (1965)

While Schweitzer put the "apocalyptic Paul" on the map, Käsemann's version of the apocalyptic Paul has proved most influential in the contemporary discussion. Käsemann began by noting the ambiguity of the term *apocalyptic* and defined it simply as denoting "the expectation of an imminent Parousia."[134] He is quick to point out that "hardly any New Testament scholar" now agrees with Schweitzer's view that Christian apocalyptic began with Jesus's burning expectation of the end—sending his disciples out on an urgent mission to Palestine and attempting to force divine intervention by entering Jerusalem, only to perish as a result.[135] Rejecting Schweitzer's failed apocalyptic Jesus, Käsemann pointed to the original disciples' central hope of "the return of Jesus in the role of the heavenly Son of Man," which derived from their Easter experience.[136]

The resurrection of Christ was "understood as the dawn of the general resurrection" and was therefore interpreted apocalyptically.[137] Jesus as the Son

---

130. Cullmann, *Christ and Time*, 242.
131. Cullmann, *Christ and Time*, 242.
132. Cullmann, *Christ and Time*, 76.
133. Cullmann, *Christ and Time*, 76.
134. Ernst Käsemann, "On the Subject of Primitive Christian Apocalyptic," in *New Testament Questions of Today*, trans. W. J. Montague (London: SCM, 1969), 109n.1.
135. Käsemann, "Christian Apocalyptic," 111. According to Käsemann, Schweitzer's apocalyptic approach "obscured rather than illuminated the true state of affairs" by departing from the presuppositions of historical criticism (113).
136. Käsemann, "Christian Apocalyptic," 114.
137. Käsemann, "Christian Apocalyptic," 114.

of Man, the exalted one, is the bearer of the last judgment and will return for judgment with heavenly glory, resulting in the general resurrection of the dead.[138] Consequently, "the name of Jesus, the final act of the governance of the world (and, consequentially, the course of history as a totality) is bound up in an eschatological whole."[139] In this way, the eschatological nature of the church finds "a particularly close similarity to the Qumran community," since the church—united in its common Easter hope—regards itself as the holy remnant, representing the eschatological new covenant on earth.[140]

Turning to consider Paul's apocalypticism specifically, Käsemann acknowledged the importance of Bultmann's interpretation, determined as it was by "its resolute placing of the apostle's present eschatology at the controlling centre of his thought."[141] But this adherence to Paul's *present* eschatology stands in tension with an apocalyptic reading of Paul, which is primarily *future* oriented. And it is not possible to deny Paul's apocalyptic character either, since his "apostolic self-consciousness is only comprehensible on the basis of his apocalyptic."[142] For Käsemann, therefore, present and future eschatological elements must be held together: "If we do not wish to do violence to the texts of his letters as we now have them, we are bound to say that there is in them a compromise between present and future eschatology."[143]

This "compromise" between present and future eschatology is most clearly evident in the resurrection of Christ. In his post-resurrection exaltation to the right hand of God, Christ saw the world-powers subjected to him, with only the lordship of death yet to be brought to an end—an end that "is identical with the end of history."[144] The resurrection of Christ is therefore presently the beginning of the general resurrection while also being the future-orientated reality "in which we can participate by hope alone."[145] However, Käsemann argued that for Paul the resurrection of Christ was not primarily concerned with the reanimation of the dead but with the reign of Christ (1 Cor 15:20–28); since Christ must reign, his people must not be left in the grip of death.[146] Presently his people are already engaged in delivering themselves over to Christ by their bodily obedience, witnessing to his lordship as Cosmocrator and anticipating

---

138. Käsemann, "Christian Apocalyptic," 115.
139. Käsemann, "Christian Apocalyptic," 115.
140. Käsemann, "Christian Apocalyptic," 116.
141. Käsemann, "Christian Apocalyptic," 131.
142. Käsemann, "Christian Apocalyptic," 131.
143. Käsemann, "Christian Apocalyptic," 131.
144. Käsemann, "Christian Apocalyptic," 134.
145. Käsemann, "Christian Apocalyptic," 134.
146. Käsemann, "Christian Apocalyptic," 135.

"the ultimate future of the reality of the Resurrection and of the untrammelled reign of Christ."[147]

For Käsemann, apocalyptic also underlies Paul's anthropology. Technical terms such as *spirit* and *flesh* do not signify the individuation of the human being but the heavenly or earthly powers that determine a person from outside, taking possession of him and locating him into one of two dualistically opposed spheres.[148] Human beings are never on their own, but are pieces of the world, determined by external powers that take possession of them and to which they must surrender. A believer's life is "from the beginning a stake in the confrontation between God and the principalities of this world."[149] In this sense, one's life mirrors the cosmic contention for the lordship of the world, and as such "man's life can only be understood apocalyptically."[150]

Concerning the apocalyptic nature of other central Pauline themes, Käsemann drew particular attention to the righteousness of God. Just as the significance of the resurrection is both present and future, so the righteousness of God is to be viewed in terms of "Paul's double eschatology."[151] The righteousness of God is his saving activity,[152] and so salvation is already present by faith and baptism, while it is also yet to be realized at the end through the parousia.[153] Furthermore, since the righteousness of God is the power of the justification of the ungodly, it is in fact "God's victory amid the opposition of the world."[154] In this sense, Käsemann is able to claim that "δικαιοσύνη θεοῦ is for Paul God's sovereignty over the world revealing itself eschatologically in Jesus."[155]

As such, Paul's understanding of the righteousness of God is not primarily focused on the individual, nor is it exclusively anthropological. Instead, the divine will for salvation is in fact directed toward the whole world.[156] This global scope of God's saving work is further evidence of Paul's apocalypticism: "His doctrine of δικαιοσύνη θεοῦ demonstrates this: God's power reaches out for the world, and the world's salvation lies in its being recaptured for the sovereignty of God."[157]

---

147. Käsemann, "Christian Apocalyptic," 135.
148. Käsemann, "Christian Apocalyptic," 136.
149. Käsemann, "Christian Apocalyptic," 136.
150. Käsemann, "Christian Apocalyptic," 136.
151. Ernst Käsemann, "'The Righteousness of God' in Paul," in *New Testament Questions of Today*, 170.
152. Käsemann, "Righteousness of God," 172.
153. Käsemann, "Righteousness of God," 170.
154. Käsemann, "Righteousness of God," 180.
155. Käsemann, "Righteousness of God," 180.
156. Käsemann, "Righteousness of God," 181.
157. Käsemann, "Righteousness of God," 181–82.

2.8 GEORGE ELDON LADD (1974)

In *The Presence of the Future*, George Eldon Ladd argued that the eschatological shape of the New Testament was best described as "inaugurated eschatology," with the kingdom of God fulfilled in Jesus, while its consummation lies ahead in the future. Ladd reacted against the likes of Albert Schweitzer, who did not reach his interpretation of the Gospels through inductive study but "by assuming that Jesus must be interpreted in terms of his environment, which Schweitzer understood to be that of Jewish apocalyptic."[158] Ladd was influenced rather by British scholarship following C. H. Dodd, who viewed eschatology as having less to do with the last things, temporally conceived, and more to do with "those things which possess finality and ultimacy in meaning."[159] In particular, the kingdom of God is not an eschatological entity found at the end of history, but the eternally present realm of God.[160] For Ladd, the kingdom of God is "timeless, eternal, transcendental, and is therefore always near and always laying its demands upon men."[161] Apocalyptic language was simply an ancient vehicle through which to convey the timeless truth about the kingdom of God.[162] Apocalyptic is "beyond history," while so-called prophetic eschatology is "within history."[163]

Ladd explored the hope of the Old Testament, demonstrating it as eschatological but also as an earthly hope; redemption always includes the earth since "Hebrew thought saw an essential unity between man and nature."[164] There is no room for the bodiless, nonmaterial, "spiritual" redemption of Greek thought.[165] The interrelation between nature and humanity means that the earth must also share in final redemption and, like humanity, must be purged of the effects of evil in order to manifest the glory of God.[166] In order to effect such purging, the natural order is expected to dissolve—not for the purpose of destruction "but to make way for a new perfect order arising out of the old imperfect one."[167] The Old Testament prophets looked ahead to the deliverance of creation from the bondage of corruption, and this is often couched in physical terms—the wilderness becoming fruitful (Isa 32:15), the desert blossoming

---

158. George Eldon Ladd, *The Presence of the Future: The Eschatology of Biblical Realism*, rev. ed. (Grand Rapids: Eerdmans, 1974), 4.
159. Ladd, *Presence of the Future*, 17.
160. Ladd, *Presence of the Future*, 17.
161. Ladd, *Presence of the Future*, 18.
162. Ladd, *Presence of the Future*, 18.
163. Ladd, *Presence of the Future*, 55.
164. Ladd, *Presence of the Future*, 59.
165. Ladd, *Presence of the Future*, 59.
166. Ladd, *Presence of the Future*, 59–60.
167. Ladd, *Presence of the Future*, 61.

(Isa 35:2), burning sands being cooled and dry places becoming springs of water (Isa 35:7)—all because the earth will be filled with the knowledge of God (Isa 11:9).[168]

Ladd raised the question as to whether such language is to be understood literally or symbolically, concluding that language about the eschatological shaking of the world, the collapse of the heavens, and so forth can be understood poetically.[169] The significance of this is that such poetic imagery provides the conceptual material for the apocalyptic literature of the New Testament, with its depictions of cosmic catastrophe, the ending of this age, and the inauguration of the age to come. Such language is grounded in the traditional language of Old Testament poetry that is used to describe the majesty of God.[170] Consequently, the symbolic nature of theophanic language warns us against woodenly literal interpretations. On the other hand, however, it is also impossible to reduce such language altogether to poetry, since "it is also an expression of a profound theology of creation and man's place in creation."[171]

Apocalyptic eschatology, then, ought to be understood "as a historical development of the prophetic eschatology," with the prophetic eschatology interpreted against the historical realities of the post-Maccabean era.[172] Both apocalyptic and prophetic eschatology depict the inbreaking of the kingdom of God, and so both are essentially catastrophic—both envisage a renewed, redeemed, and transformed order. The stark dualism found in apocalyptic is actually just a sharpening of the concept found in prophetic literature and theology.[173] But, according to Ladd, a key distinction between apocalyptic eschatology and that of the prophets was that the former ignored the concept of God's dynamic activity in the history of redemption; "the apocalypticists, contrary to the prophets, despaired of history, feeling that it was completely dominated by evil."[174] Only the future held any hope, when God would finally deliver his people from the tyranny of evil at the end of history. God is only God of the future; he is God of the present only in a theoretical capacity.[175]

According to Ladd, Jesus's message was one of prophetic hope rather than apocalypticism. The kingdom of God as God's present rule is thus the correct understanding of Jesus's preaching, rather than a future-only intervention of

---

168. Ladd, *Presence of the Future*, 61–62.
169. Ladd, *Presence of the Future*, 62.
170. Ladd, *Presence of the Future*, 62.
171. Ladd, *Presence of the Future*, 62.
172. Ladd, *Presence of the Future*, 101.
173. Ladd, *Presence of the Future*, 101.
174. Ladd, *Presence of the Future*, 101.
175. Ladd, *Presence of the Future*, 101.

God, as Schweitzer argued.[176] The coming kingdom of God is "God's dynamic reign invading the present age without transforming it into the age to come."[177] This kingdom of God works in and through human beings, but is not subject to them since it is *God's* kingdom. And the kingdom does not come as people receive it, but *has come* into history through Jesus, bringing their messianic salvation.[178] To receive this kingdom of God, believers submit themselves to God's reign and so receive the gift of the kingdom and enter into its blessings. Thus, in this way "the age of fulfillment is present, but the time of consummation still awaits the age to come."[179]

2.9 E. P. Sanders (1977)

In his seminal work *Paul and Palestinian Judaism*, E. P. Sanders declared that any right understanding of Paul's eschatology could not be left to "last place" in a systematic treatment of his theology—to do so would be to completely obscure his thought.[180] Indeed, there are no two elements of Paul's thought more certain than "his conviction that the full salvation of believers and the destruction of unbelievers lay in the near future" and "that Christians possessed the Spirit as the present guarantee of future salvation."[181]

According to Sanders, Paul affirmed a clear distinction between being saved by God's grace and being judged according to deeds, being rewarded for good deeds and punished for bad. Such is clear from three passages in the Corinthian correspondence—1 Corinthians 3:10–15; 11:29; and 2 Corinthians 5:8–11.[182] Paul's assurance of salvation did not rest on his perfect work, but neither would there be nothing held against him at the judgment—and in this, Paul was typically Jewish. To be judged on the basis of deeds and to be saved by God's gracious election was the general view in rabbinic literature. Thus, "salvation by grace is not incompatible with punishment and reward for deeds."[183] Sanders reflected this in terms of the centrality of covenant membership, such that "good deeds are the *condition* of remaining 'in' [the covenant], but they do not *earn* salvation."[184]

Sanders affirmed the existing observation that similarity between Paul's

---

176. Ladd, *Presence of the Future*, 148.
177. Ladd, *Presence of the Future*, 149.
178. Ladd, *Presence of the Future*, 194.
179. Ladd, *Presence of the Future*, 217.
180. E. P. Sanders, *Paul and Palestinian Judaism: A Comparison of Patterns of Religion* (Minneapolis: Fortress, 1977), 434.
181. Sanders, *Paul and Palestinian Judaism*, 447.
182. Sanders, *Paul and Palestinian Judaism*, 516–17.
183. Sanders, *Paul and Palestinian Judaism*, 517.
184. Sanders, *Paul and Palestinian Judaism*, 517.

eschatological conception and that of Jewish apocalypticism is general rather than detailed. Paul did not calculate the times and seasons, nor did he use visions of beasts or other apocalyptic literary conventions in his discussions of the end.[185] This led Sanders to conclude that prior to his conversion and call, Paul was not especially apocalyptically minded and therefore did not just "fit" Christ into an existing apocalyptic framework.[186] Nevertheless, "if one is tallying differences and similarities, the expectation of the parousia counts a general similarity between Paul and Palestinian Judaism."[187] There are likewise parallels in the two aeons, the opposing world powers, and the resolution with God's victory at the eschatological end.[188]

Regarding Paul's conception of the *plight* of humanity, Sanders found that Paul differed slightly from apocalyptic literature, which regarded the individual as *oppressed* during the evil aeon, unable to achieve vindication and victory until the eschatological moment. This does not quite match Paul's concept of the slavery of the individual to the evil powers and dominions.[189] Thus Sanders hesitated to understand humanity's plight, according to Paul, as directly derived from apocalypticism despite significant similarities.[190] Rather, "Paul appears to have held to a curious combination of conceptions concerning man's plight."[191] In the end, humanity's plight is not ultimately seen in the oppression of the righteous by the wicked but rather in the fact that a person is *not in Christ*.[192]

2.10 J. Christiaan Beker (1980, 1982)

The first major treatment of Paul's theology as apocalyptic came in J. Christiaan Beker's *Paul the Apostle: The Triumph of God in Life and Thought* (1980),[193] which was followed by the shorter *Paul's Apocalyptic Gospel: The Coming Triumph of God* (1982).[194] Beker's first work in particular represented the most significant apocalyptic reading of Paul since Käsemann, while the second put the first's major contributions into a more accessible form, exploring "the challenge of Paul's apocalyptic gospel for the church."[195] As indicated by the subtitles of both

---

185. Sanders, *Paul and Palestinian Judaism*, 543.
186. Sanders, *Paul and Palestinian Judaism*, 543.
187. Sanders, *Paul and Palestinian Judaism*, 543.
188. Sanders, *Paul and Palestinian Judaism*, 554.
189. Sanders, *Paul and Palestinian Judaism*, 554.
190. Sanders, *Paul and Palestinian Judaism*, 554.
191. Sanders, *Paul and Palestinian Judaism*, 554.
192. Sanders, *Paul and Palestinian Judaism*, 554.
193. J. Christiaan Beker, *Paul the Apostle: The Triumph of God in Life and Thought* (Philadelphia: Fortress, 1980).
194. J. Christiaan Beker, *Paul's Apocalyptic Gospel: The Coming Triumph of God* (Philadelphia: Fortress, 1982).
195. Beker, *Paul's Apocalyptic Gospel*, 9.

books, Beker's major concern was the triumph of God as the coherent theme of Paul's gospel. This triumph represents "the hope in the dawning victory of God and in the imminent redemption of the created order, which he inaugurated in Christ."[196] According to Beker, Paul's unique achievement was to translate the apocalyptic theme of the gospel "into the contingent particularities of the human situation."[197]

In *Paul the Apostle*, Beker located Paul's gospel in his apocalyptic worldview, which was affirmed and modified by the resurrection of Christ (ch. 8). This apocalyptic worldview also determined Paul's view of the death of Christ (ch. 9). Beker then addressed the two major power structures of death (ch. 10) and the law (ch. 11), since the death and resurrection of Christ had established their defeat. The consequences of Paul's apocalyptic gospel are explored with reference to redemption (ch. 12) and the Christian life (ch. 13). Paul's apocalyptic perspective also shaped his understanding of the church (ch. 14) and Israel (ch. 15). Beker concluded the book with a summary of its argument, demonstrating that "all elements of Paul's thought are distorted unless they are viewed from the perspective of the dawning triumph of God, which constitutes the coherent theme of Paul's gospel" (ch. 16).[198]

After surveying leading scholarship on Jewish apocalyptic literature, Beker summarized that apocalyptic revolves around three basic ideas: "(1) historical dualism; (2) universal cosmic expectation; and (3) the imminent end of the world."[199] Beker noted the deep existential concern of apocalyptic literature that "is in many respects a theology of martyrdom."[200] The apocalypticist is profoundly aware "of the discrepancy between what is and what should be" and the tension "between faithfulness to the Torah and its apparent futility."[201] He lives in hope that God will keep his promises to his people notwithstanding their present persecution in a world that seems to contradict such hope.[202]

As Schweitzer and Käsemann insisted, Beker likewise regarded Paul's apocalypticism to be "the central climate and focus of his thought, as it was for most early Christian thinkers."[203] Indeed, Paul's apocalyptic commitment shaped his temper and lifestyle with its awareness that "he is the man of the hour whose mission takes place in the last hours of world history."[204] He is an eschatological

---

196. Beker, *Paul the Apostle*, ix.
197. Beker, *Paul the Apostle*, ix.
198. Beker, *Paul the Apostle*, xi.
199. Beker, *Paul the Apostle*, 136.
200. Beker, *Paul the Apostle*, 136.
201. Beker, *Paul the Apostle*, 136.
202. Beker, *Paul the Apostle*, 136.
203. Beker, *Paul the Apostle*, 144.
204. Beker, *Paul the Apostle*, 144.

apostle positioned between the resurrection of Christ and the final resurrection of the dead.²⁰⁵ While Paul profoundly modified Jewish apocalypticism in light of the Christ-event, such modification did not lessen his apocalyptic intensity.²⁰⁶

Some of Paul's modifications of apocalyptic included his nonuse of certain traditional apocalyptic terminology and not engaging "in apocalyptic timetables, descriptions of the architecture of heaven, or accounts of demons and angels. He does not relish the rewards of the blessed or delight in the torture of the wicked."²⁰⁷ The Christ-event has strongly modified the dualistic structure of traditional apocalyptic thought.²⁰⁸ Though death is "the last enemy" (1 Cor 15:26), Paul differs from traditional apocalyptic by emphasizing the openness of the present to the future glory of God and interruption of the present by the future.²⁰⁹ The future age is already present, allowing believers now to rejoice and now claim the new creation as they live by the power of the Spirit.²¹⁰

Beker does not see in Paul as harsh a dualism as expected in typical apocalyptic thought. Israel's history is seen in a typological light with its own imprint of God's salvation. Consequently, Paul's view of the difference between the old and new is not the same as in apocalyptic Judaism, which regarded the old age as one of only darkness.²¹¹

> The era of "the old covenant" has its own (temporary) "splendor" (2 Cor. 3:7–11); the Exodus story has eschatological meaning for believers (1 Cor. 10:1–13); the privileges of Israel are real and abiding (Romans 9–11), and although Christ is the end of the law (Rom. 10:4), the law is "holy and righteous and good" and plays a necessary part in salvation-history. The past contains the footprints of the promises of God, and these promises are taken up into the new rather than cast aside.²¹²

According to Beker, Paul's understanding of hope has an apocalyptic specificity. It points forward to the object of Christian longing—namely, the victory over evil and death in the parousia of Christ.²¹³ Paul's apocalypticism is determined by the Christ-event, which negated the old order and "initiated the hope for the transformation of the creation that has gone astray and is in

---

205. Beker, *Paul the Apostle*, 145.
206. Beker, *Paul the Apostle*, 145.
207. Beker, *Paul the Apostle*, 145.
208. Beker, *Paul the Apostle*, 145.
209. Beker, *Paul the Apostle*, 145.
210. Beker, *Paul the Apostle*, 145.
211. Beker, *Paul the Apostle*, 151–52.
212. Beker, *Paul the Apostle*, 150–51.
213. Beker, *Paul the Apostle*, 149.

travail because it longs for its redemption from decay (Rom. 8:20)."[214] When the glory of God breaks into this fallen world, it will not destroy the world but "break off its present structure of death, because it aims to transform the cosmos rather than to confirm its ontological nothingness."[215] The beginning of this transformation is marked by the resurrection of Christ—its historical reality being therefore crucial to Paul, as it represents the end "in history," not simply the end "of history."[216] As such, Paul understands faith as "the ability to sustain the contradiction between present reality and future hope and to live out of that tension."[217]

Beker regarded the concept of the future resurrection of the dead as unintelligible apart from the end-time apocalyptic thought-world to which it belongs.[218] Resurrection belongs to the new age to come and is inherently part of the re-creation of all reality. "Thus, the resurrection of Christ, the coming reign of God, and the future resurrection of the dead belong together."[219] The resurrection of Christ therefore represents his enthronement to heavenly lordship and foreshadows the apocalyptic general resurrection of the dead and the transformation of the created world.[220] To ignore the apocalyptic character of the resurrection of Christ would be to turn it into something radically different—an event "in the midst of history rather than at the end of history for the sake of history's transformation."[221]

Beker likewise claimed that Paul's interpretation of the death of Christ was remarkably apocalyptic—it marked the defeat of the apocalyptic powers, signified the final judgment of the old age, and is inseparably connected to the resurrection of Christ, which is absolutely an apocalyptic-cosmic event, inaugurating the cosmic triumph of God.[222] The death of Christ overpowered the ontological powers of sin, the law, and the flesh—all of which are under the sovereign rule of death.[223] In the cross of Christ, the world itself is judged, along with the forces that rule it. It marks the finality of the old age, just as his resurrection marks the birth of the new.[224] Thus Beker regarded the death and resurrection of Christ to form together the centerpiece of Paul's apocalyptic

---

214. Beker, *Paul the Apostle*, 149.
215. Beker, *Paul the Apostle*, 149.
216. Beker, *Paul the Apostle*, 150.
217. Beker, *Paul the Apostle*, 356.
218. Beker, *Paul the Apostle*, 153.
219. Beker, *Paul the Apostle*, 153.
220. Beker, *Paul the Apostle*, 153.
221. Beker, *Paul the Apostle*, 155.
222. Beker, *Paul the Apostle*, 189.
223. Beker, *Paul the Apostle*, 189.
224. Beker, *Paul the Apostle*, 191, 206–7.

thought: "Paul's soteriological apocalyptic is determined by the theocentric focus of the death and resurrection of Christ."[225]

Following Käsemann, Beker regarded the "righteousness of God" in Paul's writings as an apocalyptic formulation, denoting the victory of God and his cosmic act of redemption.[226] God's righteousness "not only acquits the sinner but also abolishes the power of sin by transferring us to the dominion of the lordship of Christ."[227] The righteousness of God therefore inaugurates the apocalyptic destiny of creation and establishes the domain in which believers will live according to the norms of the new world.[228] Similarly, Beker described grace as an event rather than "a private line to a divine reservoir of indiscriminate graciousness that increases in proportion to the increase of evil."[229] As an event, grace marks a new epoch and dominion antithetical to the power of sin. This apocalyptic meaning of grace therefore cuts across Western, "privatistic" notions and refers to a cosmic power and the domain of our life in Christ.[230]

After addressing the eschatological significance of "in Christ" language, the Spirit, and the church, Beker turned to the problem of Israel. Contrary to popular interpretations of Paul, Beker insisted that the church does not displace Israel.[231] Indeed, Israel's strategic position in salvation-history is not limited to the past era, but it remains "a distinct entity in the future of God's purpose."[232] In this way, Paul's mission to the gentiles is related to the salvation of Israel and is not a turning away from Israel.[233] Instead, according to Beker the apostle Paul believes that Israel will enter the kingdom of God as a people once the gentile mission has been fulfilled (Rom. 11:25–26).[234] Israel remains God's special people subsequent to Christ and is not absorbed into the church—the church is not the new Israel.[235]

2.11 ANDREW LINCOLN (1981)

In his study *Paradise Now and Not Yet*, Andrew Lincoln gave attention to Paul's cosmological language and imagery as key components of his eschatological vision. In Paul's writings the message of salvation is presented through the

---

225. Beker, *Paul the Apostle*, 211.
226. Beker, *Paul the Apostle*, 262.
227. Beker, *Paul the Apostle*, 262.
228. Beker, *Paul the Apostle*, 263.
229. Beker, *Paul the Apostle*, 265.
230. Beker, *Paul the Apostle*, 265.
231. Beker, *Paul the Apostle*, 332.
232. Beker, *Paul the Apostle*, 333.
233. Beker, *Paul the Apostle*, 335.
234. Beker, *Paul the Apostle*, 335.
235. Beker, *Paul the Apostle*, 336.

language of a cosmic drama that cannot be separated out from it.[236] Such language includes vertical and horizontal referents along with spatial and temporal categories—so that "eschatology involves heaven as well as the Last Day."[237] The study of eschatology should not be restricted to the latter, as is so often the case. According to Lincoln, heaven is related to the two-age structure of Paul's eschatology, and his language about it has close ties with apocalyptic literature.[238]

Examining first the language of the heavenly Jerusalem as found in Galatians, Lincoln pointed to its rich conceptual prefiguring in Old Testament prophecy with its hopes for a new, eschatological Jerusalem.[239] He pointed out that passages such as Isaiah 2; 54:10–14; 60–62; Ezekiel 40–48; and Zechariah 12–14, which depict a new and glorified Jerusalem as the center of the world to which the nations will come in the last days, nevertheless remain strongly in continuity with Israel's national hopes centering around the earthly Jerusalem.[240] However, Isaiah 65:17–25 is a key text in which the new Jerusalem transcends earthly bounds and participates in the new heavens and new earth. This vision stands as a starting point for the later development of a heavenly Jerusalem—a concept that is barely found in embryonic form in the Old Testament.[241]

Later Judaism evidences several traditions about a glorified, earthly Jerusalem (cf. Tob 13:9ff; 14:7; Jub. 4:26; Sib. Or. V, 250ff; 414–433; Ps. Sol. 11.8; T. Levi 10.5; T. Dan 5.7, 12).[242] Lincoln drew attention to the example of 1 Enoch 90:28f, which views the new Jerusalem as a renewal of the old—the old Jerusalem is taken away, and God brings a new one, but it had not preexisted in heaven. Other similar examples of a renewed Jerusalem can be found in Qumran literature (cf. 1QM XII, 13ff; 4QpIsa^a 1, 7, 11 and the Aramaic fragments 1Q32 which describe the new Jerusalem).[243] Such texts attest to the hope for a new age with Jerusalem as the earthly capital of an earthly state.[244] Paul's concept of the heavenly Jerusalem has more in common with the apocalyptic notion of a new, eschatological Jerusalem as found in 2 Baruch and 4 Ezra, though they postdate Paul's writings. However, unlike those two texts, Galatians 4 holds no hope for the present Jerusalem since it is classed as part of the old age, which is

---

236. Andrew T. Lincoln, *Paradise Now and Not Yet: Studies in the Role of the Heavenly Dimension in Paul's Thought with Special Reference to his Eschatology*, SNTSMS 43 (Cambridge: Cambridge University Press, 1981), 5.
237. Lincoln, *Paradise Now and Not Yet*, 5.
238. Lincoln, *Paradise Now and Not Yet*, 8.
239. Lincoln, *Paradise Now and Not Yet*, 18.
240. Lincoln, *Paradise Now and Not Yet*, 18–19.
241. Lincoln, *Paradise Now and Not Yet*, 18–19.
242. Lincoln, *Paradise Now and Not Yet*, 19.
243. Lincoln, *Paradise Now and Not Yet*, 19.
244. Lincoln, *Paradise Now and Not Yet*, 19.

subject to the law, sin, and death.[245] The heavenly Jerusalem is in fact viewed as "the new age depicted in spatial terms."[246]

Lincoln turned to examine the heavenly dimension in 1 Corinthians 15, in which Paul describes both Christ and believers as heavenly.[247] Though the Corinthians could not imagine that the human body should belong to the new age, Paul asserts that the Spirit now at work in them would rule over them at the resurrection, such that their bodies would no longer be subject to weakness or perishability.[248] It is in this sense that believers' bodies will become "spiritual"—not ethereal or immaterial.[249] In the end, believers are heavenly "not because they came from heaven or are going to heaven, but because they are 'in Christ' (cf. verse 22) and share his resurrection life."[250] This means that their heavenliness is not entirely futuristic and that they will share the mode of existence that the body of Christ now possesses.[251] This is achieved through the Spirit who constitutes the link with heaven. If the Corinthians are spiritual, they are also heavenly, "for the Spirit provides a foretaste of the fullness of heavenly life."[252]

Next Lincoln addresses the heavenly-house and the third-heaven concepts found in 2 Corinthians 4:16–5:10 and 12:1–10 respectively. Paul anticipates sharing in heavenly glory and possessing the heavenly body,[253] guaranteed by the pledge of the Spirit which "reinforces the notion that heavenly embodiment is the consummation and goal of Christian existence."[254] The Spirit is the connection between present-day renewal within believers and its consummation in the heavenly body.[255] Regarding the cosmological significance of Paul's "third heaven," Lincoln remains ambivalent but suggests that Paul may simply have taken over the term as a variant designation for paradise.[256] It is not some ethereal space intended for cosmological speculation but an experience of heaven that had been opened by Christ in order to confirm Paul's hope that the heavenly man will restore paradise.[257]

---

245. Lincoln, *Paradise Now and Not Yet*, 22.
246. Lincoln, *Paradise Now and Not Yet*, 25.
247. Lincoln, *Paradise Now and Not Yet*, 33.
248. Lincoln, *Paradise Now and Not Yet*, 42.
249. Lincoln, *Paradise Now and Not Yet*, 42.
250. Lincoln, *Paradise Now and Not Yet*, 50.
251. Lincoln, *Paradise Now and Not Yet*, 51.
252. Lincoln, *Paradise Now and Not Yet*, 53–54.
253. Lincoln, *Paradise Now and Not Yet*, 65.
254. Lincoln, *Paradise Now and Not Yet*, 67.
255. Lincoln, *Paradise Now and Not Yet*, 67.
256. Lincoln, *Paradise Now and Not Yet*, 78.
257. Lincoln, *Paradise Now and Not Yet*, 84.

In Philippians 3:20–21, heaven is regarded as the state or commonwealth of believers.[258] This is the place from which Christ rules from God's right hand, and thus his commonwealth governs the believer's life.[259] The spatial dimension of heavenly reality relates to temporal elements in Paul's eschatology in that "heaven features in the proleptic enjoyment of eschatological salvation in the period between the individual's death and the Parousia."[260] But heaven is not the final goal of salvation; "the heavenly realm is not some static eternal state but rather part of the forward moving history of salvation."[261] Being with Christ in heaven is a temporary state preceding the consummation of salvation when Christ comes in glory *from* heaven. He does not take believers *back* to heaven with him but accomplishes "the redemption of the body as believers are clothed with heavenly glory (3:21)."[262]

In Colossians, resurrection is heavenly life due to union with Christ—by participating in his resurrection, believers participate in the life of the realm above.[263] Similarly, believers are dead to the sphere of sin because they are united to Christ in his death.[264] For Paul, the heavenliness of Christian existence "does not mean that real life is in some other realm and human life on earth is therefore doomed to be a shadowy inauthentic existence."[265] Rather, Paul insists on the reality of the transcendent dimension with Christ and on the fullness he expects for human life here and now. Because believers participate in the triumph of the exalted Christ over the cosmic powers, they are able to live the heavenly life within the structures of the world.[266]

Of all the letters in the Pauline corpus, Lincoln pointed to Ephesians as exhibiting the most pervasive integration of the concept of the heavenly dimension.[267] The letter's Christology focuses on Christ's exalted state in the heavenlies, which shapes the status of believers and the church. According to Lincoln, Paul's view of heaven was derived from the opening statement of Genesis—"In the beginning God created the heavens and the earth" (Gen 1:1), thus establishing the structure of created reality as composed of two major parts.[268] The concept developed from there:

---

258. Lincoln, *Paradise Now and Not Yet*, 97–99.
259. Lincoln, *Paradise Now and Not Yet*, 101.
260. Lincoln, *Paradise Now and Not Yet*, 106.
261. Lincoln, *Paradise Now and Not Yet*, 106.
262. Lincoln, *Paradise Now and Not Yet*, 106.
263. Lincoln, *Paradise Now and Not Yet*, 124.
264. Lincoln, *Paradise Now and Not Yet*, 128.
265. Lincoln, *Paradise Now and Not Yet*, 130.
266. Lincoln, *Paradise Now and Not Yet*, 130–31.
267. Lincoln, *Paradise Now and Not Yet*, 135.
268. Lincoln, *Paradise Now and Not Yet*, 140.

That part known as the heavens could be thought of in terms of the atmospheric heaven (e.g. Ps. 147:8) or firmament (e.g. Gen. 1:7, 14). As the upper part of the cosmos it also came to stand for the dwelling-place of God, pointing beyond its own createdness to the divine transcendence (e.g. Ps. 2:4). Not only so, but the upper limits of the firmament were regarded as concealing a presently invisible created spiritual order (e.g. 2 Kgs. 6:17; Job. 1:6; Zech. 3:1). . . . Here heaven had a priority as the upper and controlling element and yet in its created aspect it was involved in God's plan for the ages, for in Jahweh's acts of judgment the heavens as well as the earth are shaken (cf. Isa. 51:6; Amos 8:9; Hag. 2:6) and Isaiah 65:17 and 66:22 can speak of the creation of a new heaven and a new earth, pointing to cosmic renewal.[269]

In Ephesians, spatial (cosmic) and temporal (eschatological) categories are combined such that God has ordered history to bring about the fullness of the times and has exalted Christ to heaven as cosmic Lord. There is thus an inseparable connection between heaven and earth; "this summing up of the cosmos in Christ has its 'already' and its 'not yet' aspects."[270]

Lincoln concluded his study by acknowledging frequent correspondences between Paul's references to heaven and Jewish apocalyptic writings:

In several passages we have seen links between heaven and the general apocalyptic concept of the two ages. More specifically we found apocalyptic references for the heavenly Jerusalem (Gal. 4:26), Paradise and the third heaven (2 Cor. 12), the age to come present in heaven and entered at death (2 Cor. 5; Phil. 1:23), the hope laid up in heaven (Col. 1:5), the 'hidden-revealed' motif and the theme of glory (Col. 3:1–4), the mystery of God's cosmic plan (Eph 1:10), the session in heaven (Eph. 2:6), the heavenly temple (Eph. 2:20ff) and the cosmic battle (Eph. 6:10ff).[271]

However, it is clear to Lincoln that Paul modified the sharp contrast between the two eschatological ages that is regularly found in apocalyptic writings. The view of history as two successive, antithetical ages is inappropriate given that for Paul the Messiah had already arrived, and in him the age to come was now a present reality.[272] Though he did not write apocalypses or apocalyptic

---

269. Lincoln, *Paradise Now and Not Yet*, 140–41.
270. Lincoln, *Paradise Now and Not Yet*, 144.
271. Lincoln, *Paradise Now and Not Yet*, 169.
272. Lincoln, *Paradise Now and Not Yet*, 170.

timetables, Paul drew on apocalyptic perspectives for his thought and in this sense may be regarded as an apocalypticist.[273]

2.12 Martinus C. de Boer (1988)

In his monograph *The Defeat of Death*, Martinus C. de Boer examined the meaning of "death" in 1 Corinthians 15 and Romans as "the basic clue to any proper definition of Paul's apocalyptic eschatology."[274] At the same time, de Boer claimed that Paul's apocalyptic eschatology provides the basic clue to what *death* means in his theology. In other words, de Boer employed a recursive method by which Paul's treatment of death helps to define his apocalyptic eschatology, and his apocalyptic eschatology informs his understanding of death.[275] The term *apocalyptic eschatology* is a construct of scholars who discern conceptual affinities between Paul's eschatology and Jewish eschatological expectations that are understood as "apocalyptic."[276] In particular, de Boer focused on the eschatological dualism of the two ages—"this age" and "the age to come," which he regarded as the fundamental characteristic of all apocalyptic eschatology.[277] De Boer demonstrated Paul's personification of death as an enemy alongside the principalities and powers in 1 Corinthians 15:24–26 and as a cosmic monarch in Romans 5:14, 17, and 21. Such personification "provides *prima facie* support for the hypothesis that death is for Paul a cosmological/apocalyptic power."[278]

De Boer surveyed Jewish texts from ca. 200 BCE to ca. 100 CE that demonstrate the dualism of the two ages—that is, they exhibit apocalyptic eschatology whether or not such works are apocalypses in the literary sense.[279] For de Boer, a work is regarded "apocalyptic" in relation to the idea of divine revelation—drawing on the etymology of the word. Such revelation can be found in diverse literary forms, not just apocalypses.[280] Having surveyed the relevant Jewish texts, de Boer demonstrated three interrelated concepts of death found within them. Physical death and moral death are prefigurations of eschatological death. That is, "eschatological death is an extension or a confirmation of physical and moral death and at the same time the dualistic antithesis of eternal or eschatological life."[281] These three meanings of death are united by the theological

---

273. Lincoln, *Paradise Now and Not Yet*, 178–79.
274. Martinus C. de Boer, *The Defeat of Death: Apocalyptic Eschatology in 1 Corinthians 15 and Romans 5*, JSNTSup 22 (Sheffield: JSOT, 1988), 7.
275. De Boer, *Defeat of Death*, 7.
276. De Boer, *Defeat of Death*, 7.
277. De Boer, *Defeat of Death*, 7.
278. De Boer, *Defeat of Death*, 35.
279. De Boer, *Defeat of Death*, 40.
280. De Boer, *Defeat of Death*, 40.
281. De Boer, *Defeat of Death*, 84.

notion that death relates to the relationship of human beings to God, and in particular death "characterizes this relationship as one of *separation*."[282]

De Boer also discerned two distinct forms of Jewish apocalyptic eschatology, which he called "tracks"—cosmological apocalyptic eschatology (track 1) and forensic apocalyptic eschatology (track 2).[283] In the latter, the notion of evil angelic powers or cosmological forces is absent, downplayed, or outright rejected. Emphasis falls on human responsibility for sin and death is regarded as divine punishment for sin. The ages of Jewish apocalyptic eschatology are basically linear, temporal, and sequential.[284] In the former, the two ages are predominantly spatial, confronting each other as conflicting spheres of power. This age is controlled by suprahuman cosmological powers that dominate human beings, challenging the sovereignty of God. The emphasis falls on the subjugation of human beings to such evil powers who lead the human world into sin.[285]

Turning to 1 Corinthians 15, de Boer pointed to its Adam-Christ typology as an expression of apocalyptic eschatology with its dualistic contrast between two ages that are cosmic in scope. "Both the 'problem' (death) and the 'solution' (resurrection of the dead) are cosmically conceived."[286] By setting the two ages of Adam and Christ against each other, Paul implies that death is the dualistic antithesis of the eschatological life promised in the gospel.[287] Death is a cosmic problem that must be viewed in light of the cosmic solution—the resurrected Christ, the firstfruits of those who have fallen asleep.[288] Moreover, the reign of Christ is fundamentally concerned with the destruction of death and the resurrection of the dead—"that and nothing else."[289] Behind the reality of human death and the promise of resurrection, "there is an apocalyptic confrontation of cosmic proportions between God's Messiah and the power of death which has subjugated and alienated all human beings from God."[290]

Turning to Romans 5, de Boer claimed that the motif of death in 5:12–21 expresses the "discontinuity between the world of Adam and God, between this age and the age to come."[291] This cosmological characterization of death goes together with the similar understanding of sin. All of human history is regarded

---

282. De Boer, *Defeat of Death*, 84 (italics original).
283. De Boer, *Defeat of Death*, 84.
284. De Boer, *Defeat of Death*, 182.
285. De Boer, *Defeat of Death*, 182.
286. De Boer, *Defeat of Death*, 114.
287. De Boer, *Defeat of Death*, 114.
288. De Boer, *Defeat of Death*, 114.
289. De Boer, *Defeat of Death*, 126.
290. De Boer, *Defeat of Death*, 139.
291. De Boer, *Defeat of Death*, 169.

as a monolithic whole over which sin and death reign together as cosmological powers,[292] while the Mosaic law is unable to remedy the cosmological power of sin.[293] Thus in Romans 5:12–21 we see two conflicting orbs of cosmological power—sin and death versus righteousness and life.[294]

De Boer argued that the universality of the reign of sin and death is matched by the universality of salvation in Christ. Statements such as "'grace abounded for the many [all],' 'justification of life for all human beings,' 'the many will be made righteous,' or 'grace more than abounded' also apply equally to all humanity before Christ as to all humanity after Christ."[295] This universalism of salvation undercuts any notion of human contribution to salvation and acknowledges that the all-powerful reign of sin and death means that Adamic humanity is not able to evaluate or accept an "offer" of salvation. Rather, "grace is God's power of salvation and takes effect at God's initiative."[296] While Paul does distinguish between believers and unbelievers, such dualism is provisional. The main benefit of being a believer is the ability to know God now, to experience the Spirit and the blessings of the new age of righteousness and peace ahead of time, as it were.[297]

In the final analysis, only God is able to rescue humanity from its cosmological enslavement to sin and death:

> Against the powers of sin and death only Christ is of any avail. For the strange—and apocalyptic—import of the gospel is that God destroys the power of sin to effect death precisely at the point at which sin seems to have triumphed, in the crucifixion of Christ. In this event, the condemnation of the whole world to the reign of death is revealed. Yet in this event the whole world is also graciously rectified and placed in the realm of life.[298]

2.13 BEN WITHERINGTON (1992)

In his book *Jesus, Paul, and the End of the World*, Ben Witherington explored the degree of continuity between Jesus and Paul's eschatological thought.[299] On the question of apocalyptic, he did not find compelling evidence that either figure could be described as such—at least not in the traditional Jewish sense.

---

292. De Boer, *Defeat of Death*, 173.
293. De Boer, *Defeat of Death*, 169.
294. De Boer, *Defeat of Death*, 173.
295. De Boer, *Defeat of Death*, 174.
296. De Boer, *Defeat of Death*, 174.
297. De Boer, *Defeat of Death*, 175.
298. De Boer, *Defeat of Death*, 185.
299. Ben Witherington III, *Jesus, Paul, and the End of the World: A Comparative Study in New Testament Eschatology* (Downers Grove, IL: InterVarsity Press, 1992).

Neither Jesus nor Paul concentrate on revealing heavenly battles, scenarios or journeys. Nor is there any indication that they saw themselves as reliant on angel visitations to provide them with the substance of their revelations. Both Jesus and Paul, insofar as they talk of cosmological change at all, do not focus on this matter, but rather focus on salvation/redemption, either of the individual or of God's people.[300]

Instead, Witherington acknowledged that many who regard Jesus and Paul's worldview as apocalyptic do so because of the imminence of the end of the world that supposedly characterizes their thought.[301] But he was likewise critical of such an approach since the language of imminence "does not seem to be a *sine qua non* of apocalyptic literature, or for that matter of an apocalyptic worldview, if we accept the authors of the heavenly ascent apocalypses as examples of those who manifest such a worldview."[302] Moreover, a careful analysis of the Gospels and Pauline literature reveals that "Jesus and Paul considered the imminence of the end possible in their era but not a certainty."[303] Consequently, Witherington concluded that it would be better to say that Jesus and Paul manifest Jewish eschatological worldviews that include some apocalyptic elements, rather than apocalyptic worldviews as such.[304]

On the question of the imminence of the end, Witherington pointed especially to the "thief in the night" motif, which connotes "both possible imminence and also uncertainty about the timing of the coming of the key figure in question."[305] This, and other evidence, points to the conclusion that "neither Jesus nor Paul seem to have taught that the end of the world or the parousia of the Son of Man (which Paul calls the return of the Lord) would *definitely* come within their lifetimes or within a generation."[306] Certainly they affirm the possibility that the end might come soon and that believers ought to keep watch and be prepared, but claims that Paul taught that the return of the Lord would occur in his lifetime are overstated.[307]

According to Witherington, Paul's concept of the kingdom of God (the *basileia*) was an already and not-yet matter, but Paul did not suggest that anyone enters or inherits the *basileia* in the present.[308] However, the *power* of the *basileia*

---

300. Witherington, *Jesus, Paul, and the End of the World*, 17.
301. Witherington, *Jesus, Paul, and the End of the World*, 18.
302. Witherington, *Jesus, Paul, and the End of the World*, 18–19.
303. Witherington, *Jesus, Paul, and the End of the World*, 19.
304. Witherington, *Jesus, Paul, and the End of the World*, 19.
305. Witherington, *Jesus, Paul, and the End of the World*, 45.
306. Witherington, *Jesus, Paul, and the End of the World*, 47–48 (italics original).
307. Witherington, *Jesus, Paul, and the End of the World*, 47–48.
308. Witherington, *Jesus, Paul, and the End of the World*, 51–52, 57.

is evident in the present, along with the effects of that power on people.[309] In its present manifestation, the *basileia* is "primarily spiritual in character and effect, not material or physical."[310] It has to do with the spiritual transformation of human beings in the present, not the physical transformation of the cosmos.[311] The material transformation of people and the world, however, will occur in the future with the return of Christ, the resurrection of believers, and the renewal of the world.[312] In order to participate in that future *basileia*, it is necessary to respond to its present presence and power as manifested in Jesus and his ministry.[313] Clearly Paul did not equate the *basileia* with the present community of God. The presence of the *basileia* through God's dynamic saving activity brings forth a community, but this is not identical to the *basileia*.[314] Paul did not discuss the relationship between the *ekklesia* (the community of God's people) and the *basileia*, but it is reasonable to conclude that he never treats the two synonymously.[315] While the *basileia* changes human lives and makes the *ekklesia* possible, the focus is especially on individual transformation, while the focus of the *ekklesia* is the group that results from such individual transformations.[316]

Regarding the day of the Lord, Paul used parousia language for its royal and divine connotations, while drawing primarily on the Jewish *Yom Yahweh* (day of Yahweh) material for the conceptual background of his "day of the Lord" imagery.[317] With respect to the resurrection of the dead, Witherington pointed to Nickelsburg's observation that the idea of a general resurrection of *all* dead (not just the believing dead) is rarely found in Jewish literature prior to the end of the first century CE (with Wis 1–6 and Dan 12:2 as possible exceptions).[318] When universal resurrection is addressed, its function is the facilitation of final justice for all. By contrast, the resurrection of the righteous functions for vindication, rescue, or reward (e.g., 2 Macc 7). This is Paul's thrust in discussions about resurrection (Rom 1:4; 1 Cor 15).[319]

Regarding the so-called intermediate state, Witherington regards such a concept evident in 2 Corinthians 5:1–10, even though it is only alluded to in passing.[320] Paul found it a mixed blessing, since it involves the bliss of going and

---

309. Witherington, *Jesus, Paul, and the End of the World*, 57.
310. Witherington, *Jesus, Paul, and the End of the World*, 57–58.
311. Witherington, *Jesus, Paul, and the End of the World*, 57–58.
312. Witherington, *Jesus, Paul, and the End of the World*, 58.
313. Witherington, *Jesus, Paul, and the End of the World*, 68.
314. Witherington, *Jesus, Paul, and the End of the World*, 77.
315. Witherington, *Jesus, Paul, and the End of the World*, 82.
316. Witherington, *Jesus, Paul, and the End of the World*, 82.
317. Witherington, *Jesus, Paul, and the End of the World*, 178.
318. Witherington, *Jesus, Paul, and the End of the World*, 186.
319. Witherington, *Jesus, Paul, and the End of the World*, 186.
320. Witherington, *Jesus, Paul, and the End of the World*, 207.

being with the Lord, but also "life without a body is not life in the full sense of the word but a form of nakedness that is to some degree embarrassing and no happy final state of affairs."[321] The final resurrection of the body, rather, is the goal for believers, and this provides both the basis and the dramatic climax of salvation. "In the end, being a Christian means being like Christ not only in character here and now, but also in body and in power then and there."[322] Indeed, the resurrection is the basis of ethics, Christian living, and Christology.[323]

2.14 JÜRGEN MOLTMANN (1996)

In his major work *The Coming of God*, Jürgen Moltmann argued that Christian eschatology is not concerned with apocalyptic "final solutions" but with the new creation of all things.[324] It is "the remembered hope of the raising of the crucified Christ" and thus deals with fresh beginnings.[325] Moltmann took a decidedly christological approach to eschatology that is evident in its personal, historical, and cosmic dimensions, reframing it in light of the resurrection, so that "*in the end is the beginning.*"[326]

Rather than reducing biblical eschatology to matters relating to the human soul and its salvation or otherwise, Moltmann posed the question, "When will God show himself in his divinity to heaven and earth?" The answer is found in the promise of the coming of God so that the whole earth is full of his glory.[327] Limiting eschatology to issues related to human salvation ignores the fact that God promises to deliver all created things and to fill the new creation with peace.[328] Thus eschatology is centered around *hope*: the hope for God's glory, for the new creation of the world, for the history of human beings with the earth, and for their resurrection and eternal life.[329]

Contrary to Cullmann on the one hand and Barth on the other, Moltmann argued that the eschaton "is neither the future of time nor timeless eternity. It is God's coming and his arrival."[330] In this eschatological coming of God, God and time are linked such that his being in the world has to be thought of

---

321. Witherington, *Jesus, Paul, and the End of the World*, 207–8.
322. Witherington, *Jesus, Paul, and the End of the World*, 214.
323. Witherington, *Jesus, Paul, and the End of the World*, 214.
324. See also his *In the End—the Beginning: The Life of Hope*, trans. Margaret Kohl (Minneapolis: Fortress, 2004), and his *Ethics of Hope*, trans. Margaret Kohl (Minneapolis: Fortress, 2012).
325. Jürgen Moltmann, *The Coming of God: Christian Eschatology*, trans. Margaret Kohl (Minneapolis: Fortress, 1996), xi.
326. Moltmann, *Coming of God*, xi (italics original).
327. Moltmann, *Coming of God*, xv.
328. Moltmann, *Coming of God*, xvi.
329. Moltmann, *Coming of God*, xvi.
330. Moltmann, *Coming of God*, 22.

eschatologically, just as the future of time has to be understood theologically.[331] The advent of God does not *enter* time nor remain *outside* time; rather, the eschaton represents "a change in the transcendental conditions of time. With the coming of God's glory, future time ends and eternal time begins."[332]

On the theme of personal eschatology, Moltmann criticized the notion that life in this world is nothing more than a preparation for the life to come. That is "a refusal to live, and a religious fraud"—even "religious atheism"—since God is a lover of life.[333] Nevertheless, human resurrection is not a return to this life but an entry into eternal life. In this sense, Christ's resurrection is not a historical event but "an eschatological happening to the crucified Christ."[334] In him, the process of the resurrection of the dead has already begun, is continued in the Spirit, and will be completed in the physical raising of the dead.[335] And in the Spirit, believers experience this life now as "at once mortal *and* immortal, as at once transient *and* intransient, as at once temporal *and* eternal."[336]

Regarding the intermediate state, Moltmann affirmed an intermediate time between Christ's resurrection and the general resurrection of the dead. This is not like an empty waiting room but "is filled by the lordship of Christ over the dead and the living, and by the experience of the Spirit."[337] The dead in Christ are not separated from God, nor are they sleeping, nor are they yet risen. They are "with Christ"—but what does this mean?[338] Moltmann likened the fellowship of Christ to two semicircles—one representing the community of the living, the other the community of the dead. We who are living are unable to imagine the space of the dead in community with Christ because we have not experienced it, but death does not cause disconnection with his community; "we simply move to the other half of the circle, so to speak, and will then experience the fellowship of Christ from its other side."[339]

Concerning the fate of those without hope in Christ, Moltmann argued against annihilationism on the basis that destruction and eternal nothingness seem incompatible with the coming omnipresence of God. He likens the "disappearing" of the lost to the actions of murder squads in military dictatorships rather than to God. "The God of the Bible is the Creator, not simultaneously

---

331. Moltmann, *Coming of God*, 23.
332. Moltmann, *Coming of God*, 26.
333. Moltmann, *Coming of God*, 50.
334. Moltmann, *Coming of God*, 69.
335. Moltmann, *Coming of God*, 69.
336. Moltmann, *Coming of God*, 71 (italics original).
337. Moltmann, *Coming of God*, 104.
338. Moltmann, *Coming of God*, 105.
339. Moltmann, *Coming of God*, 106.

the Destroyer, like the Indian god Shiva."[340] On the question of universalism, Moltmann acknowledged that universal salvation *and* a double outcome of judgment are well attested biblically.[341] In favor of universalism, Moltmann pointed to the meaning of the Greek word *aiōnios* and the Hebrew *olam*, which both refer to time without a fixed end, but not "eternity" in an absolute sense.[342] On the other hand, universalism seems to make God's grace cheap grace, imposes bounds on God's freedom, and dissipates the significance of faith's decision.[343] In the end, however, Moltmann affirms a transformative type of universalism:

> In the divine Judgment all sinners, the wicked and the violent, the murderers and the children of Satan, the Devil and the fallen angels will be liberated and saved from their deadly perdition through transformation into their true, created being, because God remains true to himself, and does not give up what he has once created affirmed, or allow it to be lost.[344]

On the theme of cosmic eschatology, Moltmann asserted its necessity because "there are not two Gods, a Creator God and a Redeemer God. There is one God. It is for his sake that the unity of redemption and creation has to be thought."[345] Christian hope is not for the restoration of the original creation but for creation's final consummation. The end does correspond to the beginning—since it represents the completion of the beginning, not its replacement—but it is much more than the beginning.[346] Thus *creation ex nihilo* is completed in the eschatological *creation ex vetere*—the creation out of the old.[347]

The final section of the book addresses the theme of glory—divine eschatology. The glorification of God is the ultimate purpose of creation.[348] The glory of God expresses itself in the communication of his own fullness of life, following upon the eternal day of resurrection.[349] His glory is the feast of eternal joy, just as the Gospels regularly compare it with a wedding feast.[350] Ultimately the creation will be transfigured and glorified by the glory of God:

---

340. Moltmann, *Coming of God*, 109.
341. Moltmann, *Coming of God*, 241.
342. Moltmann, *Coming of God*, 242.
343. Moltmann, *Coming of God*, 242.
344. Moltmann, *Coming of God*, 255.
345. Moltmann, *Coming of God*, 259.
346. Moltmann, *Coming of God*, 264.
347. Moltmann, *Coming of God*, 264.
348. Moltmann, *Coming of God*, 323.
349. Moltmann, *Coming of God*, 336.
350. Moltmann, *Coming of God*, 336.

It is like a great song or a splendid poem or a wonderful dance of his fantasy, for the communication of his divine plenitude. The laughter of the universe is God's delight. It is the universal Easter laughter.[351]

2.15 J. Louis Martyn (1997)

Martyn's 1997 commentary on Galatians was the first major attempt to offer a fully "apocalyptic" exposition of one of Paul's letters.[352] He took his cue from certain vocabulary associated with apocalyptic literature and theology (not least the *apokalypt-* cognate word group) found in the letter. The relevant passages are conventionally addressed together in Martyn's excursus, "Comment #3: Apocalyptic Theology in Galatians."[353]

Martyn pointed to "the distinctly apocalyptic expression 'the present evil age'" in Galatians 1:4b as the first of numerous apocalyptic expressions in the letter.[354] The reference to this present evil age sheds light both on Paul's perception of the human plight as well as what God has accomplished in Christ to deliver humanity from the captivity of this present evil age.[355] Martyn also observed that this reference to a present evil age implies the existence of another age, and indeed the concept of *two ages* is a fundamental apocalyptic schema.[356] In the language of Galatians, the opposite counterpart of "the present evil age" is "the new creation" (Gal 6:15), which Martyn takes as a further indicator of Jewish apocalyptic dualism.[357]

The noun *apokalypsis* and the verb *apokalyptō* are found in Galatians 1:12, 15–16; 2:2; and 3:23. The references in 1:12 and 16 indicate that Paul's gospel "came into being when God apocalypsed Christ to him."[358] Thus was born Paul's christological apocalyptic as God opened his eyes to the risen Lord Jesus Christ, alongside the realization that the old cosmos in which Paul had previously lived "met its end in God's apocalypse of Jesus Christ (cf. 6:14)."[359] Paul's subsequent gospel mission was conducted under the banner of apocalypse as he waged battles for the truth of the gospel.[360]

Martyn noted the explication of the verb *apokalyptō* with the verbs *erchomai*

---

351. Moltmann, *Coming of God*, 339.
352. J. Louis Martyn, *Galatians: A New Translation with Introduction and Commentary*, AB 33A (New York: Doubleday, 1997).
353. Martyn, *Galatians*, 97–105.
354. Martyn, *Galatians*, 97.
355. Martyn, *Galatians*, 97.
356. Martyn, *Galatians*, 98.
357. Martyn, *Galatians*, 98.
358. Martyn, *Galatians*, 99.
359. Martyn, *Galatians*, 99.
360. Martyn, *Galatians*, 99.

("to come [on the scene]") and *exapostellō* "to send [into the scene]" in 4:4 and 4:6 to suggest that the usual translation of *apokalyptō* as "to reveal" or "to unveil" is not an adequate representation of its meaning in Galatians.[361] Rather, in Galatians Paul's apocalyptic is not focused on God's unveiling something previously hidden but that "God has *invaded* the present evil age by sending Christ and his Spirit into it."[362] Thus, according to Martyn, Paul's apocalyptic is more about *invasion* than *revealing*. And this invasion has created two clear epochs in which there was a time "before," the time of imprisonment, and a time "after," the time of deliverance.[363]

Martyn also regarded the "fullness of time" language found in Galatians 4:4 as a clear apocalyptic motif, corresponding to the "present evil age."[364] In this fullness of time, God sent Christ and the Spirit as an invasion into the present evil age. As with all apocalyptic thinkers, Paul viewed liberating redemption as a matter of God's invasive action rather than something that could grow out of the present scene.[365] The cross in particular is viewed by Paul as an instrument of cosmic warfare. In the event of the crucifixion of Christ, "God's war of liberation was commenced and decisively settled, making the cross the foundation of Paul's apocalyptic theology."[366] The apocalyptic death of Jesus marks the turn of the ages and is a vicarious act "for our sins." But Martyn insisted that his death is "oriented not toward personal guilt and forgiveness, but rather toward corporate enslavement and liberation."[367] It was the central deed in God's apocalyptic war that "has already freed us from the malevolent grasp of the present age."[368]

The dispatch of the Spirit of Christ into believers' hearts activates them as soldiers in the field of cosmic battle, so that the church is both God's new creation and the apocalyptic community serving in the front trenches in God's war against the powers of the present evil age.[369] This present time is therefore the juncture of the new creation and the evil age. People now exist in hotly contested territory, "a place of jungle warfare in which battles precipitated by the powers of the new creation are sometimes won (Gal 2:9; 5:10; cf. 2 Cor 2:14; 1 Thess 3:6) and sometimes lost (Gal 2:13; 5:7–8; cf. 2 Cor 2:11; Gal 2:2; 1 Thess 2:16, 18)."[370]

---

361. Martyn, *Galatians*, 99.
362. Martyn, *Galatians*, 99 (italics original).
363. Martyn, *Galatians*, 99.
364. Martyn, *Galatians*, 99.
365. Martyn, *Galatians*, 100.
366. Martyn, *Galatians*, 101.
367. Martyn, *Galatians*, 101.
368. Martyn, *Galatians*, 101.
369. Martyn, *Galatians*, 102.
370. Martyn, *Galatians*, 102.

In this arena, the Spirit and the flesh constitute an apocalyptic antinomy as two opposed orbs of power actively at war with the other. The newly invaded space in which human beings now live cannot remain unchanged.[371]

Finally, Martyn addressed potential objections to reading Galatians apocalyptically, since it contains no reference to the future coming of Christ, to the archangel's cry, the last trumpet, or to the resurrection of the dead.[372] Nor does it contain any of the imagery characteristic of apocalyptic literature. But in the absence of the so-called "grotesque characteristics of apocalyptic," such as earthquakes, beasts, and angel-warriors, Martyn aptly quipped, "The motif of an earthquake lies at the heart of this letter without being literally mentioned."[373] This earthquake represents nothing less than the redemption of the whole of creation, which had been enslaved under the power of the present evil age.[374]

2.16 DOUGLAS CAMPBELL (2009)

Douglas Campbell's *The Deliverance of God* does not focus on eschatology *per se*, but represents a rereading of Paul's entire gospel in "apocalyptic" terms, with special reference to the theme of justification, as expressed by the book's subtitle—*An Apocalyptic Rereading of Justification in Paul*.[375] Campbell did not attempt to show that Paul is an apocalypticist in the traditional sense, as several preceding scholars have sought to do (e.g., Schweitzer, Käsemann, Beker). He did not draw parallels to Jewish apocalyptic literature or theology. Indeed, Campbell did not focus on eschatology specifically except as it relates to justification and Paul's gospel in general. Instead, Campbell used apocalyptic terminology simply to refer to the vertical announcement of God's saving work in Christ.

Campbell spent considerable space critiquing what he called "justification theory," claiming it to be contractual rather than covenantal[376] and flawed by intrinsic difficulties—"problems that it seems to face by virtue of its very construction"[377]—and systematic difficulties—tensions that justification theory produces for major topics of systematic theology.[378] After exploring the questions of Judaism and conversion as they relate to justification theory,[379] Campbell

---

371. Martyn, *Galatians*, 573.
372. Martyn, *Galatians*, 105.
373. Martyn, *Galatians*, 104.
374. Martyn, *Galatians*, 105.
375. Douglas A. Campbell, *The Deliverance of God: An Apocalyptic Rereading of Justification in Paul* (Grand Rapids: Eerdmans, 2009).
376. Campbell, *Deliverance of God*, 15–29.
377. Campbell, *Deliverance of God*, 37, 36–61.
378. Campbell, *Deliverance of God*, 62–95.
379. Campbell, *Deliverance of God*, 96–166.

contended that his apocalyptic reading of Paul transcends both old and new perspectives on Paul.[380] In particular, the participatory and transformational nature of salvation, as articulated in Romans 5–8, represents an alternative soteriological account that collides with justification theory.[381]

Following Käsemann, Campbell regarded an "apocalyptic" interpretation of the righteousness of God as the "eschatological saving action of God," which infuses "the notion of righteousness as a gift *from* God with the power *of* God."[382] It focuses on the sovereignty of God, the unconditional nature of divine action in the world, robust ethical commitment of God's people, and the reality of eschatology—both in the present intervention of God and in the coming consummation.[383] While noting various problems and criticisms of his use of the term *apocalyptic*, Campbell defended the label as denoting "an approach to Paul . . . that ultimately aligns with the concerns and readings of—in this context in particular—Lou Martyn, and that therefore is in sympathy with the alternative texts and soteriological paradigm that he endorses, and sensitive to the tensions that he detects between that paradigm and Justification concerns."[384] Salvation is liberation from the evil powers rather than an assuaging of God's righteous anger at human sin. The atonement delivers humanity from its bondage to evil powers and reconstitutes it in the age to come.[385] In this sense, "the 'participatory' and the 'apocalyptic' Paul are both posited in large measure in opposition to the same underlying problem: the construal of Paul's gospel in terms of Justification."[386]

Campbell concluded the first section of his book by claiming that "*the elimination of Justification theory from Paul's interpretation is vital to his fundamental evangelical integrity.*"[387] The second part deals with some hermeneutical clarifications, such as the nature of reading and recognizing a discourse, as well as ancient distortions in reading and modern dangers.[388] The third section critiques conventional readings of Romans 1–4,[389] concluding that there are no viable solutions to the difficulties generated by the conventional construal of Romans 1–4 with its intrinsic endorsement of justification theory.[390]

---

380. Campbell, *Deliverance of God*, 167–218.
381. Campbell, *Deliverance of God*, 177, 183.
382. Campbell, *Deliverance of God*, 188 (italics original).
383. Campbell, *Deliverance of God*, 189.
384. Campbell, *Deliverance of God*, 191.
385. Campbell, *Deliverance of God*, 192.
386. Campbell, *Deliverance of God*, 192.
387. Campbell, *Deliverance of God*, 217 (italics original).
388. Campbell, *Deliverance of God*, 221–309.
389. Campbell, *Deliverance of God*, 313–466.
390. Campbell, *Deliverance of God*, 466.

Part four offers a rhetorical and apocalyptic rereading of Romans 1–4, in which Campbell claims that Romans 1–3 opposes a rival missionary by presenting the *rival's* position, which is subsequently humiliated through Socratic rhetoric. Thus, "the argument's ringing opening paragraph in 1:18–32 could well be a presentation of his *opponent's* aggressive opening proclamation—an opening that turns out to rebound onto this preacher's own head (see esp. 2:1–5; 3:19), undermining all his subsequent claims."[391] Campbell argued that by rereading Romans 1–3 as the argument of Paul's opponent, thus removing justification theory from the letter, the gospel can simply be a declaration of good news rooted in God's revelation (cf. 1:17; 3:21). All the major difficulties raised by justification theory thus disappear.[392] Part five offers a rereading of Romans 9–14, Galatians, Philippians, and beyond.[393]

Ultimately, Campbell hopes that his apocalyptic rereading of Paul will redeem Paul from his interpreters:

> It seems, then, that a thoroughgoing apocalyptic interpretation of Paul is indeed possible. And if this sweeping reinterpretation can be achieved, we will not only reinforce what is arguably an orthodox and dynamic account of Paul's gospel, but with the very same stroke we will eliminate a massive set of contradictions and tensions from the apostle's thinking, thereby going some way toward restoring if not enhancing his theological integrity. The elimination of so many interpretative problems en route should serve as a strong validation.[394]

2.17 N. T. Wright (2013)

Though N. T. Wright has addressed major eschatological themes in earlier works,[395] his 2013 magnum opus on Paul represents his mature and most up-to-date treatment of Paul's eschatology.[396] On the question of apocalypticism, Wright acknowledged both the vagueness of the term and what it is intended to mean, but also at the same time its significance as "something which Paul really does seem to have made central."[397] His chief problem with the "apocalyptic

---

391. Douglas A. Campbell, "An Apocalyptic Rereading of 'Justification' in Paul: Or, an Overview of the Argument of Douglas Campbell's *The Deliverance of God*—by Douglas Campbell," *ExpTim* 123.8 (2012): 382–93 [391].
392. Campbell, "Apocalyptic Rereading," 391.
393. Campbell, *Deliverance of God*, 765–930.
394. Campbell, *Deliverance of God*, 527–28.
395. See especially N. T. Wright, *Surprised by Hope: Rethinking Heaven, the Resurrection, and the Mission of the Church* (New York: HarperOne, 2008).
396. N. T. Wright, *Paul and the Faithfulness of God* (Minneapolis: Fortress, 2013).
397. Wright, *Paul and the Faithfulness of God*, 40.

Paul" movement is its insistence (to varying degrees) of pitting an apocalyptic worldview against any sense of covenantal and salvation-historical emphases. According to Wright, Jewish apocalyptic literature was both deeply covenantal and firmly salvation-historical,[398] and thus the Jewish sources of apocalypticism were not somehow *a priori* opposed to Jewish covenantalism. The elevation of Paul's apocalyptic instincts must not therefore *a priori* rule out "all sense of a larger narrative within which the story of Jesus the Messiah, the story of Paul himself and the story of the communities he founded. . . . That is to deJudaize the context before we even begin."[399]

The chief purpose of apocalyptic literature—either in Second-Temple Judaism or early Christianity—was "to give its hearers and readers *an alternative frame of reference within which to live their lives*, an alternative narrative to that which the world's power-brokers are putting out, an alternative symbolic universe to reshape their imagination and structure their worldview."[400] While the audience of apocalyptic literature did not expect the stars to fall from the sky, "they did expect the creator God to do extraordinary things for which comets, earthquakes and other portents might be powerful and appropriate metaphors."[401]

In concert with his previous work, Wright reaffirmed Jewish expectation of "life *after* 'life after death.'"[402] First-century Jews assumed a continuation of life of some sort after death (with the exception of the Sadducees). But far more important was "the age to come," which would involve resurrection into God's new creation after a period of being dead.[403] The strong interest in resurrection—especially among the Pharisees—was due to their belief in the creator God "whose faithfulness demanded that he not abandon this creation to chaos. This God would rescue the whole world."[404] Christian hope was of course predicated on the concrete historical fact of the resurrection of Christ, with his body having been thoroughly transformed, leaving behind the possibility of corruption and death.[405] This event was a fresh marker of time, since it announced the dawning of the new age and was "the sign of a freshly inaugurated eschatology: the end of Israel's time of desolation."[406] In this sense, Paul had to reimagine Jewish eschatology with its expectation of the resurrection of all (or at least all the faithful) at the end of history, since now a

---

398. Wright, *Paul and the Faithfulness of God*, 40.
399. Wright, *Paul and the Faithfulness of God*, 461.
400. Wright, *Paul and the Faithfulness of God*, 175 (italics original).
401. Wright, *Paul and the Faithfulness of God*, 175.
402. Wright, *Paul and the Faithfulness of God*, 113 (italics original).
403. Wright, *Paul and the Faithfulness of God*, 113.
404. Wright, *Paul and the Faithfulness of God*, 113.
405. Wright, *Paul and the Faithfulness of God*, 408.
406. Wright, *Paul and the Faithfulness of God*, 408–9.

man had been resurrected in the middle of history.[407] If Jesus of Nazareth had been raised from the dead, then "the resurrection" had come forward into the present, "with Jesus leading the way and everyone else following in due course."[408]

But Wright warned against Cullmann's famous image of D-Day and V-Day—used to illustrate Paul's inaugurated eschatology—supposing that the present time is a matter of a steady advance with the world slowly improving as God or the church engages in a mop-up operation, eliminating remaining pockets of resistance to the rule of God's Messiah.[409] Church history certainly cannot be read that way, but more importantly there is no hint of such a "progressive kingdom" in Paul's writings.[410] The last enemy of death, for example, is not progressively diminished or made a little less potent. Rather, it's final overthrow in the ultimate resurrection of the dead "will be as sudden, new and shocking as was Easter Day itself."[411] But the overthrow of the enslaving evil powers has "been inaugurated in and through the messianic events of Jesus's death and resurrection."[412] These events have achieved rescue from the present evil age, and participation in the age to come is assured for those who are "in the Messiah."[413]

Wright articulated what he termed "creational eschatology," which refers to God the creator's intention to remake the creation, "righting all wrongs and filling the world with his own presence."[414] This differed from a so-called "gnostic" eschatology in which the future sees the created order abandoned rather than rectified.[415] For this ultimate end to occur, human beings must also be "put right." Thus, "anthropological eschatology" involves the renewal and restoration of humanity as a centerpiece for the renewal of the world.[416] Each of these themes points forward to the divine judgment on the last day, which Wright labels "final eschatology."[417] In this Paul affirms basic Jewish beliefs that on a set day God will call the whole world to account and rectify it; that this will see the reconstitution of human beings through their resurrection from the dead; that this will represent the final fulfillment of the Abrahamic covenant in which God promised to bless the whole world through Abraham's

---

407. Wright, *Paul and the Faithfulness of God*, 1061.
408. Wright, *Paul and the Faithfulness of God*, 1062.
409. Wright, *Paul and the Faithfulness of God*, 548.
410. Wright, *Paul and the Faithfulness of God*, 548.
411. Wright, *Paul and the Faithfulness of God*, 548.
412. Wright, *Paul and the Faithfulness of God*, 1068.
413. Wright, *Paul and the Faithfulness of God*, 1069.
414. Wright, *Paul and the Faithfulness of God*, 926.
415. Wright, *Paul and the Faithfulness of God*, 926.
416. Wright, *Paul and the Faithfulness of God*, 926–27.
417. Wright, *Paul and the Faithfulness of God*, 936.

seed; and that the resurrection from the dead will be human beings' ultimate vindication in the legal, forensic sense.[418]

2.18 SYNTHESIS

This chapter has surveyed significant academic contributions concerning Paul's eschatology through the twentieth century to the present day. We must now begin to piece together the various strands of thought that run throughout. Our survey revealed a range of issues, reflecting the prominence they achieved through the last century to now. We will attempt to delineate these issues here and briefly canvas the main positions that scholars have adopted regarding them. The purpose of this synthesis is to sharpen our ability to interact with the history of scholarship in the following chapters by identifying the pivotal issues that will require analysis and give shape to those chapters.

2.18.1 JEWISH ANTECEDENTS

Unlike some other areas of Pauline theology (e.g., union with Christ),[419] the Jewish character of Paul's eschatology has not seriously been challenged in the past hundred years of scholarship.[420] Beginning with Schweitzer's assertion of Paul's indebtedness to late-Jewish apocalyptic, most scholars surveyed either reaffirmed Paul's Jewish eschatological antecedents (even if not late-Jewish apocalyptic, as Schweitzer) or simply accepted it as established. While Bultmann attempted to analyze Paul's cosmic treatment of the death and resurrection of Christ as indebted to pagan mystery religions and gnostic mythology, even he acknowledged the otherwise Jewish character of Paul's eschatological heritage.

The strongest point of comparison to Jewish literature and theology is that of apocalypticism, which will be addressed independently below. Other areas of comparison include Paul's two-age (or two-realm) eschatological framework, his conception of inaugurated eschatology, the resurrection of the righteous, universal judgment, the new creation, and the ultimate glory of God.

It has been observed that the two-age (or two-realm) framework can be seen in Jewish literature contemporary to Paul, and it is commonplace within an apocalyptic mindset. Indeed, for de Boer, the presence of a two-age schema is

---

418. Wright, *Paul and the Faithfulness of God*, 936.
419. See Campbell, *Paul and Union with Christ*.
420. So Frey: "There can be hardly any doubt that motifs and views of Early Christian eschatology are deeply *rooted within the Biblical tradition* and, even more, within the range of traditions and expectations developed in *Second Temple Judaism*. Thus the variety of early Christian concepts can only be understood against the background of a thorough knowledge of the variety within earlier and contemporary Jewish eschatological ideas" (Frey, "New Testament Eschatology," 26).

the key distinguishing feature of apocalypticism. But Paul's chief distinction is to assert that the age to come has already been ushered in with the resurrection of Christ and the outpouring of the Spirit. Thus, Paul's inaugurated eschatology is distinct as he views the new age coexisting with the old by the presence of the Spirit.

It is widely pointed out that Paul's expectation of the resurrection of the righteous is directly inherited from Judaism, but that Paul's distinct views about dying and rising with Christ mean that he views the righteous as having already been raised from the dead spiritually. Their physical resurrection still awaits (as in Judaism), but it is preempted by virtue of union with Christ such that believers already belong to the new age that has already dawned.

Paul shares with Judaism the concept of the universal judgment of God, but again strikes a distinct course because of the resurrection of Christ. In the resurrection of Christ, judgment has already been declared such that Christ is vindicated as righteous. So too are those who are found in Christ—thus they too can now be declared righteous, preempting the final judgment and facing it with confidence.

2.18.2 APOCALYPTICISM

Apocalypticism is the strongest element of Jewish influence on Paul discussed among key scholars. Schweitzer's depiction of Paul as an apocalyptic thinker remains largely unchallenged, though exactly what that means is widely open to interpretation. Affirmed by other early voices such as Vos and Bultmann, the "apocalyptic Paul" dawned afresh with Käsemann and was subsequently championed by Beker, de Boer, Martyn, and Campbell.

However, the two "apocalyptic Paul" eras within scholarship have quite a different nature. The earlier era, beginning with Schweitzer, was more historically oriented, seeking direct parallels between Paul and Jewish apocalyptic literature such as the Book of Enoch, the Psalms of Solomon, and the Apocalypses of Baruch and of Ezra. This led to some conclusions that were roundly rejected by later scholarship, such as Schweitzer's belief that the delay of the parousia represented a major eschatological problem for Paul to solve.

The latter era, beginning with Käsemann, was more general in its approach to the apocalyptic Paul. Rather than focusing on parallels to apocalyptic literature, these scholars tended to identify in Paul's theology certain thrusts that were arguably apocalyptic in nature, such as God's sovereignty (Käsemann), triumph (Beker), invasion (Martyn), the two ages (de Boer), and salvation (Campbell). This strongly "vertical" approach to Paul's apocalypticism has led some to deny (or at least mute) "horizontal" elements such as salvation-historical or covenantal concerns in Paul. It has also come under criticism for its vagueness and quite loose association with what scholars of Judaism would identify as apocalyptic literature and theology.

Of the scholars surveyed in this chapter, Ladd, Witherington, and Wright represent varying levels of dissent concerning the "apocalyptic Paul." Ladd viewed apocalyptic language simply as a vehicle to convey timeless truths about the kingdom of God; it did not necessarily indicate that Paul was an apocalyptic theologian. Witherington was most critical of apocalyptic approaches, concluding that the evidence for such parallels was not compelling and that the main ingredient in Paul's supposed apocalypticism—his apparent belief in the imminence of the parousia—had been overstated. And while Wright affirmed the centrality of apocalypticism for Paul, it is vague and does not contradict the clear salvation-historical and covenantal elements of his thought.

2.18.3 Two Ages and Two Realms

That Paul espoused two ages (temporally conceived) and two realms (spatially conceived) is overwhelmingly supported by scholarly consensus (notwithstanding Cullmann's three ages). None of the scholars surveyed challenge this duality, though it is sometimes perceived differently. Schweitzer, for instance, held that the new age was yet to come with the parousia, and the time between the resurrection of Christ and his return was one of eschatological tension awaiting the dawning of that new messianic age. For others, however, the new age has already come with the resurrection of Christ and the outpouring of the Spirit, and it coexists alongside the old (e.g., Vos, Barth, Cullmann, Käsemann, Ladd, Witherington, Martyn, de Boer, Campbell, Wright). Some use different terminology—such as Martyn's "present evil age" versus "new creation" (because that is the language of Galatians, Martyn's focus)—but the concepts are parallel to the old/new age/realm language used by others.

The reason these two ages can also be described as two realms is because their temporal nature—old and new—brings with them major changes in rule and authority. The old age is dominated by the forces of evil, human captivity, and death. The new age sees the overthrow of these evil forces, the liberation of humanity, and the overturning of death. In such ways, the new age is also a new realm ruled by Christ and marked by righteousness, life, and peace. As Lincoln espoused, Paul's eschatology is therefore vertical and horizontal, with temporal development perceived vertically and change in rule perceived horizontally. The heavenly Jerusalem, for instance, represents the new age in spatial terms.

2.18.4 Inaugurated Eschatology

For most scholars, Paul's two-age/two-realm schema is radically oriented around the resurrection of Christ. That event inaugurated the new age while the old age is still extant, thus creating an overlap of the ages. This is because the resurrection of the dead is an end-time event but has already occurred for Christ "in the middle of time" (Wright). Thus the end has broken into the present.

The two ages coexist in tension, and while the old age still seems dominant to natural eyes, the eyes of faith perceive that the new age has already asserted its victory, which will one day become evident to all. Cullmann's classic D-Day/V-Day analogy articulates this point, but, as Wright comments, it should not be used to understand history as steadily progressing toward final victory. There is no hint of a progressive kingdom in Paul's writings; rather, the final overthrow of death will come with the resurrection of those in Christ, which will be as sudden and shocking as was Easter Day itself.

Believers therefore find their lives determined by this eschatological tension, as their fleshly bodies yet belong to the old age, while the presence of the Spirit within them claims them for the new age. Martyn puts this most evocatively, in concert with his apocalyptic "invasion" theme: the Spirit turns people into God's soldiers deployed in the cosmic battle. Perhaps less evocatively, the life of the believer is now future-oriented (Bultmann), yet already experiences liberation from the powers (Campbell), and is defined by hope (Barth, Moltmann). Such is a certain hope, trusting in the already-accomplished victory of God in Christ, awaiting its final consummation.

2.18.5 The Importance of Eschatology

The essential importance of eschatology within Paul's theological framework is either explicitly or implicitly affirmed by all the scholars surveyed in this chapter. For Schweitzer, eschatology functions like the frame of a spiderweb; without the frame the web cannot maintain its integrity and collapses upon itself. Vos regarded Paul's theology as inextricably eschatological in nature. Cullmann affirmed the central significance of Paul's eschatology, as did Ladd, Sanders, and several others. Käsemann and his followers all interpreted Paul's gospel apocalyptically, thus recognizing the eschatological nature of his central message and its implications.[421]

But what does it mean to affirm the importance of eschatology in Paul's theological thought? Schweitzer and Vos are particularly interesting on this point. Schweitzer's analogy of the spiderweb remains powerful, since the point

---

421. As Frey comments, "there is good reason not to consider eschatology only as a final or even marginal locus of Christian theology but to see it in the centre of Christian faith" (Frey, "New Testament Eschatology," 28).

has to do with the *structure* that eschatology provides for Paul's thought. His two-age eschatological schema provides the arena in which all other theologically significant events take place. Even the death and resurrection of Christ must be fit within it. In this sense, the word *centrality* may not be entirely apt in Schweitzer's case, since Paul's eschatology is not so much central as it is all-pervasive. For Vos, Paul's theology is inextricably eschatological. Eschatology is not one item within his thought but draws in all its fundamental tenets and gives them an eschatological complexion.

2.18.6 THE ESCHATOLOGICAL CHARACTER OF THE DEATH AND RESURRECTION OF CHRIST

Regarding elements within Paul's theological thought that are eschatologically conditioned, the death and resurrection of Christ are prime examples, according to scholarship. Schweitzer and Bultmann described them as cosmic events. Vos, Barth, Moltmann, Wright, and others likewise acknowledge the eschatological character of the death and resurrection of Christ. Again, Käsemann and other similar interpreters naturally took these as major apocalyptic events and thus essentially eschatological in character.

It is important to assess the ways in which the death and resurrection of Christ are to be regarded as eschatological. The "cosmic" angle of Schweitzer and Bultmann recognizes that these events affect cosmological realities, reaching far beyond the scope of human sin and reconciliation. The death and resurrection of Christ overthrow powers and authorities and establish the reign of Christ over sin, death, and the forces of evil. The same focus is emphasized among apocalyptic interpreters, who view the death of Christ as the invasion of God, storming the threshold of the powers, and the resurrection of Christ as God's triumphant victory over them.

Another important aspect in which the death and resurrection of Christ are regarded as eschatological in nature concerns their relationship to the two-age schema of Paul's eschatology. Taken together, Christ's death and resurrection effect and mark the end of the old age and the inauguration of the new. Though the old age remains extant after the death and resurrection of Christ, its days are numbered since its power and grip over humanity have been overthrown. The death of Christ is the power of God, putting opposing powers to open shame. The resurrection inaugurated the new age and the dominion of Christ. In the resurrection of Christ, judgment day and the vindication (or justification) that comes with it have already dawned. It is thus impossible to do justice to Paul's understanding of the death and resurrection of Christ without acknowledging their inextricably eschatological nature.

2.18.7 Judgment, Annihilationism, and Universalism

As for the "last things" elements of Paul's eschatological vision, scholars acknowledge his obvious expectation of God's universal judgment of humanity on the last day. Though that day has already broken into the present through the death and resurrection of Christ, there will be a final expression of judgment subsequent to his parousia. This final judgment invokes one element of scholarly uncertainty and one of debate. The uncertainty concerns whether Paul anticipated a general resurrection of all dead for the purpose of judgment, or only a resurrection of the righteous. Paul does not appear to indicate belief in a general resurrection, which leads some such as Vos and Witherington to doubt that Paul expected such. In addition to the absence of any mention of a general resurrection in Paul's writings, it seems that wider Jewish literature does not push the idea until later in the first century.

A key issue of debate concerning the final judgment is whether it will be according to works—even for believers who are already justified by virtue of sharing in the vindication of Christ, seen in his resurrection. Sanders is the key figure here, advocating "covenantal nomism," in which believers are received into the covenant by faith, and "stay in" by works. While Wright differs in important ways, he likewise affirms Paul's insistence that human works will play a role in the judgment of the righteous. Such views have drawn considerable criticism from various quarters, and the whole question requires careful scrutiny.

Some scholars addressed what happens to those who fall on the wrong side of God's judgment. While not addressing Paul's writings specifically, Moltmann argued against annihilationism on grounds that destruction and nothingness are incompatible with the coming omnipresence of God. Such ultimate destruction is not the work of the creator God of the Bible. Moltmann was more equivocal on the question of universalism, acknowledging biblical and theological support both for universal salvation and a double outcome of judgment (positive and negative). But he finally affirmed a transformative type of universalism in which all sinners—and even the devil and fallen angels—will be liberated and saved through transformation into their true, created beings, since God does not give up on what he has created or allow it to be lost forever. Barth also explored the question of universalism, claiming that it is appropriate to hope and pray that God's compassion would result in ultimate mercy for all, even in the face of significant biblical warrant to believe the opposite.

De Boer was more direct, arguing for universalism on the grounds of Romans 5:12–21 and its apparent insistence that just as all of humanity is enslaved with Adam by the cosmological powers of sin and death, so it is liberated from them in Christ. Adamic humanity is not able to evaluate or accept an "offer" of salvation and so is reliant solely upon the decision and grace of God for salvation applied to all humanity.

2.18.8 HOPE, NEW CREATION, AND GLORY

The themes of hope, new creation, and glory resonate through much of the scholarly literature, since they are indispensable to Paul's teaching. For Barth, hope is likened to Christian faith and love in that it is the object of one's hope that is most significant, especially in the face of the not-yet-fulfilled nature of hope. Despite this nature, the believer cannot live in light of the end except in hope. For Moltmann, eschatology is centered around hope—hope for God's glory, for the new creation, and for resurrection and eternal life.

An essential element of Christian hope is the expectation of the renewal of creation. The cosmic dimensions of Paul's gospel mean that any apocalyptic interpretation necessarily includes a wider view than "personal eschatology," anticipating the restoration of all creation. According to Moltmann, limiting eschatology to human salvation ignores the fact that God has promised to deliver all created things and to fill the new creation with peace. Wright strongly affirmed "creational eschatology," reflecting God the creator's intention to remake the creation through its rectification. Humanity must be renewed and restored as an essential centerpiece of God's renewing activity, but this is set within the wider project of cosmic re-creation.

The most essential element within the renewed creation will be the glorious presence of God himself. As Wright articulated, God's intention to remake the creation involves righting all wrongs and filling the world with his own presence. And according to Moltmann, the glorification of God is the ultimate purpose of creation. The creation will ultimately be transfigured and glorified by God's own glory.

2.18.9 TIME AND ETERNITY

While most scholars surveyed here did not focus on the nature of time and eternity, the notable exceptions are Cullmann and Moltmann. While Barth regarded the destruction of death as the end of time, Cullmann resisted the notion that God is outside time and eternal life is timeless existence. Consistent with the way that God operates within a temporal framework for salvation history, his commitment to time does not end with the end of (this-)world history. Rather, Cullmann argued, eternity consists of *unlimited time*, not timelessness.

Against Cullmann on one side and Barth on the other, Moltmann claimed that the eschaton is neither the future of time nor timeless eternity. Rather, it is God's coming and his arrival. In his coming, God and time are linked, so that his being in the world must be eschatological and the future of time must be theological. God does not enter time nor remain outside it. Instead, the eschaton brings a change in the transcendental conditions of time. With the coming of God's glory, future time ends and eternal time begins.

In certain ways this discussion lies outside Paul's written concerns, but an examination of his eschatology naturally raises questions about time and eternity. Is time one of those things that God will abolish on the last day, alongside death? Is eternal life conditioned by time or is it "eternal" in a timeless sense? Or is time itself transformed and transfigured so that it continues into eternity in a renewed way?

2.19 Moving Forward

This chapter has surveyed the key scholarly voices of the past century who have most shaped our understanding of Paul's eschatological thought. Naturally there are several areas of consensus as well as issues of ongoing debate and discussion. The foregoing survey sets the stage for our forthcoming exploration of Paul's writings and their synthesis. As we examine Paul's treatment of various eschatological themes and his overall eschatological worldview, we will keep an eye open to how these interact with the scholarly issues now raised. At the conclusion of this book, we will be in a position to assess some of these issues of debate and, it is hoped, to advance the discussion.

Part 2

Exegetical Study

Chapter 3

Two Ages and Two Realms

3.1 Introduction

This chapter investigates a number of related themes that fit under the rubric of *ages and realms*. The language of *age* refers to an era or epoch. It is a defined period of time. The language of *realm* refers to a sphere of rule or influence. To exist within, or under, a certain realm is to be subject to the ruler(s) that govern(s) it. Paul's eschatological vision imagines all of reality existing under two competing realms, and these are primarily spatial in nature, for want of a better term. That is, the two realms exist "side by side," as it were, coexisting and competing for space. All people—and all spiritual beings for that matter—exist in allegiance to one realm or the other.

If it is not clear exactly how Paul's *realm theology* is regarded as an eschatological subject, the following study of texts should resolve the question. In short, the two realms exist as a result of Paul's inaugurated eschatology. With the death, resurrection, and ascension of Christ, a new realm has been established. In an important sense, this realm properly belongs to the future. But since Paul's eschatology is inaugurated, the realm has already broken into the present. Thus, two realms exist side by side, one naturally belonging to this present age, and the other belonging to the age to come, but both existing at once.

Thus, Paul's realm theology is inextricably tied to his theology of *ages*. While the notion of realm is spatial, the notion of age is temporal. This present age is one of sin and death, while the age to come is one of judgment and salvation. But again, Paul's inaugurated eschatology means that the age to come has already broken into the present, thus creating the famed "overlap of the ages," which is consistent with the eschatology of the whole of the New Testament. The future has broken into the present, creating two competing realms of authority and orienting believers to live as belonging to the age to come rather than this present age.

Included under the rubric of ages and realms are the topics of kingdom, inaugurated eschatology, elemental forces and/or spirits, spiritual warfare and weapons, visible and invisible realities, and authorities, powers, and dominions. These topics each relate to the rubric either spatially or temporally, or both. Perhaps surprising for a study of eschatology, the majority are spatial in nature, such as kingdom, elemental forces, spiritual warfare, visible and invisible forces, and authorities, powers, and dominions. As noted above, however, the spatial is created by the temporal in the sense that the breaking in of the future is the reason for which the realm theology exists.

As will become evident, the nature of Paul's realm theology is primarily combative. The two realms compete against each other, or—more in keeping with Paul's language—they are at war. Spiritual warfare therefore ensues, and believers are to don the spiritual armor at their disposal. Believers belong to the kingdom of Christ and are therefore subject to his rule, and they must resist competing forces that seek their allegiance.

The following study of texts proceeds in canonical order, with the subthemes of kingdom, inaugurated eschatology, elemental forces and/or spirits, spiritual warfare and weapons, visible and invisible realities, and authorities, powers, and dominions occurring in no particular order.

3.2 Two Ages/Realms Texts

Rom 5:19–21 ὥσπερ γὰρ διὰ τῆς παρακοῆς τοῦ ἑνὸς ἀνθρώπου ἁμαρτωλοὶ κατεστάθησαν οἱ πολλοί, οὕτως καὶ διὰ τῆς ὑπακοῆς τοῦ ἑνὸς δίκαιοι κατασταθήσονται οἱ πολλοί. 20 νόμος δὲ παρεισῆλθεν, ἵνα πλεονάσῃ τὸ παράπτωμα· οὗ δὲ ἐπλεόνασεν ἡ ἁμαρτία, ὑπερεπερίσσευσεν ἡ χάρις, 21 ἵνα ὥσπερ ἐβασίλευσεν ἡ ἁμαρτία ἐν τῷ θανάτῳ, οὕτως καὶ ἡ χάρις βασιλεύσῃ διὰ δικαιοσύνης εἰς ζωὴν αἰώνιον διὰ Ἰησοῦ Χριστοῦ τοῦ κυρίου ἡμῶν.

For just as through one man's disobedience the many were made sinners, so also through the one man's obedience the many will be made righteous. 20 The law came along to multiply the trespass. But where sin multiplied, grace multiplied even more 21 so that, just as sin reigned in death, so also grace will reign through righteousness, resulting in eternal life through Jesus Christ our Lord.

Part of a famously discussed passage (5:12–21), the various debated details of the text need not concern us at this point.[1] The element to observe concerns

---

1. Debates concerning "original sin" fall into this category. See, however, Fitzmyer for a discussion (Joseph A. Fitzmyer, *Romans*, AYB [New Haven: Yale University Press, 1993], 408–10).

the *realm* language seen in 5:21a—*just as sin reigned in death, so also grace will reign through righteousness*. The concept of reign is directly related to the notion of realm. Reigning occurs within a domain of rule.

Two realms are contrasted by way of their rulers—the personified rulers of *sin* and *grace*. Both rulers are in fact corulers over their respective realms—sin reigns *in death* (ἐν τῷ θανάτῳ), while grace rules *through righteousness* (διὰ δικαιοσύνης).

As with any ruler and realm, there is an inherent relationship between the two. A realm will be shaped by its ruler as the ruler imposes its will over its domain. As such, the realm of sin and death is characterized by their evil and darkness. All those who exist under this realm will likewise be subject to their character. Likewise, *mutatis mutandis*, the realm of grace and righteousness is characterized by their goodness and light. All those who exist under this second realm will likewise be subject to their character.[2] While the final outcome for those under the former realm is death (not stated here), so the final outcome for those under the latter realm is *eternal life through Jesus Christ our Lord* (5:21b).

The realm structure of the text then shines light on 5:19—*For just as through one man's disobedience the many were made sinners, so also through the one man's obedience the many will be made righteous*. While it is common to understand the verse as indicating a type of imputed sinfulness extended from Adam (the *one man*) to all other members of the human race, this is not the most likely reading. Given the concept of realm and dominion, Adam's disobedience most likely represents a *route* or *pathway* or *entrance* into the realm of sin and death. Adam's disobedience establishes the route through which *the many were made sinners* (5:19a). Incidentally, this reading does *not* undermine the doctrine of original sin nor the universal depravity of humanity, because the descendants of Adam have no choice but to be born under the realm of sin and death. Once Adam opened the door, as it were, to the realm of sin and death, all people became subject to its rule.

By the same token, *mutatis mutandis, so also through the one man's obedience the many will be made righteous* (5:19b). This *one man* is the new Adam, Christ, who like Adam has established a route by which the many gain access to the realm he represents. While Adam leads all humanity into the domain of sin and death, Christ leads humanity into the domain of grace and righteousness. Again, it is often asserted that this text affirms the imputation of Christ's obedience to others, but this is not the most likely reading of the text. The realm structure that contrasts the domain of sin and death with the domain of grace and righteousness suggests that Christ, like Adam, stands as the way into

---

2. Robert Jewett, *Romans: A Commentary*, Hermeneia (Minneapolis: Fortress, 2007), 389.

the realm he represents. Those who exist under this realm are characterized by righteousness because they belong to the realm of righteousness, made open to them by Christ, not by being imputed with Christ's righteousness *per se*.

This text demonstrates the essential nature of the realm structure for Paul's soteriology and eschatology. It is through membership in the realm of Christ that believers are ruled by grace and righteousness, resulting in eternal life. Their salvation depends on their membership in the realm of Christ, as does their eschatological destination.

Rom 6:12–14 Μὴ οὖν βασιλευέτω ἡ ἁμαρτία ἐν τῷ θνητῷ ὑμῶν σώματι εἰς τὸ ὑπακούειν ταῖς ἐπιθυμίαις αὐτοῦ, 13 μηδὲ παριστάνετε τὰ μέλη ὑμῶν ὅπλα ἀδικίας τῇ ἁμαρτίᾳ, ἀλλὰ παραστήσατε ἑαυτοὺς τῷ θεῷ ὡσεὶ ἐκ νεκρῶν ζῶντας καὶ τὰ μέλη ὑμῶν ὅπλα δικαιοσύνης τῷ θεῷ. 14 ἁμαρτία γὰρ ὑμῶν οὐ κυριεύσει· οὐ γάρ ἐστε ὑπὸ νόμον ἀλλὰ ὑπὸ χάριν.

Therefore do not let sin reign in your mortal body, so that you obey its desires. 13 And do not offer any parts of it to sin as weapons for unrighteousness. But as those who are alive from the dead, offer yourselves to God, and all the parts of yourselves to God as weapons for righteousness. 14 For sin will not rule over you, because you are not under the law but under grace.

The notion of realm is seen here first in the exhortation not to *let sin reign in your mortal body, so that you obey its desires* (6:12). Sin is viewed as a lord whose rule is to be rejected with respect to believers' bodies. Moreover, this potential (former) lord is not to be offered any parts of the body *as weapons for unrighteousness* (v. 13a). Like a warlord whose subjects offer themselves for battle, so sin would use believers' bodies for warfare. Where a lord reigns, there is his (its) realm of dominion; thus the language of sin reigning indicates the notion of a realm ruled by sin.

By the same token, God is regarded as the Lord of his realm. Instead of offering their body-parts to the would-be ruler of sin, believers are to offer themselves to God, *and all the parts of yourselves to God as weapons for righteousness* (v. 13b). As his subjects, living in his realm, believers owe their full allegiance to him, offering their whole selves and engaging in this warlord's battle in service to him.[3]

Furthermore, the language of weaponry (ὅπλα) implies that these two realms are engaged in battle with each other. The subjects of each realm are engaged in

---

3. James D. G. Dunn, *Romans 1–8*, WBC 38A (Dallas: Word, 1988), 337.

Two Ages and Two Realms • 69

battle as their respective warlords' weapons against each other. Sin wars against God, and God wars against sin.

The summary statement of 6:14—*For sin will not rule over you, because you are not under the law but under grace*—reminds believers that their allegiance to God, their lord, cancels sin's legitimacy as ruler over them.[4] Sin will not rule over them because they no longer belong to the realm ruled by sin. As members of God's realm, they are to offer obedience only to him. Believers are to remember who they are as members of the realm ruled by God, and they are to remain loyal to him in every respect. They must resist any temptation to follow sin again as though they are still subject to it.

> Rom 6:17–23 χάρις δὲ τῷ θεῷ ὅτι **ἦτε δοῦλοι τῆς ἁμαρτίας** ὑπηκούσατε δὲ ἐκ καρδίας εἰς ὃν παρεδόθητε τύπον διδαχῆς, 18 **ἐλευθερωθέντες δὲ ἀπὸ τῆς ἁμαρτίας ἐδουλώθητε τῇ δικαιοσύνῃ**. 19 ἀνθρώπινον λέγω διὰ τὴν ἀσθένειαν τῆς σαρκὸς ὑμῶν. ὥσπερ γὰρ παρεστήσατε τὰ μέλη ὑμῶν δοῦλα τῇ ἀκαθαρσίᾳ καὶ τῇ ἀνομίᾳ εἰς τὴν ἀνομίαν, οὕτως νῦν παραστήσατε τὰ μέλη ὑμῶν δοῦλα τῇ δικαιοσύνῃ εἰς ἁγιασμόν. 20 ὅτε γὰρ δοῦλοι ἦτε τῆς ἁμαρτίας, ἐλεύθεροι ἦτε τῇ δικαιοσύνῃ. 21 τίνα οὖν καρπὸν εἴχετε τότε; ἐφ᾽ οἷς νῦν ἐπαισχύνεσθε, τὸ γὰρ τέλος ἐκείνων θάνατος. 22 νυνὶ δὲ **ἐλευθερωθέντες ἀπὸ τῆς ἁμαρτίας δουλωθέντες δὲ τῷ θεῷ** ἔχετε τὸν καρπὸν ὑμῶν εἰς ἁγιασμόν, τὸ δὲ τέλος ζωὴν αἰώνιον. 23 τὰ γὰρ ὀψώνια τῆς ἁμαρτίας θάνατος, τὸ δὲ χάρισμα τοῦ θεοῦ ζωὴ αἰώνιος ἐν Χριστῷ Ἰησοῦ τῷ κυρίῳ ἡμῶν.
>
> *But thank God that, although **you used to be slaves of sin**, you obeyed from the heart that pattern of teaching to which you were handed over, 18 and **having been set free from sin, you became enslaved to righteousness**. 19 I am using a human analogy because of the weakness of your flesh. **For just as you offered the parts of yourselves as slaves to impurity, and to greater and greater lawlessness, so now offer them as slaves to righteousness, which results in sanctification**. 20 For when you were slaves of sin, you were free with regard to righteousness. 21 So what fruit was produced then from the things you are now ashamed of? The outcome of those things is death. 22 But now, since **you have been set free from sin and have become enslaved to God**, you have your fruit, which results in sanctification—and the outcome is eternal life! 23 For the wages of sin is death, but the gift of God is eternal life in Christ Jesus our Lord.*

---

4. "It is presupposed here as elsewhere that a person belongs constitutively to a world and lies under lordship. With baptism a change of lordship has been effected" (Ernst Käsemann, *Commentary on Romans*, trans. Geoffrey W. Bromiley [Grand Rapids: Eerdmans, 1980], 179).

The notion of realm continues throughout this text, with further detail demonstrating the nature of the two competing realms and how people interact with them. Paul refers to his readers as former *slaves of sin* (6:17a), treating sin as a personified lord whom they must obey. Indeed, although they once belonged to sin as their lord, believers *obeyed from the heart that pattern of teaching* that was used to rule over them (v. 17b). They had once *offered the parts of* themselves *as slaves to impurity, and to greater and greater lawlessness* (v. 19b). As slaves to the lord known as sin, believers also once engaged in slavery to impurity and lawlessness—which are both subsets of sin—offering their parts in service to this slavery. When they were slaves of sin, they *were free with regard to righteousness* (v. 20), meaning that they were not obligated to serve righteousness and indeed were entirely alienated from its influence. This statement demonstrates the exclusivity of each realm—to belong to the realm of sin means "freedom" from the realm of righteousness. No one can obey two masters.

On the other hand, while believers *used to be slaves of sin*, they now have been *set free from sin*, and have become *enslaved to righteousness* (vv. 17–18). Just as sin is regarded as a personified ruler over its realm of authority, so righteousness is likewise a personified ruler over its realm of authority. And instead of serving impurity and lawlessness with their parts, believers are now to *offer them as slaves to righteousness* (v. 19c). Righteousness is their new slaveowner, which is to say their new slaveowner is actually God himself (v. 22a).

While each realm has its own ruler, each also has its own outcome. The realm of sin produced its own fruit, and *the outcome of those things is death* (v. 21b). Indeed, *the wages of sin is death* (v. 23a), meaning that if one serves sin as their master, they will be paid for their labor with death. In contrast, slavery to righteousness and to God *results in sanctification* (vv. 19d, 22b) and *eternal life* (v. 22b). Moreover, while sin pays its wages with death, God *gives* (not pays) the gift of *eternal life in Christ Jesus our Lord* (v. 23b). The different outcomes of each realm reflect their rulers in their own ways. Sin and death rule their realm, so it is unsurprising that death is the final outcome for their subjects. God rules his realm, and so eternal life is the final outcome for his subjects, since righteousness brings life. Moreover, sin is the kind of master that pays what is owed to its servants, though it is a payment that no one should desire, while God is the kind of master who gives good gifts, and his gift is eternally good.

There is one item left to consider. In 6:19a, Paul says he is *using a human analogy because of the weakness of your flesh*. What exactly does he refer to as a *human analogy*, and what does it mean for our analysis of this passage? In actual fact, Paul does *not* speak of an analogy directly; this idea is supplied by translators of the term *human* (ἀνθρώπινος), which refers to something pertaining to being a person.⁵ That is, Paul says he is speaking in a human way, or, perhaps better, he is speaking of things in a way that casts them in human terms. In light of the possible uses of ἀνθρώπινος, it seems most likely that Paul is acknowledging that he has been speaking of *sin*, and its accompanying powers such as impurity and lawlessness, in a personified fashion. Sin rules over its realm, but sin is not actually a personal being. Paul speaks of it that way because it is more readily understood as such. If sin is imagined as a slaveowner who rules over his dominion, Paul's readers can easily understand why they should not obey him if they live in a different dominion under the authority of an opposing lord.⁶

This would also explain why Paul refers to the weakness of his readers' flesh (διὰ τὴν ἀσθένειαν τῆς σαρκὸς ὑμῶν). This is not meant as an insult, nor as a criticism. It is simply an acknowledgement that sometimes such images are useful in helping people to grasp abstract concepts. Paul casts the rulers of the realm of sin in human terms so that his human readers will know how to relate to it. It was once their master, but no longer. They should live accordingly and appreciate the abundant goodness of now living under a new Lord.

> Rom 8:38–39 πέπεισμαι γὰρ ὅτι οὔτε θάνατος οὔτε ζωὴ **οὔτε ἄγγελοι οὔτε ἀρχαὶ** οὔτε ἐνεστῶτα οὔτε μέλλοντα **οὔτε δυνάμεις** 39 οὔτε ὕψωμα οὔτε βάθος οὔτε τις κτίσις ἑτέρα δυνήσεται ἡμᾶς χωρίσαι ἀπὸ τῆς ἀγάπης τοῦ θεοῦ τῆς ἐν Χριστῷ Ἰησοῦ τῷ κυρίῳ ἡμῶν.

> *For I am persuaded that neither death nor life,* **nor angels nor rulers***, nor things present nor things to come,* **nor powers***, 39 nor height nor depth, nor any other created thing will be able to separate us from the love of God that is in Christ Jesus our Lord.*

The language of *rulers* and *powers* relates to the concept of realm and dominion. While such rulers and powers could easily refer to earthly, temporal institutions, their proximity to *death*, *life*, and *angels* means that they could also refer to spiritual entities that exercise authority within a spiritual domain.⁷ Either way, two things about their nature are clear. First, they are regarded as part of the created realm (8:39a); these rulers and powers do not represent some kind of uncreated opposition to God within a dualistic universe.

---

5. BDAG 80.
6. Craig S. Keener, *Romans: A New Covenant Commentary*, NCCS (Eugene, OR: Cascade, 2009), 84.
7. David G. Peterson, *Commentary on Romans*, BTCP (Nashville: Holman, 2017), 340.

Second, these rulers and powers, along with all else in creation, are powerless to separate believers *from the love of God that is in Christ Jesus our Lord* (v. 39c). This means that if the rulers and powers are spiritual in nature and govern a spiritual domain in opposition to God, then we must conclude that such a spiritual domain is unable to claim for itself anyone who belongs to God in Christ. Its opposition to the realm of God is ultimately unsuccessful, and its dominion will one day be vanquished.

Rom 13:11–14 Καὶ τοῦτο εἰδότες τὸν καιρόν, ὅτι ὥρα ἤδη ὑμᾶς ἐξ ὕπνου ἐγερθῆναι, νῦν γὰρ ἐγγύτερον ἡμῶν ἡ σωτηρία ἢ ὅτε ἐπιστεύσαμεν. 12 ἡ νὺξ προέκοψεν, ἡ δὲ ἡμέρα ἤγγικεν. **ἀποθώμεθα οὖν τὰ ἔργα τοῦ σκότους, ἐνδυσώμεθα δὲ τὰ ὅπλα τοῦ φωτός**. 13 ὡς ἐν ἡμέρᾳ εὐσχημόνως περιπατήσωμεν, μὴ κώμοις καὶ μέθαις, μὴ κοίταις καὶ ἀσελγείαις, μὴ ἔριδι καὶ ζήλῳ, 14 ἀλλ' ἐνδύσασθε τὸν κύριον Ἰησοῦν Χριστὸν καὶ τῆς σαρκὸς πρόνοιαν μὴ ποιεῖσθε εἰς ἐπιθυμίας.

Besides this, since you know the time, it is already the hour for you to wake up from sleep, because now our salvation is nearer than when we first believed. 12 The night is nearly over, and the day is near; **so let us discard the deeds of darkness and put on the armor of light**. *13 Let us walk with decency, as in the daytime: not in carousing and drunkenness; not in sexual impurity and promiscuity; not in quarreling and jealousy. 14 But put on the Lord Jesus Christ, and don't make plans to gratify the desires of the flesh.*

This text is not as clearly related to realm theology as some others, but the reference to *armor* (ὅπλα) offers a plausible possible connection to it. We have observed elsewhere that *armor*, or *weaponry* (both translate the same Greek word, ὅπλα), is associated with the ongoing battle between the two opposing realms. In Romans 6:13 (see above), we observe that the language of weaponry (ὅπλα) implies that two realms are engaged in battle with each other.[8] The subjects of each realm are engaged in battle as their respective warlords' weapons against each other. Sin wars against God, and God wars against sin.

Given such a reference, seen earlier in the same letter, it is reasonable to assume that the same kind of realm-battle imagery is at work with the reference to *the armor of light*. The *light* contrasts *the deeds of darkness* that believers are to discard (13:12b). Instead of engaging in the deeds of darkness, believers are

---

8. See also 2 Cor 6:7; 10:4; Eph 6:10–20; 1 Thess 5:8; and Thomas R. Schreiner, *Romans*, BECNT 6 (Grand Rapids: Baker, 1998), 700.

to live *as in the daytime*—the shape of which is sketched out in the following exhortations: *not in carousing and drunkenness; not in sexual impurity and promiscuity; not in quarreling and jealousy* (v. 13b).

The main distinction of this passage, when compared to Romans 6, is that the two realms are chronologically related. The realm of darkness belongs to this age, while the realm of light is yet to dawn, as seen in the phrases *the night is nearly over, and the day is near* (13:12a). This differs from the realm structure of Romans 6 in which the opposing realms coexist side by side. The realm of righteousness and grace—the realm ruled by God—is a current reality to which believers already belong.

Even though one realm currently exists, and the other is yet to come, Paul expects believers to express their allegiance to the coming realm. They are to put on *the armor of light* (v. 12b), which suggests that there is a battle being waged between the two realms, even though technically the realm of light has yet to come. Moreover, believers are to *walk with decency, as in the daytime* (v. 13a), which again suggests that they are to live in a way that expresses allegiance to the kingdom of light even though it has not yet come.

So, is it the case that the two realms coexist at the same time, next to each other, as it were, or is one yet to come? The answer, of course, is *yes*. The kingdom of light is in the first instance a future kingdom—it belongs to the age to come. But Paul's eschatology is shaped by the conviction that in Christ the future has broken into the present. This is because Christ has already been raised from the dead, anticipating the resurrection of the dead that will occur at the end of this age and at the dawn of the new age. If he has already been raised and vindicated in the face of judgment, then the age to come has already come proleptically in Christ.

It is because of this eschatological conviction that Paul can in one place refer to two competing realms and in another place refer to one realm that is about to pass and another that is about to dawn. The two realms are thus correlated spatially as well as temporally. They are "next to" each other, even while they are prior and later, respectively. Both ways of expressing his realm theology require believers to demonstrate allegiance to the realm of Christ. They are to serve as soldiers in the battle between the darkness and the light, and they are to live in keeping with the character of the realm to which they belong, spurning the deeds of darkness and putting on the Lord Jesus Christ.[9]

---

9. As Barth says, "Ours is the great possibility of *being clothed upon* with the offensive and defensive armoury which God alone can provide. We can be armed with the Lord Jesus Christ Himself" (Karl Barth, *The Epistle to the Romans*, trans. Edwin C. Hoskyns [London: Oxford University Press, 1933], 502 [italics original]).

1 Cor 2:6–8 Σοφίαν δὲ λαλοῦμεν ἐν τοῖς τελείοις, σοφίαν δὲ οὐ τοῦ αἰῶνος τούτου οὐδὲ **τῶν ἀρχόντων τοῦ αἰῶνος τούτου** τῶν καταργουμένων· 7 ἀλλὰ λαλοῦμεν θεοῦ σοφίαν ἐν μυστηρίῳ τὴν ἀποκεκρυμμένην, ἣν προώρισεν ὁ θεὸς πρὸ τῶν αἰώνων εἰς δόξαν ἡμῶν, 8 ἣν **οὐδεὶς τῶν ἀρχόντων τοῦ αἰῶνος τούτου ἔγνωκεν**· εἰ γὰρ ἔγνωσαν, οὐκ ἂν τὸν κύριον τῆς δόξης ἐσταύρωσαν.

*We do, however, speak a wisdom among the mature, but not a wisdom of this age, or of **the rulers of this age**, who are coming to nothing. 7 On the contrary, we speak God's hidden wisdom in a mystery, a wisdom God predestined before the ages for our glory. 8 **None of the rulers of this age knew this wisdom**, because if they had known it, they would not have crucified the Lord of glory.*

The rulers of this age—a phrase that occurs twice in this passage (2:6, 8)—could refer to rulers of the evil spiritual realm that is opposed to God, or it could refer to human rulers who govern earthly institutions in the physical world. Though the former is a well-established concept in Paul's writings, the latter is often assumed by interpreters due to the claim made in 2:8—*None of the rulers of this age knew this wisdom, because if they had known it, they would not have crucified the Lord of glory*. The reference to the rulers crucifying the Lord of glory is naturally understood as referring to the Jewish and Roman authorities who were responsible for the crucifixion of Jesus. But it can also be argued that even here spiritual authorities are in view—working behind the scenes, in concert with human authorities—in keeping with the biblical and Jewish apocalyptic background that sees evil supernatural figures behind such acts against God.[10] *The rulers of this age* include spiritual forces who manipulate earthly institutions in the physical world.

The passage is undeniably eschatological in nature. The human rulers who govern earthly institutions in the physical world, and the supernatural figures who stand behind them, do so in *this age* (τοῦ αἰῶνος τούτου). The term *this age* is an important one for Paul's eschatological vocabulary. In this context, it is used to underscore the ignorance of the rulers of this age; they know only the *wisdom of this age* (v. 6b), and are ignorant of the *wisdom among the mature* (vv. 6a, 8a), which is *a wisdom God predestined before the ages for our glory* (v. 7b). The wisdom of which Paul speaks is one that transcends the current age; it is not understood by the rulers of this age, and it is a *hidden wisdom* (v. 7a), preordained by God before this age began (v. 7b). Such wisdom is, therefore, eschatological in nature.

---

10. Roy E. Ciampa and Brian S. Rosner, *The First Letter to the Corinthians*, PNTC (Grand Rapids: Eerdmans, 2010), 125.

Moreover, the phrase *before the ages* (v. 7b) not only sets limits for the current age (God operated at a time prior to this current age), but it expresses the plural—*ages* (τῶν αἰώνων). This is unlikely to be merely a stylistic flurry; it points to the existence of at least one other age besides this current age. Most likely we should understand this as a subtle reference to the age to come that will supersede this current age.

Thus, while the passage refers primarily to earthly rulers rather than spiritual ones, the eschatological shape of the text establishes Paul's understanding of the limitation of this current age both in terms of God's preeminence over it and its noneternal nature. Just as this age had a beginning, so it will have an end. And when the end comes, the new age will dawn.

1 Cor 15:23–28 ἕκαστος δὲ ἐν τῷ ἰδίῳ τάγματι· ἀπαρχὴ Χριστός, ἔπειτα οἱ τοῦ Χριστοῦ ἐν τῇ παρουσίᾳ αὐτοῦ, 24 εἶτα τὸ τέλος, ὅταν παραδιδῷ τὴν βασιλείαν τῷ θεῷ καὶ πατρί, ὅταν καταργήσῃ πᾶσαν ἀρχὴν καὶ πᾶσαν ἐξουσίαν καὶ δύναμιν. 25 δεῖ γὰρ αὐτὸν βασιλεύειν ἄχρι οὗ θῇ πάντας τοὺς ἐχθροὺς ὑπὸ τοὺς πόδας αὐτοῦ. 26 ἔσχατος ἐχθρὸς καταργεῖται ὁ θάνατος· 27 πάντα γὰρ ὑπέταξεν ὑπὸ τοὺς πόδας αὐτοῦ. ὅταν δὲ εἴπῃ ὅτι πάντα ὑποτέτακται, δῆλον ὅτι ἐκτὸς τοῦ ὑποτάξαντος αὐτῷ τὰ πάντα. 28 ὅταν δὲ ὑποταγῇ αὐτῷ τὰ πάντα, τότε αὐτὸς ὁ υἱὸς ὑποταγήσεται τῷ ὑποτάξαντι αὐτῷ τὰ πάντα, ἵνα ᾖ ὁ θεὸς πάντα ἐν πᾶσιν.

But each in his own order: Christ, the firstfruits; afterward, at his coming, those who belong to Christ. 24 **Then comes the end, when he hands over the kingdom to God the Father, when he abolishes all rule and all authority and power. 25 For he must reign until he puts all his enemies under his feet. 26 The last enemy to be abolished is death.** *27 For God has put everything under his feet. Now when it says "everything" is put under him, it is obvious that he who puts everything under him is the exception. 28 When everything is subject to Christ, then the Son himself will also be subject to the one who subjected everything to him, so that God may be all in all.*

The parousia of the resurrected Christ will mark *the end, when he hands over the kingdom to God the Father, when he abolishes all rule and all authority and power* (15:24). His arrival therefore signals the end of this current age and the final consummation of the kingdom of God. The consummation of the kingdom of God is marked by Christ's handing it over to God the Father. Evidently, the Father's possession of the kingdom (or is it his assumption of command over it?) is the key moment of its consummation. At this point, *all rule and all authority and power* will be abolished (v. 24b).[11]

This last comment indicates that there are now competing authorities at work even while the kingdom of Christ has been inaugurated. Indeed, Paul adds that Christ *must reign until he puts all his enemies under his feet* (v. 25). That is, Christ is now currently reigning, even though competing authorities are still extant. His reign will not be complete until all enemies have been put under his feet.

The last of these enemies is death (v. 26). Though death has been conquered by Christ's death and resurrection, it has not yet been abolished; death continues to claim its hapless victims. This reference to the abolition of death (καταργεῖται ὁ θάνατος) helps us to see the way that the enemies of Christ are conquered yet remain active. Like death they have been defeated, but they have not yet been abolished. Their final abolition will occur at the end.

The above reading may seem compromised by the quotation of Psalm 8:6 in 15:27—*For God has put everything under his feet*. A complication is raised by the juxtaposition of this statement against 15:25—*he must reign until he puts all his enemies under his feet*. Is everything already under Christ's feet or not? The key to resolving this problem is to address the Psalm quotation. Psalm 8 concerns the wonder of human beings as part of God's creation.

1 LORD, our Lord,
 how magnificent is your name throughout the earth!
 You have covered the heavens with your majesty.
2 From the mouths of infants and nursing babies,
 you have established a stronghold
 on account of your adversaries
 in order to silence the enemy and the avenger.

3 When I observe your heavens,
 the work of your fingers,
 the moon and the stars,
 which you set in place,
4 what is a human being that you remember him,
 a son of man that you look after him?

---

11. As Mearns comments, it is "clear that Paul is deliberately concerned to impose a new order, a programmatic 'tagma,' upon the eschatological events" (Christopher L. Mearns, "Early Eschatological Development in Paul: The Evidence of 1 Corinthians," *JSNT* 22 [1984]: 27).

> 5 You made him little less than God
>   and crowned him with glory and honor.
> 6 You made him ruler over the works of your hands;
>   **you put everything under his feet:**
> 7 all the sheep and oxen,
>   as well as the animals in the wild,
> 8 the birds of the sky,
>   and the fish of the sea
>   that pass through the currents of the seas.
>
> 9 LORD, our Lord,
>   how magnificent is your name throughout the earth!

Beginning at 8:3, the psalmist wonders at the honor bestowed on human beings, who are such a small and seemingly insignificant part of God's creation. He has *made him little less than God and crowned him with glory and honor* (v. 5). In v. 6, the psalmist states that God has made man *ruler over the works of your hands* and has *put everything under his feet*. He then goes on to list the elements of God's creation that are under the authority of human beings—sheep, oxen, wild animals, birds, and fish (vv. 7–8).

Clearly Paul uses this psalm in quite a different way from its original intent. It is a psalm about humanity in general, not about the Christ in particular. And *everything under his feet* refers to humanity's delegated dominion over the earth rather than Christ's rule over competing forces and authorities such as death. But perhaps there is more to Paul's appropriation of the psalm than first meets the eye. Its christological function can be explained if Paul regards Christ's rule as the fulfillment of God's intention for humanity as a whole. As the ultimate *son of man* (Psalm 8:4), God has put everything under Christ's feet.

But according to the constraints of the psalm, this refers more to the highly dignified position with which humanity (and Christ as humanity's representative) has been bestowed. It does not mean that everything has yet been subjected to him in reality. Indeed, this point is implicit in the psalm itself, since the psalmist knew that a wild lion would not consider itself subject to man. God has put humans above lions in dignity and order, but this does not mean that every lion is going to do what a man tells him to do.

Just as the dominion of humanity over creation has been established and yet is still finding fulfillment, so the dominion of Christ over his enemies has been established but is yet to be consummated. If Paul's use of Psalm 8 is to be understood in this way, it is comfortably accommodated alongside the other claims of 1 Corinthians 15:23–28. Christ's rule is established, but it is not yet consummated. *God has put everything under his feet* (v. 27a), and yet *he must reign until he puts all his enemies under his feet* (v. 25).

The passage concludes with a reiteration of the expectation that everything will in the future become subject to Christ (and therefore is not yet subject to him in reality; v. 28a). When this full subjugation is realized, *then the Son himself will also be subject to the one who subjected everything to him* (v. 28b). This idea relates back to the previous thought that Christ will hand over the kingdom to the Father at the end (v. 24a). Christ's reign is exercised under the preeminence of the Father. It does not necessarily mean that Christ will cease to rule, as though the Father will then take over; more likely it means that Christ will continue to reign, but this occurs as the Father's *viceroy*. He has put everything under Christ's feet, but he himself remains outside the reign of Christ (v. 27). Indeed, *the Son himself will also be subject* to the Father, *so that God may be all in all* (v. 28).

2 Cor 4:17–18 τὸ γὰρ παραυτίκα ἐλαφρὸν τῆς θλίψεως ἡμῶν καθ' ὑπερβολὴν εἰς ὑπερβολὴν αἰώνιον βάρος δόξης κατεργάζεται ἡμῖν, 18 **μὴ σκοπούντων ἡμῶν τὰ βλεπόμενα ἀλλὰ τὰ μὴ βλεπόμενα·** τὰ γὰρ βλεπόμενα πρόσκαιρα, τὰ δὲ μὴ βλεπόμενα αἰώνια.

For our momentary light affliction is producing for us an absolutely incomparable eternal weight of glory. 18 **So we do not focus on what is seen, but on what is unseen.** *For what is seen is temporary, but what is unseen is eternal.*

According to this statement, we could say that Paul sees reality divided between two realms, the *seen* and the *unseen*. This distinction does not simply acknowledge that some things are invisible (like air, love, thoughts) while others are visible (like trees, people, water), and he prefers to focus on the former.[12] This would make little sense of 4:18b—*for what is seen is temporary, but what is unseen is eternal*. Clearly the *unseen* in this context must refer to spiritual entities rather than invisible, nonspiritual things. Their eternal nature indicates this.

It is unlikely, however, that Paul regards *everything* visible as temporary. People, for example, are not temporary beings according to Paul (see on 1 Cor

---

12. As Seifrid comments, "Paul should not be understood as speaking in Platonic terms. In his distinction between 'the seen' and 'the unseen,' he is not making a generalized contrast between the material world and the world of ideas" (Mark A. Seifrid, *The Second Letter to the Corinthians*, PNTC [Grand Rapids: Eerdmans, 2014], 219).

15:51–58 in §7.2, below). We are all eternal. Of course, people may appear differently after the resurrection, but they will still be themselves and, presumably, perfectly visible. Moreover, the creation itself will be renewed in the new age, meaning that at least some of what is visible now will also be visible in eternity (see on Rom 8:18–25 in §§9.2 and 10.2, below).

If Paul does not really mean that *everything* visible is temporary, what then does he mean? The simplest answer is found in 4:17—*for our momentary light affliction is producing for us an absolutely incomparable eternal weight of glory*. Indeed, the words *momentary* and *eternal* give it away. *What is seen* refers to Paul's *momentary light affliction*. Suffering persecution, abuse, beating, imprisonment, and so forth are all temporary afflictions, and they are manifested within the physical, visible world. So, Paul prefers to focus on the *absolutely incomparable eternal weight of glory* that is being produced through his temporary afflictions. This glory is currently unseen since it belongs to a different order of reality. Paul's persecutors do not see the glory that he anticipates, but he does "see" it by faith. Such glory is eternal, invisible, and cannot be compared to whatever physical afflictions to which he is temporarily subjected.

2 Cor 6:3–7 μηδεμίαν ἐν μηδενὶ διδόντες προσκοπήν, ἵνα μὴ μωμηθῇ ἡ διακονία, 4 ἀλλ' ἐν παντὶ συνιστάντες ἑαυτοὺς ὡς θεοῦ διάκονοι, ἐν ὑπομονῇ πολλῇ, ἐν θλίψεσιν, ἐν ἀνάγκαις, ἐν στενοχωρίαις, 5 ἐν πληγαῖς, ἐν φυλακαῖς, ἐν ἀκαταστασίαις, ἐν κόποις, ἐν ἀγρυπνίαις, ἐν νηστείαις, 6 ἐν ἁγνότητι, ἐν γνώσει, ἐν μακροθυμίᾳ, ἐν χρηστότητι, ἐν πνεύματι ἁγίῳ, ἐν ἀγάπῃ ἀνυποκρίτῳ, 7 ἐν λόγῳ ἀληθείας, ἐν δυνάμει θεοῦ· διὰ **τῶν ὅπλων τῆς δικαιοσύνης τῶν δεξιῶν καὶ ἀριστερῶν**

We are not giving anyone an occasion for offense, so that the ministry will not be blamed. 4 Instead, as God's ministers, we commend ourselves in everything: by great endurance, by afflictions, by hardships, by difficulties, 5 by beatings, by imprisonments, by riots, by labors, by sleepless nights, by times of hunger, 6 by purity, by knowledge, by patience, by kindness, by the Holy Spirit, by sincere love, 7 by the word of truth, by the power of God; through **weapons of righteousness for the right hand and the left**

In order not to give offense to anyone, and to protect the ministry, Paul and his partners commend themselves in several ways, listed (in part) here (6:4–7). The list consists of several types of things. Sufferings (afflictions, hardships, difficulties, beatings, imprisonments, riots, labors, sleepless nights, hunger), character and disposition (purity, knowledge, patience, kindness, sincere love), and God's provision (the Holy Spirit, the word of truth, the power of God) constitute the majority of the list of elements that commend Paul's ministry.

At the end of this list we observe something not quite like the others—*weapons of righteousness for the right hand and the left* (v. 7c). Technically, this should be categorized alongside *the Holy Spirit, the word of truth*, and *the power of God* as elements of God's provision. But unlike anything else in the list, these *weapons of righteousness* are apparently offensive in nature. They speak of the warfare element of Paul's ministry. While it appears that he is nothing but battered and bruised by the other side, and simply accepts it, he is in fact warring against the opposition. The *weapons of righteousness* are not conventional weapons, of course, and the descriptor *of righteousness* indicates the spiritual nature of Paul's battle. His mention of the *right hand and the left* may refer to the custom of wielding a sword in one hand and a shield in the other (cf. Eph 6:16–17), in which case Paul's ministry is presented "as both a spiritual offensive and a defensive endeavor."[13]

While it is not unpacked here, the reference to spiritual warfare implies Paul's realm theology. There are two realms at war with each other, and righteousness belongs firmly on one side. Paul wields his weapons of righteousness as a faithful soldier in the battle, and he himself is a weapon used by God, as a minister of God (2 Cor 6:4a).

> 2 Cor 10:3–6 ἐν σαρκὶ γὰρ περιπατοῦντες οὐ κατὰ σάρκα στρατευόμεθα, 4 τὰ γὰρ ὅπλα τῆς στρατείας ἡμῶν οὐ σαρκικὰ ἀλλὰ δυνατὰ τῷ θεῷ πρὸς καθαίρεσιν ὀχυρωμάτων, λογισμοὺς καθαιροῦντες 5 καὶ πᾶν ὕψωμα ἐπαιρόμενον κατὰ τῆς γνώσεως τοῦ θεοῦ, καὶ αἰχμαλωτίζοντες πᾶν νόημα εἰς τὴν ὑπακοὴν τοῦ Χριστοῦ, 6 καὶ ἐν ἑτοίμῳ ἔχοντες ἐκδικῆσαι πᾶσαν παρακοήν, ὅταν πληρωθῇ ὑμῶν ἡ ὑπακοή.

> *For although we live in the flesh,* **we do not wage war according to the flesh, 4 since the weapons of our warfare are not of the flesh, but are powerful through God for the demolition of strongholds. We demolish arguments 5 and every proud thing that is raised up against the knowledge of God, and we take every thought captive to obey Christ.** *6 And we are ready to punish any disobedience, once your obedience is complete.*

The nature of the spiritual warfare in which Paul is engaged is expounded here to some degree. Though living in the flesh, his is not a fleshly battle

---

13. George H. Guthrie, *2 Corinthians*, BECNT (Grand Rapids: Baker Academic, 2015), 333.

(10:3). As such, Paul does not wield fleshly weapons but weapons powered by God (v. 4). And these weapons are used *for the demolition of strongholds* (v. 4). The *stronghold* language (ὀχυρωμάτων) is intensely militaristic, normally used to indicate "a strong military installation, fortress."[14] This indicates both the strength of the opposing side and that of Paul's weaponry powered by God for the demolition of the enemy's fortresses.

While it is unlikely the only type of stronghold, Paul narrows to discuss the demolition of *arguments* in particular (v. 4). Whatever *proud thing that is raised up against the knowledge of God* is a viable target for his offensive strategy (v. 5). If arguments against the knowledge of God are strongholds, then thoughts are regarded as soldiers taken captive by the conquering army—*we take every thought captive to obey Christ* (v. 5).[15] Not only are captured soldiers now under the authority of Christ, compelled to obey him, but Paul is also *ready to punish any disobedience* (v. 6). That is, former enemies are taken captive, compelled to obey Christ, and they are disciplined to conform to their new allegiance.

While perhaps distasteful to some readers, Paul's militaristic vision of his ministry offers important insights into the nature of the spiritual conflict. His work of ministry, proclamation, and evangelism is nothing less than spiritual warfare. The enemy is active in their hostility to the plans and purposes of God, and so God empowers his servants to engage, overpower, and recruit those under the enemy's domain. The transference of people from one domain to the other is an essential piece of Paul's realm theology. It is by being transferred from the realm of evil to the realm of righteousness that people are restored and come to know Christ as their Lord and Savior.

> Gal 4:1–5 Λέγω δέ, ἐφ' ὅσον χρόνον ὁ κληρονόμος νήπιός ἐστιν, οὐδὲν διαφέρει δούλου κύριος πάντων ὤν, 2 ἀλλ' ὑπὸ ἐπιτρόπους ἐστὶν καὶ οἰκονόμους ἄχρι τῆς προθεσμίας τοῦ πατρός. 3 οὕτως καὶ ἡμεῖς, ὅτε ἦμεν νήπιοι, **ὑπὸ τὰ στοιχεῖα τοῦ κόσμου ἤμεθα δεδουλωμένοι**· 4 ὅτε δὲ ἦλθεν τὸ πλήρωμα τοῦ χρόνου, ἐξαπέστειλεν ὁ θεὸς τὸν υἱὸν αὐτοῦ, γενόμενον ἐκ γυναικός, γενόμενον ὑπὸ νόμον, 5 ἵνα τοὺς ὑπὸ νόμον ἐξαγοράσῃ, ἵνα τὴν υἱοθεσίαν ἀπολάβωμεν.
>
> *Now I say that as long as the heir is a child, he differs in no way from a slave, though he is the owner of everything. 2 Instead, he is under guardians and trustees until the time set by his father. 3 In the same way we also, when we*

---

14. BDAG 746.
15. Colin G. Kruse, *The Second Epistle of Paul to the Corinthians*, TNTC (Leicester: Inter-Varsity Press, 1987), 174–75.

*were children, **were in slavery under the elements of the world**. 4 When the time came to completion, God sent his Son, born of a woman, born under the law, 5 to redeem those under the law, so that we might receive adoption as sons.*

There is much discussion concerning the meaning of the phrase *the elements of the world* (4:3).[16] Its precise reference, however, is not our concern here. Instead, we note that it indicates a previous realm under which the *children* were treated as slaves—*when we were children, we were in slavery under the elements of the world* (v. 3). This previous realm, however, has given way to a new epoch—*when the time came to completion, God sent his Son . . . to redeem those under the law, so that we might receive adoption as sons* (vv. 4–5). The children, who were heirs, have now been redeemed and have received adoption (v. 5). They are no longer under the previous epoch that held them as slaves but under a new epoch in which they enjoy the privileges of children.

The two epochs evident in this text do not equate to the two realms of Paul's "realm theology" such as is seen in Romans 6 and other places. That realm theology involves two competing dominions that coexist alongside each other and that are engaged in conflict. The two epochs here, on the other hand, refer to two eras within salvation history. The first is an era of slavery under the law, in which the heirs of God are held in bondage, awaiting their promised redemption. The second is an era of freedom in which God's heirs are enabled to embrace their sonship and their inheritance as God's children.[17]

Gal 4:8–11 Ἀλλὰ τότε μὲν οὐκ εἰδότες θεὸν ἐδουλεύσατε τοῖς φύσει μὴ οὖσιν θεοῖς· 9 νῦν δὲ γνόντες θεόν, μᾶλλον δὲ γνωσθέντες ὑπὸ θεοῦ, πῶς ἐπιστρέφετε πάλιν ἐπὶ **τὰ ἀσθενῆ καὶ πτωχὰ στοιχεῖα** οἷς πάλιν ἄνωθεν δουλεύειν θέλετε; 10 ἡμέρας παρατηρεῖσθε καὶ μῆνας καὶ καιροὺς καὶ ἐνιαυτούς, 11 φοβοῦμαι ὑμᾶς μή πως εἰκῇ κεκοπίακα εἰς ὑμᾶς.

*But in the past, since you didn't know God, you were enslaved to things that by nature are not gods. 9 But now, since you know God, or rather have become known by God, how can you turn back again to **the weak and worthless elements**? Do you want to be enslaved to them all over again? 10 You are observing special days, months, seasons, and years. 11 I am fearful for you, that perhaps my labor for you has been wasted.*

---

16. See the detailed excursus, "Christ and the Elements of the Cosmos," in Martyn, *Galatians*, 393–406.
17. Francois Tolmie, "Living in Hope 'in the Fullness of Time,'" in van der Watt, *Eschatology of the New Testament*, 240–41.

This text follows closely on from the previous one (Gal 4:1–5), and the same two epochs are in view. Paul refers to the past (τότε) when his readers did not know God and were *enslaved to things that by nature are not gods* (v. 8). Again, as with the previous passage, the previous epoch is regarded as one of slavery. The new epoch, however, has come—*but now* (νῦν δὲ)—and it is marked by knowing God and by being known by him (v. 9a).

Paul's concern here is to warn his readers of the danger of returning to the order of things as they were when they lived under the previous epoch: *How can you turn back again to the weak and worthless elements?* (v. 9b). The disputed language of *elements* (στοιχεῖα) harks back to the previous passage (4:3), where we observed *the elements of the world* (τὰ στοιχεῖα τοῦ κόσμου).[18] His readers are at risk of becoming *enslaved to* these elements *all over again* (v. 9c). This turning back to the elements takes the shape of *observing special days, months, seasons, and years* (v. 10). In the wider context of the letter to the Galatians, the most obvious referent for this is the religious life of law-abiding Israel.[19] According to Paul, the gentile Galatians should not feel compelled to put themselves under the law, which belongs to the previous era in which God's people had not yet come to maturity.

As with the previous passage (4:1–5), the two epochs in view here refer to two eras within salvation history. The first is an era of slavery under the law, and the second is an era of freedom. To put themselves under the law, the Galatians are mistakenly choosing to be subjected to the slavery of the first era. Their mistake is one of misunderstanding their place within salvation history. They belong to the new age of the new covenant, not to the old age of the old covenant.

Eph 1:20–23 ἣν ἐνήργησεν ἐν τῷ Χριστῷ ἐγείρας αὐτὸν ἐκ νεκρῶν καὶ καθίσας ἐν δεξιᾷ αὐτοῦ ἐν τοῖς ἐπουρανίοις 21 **ὑπεράνω πάσης ἀρχῆς καὶ ἐξουσίας καὶ δυνάμεως καὶ κυριότητος καὶ παντὸς ὀνόματος ὀνομαζομένου, οὐ μόνον ἐν τῷ αἰῶνι τούτῳ ἀλλὰ καὶ ἐν τῷ μέλλοντι·** 22 καὶ πάντα ὑπέταξεν ὑπὸ τοὺς πόδας αὐτοῦ καὶ αὐτὸν ἔδωκεν κεφαλὴν ὑπὲρ πάντα τῇ ἐκκλησίᾳ, 23 ἥτις ἐστὶν τὸ σῶμα αὐτοῦ, τὸ πλήρωμα τοῦ τὰ πάντα ἐν πᾶσιν πληρουμένου.

He exercised this power in Christ by raising him from the dead and seating him at his right hand in the heavens— 21 ***far above every ruler and authority,***

---

18. Again, see the detailed excursus, "Christ and the Elements of the Cosmos," in Martyn, *Galatians*, 393–406.

19. Craig S. Keener, *Galatians*, NCBC (Cambridge: Cambridge University Press, 2018), 194–96; idem, *Galatians: A Commentary* (Grand Rapids: Baker Academic, 2019), 359–64.

power and dominion, and every title given, not only in this age but also in the one to come. 22 *And he subjected everything under his feet and appointed him as head over everything for the church,* 23 *which is his body, the fullness of the one who fills all things in every way.*

The ascension of Christ to the right hand of the Father has great implications for Paul's theology of the authority of Christ and his eschatology. This position at God's right hand is of messianic significance (cf. Ps 110:1) and puts Christ *far above every ruler and authority, power and dominion, and every title given* (Eph 1:21a). There is no need to specify whether Paul means to refer to human rulers and authorities or to spiritual rulers and authorities since it is clearly an exhaustive statement—*every ruler and authority* includes those of the human, earthly domain as well as those of the heavenly, supraearthly domain.[20]

Moreover, the position of Christ over all other authorities pertains *not only in this age but also in the one to come* (v. 21b). The striking thing about this statement is not that Paul expects Christ's reign in the age to come, but that he regards it as in effect now in the present age (τῷ αἰῶνι τούτῳ). Indeed, it is exactly this point that has led many interpreters to conclude that Ephesians displays a realized (or overrealized) eschatology when compared to other parts of the Pauline corpus in which an inaugurated eschatology is detected. And it is usually concluded, therefore, that Paul cannot be the author of Ephesians—but that point is of no interest here.

Claims of a realized (or overrealized) eschatology are perhaps made from too hasty an assessment of this text. We will unpack its details in comparison to 1 Corinthians 15:23–28, which has already been explored above. That text also refers to the reign of Christ over competing authorities, but it does so with an inaugurated-eschatological outlook. Both texts cite the same sentence from Psalm 8:6, which is another reason to consider them both together.

There are two elements in Ephesians 1:20–23 that lend it to a realized-eschatological understanding. First is that Christ is regarded as already having been seated above every ruler and authority, power and dominion. Christ is *already* preeminent over the competing forces. The second is that the quote from Psalm 8:6 says that God has already subjected everything under his feet.

We will deal with the latter element first. Paul's use of Psalm 8:6 has already

---

20. Beginning with Eph 1:3–4 and continuing through the epistle "we observe Paul's basic division of the cosmos into the 'heavenly places' (ἐπουρανίοις) and the world or universe (κόσμος). What distinguishes the heavenly places and the universe, at least in part, is the fact that the heavenly places existed sometime earlier than the universe" (Robert L. Foster, "Reoriented to the Cosmos: Cosmology & Theology in Ephesians through Philemon," in Pennington and McDonough, *Cosmology and New Testament Theology*, 108).

been discussed with reference to 1 Corinthians 15:27 (above). There it was argued that Paul regards Christ's rule as the fulfillment of God's intention for humanity as a whole. As the ultimate *son of man* (Psalm 8:4), God has put everything under Christ's feet. Yet the psalm refers to the highly dignified position with which humanity (and Christ as humanity's representative) has been bestowed. It does not mean that everything has yet been subjected to him in reality.

This reading of the psalm, and Paul's use of it here and in 1 Corinthians 15:27, mitigates the appearance of realized eschatology with respect to one of the two elements that seem to point in that direction. The other element can easily be correlated to this understanding.

Christ is regarded as already having been seated above every ruler and authority, power and dominion (Eph 1:21). Since this claim is supported by the citation of Psalm 8:6 in 1:22, it should be understood in a way that fits a correct reading of the psalm. As already argued, the psalm points to humanity's dignified status and position above other elements of creation. It does not mean that everything is already seen to be subject to humanity in reality. As such, the elevation of Christ above every ruler and authority, power and dominion, should be understood likewise.

As argued for 1 Corinthians 15:23–28 above, the dominion of humanity over creation has been established and yet is still finding fulfillment. So too the dominion of Christ over his enemies has been established but is yet to be consummated. Christ's rule is established, but it is not yet consummated.

In these ways, Ephesians 1:20–23 can be harmonized with other eschatological statements in the Pauline canon. Paul's use of Psalm 8:6 here and in 1 Corinthians 15:27 expresses inaugurated eschatology. Christ has been appointed to a position above all rulers, authorities, powers, and dominions in this age and the age to come. His preeminence in this age consists of dignity and appointment. His preeminence in the age to come will consist of the unrivaled execution of his will over all other authorities and the abolition of his enemies. The reign of Christ has begun but is not yet consummated.

Eph 2:1–3 Καὶ ὑμᾶς ὄντας νεκροὺς τοῖς παραπτώμασιν καὶ ταῖς ἁμαρτίαις ὑμῶν, 2 ἐν αἷς ποτε περιεπατήσατε **κατὰ τὸν αἰῶνα τοῦ κόσμου τούτου, κατὰ τὸν ἄρχοντα τῆς ἐξουσίας τοῦ ἀέρος, τοῦ πνεύματος τοῦ νῦν ἐνεργοῦντος ἐν τοῖς υἱοῖς τῆς ἀπειθείας**· 3 ἐν οἷς καὶ ἡμεῖς πάντες ἀνεστράφημέν ποτε ἐν ταῖς ἐπιθυμίαις τῆς σαρκὸς ἡμῶν ποιοῦντες τὰ θελήματα τῆς σαρκὸς καὶ τῶν διανοιῶν, καὶ ἤμεθα τέκνα φύσει ὀργῆς ὡς καὶ οἱ λοιποί

And you were dead in your trespasses and sins 2 in which you previously lived **according to the ways of this world, according to the ruler of the power of the air, the spirit now working in the disobedient.** *3 We too all previously lived among them in our fleshly desires, carrying out the inclinations of our flesh and thoughts, and we were by nature children under wrath as the others were also.*

The previous life of believers was characterized by spiritual death (2:1) while they walked (περιεπατήσατε) *according to the ways of this world* (v. 2a). The translation *ways of this world* is misleading for our purposes, since it translates the phrase τὸν αἰῶνα τοῦ κόσμου τούτου, which would be better rendered "the age of this world." The genitive expression *of this world* (τοῦ κόσμου τούτου) is best understood as one of apposition, in which it narrows the reference of *the age* (τὸν αἰῶνα). Since Paul believes in multiple ages, *the age of this world* indicates which age he means. The age that pertains to this world is the one according to which the spiritually dead walked.

The spiritually dead also walked *according to the ruler of the power of the air* (v. 2b). The power, or authority (τῆς ἐξουσίας), of the air seems to indicate a realm or dominion over which its *ruler* exercises control. In keeping with Paul's cosmology, this authority of the air is a spiritual domain—part of the heavenly realms—that interacts with the human world. Its ruler—most likely Satan—evidently[21] has influence over those who live according to the age of this world. This is made explicit with the following clause—*the spirit now working in the disobedient* (v. 2c). Thus, we observe an interrelationship between this world, the age or era of this world, and the spiritual domain ruled by Satan.

This interaction between the world, the age of this world, and the ruler of the authority of the air forms the context in which the spiritually dead conduct themselves. Though Satan is at work in them, they are also culpable for their actions, as the next verse indicates—*we too all previously lived among them in our fleshly desires, carrying out the inclinations of our flesh and thoughts* (v. 3). No one can claim that the devil made them do it; he is at work in them, but they also willfully do as they desire.

This text reveals several elements concerning Paul's eschatological vision. This current world, with its disobedience and fleshly indulgence, belongs to a particular eschatological age or era. It is the age of this world. And the era of this world is under the influence of a spiritual domain ruled by the evil one. He works within the disobedient as they walk according to the patterns and

---

21. Depending on how one understands the Greek syntax, Paul refers either to Satan or to an evil spirit over which the devil rules. See Hoehner's exposition for discussion (Harold W. Hoehner, *Ephesians: An Exegetical Commentary* [Grand Rapids: Baker Academic, 2002], 313–15).

attitudes of this worldly age, according to his influence, and according to their own desires.

Eph 3:8–11 ἐμοὶ τῷ ἐλαχιστοτέρῳ πάντων ἁγίων ἐδόθη ἡ χάρις αὕτη, τοῖς ἔθνεσιν εὐαγγελίσασθαι τὸ ἀνεξιχνίαστον πλοῦτος τοῦ Χριστοῦ 9 καὶ φωτίσαι πάντας τίς ἡ οἰκονομία τοῦ μυστηρίου τοῦ ἀποκεκρυμμένου ἀπὸ τῶν αἰώνων ἐν τῷ θεῷ τῷ τὰ πάντα κτίσαντι, 10 ἵνα γνωρισθῇ νῦν **ταῖς ἀρχαῖς καὶ ταῖς ἐξουσίαις ἐν τοῖς ἐπουρανίοις** διὰ τῆς ἐκκλησίας ἡ πολυποίκιλος σοφία τοῦ θεοῦ, 11 κατὰ πρόθεσιν τῶν αἰώνων ἣν ἐποίησεν ἐν τῷ Χριστῷ Ἰησοῦ τῷ κυρίῳ ἡμῶν

This grace was given to me—the least of all the saints—to proclaim to the Gentiles the incalculable riches of Christ, 9 and to shed light for all about the administration of the mystery hidden for ages in God who created all things. 10 This is so that God's multi-faceted wisdom may now be made known through the church **to the rulers and authorities in the heavens**. *11 This is according to his eternal purpose accomplished in Christ Jesus our Lord.*

Paul reflects on his responsibility *to proclaim to the Gentiles the incalculable riches of Christ* (3:8), which involves *the administration* (or "plan"; ἡ οἰκονομία) *of the mystery* that was once hidden (v. 9). The details of this mystery (or "secret"; τὸ μυστήριον) are explored elsewhere (see §15.4.1). The important point to observe here is the comment that follows—*this is so that God's multi-faceted wisdom may now be made known through the church to the rulers and authorities in the heavens* (v. 10).

There are three elements to draw out from this statement. First is the acknowledgement of *the rulers and authorities* that exist in the heavenly realms. While some of Paul's statements concerning rulers and authorities could be understood to refer to earthly, temporal authorities—such as kings and emperors—it is clear that heavenly authorities are in view here. While Paul does not describe such authorities as evil (nor as good for that matter), the fact that they are put under Christ's feet (see Eph 1:20–22) implies that they are forces that attempt to compete with the authority of Christ. Moreover, Ephesians 2:1–3 describes the influence that *the ruler of the power of the air* exercises over humanity (see on this passage above). This would seem to be a prominent example of the *rulers and authorities in the heavens* (3:9). Thus, the heavens include good and evil spiritual forces, and the latter exercise some degree of authority and dominion.[22]

---

22. Clinton E. Arnold, *Ephesians*, ZECNT (Grand Rapids: Zondervan, 2010), 78, 196.

Second is the fact that *God's multi-faceted wisdom* is to *be made known* to these rulers and authorities in the heavens (3:10). Does Paul mean to imply that they do not already know the details to which he is referring? Or does he mean that God's wisdom will be further impressed upon them in some way? The former seems most likely. There is a tradition in Judaism that not everything is known by spiritual beings, even "good" ones such as angels (cf. 1 Pet 1:12). It does not seem implausible, therefore, that opposing spiritual forces might be ignorant of God's plans and operations. Thus, through the proclamation to the gentiles of the riches of Christ, and shedding light on the once-hidden mystery of God, the opposing rulers and authorities in the spiritual realm are notified of God's multifaceted wisdom.

Third, God's wisdom is made known to the heavenly rulers and authorities *through the church* (v. 10). Being such a truncated statement, it is difficult to know what exactly Paul means by this. Probably he means that the church's very existence—consisting of both Jews and gentiles—is the means by which God's wisdom is made known to the rulers and authorities. A people have been created through Christ to belong to God, and this people consists of the descendants of Abraham—the Jews—but also those whom Abraham was promised would be blessed through him—namely, all the peoples on earth (Gen 12:1–3). While it was a mystery or secret as to how God would keep his promise to Abraham, the rulers and authorities now have their answer. Through Christ, the promise has come to pass, and the existence of the church proves it.

Eph 5:5–6 τοῦτο γὰρ ἴστε γινώσκοντες, ὅτι **πᾶς πόρνος ἢ ἀκάθαρτος ἢ πλεονέκτης, ὅ ἐστιν εἰδωλολάτρης, οὐκ ἔχει κληρονομίαν ἐν τῇ βασιλείᾳ τοῦ Χριστοῦ καὶ θεοῦ.** 6 Μηδεὶς ὑμᾶς ἀπατάτω κενοῖς λόγοις· διὰ ταῦτα γὰρ ἔρχεται ἡ ὀργὴ τοῦ θεοῦ ἐπὶ τοὺς υἱοὺς τῆς ἀπειθείας.

For know and recognize this: **Every sexually immoral or impure or greedy person, who is an idolater, does not have an inheritance in the kingdom of Christ and of God.** *6 Let no one deceive you with empty arguments, for God's wrath is coming on the disobedient because of these things.*

The kingdom of Christ and of God represents the realm of Christ's rule (5:5).[23] Naturally, Paul believes that the entire cosmos is God's domain. He is the creator and sustainer of all things, and he is the sovereign Lord over all his creation.

---

23. "In Ephesians, God not only has seated the Messiah at his right hand (1:20), but his enemies are also already beneath his feet (1:22; cf. Ps. 8:7 LXX, MT): both God and the Messiah, then, reign victorious over their enemies" (Frank Thielman, *Ephesians*, BECNT [Grand Rapids: Baker Academic, 2010], 334).

But here we see a kingdom specified that does not include all of creation. This is clear by the fact that the *sexually immoral or impure or greedy person . . . does not have an inheritance* in it (v. 5). Such people will be excluded from the kingdom of Christ because of their unrepentant rebellion against God's standards.

This kingdom of Christ and of God therefore represents a subset within God's creation. While God's will is exercised over all creation, there is a special way in which Christ rules over this kingdom. Because the kingdom excludes the unrepentant and disobedient, it can be assumed that the rule is of the nature that exists between a king and his loyal subjects. Those who have allegiance to Christ constitute his kingdom, and his rule over them is set in the context of close association rather than hostile antagonism.

In this way, though it is not stated here, the kingdom of Christ and of God is set against the realm under which the disobedient exist. Earlier we had observed that this realm is governed by competing rulers and authorities who further enhance the rebellion of the disobedient (see above on Eph 2:1–3). While the disobedient pertain to this realm, governed by forces in competition with Christ, God has not given up his natural jurisdiction over them as their creator and judge. Indeed, Paul states that *God's wrath is coming on the disobedient because of these things* (5:6). Though the disobedient do not belong to the kingdom of Christ and of God, they nevertheless belong to God's creation, and so his rule over them will be expressed in judgment. This is the kind of rule that exists over hostile antagonism rather than close association.

Eph 6:10–17 Τοῦ λοιποῦ, ἐνδυναμοῦσθε ἐν κυρίῳ καὶ ἐν τῷ κράτει τῆς ἰσχύος αὐτοῦ. 11 **ἐνδύσασθε τὴν πανοπλίαν τοῦ θεοῦ** πρὸς τὸ δύνασθαι ὑμᾶς στῆναι πρὸς τὰς μεθοδείας τοῦ διαβόλου· 12 **ὅτι οὐκ ἔστιν ἡμῖν ἡ πάλη πρὸς αἷμα καὶ σάρκα, ἀλλὰ πρὸς τὰς ἀρχάς, πρὸς τὰς ἐξουσίας, πρὸς τοὺς κοσμοκράτορας τοῦ σκότους τούτου, πρὸς τὰ πνευματικὰ τῆς πονηρίας ἐν τοῖς ἐπουρανίοις**. 13 διὰ τοῦτο ἀναλάβετε τὴν πανοπλίαν τοῦ θεοῦ, ἵνα δυνηθῆτε ἀντιστῆναι ἐν τῇ ἡμέρᾳ τῇ πονηρᾷ καὶ ἅπαντα κατεργασάμενοι στῆναι. 14 στῆτε οὖν **περιζωσάμενοι τὴν ὀσφὺν ὑμῶν ἐν ἀληθείᾳ καὶ ἐνδυσάμενοι τὸν θώρακα τῆς δικαιοσύνης** 15 καὶ ὑποδησάμενοι τοὺς πόδας ἐν ἑτοιμασίᾳ τοῦ εὐαγγελίου τῆς εἰρήνης, 16 ἐν πᾶσιν ἀναλαβόντες **τὸν θυρεὸν τῆς πίστεως**, ἐν ᾧ δυνήσεσθε πάντα τὰ βέλη τοῦ πονηροῦ τὰ πεπυρωμένα σβέσαι· 17 καὶ **τὴν περικεφαλαίαν τοῦ σωτηρίου** δέξασθε καὶ **τὴν μάχαιραν τοῦ πνεύματος**, ὅ ἐστιν ῥῆμα θεοῦ.

Finally, be strengthened by the Lord and by his vast strength. **11 Put on the full armor of God** *so that you can stand against the schemes of the devil.* **12 For our** *struggle is not against flesh and blood, but against the rulers, against the authorities, against the cosmic powers of this darkness, against evil, spiritual forces in the heavens.* 13 *For this reason* **take up the full armor of God**, *so that you may be able to resist in the evil day, and having prepared everything, to take your stand.* 14 *Stand, therefore, with* **truth like a belt around your waist, righteousness like armor on your chest**, 15 *and your feet sandaled with readiness for the gospel of peace.* 16 *In every situation take up* **the shield of faith** *with which you can extinguish all the flaming arrows of the evil one.* 17 *Take* **the helmet of salvation** *and* **the sword of the Spirit**—*which is the word of God.*

This justly famous text about spiritual warfare makes explicit many of the themes that have already been detected in the letter to the Ephesians and that resonate throughout the Pauline corpus. Paul's fullest description of competing spiritual authorities is given in 6:12—*for our struggle is not against flesh and blood, but against the rulers, against the authorities, against the cosmic powers of this darkness, against evil, spiritual forces in the heavens.* While it is plausible that elsewhere the powers and authorities could refer to earthly temporal powers—such as kings and emperors—this is explicitly denied here, since the rulers are directly contrasted with *flesh and blood* (v. 12a). These are *not* flesh-and-blood rulers. Instead, they are *cosmic powers* (τοὺς κοσμοκράτορας); they are *evil, spiritual forces in the heavens* (τὰ πνευματικὰ τῆς πονηρίας ἐν τοῖς ἐπουρανίοις).

While *our struggle is not against flesh and blood*, Paul expects an all-encompassing spiritual battle against these evil, heavenly forces. Believers are to *put on the full armor of God so that you can stand against the schemes of the devil* (v. 11). They are to *take up the full armor of God, so that you may be able to resist in the evil day, and having prepared everything, to take your stand* (v. 13). This armor is identified and listed in 6:14–17, as Paul employs imagery from the arsenal of the Roman soldier, which was well-known to everyone under Rome's authority. The armor also demonstrates compelling parallels to the armor of God as detailed in Isaiah 59 and other places.[24] Such parallels need not concern us here. The point is that the belt, chest armor, sandals, shield, helmet, and sword all point to one overwhelming reality: spiritual warfare is an inevitable feature of the life of believers. And where there is warfare, there are realms engaged in war. Thus the spiritual warfare of 6:10–17 is a direct indication of the battle that wages between the realm of Christ and that of his enemies—the rulers, authorities, cosmic powers, and evil spiritual forces in the heavens.

---

24. See Barth's excursus, "Military Metaphors in Paul's Environment," in Markus Barth, *Ephesians: Translation and Commentary on Chapters 4–6*, AB 34A (Garden City, NJ: Doubleday, 1974), 787–93.

The passage has further significance for the eschatology of Ephesians. While it is often claimed that 1:20–23 displays an (over)realized eschatology (see on this passage above), 6:10–17 mitigates such claims. Though the authorities and powers have been put under Christ's feet (1:22), the very notion of ongoing spiritual warfare demonstrates that 1:22 does *not* mean that the opposing powers have already been fully subjugated. If they had, there would be no more warfare. But since warfare continues, so 1:20–23 must be taken as an expression of inaugurated eschatology, not (over)realized eschatology. This is in keeping with the exegesis of that text (above), but the existence of ongoing spiritual warfare here proves the point. Christ has been seated above all competing powers and authorities, but those powers have not yet been abolished. Consequently, they continue to rage against the soldiers of Christ.

Col 1:13–14 ὃς ἐρρύσατο ἡμᾶς ἐκ τῆς ἐξουσίας τοῦ σκότους καὶ μετέστησεν εἰς τὴν βασιλείαν τοῦ υἱοῦ τῆς ἀγάπης αὐτοῦ, 14 ἐν ᾧ ἔχομεν τὴν ἀπολύτρωσιν, τὴν ἄφεσιν τῶν ἁμαρτιῶν

He has rescued us from the domain of darkness and transferred us into the kingdom of the Son he loves. *14 In him we have redemption, the forgiveness of sins.*

Here we observe a direct reference to the two opposing realms that constitute Paul's realm theology—*the domain of darkness* is that from which people need rescue (1:13).[25] Paul's claim is that Christ has rescued believers from this domain *and transferred us into the kingdom of the Son he loves* (v. 13). This *domain of darkness* also contrasts with the *light* mentioned in the previous verse—*the Father . . . has enabled you to share in the saints' inheritance in the light* (v. 12). This *inheritance in the light* likely parallels *the kingdom of the Son;* the inheritance is found in *the light* rather than in the darkness. And it is found in the light because believers have been transferred to the realm of light, otherwise known as the kingdom of the Son.

It is also striking that the transferal of allegiance from one realm to the other is achieved by the work of God—*he has transferred* [μετέστησεν] *us*. This has been achieved through rescue—*he has rescued us* (ἐρρύσατο ἡμᾶς). And, by implication this rescue has taken place through *redemption, the forgiveness of sins* (v. 14). Thus this text offers a concise account of the way in which Paul's realm

---

25. The domain of darkness is "the deep, cosmic, demonic personal realities capturing structures and society and people in this world systematically to thwart the good plan of God" (Scot McKnight, *The Letter to the Colossians*, NICNT (Grand Rapids: Eerdmans, 2018), 126.

theology intersects with his redemption theology. Redemption occurs through the forgiveness of sins. This forgiveness effects the rescue of God's people, and they are transferred from the domain of darkness into the kingdom of the Son.

There are obvious parallels here with the exodus account in which God rescues his people from the dominion of Egypt and, having redeemed them, establishes a covenant with them that constitutes them as a nation under God.[26] The Hebrews are transferred from the kingdom of Pharaoh to the direct rule of Yahweh. With such a clear analogy with which to compare what has happened in Christ, it is reasonable to suppose that the whole of Paul's realm theology is grounded in the exodus event. It is, after all, the most significant salvation event in the Hebrew Bible, and Paul alludes to it on occasion. New Testament authors commonly find connections between the work of Christ and the blood sacrifice of the Passover lamb, salvation by that blood, and redemption out of slavery to freedom. Paul's realm theology simply adds the notion of two dominions under which all of this occurs. Believers are redeemed by the blood of the lamb, rescued out of slavery to sin, and are transferred out of the dominion of evil to belong to the kingdom of Christ. The exodus is thus a type of which realm theology is antitype.

> Col 1:16 ὅτι ἐν αὐτῷ ἐκτίσθη τὰ πάντα
> ἐν τοῖς οὐρανοῖς καὶ ἐπὶ τῆς γῆς,
> τὰ ὁρατὰ καὶ τὰ ἀόρατα,
> **εἴτε θρόνοι εἴτε κυριότητες**
> **εἴτε ἀρχαὶ εἴτε ἐξουσίαι·**
> τὰ πάντα δι' αὐτοῦ καὶ εἰς αὐτὸν ἔκτισται
>
> *For everything was created by him,*
> *in heaven and on earth,*
> *the visible and the invisible,*
> ***whether thrones or dominions***
> ***or rulers or authorities—***
> *all things have been created through him and for him.*

Part of the so-called Christ hymn of Colossians 1:15–20, this verse refers to *thrones*, *dominions*, *rulers*, and *authorities*, all of which are regarded as created by Christ. The hymn does not limit these authorities to heavenly forces; in fact, the most likely reading is that all types of authorities are in view—heavenly and

---

26. McKnight, *Colossians*, 124–25.

earthly—given the first half of the verse—*for everything was created by him, in heaven and on earth, the visible and the invisible*. In this context, the immediately following reference to authorities is naturally understood as pertaining to both heaven and earth (visible and invisible).

The bold claim of the Christ hymn is that all such powers were created by Christ, *through him and for him*. This throws the nature of Paul's realm theology into sharp relief. Though elsewhere rulers and authorities—especially the heavenly, spiritual ones—are cast in opposition to the kingdom of Christ, this does not undermine the fact that all such entities have been created by him and exist for him. Paul is no dualist. No competing spiritual realm is, in fact, in genuine competition with Christ because in the end they are subject to their creator. They are indeed *part of* the realm of Christ—when this is understood to mean the entire created cosmos.[27]

Just as Egypt stood in opposition to God (see on 1:13 above), so too various thrones, dominions, rulers, and authorities stand in opposition to Christ. But just as Egypt was ultimately under the authority of Yahweh, even while arrogantly defying him, so too all rebellious thrones and dominions are under the authority of Christ. Their rebellion does not set up a dualistic reality in which they exist apart from the authority of Christ. Though they may resist him and reject his rule, they are ultimately under him and are subject to his rule.

Col 2:8–10 Βλέπετε μή τις ὑμᾶς ἔσται ὁ συλαγωγῶν διὰ τῆς φιλοσοφίας καὶ κενῆς ἀπάτης κατὰ τὴν παράδοσιν τῶν ἀνθρώπων, κατὰ τὰ στοιχεῖα τοῦ κόσμου καὶ οὐ κατὰ Χριστόν· 9 ὅτι ἐν αὐτῷ κατοικεῖ πᾶν τὸ πλήρωμα τῆς θεότητος σωματικῶς, 10 καὶ ἐστὲ ἐν αὐτῷ πεπληρωμένοι, ὅς ἐστιν ἡ **κεφαλὴ πάσης ἀρχῆς καὶ ἐξουσίας**.

Be careful that no one takes you captive through philosophy and empty deceit based on human tradition, based on the elements of the world, rather than Christ. 9 For the entire fullness of God's nature dwells bodily in Christ, 10 and you have been filled by him, who is **the head over every ruler and authority**.

Whatever the much-disputed *elements of the world* (τὰ στοιχεῖα τοῦ κόσμου) refers to,[28] Paul regards them as the foundation of the so-called Colossian

---

27. As Foster comments, "The major contrast between these two realities seems to be that things in the heavens remain invisible while things in the world (cosmos) are visible" (Foster, "Reoriented to the Cosmos," 114).

28. Pao summarizes interpretations into three main options, preferring the third: *elements of the physical world*—the four or five elements of the physical earth; *elemental teachings of the world*—rudimentary teachings of the world; and *elemental spirits of the world*—spiritual forces that influence daily existence (David W. Pao, *Colossians and Philemon*, ZECNT [Grand Rapids: Zondervan, 2012], 160–61).

heresy, which is his subject in Colossians 2:8–23.[29] Of more immediate interest is the claim that Christ *is the head over every ruler and authority* (v. 10). There has already been much discussion of what this motif refers to, but here it is set in a different context. In the warning and critique against the Colossian heresy, Christ's headship over every ruler and authority serves to undermine the attraction of the heresy.

Against the quest for spiritual fulfillment through *philosophy and empty deceit based on human tradition*, Paul's argument rests on the fullness of God's nature dwelling in Christ (vv. 8–9). God's nature dwells in Christ, and believers *have been filled by him* (v. 10a). The point is that if it is spiritual fulfillment the Colossians are looking for, God is in Christ and Christ is in the Colossians—there can be no greater spiritual fulfillment than that.

The Colossians have been filled by Christ, and Christ is *the head over every ruler and authority* (v. 10). If the Colossian heresy is in any way associated with competing spiritual authorities (and Paul no doubt thinks it is), then Paul's trump card is the fact that Christ is superior to them and supreme over them. Why would they waste their time pursuing lesser powers when Christ—the head over all powers—is already in them? Why would they seek fulfillment through such powers when they are already filled by Christ, in whom God's nature dwells?

Thus it is the peculiar nature of the so-called Colossian heresy that leads Paul to reflect on the indwelling nature of God in Christ, and Christ's indwelling within the Colossians, alongside the headship of Christ over every ruler and authority. No spirituality that derives its power from such spiritual authorities is any match for authentic Christian faith, since Christ is head over all powers, and Christ spiritually indwells believers. This is genuine spiritual fulfillment.

Col 2:14–15 ἐξαλείψας τὸ καθ' ἡμῶν χειρόγραφον τοῖς δόγμασιν ὃ ἦν ὑπεναντίον ἡμῖν, καὶ αὐτὸ ἦρκεν ἐκ τοῦ μέσου προσηλώσας αὐτὸ τῷ σταυρῷ· 15 ἀπεκδυσάμενος τὰς ἀρχὰς καὶ τὰς ἐξουσίας ἐδειγμάτισεν ἐν παρρησίᾳ, θριαμβεύσας αὐτοὺς ἐν αὐτῷ.

He erased the certificate of debt, with its obligations, that was against us and opposed to us, and has taken it away by nailing it to the cross. 15 **He disarmed the rulers and authorities and disgraced them publicly; he triumphed over them in him.**

---

29. See the useful discussion of the false teaching in Colossae in Douglas J. Moo, *The Letters to the Colossians and to Philemon*, PNTC (Grand Rapids: Eerdmans, 2008), 46–60.

The disarmament of *the rulers and authorities* has been achieved *in him* (ἐν αὐτῷ), meaning in Christ (2:15). While ἐν αὐτῷ could be translated *in it*, referring to the cross (the last-mentioned possible antecedent of the personal pronoun; v. 14), it more likely refers to Christ since ἐν αὐτῷ is a standard Pauline idiom to speak of God's actions in Christ.[30] Though the phrase refers to Christ, it is nevertheless by the cross of Christ in particular that God triumphs. This is made clear in v. 14, as *the certificate of debt . . . that was against us and opposed us* has been taken away by being nailed to the cross. It is in this action of nailing to the cross the certificate of debt against us that God has disarmed the rulers and authorities.

If the abolition of this certificate of debt is the way in which the rulers and authorities have been disarmed, it must mean that those powers had a vested interest in humanity's guilt and debt. Though none of this is unpacked here, the most likely reconstruction is that the rulers and authorities held humanity captive by way of their sin. The certificate of debt opposed humanity and kept all people under the captivity of the rulers and authorities. To be under the debt of sin is to be under the rule of the evil spiritual realm. But by taking away humanity's certificate of debt, God caused the rulers and authorities to lose their grip on the debtors. They were thus disarmed.

There is one final element to notice here. The rulers and authorities were not only disarmed through the cross. Literally, they were *stripped* (ἀπεκδυσάμενος). They were also publicly disgraced (ἐδειγμάτισεν ἐν παρρησίᾳ; v. 15a). It is striking that Paul uses such language about the rulers and authorities as a result of the cross, because the events surrounding the cross saw Jesus stripped and publicly disgraced. In other words, from Paul's perspective, while Jesus was physically stripped and publicly disgraced on his way to the cross, it was in fact the rulers and authorities who were spiritually stripped and disgraced. While it seemed that Jesus had been defeated at the cross, the reality is that by the cross God was victorious over the powers (for more on this, see 14.14.2.2 below).

If such was intended by Paul (and I think it was), then Colossians 2:15 represents a genuinely apocalyptic statement. If by *apocalyptic* we mean that something hidden has been revealed, then the cross represents the ultimate apocalyptic event, since its appearance was opposite to its reality. It appeared weak, but in fact wielded the power of God. It appeared as failure but was the victory of God over his enemies. Christ appeared stripped and disgraced,

---

30. Constantine R. Campbell, *Colossians and Philemon: A Handbook on the Greek Text*, BHGNT (Waco, TX: Baylor University Press, 2013), 41.

but in fact the powers were stripped and disgraced. The moment of Christ's humiliation was the moment of God's triumph.

Col 2:20–23 Εἰ ἀπεθάνετε σὺν Χριστῷ ἀπὸ τῶν στοιχείων τοῦ κόσμου, τί ὡς ζῶντες ἐν κόσμῳ δογματίζεσθε; 21 μὴ ἅψῃ μηδὲ γεύσῃ μηδὲ θίγῃς, 22 ἅ ἐστιν πάντα εἰς φθορὰν τῇ ἀποχρήσει, κατὰ τὰ ἐντάλματα καὶ διδασκαλίας τῶν ἀνθρώπων, 23 ἅτινά ἐστιν λόγον μὲν ἔχοντα σοφίας ἐν ἐθελοθρησκίᾳ καὶ ταπεινοφροσύνῃ καὶ ἀφειδίᾳ σώματος, οὐκ ἐν τιμῇ τινι πρὸς πλησμονὴν τῆς σαρκός.

If you died with Christ to the elements of this world, *why do you live as if you still belonged to the world? Why do you submit to regulations: 21 "Don't handle, don't taste, don't touch"? 22 All these regulations refer to what is destined to perish by being used up; they are human commands and doctrines. 23 Although these have a reputation for wisdom by promoting self-made religion, false humility, and severe treatment of the body, they are not of any value in curbing self-indulgence.*

The elements of this world (τῶν στοιχείων τοῦ κόσμου) are the subject of much discussion within the literature (see the note at Col 2:8–10 above), but they most likely refer to the fundamental components of earthly existence.[31] In that sense, they are not necessarily negative; they are neutral. But when these elements are elevated to the position of securing spirituality, they take on a negative significance. A parallel would be Paul's attitude to circumcision in his letter to the Galatians. Paul regards circumcision as neutral; it is neither good nor bad. But when it is regarded by some as necessary for salvation, circumcision takes on a negative significance. So too *the elements of this world* are simply the building blocks with which this world is constructed—indeed, they are necessary for human life on earth. But if they are worshiped, or if they are regarded as essential for spirituality, they become negative.

Paul regards participation with Christ in his death as putting believers to death to the elements of this world—*if you died with Christ to the elements of this world . . .* (2:20a). If *the elements of this world* are correctly understood, this cannot mean that believers will now have no use for food, drink, air, water, and other such elements of the world. It means, rather, that they will not engage such things in any inappropriate sense. To live in a way that treats the elements of the world as religious and spiritual icons is to submit to a false spirituality.

---

31. Contra Pao, *Colossians and Philemon*, 160–61.

As such, dying with Christ means dying to allegiance to any system of worship that is grounded in the elements of the world.

Thus, having died with Christ, believers ought not live *as if you still belonged to the world* (v. 20b). They ought not *submit to regulations* such as "*don't handle, don't taste, don't touch*" (v. 21), which most likely refer to ascetic practices intended for spiritual enhancement.[32] According to Paul, *all these regulations refer to what is destined to perish by being used up; they are human commands and doctrines* (v. 22). He means that regulations that involve food, drink, and other consumable elements are useless because such things are for normal human use—they *perish by being used up*. They cannot deliver spiritual fullness since they are by definition perishable. Regulations that depend on these earthly elements, therefore, are nothing but *human commands and doctrines* (v. 22b).

Paul acknowledges that such regulations enjoy *a reputation for wisdom*, but *they are not of any value in curbing self-indulgence* (v. 23). Human-made religion may indeed be popular and seem to enhance spirituality, but because it is human-made and depends on perishable elements, it is useless for genuine spiritual fulfillment. Participation with Christ means that believers have been set free from allegiance to human-made, false versions of spirituality. As having been set free, they no longer ought to submit to its assumptions and regulations.

1 Thess 5:5–8 πάντες γὰρ ὑμεῖς υἱοὶ φωτός ἐστε καὶ υἱοὶ ἡμέρας. οὐκ ἐσμὲν νυκτὸς οὐδὲ σκότους· 6 ἄρα οὖν μὴ καθεύδωμεν ὡς οἱ λοιποὶ ἀλλὰ γρηγορῶμεν καὶ νήφωμεν. 7 οἱ γὰρ καθεύδοντες νυκτὸς καθεύδουσιν καὶ οἱ μεθυσκόμενοι νυκτὸς μεθύουσιν· 8 ἡμεῖς δὲ ἡμέρας ὄντες νήφωμεν **ἐνδυσάμενοι θώρακα πίστεως καὶ ἀγάπης καὶ περικεφαλαίαν ἐλπίδα σωτηρίας**

For you are all children of light and children of the day. We do not belong to the night or the darkness. 6 So then, let us not sleep, like the rest, but let us stay awake and be self-controlled. 7 For those who sleep, sleep at night, and those who get drunk, get drunk at night. 8 But since we belong to the day, let us be self-controlled and **put on the armor of faith and love, and a helmet of the hope of salvation.**

This text presents a strong contrast between light and darkness, day and night. Believers *are children of light and children of the day* and *do not belong to the night or the darkness* (5:5). These metaphors clearly represent two different

---

32. Robert W. Wall, *Colossians and Philemon*, IVPNTC (Downers Grove, IL: InterVarsity Press, 1993), 126.

realms between which all of humanity is divided. As clearly different as day and night, light and darkness, so believers belong to a realm that is starkly different from its opposite counterpart.

As such, believers are to live in a way that is appropriate for the daytime. Rather than sleep, which belongs to the night, Paul says *let us stay awake and self-controlled* (v. 6). Sleeping happens at night, and drunkenness happens at night (v. 7). But since believers *belong to the day*, they are to *be self-controlled and put on the armor of faith and love, and a helmet of the hope of salvation* (v. 8). While staying awake is an obvious implication of belonging to the day, the other exhortations are less obviously so. Self-control makes sense, since drunkenness happens at night—it is the time when self-control can be lacking. But the armor of faith and love, and the helmet of the hope of salvation is not clearly associated with daytime in particular. How do these things relate to believers belonging to the day?

Most likely the armor and helmet relate to the opposition between the two realms. Day and night, light and darkness are not only opposite in nature; they are opposed to one another. Thus, those who belong to the day are to be prepared for battle. Their armor (or "breastplate"; θώρακα) of faith and love, and their helmet of the hope of salvation no doubt reflect core characteristics of the realm of the day.[33] The day is characterized by faith, love, and the hope of salvation, and so its soldiers go into battle carrying these attributes with them.

2 Tim 4:1–2 Διαμαρτύρομαι ἐνώπιον τοῦ θεοῦ καὶ Χριστοῦ Ἰησοῦ τοῦ μέλλοντος κρίνειν ζῶντας καὶ νεκρούς, καὶ **τὴν ἐπιφάνειαν αὐτοῦ καὶ τὴν βασιλείαν αὐτοῦ**· 2 κήρυξον τὸν λόγον, ἐπίστηθι εὐκαίρως ἀκαίρως, ἔλεγξον, ἐπιτίμησον, παρακάλεσον, ἐν πάσῃ μακροθυμίᾳ καὶ διδαχῇ.

*I solemnly charge you before God and Christ Jesus, who is going to judge the living and the dead, and **because of his appearing and his kingdom**: 2 Preach the word; be ready in season and out of season; rebuke, correct, and encourage with great patience and teaching.*

The language of charging (διαμαρτύρομαι) belongs to the law court, and Paul's charge to Timothy is issued *before God and Christ Jesus* (4:1a), which establishes the seriousness of the charge. God the Father and Jesus Christ stand as the judges in this court of law. Indeed, in his capacity as judge, Christ Jesus

---

33. The imagery is derived not only from the Roman soldier but from Isaiah 59:17: "He put on righteousness as a breastplate and placed a helmet of salvation on his head" (Jeffrey A. D. Weima, *1–2 Thessalonians*, BECNT [Grand Rapids: Baker Academic, 2014], 363).

is going to judge the living and the dead (v. 1b). Christ will exercise judgment of both the living and the dead because his judgment pertains to the age to come; it is not limited to those who are alive in this present age when he comes. Even those who have passed will come under the purview of his judgment.

The judgment of Christ is *because of his appearing and his kingdom* (v. 1c). In fact, the translation *because* is supplied, since there is no causal relationship explicit in the Greek text (the conjunction is καί). Nevertheless, a causal relationship (*because*) seems entirely plausible[34] (and the accusatives τὴν ἐπιφάνειαν and τὴν βασιλείαν might imply the preposition κατά), but the expression might also indicate a straightforward temporal relation—Christ will judge the living and dead *at the time of his appearing and his kingdom*. Admittedly, the relationship of clauses is ambiguous. However, it is clear that there *is* a relationship—the judgment exercised by Christ is related to his coming and to his kingdom. The *coming* of Christ is explored below (see ch. 4), but his kingdom is of interest here.

The kingdom of Christ implies the rule of Christ. He is the promised king of Israel, and his kingdom is the expression of his governing rule. As ruler of his kingdom, it is his prerogative to execute judgment over his people. Thus, his judgment of the living and the dead is grounded, in part, on his rightful position as king over his kingdom.

In view of the coming of Christ and in view of his kingdom, Timothy is charged to *preach the word* (v. 2a). He is to *correct,* rebuke, *and encourage with great patience and teaching* (v. 2b). This duty is no doubt related to the fact of Christ's judgment and the coming of his kingdom. Timothy's responsibilities involve preparing believers for the kingdom of Christ. The king is coming, and they must be ready to meet him. So Timothy must preach the word to that end.

Though it is not stated here, Paul's kingdom theology is related to his realm theology. Indeed, a kingdom is simply a type of realm. It is the sphere of Christ's rule, under which his people exist and live. It is the realm of Christ. Additionally, the notion of a kingdom implies a "non-kingdom." That is, the kingdom of Christ does not extend over those who share no allegiance to its king. While Christ is Lord over all creation, his kingdom is a subset within creation; it reaches only as far as allegiance to him exists. Those who reject the rule of the king are not part of his kingdom, even though in the end they are still under his rule as the sovereign creator.

And where there is a "non-kingdom," so there is an alternate realm. Anything and anyone who does not belong to the kingdom of Christ is part of another realm, complete with its own rulers and structures. Thus, it is not possible to

---

34. William D. Mounce, *Pastoral Epistles*, WBC 46 (Grand Rapids: Zondervan Academic, 2016), 571.

posit a kingdom of Christ without at the same time positing an opposing realm or kingdom that rejects Christ. By Timothy's preaching, and his attendant duties, he further reinforces believers' membership in the kingdom of Christ, which in turn further distances them from the opposing kingdom or realm.

Titus 2:11–13 Ἐπεφάνη γὰρ ἡ χάρις τοῦ θεοῦ σωτήριος πᾶσιν ἀνθρώποις 12 παιδεύουσα ἡμᾶς, ἵνα ἀρνησάμενοι τὴν ἀσέβειαν καὶ τὰς κοσμικὰς ἐπιθυμίας σωφρόνως καὶ δικαίως καὶ εὐσεβῶς ζήσωμεν **ἐν τῷ νῦν αἰῶνι**, 13 προσδεχόμενοι τὴν μακαρίαν ἐλπίδα καὶ ἐπιφάνειαν τῆς δόξης τοῦ μεγάλου θεοῦ καὶ σωτῆρος ἡμῶν Ἰησοῦ Χριστοῦ

*For the grace of God has appeared, bringing salvation for all people, 12 instructing us to deny godlessness and worldly lusts and to live in a sensible, righteous, and godly way **in the present age**, 13 while we wait for the blessed hope, the appearing of the glory of our great God and Savior, Jesus Christ.*

The present age (τῷ νῦν αἰῶνι) is the period through which believers must wait for the blessed hope, the appearing of the glory of our great God and Savior, Jesus Christ (v. 13). Various other details of this passage are discussed below (see §4.2; 12.2), but of interest here is the nature of *the present age*.

Salvation has come with *the grace of God* (v. 11), and this grace instructs believers *to deny godlessness and worldly lusts and to live in a sensible, righteous, and godly way in the present age* (v. 12). These verses imply several characteristics of *the present age*. First, it is a period in which salvation is needed and provided. As such, it is an age in which people are by default enslaved. They need rescue from their enslaving forces. This rescue has been provided with the appearing of the grace of God. Second, *the present age* is a period in which believers require (and receive) instruction to live against its values. They are *to deny godlessness* and its attendant vices and instead live in a godly way, which involves waiting for Christ (vv. 12–13). Though it is not stated here, the text implies that *the appearing of the glory* of Christ will usher in the age to come. This is implied by the fact that this present age involves waiting for him. If the present age is one of waiting, then the end of waiting is also the end of the age.

Thus, the present age is a penultimate era whose default values are opposed to values consistent with the appearing of Christ.[35] Believers are to live in this present age in a way that anticipates the age to come. Their conduct is to match

---

35. I. Howard Marshall, *A Critical and Exegetical Commentary on The Pastoral Epistles*, ICC (London: T&T Clark, 1999), 271–72.

their expectation of the appearing of the glory of Christ, and it is to reject the default values of the present age, from whose ruling powers they have already received salvation.

3.3 Summary

This chapter has investigated all texts belonging to the Pauline corpus that relate to the rubric of ages and realms. As claimed in the introduction to this chapter, Paul's eschatological vision imagines all of reality existing under two competing realms, and these are primarily spatial in nature. The two realms exist side by side, coexisting and competing for space. All people—and all spiritual beings for that matter—exist in allegiance to one realm or the other.

A number of passages refer to one or more of the ages or eras that constitute Paul's eschatological outlook (Rom 13:11–14; 1 Cor 2:6–8; 5:23–28; 2 Cor 4:17–18; Gal 4:1–5; 4:8–11; Titus 2:11–13). The present age is visible and temporary (2 Cor 4:17–18), and it is characterized by worldly lusts that believers must deny while waiting for Christ (Rom 13:11–14; Titus 2:11–13). The earthly rulers of this age crucified the Lord of glory since they did not know the wisdom of God that was predestined before the ages (1 Cor 2:6–8). While one era spells slavery under the elements of the world, the other spells freedom for the children of God (Gal 4:1–5).

As indicated in the introduction to this chapter, Paul's realm theology derives from his inaugurated eschatology. With the death, resurrection, and ascension of Christ, a new realm has been established. In an important sense, this realm properly belongs to the future. But since Paul's eschatology is inaugurated, the realm has already broken into the present. Thus, two realms exist side by side—one naturally belonging to this present age, and the other belonging to the age to come—but both existing at once.

The notion of realm is seen in several passages (e.g., Rom 5:19–21; 6:12–14; 6:17–23; 2 Cor 4:17–18; Eph 2:1–3; Col 1:13; 1 Thess 5:5–8). One realm is ruled by sin and death, while the other is ruled by grace and righteousness (Rom 5:19–21). Membership in the latter realm requires fidelity to its values and principles (6:12–14), while membership to the former spells slavery (6:17–23). These two realms are also distinct as seen and unseen (2 Cor 4:17–18). The ruler of the air has influence over those living according to the ways of the world (Eph 2:1–3), while believers have been rescued from the domain of darkness and transferred into the kingdom of the Son (Col 1:13–14). They have become children of the day and no longer belong to the night (1 Thess 5:5–8).

The opposing realm is governed by its rulers, authorities, and powers (e.g., Rom 6:12–14; 6:17–23; 8:38–39; 1 Cor 2:6–8; 15:23–28; Eph 1:20–23; 2:1–3;

3:8–11; Col 1:16; 2:9–10; 2:14–15). These rulers include sin (Rom 6:12–14; 6:17–23), death (1 Cor 15:26), Satan (Eph 2:2), other heavenly powers (Eph 3:10), as well as human institutional authorities (1 Cor 2:6–8). These rulers and authorities have been created by Christ and exist for him (Col 1:16). Thus they are powerless to separate believers from the love of God that is in Christ Jesus (Rom 8:38–39), having been disarmed and disgraced by the cross of Christ (Col 2:15). They have been assigned a position under the feet of Christ (Eph 1:20–22) and will be abolished in the end (1 Cor 15:23–28).

Paul's realm theology includes the kingdom of Christ (1 Cor 15:23–28; Eph 5:5–6; 2 Tim 4:1–2). Christ is the king who rules over his realm or kingdom. And though Christ is the sovereign creator of all things, his kingdom consists of those who acknowledge his rule and who demonstrate allegiance to him. As ruler of his kingdom, Christ will exercise judgment over it (2 Tim 4:1–2), and the disobedient and unrepentant have no inheritance in it (Eph 5:5–6). Christ will hand his kingdom over to his Father once all competing rulers and powers are abolished (1 Cor 15:23–28).

The two realms are engaged in warfare against one another (2 Cor 10:3–6; Eph 6:10–17; Col 2:14–15), which means that believers are to wear armor appropriate for spiritual battle (Rom 13:11–14; 2 Cor 6:3–7; 10:3–6; Eph 6:10–17; 1 Thess 5:5–8), and they are to *be* weapons for righteousness (Rom 6:12–14).

The rubric of age and realm gives shape to Paul's overall eschatological vision of reality. All reality is shaped by two ages and two realms. The breaking into the present of the age to come has created a realm of righteousness to which believers in Christ now belong. They have been transferred out of the present evil age and realm and exist under the future (but present) age and realm. This reality has deeply significant consequences for the ways in which believers must conduct themselves. They no longer belong to the realm ruled by sin, death, and the devil, and as such are to show no allegiance to it. Rather, as people who belong to Christ, they are to live according to the values of his realm—according to righteousness, grace, and godliness.

The eschatological elements to be discussed in the following chapters must be understood in light of this two-realm and two-age structure. The two realms and ages provide the context for all else that follows.

CHAPTER 4

THE PAROUSIA

4.1 INTRODUCTION

This chapter explores the texts in the Pauline corpus that deal with the coming, or *parousia*, of Christ. The technical Greco-Roman understanding of the term *parousia* was that of the public ceremonial arrival of a ruling dignitary.[1] The term was also used "to denote the 'appearance' or 'manifestation' of a divinity" (since the Caesars were increasingly regarded as divinized in Paul's day).[2] Included under this rubric are references to the parousia of Christ, the revelation of Christ,[3] the appearing of Christ, his descending from heaven, and the day of the Lord. Each of these notions point to the same expectation—that Christ will return from heaven in an event that will mark the end of this present age and will usher in the age to come.

It will become evident that believers are to await the arrival of Christ for several reasons. As the event that will bring this age to an end, his presence will also mark the end of believers' suffering and the end of death. The dead will be raised and will be with Christ. The parousia of Christ will also bring his righteous judgment, destroying evil and rewarding faithfulness. And the arrival of Christ will usher in the new age in which righteousness and grace will reign unabated.

As with the previous chapter, the following study of texts proceeds in canonical order, with references to Christ's coming, his revelation, his appearing, and his descent from heaven occurring in no particular order.

4.2 PAROUSIA TEXTS

1 Cor 1:6–8 καθὼς τὸ μαρτύριον τοῦ Χριστοῦ ἐβεβαιώθη ἐν ὑμῖν, 7 ὥστε ὑμᾶς μὴ ὑστερεῖσθαι ἐν μηδενὶ χαρίσματι ἀπεκδεχομένους **τὴν ἀποκάλυψιν**

---

1. Charles A. Gieschen, "Christ's Coming and the Church's Mission in 1 Thessalonians," *CTQ* 76.1–2 (Jan 2012): 44.
2. Wright, *Paul and the Faithfulness of God*, 1082.
3. This is a well-recognized second term that is descriptive of the eschatological coming of Christ (Vos, *Pauline Eschatology*, 77).

τοῦ κυρίου ἡμῶν Ἰησοῦ Χριστοῦ· 8 ὃς καὶ βεβαιώσει ὑμᾶς ἕως τέλους ἀνεγκλήτους ἐν τῇ ἡμέρᾳ τοῦ κυρίου ἡμῶν Ἰησοῦ Χριστοῦ.

In this way, the testimony about Christ was confirmed among you, 7 so that you do not lack any spiritual gift as you eagerly wait for **the revelation of our Lord Jesus Christ***. 8 He will also strengthen you to the end, so that you will be blameless in* **the day of our Lord Jesus Christ***.*

Found in the opening thanksgiving of 1 Corinthians (1:4–9), Paul affirms the provision of every spiritual gift for the Corinthian believers as they *eagerly wait for the revelation of our Lord Jesus Christ* (v. 7). Given the concerns of the letter, it is possible that their eager waiting (ἀπεκδεχομένους) is meant slightly ironically, or at least with an exhortatory intention. In any case, Paul points the Corinthians to the revelation (ἀποκάλυψιν) of Christ.

It is clear that this revelation of Christ refers to his parousia, as the next verse mentions *the end* and *the day of our Lord Jesus Christ* (v. 8). But, as Kraus observes, this is the only place in Paul's letters where ἀποκάλυψις is used to denote the parousia.[4] Christ will strengthen the Corinthians to the end, which will ensure their blamelessness on that day.

We see at least three pastoral issues related to Christ's parousia here. First is the expectation that believers will eagerly await his arrival (v. 7); anticipation of the return of Christ is to shape the mindset of believers in this period between his ascension and parousia. Second, Christ himself will strengthen believers as the end approaches (v. 8a); maturity and growth are required for faithful living in this interim period, and such growth is stimulated by Christ. Third, this will prepare them for the day of Christ; they will be found blameless (v. 8b).

Paul's affirmation that the Corinthians will be found blameless on the day of Christ presupposes that it will be a day of judgment. Yet their anticipated blameless status means that this day of judgment is one they may look forward to rather than dread.

1 Cor 4:4–5 οὐδὲν γὰρ ἐμαυτῷ σύνοιδα, ἀλλ᾽ οὐκ ἐν τούτῳ δεδικαίωμαι, ὁ δὲ ἀνακρίνων με κύριός ἐστιν. 5 **ὥστε μὴ πρὸ καιροῦ τι κρίνετε ἕως ἂν ἔλθῃ ὁ κύριος, ὃς καὶ φωτίσει τὰ κρυπτὰ τοῦ σκότους καὶ φανερώσει τὰς βουλὰς τῶν καρδιῶν**· καὶ τότε ὁ ἔπαινος γενήσεται ἑκάστῳ ἀπὸ τοῦ θεοῦ.

---

4. Wolfgang Kraus and Martin Kraus, "On Eschatology in Paul's First Epistle to the Corinthians," in van der Watt, *Eschatology of the New Testament*, 198.

> *For I am not conscious of anything against myself, but I am not justified by this. It is the Lord who judges me.* **5 *So don't judge anything prematurely, before the Lord comes, who will both bring to light what is hidden in darkness and reveal the intentions of the hearts.*** *And then praise will come to each one from God.*

In this chapter dealing with the true nature of apostleship, Paul insists that he does not care if the Corinthians judge him, and he does not even judge himself (4:3), as it is the Lord who evaluates him (v. 4). This leads to Paul's exhortation not to *judge anything prematurely before the Lord comes* (v. 5a). Paul implicitly affirms that judgment belongs to the Lord and not to people, and the reason given here is that at his coming he will *reveal the intentions of the hearts* (v. 5b). As a result of such exposure, God will praise people as appropriate (v. 5c).

While Jesus is not named, *the Lord* (κύριος) always refers to Christ in Paul's writings, except in some Old Testament quotations.[5] Thus we see that judgment will occur at the coming of Christ. His coming will be revelatory, laying open the motivations and intentions of human hearts. It is only at this point that people will be judged properly, since only Christ is able to bring to light what is left hidden to mere human and earthly perception.[6]

In a context in which Paul's readers are prone to judge him, Paul asserts that Christ is the only true judge, and fitting praise then comes from God. As such, any human praise or judgment is provisional at best and will no doubt often be found inaccurate since our knowledge of hearts is partial until that day.

1 Cor 15:20–26 Νυνὶ δὲ Χριστὸς ἐγήγερται ἐκ νεκρῶν ἀπαρχὴ τῶν κεκοιμημένων. 21 ἐπειδὴ γὰρ δι' ἀνθρώπου θάνατος, καὶ δι' ἀνθρώπου ἀνάστασις νεκρῶν. 22 ὥσπερ γὰρ ἐν τῷ Ἀδὰμ πάντες ἀποθνῄσκουσιν, οὕτως καὶ ἐν τῷ Χριστῷ πάντες ζῳοποιηθήσονται. 23 **ἕκαστος δὲ ἐν τῷ ἰδίῳ τάγματι· ἀπαρχὴ Χριστός, ἔπειτα οἱ τοῦ Χριστοῦ ἐν τῇ παρουσίᾳ αὐτοῦ,** 24 εἶτα τὸ τέλος, ὅταν παραδιδῷ τὴν βασιλείαν τῷ θεῷ καὶ πατρί, ὅταν καταργήσῃ πᾶσαν ἀρχὴν καὶ πᾶσαν ἐξουσίαν καὶ δύναμιν. 25 δεῖ γὰρ αὐτὸν βασιλεύειν ἄχρι οὗ θῇ πάντας τοὺς ἐχθροὺς ὑπὸ τοὺς πόδας αὐτοῦ. 26 ἔσχατος ἐχθρὸς καταργεῖται ὁ θάνατος

---

5. Paul sometimes understands "the Lord" in Old Testament citations as referring to Christ (e.g., Rom 10:13; cf. 10:9) and at other times as referring to the Father (e.g., 2 Cor 6:17; cf. 6:16). In yet other instances, the precise referent is left unspecified.

6. Paul Gardner, *1 Corinthians*, ZECNT (Grand Rapids: Zondervan, 2018), 195.

But as it is, Christ has been raised from the dead, the firstfruits of those who have fallen asleep. 21 For since death came through a man, the resurrection of the dead also comes through a man. 22 For just as in Adam all die, so also in Christ all will be made alive. 23 **But each in his own order: Christ, the first fruits; afterward, at his coming, those who belong to Christ.** *24 Then comes the end, when he hands over the kingdom to God the Father, when he abolishes all rule and all authority and power. 25 For he must reign until he puts all his enemies under his feet. 26 The last enemy to be abolished is death.*

In his glorious exposition concerning the resurrection of the dead in 1 Corinthians 15, Paul clearly connects the parousia of Christ with the resurrection of those who belong to him. Christ has been raised from the dead as the firstfruits of those who have *fallen asleep* (v. 20), and at his arrival (ἐν τῇ παρουσίᾳ αὐτοῦ) those in Christ will also be resurrected (v. 23).

Following the parousia of Christ, *then comes the end* (εἶτα τὸ τέλος; v. 24a), which must refer to the eschatological end of this current age. There are two *when* (ὅταν) clauses correlated with this end: it is *when he hands over the kingdom to God the Father*, and *when he abolishes all rule and all authority and power* (vv. 24b, c).

Paul reasons that Christ must reign *until he puts all his enemies under his feet* (v. 25), and the last enemy to be abolished is death (v. 26).[7] In other words, with the resurrection of the dead, death is abolished. And with the abolition of death, the last enemy of Christ is nullified. This is the point at which the kingdom may be handed over to the Father, since it is necessary for Christ to reign until death is vanquished. With the resurrection, following the parousia, Christ has fulfilled the necessary parameters of his reign.

These events will be further explored later (see §14.14.3.1). Here we simply note the apparent timetable that Paul lays forth: the parousia is followed by the resurrection of those in Christ, which is followed by *the end*, at which time Christ hands the kingdom over to the Father and abolishes all competing powers.

---

7. The present indicative καταργεῖται has caused problems for some interpreters (e.g., Gordon D. Fee, *The First Epistle to the Corinthians*, rev. ed., NICNT [Grand Rapids: Eerdmans, 2014], 838; it "is somewhat puzzling"—in what sense is the last enemy *being destroyed*?). But as elsewhere (cf. Rom 8:30), a simple solution is found through an appreciation of verbal aspect. The imperfective aspect of the present καταργεῖται does not necessarily convey a present continuous action ("is being destroyed"). Rather, it may simply be read gnomically so that Paul is making a general statement about reality without any temporal location identified (see Constantine R. Campbell, *Basics of Verbal Aspect in Biblical Greek* [Grand Rapids: Zondervan, 2008], 65–66).

Phil 3:18–21 πολλοὶ γὰρ περιπατοῦσιν οὓς πολλάκις ἔλεγον ὑμῖν, νῦν δὲ καὶ κλαίων λέγω, τοὺς ἐχθροὺς τοῦ σταυροῦ τοῦ Χριστοῦ, 19 ὧν τὸ τέλος ἀπώλεια, ὧν ὁ θεὸς ἡ κοιλία καὶ ἡ δόξα ἐν τῇ αἰσχύνῃ αὐτῶν, οἱ τὰ ἐπίγεια φρονοῦντες. 20 ἡμῶν γὰρ τὸ πολίτευμα ἐν οὐρανοῖς ὑπάρχει, ἐξ οὗ καὶ **σωτῆρα ἀπεκδεχόμεθα κύριον Ἰησοῦν Χριστόν**, 21 ὃς μετασχηματίσει τὸ σῶμα τῆς ταπεινώσεως ἡμῶν σύμμορφον τῷ σώματι τῆς δόξης αὐτοῦ κατὰ τὴν ἐνέργειαν τοῦ δύνασθαι αὐτὸν καὶ ὑποτάξαι αὐτῷ τὰ πάντα.

*For I have often told you, and now say again with tears, that many live as enemies of the cross of Christ. 19 Their end is destruction; their god is their stomach; their glory is in their shame. They are focused on earthly things, 20 but our citizenship is in heaven, and **we eagerly wait for a Savior from there, the Lord Jesus Christ**. 21 He will transform the body of our humble condition into the likeness of his glorious body, by the power that enables him to subject everything to himself.*

Paul contrasts the enemies of the cross of Christ with those who eagerly await his coming. While their end is destruction (3:19a), the believers' citizenship is in heaven (v. 20)—rather than face destruction, they will live with the full rights of heavenly citizenship.[8] While their god is their stomach (v. 19a), referring to the idolatry of self-centered desire and appetite, believers eagerly await their Lord Jesus Christ (v. 20b). Immediate gratification contrasts patient waiting. While their glory is in their shame (v. 19a), referring to glorying in things that ought to be regarded shameful, believers will be transformed into the likeness of Christ's glorious body (v. 21a). While they are focused on earthly things (v. 19b), believers look to these heavenly blessings.

As in 1 Corinthians 1:7, Paul depicts eager expectation (ἀπεκδεχόμεθα) for the coming of the Lord Jesus Christ, the *Savior* (3:20b).[9] He will come from the heavens (οὐρανοῖς), the location in which believers' citizenship is grounded. Upon his arrival from the heavens, Christ will effect the transformation of *the body of our humble condition into the likeness of his glorious body* (v. 21a). Though Paul does not use the language of resurrection here, the transformation from

---

8. "In contrast to the allegiance of Roman Philippians to their governing power, their *politeuma* (τὸ πολίτευμα, *citizenship*), in Rome, Paul sets forth the parallel and opposing claim of Christians that their governing power, their *politeuma*, is in heaven" (G. Walter Hansen, *The Letter to the Philippians*, PNTC [Grand Rapids: Eerdmans, 2009], 269).

9. Paul's use of the term *Savior* to describe Christ sets him in direct opposition to Caesar, the imperial "savior" (Richard A. Horsley, *Paul and Empire: Religion and Power in Roman Imperial Society* [Harrisburg, PA: Trinity Press International, 1997], 141).

humility to glory strongly parallels 1 Corinthians 15:42–49, which deals with the resurrection of the dead in Christ (see §7.2).

This transformation is effected *by the power that enables him to subject everything to himself* (v. 21b), thus creating an implicit connection between resurrection and rule; the same power by which Christ raises the dead is that which enables him to rule over everything. In 1 Corinthians 15:20–26, we observe a similar connection, in which the last enemy to be abolished is death. By nullifying death through the resurrection of the dead, Christ puts this last enemy under his feet. We do not see these ideas spelled out in Philippians 3:21, but they are arguably present in compressed form.

> Col 3:1 Εἰ οὖν συνηγέρθητε τῷ Χριστῷ, τὰ ἄνω ζητεῖτε, οὗ ὁ Χριστός ἐστιν ἐν δεξιᾷ τοῦ θεοῦ καθήμενος· 2 τὰ ἄνω φρονεῖτε, μὴ τὰ ἐπὶ τῆς γῆς. 3 ἀπεθάνετε γὰρ καὶ ἡ ζωὴ ὑμῶν κέκρυπται σὺν τῷ Χριστῷ ἐν τῷ θεῷ· 4 ὅταν ὁ Χριστὸς φανερωθῇ, ἡ ζωὴ ὑμῶν, τότε καὶ ὑμεῖς σὺν αὐτῷ **φανερωθήσεσθε ἐν δόξῃ.**
>
> *So if you have been raised with Christ, seek the things above, where Christ is, seated at the right hand of God. 2 Set your minds on things above, not on earthly things. 3 For you died, and your life is hidden with Christ in God. 4* **When Christ, who is your life, appears, then you also will appear with him in glory.**

Drawing on the central theme of participation with Christ, Paul affirms that believers have died with Christ (2:20) and have been raised with him (3:1). Now the life of the believer *is hidden with Christ in God* (v. 3), which refers to the "believers' union with Christ as sharing in his position and status as hidden in God."[10] Believers hid with Christ in God will also be revealed with him in glory (v. 4).

The passage refers to Christ's current position as one of hiddenness (κέκρυπται), while in his parousia he is revealed (φανερωθῇ). Interestingly, the counterpart of κρύπτω ("to hide") is not ἀποκαλύπτω ("to reveal"), as we might expect, but φανερόω ("to become visible," "to become known").[11] Given the lexical synonymity between ἀποκαλύπτω and φανερόω, it is reasonable to regard this text as apocalyptic in nature. Indeed, its apocalyptic essence goes well beyond lexical matters since the transition from hiddenness to visibility is a central notion of apocalypticism.

---

10. Campbell, *Paul and Union with Christ*, 222.
11. BDAG 1048.

Participation with Christ means that at his parousia believers will be revealed with him in glory. This idea differs from 1 Thessalonians 4:17, where Paul states that those believers still alive will meet the Lord in the air at his appearance; here, believers are hid with Christ and will be revealed with him at his appearance. This expresses Paul's apocalyptic vision of the Christian life in participation with Christ: the spiritual reality of having died and risen with Christ is *hidden* in this world; it is an unseen existence. But believers' sharing in Christ will one day no longer remain hidden—it will be revealed for all to see. This revelation will be glorious, in contrast to the current experience of those in Christ.

1 Thess 1:9–10 αὐτοὶ γὰρ περὶ ἡμῶν ἀπαγγέλλουσιν ὁποίαν εἴσοδον ἔσχομεν πρὸς ὑμᾶς, καὶ πῶς ἐπεστρέψατε πρὸς τὸν θεὸν ἀπὸ τῶν εἰδώλων δουλεύειν θεῷ ζῶντι καὶ ἀληθινῷ 10 καὶ **ἀναμένειν τὸν υἱὸν αὐτοῦ ἐκ τῶν οὐρανῶν**, ὃν ἤγειρεν ἐκ τῶν νεκρῶν, Ἰησοῦν τὸν ῥυόμενον ἡμᾶς ἐκ τῆς ὀργῆς τῆς ἐρχομένης.

For they themselves report what kind of reception we had from you: how you turned to God from idols to serve the living and true God 10 and **to wait for his Son from heaven***, whom he raised from the dead—Jesus, who rescues us from the coming wrath.*

Paul commends the Thessalonians for their turning from idolatry to serve the true God and to wait for his Son from heaven.[12] Waiting is affirmed as an aspect of the commendable Christian life; indeed, "the expectation of the *parousia* has a transformative effect on the present lifestyle of believers."[13] This does not necessarily mean that the Thessalonians expected Christ to come during their lifetimes, as many have supposed. The only thing that can be deduced with confidence is their expectation that Christ *may* return within their lifetimes. The posture of the Christian life is to await the arrival of Christ.

The Son of God will come from heaven, having been raised from the dead. The clause about resurrection is unlikely just an aside (1:10b); the reason the Son will come from heaven is because he has been raised from the dead. In this

---

12. The language of "'Son,' 'heavens,' and the context of end-time judgment in 1:10 indicates that Paul is alluding to the 'one like a son of man' scene in Daniel 7:9–14, an apocalyptic text that prominently influenced Jesus and early Christian eschatological expectations (e.g., Matt 25:31–46)" (Gieschen, "Christ's Coming and the Church's Mission," 40–41).

13. Pieter G. R. de Villiers, "In the Presence of God: The Eschatology of 1 Thessalonians," in van der Watt, *Eschatology of the New Testament*, 316.

respect, the notion of the resurrection of Jesus may be understood to include his ascension.

Furthermore, waiting for the Son from heaven is related to rescue from the coming wrath (v. 10c). The coming of Christ is associated with this coming wrath, apparently correlating his parousia with final judgment. The focus here, however, is that the Son will rescue believers from this wrath. Thus, waiting for the parousia is a double-edged sword, for with it comes the judgment of God, but also rescue from his wrath.

1 Thess 2:19–20 τίς γὰρ ἡμῶν ἐλπὶς ἢ χαρὰ ἢ στέφανος καυχήσεως–ἢ οὐχὶ καὶ ὑμεῖς–ἔμπροσθεν τοῦ κυρίου ἡμῶν Ἰησοῦ ἐν τῇ αὐτοῦ παρουσίᾳ; 20 ὑμεῖς γάρ ἐστε ἡ δόξα ἡμῶν καὶ ἡ χαρά.

*For who is our hope or joy or crown of boasting **in the presence of our Lord Jesus at his coming**? Is it not you? 20 Indeed you are our glory and joy!*

Paul affirms that believers will be in the presence of the Lord Jesus at his parousia. It is striking that he regards the Thessalonians as his *hope, joy,* and *crown of boasting* before (ἔμπροσθεν) the Lord. Clearly Paul regards the arrival of the Lord as a celebratory moment in which he will share glory and joy (2:20).[14]

The celebratory moment is also communal, since the Thessalonians themselves are Paul's hope, joy, and source of boasting. This probably reflects Paul's anticipation that the Thessalonians will stand together with Paul before the Lord at his arrival. Their presence with Jesus is Paul's crown and joy.

1 Thess 3:13 εἰς τὸ στηρίξαι ὑμῶν τὰς καρδίας ἀμέμπτους ἐν ἁγιωσύνῃ ἔμπροσθεν τοῦ θεοῦ καὶ πατρὸς ἡμῶν ἐν τῇ **παρουσίᾳ τοῦ κυρίου ἡμῶν Ἰησοῦ μετὰ πάντων τῶν ἁγίων αὐτοῦ**, [ἀμήν].

*May he make your hearts blameless in holiness before our God and Father at **the coming of our Lord Jesus with all his saints**. Amen.*

While 1 Thessalonians 2:19 speaks of being in the presence (ἔμπροσθεν) of Christ at his parousia, here Paul refers to the presence (ἔμπροσθεν) of God the Father. This too occurs at the parousia of Christ, thus demonstrating that it will not only usher believers into the presence of Christ but into the presence of the Father.

---

14. Gene L. Green, *The Letters to the Thessalonians*, PNTC (Grand Rapids: Eerdmans, 2002), 154–55.

Paul prays for the Thessalonians that the Lord would strengthen their hearts for blamelessness in holiness. This prayer is offered with a view to the parousia of Christ, so that the believers would be prepared to stand before God the Father in holiness (for more on this, see §6.2 below).

The phrase *with all his saints* (μετὰ πάντων τῶν ἁγίων αὐτοῦ) likely means that these saints will accompany the Lord Jesus when he comes. While the phrase could refer to the saints being in the presence of God the Father alongside the Thessalonians (i.e., *May he make your hearts blameless in holiness* together with all his saints *before our God and Father*), the position of the phrase strongly suggests the former option.

So, who are these saints who accompany the Lord Jesus at his arrival? Since his *saints* are *holy ones* (τῶν ἁγίων αὐτοῦ), it is possible that Paul is referring to angels (or both).[15] However, given that Paul's usual referents for *holy ones* or *saints* are people in Christ, angels seem an unlikely referent here. Instead, if we take our cue from 4:16–17, these saints may be *the dead in Christ* who will rise first at the parousia. After the resurrection of the dead in Christ, those still living *will be caught up together with them in the clouds to meet the Lord in the air* (4:17; see below for more on this verse). In other words, the saints who accompany Jesus at his arrival (3:13) could be the resurrected dead in Christ who will proceed those still alive when he comes. Paul imagines the Thessalonians standing in the presence of God at Christ's coming, together with all those who have been raised from the dead.

1 Thess 4:15–18 Τοῦτο γὰρ ὑμῖν λέγομεν ἐν λόγῳ κυρίου, ὅτι ἡμεῖς οἱ ζῶντες οἱ περιλειπόμενοι εἰς τὴν παρουσίαν τοῦ κυρίου οὐ μὴ φθάσωμεν τοὺς κοιμηθέντας· 16 ὅτι αὐτὸς ὁ κύριος ἐν κελεύσματι, ἐν φωνῇ ἀρχαγγέλου καὶ ἐν σάλπιγγι θεοῦ, καταβήσεται ἀπ' οὐρανοῦ καὶ οἱ νεκροὶ ἐν Χριστῷ ἀναστήσονται πρῶτον, 17 ἔπειτα ἡμεῖς οἱ ζῶντες οἱ περιλειπόμενοι ἅμα σὺν αὐτοῖς ἁρπαγησόμεθα ἐν νεφέλαις εἰς ἀπάντησιν τοῦ κυρίου εἰς ἀέρα· καὶ οὕτως πάντοτε σὺν κυρίῳ ἐσόμεθα. 18 Ὥστε παρακαλεῖτε ἀλλήλους ἐν τοῖς λόγοις τούτοις.

For we say this to you by a word from the Lord: We who are still alive **at the Lord's coming** *will certainly not precede those who have fallen asleep.* *16 For* **the Lord himself will descend from heaven with a shout, with the archangel's voice, and with the trumpet of God**, *and the dead in Christ will rise first. 17* **Then we who are still alive, who are left, will be caught**

---

15. See Gary S. Shogren, *1 & 2 Thessalonians*, ZECNT (Grand Rapids: Zondervan, 2012), 145–46.

up together with them in the clouds to meet the Lord in the air, and so we will always be with the Lord. 18 Therefore encourage one another with these words.

Paul's major concern here is to give assurance to the Thessalonians that those who have *fallen asleep* in Christ will not be disadvantaged when the Lord arrives.[16] Those still alive at the parousia of the Lord (τὴν παρουσίαν τοῦ κυρίου) will have no advantage over those already dead (4:15). Paul then offers a vivid image of what will take place: the Lord will descend from heaven accompanied by a *shout* (ἐν κελεύσματι), the sound or voice of an archangel (ἐν φωνῇ ἀρχαγγέλου), and the trumpet of God (ἐν σάλπιγγι θεοῦ; v. 16a).[17] Whether or not these audible elements are meant to be understood literally, it is clear that Paul believes the event will be dramatic—the Lord's descent from heaven will be heralded.[18]

At the parousia, *the dead in Christ will rise first* (v. 16b). Following the resurrection of the dead, *we who are still alive, who are left, will be caught up together with them in the clouds* (v. 17a), indicating the gathering together of the living and the (formerly) dead in Christ. This is why there is no advantage or disadvantage for the living or dead; both groups will be together *in the clouds*.[19] They will then *meet the Lord in the air* and will always be with him (v. 17b).

The phrase *will be caught up*, translating ἁρπαγησόμεθα (rendered in the Latin Vulgate *rapiemur*, thus "rapture"), is infamously responsible for so-called *rapture* theology. However, uses of ἁρπάζω have been observed in numerous epitaphs, such as those of Lucian, Plutarch, Seneca, Ovid, Cicero, Horace, and Pliny, in which the deceased are said to have been "snatched up" by death. Thus, Gieschen observes, "In what appears to be a wonderful twist on this common

---

16. According to Gieschen, Paul was not the originator of the language that Christians who have physically died are "asleep" (1 Thess 4:13, 14). He writes: "He probably used language that was already part of the oral Gospel tradition with which he was familiar (e.g., Matt 9:24; Mark 5:39; Luke 8:52; John 11:11–13)." He adds further that "sleep" is not a euphemism used to soften the harsh reality of death, but is used by Paul "to communicate the mystery that those who physically die in Christ continue to live on even though their heart and brain activity cease" (Gieschen, "Christ's Coming and the Church's Mission," 46–47).

17. As Scott points out, the "sound of the trumpet" is a herald of the Messiah and/or the end in the literature of both Late Judaism (4 Ezra 6.26; Sib. Or. 4.173–74; Ps. Sol. 11.1; Apoc. Ab. 31) and the Talmudic scholars. J. Julius Scott, "Paul and Late-Jewish Eschatology—A Case Study, 1 Thessalonians 4:13–18 and 2 Thessalonians 2:1–12," *JETS* 15.2 (1972): 138.

18. "Against all rapture doctrines that assert a secret coming of Christ that brings about a secret exit of the church, be they pre-tribulation, mid-tribulation, or post-tribulation variations of the rapture, Paul writes here of a very public triumphal coming" (Gieschen, "Christ's Coming and the Church's Mission," 48).

19. Madigan and Levenson here detect an echo of the apocalyptic vision of Daniel 7, in which a quasi-human figure is ferried along by the clouds of heaven. Paul draws on this Jewish apocalyptic tradition "to dramatize the nearness of the dominion of God and to reassure the Thessalonians that they will share in that everlasting kingdom" (Kevin J. Madigan and Jon D. Levenson, *Resurrection: The Power of God for Christians and Jews* [New Haven: Yale University Press, 2008], 28).

usage, Paul uses this same verb here to emphasize that we will be snatched up, not by death, but by the living Jesus unto eternal resurrected life with him."[20]

Paul obviously expects that the instruction about these events will be encouraging to the Thessalonians (v. 18).

1 Thess 5:1–4 Περὶ δὲ τῶν χρόνων καὶ τῶν καιρῶν, ἀδελφοί, οὐ χρείαν ἔχετε ὑμῖν γράφεσθαι, 2 αὐτοὶ γὰρ ἀκριβῶς οἴδατε ὅτι **ἡμέρα κυρίου ὡς κλέπτης ἐν νυκτὶ οὕτως ἔρχεται**. 3 ὅταν λέγωσιν, εἰρήνη καὶ ἀσφάλεια, τότε αἰφνίδιος αὐτοῖς ἐφίσταται ὄλεθρος ὥσπερ ἡ ὠδὶν τῇ ἐν γαστρὶ ἐχούσῃ, καὶ οὐ μὴ ἐκφύγωσιν. 4 ὑμεῖς δέ, ἀδελφοί, οὐκ ἐστὲ ἐν σκότει, **ἵνα ἡ ἡμέρα ὑμᾶς ὡς κλέπτης καταλάβῃ**

*About the times and the seasons: Brothers and sisters, you do not need anything to be written to you. 2 For you yourselves know very well that **the day of the Lord will come just like a thief in the night**. 3 When they say, "Peace and security," then sudden destruction will come upon them, like labor pains on a pregnant woman, and they will not escape. 4 But you, brothers and sisters, are not in the dark, **for this day to surprise you like a thief**.*

Given the context (e.g., 1 Thess 4:15–18), the *day of the Lord* must here be understood as the day of the Lord's coming. And this day *will come just like a thief in the night* (5:2), which appears to be a clear reference to Jesus's teaching that the Son of Man will come like an unexpected thief (Matt 24:36–44; Luke 12:35–40).[21]

The image of a thief in the night serves two purposes here. First, in keeping with Jesus's teaching about the coming of the Son of Man, no one knows when it will take place. It is impossible to predict. Second, while the timing is unknown, the expectation of the coming of the Son of Man is nevertheless certain. Paul assures his readers that since they are not in the dark (unlike those he describes in 1 Thess 5:3), the coming of the day of the Lord need not surprise them (5:4). Thus, the correct way for believers to anticipate the day of the Lord is to expect it at any time.

Finally, that day will bring sudden destruction on those who do not expect it (v. 3). The imagery of labor pains may have as many as three inferences. First, going into labor can hardly be surprising to a pregnant woman—it is expected—yet the timing often comes as a surprise. Second, labor pains are inevitable for the pregnant woman, and so is the coming of the Son of Man.

---

20. Gieschen, "Christ's Coming and the Church's Mission," 48.
21. Gieschen, "Christ's Coming and the Church's Mission," 51; Richard N. Longenecker, "The Nature of Paul's Early Christology," *NTS* 31 (1985): 91.

Third, once labor begins, the process takes over, and it is impossible to reverse it. So, the coming of the Son of Man will set into motion a series of events that cannot be interrupted (see 4:15–18). This notion is underscored by Paul's mention that *they will not escape* (5:3c). Once the day of the Lord comes, it is too late to avoid it.

> 2 Thess 1:5–10 ἔνδειγμα τῆς δικαίας κρίσεως τοῦ θεοῦ εἰς τὸ καταξιωθῆναι ὑμᾶς τῆς βασιλείας τοῦ θεοῦ, ὑπὲρ ἧς καὶ πάσχετε, 6 εἴπερ δίκαιον παρὰ θεῷ ἀνταποδοῦναι τοῖς θλίβουσιν ὑμᾶς θλῖψιν 7 καὶ ὑμῖν τοῖς θλιβομένοις ἄνεσιν μεθ' ἡμῶν, **ἐν τῇ ἀποκαλύψει τοῦ κυρίου Ἰησοῦ ἀπ' οὐρανοῦ μετ' ἀγγέλων δυνάμεως αὐτοῦ** 8 ἐν πυρὶ φλογός, διδόντος ἐκδίκησιν τοῖς μὴ εἰδόσιν θεὸν καὶ τοῖς μὴ ὑπακούουσιν τῷ εὐαγγελίῳ τοῦ κυρίου ἡμῶν Ἰησοῦ, 9 οἵτινες δίκην τίσουσιν ὄλεθρον αἰώνιον ἀπὸ προσώπου τοῦ κυρίου καὶ ἀπὸ τῆς δόξης τῆς ἰσχύος αὐτοῦ, 10 **ὅταν ἔλθῃ ἐνδοξασθῆναι ἐν τοῖς ἁγίοις αὐτοῦ καὶ θαυμασθῆναι ἐν πᾶσιν τοῖς πιστεύσασιν**, ὅτι ἐπιστεύθη τὸ μαρτύριον ἡμῶν ἐφ' ὑμᾶς, ἐν τῇ ἡμέρᾳ ἐκείνῃ.

> *It is clear evidence of God's righteous judgment that you will be counted worthy of God's kingdom, for which you also are suffering, 6 since it is just for God to repay with affliction those who afflict you 7 and to give relief to you who are afflicted, along with us.* ***This will take place at the revelation of the Lord Jesus from heaven with his powerful angels****, 8 when he takes vengeance with flaming fire on those who don't know God and on those who don't obey the gospel of our Lord Jesus. 9 They will pay the penalty of eternal destruction from the Lord's presence and from his glorious strength 10* ***on that day when he comes to be glorified by his saints and to be marveled at by all those who have believed****, because our testimony among you was believed.*

Believers who suffer for God's kingdom can be assured that those afflicting them will know the justice of God *at the revelation* [ἐν τῇ ἀποκαλύψει] *of the Lord Jesus*. It is also at this revelation that the afflicted will know relief (1:7). The revelation of the Lord Jesus is *from heaven* (ἀπ' οὐρανοῦ), most likely indicating heaven as the "location" from which he comes (v. 10). He will be accompanied by powerful angels and will execute *vengeance with flaming fire* on unbelievers (for more on this, see §6.2 below).[22]

---

22. Reference to powerful angels and flaming fire are theophanic motifs, traditionally associated with God but here ascribed to Christ (Exod 19:18; Deut 5:4; Dan 7:9–10, but esp. Isa 66:15–16); see Pieter G. R. de Villiers, "The Glorious Presence of the Lord: The Eschatology of 2 Thessalonians," in van der Watt, *Eschatology of the New Testament*, 338.

The coming of Christ is not, of course, only a negative occurrence. On the day he comes, he will *be glorified by his saints* and *marveled at by all those who have believed* (v. 10). The positive counterpart of receiving his vengeance and the penalty of eternal destruction is to engage in the glorification of, and marveling in, the Lord. Both parties—unbelievers and believers—will experience the Lord's glorious strength on that day, but in dramatically differing ways. The former will experience it through their overthrow and reception of vengeance. The latter will experience it through the reversal of their afflictions and through witnessing the final judgment and destruction of their opponents.

2 Thess 2:1–2 Ἐρωτῶμεν δὲ ὑμᾶς, ἀδελφοί, **ὑπὲρ τῆς παρουσίας τοῦ κυρίου ἡμῶν Ἰησοῦ Χριστοῦ καὶ ἡμῶν ἐπισυναγωγῆς ἐπ᾽ αὐτὸν** 2 εἰς τὸ μὴ ταχέως σαλευθῆναι ὑμᾶς ἀπὸ τοῦ νοὸς μηδὲ θροεῖσθαι, μήτε διὰ πνεύματος μήτε διὰ λόγου μήτε δι᾽ ἐπιστολῆς ὡς δι᾽ ἡμῶν, ὡς ὅτι ἐνέστηκεν ἡ ἡμέρα τοῦ κυρίου

Now concerning **the coming of our Lord Jesus Christ and our being gathered to him**: *We ask you, brothers and sisters, 2 not to be easily upset or troubled, either by a prophecy or by a message or by a letter supposedly from us, alleging that the day of the Lord has come.*

These verses provide a clear correlation between *the coming of our Lord Jesus Christ* and *the day of the Lord*, with no apparent difference meant by the two appellations except that the former refers to an event, while the latter refers to the day on which that event occurs.

We also note that the coming (or arrival) of Christ will include *our being gathered to him* (2:1). This notion has a clear parallel in Paul's first letter to the Thessalonians, in which he comforts them concerning the dead in Christ. Still-living believers *will be caught up together with them* [i.e., the dead in Christ] *in the clouds to meet the Lord in the air* (1 Thess 4:17). The arrival of Christ will involve a gathering of all his people. It is as his gathered people that believers will glorify and marvel at him (2 Thess 1:10).

Nevertheless, the arrival of the Lord Jesus Christ is apparently a topic of some consternation for the Thessalonians—not its reality or its implications, but its timing. Paul exhorts his readers not to become upset by any claims *that the day of the Lord has come* (2:2; cf. 1 Thess 5:1–3). He anticipates that such a claim might be made by a prophecy, a message, or even a letter falsely attributed to Paul and his cohort.[23]

---

23. See G. K. Beale, *1–2 Thessalonians*, IVPNTC (Downers Grove, IL: InterVarsity Press, 2003), 199–203.

That Paul exhorts the Thessalonians in this way implies several things. First, they have a clear expectation of the arrival of Christ, given to them through Paul's own teaching (2:5). Second, the Thessalonians accept the possibility that Christ's arrival could occur at any time (cf. 1 Thess 5:2). Third, they seem anxious that they might somehow miss the arrival of Christ, hence Paul's warning that they need not worry in this way. Fourth, Paul anticipates that other teachers may attempt to deceive believers regarding the timing of Christ's arrival.

2 Thess 2:8 καὶ τότε ἀποκαλυφθήσεται ὁ ἄνομος, ὃν ὁ κύριος Ἰησοῦς ἀνελεῖ τῷ πνεύματι τοῦ στόματος αὐτοῦ καὶ καταργήσει τῇ ἐπιφανείᾳ τῆς παρουσίας αὐτοῦ

And then the lawless one will be revealed. **The Lord Jesus will destroy him with the breath of his mouth and will bring him to nothing at the appearance of his coming**.

The "lawless one" is discussed from 2:3–7; he *exalts himself* and *sits in God's temple, proclaiming that he himself is God* (v. 4). Paul's readers may have understood this description to point to certain pagan kings known from the Old Testament, to the Seleucid king Antiochus IV Epiphanes, or to the Roman emperor Caligula, who attempted to set up a statue of himself in the Jewish temple in AD 40, asserting his divinity.[24] The "lawless one" is therefore a type of rebellious, self-exalting leadership figure who desires to be worshiped in God's place.

The typological lawless one will be destroyed by the Lord Jesus *with the breath of his mouth*. This imagery comes from Isaiah 11:4 (LXX), in which the Messiah *will strike the earth with the word of his mouth and with the breath of his lips he will destroy the wicked* (author's transl.). Though Paul does not refer to Jesus as the Christ here, his allusion to Isaiah 11:4 indicates that he regards the destruction of the lawless one as a messianic accomplishment.

Christ *will bring him to nothing at the appearance of his coming* (2 Thess 2:8b). The phrase *bring him to nothing* translates καταργήσει. Though the word can indicate the annihilation of an entity,[25] it more likely here conveys the sense of nullification.[26] The lawless one had set himself up as an object of (false) worship (v. 4), and his destruction will obviously entail the loss of his power and status.

This will occur *at the appearance of [Christ's] coming*. The translation

---

24. Andy Johnson, *1 and 2 Thessalonians*, THNTC (Grand Rapids: Eerdmans, 2016), 188–90.
25. BDAG 525, §3.
26. BDAG 525, §2.

appearance (CSB, ESV) should not be understood in the sense of a *mere appearance* of his coming—that is, as an apparition or image rather than a physical, concrete reality. In ancient literature, the word translated *appearance* (ἐπιφανείᾳ) refers to the "sudden manifestation of a hidden divinity."[27] Thus, Paul refers to the manifestation of the divine Jesus at his coming. This is further confirmed by the fact that Paul expects Christ to destroy the lawless one with the breath of his mouth; clearly a concrete, real presence of the Lord is expected for this act of judgment (cf. 1:9).

1 Tim 6:13–14 παραγγέλλω σοι ἐνώπιον τοῦ θεοῦ τοῦ ζῳογονοῦντος τὰ πάντα καὶ Χριστοῦ Ἰησοῦ τοῦ μαρτυρήσαντος ἐπὶ Ποντίου Πιλάτου τὴν καλὴν ὁμολογίαν, 14 τηρῆσαί σε τὴν ἐντολὴν ἄσπιλον ἀνεπίλημπτον μέχρι τῆς ἐπιφανείας τοῦ κυρίου ἡμῶν Ἰησοῦ Χριστοῦ

In the presence of God, who gives life to all, and of Christ Jesus, who gave a good confession before Pontius Pilate, **I charge you 14 to keep this command without fault or failure until the appearing of our Lord Jesus Christ.**

This text is loaded with legal language as Paul charges (παραγγέλλω) Timothy *in the presence of God* (ἐνώπιον τοῦ θεοῦ), evoking a binding instruction[28] issued before those who will judge Timothy's obedience (6:13). While God is the one who *gives life to all*, Christ Jesus is the one having testified (μαρτυρήσαντος) *a good confession before Pontius Pilate* (v. 13). The language of testimony also evokes juridical overtones, presenting Christ as a witness (as well as judge) in this courtroom scene.

The charge issued to Timothy is *to keep this command without fault or failure* (v. 14), apparently referring back to the imperative(s) *fight the good fight of the faith* and/or *take hold of the eternal life to which were called* (v. 12). And Timothy is to keep this command *until the appearing of our Lord Jesus Christ* (v. 14). As with 2 Thessalonians 2:8 (see above), the word translated *appearing* (ἐπιφάνεια) refers to the "sudden manifestation of a hidden divinity."[29] Thus Paul refers to the manifestation of the divine Jesus at his coming. This utterance implies at least three things.

First, Timothy's obligation will come to an end with the appearance of Christ. His charge is only in effect for the period preceding the coming of Christ—no doubt because Christ's coming will signal the end of this current

---
27. BDAG 385.
28. BDAG 760: "To make an announcement about someth. that must be done."
29. BDAG 385.

eschatological era, and with it the end of the ministry of the gospel. Second, given the first point, Paul accepts the possibility that Christ's appearing may occur during Timothy's lifetime (though he does not assert that it will). But given that Paul does not charge Timothy "until death," it is clear that he does not necessarily expect Timothy's death to occur before the appearance of Christ. Third, it is possible to understand the appearance of Christ as the point at which Timothy will be judged according to how well he has kept Paul's charge. This is not stated, but given that Timothy is charged before God and Christ, it follows that Christ's coming can be seen as the culmination, and therefore the assessment, of the charge.

Thus, it seems appropriate to view *the appearing of our Lord Jesus Christ* with juridical overtones, as part of the courtroom scenario in which Paul charges Timothy with this binding imperative. The appearing of Christ marks both the completion of Timothy's responsibility and the assessment of his performance.

2 Tim 4:1–2 Διαμαρτύρομαι ἐνώπιον τοῦ θεοῦ καὶ Χριστοῦ Ἰησοῦ τοῦ μέλλοντος κρίνειν ζῶντας καὶ νεκρούς, καὶ **τὴν ἐπιφάνειαν αὐτοῦ καὶ τὴν βασιλείαν αὐτοῦ**· 2 κήρυξον τὸν λόγον, ἐπίστηθι εὐκαίρως ἀκαίρως, ἔλεγξον, ἐπιτίμησον, παρακάλεσον, ἐν πάσῃ μακροθυμίᾳ καὶ διδαχῇ

*I solemnly charge you before God and Christ Jesus, who is going to judge the living and the dead, and **because of his appearing and his kingdom**: 2 Preach the word; be ready in season and out of season; rebuke, correct, and encourage with great patience and teaching.*

As with 1 Timothy 6:14 and 2 Thessalonians 2:8 (above), the word translated *appearing* (ἐπιφάνεια) refers to the "sudden manifestation of a hidden divinity."[30] Thus, Paul refers to the manifestation of the divine Jesus at his coming. It is possible that Jesus's *first* coming is in view here at 2 Timothy 4:1, given that the same word, ἐπιφάνεια, is used with reference to Christ's earthly ministry earlier in this letter (1:10). But the context strongly favors Jesus's eschatological *appearing* (ἐπιφάνεια) in 4:1. Christ *is going to judge the living and the dead*; read against this, his *appearing* is most naturally understood in relation to said judgment, which will occur at his future coming.

This passage is in several respects parallel to 1 Timothy 6:13–14. Overtones of a juridical setting are heard: Paul uses the language of a solemn charge (διαμαρτύρομαι), which is issued *before God and Christ Jesus*, viewing them as

---

30. BDAG 385.

the witnesses and judges of this charge. The appearing of Christ is here tied explicitly to the theme of judgment (which is only implied in 1 Tim 6:13–14), since he will *judge the living and the dead* (4:1).

The connection of Christ's appearing with judgment implies that Timothy's faithfulness to Paul's charge will be assessed by Christ at his coming. He will judge the living and the dead, so that whether or not Timothy lives to see Christ's return in his lifetime, or will be dead in Christ, his faithfulness will nevertheless come under the judgment of Christ.

Unlike 1 Timothy 6:12–14, the appearing of Christ is coupled with mention of his kingdom. It seems that Paul regards both Christ's coming *and* his kingdom as keeping Timothy accountable to keep the charge to preach the word (2 Tim 4:2). There is also an implicit connection between the two, such that Christ's appearing is coupled with his kingdom. Most likely this means that Christ's kingdom will be made manifest alongside Christ himself.

2 Tim 4:6–8 Ἐγὼ γὰρ ἤδη σπένδομαι, καὶ ὁ καιρὸς τῆς ἀναλύσεώς μου ἐφέστηκεν. 7 τὸν καλὸν ἀγῶνα ἠγώνισμαι, τὸν δρόμον τετέλεκα, τὴν πίστιν τετήρηκα· 8 λοιπὸν ἀπόκειταί μοι ὁ τῆς δικαιοσύνης στέφανος, ὃν ἀποδώσει μοι ὁ κύριος ἐν ἐκείνῃ τῇ ἡμέρᾳ, ὁ δίκαιος κριτής, οὐ μόνον δὲ ἐμοὶ ἀλλὰ καὶ **πᾶσιν τοῖς ἠγαπηκόσιν τὴν ἐπιφάνειαν αὐτοῦ**.

For I am already being poured out as a drink offering, and the time for my departure is close. 7 I have fought the good fight, I have finished the race, I have kept the faith. 8 There is reserved for me the crown of righteousness, which the Lord, the righteous Judge, will give me on that day, and not only to me, but to **all those who have loved his appearing***.*

Reflecting on the end of his life and ministry, Paul expects his *departure* to come soon (4:6). He has *fought the good fight, finished the race,* and *kept the faith* (v. 7). In keeping with the *race* metaphor, he looks forward to *the crown of righteousness* that will be given to him *on that day* (v. 8). *The crown of righteousness* given to Paul on the day of judgment (see §6.2, below) is seen as a reward for his faithfulness in finishing the race (vv. 7–8). But he adds that this crown will be awarded *not only to me, but to all those who have loved his appearing* (v. 8).

The language of *appearing* (ἐπιφάνεια) refers to the "sudden manifestation of a hidden divinity."[31] Elsewhere Paul uses the language to refer to the manifestation of the divine Jesus at his future coming (e.g., 4:1; 2 Thess 2:8; 1 Tim

---

31. BDAG 385.

6:14; Titus 2:13), though there is one instance in which it refers to Jesus's earthly life and ministry (2 Tim 1:10). Does the *appearing* here refer to Jesus's previous or future coming?

The context strongly suggests an eschatological future *appearing*, given the judgment-day scenario of 4:8. But one factor may point to the *first* appearing of Christ in his earthly life and ministry—the phrase *all those who have loved (his appearing)*. *Those who have loved* translates the Greek perfect substantival participle τοῖς ἠγαπηκόσιν. The past temporal reference expressed in this translation suggests that the object of their love was the first appearance of Christ. They loved Jesus, who became known to them through his life and ministry (whether or not they personally knew Jesus, or were simply taught about him).

However, this translation may not accurately reflect the meaning of the Greek participle. While traditional analyses of the Greek verbal system retain an element of past temporal reference in default translations of perfect participles, more recent research has demonstrated that the "perfect participle most often expresses contemporaneous temporal reference in relation to its principal verb in a similar fashion to the present participle."[32] I have argued that this is due to the imperfective aspect of Greek perfect verbs. But even if this explanation is not accepted, it remains a fact that most perfect participles nevertheless express contemporaneous temporal reference, even substantival participles.[33] While many substantival perfect participles convey past temporal reference, these normally involve certain types of lexemes,[34] which are not relevant in this case. As such, τοῖς ἠγαπηκόσιν could be translated *to those who love*. That is, *all those who love his appearing* will receive the crown of righteousness.

While most major translations adopt the past temporal translation (e.g, CSB, NIV, ESV), the KJV reads, *all them also that love his appearing*. Given the possibility of such a translation of the Greek participle, together with the judgment-day context, it is preferable to understand this *appearing* as Christ's future eschatological parousia.

If that is correct, Paul is saying that on that day all who love to see Jesus's appearing will be given the crown of righteousness. The appearance of Christ will itself sort people according to their response to it. Many will not be glad to see Christ at the judgment. But others, like Paul, will indeed be glad because of their relationship with him and their confidence in the face of the righteous judge.

---

32. Constantine R. Campbell, *Verbal Aspect and Non-Indicative Verbs: Further Soundings in the Greek of the New Testament*, SBG 15 (New York: Peter Lang, 2008), 26.
33. Campbell, *Verbal Aspect and Non-Indicative Verbs*, 44–47.
34. Campbell, *Verbal Aspect and Non-Indicative Verbs*, 45–46.

Titus 2:11–13 Ἐπεφάνη γὰρ ἡ χάρις τοῦ θεοῦ σωτήριος πᾶσιν ἀνθρώποις 12 παιδεύουσα ἡμᾶς, ἵνα ἀρνησάμενοι τὴν ἀσέβειαν καὶ τὰς κοσμικὰς ἐπιθυμίας σωφρόνως καὶ δικαίως καὶ εὐσεβῶς ζήσωμεν ἐν τῷ νῦν αἰῶνι, 13 προσδεχόμενοι τὴν μακαρίαν ἐλπίδα καὶ ἐπιφάνειαν τῆς δόξης τοῦ μεγάλου θεοῦ καὶ σωτῆρος ἡμῶν Ἰησοῦ Χριστοῦ

For the grace of God has appeared, bringing salvation for all people, 12 instructing us to deny godlessness and worldly lusts and to live in a sensible, righteous, and godly way in the present age, 13 while we wait for **the blessed hope, the appearing of the glory of our great God and Savior, Jesus Christ.**

Paul describes godly living between two *appearings*. First, *the grace of God has appeared* [ἐπεφάνη], *bringing salvation for all people* (2:11). This grace of God instructs believers to live in a godly way in the present age. And such living involves waiting for *the appearing* [ἐπιφάνειαν] *of the glory of our great God and Savior, Jesus Christ* (2:13).

Unlike previous *appearing* texts (2 Thess 2:8; 1 Tim 6:14; 2 Tim 4:1), here Paul does not explicitly posit Jesus as its subject. In the first instance, *the grace of God* appeared; in the second it is *the glory of our great God and Savior* that will appear. Nevertheless, there is little doubt that these two appearances refer to Christ's first and second comings.

The question remains, however, as to why Paul uniquely posits abstract subjects of the appearance language rather than simply say that Christ appeared or will appear, as he does elsewhere. Its rhetorical effect is to underscore two essential qualities that accompany the two comings of Christ. His first coming is characterized by the grace of God, issuing in salvation and instruction for godly living.[35] But his second coming is characterized by the glory of this God and Savior. Grace and glory are poignant descriptions of Christ's first and second comings. They not only characterize the mode of each coming but point to the purpose of each. Christ's first coming was to save all people. His second coming will be for the manifestation of his glory and all that entails.

4.3 Summary

This chapter has engaged the Pauline texts pertaining to the parousia of Christ. Contrary to popular perceptions of this event, Paul does not use the language of the *return* of Christ. Instead the event is cast as his *presence* or *arrival*

---

35. Andreas J. Köstenberger, *Commentary on 1–2 Timothy & Titus*, BTCP (Nashville: Holman, 2017), 340–41.

(ἡ παρουσία), his *revelation* (ἡ ἀποκάλυψις), his *appearing* (φανερόω), and his *descent* (καταβαίνω), all of which signal *the day of the Lord* (ἡ ἡμέρα τοῦ κυρίου).

Believers are to eagerly await the revelation of the Lord Jesus Christ (1 Cor 1:7; Titus 2:13), and they will be strengthened to the end in order to be blameless in the day of Christ (1 Cor 1:8; 1 Thess 3:13). Those charged with the responsibilities of ministry are to fulfill their charge in light of the expected appearing of Christ (1 Tim 6:13–14; 2 Tim 4:1–2). Though the coming day of the Lord is expected, its timing is unknown (1 Thess 5:1–4). At his arrival from heaven (Phil 3:20; 1 Thess 1:10), the dead in Christ will be raised (1 Cor 15:20–23; 1 Thess 4:16), while the living will meet the Lord in the air (1 Thess 4:17). All in Christ will stand in his presence (1 Thess 2:19), having been gathered to him (2 Thess 2:1), and will appear with him in glory (Col 3:4).

On that day Christ will bring to light the hidden intentions of the heart, leading both to judgment and to praise (1 Cor 4:4–5). The presence of Christ will mark the destruction of the lawless one and Christ's vengeance against those who have afflicted his people, who will in turn marvel at him and ascribe him glory (2 Thess 1:5–10; 2:8). Those who have loved his appearing will be awarded the crown of righteousness (2 Tim 4:8).

The parousia of Christ therefore functions in three broad ways in Paul's thought. First, it is the event of expectation for believers in this present age. They are to live in anticipation of his arrival. Second, the parousia of Christ will bring the end of the age, the resurrection of the dead, and his presence among his people. Third, the parousia of Christ will inaugurate final judgment as he punishes his enemies and shares his glorify with those who belong to him.

CHAPTER 5

The Last Day

5.1 Introduction

Paul never speaks of the eschaton. At least, he does not speak of the eschaton by use of the word ἔσχατος. There are, however, several other ways in which Paul refers to the eschaton—*the end*—without it. Language that directly points to the eschaton includes *the day of wrath, the day, the hour*, and *the end* (τέλος, not ἔσχατος). Even uses of these terms, however, are sparse. This does not mean that Paul is disinterested in the eschaton. He is, rather, significantly shaped by his conviction that a final day is coming. These terms point directly to that final day, but they do not tell the whole story.

5.2 Last-Day Texts

Rom 2:5 κατὰ δὲ τὴν σκληρότητά σου καὶ ἀμετανόητον καρδίαν **θησαυρίζεις σεαυτῷ ὀργὴν ἐν ἡμέρᾳ ὀργῆς** καὶ ἀποκαλύψεως δικαιοκρισίας τοῦ θεοῦ

*Because of your hardened and unrepentant heart **you are storing up wrath for yourself in the day of wrath**, when God's righteous judgment is revealed.*

This is Paul's only use of the phrase *the day of wrath* (ἡμέρα ὀργῆς). It is more common simply to refer to *the day* (e.g., Rom 13:12; 2 Thess 1:10), but since the context addresses God's righteous judgment, the descriptor *of wrath* is appropriately supplied. As the wider context demonstrates, *the day* is not one solely of wrath (see 2:6–8), but it is so described here to underscore the fact that it will bring wrath to those who *are storing up wrath* for themselves.

The notion of *storing up wrath* conveys an expectation of delayed judgment of sin. That is, sinners do not experience the full consequences of their actions until God's righteous judgment is revealed. This serves as an implicit warning that sinners will not get away with what they have done in the end. They might think they are able to sin without consequence or reprimand, but in fact the day is coming in which reckoning will occur.¹ This may explain why Paul uses the word *revealed* (ἀποκαλύψεως) of God's righteous judgment; it may appear absent while evil people seem to get away with their crimes, but on that day judgment will be *revealed*.

Finally, stored-up wrath is for those with a *hardened and unrepentant heart* (2:5). It is not for all sinful people, which, according to Romans 3:23, includes all people. It is only for those who refuse to repent for their sins and live accordingly.

Rom 2:14–16 ὅταν γὰρ ἔθνη τὰ μὴ νόμον ἔχοντα φύσει τὰ τοῦ νόμου ποιῶσιν, οὗτοι νόμον μὴ ἔχοντες ἑαυτοῖς εἰσιν νόμος· 15 οἵτινες ἐνδείκνυνται τὸ ἔργον τοῦ νόμου γραπτὸν ἐν ταῖς καρδίαις αὐτῶν, συμμαρτυρούσης αὐτῶν τῆς συνειδήσεως καὶ μεταξὺ ἀλλήλων τῶν λογισμῶν κατηγορούντων ἢ καὶ ἀπολογουμένων, 16 **ἐν ἡμέρᾳ ὅτε κρίνει ὁ θεὸς τὰ κρυπτὰ τῶν ἀνθρώπων κατὰ τὸ εὐαγγέλιόν μου διὰ Χριστοῦ Ἰησοῦ.**

So, when Gentiles, who do not by nature have the law, do what the law demands, they are a law to themselves even though they do not have the law. 15 They show that the work of the law is written on their hearts. Their consciences confirm this. Their competing thoughts either accuse or even excuse them 16 **on the day when God judges what people have kept secret, according to my gospel through Christ Jesus.**

Extended discussion of this passage is offered below (see §6.2), but here it is noted that God's judgment occurs *on the day* (2:16). As seen elsewhere, *the day* is the point at which judgment will take place, including the uncovering of *what people have kept secret*. On what this phrase means, see §6.2 below.

Rom 13:11–14 Καὶ τοῦτο εἰδότες τὸν καιρόν, ὅτι **ὥρα ἤδη ὑμᾶς ἐξ ὕπνου ἐγερθῆναι**, νῦν γὰρ ἐγγύτερον ἡμῶν ἡ σωτηρία ἢ ὅτε ἐπιστεύσαμεν. 12 ἡ νὺξ προέκοψεν, **ἡ δὲ ἡμέρα ἤγγικεν**. ἀποθώμεθα οὖν τὰ ἔργα τοῦ σκότους, ἐνδυσώμεθα δὲ τὰ ὅπλα τοῦ φωτός. 13 **ὡς ἐν ἡμέρᾳ εὐσχημόνως περιπατήσωμεν**, μὴ κώμοις καὶ μέθαις, μὴ κοίταις καὶ ἀσελγείαις, μὴ ἔριδι καὶ ζήλῳ, 14 ἀλλ' ἐνδύσασθε τὸν κύριον Ἰησοῦν Χριστὸν καὶ τῆς σαρκὸς πρόνοιαν μὴ ποιεῖσθε εἰς ἐπιθυμίας.

---

1. As Moo indicates, the metaphor of "storing up" normally refers to something positive; thus it here expresses an irony: "The recalcitrant sinner is storing up for himself not blessing or life but wrath" (Douglas J. Moo, *The Epistle to the Romans*, NICNT [Grand Rapids: Eerdmans, 1996], 134).

> *Besides this, since you know the time,* **it is already the hour for you to wake up from sleep**, *because now our salvation is nearer than when we first believed. 12 The night is nearly over,* **and the day is near**; *so let us discard the deeds of darkness and put on the armor of light. 13* **Let us walk with decency, as in the daytime**: *not in carousing and drunkenness; not in sexual impurity and promiscuity; not in quarreling and jealousy. 14 But put on the Lord Jesus Christ, and don't make plans to gratify the desires of the flesh.*

This passage employs a collocation of temporal indicators: *the time, the hour, the night,* and *the day* (13:11–12; *daytime* in v. 13 is literally "day" [ἡμέρα]). *The time* and *the hour* refer to present reality: Paul says *you know the time* and *it is already* (or "now"; ἤδη) *the hour for you to wake up from sleep* (v. 11). The language of waking from sleep has apocalyptic overtones, with its warning for readiness in expectation of the imminent day. The following clause further heightens such imminence: *now our salvation is nearer than when we first believed* (v. 11). Salvation drawing *nearer* (ἐγγύτερον) underscores the fact that this current hour is passing—*the time* is not of indefinite extent.

The hour is viewed as part of *the night*, which *is nearly over* and is set in contrast to *the day*, which *is near* (v. 12). Thus the fundamental contrast is between *the night* and *the day*. Since *the night* is correlated with this present time (*you know the time; it is already the hour*, v. 11; *the night is nearly over*, v. 12), *the day* is most likely also regarded as an epoch or era rather than as a single, literal "day." The nearing day is an era filled with light, in contrast to the era of the night, filled with darkness.

As such, Paul exhorts his readers to live as though the day were about to dawn. They are to *discard the deeds of darkness and put on the armor of light* (v. 12). Some of the *deeds of darkness* are articulated in a short vice-list—*carousing and drunkenness, sexual impurity and promiscuity,* and *quarreling and jealousy* (v. 13). On the other hand, putting on *the armor of light* is correlated with walking with decency *as in the daytime* (or "day"; v. 13) and putting on *the Lord Jesus Christ* (v. 14a). Those walking as in the day are not to *make plans to gratify the desires of the flesh* (v. 14b).

This passage evokes an image of the last vestiges of night giving way to daybreak. It is close enough to dawn that a little predawn light may be sensed faintly. Such an image holds several strengths for Paul's communicative purposes. First, it is self-evident that some activities naturally belong to the night, while others belong to the day. Sleeping, for example, is a nocturnal activity, but Paul exhorts his readers to *wake up from sleep* (v. 11), like a person who rises before dawn in preparation for the day ahead.[2] The early riser does not

---

2. As Thielman notes, those living in ancient Roman cities rose early before daybreak in order to take advantage of the daylight (Frank Thielman, *Romans*, ZECNT [Grand Rapids: Zondervan, 2018], 614).

wake before dawn in order to engage further in nocturnal activities but to begin their day. The fact that it may technically still be nighttime when they wake does not alter this fact. Having slept already, the early riser treats their subsequent time as though daytime. Thus, when Paul exhorts his readers to *walk with decency, as in the daytime* (v. 13), he is not endorsing a fiction ("it is in fact nighttime, but please pretend that it is daytime"). Rather, he draws on phenomenological experience to exhort daytime living now that the night has virtually come to an end.

Second, the image of night giving way to daybreak conveys absolute certainty of what is to come.[3] No one rising from their slumber in darkness doubts that the new day will soon dawn. It is an inevitable fact. Thus, Paul's image addresses potential objections that may arise from doubts that the work of Christ has actually changed anything. Having woken from sleep, the believer may complain that it is still night—where is this day that was promised? Paul's image acknowledges that, yes, it is still nighttime, but the day is inevitably approaching.

Third, the image conveys this current situation as an *hour*, which is obviously a subcomponent of the night. This current period represents the final fraction of the night. Thus the image underscores the eschatological drama of the period following the ascension of Christ. Not only is this the final period before daybreak, but it is passing by quickly—*our salvation is nearer than when we first believed* (v. 11).

1 Cor 15:23–28 ἕκαστος δὲ ἐν τῷ ἰδίῳ τάγματι· ἀπαρχὴ Χριστός, ἔπειτα οἱ τοῦ Χριστοῦ ἐν τῇ παρουσίᾳ αὐτοῦ, 24 **εἶτα τὸ τέλος, ὅταν παραδιδῷ τὴν βασιλείαν τῷ θεῷ καὶ πατρί,** ὅταν καταργήσῃ πᾶσαν ἀρχὴν καὶ πᾶσαν ἐξουσίαν καὶ δύναμιν. 25 δεῖ γὰρ αὐτὸν βασιλεύειν ἄχρι οὗ θῇ πάντας τοὺς ἐχθροὺς ὑπὸ τοὺς πόδας αὐτοῦ. 26 ἔσχατος ἐχθρὸς καταργεῖται ὁ θάνατος· 27 πάντα γὰρ ὑπέταξεν ὑπὸ τοὺς πόδας αὐτοῦ. ὅταν δὲ εἴπῃ ὅτι πάντα ὑποτέτακται, δῆλον ὅτι ἐκτὸς τοῦ ὑποτάξαντος αὐτῷ τὰ πάντα. 28 ὅταν δὲ ὑποταγῇ αὐτῷ τὰ πάντα, τότε αὐτὸς ὁ υἱὸς ὑποταγήσεται τῷ ὑποτάξαντι αὐτῷ τὰ πάντα, ἵνα ᾖ ὁ θεὸς πάντα ἐν πᾶσιν.

But each in his own order: Christ, the firstfruits; afterward, at his coming, those who belong to Christ. 24 **Then comes the end, when he hands over the kingdom to God the Father, when he abolishes all rule and all authority**

---

3. The timing of the parousia is not the point, but rather its certainly is; "the time of the appearing is subordinate to the fact of the appearing" (Everett F. Harrison, "Romans," in *The Expositors Bible Commentary: Romans, 1 Corinthians, 2 Corinthians, Galatians* [Grand Rapids: Zondervan, 1976], 142).

and power. 25 *For he must reign until he puts all his enemies under his feet.* 26 *The last enemy to be abolished is death.* 27 *For God has put everything under his feet. Now when it says "everything" is put under him, it is obvious that he who puts everything under him is the exception.* 28 *When everything is subject to Christ, then the Son himself will also be subject to the one who subjected everything to him, so that God may be all in all.*

As discussed above (see §4.2), this passage outlines a sequence of events beginning with the parousia of Christ. *At his coming*, believers (*those who belong to Christ*) will be resurrected just as Christ has been as *the firstfruits* of the resurrection (15:23). *Then comes the end* with Christ's handing over *the kingdom to God the Father* and the abolition of *all rule and all authority and power* (v. 24).[4] Since death is *the last enemy* (v. 26), the resurrection of the dead signals its final defeat. And with the defeat of the last enemy, *everything is subject to Christ* (v. 28).

Arguably the most curious element of this passage is the notion of handing *over the kingdom to God the Father* (v. 24). It is unclear what is envisaged here,[5] but at least one observation may be made. There is a mutuality with respect to the subjection of all things. *God has put everything under the Son's feet*, with the obvious exception of God himself (v. 27). Once all has been subject to Christ, the Son *hands over the kingdom to God the Father* (v. 24). The Father establishes the kingdom for the Son, and the Son returns the kingdom to the Father. The result of this mutuality is that *God may be all in all*.

1 Thess 5:1–4 Περὶ δὲ τῶν χρόνων καὶ τῶν καιρῶν, ἀδελφοί, οὐ χρείαν ἔχετε ὑμῖν γράφεσθαι, 2 αὐτοὶ γὰρ ἀκριβῶς οἴδατε ὅτι **ἡμέρα κυρίου ὡς κλέπτης ἐν νυκτὶ οὕτως ἔρχεται.** 3 ὅταν λέγωσιν, εἰρήνη καὶ ἀσφάλεια, τότε αἰφνίδιος αὐτοῖς ἐφίσταται ὄλεθρος ὥσπερ ἡ ὠδὶν τῇ ἐν γαστρὶ ἐχούσῃ, καὶ οὐ μὴ ἐκφύγωσιν. 4 ὑμεῖς δέ, ἀδελφοί, οὐκ ἐστὲ ἐν σκότει, **ἵνα ἡ ἡμέρα ὑμᾶς ὡς κλέπτης καταλάβῃ**

About the times and the seasons: Brothers and sisters, you do not need anything to be written to you. 2 For you yourselves know very well that **the day of the**

---

4. Some interpreters find room here to posit an intermediate kingdom between the parousia and the final resurrection of the dead (the millennial kingdom; cf. Rev 20:4–6). For a helpful summary of the issues, and an argument against this view, see David E. Garland, *1 Corinthians*, BECNT (Grand Rapids: Baker Academic, 2003), 710.

5. Though, as Lewis rightly acknowledges, it symbolizes "the final and full sovereignty of God" (Scott M. Lewis, *"So That God May Be All in All": The Apocalyptic Message of 1 Corinthians 15,12–34*, Tesi Gregoriana Serie Teologia 42 [Rome: Pontifical Gregorian University Press, 1998], 55).

Lord will come just like a thief in the night. 3 When they say, "Peace and security," then sudden destruction will come upon them, like labor pains on a pregnant woman, and they will not escape. 4 But you, brothers and sisters, are not in the dark, **for this day to surprise you like a thief.**

As indicated above (§4.2), the "day of the Lord" must here be understood as the day of the Lord's coming. This day *will come just like a thief in the night* (5:2), and Paul's language here alludes to Jesus's teaching that the Son of Man will come like an unexpected thief (Matt 24:36–44; Luke 12:35–40).[6]

While the timing of this day is unknown, the expectation of its arrival is certain. It ought not to be a surprise to those who are not in the dark (1 Thess 5:4). But to those who are surprised by its coming, the day of the Lord will bring sudden and inescapable destruction (v. 3).

2 Thess 1:5–10 ἔνδειγμα τῆς δικαίας κρίσεως τοῦ θεοῦ εἰς τὸ καταξιωθῆναι ὑμᾶς τῆς βασιλείας τοῦ θεοῦ, ὑπὲρ ἧς καὶ πάσχετε, 6 εἴπερ δίκαιον παρὰ θεῷ ἀνταποδοῦναι τοῖς θλίβουσιν ὑμᾶς θλῖψιν 7 καὶ ὑμῖν τοῖς θλιβομένοις ἄνεσιν μεθ' ἡμῶν, ἐν τῇ ἀποκαλύψει τοῦ κυρίου Ἰησοῦ ἀπ' οὐρανοῦ μετ' ἀγγέλων δυνάμεως αὐτοῦ 8 ἐν πυρὶ φλογός, διδόντος ἐκδίκησιν τοῖς μὴ εἰδόσιν θεὸν καὶ τοῖς μὴ ὑπακούουσιν τῷ εὐαγγελίῳ τοῦ κυρίου ἡμῶν Ἰησοῦ, 9 οἵτινες δίκην τίσουσιν ὄλεθρον αἰώνιον ἀπὸ προσώπου τοῦ κυρίου καὶ ἀπὸ τῆς δόξης τῆς ἰσχύος αὐτοῦ, 10 **ὅταν ἔλθῃ ἐνδοξασθῆναι ἐν τοῖς ἁγίοις αὐτοῦ καὶ θαυμασθῆναι ἐν πᾶσιν τοῖς πιστεύσασιν**, ὅτι ἐπιστεύθη τὸ μαρτύριον ἡμῶν ἐφ' ὑμᾶς, **ἐν τῇ ἡμέρᾳ ἐκείνῃ**.

It is clear evidence of God's righteous judgment that you will be counted worthy of God's kingdom, for which you also are suffering, 6 since it is just for God to repay with affliction those who afflict you 7 and to give relief to you who are afflicted, along with us. This will take place at the revelation of the Lord Jesus from heaven with his powerful angels, 8 when he takes vengeance with flaming fire on those who don't know God and on those who don't obey the gospel of our Lord Jesus. 9 They will pay the penalty of eternal destruction from the Lord's presence and from his glorious strength 10 **on that day when he comes to be glorified by his saints and to be marveled at by all those who have believed**, *because our testimony among you was believed.*

---

6. Leon Morris, *The First and Second Epistles to the Thessalonians*, rev. ed., NICNT (Grand Rapids: Eerdmans, 1991), 150.

The discussion of this passage above established that *the revelation of the Lord Jesus from heaven* will bring relief to those afflicted for God's kingdom, as well as vengeance on, and eternal destruction of, *those who don't know God* (1:7–9; see §4.2). This will occur *on that day when he comes to be glorified by his saints* (v. 10).

Here we see that the eschatological *day* is marked by the coming of Christ, which is also described as *the revelation of the Lord Jesus from heaven* (1:7, 10). Indeed, it is the coming of Christ—his revelation from heaven—that establishes the *day* for what it is. It is the eschatological era ushered in by the Lord's coming and appearance. As noted above, the coming of Christ will bring vengeance for some and relief for others. But *that day* will also be characterized by Christ's reception in glory—he will be *glorified by his saints* and *marveled at by all those who have believed* (v. 10).[7] Thus, the *day* is a multifaceted one. The presence of Christ will be glorious, with his *glorious strength* being exerted for the punishment of evil and the restoration of the faithful.

2 Thess 2:1–3 Ἐρωτῶμεν δὲ ὑμᾶς, ἀδελφοί, ὑπὲρ τῆς παρουσίας τοῦ κυρίου ἡμῶν Ἰησοῦ Χριστοῦ καὶ ἡμῶν ἐπισυναγωγῆς ἐπ' αὐτὸν 2 εἰς τὸ μὴ ταχέως σαλευθῆναι ὑμᾶς ἀπὸ τοῦ νοὸς μηδὲ θροεῖσθαι, μήτε διὰ πνεύματος μήτε διὰ λόγου μήτε δι' ἐπιστολῆς ὡς δι' ἡμῶν, ὡς ὅτι **ἐνέστηκεν ἡ ἡμέρα τοῦ κυρίου**· 3 μή τις ὑμᾶς ἐξαπατήσῃ κατὰ μηδένα τρόπον. **ὅτι ἐὰν μὴ ἔλθῃ ἡ ἀποστασία πρῶτον καὶ ἀποκαλυφθῇ ὁ ἄνθρωπος τῆς ἀνομίας**, ὁ υἱὸς τῆς ἀπωλείας

Now concerning the coming of our Lord Jesus Christ and our being gathered to him: We ask you, brothers and sisters, 2 not to be easily upset or troubled, either by a prophecy or by a message or by a letter supposedly from us, **alleging that the day of the Lord has come***. 3 Don't let anyone deceive you in any way.* **For that day will not come unless the apostasy comes first and the man of lawlessness is revealed***, the man doomed to destruction.*

As discussed above, this text demonstrates a clear correlation between *the coming of our Lord Jesus Christ* and *the day of the Lord*, with no apparent difference meant by the two appellations except that the former refers to an event, while the latter refers to the day on which that event occurs (see §4.2 above).

---

7. There may be an echo of Ps 89:5–7 here, in which God is praised and feared *in the council of the holy ones* (Ernest Best, *The First and Second Epistles to the Thessalonians*, BNTC [Peabody: Hendrickson, 1972], 264–65).

Also as discussed above, Paul anticipates that some deceivers may allege *that the day of the Lord has come*, and he likewise anticipates that the Thessalonians may be *troubled* by such allegations (2:2; see §4.2).

Here we see that *that day will not come unless the apostasy comes first and the man of lawlessness is revealed* (v. 3). Paul elaborates on *the man of lawlessness* in vv. 3–9 and seems to describe *the apostasy* in v. 10–12. *The man of lawlessness* may allude to Caligula's sacrilegious self-exaltation in the Jewish temple in AD 40, establishing a type of leader who desires to be worshiped in God's place (see §4.2 above). But regardless of possible historical antecedents such as Caligula, Pompey, or Antiochus IV Epiphanes, this lawless one "is the embodiment, but also the climax of the traditional expectation of the eschatological adversary of God."[8] If vv. 10–12 describes *the apostasy* of v. 3, it seems that *the man of lawlessness* deceives those who *did not accept the love of the truth* (vv. 9–10), leading to their condemnation (vv. 11–12).

Beyond these details, it is difficult to know how Paul envisaged these events. However, it seems clear that he expects the coming of *the man of lawlessness* and the accompanying *apostasy* to be self-evident, otherwise they could not function as signposts for the coming of *that day*. As Paul reassures his readers, *that day will not come unless the apostasy comes first and the man of lawlessness is revealed* (v. 3). They could hardly be reassured that the day has not yet come if they were not able to ascertain that *the man of lawlessness* had not yet come. Thus, while we are unable to ascertain exactly what Paul means by *the man of lawlessness* and *the apostasy*, it is very likely that his original readers were able to discern his meaning.

2 Tim 4:6–8 Ἐγὼ γὰρ ἤδη σπένδομαι, καὶ ὁ καιρὸς τῆς ἀναλύσεώς μου ἐφέστηκεν. 7 τὸν καλὸν ἀγῶνα ἠγώνισμαι, τὸν δρόμον τετέλεκα, τὴν πίστιν τετήρηκα· 8 λοιπὸν ἀπόκειταί μοι ὁ τῆς δικαιοσύνης στέφανος, ὃν ἀποδώσει μοι ὁ κύριος ἐν ἐκείνῃ τῇ ἡμέρᾳ, ὁ δίκαιος κριτής, οὐ μόνον δὲ ἐμοὶ ἀλλὰ καὶ πᾶσιν τοῖς ἠγαπηκόσιν τὴν ἐπιφάνειαν αὐτοῦ.

For I am already being poured out as a drink offering, and the time for my departure is close. 7 I have fought the good fight, I have finished the race, I have kept the faith. 8 **There is reserved for me the crown of righteousness, which the Lord, the righteous Judge, will give me on that day, and not only to me, but to all those who have loved his appearing.**

---

8. Villiers, "Eschatology of 2 Thessalonians," 353.

Reflecting on the end of his life and ministry, Paul expects his *departure* to come soon (4:6). He has *fought the good fight, finished the race,* and *kept the faith* (v. 7). In keeping with the *race* metaphor, he looks forward to *the crown of righteousness* that will be given to him *on that day* (v. 8). The language of the *day* is clearly associated with judgment, since on that day *the crown of righteousness* is given by *the Lord, the righteous Judge* (v. 8).[9] This implies a day of judgment, with Paul's faithfulness being rewarded by the Lord. And it obviously entails the presence of the Lord. Thus, *that day* is a day of the Lord's presence, judgment, and reward for the faithful.[10]

5.3 Summary

This chapter has investigated texts related to the last day, including *the day of wrath* (ἡ ἡμέρα ὀργῆς), *the day* (ἡ ἡμέρα), *the hour* (ἡ ὥρα), and *the end* (τὸ τέλος). A day of wrath is coming in which God's righteous judgment will be revealed (Rom 2:5). On that day, God will judge what people have kept secret (v. 16). Since the day is near, and the night is nearly over, it is the hour to wake up from sleep and live as in the daytime (13:11–14). Believers ought not be surprised by the coming of the day of the Lord, though it will come like a thief in the night (1 Thess 5:1–4). On the day that Christ comes, he will be glorified by his saints (2 Thess 1:10), and those who have loved his coming will receive from him a crown of righteousness (2 Tim 4:8). But believers ought not be deceived into thinking that the day of the Lord has already come. It will not come until the man of lawlessness has been revealed (2 Thess 2:1–3). Then, after the coming of Christ comes the end, when all rule and authority is abolished, and he hands over the kingdom to God the Father (1 Cor 15:24–25).

The concept of the day of the Lord has a rich history through Jewish writings and theology and is no doubt in the background of Paul's use of *day* terminology. As Burkeen summarizes, the day of the Lord represents "the division between the transcendent heaven and the earth, as well as the division between this aeon and the future aeon."[11] It refers to the end of this aeon and the beginning of the new aeon. "The Day will bring about the destruction of the fallen angelic beings which have brought evil into the world."[12] Motifs from

---

9. For more on the significance of "the day" in 2 Timothy, see the excursus in Luke Timothy Johnson, *The First and Second Letters to Timothy: A New Translation with Introduction and Commentary*, AYB (New Haven: Yale University Press, 2008), 433–37.

10. Johnson observes that "2 Timothy is also at least as future-oriented, communal, and apocalyptic in its eschatology as those undisputed letters we have surveyed." There is nothing to suggest a diminished eschatological expectation (Johnson, *First and Second Letters to Timothy*, 435).

11. W. Howard Burkeen, "The Parousia of Christ in the Thessalonian Correspondence" (PhD diss., University of Aberdeen, 1979), 217.

12. Burkeen, "Parousia of Christ," 217.

Old Testament theophanies and from the day-of-Yahweh tradition are applied to Jesus as the messianic figure who was raised by the power of the Father and "who is to come at the end of the age for the completion of the judgment and salvation of the world."[13] According to Burkeen, Paul modifies the traditional Jewish concept of the day of the Lord in two key ways. While the day of the Lord portrayed God himself as its figure and coming one, Paul sees Christ in that role. And while the tradition sees the day of the Lord as the time when God would overcome the forces of evil, Paul proclaims that they have already been decisively defeated.[14]

Since our study is Paul's *eschatology*, it is striking how few explicit references to the *end* are to be found in the Pauline canon. Only in seven texts do we see mention of the end, the day, or the hour. Indeed, only one of these refers to *the end* explicitly, and this uses the word τέλος, not ἔσχατος (1 Cor 15:24). While ἔσχατος occurs six times in the Pauline canon, none of these refer to *the end* in an eschatological sense. Rather, they refer to the apostles in last place (1 Cor 4:9), Paul as the last eyewitness of the resurrection (1 Cor 15:8), death as the last enemy (v. 26), Christ as the last Adam (v. 45), the last trumpet (v. 52), and the last days—which refer to this age, not the end of the age (2 Tim 3:1). While mention of the last enemy and the last trumpet are of course eschatological notions, the word ἔσχατος is nevertheless not meant for "the eschatological end." Thus, Paul's eschatology is strikingly free of the eschaton, in one manner of speaking.

But, of course, the end is assumed in myriad ways in Paul's thinking, and there are several other ways in which it is indicated. Reference to the coming of Christ, judgment, resurrection, eternal life, inheritance, the new creation, hope, and so forth all assume a final day, even if such language is rare. Indeed, the entire shape of Paul's inaugurated eschatology arises from his conviction that the end has broken into the present. In particular, the resurrection of Christ points to this, since the resurrection of the righteous belongs to the last day. Since he has already been raised, the day has already come with Christ. Thus, the end has broken into the present, creating the overlap of the ages that characterizes Paul's inaugurated eschatology.

---

13. Burkeen, "Parousia of Christ," 221. See also Paul R. Williamson, *Death and the Afterlife: Biblical Perspectives on Ultimate Questions*, NSBT 44 (London: Apollos, 2017), 98.
14. Burkeen, "Parousia of Christ," 221–22.

CHAPTER 6

JUDGMENT

6.1 Introduction

The expectation of final judgment is a central theme of biblical eschatology, of Second Temple Judaism, and, of course, for Paul. It is an indispensable feature of Paul's hope for the future, as he expects evil to be judged and justice to prevail. According to Paul, judgment will be universal, and the evil that has yet gone unpunished will not escape God's wrath, just as glory awaits those who have patiently endured in the pursuit of righteousness. Paul insists that God's judgment is just, and there is no way to be excused from it—for even our consciences condemn us.

While all people are initially subject to his wrath, God declares righteous those who trust in the blood of Christ. They will be held blameless on the day of judgment, though they will nevertheless need to give an account for what they have done. Christ himself will stand as judge of the living and the dead.

In the end, judgment is ultimately concerned with the eradication of evil and the final establishment of righteousness and peace. It is a necessary precursor to the promised renewal of creation.

Future judgment holds several implications for life here and now, including its motivation toward godly living. It also offers security and hope in the face of injustice, and puts human opinion into perspective.

This chapter traces the theme of final judgment by exploring relevant references to *judgment, wrath, anger, blamelessness, the judgment seat of Christ, destruction, salvation,* and other concepts that are clearly related to the event of final assessment.

6.2 Judgment Texts

Rom 2:1–11 Διὸ ἀναπολόγητος εἶ, ὦ ἄνθρωπε πᾶς ὁ κρίνων· ἐν ᾧ γὰρ κρίνεις τὸν ἕτερον, σεαυτὸν κατακρίνεις, τὰ γὰρ αὐτὰ πράσσεις ὁ κρίνων. 2 οἴδαμεν δὲ ὅτι τὸ κρίμα τοῦ θεοῦ ἐστιν κατὰ ἀλήθειαν ἐπὶ τοὺς τὰ τοιαῦτα πράσσοντας. 3 λογίζῃ δὲ τοῦτο, ὦ ἄνθρωπε ὁ κρίνων τοὺς τὰ τοιαῦτα πράσσοντας καὶ ποιῶν αὐτά, ὅτι σὺ ἐκφεύξῃ τὸ κρίμα τοῦ θεοῦ; 4 ἢ τοῦ πλούτου τῆς χρηστότητος αὐτοῦ καὶ τῆς ἀνοχῆς καὶ τῆς μακροθυμίας καταφρονεῖς, ἀγνοῶν ὅτι τὸ χρηστὸν τοῦ θεοῦ εἰς μετάνοιάν σε ἄγει; 5 κατὰ δὲ τὴν σκληρότητά σου καὶ ἀμετανόητον καρδίαν **θησαυρίζεις σεαυτῷ ὀργὴν ἐν ἡμέρᾳ ὀργῆς καὶ ἀποκαλύψεως δικαιοκρισίας τοῦ θεοῦ** 6 ὃς ἀποδώσει ἑκάστῳ κατὰ τὰ ἔργα αὐτοῦ· 7 τοῖς μὲν καθ᾽ ὑπομονὴν ἔργου ἀγαθοῦ δόξαν καὶ τιμὴν καὶ ἀφθαρσίαν ζητοῦσιν ζωὴν αἰώνιον, 8 **τοῖς δὲ ἐξ ἐριθείας καὶ ἀπειθοῦσιν τῇ ἀληθείᾳ πειθομένοις δὲ τῇ ἀδικίᾳ ὀργὴ καὶ θυμός**. 9 θλῖψις καὶ στενοχωρία ἐπὶ πᾶσαν ψυχὴν ἀνθρώπου τοῦ κατεργαζομένου τὸ κακόν, Ἰουδαίου τε πρῶτον καὶ Ἕλληνος· 10 δόξα δὲ καὶ τιμὴ καὶ εἰρήνη παντὶ τῷ ἐργαζομένῳ τὸ ἀγαθόν, Ἰουδαίῳ τε πρῶτον καὶ Ἕλληνι· 11 οὐ γάρ ἐστιν προσωπολημψία παρὰ τῷ θεῷ.

Therefore, every one of you who judges is without excuse. For when you judge another, **you condemn yourself, since you, the judge, do the same things**. *2 We know that* **God's judgment on those who do such things is based on the truth**. *3 Do you really think—anyone of you who judges those who do such things yet do the same—***that you will escape God's judgment?*** *4 Or do you despise the riches of his kindness, restraint, and patience, not recognizing that God's kindness is intended to lead you to repentance? 5 Because of your hardened and unrepentant heart* **you are storing up wrath for yourself in the day of wrath, when God's righteous judgment is revealed**. *6 He will repay each one according to his works: 7 eternal life to those who by persistence in doing good seek glory, honor, and immortality; 8 but* **wrath and anger to those who are self-seeking and disobey the truth while obeying unrighteousness**. *9 There will be affliction and distress for every human being who does evil, first to the Jew, and also to the Greek; 10 but glory, honor, and peace for everyone who does what is good, first to the Jew, and also to the Greek. 11 For there is no favoritism with God.*

Having established the depravity and guilt of the gentile world (1:18–32), Paul now shifts to the judgment of Jews who stand in judgment over gentiles. Though there is no doubt about gentile guilt in Paul's mind, there is also no grounds for others to judge them when they themselves *do the same things* (2:1). Their judgment of others leads to their own condemnation, since *God's judgment . . . is based on truth* (2:2). That is, God's judgment is not based on favoritism (v. 11), but on the reality of how people conduct themselves.

Those who judge others yet do the same things will not *escape God's judgment* (v. 3). At this point, the tables have turned away from gentile guilt to the hypocrisy of Jewish judgment of the gentiles. Not only do the Jews condemn themselves since they *do the same things* as the gentiles (2:1), but they apparently *despise the riches of* God's *kindness*, which *is intended to lead* them *to repentance* (v. 4). That is, God patiently restrains himself from exercising his wrath against their hypocrisy. This patience ought not to be interpreted as blessing that comes as a reward for faithful living. Rather, it is holding off God's just judgment in order to allow repentance for their hypocrisy.

Sadly, however, their *hardened and unrepentant heart* means that they *are storing up wrath* for themselves *in the day of wrath, when God's righteous judgment is revealed* (v. 5). As discussed above (see §5.2), this is Paul's only use of the phrase *the day of wrath* (ἡμέρα ὀργῆς). It is more common simply to refer to *the day* (Rom 13:12; 2 Thess 1:10), but since the context addresses God's righteous judgment, the descriptor *of wrath* is appropriately supplied. It is clear that *the day* is not one solely of wrath (Rom 2:6–8), but it is so described here to underscore the fact that it will bring wrath to those who *are storing up wrath* for themselves.

Furthermore, the notion of *storing up wrath* conveys an expectation of delayed judgment of sin (v. 5). That is, the hypocrites will not experience the full consequences of their actions until God's righteous judgment is revealed. This serves as an implicit warning that hypocrites will not get away with their deeds in the end. They might think they are able to sin without consequence or reprimand, but in fact the day is coming in which reckoning will occur. This may explain why Paul uses the word *revealed* (ἀποκάλυψις) of God's righteous judgment; it may appear absent while the hypocrites seem to get away with (gentile-like) sin, but on that day judgment will be *revealed*.

God's righteous judgment will be revealed when *he will repay each one according to his works* (v. 6; see Ps 62:12b). If Psalm 62 is the correct background for this citation (it could also come from Prov 24:12),[1] God's judgment according to works is an expression of his faithful love (Ps 62:12a). David, like Paul, has critiqued the hypocrisy observed around him: *they bless with their mouths, but they curse inwardly* (62:4). But David's refuge is in God (v. 7) in the face of oppression (vv. 3, 10). In this context, judgment according to works is comforting since people are assessed according to their deeds rather than their appearance. The problem with hypocrites is that they pass themselves off as something they are not, and often the world goes along with the false perception. Judgment according to works sets the record straight.

This point is expanded in the following verses. *Eternal life* will be awarded *to those who by persistence in doing good seek glory, honor, and immortality* (Rom 2:7).

---

1. Colin G. Kruse, *Paul's Letter to the Romans*, PNTC (Grand Rapids: Eerdmans, 2012), 124.

But *wrath and anger* will be due *to those who are self-seeking and disobey the truth while obeying unrighteousness* (v. 8). While these verses are the subject of much debate within Pauline scholarship since they seem to endorse a "works righteousness" that Paul later firmly disavows (e.g., Rom 3:27–31; 4:1–8), it is important to remember the context. Paul is critiquing Jewish hypocrites. Against hypocrisy, Paul asserts that judgment will not be based on appearance or Jewish privilege but on works. God's righteous judgment will be *righteous* because it will look beyond façades to the inner truth (2:16).

The next two verses form an inverted parallel to 2:7–8, with *affliction and distress* for those who do *evil* (v. 9) and *glory, honor, and peace for everyone who does what is good* (v. 10). The additional element in both verses is the phrase *first to the Jew, and also to the Greek*. While this phrase speaks to a theological priority (cf. 1:16), in this context it underscores the equality of both Jew and Greek in the face of God's judgment. Jews are not exempt from scrutiny just because the gentiles are self-evidently guilty before God. Jewish hypocrites may not be self-evidently guilty, but their guilt remains nonetheless. This is finally confirmed by the following verse: *For there is no favoritism with God* (2:11). In the face of God's righteous judgment, Jews have no advantage over gentiles. Both will be judged according to their works, not according to favoritism, ethnic status, appearance, or human opinion.[2]

Rom 2:14–16 ὅταν γὰρ ἔθνη τὰ μὴ νόμον ἔχοντα φύσει τὰ τοῦ νόμου ποιῶσιν, οὗτοι νόμον μὴ ἔχοντες ἑαυτοῖς εἰσιν νόμος· 15 οἵτινες ἐνδείκνυνται τὸ ἔργον τοῦ νόμου γραπτὸν ἐν ταῖς καρδίαις αὐτῶν, συμμαρτυρούσης αὐτῶν τῆς συνειδήσεως καὶ μεταξὺ ἀλλήλων τῶν λογισμῶν κατηγορούντων ἢ καὶ ἀπολογουμένων, 16 **ἐν ἡμέρᾳ ὅτε κρίνει ὁ θεὸς τὰ κρυπτὰ τῶν ἀνθρώπων** κατὰ τὸ εὐαγγέλιόν μου διὰ Ἰησοῦ Χριστοῦ.

So, when Gentiles, who do not by nature have the law, do what the law demands, they are a law to themselves even though they do not have the law. 15 They show that the work of the law is written on their hearts. Their consciences confirm this. Their competing thoughts either accuse or even excuse them 16 **on the day when God judges what people have kept secret***, according to my gospel through Christ Jesus.*

---

2. Wright points to the impartiality of God as judge within Jewish tradition (e.g., Sir 35:15; see N. T. Wright, "The Letter to the Romans," in *The New Interpreter's Bible: Volume Ten—Acts, Introduction to Epistolary Literature, Romans, 1 Corinthians* [Nashville: Abingdon, 2002], 440). See also Jouette M. Bassler, *Divine Impartiality: Paul and a Theological Axiom*, SBLDS 59 (Chico, CA: Scholars Press, 1982); idem, "Divine Impartiality in Paul's Letter to the Romans," *NovT* 26 (1984): 43–58.

Though God's judgment of *what people have kept secret* can be understood generically to refer to the unveiling of secret sins, the context suggests a more specific reference. Paul speaks of gentiles becoming *a law to themselves even though they do not have the law* (2:14). This refers to an inherent moral compass that leads them to *do what the law demands* even though they *do not by nature have the law* (v. 14). The absence of the "external" law is juxtaposed with the presence of an "internal" law.

There are several further indicators of this "internal" moral compass. The gentiles, who do not have the "external" law, *show that the work of the law is written on their hearts* (v. 15a). The works of the law being *written on their hearts* obviously refers to a kind of internal morality (see also Jer 31:33). Moreover, *their consciences confirm this* (Rom 2:15b). Furthermore, Paul draws attention to their inner thought world: *their competing thoughts either accuse or even excuse them* (v. 15c). That is, their consciences can accuse them inwardly when they do things that they consider wrong or immoral. But their consciences can also *excuse them*, if gentiles do things that they do not consider to be wrong or immoral (even if the "external" law regards them so).[3]

Set against this context, God's judgment of *what people have kept secret* (v. 16) most likely refers to these inner moral issues. That is, God will judge gentiles with a view to their inner moral compasses. He will assess the hidden factors that constitute every person's inner world. This means that the generic reading of 2:16—that God will unveil secret sins—though no doubt theologically correct, is not the intended meaning here. It refers to God's assessment of people's inner world; how they live in response to what is written on their hearts, what their consciences dictate, and how their thoughts accuse or excuse them.

Finally, Paul regards God's judgment of people's inner moral compass as *according to* his *gospel through Christ Jesus* (v. 16). It is unclear exactly what in this text Paul sees as according to the gospel. He could simply mean that the coming of judgment is according to the gospel—God will one day judge all for their sins, but through faith in Jesus Christ Jew and gentile will be saved. Or Paul could mean that the judgment of things *kept secret* is according to the gospel. The former is most likely, since Paul elsewhere affirms the judgment of God as an essential part of his message (e.g., Rom 3:19). It is unnecessary to find a more specific referent.

---

3. As for the identity of the gentiles Paul has in mind, Bird is likely correct to argue that he is here speaking cryptically about Christian gentiles, "who, by their obedience as enabled through the Spirit, fulfilled the law and thus shame an imaginary Jewish opponent" (Michael F. Bird, *Romans*, SGBC [Grand Rapids: Zondervan, 2016], 78).

Rom 2:28–29 οὐ γὰρ ὁ ἐν τῷ φανερῷ Ἰουδαῖός ἐστιν οὐδὲ ἡ ἐν τῷ φανερῷ ἐν σαρκὶ περιτομή, 29 ἀλλ' ὁ ἐν τῷ κρυπτῷ Ἰουδαῖος, καὶ περιτομὴ καρδίας ἐν πνεύματι οὐ γράμματι, **οὗ ὁ ἔπαινος οὐκ ἐξ ἀνθρώπων ἀλλ' ἐκ τοῦ θεοῦ.**

A person is not a Jew who is one outwardly, and true circumcision is not something visible in the flesh. 29 On the contrary, a person is a Jew who is one inwardly, and circumcision is of the heart—by the Spirit, not by the letter. ***That person's praise is not from people, but from God.***

While this text does not speak directly of judgment, it is implied. According to Paul, a true Jew *is one inwardly,* with *circumcision . . . of the heart—by the Spirit* (2:29). Such a person will not be praised by people but will be praised by God. In order to receive praise from God, some kind of assessment is necessary. And such assessment most likely occurs on the day of judgment.[4]

If this is correct, it is clear that judgment does not have only negative outcomes. Some people will receive praise from God on that day. Since Paul refers to circumcision of the heart by the Spirit (v. 29), it seems that Paul has believers in mind. The Spirit is the indisputable sign of belonging to Christ (8:9), and so Paul believes that those circumcised by the Spirit are declared righteous through faith in Jesus Christ (3:22). As such, the outcome of judgment will be positive rather than negative. It can even be referred to as praise from God.

Rom 3:1–6 Τί οὖν τὸ περισσὸν τοῦ Ἰουδαίου ἢ τίς ἡ ὠφέλεια τῆς περιτομῆς; 2 πολὺ κατὰ πάντα τρόπον. πρῶτον μὲν [γὰρ] ὅτι ἐπιστεύθησαν τὰ λόγια τοῦ θεοῦ. 3 τί γάρ; εἰ ἠπίστησάν τινες, μὴ ἡ ἀπιστία αὐτῶν τὴν πίστιν τοῦ θεοῦ καταργήσει; 4 μὴ γένοιτο· γινέσθω δὲ ὁ θεὸς ἀληθής, πᾶς δὲ ἄνθρωπος ψεύστης, καθὼς γέγραπται,

ὅπως ἂν δικαιωθῇς ἐν τοῖς λόγοις σου
*καὶ **νικήσεις ἐν τῷ κρίνεσθαί σε**.*

5 εἰ δὲ ἡ ἀδικία ἡμῶν θεοῦ δικαιοσύνην συνίστησιν, τί ἐροῦμεν; **μὴ ἄδικος ὁ θεὸς ὁ ἐπιφέρων τὴν ὀργήν;** κατὰ ἄνθρωπον λέγω. 6 μὴ γένοιτο· ἐπεὶ **πῶς κρινεῖ ὁ θεὸς τὸν κόσμον;**

So what advantage does the Jew have? Or what is the benefit of circumcision? 2 Considerable in every way. First, they were entrusted with the very words of

---

4. Solomon Andria, *Romans*, ABCS (Nairobi: Hippo, 2012), 60.

> God. **3** What then? If some were unfaithful, will their unfaithfulness nullify God's faithfulness? **4** Absolutely not! Let God be true, even though everyone is a liar, as it is written:
>
>> That you may be justified in your words
>> and **triumph when you judge**.
>
> **5** But if our unrighteousness highlights God's righteousness, what are we to say? I am using a human argument: **Is God unrighteous to inflict wrath? 6 Absolutely not! Otherwise, how will God judge the world?**

Paul draws on Psalm 51:4 to assert the righteousness of God's judgment.[5] God is true and will be *justified in* his *words* (Rom 3:4). His judgment will be his *triumph* (3:4). This righteousness is set against the unfaithfulness and untrustworthiness of others (v. 3). In contrast to unfaithful Jews, God's righteousness is accentuated.

He then anticipates a possible false conclusion that could arise from the accentuation of God's righteousness: *If our unrighteousness highlights God's righteousness. . . . Is God unrighteous to inflict wrath?* (v. 5). That is, if human unrighteousness serves to amplify God's righteousness, is it unfair to punish unrighteousness? After all, it ultimately serves a greater good. Ironically then, is God *unrighteous to inflict wrath* on people who accentuate his righteousness through their unrighteousness?

The question is a clever piece of trickery that tries to use God's righteousness against him. His infliction of wrath must be unjust since it punishes unrighteousness that, as has been established, amplifies God's righteousness. But Paul's immediate answer to the question is *Absolutely not!* (μὴ γένοιτο; v. 6a). And the reason he gives for this response is *otherwise, how will God judge the world?* (v. 6b).

What exactly does this response mean to Paul? The question attempts to undermine the validity of God's judgment, and his response is to say, "But then God could not judge the world"! Mostly likely Paul is simply rejecting the premise of the question. The premise undermines the authority of God to judge: Is it right for God to judge? But Paul's response corrects the premise:

---

5. Regarding Psalm 51, Moule exclaims, "The whole Scripture contains no more impassioned, yet no more profound and deliberate, utterance of the eternal truth that God is always in the right or He would be no God at all; that it is better, and more reasonable, to doubt anything than to count His righteousness, whatever cloud surrounds it, and whatever lightning bursts the cloud" (H. C. G. Moule, *The Epistle to the Romans*, new ed. [London: Pickering & Inglis, n.d.], 81).

it is simply a fact that God will judge the world. This is nonnegotiable; God *is* judge. Since we know for a fact that God will judge the world, the premise of the question must be rejected.

Through this brief interchange with Paul's imaginary interlocutor, we see how deeply ingrained is the assumption that God will judge the world. This belief exists at the level of presupposition, and for Paul it is absolutely nonnegotiable. It is a simple fact that God will judge the world.

> Rom 3:19 Οἴδαμεν δὲ ὅτι ὅσα ὁ νόμος λέγει τοῖς ἐν τῷ νόμῳ λαλεῖ, ἵνα **πᾶν στόμα φραγῇ καὶ ὑπόδικος γένηται πᾶς ὁ κόσμος τῷ θεῷ·** 20 διότι ἐξ ἔργων νόμου οὐ δικαιωθήσεται πᾶσα σὰρξ ἐνώπιον αὐτοῦ, διὰ γὰρ νόμου ἐπίγνωσις ἁμαρτίας.
>
> *Now we know that whatever the law says, it speaks to those who are subject to the law, so that **every mouth may be shut and the whole world may become subject to God's judgment**. 20 For no one will be justified in his sight by the works of the law, because the knowledge of sin comes through the law.*

Following his devastating assessment of Jews and gentiles under sin (3:9–18), Paul concludes that *the whole world* is *subject to God's judgment* (3:19c). This is on the basis that the law silences every mouth (v. 19b). The law condemns humanity because it reveals the extent of sin (v. 20).

Though Paul has established that Jews and gentiles are all under sin (v. 9), it is not entirely clear how the law silences *every mouth* and puts the *whole world* under judgment, since the law belongs to Israel. The gentile world on the whole does not know the law, and as such it is not clear how gentiles, along with Jews, are condemned by the law. Indeed, Paul even says that the law *speaks to those who are subject to the law* (v. 19), and gentiles are not self-evidently subject to it.[6]

It is likely that Paul somehow regards the law as having universal scope. Even though it is the law of Israel, it nevertheless declares God's character and his expectations for humanity. However, Paul nowhere states this, and in fact his writings underscore the importance of gentile freedom from the law. Whatever the solution to this problem—which is beyond our interest here—Paul regards the whole world, both Jew and gentile, as subject to God's judgment.

---

6. A common solution is expressed by Thielman: "If the Jews, who had the privilege of being God's covenantal and elect people, could not keep the law, then it follows that no one, including the gentiles can" (Thielman, *Romans*, 168). The problem with this interpretation, however, is that Paul has just stressed in the previous chapter that a gentile who does not even know the law may, in theory (or by the power of the Spirit) fulfill the law even while the Jewish custodians of the law fail to keep it.

The judgment of God renders Jews and gentiles of equal status, since all are under sin and are accountable to God for it.

Rom 5:8–10 συνίστησιν δὲ τὴν ἑαυτοῦ ἀγάπην εἰς ἡμᾶς ὁ θεός, ὅτι ἔτι ἁμαρτωλῶν ὄντων ἡμῶν Χριστὸς ὑπὲρ ἡμῶν ἀπέθανεν. 9 πολλῷ οὖν μᾶλλον δικαιωθέντες νῦν ἐν τῷ αἵματι αὐτοῦ **σωθησόμεθα δι' αὐτοῦ ἀπὸ τῆς ὀργῆς.** 10 εἰ γὰρ ἐχθροὶ ὄντες κατηλλάγημεν τῷ θεῷ διὰ τοῦ θανάτου τοῦ υἱοῦ αὐτοῦ, πολλῷ μᾶλλον καταλλαγέντες σωθησόμεθα ἐν τῇ ζωῇ αὐτοῦ

But God proves his own love for us in that while we were still sinners, Christ died for us. 9 How much more then, since we have now been declared righteous by his blood, **will we be saved through him from wrath**. *10 For if, while we were enemies, we were reconciled to God through the death of his Son, then how much more, having been reconciled, will we be saved by his life.*

In this text we observe a number of tightly packed ideas with a logical progression from one to the next. The love of God has led to Christ's death for sinners (5:8). This death for sinners has led to being *declared righteous by his blood*, which in turns means that they will *be saved through him from wrath* (v. 9). The logical progression is reiterated in v. 10, in which Paul employs the technique of *qal wahomer* (a Jewish "how much greater" type of argument; also seen in 5:9).[7] If, having been God's enemies, believers have been reconciled to God through the death of Christ, *how much more, having been reconciled, will we be saved by his life* (v. 10).

There are several interesting parallels between the three verses. *While we were still sinners* (v. 8) parallels *while we were enemies* (v. 10a); *declared righteous by his blood* (v. 9a) parallels *reconciled to God through the death of his Son* (v. 10b); *saved through him from wrath* (v. 9b) parallels *saved by his life* (v. 10c). The first two couplets are straightforward, with the parallels between each pair quite transparent. The third couplet, however, is less transparent. Obviously a parallel is intended, with its *saved through/saved by* language, but the parallel between *from wrath* and *his life* is perplexing.

The parallel between *saved . . . from wrath* and *saved by his life* is a negative/positive contrast, with *wrath* as the fate from which sinners are saved and *his life* the means by which they are saved. The question is, in what sense does *his life* save them from wrath? Paul has already made clear—even in this short text—the role that Christ's *death* plays in salvation: *Christ died for us* (v. 8);

---

7. C. E. B. Cranfield, *The Epistle to the Romans*, 2 vols., ICC (London: T&T Clark, 1975), 265–66.

we have now been declared righteous by his blood (v. 9); *we were reconciled to God through the death of his Son* (v. 10). But what about his *life*?

There are only two options. First, Paul refers to Christ's life of obedience to his heavenly Father—a life that makes possible his sacrificial death for sin. In the second option, Paul refers to Christ's resurrection. While both are possible theologically, the latter option is the strongest in this context. There is an implied temporal order to the events described in v. 10—*we were reconciled; having been reconciled; will . . . be saved*. We know that the reconciliation occurs through the death of Christ, so it follows that the salvation *subsequent to* reconciliation involves the life that is *subsequent to* the death of Christ—that is, his resurrection life. This would fit other statements that appear to connect the resurrection of Christ with salvation, such as Romans 4:25: *He was delivered up for our trespasses and raised for our justification.*

Finally, in this text there is an interesting temporal correlation between the elements of salvation and the death and resurrection of Christ. The declaration of righteousness (δικαιωθέντες) has already occurred (5:9), as has reconciliation with God (κατηλλάγημεν; v. 10). Both elements are connected to the death of Christ (*declared righteous by his blood; reconciled to God through the death of his Son*). But both references to salvation are future referring (σωθησόμεθα; vv. 9, 10), and the latter is connected to the resurrection of Christ (*will . . . be saved by his life*; v. 10). There is thus an *analeptic*[8] function for the death of Christ, and a *proleptic* function for his resurrection. While the analeptic facts of righteousness and reconciliation have bearing on judgment day, it is the proleptic resurrection that will save believers from wrath on that day. In this way, believers may enjoy assurance as the day approaches, since their salvation from wrath is as certain as Christ's resurrection from the dead.

Rom 9:19–24 Ἐρεῖς μοι οὖν, Τί οὖν ἔτι μέμφεται; τῷ γὰρ βουλήματι αὐτοῦ τίς ἀνθέστηκεν; 20 ὦ ἄνθρωπε, μενοῦνγε σὺ τίς εἶ ὁ ἀνταποκρινόμενος τῷ θεῷ; μὴ ἐρεῖ τὸ πλάσμα τῷ πλάσαντι, Τί με ἐποίησας οὕτως; 21 ἢ οὐκ ἔχει ἐξουσίαν ὁ κεραμεὺς τοῦ πηλοῦ ἐκ τοῦ αὐτοῦ φυράματος ποιῆσαι ὃ μὲν εἰς τιμὴν σκεῦος ὃ δὲ εἰς ἀτιμίαν; 22 **εἰ δὲ θέλων ὁ θεὸς ἐνδείξασθαι τὴν ὀργὴν καὶ γνωρίσαι τὸ δυνατὸν αὐτοῦ ἤνεγκεν ἐν πολλῇ μακροθυμίᾳ σκεύη ὀργῆς κατηρτισμένα εἰς ἀπώλειαν**, 23 καὶ ἵνα γνωρίσῃ τὸν πλοῦτον τῆς δόξης αὐτοῦ ἐπὶ σκεύη ἐλέους ἃ προητοίμασεν εἰς δόξαν; 24 οὓς καὶ ἐκάλεσεν ἡμᾶς οὐ μόνον ἐξ Ἰουδαίων ἀλλὰ καὶ ἐξ ἐθνῶν

---

8. "Analeptic" is the adjectival form of *analepsis*, here used as "a literary technique that involves interruption of the chronological sequence of events by interjection of events or scenes of earlier occurrence" ("Analepsis," Merriam-Webster, www.merriam-webster.com).

You will say to me, therefore, "Why then does he still find fault? For who can resist his will?" 20 But who are you, a mere man, to talk back to God? Will what is formed say to the one who formed it, "Why did you make me like this?" 21 Or has the potter no right over the clay, to make from the same lump one piece of pottery for honor and another for dishonor? 22 **And what if God, wanting to display his wrath and to make his power known, endured with much patience objects of wrath prepared for destruction?** *23 And what if he did this to make known the riches of his glory on objects of mercy that he prepared beforehand for glory— 24 on us, the ones he also called, not only from the Jews but also from the Gentiles?*

While addressing Israel's rejection of Christ (9:1–5), Paul argues that God has always created a people through election (vv. 6–13). This then leads to a defense of God's justice, since he shows mercy to whom he chooses, while others he hardens (vv. 14–18). The heart of the objection to God's election is seen in v. 19: *Why then does he still find fault? For who can resist his will?* If God's sovereign choice means that no one can alter their ultimate destiny, why should God judge people at all?

The nub of Paul's response is to affirm that God is God and people are not: *But who are you, a mere man, to talk back to God? Will what is formed say to the one who formed it, "Why did you make me like this?"* (v. 20). What right does a man have to question God, his maker? The God-ness of God is seen in the simple fact that he is the creator, while humans are his creation. And as creator, God has absolute authority to do as he pleases with what he has made: *Or has the potter no right over the clay, to make from the same lump one piece of pottery for honor and another for dishonor?* (v. 21).

Then Paul digs deeper to ponder the will of God in all this: *And what if God, wanting to display his wrath and to make his power known, endured with much patience objects of wrath prepared for destruction?* (v. 22). In other words, God has made one piece of pottery for honor and another for dishonor (v. 21), for the purpose of making his wrath and power known, and *to make known the riches of his glory on objects of mercy that he prepared beforehand for glory* (v. 23).

According to this line of argument, God's wrath in judgment has a revelatory purpose: it is ultimately about God being God—in creation and in judgment. *Objects of wrath prepared for destruction* serve to display God's wrath and power (v. 22).[9] By the same token, *objects of mercy* serve to display his glory (v. 23).

---

9. "God works with those who are not in positive relationship with him to display in greater degree his own nature and power" (Moo, *Romans*, 606).

Rom 14:10–12 σὺ δὲ τί κρίνεις τὸν ἀδελφόν σου; ἢ καὶ σὺ τί ἐξουθενεῖς τὸν ἀδελφόν σου; **πάντες γὰρ παραστησόμεθα τῷ βήματι τοῦ θεοῦ**, 11 γέγραπται γάρ,

ζῶ ἐγώ, λέγει κύριος, ὅτι ἐμοὶ κάμψει πᾶν γόνυ
καὶ πᾶσα γλῶσσα ἐξομολογήσεται τῷ θεῷ.

12 ἄρα οὖν ἕκαστος ἡμῶν περὶ ἑαυτοῦ λόγον δώσει τῷ θεῷ. 13 Μηκέτι οὖν ἀλλήλους κρίνωμεν·

But you, why do you judge your brother or sister? Or you, why do you despise your brother or sister? **For we will all stand before the judgment seat of God.** *11 For it is written,*

As I live, says the Lord,
every knee will bow to me,
and every tongue will give praise to God.

12 So then, **each of us will give an account of himself to God**. *13 Therefore, let us no longer judge one another.*

The notion of judging one another is nullified by the fact that *we will all stand before the judgment seat of God* (14:10). That God is judge of all undercuts any sense in which believers ought to act as judges with respect to one another—the duty of judgment belongs to God and not to the *brother or sister*.[10]

Not only is the role of judge occupied by God alone, but the application of his judgment to all implies that everyone will have reason to be judged. No believers are exempt or above judgment, including Paul the great apostle. Rather, *each of us will give an account of himself to God* (v. 12).

The word translated *judgment seat* (βῆμα) refers to "a dais or platform that required steps to ascend."[11] According to BDAG, "a magistrate would address an assembly from a chair placed on the structure."[12] Thus the image evoked is one of all people standing trial in the magistrate's court. It is a serious and solemn image, intended to impress gravitas and sobriety upon Paul's readers.

This judgment scene will involve deference, with every knee bowing to God and every tongue giving praise to him (v. 11). And in keeping with courtroom

---

10. Barth, *Romans*, 514–15.
11. BDAG 175, §3.
12. BDAG 175, §3.

expectations, *each of us will give an account of himself to God* (v. 12). Given the context, this account given to God is clearly meant to resemble the testimony of a defendant. Each person will be subject to trial and therefore subject to the magistrate's verdict.

Since God is clearly the one seated upon his *judgment seat*, there is no room for others to judge one another. This reality frames the text, with 14:10 asking, *Why do you judge your brother or sister?* and with the conclusion of v. 13a, *Therefore, let us no longer judge one another.*

1 Cor 1:6–8 καθὼς τὸ μαρτύριον τοῦ Χριστοῦ ἐβεβαιώθη ἐν ὑμῖν, 7 ὥστε ὑμᾶς μὴ ὑστερεῖσθαι ἐν μηδενὶ χαρίσματι ἀπεκδεχομένους τὴν ἀποκάλυψιν τοῦ κυρίου ἡμῶν Ἰησοῦ Χριστοῦ· 8 ὃς καὶ βεβαιώσει ὑμᾶς ἕως τέλους ἀνεγκλήτους ἐν τῇ ἡμέρᾳ τοῦ κυρίου ἡμῶν Ἰησοῦ Χριστοῦ.

In this way, the testimony about Christ was confirmed among you, 7 so that you do not lack any spiritual gift as you eagerly wait for the revelation of our Lord Jesus Christ. 8 He will also strengthen you to the end, **so that you will be blameless in the day of our Lord Jesus Christ***.*

As discussed above (see §4.2 above), this passage connects the *revelation of our Lord Jesus Christ* (1:7) with *the end*, and *the day of our Lord Jesus Christ* (v. 8). Three pastoral issues are related to the revelation of Christ. First is the expectation that believers will eagerly await his return (v. 7); anticipation of the return of Christ is to shape the mindset of believers in this period between his ascension and parousia. Second, Christ himself will strengthen believers as the end approaches (v. 8a); maturity and growth is required for faithful living in this interim period, and such growth is stimulated by Christ. Third, this will prepare them for the day of Christ; they will be found blameless (v. 8b).

Paul presupposes that *the day of our Lord Jesus Christ* will be a day of judgment, since his encouragement to the Corinthians is that they *will be blameless* on that day. But as the letter makes clear, the Corinthians are not without blame. Paul addresses several areas in which the Corinthians have failed, are living according to worldly wisdom, and even behave worse than unbelievers. Nevertheless, Paul can assert their blameless status on the day of Christ.

No doubt this is because Christ will strengthen them to the end.[13] Whatever

---

13. Thiselton acknowledges that the relative pronoun ὅς at the beginning of v. 8 could refer to *God* or to *Christ*, citing Weiss, Conzelmann, and Fee in favor of the former and Origen, Chrysostom, and Meyer in favor of the latter. Remaining uncommitted himself, Thiselton states that linguistic arguments favor *Christ*, while theological arguments favor *God* (Anthony C. Thistleton, *The First Epistle to the Corinthians: A Commentary*

else is involved in making the Corinthians blameless (justification, sanctification, etc.), it is Christ himself who enables the Corinthians to stand blameless on the day of Christ. Since it is the day of *Christ*, it is comforting that he is also the one who prepares believers to stand on that day.

1 Cor 4:3–5 ἐμοὶ δὲ εἰς ἐλάχιστόν ἐστιν, ἵνα ὑφ' ὑμῶν ἀνακριθῶ ἢ ὑπὸ ἀνθρωπίνης ἡμέρας· ἀλλ' οὐδὲ ἐμαυτὸν ἀνακρίνω. 4 οὐδὲν γὰρ ἐμαυτῷ σύνοιδα, ἀλλ' οὐκ ἐν τούτῳ δεδικαίωμαι, ὁ δὲ ἀνακρίνων με κύριός ἐστιν. 5 ὥστε μὴ πρὸ καιροῦ τι κρίνετε ἕως ἂν ἔλθῃ ὁ κύριος, **ὃς καὶ φωτίσει τὰ κρυπτὰ τοῦ σκότους καὶ φανερώσει τὰς βουλὰς τῶν καρδιῶν**· καὶ τότε ὁ ἔπαινος γενήσεται ἑκάστῳ ἀπὸ τοῦ θεοῦ.

It is of little importance to me that I should be judged by you or by any human court. In fact, I don't even judge myself. 4 For I am not conscious of anything against myself, but I am not justified by this. **It is the Lord who judges me.** *5 So don't judge anything prematurely, before the Lord comes,* **who will both bring to light what is hidden in darkness and reveal the intentions of the hearts**. *And then praise will come to each one from God.*

Reflecting on his role as a manager of the mysteries of God (4:1–2), Paul explores the assessment of his performance. He does not care if he is judged by the Corinthians or by any human court, and he does not even trust his own assessment of himself (v. 4). Whatever his opinion of himself, he is not justified by it; the central point is that *it is the Lord who judges me* (v. 4). Paul views this judgment as occurring in the future, as indicated by reference to the coming of the Lord (v. 5).

Because judgment belongs to the Lord and will occur when the Lord comes, believers should not *judge anything prematurely* (v. 5a). This is not only because judgment belongs to the Lord and not to believers, but also because humans are not able to assess one another accurately, especially not now.[14] When the Lord comes, he *will both bring to light what is hidden in darkness and reveal the intention of the hearts* (v. 5b). The Lord himself is able to judge the hidden things that are beyond human ability to perceive.

---

on the Greek Text, NIGTC [Grand Rapids: Eerdmans, 2000], 101 [and n. 88]). However, with Christ as the nearest possible antecedent at the end of v. 7, he is the most natural candidate for the subject of ὅς in v. 8, contra Brookins and Longenecker, who take the relative pronoun to have demonstrative rather than relative force here (Timothy A. Brookins and Bruce W. Longenecker, *1 Corinthians 1–9: A Handbook on the Greek Text*, BHGNT [Waco, TX: Baylor University Press, 2016], 10).

14. "If the Corinthians pronounce judgment on Paul, they are not only being presumptuous but also acting prematurely" (Richard B. Hays, *First Corinthians*, Interpretation [Louisville: Westminster John Knox, 1997], 67).

While *what is hidden in darkness* could refer to sins conducted in secret, given the parallel phrase that follows it—*and reveal the intentions of the hearts*—it most likely refers to hidden intentions, motivations, secret longings, and so forth. In this way, *what is hidden in darkness* and *the intentions of the hearts* are in synonymous parallelism with the latter offering a more specific referent, shifting from the metaphor of *darkness* to what is hidden in *hearts*.

Finally, Paul states that *praise will come to each one from God* (v. 5c). This reiterates the point that judgment belongs to the Lord and not to humans. But it also demonstrates that judgment is not only negative. Once the intentions of hearts are revealed, praise will be extended as appropriate. This also implies that not everything *hidden in darkness* is negative, notwithstanding the fact that the metaphor of *darkness* is almost universally negative. Rather, the intentions of hearts can be good, which is important to remember for someone like Paul, who is constantly misjudged and accused of various false motives. Whatever the Corinthians think of him, the intentions of his heart will be seen for what they are on that day. And Paul anticipates praise from God for his faithfulness.

2 Cor 5:8–10 θαρροῦμεν δὲ καὶ εὐδοκοῦμεν μᾶλλον ἐκδημῆσαι ἐκ τοῦ σώματος καὶ ἐνδημῆσαι πρὸς τὸν κύριον. 9 διὸ καὶ φιλοτιμούμεθα, εἴτε ἐνδημοῦντες εἴτε ἐκδημοῦντες, εὐάρεστοι αὐτῷ εἶναι. 10 **τοὺς γὰρ πάντας ἡμᾶς φανερωθῆναι δεῖ ἔμπροσθεν τοῦ βήματος τοῦ Χριστοῦ, ἵνα κομίσηται ἕκαστος τὰ διὰ τοῦ σώματος πρὸς ἃ ἔπραξεν, εἴτε ἀγαθὸν εἴτε φαῦλον.**

In fact, we are confident, and we would prefer to be away from the body and at home with the Lord. 9 Therefore, whether we are at home or away, we make it our aim to be pleasing to him. 10 ***For we must all appear before the judgment seat of Christ, so that each may be repaid for what he has done in the body, whether good or evil.***

When in Corinth, Paul faced the Roman governor Gallio (Acts 18:12), who sat on Corinth's impressive judgment seat (βῆμα). But Paul sees the judgment seat of Christ as of far greater significance. Moreover, Christ is the true judge of all, not whichever man has temporary authority over the city.

The universality of the judgment of Christ is clear, Paul including himself in its scope. The language of being *repaid* [κομίζω] *for what* is *done in the body* (2 Cor 5:10) has the sense of receiving something as recompense, as though wages for work performed.[15] Whatever is done, *whether good or evil*, will receive

---

15. BDAG 557, §3.

wages in keeping with the nature of the deed. This text therefore strongly contributes to Paul's theology of "judgment according to works" and the notion of reward.[16]

The phrase *what he has done in the body* is likely not meant to focus on physical deeds as opposed to mental and spiritual ones. Rather, it connects to the context in which Paul is addressing life *at home in the body* (v. 6) compared to being *away from the body and at home with the Lord* (v. 8). In other words, *what he has done in the body* refers to deeds performed during this life, before death. Even though Paul is concerned to please the Lord *whether we are at home or away* (i.e., whether alive or dead; v. 9), judgment only pertains to actions performed while living.

Gal 6:7–9 Μὴ πλανᾶσθε, θεὸς οὐ μυκτηρίζεται. ὃ γὰρ ἐὰν σπείρῃ ἄνθρωπος, τοῦτο καὶ θερίσει· 8 ὅτι ὁ σπείρων εἰς τὴν σάρκα ἑαυτοῦ ἐκ τῆς σαρκὸς θερίσει φθοράν, ὁ δὲ σπείρων εἰς τὸ πνεῦμα ἐκ τοῦ πνεύματος θερίσει ζωὴν αἰώνιον. 9 τὸ δὲ καλὸν ποιοῦντες μὴ ἐγκακῶμεν, καιρῷ γὰρ ἰδίῳ θερίσομεν μὴ ἐκλυόμενοι.

Don't be deceived: God is not mocked. For whatever a person sows he will also reap, 8 because **the one who sows to his flesh will reap destruction from the flesh, but the one who sows to the Spirit will reap eternal life from the Spirit**. *9 Let us not get tired of doing good, for we will reap at the proper time if we don't give up.*

While reaping what one sows could easily be understood in a noneschatological way, just as the same idiom is used today, the reference to *eternal life* (6:8) indicates the eschatological concern here. Given the reference to *eternal life*, it is natural to understand *destruction* likewise as an eschatological fate. It is also natural then to read *for we will reap at the proper time* as a reference to the outcome of eschatological judgment, with *the proper time* indicating the moment of judgment (v. 9).

There is a binary set of oppositions presented as the possible outcomes of judgment—*destruction* and *eternal life*—and these are understood as resulting from *whatever a person sows* (v. 7). The sowing metaphor seems clearly to refer to the way a person lives, and yet Paul's warning does not advocate salvation by works.[17] He has argued against such a position throughout the letter to this

---

16. Linda L. Belleville, *2 Corinthians*, IVPNTC (Downers Grove, IL: InterVarsity Press, 1996), 142–43.
17. "Human works that please the Spirit are indeed necessary for final salvation, and the very fact that Paul sets forth two options before his readers makes clear that he does not assume that all those he addressees

point. How then should this text be understood? Paul employs the sowing metaphor to contrast two alternate orientations. The contrast between *the flesh* and *the Spirit* has been in view since 5:16—to *walk by the Spirit* is to reject *the desire of the flesh*. Indeed, *the flesh desires what is against the Spirit, and the Spirit desires what is against the flesh; these are opposed to each other* (v. 17). The flesh and the Spirit therefore represent two mutually exclusive orientations, with *the works of the flesh* (vv. 19–21) contrasted with *the fruit of the Spirit* (vv. 22–23). These two orientations, then, have direct consequences for the way people live.

But these consequences apparently flow out of the preexisting orientations. That is, if people live according to the flesh, the works of the flesh will become evident in their lives. But if people walk by the Spirit, the fruit of the Spirit will become evident in their lives. In other words, the manifest evidences of either the flesh or the Spirit are exactly that—evidences. They are "symptoms" of an underlying reality. With that in mind, *the one who sows to his flesh* is a person who lives according to the flesh; sowing to the flesh is acting in line with their flesh-orientation. Likewise, *the one who sows to the Spirit* is a person who lives according to the Spirit, with the Spirit as their orientation. Thus, while judgment takes into account one's deeds—what one sows—it is ultimately concerned with orientation and allegiance. The person whose life demonstrates allegiance to the flesh will reap destruction. The one whose life evidences allegiance to the Spirit will reap eternal life.

The sowing metaphor pictures a "harvest" that grows out of what was sown. This implies that the two outcomes of judgment—destruction and eternal life—are inevitable consequences of what was sown. According to this metaphor, judgment is less concerned with deciding one's fate, and more concerned with recognizing reality. Perhaps that is why this text does not explicitly refer to God's role in judgment; the sowing and reaping metaphor does not require it. A person's eternal destiny is decided by their allegiance either to the flesh or to the Spirit, and that allegiance is recognized by their deeds.

Eph 2:1–3 Καὶ ὑμᾶς ὄντας νεκροὺς τοῖς παραπτώμασιν καὶ ταῖς ἁμαρτίαις ὑμῶν, 2 ἐν αἷς ποτε περιεπατήσατε κατὰ τὸν αἰῶνα τοῦ κόσμου τούτου, κατὰ τὸν ἄρχοντα τῆς ἐξουσίας τοῦ ἀέρος, τοῦ πνεύματος τοῦ νῦν ἐνεργοῦντος ἐν τοῖς υἱοῖς τῆς ἀπειθείας· 3 ἐν οἷς καὶ ἡμεῖς πάντες ἀνεστράφημέν ποτε ἐν ταῖς ἐπιθυμίαις τῆς σαρκὸς ἡμῶν ποιοῦντες τὰ θελήματα τῆς σαρκὸς καὶ τῶν διανοιῶν, καὶ **ἤμεθα τέκνα φύσει ὀργῆς ὡς καὶ οἱ λοιποί**

---

will necessarily produce those works. But Paul's teaching elsewhere in this very letter justifies our claiming that these works are the effect of faith and are produced in and through the Spirit" (Douglas J. Moo, *Galatians*, BECNT [Grand Rapids: Baker Academic, 2013], 387).

And you were dead in your trespasses and sins 2 in which you previously lived according to the ways of this world, according to the ruler of the power of the air, the spirit now working in the disobedient. 3 We too all previously lived among them in our fleshly desires, carrying out the inclinations of our flesh and thoughts, and **we were by nature children under wrath as the others were also***.*

The *you* and *we* of this passage most likely refer to gentiles (*you*) and Jews (*we*). Paul describes his gentile readers' former way of life as spiritual death *in your trespasses and sins* (2:1). Though *dead*, they *lived according to the ways of this world* and according to demonic influence (v. 2). Jews also *lived among them in our fleshly desires* and with gentiles *were by nature children under wrath* (v. 3).

The description of *children under wrath* is peculiar. Why does Paul describe rebellious humanity as *children* in this context? It is a universally negative context—gravely negative—so the familial term jars against it. The tension, however, is resolved if we understand τέκνα φύσει ὀργῆς to mean *by nature children of wrath*. This takes ὀργῆς (*wrath*) as a genitive of source or a genitive of relationship.[18] Taken this way, *children* becomes a negative term in keeping with the context. To be *children of wrath* imagines human beings as the offspring of evil. Such children are born to share in the destiny of their progenitor.

Eph 5:5–6 τοῦτο γὰρ ἴστε γινώσκοντες, ὅτι πᾶς πόρνος ἢ ἀκάθαρτος ἢ πλεονέκτης, ὅ ἐστιν εἰδωλολάτρης, οὐκ ἔχει κληρονομίαν ἐν τῇ βασιλείᾳ τοῦ Χριστοῦ καὶ θεοῦ. 6 Μηδεὶς ὑμᾶς ἀπατάτω κενοῖς λόγοις· διὰ ταῦτα γὰρ ἔρχεται ἡ ὀργὴ τοῦ θεοῦ ἐπὶ τοὺς υἱοὺς τῆς ἀπειθείας.

For know and recognize this: Every sexually immoral or impure or greedy person, who is an idolater, does not have an inheritance in the kingdom of Christ and of God. 6 Let no one deceive you with empty arguments, **for God's wrath is coming on the disobedient because of these things***.*

Sexual immorality, impurity, and greed are incompatible with *the kingdom of Christ and of God* (5:5). Such people do not have an inheritance in it (for more on the "inheritance," see §9.2 below). The threat of deception with *empty arguments* (v. 6a) probably concerns the gravity of such sins. Paul may have imagined false teachers claiming that impurity or greed are not as serious as

---

18. Andreas J. Köstenberger, Benjamin L. Merkle, and Robert L. Plummer, *Going Deeper with New Testament Greek: An Intermediate Study of the Grammar and Syntax of the New Testament* (Nashville: B&H Academic, 2016), 92–94.

he says.[19] That's why he adds *for God's wrath is coming on the disobedient because of these things* (v. 6b). The gravity of these sins, and those like them, are obvious in God's view—evidenced by the fact that his wrath is coming because of them.

The warning not to be deceived is a natural one in light of Paul's message of salvation by grace (2:8–9). Believers can be tempted to think that, because salvation is by grace, these sins are not so grievous—since all can be forgiven. Paul's point, however, is that such is a misunderstanding and a deception. God's wrath is dreadful, and it is coming because of sin. Forgiveness of sins is not therefore a reason to take sin flippantly. It is certainly not a reason to continue willfully in such dire rebellion. Paul's warning means that anyone who continues in their immoral ways without repentance will remain under the wrath of God.

Eph 6:6–8 μὴ κατ' ὀφθαλμοδουλίαν ὡς ἀνθρωπάρεσκοι ἀλλ' ὡς δοῦλοι Χριστοῦ ποιοῦντες τὸ θέλημα τοῦ θεοῦ ἐκ ψυχῆς, 7 μετ' εὐνοίας δουλεύοντες ὡς τῷ κυρίῳ καὶ οὐκ ἀνθρώποις, 8 εἰδότες ὅτι **ἕκαστος ἐάν τι ποιήσῃ ἀγαθόν**, τοῦτο κομίσεται παρὰ κυρίου εἴτε δοῦλος εἴτε ἐλεύθερος.

*Don't work only while being watched, as people-pleasers, but as slaves of Christ, do God's will from your heart. 7 Serve with a good attitude, as to the Lord and not to people, 8 knowing that **whatever good each one does, slave or free, he will receive this back from the Lord**.*

Found in the household code, this exhortation to *serve with a good attitude* is directed toward slaves (6:7). Their service is to be *as to the Lord and not to people*, which helps to explain why slaves ought to work with such an attitude (v. 7). It also motivates them to do so, since their heavenly Lord will reward their service: *whatever good each one does . . . he will receive this back from the Lord* (v. 8).

Such reward is most likely to be understood as eschatological rather than received during the course of life. While Paul does not explicitly tie the exhortation and encouragement to the day of the Lord or some other such notion, there are some implicit indicators pointing in that direction. The future tense, *he will receive* (κομίσεται), does not resolve the issue, since the future reference could point to a later point in a slave's life or to the eschaton. But alongside the statement issued toward masters, *there is no favoritism with him* (v. 9), it implies eschatological judgment. The concept of God's lack of favoritism is specifically linked to eschatological judgment in various contexts (e.g., Rom 2:11).

This text is striking for a few reasons. First, slaves by definition were not

---

19. Andrew T. Lincoln, *Ephesians*, WBC 42 (Dallas: Word, 1990), 325–26.

owed wages or reward—they were bondservants. But their real master is their Lord in heaven, and this master *does* reward such slaves of Christ (Eph 6:6). This implies that the slave of Christ is really no slave at all.

Second, the wages or reward promised for the *good each one does* is for *slave or free* (v. 8). Though addressing slaves directly, Paul's encouragement is not limited to slaves. The fact of reward from the Lord is universal. This notion is underscored when Paul switches to address slave masters: they too have a master in heaven, who will keep them accountable for the way they treat their slaves (v. 9).

Third, the prospect of judgment is only positive in this context. When addressing the slaves, Paul does not warn them of the negative aspects of judgment, but simply encourages them that the Lord's judgment will involve reward for the good they have done (cf. Col 3:25). On the other hand, slave masters are under the implicit threat of negative judgment.

Fourth, given the previous point, judgment implicitly equalizes the relationship between slaves and their masters.[20] Though Paul nowhere explicitly undermines the institution of slavery, the fact of eschatological judgment implicitly undermines it—at least in the sense of putting both slave and master under the same Lord and rewarding or punishing both according to their deeds. The institutional privilege of master over their slaves will not stand on that day. There is one heavenly master, and all are subject to him.

Finally, it is noteworthy that it is only here, addressing slaves and masters, that Paul invokes eschatological judgment within the household code. Though the reference to Christ presenting the church to himself as holy and blameless may imply a judgment setting (Eph 5:27), it does not form part of the explicit instruction for husbands and wives, parents and children. Only to slaves and masters does Paul set his exhortations in the light of the eschaton.

Perhaps one reason for this is that the instructions to the other members of the household offer benefits for life now. Husbands and wives may live together in harmony; parents and children will go well. But what benefit does the slave enjoy for his faithful service? None that Paul anticipates in this life. Thus, his hope is cast to the future. The faithful slave will one day be rewarded for his work conducted with a good attitude.

Col 3:5–7 Νεκρώσατε οὖν τὰ μέλη τὰ ἐπὶ τῆς γῆς, πορνείαν ἀκαθαρσίαν πάθος ἐπιθυμίαν κακήν, καὶ τὴν πλεονεξίαν, ἥτις ἐστὶν εἰδωλολατρία, 6 δι'

---

20. Ernest Best, *A Critical and Exegetical Commentary on Ephesians*, ICC (London: T&T Clark, 1998), 580; it is "suggestive of some kind of equality."

ἃ ἔρχεται ἡ ὀργὴ τοῦ θεοῦ [ἐπὶ τοὺς υἱοὺς τῆς ἀπειθείας]. 7 ἐν οἷς καὶ ὑμεῖς περιεπατήσατέ ποτε, ὅτε ἐζῆτε ἐν τούτοις

Therefore, put to death what belongs to your earthly nature: sexual immorality, impurity, lust, evil desire, and greed, which is idolatry. 6 Because of these, **God's wrath is coming upon the disobedient***, 7 and you once walked in these things when you were living in them.*

This text is parallel to Ephesians 5:5–6 (see above), but with some important differences. The vice list is more or less parallel to that of the latter passage, mentioning *sexual immorality* (πορνεία), *impurity* (ἀκαθαρσία), and *greed* (πλεονεξία), with both texts equating the latter with idolatry (εἰδωλολατρία).

While this text also mentions *lust* (πάθος) and *evil desire* (ἐπιθυμία κακή), which are not found in Ephesians 5:5–6, the chief distinction between the two vice lists is that Colossians treats the vices as abstract sins, while Ephesians refers to *people* who are characterized by them (πᾶς πόρνος ἢ ἀκάθαρτος ἢ πλεονέκτης, ὅ ἐστιν εἰδωλολάτρης). Ephesians 5:5 simply states such people do not have an inheritance in the kingdom of Christ and of God. On the other hand, Colossians 3:5 recognizes that these abstract sins belong to believers' *earthly nature*, and as such they are to *put* them *to death*, in keeping with the theme of having died with Christ (2:20).

The two passages are virtually identical in what follows: *Because of these, God's wrath is coming upon the disobedient* (Col 3:6; Eph 5:6b), though the phrase translated *upon the disobedient* (lit., *upon the sons of disobedience*; ἐπὶ τοὺς υἱοὺς τῆς ἀπειθείας) in Colossians 3:6 is likely a scribal emendation to shore up the parallel with Ephesians 5:6b.[21] Following this, Colossians adds *and you once walked in these things when you were living in them* (3:7), which is not found in Ephesians.

The strongest parallel between the two passages, then, is the declaration that God's wrath is coming because of sin. Though the sons of disobedience are the objects of his wrath, they are not directly the cause; it is *sin* that prompts God's wrath rather than some innate feature of disobedient people. This is underscored in the Colossians text, which affirms that believers once *walked* and *lived in* such sins (v. 7), yet they are no longer the objects of wrath. Even now as they are exhorted to put to death these sins belonging to the earthly nature (v. 5), they are not condemned for them. No doubt this is because they

---

21. Murray J. Harris, *Colossians and Philemon*, EGGNT (Grand Rapids: Eerdmans, 1991), 148; Campbell, *Colossians and Philemon*, 52–53.

now seek to be sons and daughters of *obedience* rather than *disobedience*, even if their obedience is not yet complete.

1 Thess 1:9–10 αὐτοὶ γὰρ περὶ ἡμῶν ἀπαγγέλλουσιν ὁποίαν εἴσοδον ἔσχομεν πρὸς ὑμᾶς, καὶ πῶς ἐπεστρέψατε πρὸς τὸν θεὸν ἀπὸ τῶν εἰδώλων δουλεύειν θεῷ ζῶντι καὶ ἀληθινῷ 10 καὶ ἀναμένειν τὸν υἱὸν αὐτοῦ ἐκ τῶν οὐρανῶν, ὃν ἤγειρεν ἐκ τῶν νεκρῶν, Ἰησοῦν τὸν ῥυόμενον ἡμᾶς ἐκ τῆς ὀργῆς τῆς ἐρχομένης.

For they themselves report what kind of reception we had from you: how you turned to God from idols to serve the living and true God 10 and to wait for his Son from heaven, whom he raised from the dead—Jesus, who rescues us from the coming wrath.

As discussed above (see §4.2), the coming of Jesus is a double-edged sword in that it ushers in the judgment of God but also the rescue from his wrath. There is also a double aspect to this rescue: the Thessalonians have *turned to God from idols to serve the living and true God*—that is, they have repented—and they are rescued by Jesus *from the coming wrath*. Both elements apparently must be held together: repentance *and* the saving work of Jesus. It is implied, therefore, that rescue from the coming wrath will not occur for those who have not turned to God in repentance.

Furthermore, the rescuing work of Jesus does not spare believers from judgment, as clearly indicated elsewhere. Believers will face judgment and give an account for what they have done. But *from the coming wrath*, believers will indeed be spared.[22] Since there is no condemnation for those in Christ Jesus (Rom 8:1), there will be no punishment of wrath following judgment.

Paul does not here spell out exactly how Jesus *rescues us from the coming wrath*, though it is natural to associate it with his coming from heaven, and it is possible that the reference to Jesus's resurrection is intended to be associated with it too. Certainly Paul elsewhere connects Jesus's resurrection to salvation (e.g., Rom 4:25, where Paul connects the resurrection with believers' justification). If a similar connection is implied here, Paul cites the resurrection as the *means* of rescue from the coming wrath, while the coming of the Son from heaven is the *occasion* for it.

---

22. "The Thessalonians believers were undergoing persecution at this time and are here assured not only of their own liberation (1 Thess 5:9) but also of the judgment of God that will come upon those who afflict them (2 Thess 1:6–10). Whatever the agony and shame of the present, in the end God will reverse their fortunes" (Green, *Letters to the Thessalonians*, 111).

1 Thess 3:13 εἰς τὸ στηρίξαι ὑμῶν τὰς καρδίας ἀμέμπτους ἐν ἁγιωσύνῃ ἔμπροσθεν τοῦ θεοῦ καὶ πατρὸς ἡμῶν ἐν τῇ παρουσίᾳ τοῦ κυρίου ἡμῶν Ἰησοῦ μετὰ πάντων τῶν ἁγίων αὐτοῦ, [ἀμήν].

May he make your hearts blameless in holiness before our God and Father at the coming of our Lord Jesus with all his saints. Amen.

Part of Paul's prayer for the Thessalonian church (3:11–13), this petition asks the Lord (v. 12) to *make* their *hearts blameless in holiness for our God and Father* (v. 13). The Lord mentioned in v. 12, who is also the subject of the petitioned action in v. 13, most likely refers to Jesus, since he is called "our Lord Jesus" in v. 11 and v. 13b.[23] Paul requests that Jesus will prepare the Thessalonians to be *blameless* [ἀμέμπτους] *in holiness* [ἐν ἁγιωσύνῃ] *before our God and Father.*

While *before* (ἔμπροσθεν) could by itself mean "in the sight of," or some other such notion, this use has connotations of judgment. This is especially so given that it is positioned *at the coming of our Lord Jesus* (for more on this, see §4.2 above). Thus, this is clearly a scenario in which the coming of Jesus ushers in God's judgment, in which believers will appear before God. And yet the one who ushers in God's judgment is also the one who will prepare believers' hearts for that same judgment.

1 Thess 5:9–10 ὅτι οὐκ ἔθετο ἡμᾶς ὁ θεὸς εἰς ὀργὴν ἀλλὰ εἰς περιποίησιν σωτηρίας διὰ τοῦ κυρίου ἡμῶν Ἰησοῦ Χριστοῦ 10 τοῦ ἀποθανόντος ὑπὲρ ἡμῶν, ἵνα εἴτε γρηγορῶμεν εἴτε καθεύδωμεν ἅμα σὺν αὐτῷ ζήσωμεν.

*For **God did not appoint us to wrath, but to obtain salvation through our Lord Jesus Christ**, 10 who died for us, so that whether we are awake or asleep, we may live together with him.*

Sidestepping the vexed issue of what it means that God *appoints* people either to wrath or to salvation, for our purposes it is noteworthy that these two outcomes of wrath and salvation—and these alone—are juxtaposed. They are clearly meant as a pair of binary opposites. All people are appointed either to wrath or to salvation.

While God's judgment is not explicitly mentioned—nor the common indicators that often accompany it, such as "the day" or "the coming of Christ"—it is nevertheless in view. It would be obvious to Paul's readers that the binary

---

23. Weima, *1–2 Thessalonians*, 238.

opposition of *wrath* and *salvation* are meant as the two outcomes of God's judgment.

The obtainment of salvation is *through our Lord Jesus Christ, who died for us*, implying that it is through his death that people are able to receive salvation. Salvation through Christ connects to Paul's metatheme of union with Christ, in which διὰ . . . Χριστοῦ indicates the instrumentality of Christ in the saving work of God.[24] Thus we see that while God appoints believers to salvation, Christ is instrumental in accomplishing their salvation through his death.

The final outcome of God's appointment, however, is not salvation itself. Rather, the final outcome is what salvation makes possible, namely, that *we may live together with him* (5:10). While it is a perfectly acceptable assumption that Paul would regard life *with Christ* as inclusive of life *with God*, that is not his focus here. He specifies life *with Christ*—the last-mentioned person and therefore the most likely antecedent of the prepositional phrase, *with him* (σὺν αὐτῷ). This specific focus on life with Christ is probably due to Paul's interest in this letter of believers being with Christ when he comes, *whether we are awake or asleep* (v. 10; cf. 4:15–17).

This text indicates a binary opposition of two possible outcomes of God's judgment—either wrath or salvation. Salvation is issued through Christ, who secured it by his death, resulting in life with him for all in Christ, whether or not they are alive when he comes.

2 Thess 1:5–10 ἔνδειγμα **τῆς δικαίας κρίσεως τοῦ θεοῦ** εἰς τὸ καταξιωθῆναι ὑμᾶς τῆς βασιλείας τοῦ θεοῦ, ὑπὲρ ἧς καὶ πάσχετε, 6 εἴπερ **δίκαιον παρὰ θεῷ ἀνταποδοῦναι τοῖς θλίβουσιν ὑμᾶς θλῖψιν** 7 καὶ ὑμῖν τοῖς θλιβομένοις ἄνεσιν μεθ' ἡμῶν, ἐν τῇ ἀποκαλύψει τοῦ κυρίου Ἰησοῦ ἀπ' οὐρανοῦ μετ' ἀγγέλων δυνάμεως αὐτοῦ 8 **ἐν πυρὶ φλογός, διδόντος ἐκδίκησιν** τοῖς μὴ εἰδόσιν θεὸν καὶ τοῖς μὴ ὑπακούουσιν τῷ εὐαγγελίῳ τοῦ κυρίου ἡμῶν Ἰησοῦ, 9 **οἵτινες δίκην τίσουσιν ὄλεθρον αἰώνιον ἀπὸ προσώπου τοῦ κυρίου καὶ ἀπὸ τῆς δόξης τῆς ἰσχύος αὐτοῦ**, 10 ὅταν ἔλθῃ ἐνδοξασθῆναι ἐν τοῖς ἁγίοις αὐτοῦ καὶ θαυμασθῆναι ἐν πᾶσιν τοῖς πιστεύσασιν, ὅτι ἐπιστεύθη τὸ μαρτύριον ἡμῶν ἐφ' ὑμᾶς, ἐν τῇ ἡμέρᾳ ἐκείνῃ.

*It is clear evidence of **God's righteous judgment** that you will be counted worthy of God's kingdom, for which you also are suffering, 6 since **it is just for God to repay with affliction those who afflict you** 7 and to give relief to you who are afflicted, along with us. This will take place at the revelation of the Lord*

---

24. Campbell, *Paul and Union with Christ*, 248.

*Jesus from heaven with his powerful angels, 8 when **he takes vengeance with flaming fire** on those who don't know God and on those who don't obey the gospel of our Lord Jesus. 9 **They will pay the penalty of eternal destruction from the Lord's presence and from his glorious strength** 10 on that day when he comes to be glorified by his saints and to be marveled at by all those who have believed, because our testimony among you was believed.*

This text has already been discussed with reference to the revelation and coming of Christ (see §4.2) and the day of the Lord (see §5.2). On this occasion, we focus on the text's strong theme of judgment.

As discussed above (see §4.2), believers who suffer for God's kingdom can be assured that those afflicting them will know the justice of God *at the revelation* [τῇ ἀποκαλύψει] *of the Lord Jesus*. He will be accompanied by powerful angels and will execute *vengeance with flaming fire* on unbelievers (vv. 7–8).

The objects of his vengeance are described as *those who don't know God* and as *those who don't obey the gospel of our Lord Jesus* (v. 8)—two descriptions of the same group of people. For Paul the latter description probably determines the former; that is, those who do not obey the gospel of Christ reveal themselves as those who do not know God. Unbelievers will *pay the penalty of eternal destruction from the Lord's presence and from his glorious strength* (v. 9). Paul does not indicate whether he sees this *eternal destruction* (ὄλεθρον αἰώνιον) as an ongoing state of *being destroyed*—an eternal process of deconstruction—or that, once destroyed, these people will remain so for eternity.

There is further ambiguity regarding the Lord's relationship to this penalty of eternal destruction. Paul says it is *from the Lord's presence*, literally, *from the face of the Lord* (ἀπὸ προσώπου τοῦ κυρίου). The key question is what the ἀπό (*from*) indicates. It can be understood to indicate that this eternal destruction occurs *away from* the Lord's presence (so NIV, ESV), in which case eternal destruction seems to result from alienation from the Lord. It also implies a passive relationship between the Lord and this eternal destruction. On the other hand, the ἀπό can indicate source, such that eternal destruction *comes from* the Lord's presence (so CSB). These two readings are more or less opposite, with the former implying that absence from the Lord is the penalty for unbelievers, while the latter implies that their penalty is received actively from the Lord's presence. According to BDAG, both readings are possible for the preposition ἀπό. For the *away from* reading, ἀπό can "indicate distance fr. a point, away from . . . far fr. someone."[25] Indeed, BDAG lists 2 Thessalonians 1:9 under this

---

25. BDAG 106, §4.

category of usage. For the *comes from* reading, this is also possible, as ἀπό can "indicate origin or source."²⁶ Thus, the preposition ἀπό itself does not seem determinative.

While the preposition may not resolve the question, the wider context favors one option more readily than the other. The text cited (2 Thess 1:5–10) focuses on the coming of the Lord. The Lord Jesus will be revealed from heaven (v. 7) and will come to be glorified by his saints (v. 10). That is, the text is primarily interested in the presence of the Lord and what it will entail. It thus seems more natural to understand *eternal destruction* as resulting from the presence of the Lord rather than from his absence. The point is what will happen in the *presence* of the Lord, not what will happen *away from* his presence. As such, the *comes from* understanding is a more natural fit in the context than is the *away from* reading: the penalty of eternal destruction will *come from* the face of the Lord—"It is the Lord Jesus who will punish with everlasting destruction."²⁷

This understanding also makes better sense of the immediately following phrase, *and from his glorious strength* (v. 9). The reference to the Lord's strength more naturally fits a context in which his enemies are overthrown and subjected to punishment in an active sense. If the Lord's absence were in view, the reference to his strength would have little significance.

Finally, the previous verse has already indicated an active wielding of vengeance on unbelievers: *when he takes vengeance with flaming fire on those who don't know God and on those who don't obey the gospel of our Lord Jesus* (v. 8). This *vengeance with flaming fire* is not executed in the Lord's absence but as a result of his revelation from heaven (v. 7). Since the penalty of eternal destruction is discussed immediately following this active execution of vengeance (vv. 8–9), it is most natural to understand it as a related occurrence in which the presence of the Lord effects the eternal penalty for unbelievers.

God's righteous judgment will result in relief for those unjustly afflicted in this life, and it will release the vengeance of God upon the perpetrators of such injustices. This is a fierce text that leaves no room for doubt concerning the fate of those who do not know God and do not obey the gospel of Christ.

1 Tim 5:24–25 Τινῶν ἀνθρώπων αἱ ἁμαρτίαι πρόδηλοί εἰσιν προάγουσαι εἰς κρίσιν, τισὶν δὲ καὶ ἐπακολουθοῦσιν· 25 ὡσαύτως καὶ τὰ ἔργα τὰ καλὰ πρόδηλα, καὶ τὰ ἄλλως ἔχοντα κρυβῆναι οὐ δύνανται.

---

26. BDAG 106, §3.
27. Villiers, "Eschatology of 2 Thessalonians," 338.

Some people's sins are obvious, preceding them to judgment, but the sins of others surface later. *25 Likewise, good works are obvious, and those that are not obvious cannot remain hidden.*

The image of sins *preceding* people *to judgment* is an interesting notion (5:24b). We can grasp its general sense since it modifies the first clause, *some people's sins are obvious* (v. 24a). Evidently, these sins are *so* obvious, they go ahead of the person to judgment. Even so, the precise meaning is not immediately apparent. The image of sins *preceding* someone *to judgment* is most likely a rhetorical device that Paul uses to underscore the obvious nature of some sins. It is not as though these sins can *literally* precede their perpetrator to judgment—what would that mean? After all, Paul believes in a day of judgment that will come at some point in the future. It is not a location that can be reached by an advance party ahead of schedule. The day of judgment is a *day*, not a place. So unless these sins can time travel into the future, they cannot literally precede someone to the judgment.

As a rhetorical device, then, what does this image convey? It may mean that, like an advance party, these sins *announce* someone's imminent arrival. The sinner can be seen coming at a distance, as it were, since his obvious sins announce his impending judgment. This would seem to fit with the next phrase, *but the sins of others surface later* (v. 24c). Literally, the sins of others *follow* (ἐπακολουθέω) them, as opposed to the aforementioned sins that precede their perpetrators. This seems to convey the notion that the sins of these others will "catch up to them." These sins have not gone ahead, announcing the imminent judgment of their perpetrators, but are more subtle. It is only when their perpetrators stand in judgment that such sins are revealed.

Such a reading of the text raises the question, to whom are these sins obvious? To whom are other sins later revealed? The same questions pertain to the following verse: *likewise, good works are obvious, and those that are not obvious cannot remain hidden* (v. 25). To whom are these good deeds obvious? From whom will hidden good deeds be revealed? Since Paul believes that God sees the heart and always knows people's sins, it would make little sense for some sins to be *obvious* to God, while others will be revealed later. By the same token, good works cannot be hidden from God, who sees and knows all. Thus, the only logical conclusion is that Paul envisions that other people (and perhaps other spiritual beings) will witness all that is revealed at the judgment.[28]

---

28. Knight sees the whole significance of this text in relation to the laying on of hands (ordination) to appoint elders in 5:22. While this makes sense to a point, the interruption of the apparently unrelated 5:23 weakens the potential connection between 5:22 and 5:24–25 (George W. Knight, *The Pastoral Epistles: A Commentary on the Greek Text*, NIGTC [Grand Rapids: Eerdmans, 1992], 240–41).

No one will be surprised by the obvious sins that herald a sinner's forthcoming judgment, and the sins not yet obvious will be revealed. The same applies to good works. The judgment will reveal hidden good deeds and make them known to all. In this way, judgment is seen as having revelatory significance. Since none of these things will surprise God who sees all, the judgment reveals currently hidden realities to others, both good and evil.

2 Tim 2:10–13 διὰ τοῦτο πάντα ὑπομένω διὰ τοὺς ἐκλεκτούς, ἵνα καὶ αὐτοὶ σωτηρίας τύχωσιν τῆς ἐν Χριστῷ Ἰησοῦ μετὰ δόξης αἰωνίου.
11 πιστὸς ὁ λόγος·

>εἰ γὰρ συναπεθάνομεν,
>καὶ συζήσομεν·
>12 εἰ ὑπομένομεν,
>καὶ συμβασιλεύσομεν·
>εἰ ἀρνησόμεθα,
>κἀκεῖνος ἀρνήσεται ἡμᾶς·
>13 εἰ ἀπιστοῦμεν,
>ἐκεῖνος πιστὸς μένει,
>ἀρνήσασθαι γὰρ ἑαυτὸν οὐ δύναται.

This is why I endure all things for the elect: so that they also may obtain salvation, which is in Christ Jesus, with eternal glory. 11 ***This saying is trustworthy:***

> ***For if we died with him,***
> ***we will also live with him;***
> 12 ***if we endure,***
> ***we will also reign with him;***
> ***if we deny him,***
> ***he will also deny us;***
> 13 ***if we are faithless,***
> ***he remains faithful,***
> ***for he cannot deny himself.***

While judgment is not explicitly mentioned here, the obtainment of salvation is elsewhere understood as an outcome of judgment. Furthermore, the series of conditional sentences in 2:11–13 implies judgment, with the conditions leading to certain outcomes through a process of evaluation.

A jarring element of this text is the juxtaposition of the language of election (*I endure all things for the elect*; 2:10a) with the conditionality that runs throughout. Paul endures *so that* the elect *may obtain salvation* (v. 10b), which suggests that their salvation rests on Paul's efforts, even though the elect are, by definition, already chosen by God for salvation. Moreover, the elect will *live with* Christ, *if* they *died with him* (v. 11), and they *will also reign with him* *if* they *endure* (v. 12a).

However the tension between election and conditionality is understood (and this is not the place to address the issue further), some observations concerning judgment may be made. First, the positive outcomes of judgment include *salvation* (v. 10b), living with Christ (v. 11), and reigning with him (v. 12a).

Salvation is *in Christ Jesus* (ἐν Χριστῷ Ἰησοῦ), meaning that "salvation is conditioned by Christ."[29] That is, the salvation to be obtained is of a "specifically Christian character."[30] This salvation is also conditioned by *eternal glory* (v. 10c). Beyond its eternal character, further description of such glory is not offered, though v. 12a may provide further insight.

The first of the four couplets in 2:11–13 indicates that dying with Christ will result in living with him (v. 11). While this could point to spiritual life with Christ in the present time, it is most likely eschatological life that is meant, since the remaining three couplets are clearly eschatological in focus. As such, it is possible that having *died with him* (συναπεθάνομεν) here refers to physical death—that is, dying as a Christian. But Paul elsewhere speaks of dying with Christ in a spiritual manner (e.g., Rom 6:5–8). And if physical death were meant, he would not likely have used the aorist tense-form (συναπεθάνομεν). So, Paul's point is that the person who has spiritually died with Christ in this life will live with him in the life to come.

The second couplet is more obviously eschatological in nature, indicating that those who endure *will also reign with him* (v. 12a). Enduring refers to the struggle and suffering of the Christian life and is parallel to dying with Christ. The endurance of suffering will give way to a reversal of situation in which believers will reign with Christ—in parallel to living with him. Reigning with Christ connects with the *eternal glory* mentioned in v. 10c. The cosmic rule of Christ, which is eternal and glorious in nature, is shared with believers who have endured with him.

The third couplet changes direction, indicating a negative outcome following the negative condition: *if we deny him, he will also deny us* (v. 12b). In contrast

---

29. Campbell, *Paul and Union with Christ*, 93.
30. Donald Guthrie, *The Pastoral Epistles*, TNTC, 2nd ed. (Leicester: Inter-Varsity Press, 1990), 156.

to the faithful endurance of the Christian life, those who reject Christ will be rejected by him. This result implies a process of judgment in which one's denial of Christ is evaluated and rewarded accordingly.

The fourth couplet is the most ambiguous, since it is unclear whether the result of faithlessness is condemnation or mercy at judgment: *if we are faithless, he remains faithful* (v. 13a). Clearly human faithlessness is negative, but does Christ's faithfulness mean that he will reject the faithless (parallel to denying those who deny him; v. 12b)? Or does it mean he will *not* reject the faithless?

Even the following addendum does not clarify the meaning: *for he cannot deny himself* (v. 13b). This could mean that Christ must deny the faithless because *he cannot deny himself*—faithlessness would then be understood as a denial of Christ, but Christ cannot tolerate that without denying himself. Or it could mean that Christ must honor his commitment to believers even when they are faithless because to renege his commitment to them would be to deny himself.

On the face of it, the negative solution seems more likely, given the structure of the four couplets. This would make the first two couplets positive (*we will also live with him*, v. 11b; *we will also reign with him*, v. 12a) and the second two negative (*he will also deny us*, v. 12b; *he remains faithful*, v. 13a).

But it is also possible that a deliberate flouting of structural expectation could serve to underscore the grace of Christ. While we should expect a negative final couplet, especially as a result of faithlessness, perhaps the point is that even in the face of faithlessness, Christ is merciful. He remains committed to his people even though they fail him.

Such a reading would understand faithlessness as qualitatively different from denial of Christ. Permanent denial of Christ severs any connection to him. But faithlessness could be understood to refer to a failure of faith or to imperfect faith rather than a complete absence of faith. An example can be found in the cry, "I do believe; help my unbelief!" (Mark 9:24).

However, this possibility ought to be weighed against Paul's almost universally negative use of the ἀπιστέω/ἀπιστία word group (note especially Rom 3:3).[31] The only possible use that might support a positive reading is found in Paul's reflection on his own history: *even though I was formerly a blasphemer, a persecutor, and an arrogant man. But I received mercy because I acted out of ignorance in unbelief* (ἀπιστίᾳ; 1 Tim 1:13). Here we see a direct connection between Paul's unbelief and the reception of God's mercy. Moreover, Paul's

---

31. See also Rom 4:20; 11:20, 23; 1 Cor 6:6; 7:12–15; 10:27; 14:22–24; 2 Cor 4:4; 6:14–15; 1 Tim 1:13; 5:8; Titus 1:15.

lack of faith was not a total absence of faith in God, but a mistaken faith; or, perhaps better, a misplaced faith. Nevertheless, if Paul had persisted in such unbelief, he would no doubt have come under God's condemnation—just as he expects will be the fate of the zealous Jewish leaders who likewise reject Christ.

Putting all this together, it seems most likely that the fourth couplet is negative after all. And so we see that at the judgment those who have died with Christ will be awarded life with him. Those who endure will reign with him. Those who deny Christ will be denied by him. And the faithless will likewise be found on the wrong side of Christ, since he cannot deny himself.

2 Tim 4:1–2 Διαμαρτύρομαι ἐνώπιον τοῦ θεοῦ καὶ Χριστοῦ Ἰησοῦ τοῦ μέλλοντος κρίνειν ζῶντας καὶ νεκρούς, καὶ τὴν ἐπιφάνειαν αὐτοῦ καὶ τὴν βασιλείαν αὐτοῦ· 2 κήρυξον τὸν λόγον, ἐπίστηθι εὐκαίρως ἀκαίρως, ἔλεγξον, ἐπιτίμησον, παρακάλεσον, ἐν πάσῃ μακροθυμίᾳ καὶ διδαχῇ.

I solemnly charge you before God and Christ Jesus, who is going to judge the living and the dead, *and because of his appearing and his kingdom: 2 Preach the word; be ready in season and out of season; rebuke, correct, and encourage with great patience and teaching.*

As discussed above (see §6.2), overtones of a juridical setting are heard in this text: Paul uses the language of a solemn charge (διαμαρτύρομαι), which is issued *before God and Christ Jesus*, viewing them as the witnesses and judges of this charge. Of the two, Christ is singled out as the one *who is going to judge the living and the dead* (4:1). Christ will judge the living and the dead, so that whether Timothy lives to see Christ's return in his lifetime or will be dead in Christ, his faithfulness will nevertheless come under the judgment of Christ. Evidently, Timothy's responsibility to *preach the word, rebuke, correct, and encourage* (v. 2) will be included in the purview of judgment, along with his entire life.[32]

2 Tim 4:6–8 Ἐγὼ γὰρ ἤδη σπένδομαι, καὶ ὁ καιρὸς τῆς ἀναλύσεώς μου ἐφέστηκεν. 7 τὸν καλὸν ἀγῶνα ἠγώνισμαι, τὸν δρόμον τετέλεκα, τὴν πίστιν τετήρηκα· 8 λοιπὸν ἀπόκειταί μοι ὁ τῆς δικαιοσύνης στέφανος, ὃν ἀποδώσει μοι ὁ κύριος ἐν ἐκείνῃ τῇ ἡμέρᾳ, ὁ δίκαιος κριτής, οὐ μόνον δὲ ἐμοὶ ἀλλὰ καὶ πᾶσιν τοῖς ἠγαπηκόσιν τὴν ἐπιφάνειαν αὐτοῦ.

---

32. Philip H. Towner, *1–2 Timothy & Titus*, IVPNTC (Downers Grove, IL: InterVarsity Press, 1994), 203.

> *For I am already being poured out as a drink offering, and the time for my departure is close. 7 I have fought the good fight, I have finished the race, I have kept the faith. 8* ***There is reserved for me the crown of righteousness, which the Lord, the righteous Judge, will give me on that day****, and not only to me, but to all those who have loved his appearing.*

This text has already been discussed with reference to the *appearing* of Christ (see §4.2 above) on *that day* (see §5.2 above). Now our interest is focused on its theme of judgment. Paul has *fought the good fight, finished the race*, and *kept the faith* (4:7). In keeping with the *race* metaphor, he looks forward to *the crown of righteousness* that will be given to him by *the Lord, the righteous Judge* (v. 8). The collocation of righteousness language (*the crown of righteousness; the righteous Judge*), not to mention *Judge* itself, invokes a judgment scenario, since for Paul righteousness is primarily a forensic category. Moreover, the anticipation of award implies an event of evaluation and appropriate recompense.

Only the positive aspect of judgment is in view here, with no mention of divine retribution or vengeance upon those who do not love the appearing of Christ (see §4.2 above). Paul anticipates the reception of the crown of righteousness, which is reserved for him ahead of time. The crown connects to the race imagery, implying that it is a reward for Paul having finished the race.[33] But this is mitigated by two factors. First, it is a crown of *righteousness*, given by the *righteous* Judge. Given Paul's theology of sharing the righteousness of Christ through union with him, we might infer that this crown of righteousness is shared with him by the one who is righteous. As much as it is a reward for finishing the race, it is also a gift given by the one who bestows righteousness on his people. Second, the only qualification that Paul explicitly states in this text is loving the appearing of Christ. The crown of righteousness will be given to all who love his appearing (see §4.2 above). While there is an *implicit* connection between finishing the race and the crown of righteousness, there is an *explicit* anticipation that loving Christ's appearing will result in the gift of the crown. Again, this suggests that the crown is less a reward for one's performance and more a result of being relationally connected to Christ.

Putting these elements together, it seems that Paul anticipates a day of judgment that will be immensely positive for those who are in loving relation

---

33. The crown is "the garland wreath that is placed on the heads of winners of athletic contests, and the sign of the honor they have won by their exploits (Herodotus, *Histories* 8.59; Diodorus Siculus, *Library of History* 20.84.3). By extension, the crown becomes metaphorical for all forms of being honored or rewarded (1 Cor 9:25; Phil 4:1; 1 Thess 2:19; 1 Pet 5:4; Rev 2:10; James 1:12)" (Johnson, *First and Second Letters to Timothy*, 366).

with Christ, the righteous Judge. Having fought the good fight, finishing the race, and keeping the faith, Paul anticipates a share in Christ's own righteousness along with all others who will love his appearing on that day.

6.3 SUMMARY

Judgment is a central theme of Paul's eschatological expectation. God's judgment cannot be escaped, with his wrath and anger stored up for the disobedient, while glory, honor, and peace await those who do what is good (Rom 2:1–11; Eph 5:5–6; Col 3:5–7; 1 Tim 5:24–25). Judgment is viewed as reaping what has been sown—either destruction reaped from sowing according to the flesh, or eternal life reaped from sowing according to the Spirit (Gal 6:7–9). It also takes into account the role of conscience, and it exposes what is kept secret (Rom 2:14–16; 1 Cor 4:3–5).

While all people begin as children under wrath by nature (Eph 2:1–3), believers are saved from God's wrath, since they have been declared righteous by the blood of Christ (Rom 5:8–10; 1 Thess 1:9–10; 5:9–10), and they will be held blameless in the day of Christ (1 Cor 1:6–8; 1 Thess 3:13).

Anticipating objections to the contrary, Paul is adamant that God's judgment of the world is righteous (Rom 3:1–6; 9:19–24). The whole world is subject to his judgment (3:19), and all people will stand before the judgment seat of God to give an account of themselves to him (14:10–12). More specifically, it is Christ himself who will judge the living and the dead (2 Tim 4:1–2, 8).

The reality of God's judgment means that Paul does not give much stock to human judgment—even his own judgment of himself (1 Cor 4:3–5). It also enables believers to work in all situations as to the Lord, expecting due recompense from him, whether or not they are justly treated in this life (Eph 6:6–8). Moreover, believers are able to endure unjust treatment, knowing that God will exact justice upon those who afflict them (2 Thess 1:5–10).

Clearly, judgment is a fundamental component of Paul's eschatological vision. It is the future event that will determine all subsequent reality for humanity, dividing all people toward their eternal destinations. While all humans are born under wrath, Christ saves those who have been made righteous by his blood. But even these will not escape the scrutiny of God's judgment, giving an account for the deeds done in the body.

Judgment does not only shape the future; it also shapes the present. The specter of forthcoming judgment is used by Paul to encourage obedience; indeed, fear of judgment is regarded as a healthy motivation for believers to abstain from worldly indulgences. Furthermore, the notion of reward at judgment is also held out as motivation. Believers can live in faithful allegiance to Christ, knowing that he will reward their devotion, come what may in their current situation. The hopeful expectation of judgment also affects daily life with respect to Paul's attitude to human opinion, work, recompense, and justice.

Above all, judgment is concerned with putting the world to rights. Though its implications for individuals is stressed in several contexts, Paul is clear that its wider implications shape the destiny of the whole world. With Christ as Lord over all creation, judgment is the necessary means of expressing his rule. It is how Christ will exert righteousness and establish peace over all.

CHAPTER 7

Resurrection

7.1 Introduction
The resurrection of Jesus is an event of central importance for Paul's eschatological understanding. It is the firstfruits of the resurrection of the dead that will occur on the last day. Christ has defeated death, so that all who participate in his death and resurrection now will be raised by God in the future on that last day. Moreover, the future resurrection of believers will follow the pattern of Christ's resurrection, with their bodies becoming glorious, incorruptible, and no longer subject to death. They will be raised by the same Spirit of God who raised Jesus from the dead.

The future bodily resurrection of believers affects their lives now in several ways, as they consider themselves alive to God in Christ, as they face dangers and threats of various kinds, and as they share in the sufferings of Christ. The hope of resurrection also comforts those who grieve for those who have already fallen asleep.

Future, physical resurrection is not the only kind found in the Pauline corpus, however, as a present, spiritual resurrection with Christ is also found. This is affirmed as a key element of believers' participation with Christ, who are said to have died and risen with him. This kind of resurrection is regarded as *real*, though spiritual, in nature. It anticipates the future, bodily resurrection to come but also has important consequences now. Those made alive with Christ experience new life in Christ, the forgiveness of sins, and reconciliation with God. They are to live in light of their raised status, thinking of things above and putting to death whatever belonged to the old self, who has now been crucified and freed from sin.

This chapter explores the resurrection of believers, taking note of the language of *resurrection*, *being made alive*, *the redemption of our bodies*, *being raised up*, and other expressions that point to the concept.

7.2 Resurrection Texts
Rom 6:4–11 συνετάφημεν οὖν αὐτῷ διὰ τοῦ βαπτίσματος εἰς τὸν θάνατον, ἵνα ὥσπερ ἠγέρθη Χριστὸς ἐκ νεκρῶν διὰ τῆς δόξης τοῦ πατρός, οὕτως καὶ

ἡμεῖς ἐν καινότητι ζωῆς περιπατήσωμεν. 5 **εἰ γὰρ σύμφυτοι γεγόναμεν τῷ ὁμοιώματι τοῦ θανάτου αὐτοῦ, ἀλλὰ καὶ τῆς ἀναστάσεως ἐσόμεθα·** 6 τοῦτο γινώσκοντες ὅτι ὁ παλαιὸς ἡμῶν ἄνθρωπος συνεσταυρώθη, ἵνα καταργηθῇ τὸ σῶμα τῆς ἁμαρτίας, τοῦ μηκέτι δουλεύειν ἡμᾶς τῇ ἁμαρτίᾳ· 7 ὁ γὰρ ἀποθανὼν δεδικαίωται ἀπὸ τῆς ἁμαρτίας. 8 **εἰ δὲ ἀπεθάνομεν σὺν Χριστῷ, πιστεύομεν ὅτι καὶ συζήσομεν αὐτῷ,** 9 εἰδότες ὅτι Χριστὸς ἐγερθεὶς ἐκ νεκρῶν οὐκέτι ἀποθνῄσκει, θάνατος αὐτοῦ οὐκέτι κυριεύει. 10 ὃ γὰρ ἀπέθανεν, τῇ ἁμαρτίᾳ ἀπέθανεν ἐφάπαξ· ὃ δὲ ζῇ, ζῇ τῷ θεῷ. 11 οὕτως καὶ ὑμεῖς λογίζεσθε ἑαυτοὺς εἶναι νεκροὺς μὲν τῇ ἁμαρτίᾳ ζῶντας δὲ τῷ θεῷ ἐν Χριστῷ Ἰησοῦ.

*Therefore we were buried with him by baptism into death, in order that, just as Christ was raised from the dead by the glory of the Father, so we too may walk in newness of life. 5 **For if we have been united with him in the likeness of his death, we will certainly also be in the likeness of his resurrection.** 6 For we know that our old self was crucified with him so that the body ruled by sin might be rendered powerless so that we may no longer be enslaved to sin, 7 since a person who has died is freed from sin. 8 **Now if we died with Christ, we believe that we will also live with him**, 9 because we know that Christ, having been raised from the dead, will not die again. Death no longer rules over him. 10 For the death he died, he died to sin once for all time; but the life he lives, he lives to God. 11 So, you too consider yourselves dead to sin and alive to God in Christ Jesus.*

In this passage firmly laden with participation theology,[1] Paul affirms that those who participate in the death of Christ will also participate in his resurrection—*for if we have been united with him in the likeness of his death, we will certainly also be in the likeness of his resurrection* (v. 5). The *likeness of his death* refers to being buried with Christ by baptism into death (v. 4), while the *likeness of his resurrection* points forward to the future bodily resurrection of believers. The point is clear: participation in death guarantees participation in resurrection.

This idea is expanded in the following verses, with reference to the crucifixion of the *old self*, which results in becoming *freed from sin* (vv. 6–7). Then the connection between death and resurrection is again affirmed—*now if we died with Christ, we believe that we will also live with him* (v. 8). Christ's death means that death can no longer rule over him (v. 9b), and it was a death *to sin once for all time*, which means that his new life is lived to God (v. 10).

---

1. See Campbell, *Paul and Union with Christ*, 333–43, for a detailed discussion.

This, then, means that believers who are in Christ, sharing in his death and resurrection, are to consider themselves *dead to sin and alive to God in Christ Jesus* (v. 11). In other words, the spiritual reality of participation in Christ's death and resurrection has implications for life here and now.[2] Like Christ, believers are now *dead to sin and alive to God*; they are therefore to think of themselves as such and live accordingly.

This passage looks forward to the future resurrection of believers, and it demonstrates the inextricable tie between participation with Christ and this future hope. Because believers participate in the death of Christ, they will share in the future, bodily resurrection, since that is the ultimate fulfillment of their sharing in Christ's resurrection.

Rom 8:11 εἰ δὲ τὸ πνεῦμα τοῦ ἐγείραντος τὸν Ἰησοῦν ἐκ νεκρῶν οἰκεῖ ἐν ὑμῖν, ὁ ἐγείρας Χριστὸν ἐκ νεκρῶν ζῳοποιήσει καὶ τὰ θνητὰ σώματα ὑμῶν διὰ τοῦ ἐνοικοῦντος αὐτοῦ πνεύματος ἐν ὑμῖν.

*And if the Spirit of him who raised Jesus from the dead lives in you, then **he who raised Christ from the dead will also bring your mortal bodies to life** through his Spirit who lives in you.*

In a context saturated with the benefits of the Spirit, Paul reflects on the Spirit's role in the resurrection of the dead. While the phrase *bring your mortal bodies to life* could, in itself, refer to spiritual renewal of the living, the context points to the resurrection of the dead. The raising of Jesus from the dead is twice mentioned, and clearly a parallel is implied between his resurrection and the bringing to life of mortal bodies.

The Spirit plays an instrumental role in resurrection but is not regarded as the ultimate agent of it. First described as *the Spirit of him who raised Jesus from the dead*, the *him* refers to God the Father;[3] he is one who raised Jesus from death. This is again the case in the clause *then he who raised Christ from the dead will also bring your mortal bodies to life*. The agent of Christ's resurrection is again God the Father, but this time the instrumentality of the Spirit is directly referenced, *through his Spirit who lives in you*.

The point is that the Spirit who lives in believers is the same Spirit who served as God's instrument in raising Jesus from the dead. Just as God raised Jesus through the Spirit, so he will bring believers' mortal bodies to resurrection life.

---

2. Campbell, *Paul and Union with Christ*, 115–16.
3. There is no personal pronoun in the Greek clause τὸ πνεῦμα τοῦ ἐγείραντος τὸν Ἰησοῦν ἐκ νεκρῶν, but the translation helpfully renders the substantival genitive participle τοῦ ἐγείραντος.

In case there is any doubt about the feasibility of the resurrection of the dead, Paul demonstrates that it is just as feasible as Christ's own resurrection from the dead, since both are powered by the Spirit who lives in believers.[4] If Christ has been raised, as believers affirm, then they too will be raised by the Spirit of God.

> Rom 8:18–25 Λογίζομαι γὰρ ὅτι οὐκ ἄξια τὰ παθήματα τοῦ νῦν καιροῦ πρὸς τὴν μέλλουσαν δόξαν ἀποκαλυφθῆναι εἰς ἡμᾶς. 19 ἡ γὰρ ἀποκαραδοκία τῆς κτίσεως τὴν ἀποκάλυψιν τῶν υἱῶν τοῦ θεοῦ ἀπεκδέχεται. 20 τῇ γὰρ ματαιότητι ἡ κτίσις ὑπετάγη, οὐχ ἑκοῦσα ἀλλὰ διὰ τὸν ὑποτάξαντα, ἐφ' ἐλπίδι 21 ὅτι καὶ αὐτὴ ἡ κτίσις ἐλευθερωθήσεται ἀπὸ τῆς δουλείας τῆς φθορᾶς εἰς τὴν ἐλευθερίαν τῆς δόξης τῶν τέκνων τοῦ θεοῦ. 22 οἴδαμεν γὰρ ὅτι πᾶσα ἡ κτίσις συστενάζει καὶ συνωδίνει ἄχρι τοῦ νῦν· 23 **οὐ μόνον δέ, ἀλλὰ καὶ αὐτοὶ τὴν ἀπαρχὴν τοῦ πνεύματος ἔχοντες, ἡμεῖς καὶ αὐτοὶ ἐν ἑαυτοῖς στενάζομεν υἱοθεσίαν ἀπεκδεχόμενοι, τὴν ἀπολύτρωσιν τοῦ σώματος ἡμῶν**. 24 τῇ γὰρ ἐλπίδι ἐσώθημεν· ἐλπὶς δὲ βλεπομένη οὐκ ἔστιν ἐλπίς· ὃ γὰρ βλέπει τίς ἐλπίζει; 25 εἰ δὲ ὃ οὐ βλέπομεν ἐλπίζομεν, δι' ὑπομονῆς ἀπεκδεχόμεθα.

> *For I consider that the sufferings of this present time are not worth comparing with the glory that is going to be revealed to us. 19 For the creation eagerly waits with anticipation for God's sons to be revealed. 20 For the creation was subjected to futility—not willingly, but because of him who subjected it—in the hope 21 that the creation itself will also be set free from the bondage to decay into the glorious freedom of God's children. 22 For we know that the whole creation has been groaning together with labor pains until now. 23* ***Not only that, but we ourselves who have the Spirit as the firstfruits—we also groan within ourselves, eagerly waiting for adoption, the redemption of our bodies****. 24 Now in this hope we were saved, but hope that is seen is not hope, because who hopes for what he sees? 25 Now if we hope for what we do not see, we eagerly wait for it with patience.*

The phrase *the redemption of our bodies* is not as clear a reference to resurrection as others, but in this context it surely points to the hope of resurrection. The widest context draws a contrast between present suffering and future glory (8:18). Within that scope, Paul focuses on the relation of creation to the fate of humanity, as it anticipates the revelation of God's sons (v. 19). Subjected to futility, creation *will also be set free from the bondage to decay* when God's

---

4. Käsemann, *Romans*, 224–25.

children are finally revealed (v. 21). The anticipation of creation is depicted as a woman in childbirth, *groaning . . . with labor pains*, as she waits for these children to be birthed (v. 22).

The focus then switches to the children waiting to be born, who *groan within ourselves, eagerly waiting for adoption* (v. 23). The reference to adoption (lit., "sonship"; υἰοθεσία)[5] is a twist on the image of natural labor and childbirth employed in the previous verse (v. 22). While it contorts the image of childbirth, adoption harks back to the theme already established in 8:14–17, especially 8:15: *you received the Spirit of adoption, by whom we cry out, "Abba, Father!"* In keeping with Roman law, Paul stresses the point that adopted children are, in every sense, *genuine* children of God, with all the privileges of status and inheritance that natural-born children enjoy. Paul probably uses adoption imagery alongside natural-childbirth imagery in vv. 22–23 because adopted children are to be regarded legitimate in every way.

Given the image of labor pains and groaning, then, the eager waiting obviously anticipates the event of childbirth, and it is in this context that *the redemption of our bodies* should be understood (v. 23). This *redemption of our bodies* is the awaited childbirth.

As such, *the redemption of our bodies* is naturally to be understood as bodily resurrection. Just as childbirth produces a living, breathing human being with an independent body, so creation will give birth to living, breathing human beings with independent, resurrected bodies. It is this prospect of future, bodily resurrection in which believers hope and for which they patiently wait (vv. 24–25).

1 Cor 6:13–14 τὰ βρώματα τῇ κοιλίᾳ καὶ ἡ κοιλία τοῖς βρώμασιν, ὁ δὲ θεὸς καὶ ταύτην καὶ ταῦτα καταργήσει. τὸ δὲ σῶμα οὐ τῇ πορνείᾳ ἀλλὰ τῷ κυρίῳ, καὶ ὁ κύριος τῷ σώματι· 14 **ὁ δὲ θεὸς καὶ τὸν κύριον ἤγειρεν καὶ ἡμᾶς ἐξεγερεῖ διὰ τῆς δυνάμεως αὐτοῦ.**

"Food is for the stomach and the stomach for food," and God will do away with both of them. However, the body is not for sexual immorality but for the Lord, and the Lord for the body. 14 **God raised up the Lord and will also raise us up by his power.**

---

5. Jewett prefers the literal language of "sonship" here as opposed to "adoption," despite its chauvinistic implications, since the link with "the revelation of the sons of God" in 8:19 is otherwise obscured (Jewett, *Romans*, 519n.109). For more on υἰοθεσία, see G. H. R. Horsley, "καθ' υἱοθεσίαν," in *New Documents Illustrating Early Christianity* 4, ed. G. H. R. Horsley (Macquarie University, Sydney: Ancient History Documentary Research Center, 1979), 173.

Found in the context of addressing the inappropriateness of sexual immorality, Paul argues against it in this text on the basis of what *the body* is for. The analogy of food and the stomach sets up the argument: *"Food is for the stomach and the stomach for food"* (6:13a). The point is, of course, that food and the stomach are made for each other; food that is not eaten does not fulfill its purpose, nor does an empty stomach. The two things go together by design.

Having made that straightforward point, Paul then claims that, likewise, *the body is not for sexual immorality but for the Lord, and the Lord for the body* (v. 13b). Countering Corinthian cultural expectations, the body is not for sexual gratification outside the covenant of marriage. This half of the claim would not have been surprising, given Paul's Jewish background. The second half, however, would have stood out: the body is *for the Lord, and the Lord for the body*. Just as food and stomach fulfill each other's purpose, so the body and the Lord are meant for each other. This idea is striking because it is not immediately transparent, but also because, whatever it means, it is obvious that it elevates the status of the body to one of extreme importance.

If the body is for the Lord, and the Lord for the body, Paul must view the body as occupying a central role in the relationship between believers and Christ (who is understood as "the Lord," as v. 14 clarifies). Relationship with Christ is not merely personal and spiritual; it is physical and bodily in a significant sense. Moreover, the centrality of the body for relationship with Christ implies the enduring significance of the body. Unlike food and stomach—of which Paul says, *God will do away with both of them*—the body will not be done away with; it will be raised immortal (notwithstanding the absence of its stomach!). And this sets up the following verse, *God raised up the Lord and will also raise us up by his power* (v. 14). The body will be immortal because God will *raise us up* (ἡμᾶς ἐξεγερεῖ). Paul correlates believers' resurrection with that of Christ, implying that it will be the same kind of resurrection as his (cf. 1 Cor 15:20–23), with an immortal, glorious body.[6] It is God's *power* that raised Christ and will raise the dead in Christ.

In his argument against sexual immorality, Paul's elevation of the body pushes against a cavalier attitude that views as unimportant what is done in the body. The body's purpose is found in relationship with Christ. And this is underscored by the expectation that the body will be raised as Christ was raised—to be with him forevermore.

---

6. As Morris aptly quips, "Food is for the stomach and the stomach for food, and the end of both is destruction. The body is for the Lord and the Lord for the body, and resurrection is the destiny of both" (Leon Morris, *The First Epistle of Paul to the Corinthians: An Introduction and Commentary*, TNTC, 2nd ed. [Leicester: Inter-Varsity Press, 1985], 97).

1 Cor 15:12–19 Εἰ δὲ Χριστὸς κηρύσσεται ὅτι ἐκ νεκρῶν ἐγήγερται, **πῶς λέγουσιν ἐν ὑμῖν τινες ὅτι ἀνάστασις νεκρῶν οὐκ ἔστιν;** 13 εἰ δὲ ἀνάστασις νεκρῶν οὐκ ἔστιν, οὐδὲ Χριστὸς ἐγήγερται· 14 εἰ δὲ Χριστὸς οὐκ ἐγήγερται, κενὸν ἄρα τὸ κήρυγμα ἡμῶν, κενὴ καὶ ἡ πίστις ὑμῶν· 15 εὑρισκόμεθα δὲ καὶ ψευδομάρτυρες τοῦ θεοῦ, ὅτι ἐμαρτυρήσαμεν κατὰ τοῦ θεοῦ ὅτι ἤγειρεν τὸν Χριστόν, ὃν οὐκ ἤγειρεν εἴπερ ἄρα νεκροὶ οὐκ ἐγείρονται. 16 **εἰ γὰρ νεκροὶ οὐκ ἐγείρονται, οὐδὲ Χριστὸς ἐγήγερται·** 17 εἰ δὲ Χριστὸς οὐκ ἐγήγερται, ματαία ἡ πίστις ὑμῶν, ἔτι ἐστὲ ἐν ταῖς ἁμαρτίαις ὑμῶν, 18 ἄρα καὶ οἱ κοιμηθέντες ἐν Χριστῷ ἀπώλοντο. 19 εἰ ἐν τῇ ζωῇ ταύτῃ ἐν Χριστῷ ἠλπικότες ἐσμὲν μόνον, ἐλεεινότεροι πάντων ἀνθρώπων ἐσμέν.

Now if Christ is proclaimed as raised from the dead, **how can some of you say, "There is no resurrection of the dead"**? *13 If there is no resurrection of the dead, then not even Christ has been raised; 14 and if Christ has not been raised, then our proclamation is in vain, and so is your faith. 15 Moreover, we are found to be false witnesses about God, because we have testified wrongly about God that he raised up Christ—whom he did not raise up, if in fact the dead are not raised. 16* **For if the dead are not raised, not even Christ has been raised**. *17 And if Christ has not been raised, your faith is worthless; you are still in your sins. 18 Those, then, who have fallen asleep in Christ have also perished. 19 If we have put our hope in Christ for this life only, we should be pitied more than anyone.*

The first of five texts to be discussed from this chapter brimming with resurrection theology, the central point here is that Christ's resurrection must be understood in light of a theology of the resurrection of the dead. The topic is raised since *some of you say, "There is no resurrection of the dead"* (15:12). Paul's response is that *if there is no resurrection of the dead, then not even Christ has been raised* (v. 13). To claim that Christ has not been raised if there is no resurrection of the dead only makes sense if Christ's resurrection is understood as part of the wider resurrection of the dead. Thus, if there is no wider resurrection, Christ must not have been raised (because his resurrection is an anticipation of it). The point is then reiterated in v. 16, *For if the dead are not raised, not even Christ has been raised.*

Paul goes on to reflect on the pastoral implications that follow from a denial of resurrection. His proclamation (κήρυγμα) would be in vain, and so would the Corinthians' faith (v. 14). The apostles would have misrepresented God (v. 15), and all would still be in their sins (v. 17). Moreover, the dead in Christ would have been lost (v. 18), and believers are to be pitied if their hope in the resurrection is unfounded (v. 19). As Barrett writes, "If Christ was not raised, Christians would only be bearing about in their body the dying of Jesus (2 Cor 4:10), without any prospect that his life also might be manifest in them. They would not merely be pursuing a figment of their imagination, but embracing death."[7]

The connection between the resurrection of Christ and the resurrection of believers is explored explicitly in the next text under discussion (15:20–23; see below). For now, it is important simply to recognize that the reality of Christ's resurrection answers the Corinthians' claim that there is no resurrection of the dead. There cannot be one without the other, since the resurrection of Christ is part of the general resurrection to follow.

1 Cor 15:20–23 Νυνὶ δὲ Χριστὸς ἐγήγερται ἐκ νεκρῶν ἀπαρχὴ τῶν κεκοιμημένων. 21 ἐπειδὴ γὰρ δι' ἀνθρώπου θάνατος, καὶ δι' ἀνθρώπου ἀνάστασις νεκρῶν. 22 **ὥσπερ γὰρ ἐν τῷ Ἀδὰμ πάντες ἀποθνῄσκουσιν, οὕτως καὶ ἐν τῷ Χριστῷ πάντες ζῳοποιηθήσονται.** 23 ἕκαστος δὲ ἐν τῷ ἰδίῳ τάγματι· ἀπαρχὴ Χριστός, ἔπειτα οἱ τοῦ Χριστοῦ ἐν τῇ παρουσίᾳ αὐτοῦ

But as it is, Christ has been raised from the dead, the firstfruits of those who have fallen asleep. 21 For since death came through a man, the resurrection of the dead also comes through a man. 22 ***For just as in Adam all die, so also in Christ all will be made alive****. 23 But each in his own order: Christ, the firstfruits; afterward, at his coming, those who belong to Christ.*

Following the point that Christ's resurrection is inextricably linked to the general resurrection of the dead (15:12–19, see above), Paul now draws out that link explicitly. Christ has indeed been raised and is *the firstfruits of those who have fallen asleep* (v. 20). The harvest imagery of *firstfruits* was well-known and immediately understood. The firstfruits of the harvest does not indicate the type and quality of the harvest to come, but it announces the imminence of what is to come. As the *firstfruits of those who have fallen asleep*, Christ reveals the type and quality of the resurrection. His resurrection was bodily, and so the resurrection of believers will be bodily. His resurrection body is immortal and incorruptible, and so the resurrection body of believers will be immortal and incorruptible. He will never again face death; so too believers will never again be subject to death (vv. 50–55). And his resurrection announces the imminence of what is to come. Those who have fallen asleep will surely rise, as he has risen. It is as certain as the harvest that follows the firstfruits.

---

7. C. K. Barrett, *The First Epistle to the Corinthians*, BNTC (Peabody, MA: Hendrickson, 1968), 350.

The theological grounding for Christ as firstfruits is found in Paul's "second Adam" Christology: *For since death came through a man, the resurrection of the dead also comes through a man. For just as in Adam all die, so also in Christ all will be made alive* (vv. 21–22; cf. Rom 5:12–21). Christ reverses the effect of Adam's introduction of death to the human world by being the one through whom resurrection comes (v. 21). Those who share solidarity in the realm of Adam (*in Adam*) will die, but those who share solidarity in the realm of Christ (*in Christ*) *will be made alive* (v. 22).[8] Being *made alive* is obviously another way to refer to physical resurrection, given the theme of the chapter at large and the language of Christ having *been raised from the dead* (v. 20).

Paul then returns to the notion of *firstfruits*: Christ must be raised first and afterward, *at his coming, those who belong to Christ* (v. 23). This statement adds two more elements to the discussion. First, when Paul speaks of the resurrection of the dead, he is only here referring to *those who belong to Christ* (ἔπειτα οἱ τοῦ Χριστοῦ). This clarifies the potentially ambiguous *in Christ* qualification in v. 22. It is not a universal qualification parallel to *in Adam* (since all people are first in Adam). Only those *of Christ* (οἱ τοῦ Χριστοῦ) are in Christ, and only they will be raised like him.

Second, those in Christ will be raised *at his coming* (ἐν τῇ παρουσίᾳ αὐτοῦ; v. 23). This is the first reference in the chapter to *when* the dead will be raised (see §4.2 above). It also implies that the coming of Christ will be instrumental in raising the dead. His coming is not merely the occasion of resurrection but its means. And so we begin to see the timeline for resurrection. Christ the firstfruits has already been raised. Later, at his coming, the anticipated harvest will follow, as the dead in Christ are raised with him and through him.

1 Cor 15:29–34 Ἐπεὶ τί ποιήσουσιν οἱ βαπτιζόμενοι ὑπὲρ τῶν νεκρῶν; εἰ **ὅλως νεκροὶ οὐκ ἐγείρονται, τί καὶ βαπτίζονται ὑπὲρ αὐτῶν;** 30 τί καὶ ἡμεῖς κινδυνεύομεν πᾶσαν ὥραν; 31 καθ' ἡμέραν ἀποθνῄσκω, νὴ τὴν ὑμετέραν καύχησιν, ἣν ἔχω ἐν Χριστῷ Ἰησοῦ τῷ κυρίῳ ἡμῶν. 32 εἰ κατὰ ἄνθρωπον ἐθηριομάχησα ἐν Ἐφέσῳ, τί μοι τὸ ὄφελος; εἰ **νεκροὶ οὐκ ἐγείρονται, Φάγωμεν καὶ πίωμεν, αὔριον γὰρ ἀποθνῄσκομεν.** 33 μὴ πλανᾶσθε·

Φθείρουσιν ἤθη χρηστὰ ὁμιλίαι κακαί.

34 ἐκνήψατε δικαίως καὶ μὴ ἁμαρτάνετε, ἀγνωσίαν γὰρ θεοῦ τινες ἔχουσιν, πρὸς ἐντροπὴν ὑμῖν λαλῶ.

---

8. Campbell, *Paul and Union with Christ*, 142.

Otherwise what will they do who are being baptized for the dead? **If the dead are not raised at all, then why are people baptized for them?** *30 Why are we in danger every hour? 31 I face death every day, as surely as I may boast about you, brothers and sisters, in Christ Jesus our Lord. 32 If I fought wild beasts in Ephesus as a mere man, what good did that do me?* **If the dead are not raised, Let us eat and drink, for tomorrow we die.** *33 Do not be deceived: "Bad company corrupts good morals." 34 Come to your senses and stop sinning; for some people are ignorant about God. I say this to your shame.*

Our third text from 1 Corinthians 15 draws further implications from the falsehood that there is no resurrection of the dead (cf. 15:12–19). The most notorious issue for interpretation of this passage is what Paul means by baptism for the dead (v. 29). Some have argued that baptism for the dead simply refers to regular baptistic practice, with *the dead* meaning the spiritually dead. People are baptized because of the reality of spiritual death. Upon conversion, baptism symbolizes their resurrection from the dead.[9] This reading is attractive because it would mean that Paul is not saying anything out of the ordinary. The point would be: Why do people get baptized at all if there is no resurrection from the dead? The symbol itself would become meaningless. But this reading struggles to account for the preposition ὑπέρ ("for, in behalf of, for the sake of").[10] This baptism is *for the dead* (ὑπὲρ τῶν νεκρῶν). While this is not the place for a detailed discussion of the preposition ὑπέρ,[11] if its use here is more or less in line with its most common functions, baptism *for the dead* seems to imply the performance of the rite on behalf of people who are already dead.

The chief problem for such a reading is its theological difficulty. How could Paul endorse such an activity when he clearly believes that death is the point after which it is too late to be reconciled to God? A person must accept Christ in this life and be baptized; there can be no room for a "baptism for the dead." Perhaps the key lies with the word *endorse*. While Paul does not condemn this practice, neither does he necessarily endorse it. Perhaps the Corinthians had known or practiced a baptism for the dead. Paul's point would be that such a practice—whether they

---

9. So Ciampa and Rosner, *First Letter to the Corinthians*, 784.

10. BDAG 1030, §A.1. Ciampa and Rosner point to the second definition of ὑπέρ listed in BDAG (§A.2) as a "marker of the moving cause or reason," so that these believers are baptized on account of the dead who will be raised in glory; that is, "They have heard about these dead being raised up (to new life and glory) and . . . they want to be part of that group" (Ciampa and Rosner, *First Letter to the Corinthians*, 784). While this reading is possible, it requires reading "dead being raised up" into "the dead," when it is more straightforward to read "the dead" as dead.

11. Brookins and Longenecker outline the main options clearly without deciding on any of them (Timothy A. Brookins and Bruce W. Longenecker, *1 Corinthians 10–16: A Handbook on the Greek Text*, BHGNT [Waco, TX: Baylor University Press, 2016], 161–62).

endorsed it or not—makes no sense at all if there is no resurrection. Those who have died have no hope in the age to come because they will simply remain dead. In any case, whatever the correct understanding of the baptism for the dead,[12] Paul's main point remains clear: without resurrection, it makes no sense.

Then Paul moves to some personal and ministry implications. He faces danger every hour (v. 30), and death every day (v. 31). He fought *wild beasts in Ephesus* (v. 32). But none of that stands to reason if there is no resurrection. Risking his life for the sake of Christ can only be reasonable if the dead are raised. Furthermore, *if the dead are not raised*, life itself is meaningless: *let us eat and drink, for tomorrow we die* (v. 32; Isa 22:13). Since death is the end, and it is coming, there is no option but to live for present comforts.

Finally, the section concludes with an exhortation: *Do not be deceived: "Bad company corrupts good morals"* (v. 34). This warning presumably means that the *bad company* of falsehood will adversely affect the Corinthians' morality. This reaches clearer exposition in the following verse: *Come to your senses and stop sinning; for some people are ignorant about God* (v. 34). Ignorance of God has moral implications. They are to stop sinning by coming to their senses. By understanding the truth about the resurrection of the dead, the Corinthians ought to engage no longer in the sinful practices that arise from mistaken belief.

1 Cor 15:35–50 Ἀλλ' ἐρεῖ τις· **πῶς ἐγείρονται οἱ νεκροί; ποίῳ δὲ σώματι ἔρχονται;** 36 ἄφρων, σὺ ὃ σπείρεις, οὐ ζωοποιεῖται ἐὰν μὴ ἀποθάνῃ· 37 καὶ ὃ σπείρεις, οὐ τὸ σῶμα τὸ γενησόμενον σπείρεις ἀλλὰ γυμνὸν κόκκον εἰ τύχοι σίτου ἤ τινος τῶν λοιπῶν· 38 ὁ δὲ θεὸς δίδωσιν αὐτῷ σῶμα καθὼς ἠθέλησεν, καὶ ἑκάστῳ τῶν σπερμάτων ἴδιον σῶμα. 39 οὐ πᾶσα σὰρξ ἡ αὐτὴ σὰρξ ἀλλ' ἄλλη μὲν ἀνθρώπων, ἄλλη δὲ σὰρξ κτηνῶν, ἄλλη δὲ σὰρξ πτηνῶν, ἄλλη δὲ ἰχθύων. 40 καὶ σώματα ἐπουράνια, καὶ σώματα ἐπίγεια· ἀλλ' ἑτέρα μὲν ἡ τῶν ἐπουρανίων δόξα, ἑτέρα δὲ ἡ τῶν ἐπιγείων. 41 ἄλλη δόξα ἡλίου, καὶ ἄλλη δόξα σελήνης, καὶ ἄλλη δόξα ἀστέρων· ἀστὴρ γὰρ ἀστέρος διαφέρει ἐν δόξῃ. 42 **Οὕτως καὶ ἡ ἀνάστασις τῶν νεκρῶν. σπείρεται ἐν φθορᾷ, ἐγείρεται ἐν ἀφθαρσίᾳ·** 43 σπείρεται ἐν ἀτιμίᾳ, ἐγείρεται ἐν δόξῃ· σπείρεται ἐν ἀσθενείᾳ, ἐγείρεται ἐν δυνάμει· 44 **σπείρεται σῶμα ψυχικόν, ἐγείρεται σῶμα πνευματικόν.** Εἰ ἔστιν σῶμα ψυχικόν, ἔστιν καὶ πνευματικόν. 45 οὕτως καὶ γέγραπται, ἐγένετο ὁ πρῶτος ἄνθρωπος Ἀδὰμ εἰς ψυχὴν ζῶσαν, ὁ ἔσχατος Ἀδὰμ εἰς πνεῦμα ζῳοποιοῦν. 46 ἀλλ' οὐ πρῶτον τὸ πνευματικὸν ἀλλὰ τὸ ψυχικόν, ἔπειτα τὸ πνευματικόν. 47 ὁ πρῶτος ἄνθρωπος ἐκ γῆς χοϊκός, ὁ δεύτερος ἄνθρωπος ἐξ οὐρανοῦ. 48 οἷος ὁ χοϊκός,

---

12. See Ciampa and Rosner for a helpful survey of the issues (*First Letter to the Corinthians*, 780–86).

τοιοῦτοι καὶ οἱ χοϊκοί, καὶ οἷος ὁ ἐπουράνιος, τοιοῦτοι καὶ οἱ ἐπουράνιοι· 49 καὶ καθὼς ἐφορέσαμεν τὴν εἰκόνα τοῦ χοϊκοῦ, φορέσομεν καὶ τὴν εἰκόνα τοῦ ἐπουρανίου.

50 Τοῦτο δέ φημι, ἀδελφοί, ὅτι σὰρξ καὶ αἷμα βασιλείαν θεοῦ κληρονομῆσαι οὐ δύναται οὐδὲ ἡ φθορὰ τὴν ἀφθαρσίαν κληρονομεῖ.

*But someone will ask, "**How are the dead raised? What kind of body will they have when they come?**" 36 You fool! What you sow does not come to life unless it dies. 37 And as for what you sow—you are not sowing the body that will be, but only a seed, perhaps of wheat or another grain. 38 But God gives it a body as he wants, and to each of the seeds its own body. 39 Not all flesh is the same flesh; there is one flesh for humans, another for animals, another for birds, and another for fish. 40 There are heavenly bodies and earthly bodies, but the splendor of the heavenly bodies is different from that of the earthly ones. 41 There is a splendor of the sun, another of the moon, and another of the stars; in fact, one star differs from another star in splendor. 42 **So it is with the resurrection of the dead: Sown in corruption, raised in incorruption;** 43 **sown in dishonor, raised in glory; sown in weakness, raised in power;** 44 **sown a natural body, raised a spiritual body.** If there is a natural body, there is also a spiritual body. 45 So it is written, The first man Adam became a living being; the last Adam became a life-giving spirit. 46 However, the spiritual is not first, but the natural, then the spiritual.*

47 The first man was from the earth, a man of dust; the second man is from heaven. 48 Like the man of dust, so are those who are of the dust; like the man of heaven, so are those who are of heaven. 49 And just as we have borne the image of the man of dust, we will also bear the image of the man of heaven. 50 What I am saying, brothers and sisters, is this: Flesh and blood cannot inherit the kingdom of God, nor can corruption inherit incorruption.

The fourth text from 1 Corinthians 15 is of central theological significance for understanding the resurrection of the dead in Paul's writings. It is a long and complex text, so will require several steps of analysis.

First, Paul begins to address the anticipated questions, *"How are the dead raised? What kind of body will they have when they come?"* (15:35). Imagining that Paul's interlocutors now accept the chief point running through the three previously examined texts (vv. 12–19, 20–23, 29–34), namely, that the resurrection of the dead is a certain future prospect because of the prior resurrection of Christ, they now move to consider what resurrection will entail. What will the resurrection body *be*?

After insulting his imaginary interlocutor—*you fool!* (ἄφρων)—Paul begins to answer the question by drawing on the image of a seed, *what you sow does not come to life unless it dies* (v. 36), indicating that death must of course precede resurrection. Moreover, just as a seed that is sown does not remain just a seed, so *you are not sowing the body that will be, but only a seed* (v. 37). That is, the resurrection body will have the sort of relation to the dead body as wheat has to its seed. The seed, when it dies, comes to life as a harvest grain.

Having established the seed metaphor, Paul now uses it to reflect on the realities of different "bodies" for different elements of creation. *God gives it a body as he wants, and to each of the seeds its own body* (v. 38). This refers back to the seed that produces wheat or another grain (v. 37). Whatever each seed produces is determined by God's design. He then moves forward to apply the same principle beyond harvest crops to humans, animals, birds, and fish (v. 39). It applies even to celestial entities—the sun, moon, and stars (vv. 40–41).

All of this serves to set up the following point that ultimately answers the question raised at v. 35:

> So it is with the resurrection of the dead: Sown in corruption, raised in incorruption; sown in dishonor, raised in glory; sown in weakness, raised in power; sown a natural body, raised a spiritual body. If there is a natural body, there is also a spiritual body (vv. 42–44).

The body that is sown is corrupted, dishonorable, weak, and natural. But the resurrected body will be incorruptible, glorious, powerful, and spiritual. The contrast between *natural* and *spiritual* bodies makes room for some confusion, since the latter could be taken to mean that Paul does not envisage a physical, bodily resurrection but rather some kind of noncorporeal, ethereal spirit. But such a conclusion does not fit what has been seen in this chapter so far. The immediately previous verses are concerned with *bodies*, and so a spiritual body must be a *body*, not a disembodied spirit. Moreover, Christ's resurrection as the firstfruits of the future resurrection of those in Christ (vv. 20–23) directly points to a physical, bodily resurrection. The firstfruits announce the type of harvest that is to come. Since Christ's resurrected body was physical (notwithstanding its unusual qualities), so too those in Christ will be resurrected physically and bodily.

Paul then returns to his "second Adam" Christology (cf. vv. 22–23) in order to contrast three elements (vv. 45–47). First, the original Adam *became a living being; the last Adam became a life-giving spirit* (v. 45). This point contrasts the association that each Adam has with life; the first Adam received life through the gift of God (this is not stated, but is assumed from Gen 2), while Christ bestows life. Implicitly then, Paul points to the superiority of Christ over Adam when it comes to their life-giving ability. Adam cannot grant life to others; he is a recipient of life along with everyone else. But Christ can grant life to others—he will make others live when they are raised from the dead.

The second point of contrast is that the natural precedes the spiritual (v. 46). This apparently draws on the order inherit to the seed-wheat analogy; the harvest of wheat is better than the seed, but the seed must come first in order that the harvest may follow. So too the natural body must come first, *then the spiritual*.

The third point of contrast is one of origins. *The first man was from the earth, a man of dust* (v. 47a)—a more explicit allusion to Genesis 2. However, *the second man is from heaven* (v. 47b). The purpose of this point of contrast is not simply to further underscore the supremacy of Christ but to provide further grounding to what Christ can do for believers. This is unfolded in the following verse (v. 48).

The points of contrast between the two Adams are now applied to humanity at large (vv. 48–49). *Those who are of the dust* are *like the man of dust* (v. 48a). This no doubt refers to those *in Adam* (v. 22a); like Adam himself, those *in Adam all die*. The man of dust has no life in himself and is thereby powerless to bestow life on other men and women of dust (cf. v. 45). On the other hand, *those who are of heaven* are *like the man of heaven* (v. 48b). This probably means that those *in Christ* will all *be made alive* (v. 22b), just as Christ was made alive.

Furthermore, just as those in Adam *have borne the image of the man of dust, we will also bear the image of the man of heaven* (v. 49). This is the first mention of *image* language (εἰκών) in the chapter, so there is not much to help us understand Paul on this point. On the one hand, he may simply be anticipating what is to follow—that those in Christ will be changed, exchanging the corruptible for the incorruptible, and so forth (vv. 51–53). On the other hand, it is possible that Paul is drawing on his broader theology of *image*, as developed elsewhere (e.g., Rom 8:29; 2 Cor 4:4; Col 1:15; 3:10).

The latter option seems preferable. It is difficult to encounter *image* language (εἰκών) without recalling Paul's other uses of the term, let alone the wider biblical theology that surrounds it. Of particular interest is Romans 8:29: *For those he foreknew he also predestined to be conformed to the image* [εἰκών] *of his Son, so that he would be the firstborn among many brothers and sisters*. Here we see conformity to the image of Christ alongside reference to the resurrection (*the firstborn among many brothers and sisters*). Moreover, conformity to the image of the Son enables (*so that*) believers to become his brothers and sisters.

Putting these things together, Romans 8:29 indicates that conformity to the image of Christ is connected to resurrection, and it means that believers may be regarded as his siblings. While these insights are not found directly in 1 Corinthians 15:49, they shed some light on Paul's theology of image and its connection to resurrection. Sharing the image of Christ is bound up with resurrection from the dead and enables membership in the divine family.

The climactic conclusion to Paul's lengthy argumentation comes next, flagged by the *meta-comment, What I am saying . . .* (v. 50a).[13] The important proposition following the meta-comment is that *flesh and blood cannot inherit the kingdom of God, nor can corruption inherit incorruption* (v. 50b). The inheritance of the kingdom of God seems to be the conclusion that Paul has been driving at all along. The natural, flesh-and-blood, corruptible body is not fit for the kingdom of God. Anyone who would inherit the kingdom must therefore be resurrected with a spiritual, incorruptible body like that of Christ.

The notion of *inheritance* also connects to the *image* language of the previous verse (v. 49). We have already established that conformity to the *image* of Christ enables membership in the divine family (see above), and *inheritance* is inherently a familial concept. Thus, anyone who would wish to inherit the kingdom of God must bear the image of the man of heaven (v. 49). Without that token of familial membership, no one is able to receive the heavenly inheritance.

> 1 Cor 15:51–58 ἰδοὺ μυστήριον ὑμῖν λέγω· πάντες οὐ κοιμηθησόμεθα, πάντες δὲ ἀλλαγησόμεθα, 52 ἐν ἀτόμῳ, ἐν ῥιπῇ ὀφθαλμοῦ, ἐν τῇ ἐσχάτῃ σάλπιγγι· σαλπίσει γὰρ καὶ **οἱ νεκροὶ ἐγερθήσονται ἄφθαρτοι καὶ ἡμεῖς ἀλλαγησόμεθα**. 53 δεῖ γὰρ τὸ φθαρτὸν τοῦτο ἐνδύσασθαι ἀφθαρσίαν καὶ τὸ θνητὸν τοῦτο ἐνδύσασθαι ἀθανασίαν. 54 ὅταν δὲ τὸ φθαρτὸν τοῦτο ἐνδύσηται ἀφθαρσίαν καὶ τὸ θνητὸν τοῦτο ἐνδύσηται ἀθανασίαν, τότε γενήσεται ὁ λόγος ὁ γεγραμμένος,
>
> κατεπόθη ὁ θάνατος εἰς νῖκος.
> 55 ποῦ σου, θάνατε, τὸ νῖκος;
> ποῦ σου, θάνατε, τὸ κέντρον;
>
> 56 τὸ δὲ κέντρον τοῦ θανάτου ἡ ἁμαρτία, ἡ δὲ δύναμις τῆς ἁμαρτίας ὁ νόμος·
> 57 τῷ δὲ θεῷ χάρις τῷ διδόντι ἡμῖν τὸ νῖκος διὰ τοῦ κυρίου ἡμῶν Ἰησοῦ

---

13. A *meta-comment* is "when a speaker stops saying what they are saying in order to comment on what is *going* to be said, speaking abstractly about it, e.g. '*I want you to know that . . .*', 'Don't you know that . . .'" The effect of the meta-comment "is to slow down the flow of the text, and to attract the reader's attention to some important proposition that follows" (Steven E. Runge, *The Lexham Discourse Greek New Testament: Introduction* [Bellingham, WA: Lexham, 2008], n.p.).

Χριστοῦ. 58 Ὥστε, ἀδελφοί μου ἀγαπητοί, ἑδραῖοι γίνεσθε, ἀμετακίνητοι, περισσεύοντες ἐν τῷ ἔργῳ τοῦ κυρίου πάντοτε, εἰδότες ὅτι ὁ κόπος ὑμῶν οὐκ ἔστιν κενὸς ἐν κυρίῳ.

Listen, I am telling you a mystery: We will not all fall asleep, but we will all be changed, 52 in a moment, in the twinkling of an eye, at the last trumpet. For the trumpet will sound, and **the dead will be raised incorruptible, and we will be changed***. 53 For this corruptible body must be clothed with incorruptibility, and this mortal body must be clothed with immortality. 54 When this corruptible body is clothed with incorruptibility, and this mortal body is clothed with immortality, then the saying that is written will take place:*

> *Death has been swallowed up in victory.*
> *55 Where, death, is your victory?*
> *Where, death, is your sting?*

56 The sting of death is sin, and the power of sin is the law. 57 But thanks be to God, who gives us the victory through our Lord Jesus Christ!
58 Therefore, my dear brothers and sisters, be steadfast, immovable, always excelling in the Lord's work, because you know that your labor in the Lord is not in vain.

The fifth and final text to be explored from 1 Corinthians 15 presents the climactic conclusion to the entire argument. Paul begins by describing how he imagines the transformation of the body from mortal to immortal (15:51–53). He then ends with doxology and exhortation (vv. 54–58).

The *mystery* he imparts is that *we will not all fall asleep, but we will all be changed* (v. 51). This reflects Paul's anticipation that Christ's coming will be met by believers who are still living (cf. 1 Thess 4:15–17). While 1 Thessalonians 4:13–18 affirms that those who have fallen asleep will not be disadvantaged when Christ comes, 1 Corinthians 15:51 affirms that those who are still living will not be disadvantaged either. Given the seed imagery employed earlier (vv. 35–44), one might wonder whether the living will receive the resurrection body since Paul had affirmed that *what you sow does not come to life unless it dies* (v. 36). If the believer is living when Christ comes and so will not taste death, how will the seed sprout since it has not been sown? Paul does not answer that question but simply affirms that the living *will all be changed*. Any problem caused by the seed imagery should be mitigated by the fact that it is just an image after all.

The change will occur *in a moment, in the twinkling of an eye, at the last trumpet* (v. 52a). It is obviously an instantaneous transformation that Paul envisages rather than a drawn-out metamorphosis. There will be no cocoon, hibernation, or somnolency. The event will therefore be one of transcendent power rather than naturally occurring processes.

The last trumpet *will sound, and the dead will be raised incorruptible, and we will be changed* (v. 52b). Trumpet imagery is found in 1 Thessalonians 4:16, further consolidating that letter's link to 1 Corinthians 15 and to Paul's resurrection teaching in general: *For the Lord himself will descend from heaven with a shout, with the archangel's voice, and with the trumpet of God, and the dead in Christ will rise first.* Whether or not this is to be taken literally, with an actual trumpet sound to be heard, is beside the point. It is an image of a dramatic, triumphant announcement, heralding the cataclysmic events of the coming of Christ and the resurrection of the dead in Christ.

The dead will be raised incorruptible, and we will be changed (1 Cor 15:52b). The importance of this transformation is again underscored in the following verse, *for this corruptible body must be clothed with incorruptibility* (v. 53), repeating the essence of Paul's argument in vv. 35–50. But when this actually takes place, Paul anticipates the final victory cry (vv. 54–55):

> *Death has been swallowed up in victory.*
> *Where, death, is your victory?*
> *Where, death, is your sting?*

When the mortal body is transformed into an incorruptible, immortal body, death will have been conquered. It will be *swallowed up in victory*. And in keeping with the taunts of the victorious toward their conquered enemy, *Where, death, is your victory? Where, death, is your sting?* On that day, death will have been extinguished from the experience of humanity once and for all.

There is, however, some difficulty associated with death's *sting*, as unfolded in the following verse, *the sting of death is sin, and the power of sin is the law* (v. 56). The chief question is what exactly is meant by *the sting of death*. We are told that *the sting of death is sin*, but what does this mean?

Traditionally *the sting of death* has been understood in a subjective sense—that *sin* brings a subjective experience of pain or *sting*. But this seems to reverse the expectation set forth from biblical theology, in which *death* is the painful result of *sin*. That is, the wages of sin is death (Rom 6:23); once sin is engaged, the futility and agony of death is consequently guaranteed (Gen 3). However, it is possible to explain Paul's wording in the reverse manner, notwithstanding the expected order of sin leading to death, so that sin is nevertheless regarded as its own painful consequence. After all, once subjected to death, people are locked into a life of sin, and such a life is one of thorns and thistles.

While such an understanding is possible, it is better to retain the expectation set forth in biblical theology—that sin leads to death. This then raises the question, again, of what it means to say, *the sting of death is sin*. The most likely answer is to reinterpret what *sting* (κέντρον) means. While this word can refer to the subjective sensation of pain or a sting,[14] it can also be used for the *objective* sting used by certain creatures to inflict venom into its prey or adversary.[15] A bee's *sting* is its *stinger*.

If the *stinger* of death is sin, this phrase immediately becomes intelligible. Paul imagines death as a creature or beast, who attacks its prey through the stinger of sin. Once a person is "stung" by sin, death has claimed him. Just as Adam sinned and was sentenced to death, so all who sin are now under the domain of death.

This reading is confirmed by 1 Corinthians 15:56b, *and the power of sin is the law*. The point here is that the law fuels sin's capacity in that it convicts people of their sin, as Paul argues elsewhere. In fact, Romans 7:7–13 offers an extended treatment of these precise issues:

> What should we say then? Is the law sin? Absolutely not! On the contrary, I would not have known sin if it were not for the law. For example, I would not have known what it is to covet if the law had not said, Do not covet. 8 And sin, seizing an opportunity through the commandment, produced in me coveting of every kind. For apart from the law sin is dead. 9 Once I was alive apart from the law, but when the commandment came, sin sprang to life again 10 and I died. The commandment that was meant for life resulted in death for me. 11 For sin, seizing an opportunity through the commandment, deceived me, and through it killed me. 12 So then, the law is holy, and the commandment is holy and just and good. 13 Therefore, did what is good become death to me? Absolutely not! On the contrary, sin, in order to be recognized as sin, was producing death in me through what is good, so that through the commandment, sin might become sinful beyond measure.

---

14. BDAG notes an epitaph that mentions the deceased's "unceasing sting" (κέντρον ἄπαυστον) because of his death (BDAG 539, §1).

15. This is the predominant use of the word, with the two major categories of usage being "1. the sting of an animal," and "2. a pointed stick that serves the same purpose as a whip" (BDAG 539, §§1–2).

We see the connection between the law and sin very clearly here: *I would not have known sin if it were not for the law* (Rom 7:7); sin *produced in me coveting of every kind* (v. 8); *when the commandment came, sin sprang to life again* (v. 9). But the clinching statement is *for sin, seizing an opportunity through the commandment, deceived me, and through it killed me* (v. 11). Paul views sin as a power that takes advantage of the law to strengthen its position. And through the law, sin kills its victims. Going back to 1 Corinthians 15:56, *the power of sin is the law* must be understood in the way outlined immediately above, in Romans 7:7–13. The law empowers sin to do what it does. And sin, together with the law, brings death.

All of this suggests that *the sting of death* should be understood as *the stinger of death*. Sin is death's instrument—once infected by sin, a person will surely die.

Returning now to the wider passage at hand, the penultimate item is doxological: *But thanks be to God, who gives us the victory through our Lord Jesus Christ!* (1 Cor 15:57). The victory over death comes through victory over its stinger—sin. Since Christ has dealt with sin through his death, he has therefore overcome death. This is the deeper logic that undergirds Paul's thinking throughout the section: once sin has been defeated, death has been defeated. Without sin, its stinger, death has become powerless and can no longer keep people captive under its domain. Like a bee without a stinger, it is harmless. Indeed, like a bee who has lost its stinger, death is bound to die.

This leads to the exhortatory conclusion of the passage, *Therefore, my dear brothers and sisters, be steadfast, immovable, always excelling in the Lord's work, because you know that your labor in the Lord is not in vain* (v. 58). There is some debate concerning the scope of *the Lord's work* and *labor in the Lord*. I have argued elsewhere that these phrases refer to "work conducted for the cause of Christ" and "Christian service conducted for the cause and purposes of the Lord."[16] While others may argue for a broader scope, inclusive of any work performed as a Christian, the scope is not our primary interest here.

Rather, the key point of observation is that this exhortation comes at the end of such a lengthy and significant discussion concerning resurrection. The exhortation to remain steadfast in the Lord's work is supported by the encouragement that *your labor in the Lord is not in vain*. The clear implication is that resurrection from the dead overturns the vanity of labor. While Qoheleth (in) famously despaired of the meaninglessness and vanity of all one's toil conducted under the sun (e.g., Eccl 2:18–23), the resurrection of the dead overturns

---

16. Campbell, *Paul and Union with Christ*, 158–59.

vanity.[17] This is because death is not the end. Death does not forever undo the significance of one's work. In resurrected life, *labor in the Lord* retains its value. Indeed, as Paul's many references to judgment (both positive and negative; see ch. 6) indicate, believers will be held accountable for the work they have done or not done, as the case may be.

One's labor in the Lord will be of eternal significance because of the resurrection of the dead. As such, believers ought to be steadfast, immovable, and always excelling in the Lord's work. Its importance and fruit will follow believers into their resurrection lives and eternal glory.

2 Cor 4:11–14 ἀεὶ γὰρ ἡμεῖς οἱ ζῶντες εἰς θάνατον παραδιδόμεθα διὰ Ἰησοῦν, ἵνα καὶ ἡ ζωὴ τοῦ Ἰησοῦ φανερωθῇ ἐν τῇ θνητῇ σαρκὶ ἡμῶν. 12 ὥστε ὁ θάνατος ἐν ἡμῖν ἐνεργεῖται, ἡ δὲ ζωὴ ἐν ὑμῖν. 13 ἔχοντες δὲ τὸ αὐτὸ πνεῦμα τῆς πίστεως κατὰ τὸ γεγραμμένον, Ἐπίστευσα, διὸ ἐλάλησα, καὶ ἡμεῖς πιστεύομεν, διὸ καὶ λαλοῦμεν, 14 εἰδότες ὅτι **ὁ ἐγείρας τὸν κύριον Ἰησοῦν καὶ ἡμᾶς σὺν Ἰησοῦ ἐγερεῖ** καὶ παραστήσει σὺν ὑμῖν.

For we who live are always being given over to death for Jesus's sake, so that Jesus's life may also be displayed in our mortal flesh. 12 So then, death is at work in us, but life in you. 13 And since we have the same spirit of faith in keeping with what is written, I believed, therefore I spoke, we also believe, and therefore speak. 14 For we know that **the one who raised the Lord Jesus will also raise us with Jesus** *and present us with you.*

The wider context contrasts the frailty of human life with the enduring treasure of the gospel (4:7–10). Paul and his companions *are always being given over to death for Jesus's sake* (v. 11a), meaning that their ministry is one of suffering, persecution, and impending death. But this is *so that Jesus's life may also be displayed in our mortal flesh* (v. 11b), indicating that the life-giving fruit of Jesus's resurrected life will be evident in them, even in their *mortal flesh*.

Paul's pastoral ministry to the Corinthians, then, means that *death is at work in us, but life in you* (v. 12). Paul and his companions suffer in every way for the Corinthians' sake, and their suffering produces spiritual life in the latter. Paul's ministry is fueled by faith—*we also believe, and therefore speak* (v. 13b), the point being that their faith will promote speaking regardless of the consequences.

Moreover, Paul's faith holds to the hope of resurrection, as the following

---

17. The fact that Greek Qoheleth uses the word ματαιότης (*futile*), while Paul uses κενός (*in vain*) is hardly significant. The two words are synonyms, and even with the different vocabulary, the conceptual parallel to Qoheleth seems unavoidable.

verse indicates: *For we know that the one who raised the Lord Jesus will also raise us with Jesus and present us with you* (v. 14). The significance of resurrection in this context is that Paul is *always being given over to death for Jesus's sake* (v. 11), but death is not the final outcome. He is able to accept death for Jesus's sake because he holds to the hope of resurrection.

Paul draws on Jesus's resurrection for his hope in his own resurrection, stating that *the one who raised the Lord Jesus will also raise us* (v. 14a). The same God who raised Jesus from the dead, thus demonstrating his power to do so, is able to effect the same in others. An implicit theological connection also exists between Jesus's resurrection and those to follow, which Paul develops elsewhere (e.g., 1 Cor 15:45–49).[18] The fact of his resurrection secures that of his followers.

Furthermore, resurrection will lead to presentation—*and present us with you* (2 Cor 4:14b). This presumably refers to their presentation for judgment. Following resurrection, believers will be put forward to give an account to God for what they have done in this life. Notably, Paul envisages this presentation involving *us with you* (v. 14b). Whatever may happen in the course of their lives, whether together or apart, whether Paul dies sooner or later, he will be reunited with the Corinthian believers at their presentation together following resurrection.

2 Cor 5:1–10 Οἴδαμεν γὰρ ὅτι ἐὰν ἡ ἐπίγειος ἡμῶν οἰκία τοῦ σκήνους καταλυθῇ, οἰκοδομὴν ἐκ θεοῦ ἔχομεν, οἰκίαν ἀχειροποίητον αἰώνιον ἐν τοῖς οὐρανοῖς. 2 καὶ γὰρ ἐν τούτῳ στενάζομεν τὸ οἰκητήριον ἡμῶν τὸ ἐξ οὐρανοῦ ἐπενδύσασθαι ἐπιποθοῦντες, 3 εἴ γε καὶ ἐκδυσάμενοι οὐ γυμνοὶ εὑρεθησόμεθα. 4 καὶ γὰρ οἱ ὄντες ἐν τῷ σκήνει στενάζομεν βαρούμενοι, ἐφ' ᾧ οὐ θέλομεν ἐκδύσασθαι ἀλλ' ἐπενδύσασθαι, ἵνα καταποθῇ τὸ θνητὸν ὑπὸ τῆς ζωῆς. 5 ὁ δὲ κατεργασάμενος ἡμᾶς εἰς αὐτὸ τοῦτο θεός, ὁ δοὺς ἡμῖν τὸν ἀρραβῶνα τοῦ πνεύματος. 6 Θαρροῦντες οὖν πάντοτε καὶ εἰδότες ὅτι ἐνδημοῦντες ἐν τῷ σώματι ἐκδημοῦμεν ἀπὸ τοῦ κυρίου· 7 διὰ πίστεως γὰρ περιπατοῦμεν, οὐ διὰ εἴδους· 8 θαρροῦμεν δὲ καὶ εὐδοκοῦμεν μᾶλλον ἐκδημῆσαι ἐκ τοῦ σώματος καὶ ἐνδημῆσαι πρὸς τὸν κύριον. 9 διὸ καὶ φιλοτιμούμεθα, εἴτε ἐνδημοῦντες εἴτε ἐκδημοῦντες, εὐάρεστοι αὐτῷ εἶναι. 10 τοὺς γὰρ πάντας ἡμᾶς φανερωθῆναι δεῖ ἔμπροσθεν τοῦ βήματος τοῦ Χριστοῦ, ἵνα κομίσηται ἕκαστος τὰ διὰ τοῦ σώματος πρὸς ἃ ἔπραξεν, εἴτε ἀγαθὸν εἴτε φαῦλον.

---

18. For an extended discussion of the connections and differences between 1 and 2 Corinthians regarding resurrection, see Martin's helpful excursus on resurrection in 2 Corinthians (Ralph P. Martin, *2 Corinthians*, 2nd ed., WBC 40 [Grand Rapids: Zondervan, 2014], 427–56).

For we know that if our earthly tent we live in is destroyed, we have a building from God, an eternal dwelling in the heavens, not made with hands. 2 Indeed, we groan in this tent, desiring to put on our heavenly dwelling, 3 since, when we have taken it off, we will not be found naked. 4 Indeed, we groan while we are in this tent, burdened as we are, because we do not want to be unclothed but clothed, so that mortality may be swallowed up by life. 5 Now the one who prepared us for this very purpose is God, who gave us the Spirit as a down payment. 6 So we are always confident and know that while we are at home in the body we are away from the Lord. 7 For we walk by faith, not by sight. 8 In fact, we are confident, and we would prefer to be away from the body and at home with the Lord. 9 Therefore, whether we are at home or away, we make it our aim to be pleasing to him. 10 For we must all appear before the judgment seat of Christ, so that each may be repaid for what he has done in the body, whether good or evil.

While this passage does not address resurrection explicitly, it is presupposed. The central theme is the *eternal dwelling* (5:1), also called *our heavenly dwelling* (v. 2). Perhaps not immediately obvious is the fact that Paul uses such descriptions to refer to the believers' heavenly body. This becomes clear in contrast to such language as *our earthly tent* (v. 1), which can be taken off (v. 3), leaving believers *unclothed* (v. 4). In context, the taking off of such a tent is a reference to death—the shedding of the earthly body. Paul becomes more specific in the verses that follow, equating *this tent* (v. 2) with being *at home in the body*, which is to be *away from the Lord* (v. 6). And Paul would prefer *to be away from the body and at home with the Lord* (v. 8).

Paul imagines that *our earthly tent* will be *destroyed* (v. 1a), but in that event, *we have a building from God, an eternal dwelling in the heavens, not made with hands* (v. 1b). This belief factors into the wider context of Paul's suffering in ministry. He always carries the death of Jesus in his body, being given over to death (4:10–11). But the heavenly body offers him hope in the face of earthly destruction.[19]

Life in the current body is one of *groaning* (5:2, 4) in expectation of the better, heavenly body. Interestingly, Paul implies that the intermediate state between death and resurrection will not be one of being *found naked* (v. 3); *we do not want to be unclothed but clothed, so that mortality may be swallowed up by life* (v. 4). It is unclear whether Paul imagines some kind of corporeal

---

19. Barnett writes: "To our minds this present existence is solid and real, whereas our coming existence seems shadowy and insubstantial. Paul teaches us that the reverse is true" (Paul Barnett, *The Message of 2 Corinthians*, BST [Leicester: Inter-Varsity Press, 1988], 98).

experience *before* the full resurrection of the body, or rather only a *temporary* disembodiment before resurrection. If the former, it is not clear at all what this would mean. Is it some kind of temporary, pre-resurrection body? If so, there does not appear to be any further evidence for such a thing in Paul's writings (nor anywhere else in the NT). If the latter, it would hardly explain Paul's desire to leave the earthly body, apparently giving preference to a disembodied state that is nevertheless *with the Lord* (v. 8). Presumably being *with the Lord* is enough reason to prefer death over earthly life, even if it is a disembodied existence for the time being.

Whatever the intermediate situation, Paul is clear that all will ultimately lead to *the judgment seat of Christ, so that each may be repaid for what he has done in the body, whether good or evil* (v. 10; for more on the judgment theme of this verse, see §6.2 above). The (full) resurrection body (here implied) is necessary for judgment, in keeping with Paul's other references to resurrection and judgment. Following bodily resurrection comes judgment. And, interestingly, this judgment is concerned with *what he has done in the body*. The current corporeal experience is the subject of judgment, which will occur once believers are ensconced in their resurrection bodies.

Eph 2:1–7 Καὶ ὑμᾶς ὄντας νεκροὺς τοῖς παραπτώμασιν καὶ ταῖς ἁμαρτίαις ὑμῶν, 2 ἐν αἷς ποτε περιεπατήσατε κατὰ τὸν αἰῶνα τοῦ κόσμου τούτου, κατὰ τὸν ἄρχοντα τῆς ἐξουσίας τοῦ ἀέρος, τοῦ πνεύματος τοῦ νῦν ἐνεργοῦντος ἐν τοῖς υἱοῖς τῆς ἀπειθείας· 3 ἐν οἷς καὶ ἡμεῖς πάντες ἀνεστράφημέν ποτε ἐν ταῖς ἐπιθυμίαις τῆς σαρκὸς ἡμῶν ποιοῦντες τὰ θελήματα τῆς σαρκὸς καὶ τῶν διανοιῶν, καὶ ἤμεθα τέκνα φύσει ὀργῆς ὡς καὶ οἱ λοιποί· 4 ὁ δὲ θεὸς πλούσιος ὢν ἐν ἐλέει, διὰ τὴν πολλὴν ἀγάπην αὐτοῦ ἣν ἠγάπησεν ἡμᾶς, 5 καὶ ὄντας ἡμᾶς νεκροὺς τοῖς παραπτώμασιν συνεζωοποίησεν τῷ Χριστῷ,—χάριτί ἐστε σεσῳσμένοι—6 καὶ συνήγειρεν καὶ συνεκάθισεν ἐν τοῖς ἐπουρανίοις ἐν Χριστῷ Ἰησοῦ, 7 ἵνα ἐνδείξηται ἐν τοῖς αἰῶσιν τοῖς ἐπερχομένοις τὸ ὑπερβάλλον πλοῦτος τῆς χάριτος αὐτοῦ ἐν χρηστότητι ἐφ' ἡμᾶς ἐν Χριστῷ Ἰησοῦ.

And you were dead in your trespasses and sins 2 in which you previously lived according to the ways of this world, according to the ruler of the power of the air, the spirit now working in the disobedient. 3 We too all previously lived among them in our fleshly desires, carrying out the inclinations of our flesh and thoughts, and we were by nature children under wrath as the others were also. 4 **But God, who is rich in mercy, because of his great love that he had for us, 5 made us alive with Christ even though we were dead in** *trespasses. You are saved by grace! 6 **He also raised us up with him and seated us with him in the heavens in Christ Jesus**, 7 so that in the coming ages he might display the immeasurable riches of his grace through his kindness to us in Christ Jesus.*

The first three verses in this text depict a dark picture of spiritual deadness. People were dead in their transgressions and sins in which they walked (περιεπατήσατε) after the ways of the world, following the evil one (*the ruler of the power of the air*), and gratifying their ungodly desires (2:1–3). The spiritually dead *were by nature under wrath* (v. 3b).

This portrayal of spiritual deadness provides the backdrop for the remarkable claim that God, because of his mercy and love, has *made us alive with Christ even though we were dead in trespasses* (vv. 4–5). This spiritual resurrection with Christ is accompanied by a spiritual ascension as well—*he also raised us up with him and seated us with him in the heavens in Christ Jesus* (v. 6).

It is this participation in Christ's resurrection and ascension that underpins the entire argument that salvation is by grace (vv. 5b, 8). Since people are naturally children of wrath and spiritually dead, it takes the intervention of God to make them alive—this is salvation by grace, not by works.

The question this text raises (and traditionally has raised for Pauline scholarship) is how the author can square this apparently *present* resurrection of believers with the *future* resurrection expectation in the undisputed Pauline epistles. Indeed, this apparent tension has contributed to scholarly doubts about the authenticity of Ephesians (and Colossians; see on Col 3:1–4 below).

But such reactions are unnecessary. Just as it is clear that being "dead" (2:1, 5) is meant spiritually—with the spiritually dead still able to walk, live, and carry out their desires—so believers are made alive *spiritually*.[20] There is no hint here that Paul claims a physical, bodily resurrection for believers ahead of time. No, the entire passage is concerned with the spiritual fate of people who were once dead and now have been made alive in terms of their relationship with God.

Perhaps it may be asked, what does it mean to be "spiritually resurrected"? This is not the place to explore the full implications of such a notion, but it is worth noting that it may only be answered in relation to participation with Christ—a subject worthy of its own book.[21]

The idea of spiritual resurrection can easily be correlated with the expectation

---

20. Hoehner, *Ephesians*, 330.
21. See my *Paul and Union with Christ*.

of a future bodily resurrection. In Romans 6, for example, the anticipation of future resurrection allows Paul to speak of walking in the newness of life now (v. 4) and being alive to God (v. 11). That is, before physical resurrection has occurred, believers are nonetheless able to live a new life in relation to God because of their union with the resurrected Christ. Such a notion is not far removed from that found in Ephesians 2.

> Phil 1:21–26 ἐμοὶ γὰρ τὸ ζῆν Χριστὸς καὶ τὸ ἀποθανεῖν κέρδος. 22 εἰ δὲ τὸ ζῆν ἐν σαρκί, τοῦτό μοι καρπὸς ἔργου, καὶ τί αἱρήσομαι οὐ γνωρίζω. 23 συνέχομαι δὲ ἐκ τῶν δύο, τὴν ἐπιθυμίαν ἔχων εἰς τὸ ἀναλῦσαι καὶ σὺν Χριστῷ εἶναι, πολλῷ μᾶλλον κρεῖσσον· 24 τὸ δὲ ἐπιμένειν τῇ σαρκὶ ἀναγκαιότερον δι' ὑμᾶς. 25 καὶ τοῦτο πεποιθὼς οἶδα ὅτι μενῶ καὶ παραμενῶ πᾶσιν ὑμῖν εἰς τὴν ὑμῶν προκοπὴν καὶ χαρὰν τῆς πίστεως, 26 ἵνα τὸ καύχημα ὑμῶν περισσεύῃ ἐν Χριστῷ Ἰησοῦ ἐν ἐμοὶ διὰ τῆς ἐμῆς παρουσίας πάλιν πρὸς ὑμᾶς.

> *For me, to live is Christ and to die is gain. 22 Now if I live on in the flesh, this means fruitful work for me; and I don't know which one I should choose. 23 I am torn between the two. I long to depart and be with Christ—which is far better—24 but to remain in the flesh is more necessary for your sake. 25 Since I am persuaded of this, I know that I will remain and continue with all of you for your progress and joy in the faith, 26 so that, because of my coming to you again, your boasting in Christ Jesus may abound.*

This text does not deal with resurrection per se, but it is relevant to the question of the intermediate state preceding resurrection. Paul clearly sees death as preferable to this life on earth: *For me, to live is Christ and to die is gain* (1:21), and *I long to depart and be with Christ—which is far better* (v. 23). But he also sees that *if I live on in the flesh, this means fruitful work for me* (v. 22a), and *to remain in the flesh is more necessary for your sake* (v. 24). While death is personally preferable, remaining in life is beneficial to others who will gain from Paul's continued ministry among them. Paul is persuaded that he will go on for exactly that reason—*I will remain and continue with all of you for your progress and joy in the faith* (v. 25).

Clearly, for Paul, being with Christ is better than remaining alive in this world. But it is not clear whether Paul is contrasting this life on earth with the so-called intermediate state prior to resurrection or to resurrection life itself. Of course, the latter is preferable in comparison to this life; resurrection life is the glorious, eternal reality that Paul longs for. But what about the former?

Is Paul saying that a disembodied intermediate state, prior to resurrection, is preferable to this life?

Paul's language conveys a sense of immediacy in that he apparently expects to *be with Christ* instantly upon death. There is no hint of expectation of an intervening period between death and being with Christ. If Paul *does* expect some kind of interval—whether it be one of "soul sleep," or some other thing—he offers no clue in such a direction. Thus, it is reasonable to conclude that Paul expects to be in the direct presence of Christ at the point of death.[22]

Putting these observations together, Paul may believe in an intermediate state, prior to bodily resurrection, in which he will consciously be with Christ. This will occur immediately upon death and is far better than this present life. While we may safely assume that the *best* future reality will be one of resurrected presence with Christ, this (apparently disembodied) intermediate state is nevertheless better than embodied life now. For Paul, the main advantage of embodied life now is the capacity to do meaningful work that will benefit others.

Phil 3:10–11 τοῦ γνῶναι αὐτὸν καὶ τὴν δύναμιν τῆς ἀναστάσεως αὐτοῦ καὶ κοινωνίαν παθημάτων αὐτοῦ, συμμορφιζόμενος τῷ θανάτῳ αὐτοῦ, 11 εἴ πως καταντήσω εἰς τὴν ἐξανάστασιν τὴν ἐκ νεκρῶν.

My goal is to know him and the power of his resurrection *and the fellowship of his sufferings, being conformed to his death, 11* ***assuming that I will somehow reach the resurrection from among the dead.***

Having compared the surpassing value of knowing Christ to his credentials in Judaism, and the loss of all things compared to gaining Christ (3:7–8), Paul now reflects further on knowing Christ in his death and resurrection.

Though he already knows Christ (v. 8), Paul's goal remains *to know him* (v. 10a). In this context, knowing Christ is apparently related to participating in his resurrection, sufferings, and death. He wants to know Christ *and the power of his resurrection and the fellowship of his sufferings, being conformed to this death* (v. 10).

Knowing the power of Christ's resurrection most likely refers to the power of new life that his resurrection brings. Christ's resurrection conquers sin and death and achieves an immortal, glorious heavenly body (e.g., 1 Cor 15:42–49).

---

22. Silva writes, "It is hardly credible that Paul would have viewed the choice [about whether to remain or to depart] as difficult as he describes it if leaving the work of the gospel did not in fact entail his being in the presence of Christ" (Moisés Silva, *Philippians*, 2nd ed., BECNT [Grand Rapids: Baker Academic, 2005], 74).

To know this power is to participate in and benefit from the resurrected Christ's gift of life. To know Christ also involves fellowship in his sufferings and conformity to his death (Phil 3:10). While these items invite further reflection, they cannot be engaged here.[23]

It is the following verse that causes some consternation—*assuming that I will somehow reach the resurrection from among the dead* (v. 11). The consternation comes from the two Greek words here translated *assuming . . . somehow* (εἴ πως). One way to understand the verse is to posit a degree of contingency with which Paul speaks of his own resurrection from the dead. The participle εἴ normally conveys some degree of contingency, but does not necessarily indicate any insecurity in Paul's mind.[24] In other words, the use of εἰ (often translated *if*) does not mean that Paul is unsure *if* he will reach resurrection. Indeed, other translations opt for a less contingent rendering of the particle. The ESV translates the first half of the verse, *that by any means possible*, while the NIV has *and so, somehow . . .*

In combination with εἰ, the indefinite particle πώς (not to be confused with the interrogative πῶς) conveys the sense of *somehow*.[25] Again, this need not imply any sort of insecurity or ambiguity as to whether Paul really will be resurrected. Rather, it most likely conveys that Paul does not know exactly *how* he will reach the resurrection from among the dead. That is, the physical and biological processes of Paul's resurrection is somewhat of a mystery—as it remains to this day.

Phil 3:18–21 πολλοὶ γὰρ περιπατοῦσιν οὓς πολλάκις ἔλεγον ὑμῖν, νῦν δὲ καὶ κλαίων λέγω, τοὺς ἐχθροὺς τοῦ σταυροῦ τοῦ Χριστοῦ, 19 ὧν τὸ τέλος ἀπώλεια, ὧν ὁ θεὸς ἡ κοιλία καὶ ἡ δόξα ἐν τῇ αἰσχύνῃ αὐτῶν, οἱ τὰ ἐπίγεια φρονοῦντες. 20 ἡμῶν γὰρ τὸ πολίτευμα ἐν οὐρανοῖς ὑπάρχει, ἐξ οὗ καὶ σωτῆρα ἀπεκδεχόμεθα κύριον Ἰησοῦν Χριστόν, 21 ὃς **μετασχηματίσει τὸ σῶμα τῆς ταπεινώσεως ἡμῶν σύμμορφον τῷ σώματι τῆς δόξης αὐτοῦ** κατὰ τὴν ἐνέργειαν τοῦ δύνασθαι αὐτὸν καὶ ὑποτάξαι αὐτῷ τὰ πάντα.

For I have often told you, and now say again with tears, that many live as enemies of the cross of Christ. 19 Their end is destruction; their god is their stomach; their glory is in their shame. They are focused on earthly things, 20 but our citizenship is in heaven, and we eagerly wait for a Savior from there, the Lord Jesus Christ. 21 **He will transform the body of our humble condition**

---

23. See, e.g., Campbell, *Paul and Union with Christ*, 233–34.
24. Compare the differing uses outlined in BDAG 277–79.
25. BDAG 279, §6.n.

into the likeness of his glorious body, by the power that enables him to subject everything to himself.

In contrast to the enemies of the cross of Christ, who are focused on earthly things and whose end is destruction (3:18–19), Paul says *our citizenship is in heaven* (v. 20a). Believers do not belong to this world but to the world to come, and so *we eagerly wait for a Savior from there, the Lord Jesus Christ* (v. 20b).

When Christ comes, *he will transform the body of our humble condition into the likeness of his glorious body* (v. 21a). As noted previously, Paul does not use the language of resurrection here, but the transformation from humility to glory strongly parallels 1 Corinthians 15:42–49, which deals with the resurrection of the dead in Christ (see §4.2). Though the word translated *transform* (μετασχηματίζω) is not found in 1 Corinthians 15, the concept is readily observed: the perishable becomes imperishable (15:42); the dishonorable and weak body is raised in glory and power (v. 43); and the natural body becomes a spiritual body (v. 44).[26] These transformations obviously correlate well to the idea that *the body of our humble condition* will be transformed *into the likeness of his glorious body* (Phil 3:21). Moreover, *the likeness of his glorious body* parallels 1 Corinthians 15:49—*And just as we have borne the image of the man of dust, we will also bear the image of the man of heaven*. Bearing *the image of the man of heaven* sounds very much like sharing in *the likeness of his glorious body*.

The point is not to draw parallels with 1 Corinthians 15:42–49, but to demonstrate that the transformation of the body is, for Paul, a result of resurrection. The absence of resurrection language from this passage does not preclude the presence of resurrection theology. It is through the resurrection that such transformation is able to take place. It is also notable that the Lord Jesus Christ is the agent of this transformation. While other passages refer to God as the one who raises the dead (e.g., Rom 8:11; 1 Cor 6:14; 15:15; 2 Cor 4:14), this passage stands out in attributing Jesus with the responsibility of effecting the resurrected transformation of lowly bodies.

As discussed above (§4.2), this transformation is effected *by the power that enables him to subject everything to himself* (Phil 3:21b), thus creating an implicit connection between resurrection and rule. The same power by which Christ raises the dead is that which enables him to rule over everything. In 1 Corinthians 15:20–26, we observe a similar connection, in which the last enemy to be abolished is death. By nullifying death through the resurrection of the dead, Christ is able to put this last enemy under his feet. We do not see

---

26. Markus Bockmuehl, *The Epistle to the Philippians*, BNTC (Peabody, MA: Hendrickson, 1998), 236.

these ideas spelled out in Philippians 3:21, but they are arguably present in compressed form.

Thus, while this text does not mention resurrection, the concept is an essential element undergirding Paul's thought. Resurrection effects the transformation of the body, which is powered by Christ's defeat of death through his own resurrection. The resurrection of Jesus is, indeed, the force that enables Christ to come from heaven as *Savior*.

> Col 1:18 καὶ αὐτός ἐστιν ἡ κεφαλὴ τοῦ σώματος τῆς ἐκκλησίας·
> ὅς ἐστιν ἀρχή,
> **πρωτότοκος ἐκ τῶν νεκρῶν,**
> ἵνα γένηται ἐν πᾶσιν αὐτὸς πρωτεύων,

He is also the head of the body, the church;
he is the beginning,
the firstborn from the dead,
so that he might come to have
first place in everything.

An essential factor of Christ's headship of the church is his status as *the firstborn from the dead* (1:18c). Parallel to 1:15, in which Christ is described as *the firstborn over all creation*, the language of *firstborn* (πρωτότοκος) is rare in the Pauline canon, with the only use outside Colossians found in Romans 8:29: *For those he foreknew he also predestined to be conformed to the image of his Son, so that he would be the firstborn* [πρωτότοκος] *among many brothers and sisters*.

This text is somewhat parallel to Romans 8:29 in that both texts use the *firstborn* language to refer to Christ's status within the church. While the Romans text keeps the firstborn imagery in its natural familial habitat (*firstborn among many brothers and sisters*), Colossians 1:18 employs it with reference to the resurrection of the dead. In this way, it also finds a parallel with the *firstfruits* imagery of 1 Corinthians 15:20–23. This imagery draws on the early budding fruit of the harvest that reveals both the nature of the harvest to come as well as the imminence of its coming (see above). In similar fashion, *the firstborn from the dead* points to the coming of "the latter-born from the dead," as it were. Christ is the first to rise but will not be the only one to do so.

Unlike the firstfruits imagery of 1 Corinthians 15:20–23, however, the *firstborn* terminology also implies status (in keeping with the parallel in Col 1:15). This is known by the usual connotation in the ancient world that the firstborn is the rightful heir of his father's estate and enjoys preeminent status among siblings.[27] That is, while the *firstborn* language naturally evokes temporal order (he is *first* born), it also evokes preeminence (he is *first* among others).[28] And this is confirmed in the wording that follows—*so that he might come to have first place in everything* (v. 18d).

It is unclear whether the result (or possibly purpose) clause[29] *so that he might come to have first place in everything* (ἵνα γένηται ἐν πᾶσιν αὐτὸς πρωτεύων; v. 18d) modifies the claims of all three previous lines—*he is also the head of the body, the church* (v. 18a); *he is the beginning* (v. 18b); *the firstborn from the dead* (v. 18c)—or just the third (v. 18c). While the language of preeminence (πρωτεύω) seems to favor the latter option, given the discussion above about the firstborn's priority of rank, the former option is nevertheless entirely plausible. This is because the language of *head of the body* (v. 18a) and *the beginning* (v. 18b) can easily be seen in terms of preeminence too. And since v. 18c lacks any kind of verb (let alone an indicative) from which to subordinate the result (or purpose?) clause (ἵνα γένηται . . .), it is probably preferable to understand it as modifying all three elements (i.e., vv. 18a, b, and c).

As such, it is most likely that v. 18c only plays a contributing role in establishing the preeminence of Christ in everything. Nevertheless, the church is created through his resurrection, and all its members will be raised like him as "latter-borns." In this way, Christ's resurrection as the firstborn has a special relationship to the other elements, since without it there would be no church of which he could be head.

Col 2:11–13 Ἐν ᾧ καὶ περιετμήθητε περιτομῇ ἀχειροποιήτῳ ἐν τῇ ἀπεκδύσει τοῦ σώματος τῆς σαρκός, ἐν τῇ περιτομῇ τοῦ Χριστοῦ, 12 **συνταφέντες αὐτῷ ἐν τῷ βαπτισμῷ, ἐν ᾧ καὶ συνηγέρθητε** διὰ τῆς πίστεως τῆς ἐνεργείας τοῦ θεοῦ τοῦ ἐγείραντος αὐτὸν ἐκ νεκρῶν· 13 καὶ ὑμᾶς νεκροὺς ὄντας τοῖς παραπτώμασιν καὶ τῇ ἀκροβυστίᾳ τῆς σαρκὸς ὑμῶν, **συνεζωοποίησεν ὑμᾶς σὺν αὐτῷ**, χαρισάμενος ἡμῖν πάντα τὰ παραπτώματα.

*You were also circumcised in him with a circumcision not done with hands, by putting off the body of flesh, in the circumcision of Christ, 12 when **you were buried with him in baptism, in which you were also raised** with him through faith in the working of God, who raised him from the dead. 13 And*

---

27. Michael F. Bird, *Colossians and Philemon: A New Covenant Commentary*, NCCS (Eugene, OR: Cascade, 2009), 52.

28. For example, Israel is described as the firstborn (Exod 4:22), as is the future Davidic king (Ps 89:27), and Wisdom (Prov 8:22); see McKnight, *Colossians*, 149.

29. Campbell, *Colossians and Philemon*, 15.

when you were dead in trespasses and in the uncircumcision of your flesh, **he made you alive with him** *and forgave us all our trespasses.*

Being buried with Christ (2:12) obviously implies death with Christ (cf. Rom 6:3–4) and refers to a spiritual participation in his death and burial.[30] It does not refer to the physical death of believers, who would not be able to read Paul's words to them otherwise. By the same token, then, being raised with Christ in this verse must also be understood from a spiritual perspective. This is confirmed in the following verse, in which the states of spiritual deadness and life are contrasted vis-à-vis trespasses and the forgiveness of trespasses (Col 2:13). While the guilt of their transgressions had left them in the state of spiritual death, being made alive with Christ is directly correlated with the forgiveness of believers' trespasses.

Spiritual resurrection occurs through participation with Christ (*you were also raised with him*),[31] which is mediated *through faith in the working of God*. The success of participation with Christ by faith in God is grounded in the fact that God has already raised Christ from the dead (v. 12). Having done so, God has proven himself worthy of believers' trust—he had the power to effect the resurrection of Christ and thus can be trusted to raise believers also. Faith in this ability of God brings about believers' participation in Christ's death and resurrection. And this in turn results in the forgiveness of their trespasses.

There are several points of connection here with Romans 6:4–11 (see above), including the relationship between burial with Christ and baptism, the necessary precursor of Christ's resurrection, and the hope of resurrection that comes from them. In Romans 6, however, resurrection is a future hope, referring to the bodily resurrection of believers at the coming of Christ. In contrast, this text looks to a present, spiritual resurrection that has already taken place for those with faith in God.

This difference between Romans 6 and Colossians 2 should not be overplayed. The notions of present, spiritual resurrection and future, bodily resurrection are easily correlated. Spiritual resurrection anticipates its bodily counterpart, bringing the forgiveness of sins, new life with Christ, and relationship with God. The resurrection of the body will be the fulfillment and completion of what has begun with spiritual resurrection.

Col 3:1–4 Εἰ οὖν συνηγέρθητε τῷ Χριστῷ, τὰ ἄνω ζητεῖτε, οὗ ὁ Χριστός ἐστιν ἐν δεξιᾷ τοῦ θεοῦ καθήμενος· 2 τὰ ἄνω φρονεῖτε, μὴ τὰ ἐπὶ τῆς γῆς.

---

30. Campbell, *Paul and Union with Christ*, 235.
31. Campbell, *Paul and Union with Christ*, 197–98, 225.

3 ἀπεθάνετε γὰρ καὶ ἡ ζωὴ ὑμῶν κέκρυπται σὺν τῷ Χριστῷ ἐν τῷ θεῷ· 4 ὅταν ὁ Χριστὸς φανερωθῇ, ἡ ζωὴ ὑμῶν, τότε καὶ ὑμεῖς σὺν αὐτῷ φανερωθήσεσθε ἐν δόξῃ.

So if you have been raised with Christ, seek the things above, where Christ is, seated at the right hand of God. 2 Set your minds on things above, not on earthly things. 3 For you died, and your life is hidden with Christ in God. 4 When Christ, who is your life, appears, then you also will appear with him in glory.

The conditional sentence *if you have been raised with Christ, seek the things above* (3:1) should not deter us from the fact that Paul assumes its protasis to be true; having been raised with Christ is a necessary corollary of believers' participation with Christ. It would hardly do to issue exhortations (*seek the things above*; *set your minds on things above*; vv. 1–2) based on the notion if Paul did not regard resurrection with Christ as a preexisting condition.[32]

Just as believers have already died with Christ (2:20), so they have now been raised with him (3:1). And since this death with Christ is clearly of a spiritual nature (otherwise Paul's readers would not be reading his letter addressed to them, since they would be dead), so their resurrection with Christ is of a spiritual nature. As with Ephesians 2:5–6, this text does not therefore contradict other Pauline statements that regard resurrection as a future event yet to come. Future resurrection will be physical and bodily, while present resurrection is spiritual in nature, as an outworking of our participation with Christ.

Believers have already died, and their lives are *hidden with Christ in God* (Col 3:3). The following statement seems to point to the physical resurrection that Paul envisions elsewhere—*When Christ, who is your life, appears, then you also will appear with him in glory* (v. 4). Though physical resurrection is not explicitly referenced, it is implied in the notion of appearing with (the resurrected) Christ when he comes in glory.

1 Thess 4:13–18 Οὐ θέλομεν δὲ ὑμᾶς ἀγνοεῖν, ἀδελφοί, περὶ τῶν κοιμωμένων, ἵνα μὴ λυπῆσθε καθὼς καὶ οἱ λοιποὶ οἱ μὴ ἔχοντες ἐλπίδα. 14 εἰ γὰρ πιστεύομεν ὅτι Ἰησοῦς ἀπέθανεν καὶ ἀνέστη, οὕτως καὶ ὁ θεὸς τοὺς κοιμηθέντας διὰ τοῦ Ἰησοῦ ἄξει σὺν αὐτῷ. 15 Τοῦτο γὰρ ὑμῖν λέγομεν ἐν λόγῳ κυρίου, ὅτι ἡμεῖς οἱ ζῶντες οἱ περιλειπόμενοι εἰς τὴν παρουσίαν τοῦ κυρίου οὐ μὴ φθάσωμεν τοὺς κοιμηθέντας· 16 ὅτι αὐτὸς ὁ κύριος ἐν

---

32. Campbell, *Paul and Union with Christ*, 236.

κελεύσματι, ἐν φωνῇ ἀρχαγγέλου καὶ ἐν σάλπιγγι θεοῦ, καταβήσεται ἀπ' οὐρανοῦ καὶ **οἱ νεκροὶ ἐν Χριστῷ ἀναστήσονται πρῶτον**, 17 ἔπειτα ἡμεῖς οἱ ζῶντες οἱ περιλειπόμενοι ἅμα σὺν αὐτοῖς ἁρπαγησόμεθα ἐν νεφέλαις εἰς ἀπάντησιν τοῦ κυρίου εἰς ἀέρα· καὶ οὕτως πάντοτε σὺν κυρίῳ ἐσόμεθα. 18 Ὥστε παρακαλεῖτε ἀλλήλους ἐν τοῖς λόγοις τούτοις.

We do not want you to be uninformed, brothers and sisters, concerning those who are asleep, so that you will not grieve like the rest, who have no hope. 14 **For if we believe that Jesus died and rose again, in the same way, through Jesus, God will bring with him those who have fallen asleep.** *15 For we say this to you by a word from the Lord: We who are still alive at the Lord's coming will certainly not precede those who have fallen asleep. 16 For the Lord himself will descend from heaven with a shout, with the archangel's voice, and with the trumpet of God, and* **the dead in Christ will rise first***. 17 Then we who are still alive, who are left, will be caught up together with them in the clouds to meet the Lord in the air, and so we will always be with the Lord. 18 Therefore encourage one another with these words.*

Offered as words of encouragement (4:18), Paul informs his readers of the fate of *those who are asleep*, for the purpose of shaping their grief—*so that you will not grieve like the rest, who have no hope* (v. 13). Since the discussion is intended to affect their *grief*, it is obvious that *sleep* is a metaphor for death. The rest of humanity has *no hope* in the face of death, but believers may grieve with the hope of the resurrection of the dead.

This hope is grounded in the events of Jesus's death and resurrection—*For if we believe that Jesus died and rose again, in the same way, through Jesus, God will bring with him those who have fallen asleep* (v. 14). If they have confidence in the factuality of Christ's death and resurrection, the Thessalonians can have assurance that God will raise the dead *in the same way*.

Clearly God is the agent of resurrection—*God will bring with him those who have fallen asleep* (v. 14c)—but is Christ spoken of as being instrumental of resurrection? The question revolves around how to understand the prepositional phrase, *through Jesus* (διὰ τοῦ Ἰησοῦ; v. 14b). In the CSB translation above, an instrumental reading is adopted, placing this phrase before the phrase *those who have fallen asleep*: *through Jesus, God will bring with him those who have fallen asleep*. But the Greek phrases are found in the reverse order: ὁ θεὸς τοὺς κοιμηθέντας διὰ τοῦ Ἰησοῦ ἄξει σὺν αὐτῷ. This ordering is preserved in the previous version of the CSB translation: *God will bring with Him those who have fallen asleep through Jesus* (HCSB). In the latter translation, which better preserves the Greek word order, the phrase *through Jesus* (διὰ τοῦ Ἰησοῦ) modifies *those who have fallen asleep* rather than the action of God. That is, believers have *fallen asleep through Jesus*, indicating that somehow they have died through him. So the two recensions of the (H)CSB translation offer important alternative ways to read the verse.

Though word order is against it, the revised CSB translation is probably better than its predecessor here. First, it is not entirely clear what it means to say *those who have fallen asleep through Jesus* (HCSB). Falling asleep (dying) *in* Christ makes perfect sense for Paul, but dying *through* Christ is awkward, even for him. Second, the instrumentality of Christ, who performs actions of which God is the ultimate agent, is an extremely common concept for Paul. And it is very often communicated through the preposition διά (*through*).[33] These two factors increase the likelihood that *through Jesus* should be understood as modifying the action of God in bringing *those who have fallen asleep* with Jesus. As the CSB expresses it, *through Jesus, God will bring with him those who have fallen asleep* (v. 14c).

What, then, does the instrumentality of Jesus involve, with respect to God's bringing the dead with Christ? Since his death and resurrection have just been referenced (v. 14a), it follows that they constitute the way in which Jesus is instrumental in the resurrection of the dead. It is because of, and through, his death and resurrection that God will raise the dead in Christ.

The remainder of this text affirms the place of the dead in Christ at his parousia (see §4.2 above). When he descends from heaven with a shout, *the dead in Christ will rise first* (v. 16). Then they will be joined by believers still living when Christ comes (v. 17).

2 Tim 1:9–10 τοῦ σώσαντος ἡμᾶς
    καὶ καλέσαντος κλήσει ἁγίᾳ,
    οὐ κατὰ τὰ ἔργα ἡμῶν
    ἀλλὰ κατὰ ἰδίαν πρόθεσιν καὶ χάριν,
    τὴν δοθεῖσαν ἡμῖν ἐν Χριστῷ Ἰησοῦ
    πρὸ χρόνων αἰωνίων,
10 φανερωθεῖσαν δὲ νῦν
    διὰ τῆς ἐπιφανείας τοῦ σωτῆρος ἡμῶν Χριστοῦ Ἰησοῦ,
    καταργήσαντος μὲν τὸν θάνατον
    φωτίσαντος δὲ ζωὴν καὶ ἀφθαρσίαν διὰ τοῦ εὐαγγελίου

---

33. See Campbell, *Paul and Union with Christ*, 237–66.

He has saved us and called us with a holy calling, not according to our works, but according to his own purpose and grace, which was given to us in Christ Jesus before time began. 10 This has now been made evident through the appearing of our Savior Christ Jesus, **who has abolished death and has brought life and immortality to light through the gospel.**

The resurrection of the dead is implied by the abolition (καταργέω) of death and the gift of *life and immortality* (1:10).[34] It is not Christ's own life and immortality in view, since these things have been brought *to light through the gospel*; rather, the proclamation of the gospel offers life and immortality to those who receive it. This is also evident in the previous verse, which refers to the salvation and calling of believers, according to God's purpose and grace (v. 9). With an emphasis on what has been *given to us in Christ Jesus*, it is clear that *life and immortality* are included in what has been given.

It is due to his abolition of death and gifts of life and immortality that Christ Jesus is described as *our Savior* (v. 10a). This is no mere moniker or honorific title; he is Savior because he brings life and immortality to others who would otherwise remain under the sentence of death.

2 Tim 2:16–18 τὰς δὲ βεβήλους κενοφωνίας περιΐστασο· ἐπὶ πλεῖον γὰρ προκόψουσιν ἀσεβείας 17 καὶ ὁ λόγος αὐτῶν ὡς γάγγραινα νομὴν ἕξει. ὧν ἐστιν Ὑμέναιος καὶ Φίλητος, 18 οἵτινες περὶ τὴν ἀλήθειαν ἠστόχησαν, **λέγοντες τὴν ἀνάστασιν ἤδη γεγονέναι**, καὶ ἀνατρέπουσιν τήν τινων πίστιν.

Avoid irreverent and empty speech, since those who engage in it will produce even more godlessness, 17 and their teaching will spread like gangrene. Hymenaeus and Philetus are among them. 18 They have departed from the truth, **saying that the resurrection has already taken place**, *and are ruining the faith of some.*

In a context of charging his disciple Timothy to be an approved worker (2:15), Paul warns him to avoid the kind of speech exemplified by false teachers such as Hymenaeus and Philetus. Their falsehood includes *saying that the resurrection has already taken place* (v. 18). Paul himself affirms that *spiritual* resurrection has already occurred for those in Christ (e.g., Eph 2:5–6). But this spiritual reality

---

34. "When those who belong to Christ are resurrected, the last aspect 'death,' physical death itself, will also be abolished (cf. 1 Cor 15:26, using the same verb as here), and this, too, will occur on the basis of Christ's decisive work" (Knight, *Pastoral Epistles*, 376).

is to be clearly differentiated from *physical* resurrection, otherwise his allegation against Hymenaeus and Philetus makes little sense. The physical resurrection that Paul evokes is no doubt the eschatological resurrection expected prior to judgment. The error of the false teachers is not their affirmation of resurrection but their locating it at the wrong time.[35] They say it *has already taken place* (ἤδη γεγονέναι; 2:18). Clearly Paul does not agree. It is yet to come.

While such an error is evidently a serious one in Paul's mind—a departure from the truth, in fact—it is perhaps understandable, since Paul proclaims, only a few verses earlier, that Christ *has abolished death and has brought life and immortality to light* (1:10). Hearers of such a message, which is no doubt representative of his preaching ministry, might get the impression that resurrection has come, since death has already been abolished.

And yet Paul regards the error as serious, and this is probably due to the eschatological nature of resurrection. To say that the resurrection has come is to say that the end of the aeon has also come, along with the coming of Christ and the judgment that is to follow. By incorrectly positioning the resurrection, these false teachers have inadvertently gotten their entire eschatological timetable wrong. Such a mistake would create dire consequences both for theology and for Christian living.

7.3 Summary

There can be no more central theme for Paul's eschatology than the resurrection of the dead. Christ stands as the firstfruits of what will come for all in Christ; his resurrection is the conquering of death that is shared by all in him, and it marks the inauguration of the new age. It also declares the vindication of Christ after the sentence of death.

The resurrection of Jesus stands as the proof that God will raise the believing dead to bodily resurrection, and it is the template for their resurrection (Rom 6:5; 1 Cor 6:14; 15:20–23; Col 1:18). While believers are sown in corruption, dishonor, and weakness with a natural body, like Christ they will be raised incorruptible, in glory, and in power with a spiritual body (1 Cor 15:35–50; Phil 3:21). When the corruptible body is clothed with incorruptibility, then death will have been swallowed up in victory (1 Cor 15:51–58). It is their resurrection to an incorruptible, glorious body that enables believers to participate in the eschaton. Their resurrected bodies will be fit for the new age in a way that their pre-resurrected bodies could only anticipate.

The Spirit of God who raised Jesus from the dead will raise believers' mortal

---

35. For a useful survey of the possible versions of this error, see Marshall, *Pastoral Epistles*, 752–54.

bodies to life (Rom 8:11; 2 Cor 4:14). And this Spirit serves as the firstfruits of the new creation and as a down payment of believers' participation in it, causing them eagerly to await the redemption of their bodies (Rom 8:23–24; 2 Cor 5:1–10).

The hope of future resurrection holds several implications for the present life. Believers are to consider themselves dead to sin and alive to God in Christ because they will be found in the likeness of Christ's resurrection (Rom 6:4–11). For Paul, it also means that he can face dangers and death every day, knowing that such threats are not ultimate (1 Cor 15:30–32). It enables him to share in the sufferings of Christ as he assumes he will reach the resurrection from among the dead (Phil 3:10–11). Resurrection also offers comfort in the face of grief, since believers will not grieve as those without hope (1 Thess 4:13–18).

The Pauline corpus also refers to *spiritual* resurrection in this present age—that is, being raised *now* rather than in the future (Eph 2:5–6; Col 2:13–14; 3:1). These texts have traditionally given rise to claims of pseudonymity since they imagine a resurrection in the present rather than the future—the latter being (the "genuine") Paul's universal expectation. But these texts do not contradict the expectation of future, bodily resurrection if they are understood to refer to a present *spiritual* resurrection in anticipation of its corresponding future *physical* counterpart. Ephesians 2:5–6 and Colossians 2:13–14; 3:1 clearly do not imagine a present physical resurrection but a resurrection that is achieved by virtue of believers' participation with Christ. Since he has been raised, believers are spiritually so raised with him now. They will be physically raised at the coming of Christ.

The notions of present, spiritual resurrection and future, bodily resurrection are easily correlated. Spiritual resurrection anticipates its bodily counterpart, bringing the forgiveness of sins, new life with Christ, and relationship with God. The resurrection of the body will be the fulfillment and completion of what has begun with spiritual resurrection.

CHAPTER 8

ETERNAL LIFE

8.1 Introduction

This chapter examines Paul's expectation of eternal life. Eternal life is the hope of those who suffer with Christ, who trust in him, and who seek to throw off the desires of the flesh. It comes as a consequence of dying and rising with Christ and depends on faith in Christ, which entails the putting to death the deeds of the body and sowing according to the Spirit. Eternal life follows from the resurrection of the dead, since believers' bodies will be made imperishable and impervious to death. Resurrection bodies are the necessary vehicles for eternal life, which will be shaped by God's reign of righteousness and unending relationship with Christ.

8.2 Eternal-Life Texts

Rom 5:19–21 ὥσπερ γὰρ διὰ τῆς παρακοῆς τοῦ ἑνὸς ἀνθρώπου ἁμαρτωλοὶ κατεστάθησαν οἱ πολλοί, οὕτως καὶ διὰ τῆς ὑπακοῆς τοῦ ἑνὸς δίκαιοι κατασταθήσονται οἱ πολλοί. 20 νόμος δὲ παρεισῆλθεν, ἵνα πλεονάσῃ τὸ παράπτωμα· οὗ δὲ ἐπλεόνασεν ἡ ἁμαρτία, ὑπερεπερίσσευσεν ἡ χάρις, 21 ἵνα ὥσπερ ἐβασίλευσεν ἡ ἁμαρτία ἐν τῷ θανάτῳ, **οὕτως καὶ ἡ χάρις βασιλεύσῃ διὰ δικαιοσύνης εἰς ζωὴν αἰώνιον διὰ Ἰησοῦ Χριστοῦ τοῦ κυρίου ἡμῶν.**

*For just as through one man's disobedience the many were made sinners, so also through the one man's obedience the many will be made righteous. 20 The law came along to multiply the trespass. But where sin multiplied, grace multiplied even more 21 so that, **just as sin reigned in death, so also grace will reign through righteousness, resulting in eternal life through Jesus Christ our Lord.***

Found at the end of the extended contrast between Adam and Christ (5:12–21), this text moves from the contrast between the *one man's disobedience* and the other *man's obedience* (v. 19), to the contrast between the multiplication of sin and the multiplication of grace (v. 20), to the contrast between sin reigning in death and grace reigning *through righteousness, resulting in eternal life* (v. 21).

Of particular significance is the language of *reigning* (βασιλεύω). This is explored further above (see §3.2), but here we simply note that *sin* and *grace* are personified as powers that rule their respective domains. Sin reigns in the realm of death, and grace reigns in the realm of eternal life.

Conceived this way, eternal life is viewed not simply as a state into which believers will enter but rather is a domain in which they will live. Just as those under the rule of sin live in the shadow of death—in a reality determined and defined by it—so believers will live in the light of eternal life.

The fitting climax to the Adam-Christ discourse of 5:12–21 is that grace will reign in the realm of eternal life *through Jesus Christ our Lord* (v. 21). This realm of eternal life comes into being through the person and work of Christ; "Christ is the agent and source of eternal life."[1]

Rom 6:21–23 τίνα οὖν καρπὸν εἴχετε τότε; ἐφ' οἷς νῦν ἐπαισχύνεσθε, τὸ γὰρ τέλος ἐκείνων θάνατος. 22 νυνὶ δὲ ἐλευθερωθέντες ἀπὸ τῆς ἁμαρτίας δουλωθέντες δὲ τῷ θεῷ ἔχετε τὸν καρπὸν ὑμῶν εἰς ἁγιασμόν, τὸ δὲ τέλος **ζωὴν αἰώνιον**. 23 **τὰ γὰρ ὀψώνια τῆς ἁμαρτίας θάνατος, τὸ δὲ χάρισμα τοῦ θεοῦ ζωὴ αἰώνιος ἐν Χριστῷ Ἰησοῦ τῷ κυρίῳ ἡμῶν.**

So what fruit was produced then from the things you are now ashamed of? The outcome of those things is death. 22 But now, since you have been set free from sin and have become enslaved to God, you have your fruit, which results in sanctification—and the outcome is **eternal life!** *23* **For the wages of sin is death, but the gift of God is eternal life in Christ Jesus our Lord.**

Eternal life is viewed as the outcome (τέλος) of sanctification, which in turn is produced from the fruit of believers' lives (v. 22b). This is presented in contrast to death, which is the outcome (τέλος) of *the things you are now ashamed of* (v. 21), referring to their lives lived under the dominion of sin (v. 22a).

Framed this way, Paul could be understood to mean that eternal life is contingent upon fruit that leads to sanctification. In other words, it would be the reward or wages of sanctification. But this is directly countered in 6:23—*For the wages of sin is death, but the gift of God is eternal life in Christ Jesus our Lord*. Note the parallel of *wages* and *gift*. Death is the "reward" for sin, but eternal

---

1. Campbell, *Paul and Union with Christ*, 242.

life is *the gift of God*. This clarifies that, notwithstanding the presentation of 6:22, eternal life is not earned or rewarded; instead, it is *given*.[2]

How, then, should 6:22 be understood? The clue is found in the freedom/slavery language—*you have been set free* [ἐλευθερόω] *from sin and have become enslaved* [δουλόω] *to God*. This language is directly related to the realm and dominion motif found in this passage (see §3.2 above). Those who are enslaved by sin, living under its authority and in its domain, are only able to produce fruit in keeping with its dominion—fruit that leads to death. On the other hand, those who *have been set free from sin and have become enslaved to God* are no longer under sin's authority. Instead they are now under the rule of a new master. And just as those under sin produced fruit in keeping with that domain, so those under God will produce fruit in keeping with sanctification. In other words, Paul does not depict a kind of "eternal life by works" theology, but "eternal life by *allegiance*." Those who belong to God are under his rule, live in his domain, and will produce fruit in accord with that reality. The result of becoming enslaved to God is eternal life, which is itself the gift of God.

Finally, we observe that this gift of eternal life is *in Christ Jesus our Lord* (v. 23b). While there are several possible ways to understand this prepositional phrase (ἐν Χριστῷ Ἰησοῦ τῷ κυρίῳ ἡμῶν), I have argued elsewhere that an instrumental reading fits best: "Christ is the instrument through which God liberates believers from sin, which enables their slavery to God, the fruit of which is eternal life."[3] This ought not exclude a participatory sense of being "in Christ," but rather it views Christ as the personal instrument who achieves God's will through communion with the Father and communion with those who belong to Christ.

Rom 8:10–13 εἰ δὲ Χριστὸς ἐν ὑμῖν, τὸ μὲν σῶμα νεκρὸν διὰ ἁμαρτίαν τὸ δὲ πνεῦμα ζωὴ διὰ δικαιοσύνην. 11 εἰ δὲ τὸ πνεῦμα τοῦ ἐγείραντος τὸν Ἰησοῦν ἐκ νεκρῶν οἰκεῖ ἐν ὑμῖν, ὁ ἐγείρας Χριστὸν ἐκ νεκρῶν ζῳοποιήσει καὶ τὰ θνητὰ σώματα ὑμῶν διὰ τοῦ ἐνοικοῦντος αὐτοῦ πνεύματος ἐν ὑμῖν. 12 Ἄρα οὖν, ἀδελφοί, ὀφειλέται ἐσμὲν οὐ τῇ σαρκὶ τοῦ κατὰ σάρκα ζῆν, 13 εἰ γὰρ κατὰ σάρκα ζῆτε, μέλλετε ἀποθνῄσκειν· εἰ δὲ πνεύματι τὰς πράξεις τοῦ σώματος θανατοῦτε, ζήσεσθε.

Now if Christ is in you, the body is dead because of sin, **but the Spirit gives life** *because of righteousness. 11* **And if the Spirit of him who raised Jesus**

---

2. Peterson, *Romans*, 278.
3. Campbell, *Paul and Union with Christ*, 76.

from the dead lives in you, then he who raised Christ from the dead will also bring your mortal bodies to life through his Spirit who lives in you. 12 So then, brothers and sisters, we are not obligated to the flesh to live according to the flesh, 13 because if you live according to the flesh, you are going to die. But if by the Spirit you put to death the deeds of the body, you will live.

While *life* (ζωή) in 8:10 could be interpreted as referring to spiritual renewal, the bodily resurrection of the dead comes into view in v. 11—*And if the Spirit of him who raised Jesus from the dead lives in you, then he who raised Christ from the dead will also bring your mortal bodies to life through his Spirit who lives in you.* As noted previously (see §7.2 above), the phrase *bring your mortal bodies to life* could, in itself, refer to spiritual renewal of the living, but the context points to the resurrection of the dead. The raising of Jesus from the dead is twice mentioned in v. 11, and clearly a parallel is implied between his resurrection and the bringing to life of mortal bodies.

The role of the Spirit in bringing forth resurrection is explored in the previous treatment of this text (§7.2). It is worth reiterating here, however, that the Spirit who lives in believers is the same Spirit who served as God's instrument in raising Jesus from the dead. Just as God raised Jesus through the Spirit, so he will bring believers' mortal bodies to resurrection life (v. 11).

This then informs our reading of the final sentence of the text—*But if by the Spirit you put to death the deeds of the body, you will live* (v. 13b). The verb *you will live* (ζήσεσθε) must refer to resurrection life, if our reading of v. 11 is correct.[4] Since v. 11 refers to the bodily resurrection of believers through the Spirit, so *by the Spirit . . . you will live* refers to resurrected life (v. 13). But whereas the Spirit effects bodily resurrection in v. 11, in v. 13b Paul refers to the role of the Spirit in putting *to death the deeds of the body*. In other words, the Spirit's role in bringing forth life is not restricted to the revivification of the flesh. Rather, the Spirit also works in the pre-resurrection life of believers to bring death—the death of deeds that belong to the spiritually dead body (v. 13b; cf. v. 10).

This then presupposes that the putting to death of the deeds of the body is a necessary precondition for resurrected life. This is reinforced by the preceding claim that *if you live according to the flesh, you are going to die* (v. 13a). The reference to death here must refer to spiritual death; that is, the opposite of resurrection life. This is because it is taken for granted that all are already sentenced to physical death. Paul's point, rather, is that living according to the flesh will result in condemnation at the judgment.

---

4. Dunn, *Romans 1–8*, 449.

And so, it seems that putting to death the deeds of the body—*not* living according to the flesh—is necessary to receive resurrected life. But the key here is to recognize that such putting to death is accomplished *by the Spirit* (v. 13b). The Spirit is instrumental for living a transformed life, just as he is instrumental in the resurrection of mortal bodies. As such, this text is not endorsing an "eternal life by right living" so much as an "eternal life by the power of the Spirit." It is eternal life by allegiance to the Spirit rather than to the flesh.

Gal 6:7–8 Μὴ πλανᾶσθε, θεὸς οὐ μυκτηρίζεται. ὃ γὰρ ἐὰν σπείρῃ ἄνθρωπος, τοῦτο καὶ θερίσει· 8 ὅτι ὁ σπείρων εἰς τὴν σάρκα ἑαυτοῦ ἐκ τῆς σαρκὸς θερίσει φθοράν, ὁ δὲ σπείρων εἰς τὸ πνεῦμα ἐκ τοῦ πνεύματος θερίσει ζωὴν αἰώνιον.

Don't be deceived: God is not mocked. For whatever a person sows he will also reap, 8 because the one who sows to his flesh will reap destruction from the flesh, but **the one who sows to the Spirit will reap eternal life from the Spirit**.

The agricultural metaphor of sowing and reaping is used to convey the idea that eschatological judgment is determined by one's orientation now—either in allegiance to the flesh or in allegiance to the Spirit. As argued earlier (§6.2 above), *the one who sows to the Spirit* is a person who lives according to the Spirit, with the Spirit as her orientation. Thus, while judgment takes into account one's deeds—what one sows—it is ultimately concerned with orientation and allegiance. The person whose life demonstrates allegiance to the flesh will reap destruction. The one whose life evidences allegiance to the Spirit will reap eternal life.

Here we note that *eternal life* (ζωὴ αἰώνιος) is juxtaposed with *destruction* (φθορά; 6:8). This could easily be used to defend the notion of eschatological annihilation, since φθορά (*destruction*) can indicate the "total destruction of an entity."[5] But it can also refer to corruption and ruination rather than annihilation.[6] In any case, just as destruction comes *from the flesh* (ἐκ τῆς σαρκός), so eternal life comes *from the Spirit* (ἐκ τοῦ πνεύματος).

Thus, eternal life is viewed as emanating from the Spirit, in keeping with a life lived in allegiance to the Spirit. In this way, eternal life is simply the expected (and intended) *telos* of life kept in step with the Spirit (5:25).

---

5. BDAG 1055, §5.
6. BDAG 1054–55. According to deSilva, "while often appropriately translated 'destruction,' the word denotes the postmortem decay or corruption that befalls flesh in its normal, physical sense" (David A. deSilva, *Galatians: A Handbook on the Greek Text*, BHGNT [Waco, TX: Baylor University Press, 2014], 136).

1 Thess 5:9–10 ὅτι οὐκ ἔθετο ἡμᾶς ὁ θεὸς εἰς ὀργὴν ἀλλὰ εἰς περιποίησιν σωτηρίας διὰ τοῦ κυρίου ἡμῶν Ἰησοῦ Χριστοῦ 10 **τοῦ ἀποθανόντος ὑπὲρ ἡμῶν, ἵνα εἴτε γρηγορῶμεν εἴτε καθεύδωμεν ἅμα σὺν αὐτῷ ζήσωμεν.**

For God did not appoint us to wrath, but to obtain salvation through our Lord Jesus Christ, 10 **who died for us, so that whether we are awake or asleep, we may live together with him***.*

As noted previously (see §6.2 above), God *appoints* people either to wrath or to salvation, and the latter is *through our Lord Jesus Christ, who died for us*, implying that it is through his death that people are able to receive salvation. The final outcome of God's appointment, however, is not salvation itself. Rather, the final outcome is what salvation makes possible, namely, that *we may live together with him* (5:10).

Though such life is not described as *eternal* life, the context clearly assumes as much. It is the outcome of salvation, and Paul's readers would no doubt understand living *with him* in this way. But the expression *we may live together with him* underscores the relational nature of eternal life.[7] It is not simply life without end; it is, rather, life lived in harmonious relationship and fellowship with Christ.

1 Tim 1:15–16 πιστὸς ὁ λόγος καὶ πάσης ἀποδοχῆς ἄξιος, ὅτι Χριστὸς Ἰησοῦς ἦλθεν εἰς τὸν κόσμον ἁμαρτωλοὺς σῶσαι, ὧν πρῶτός εἰμι ἐγώ. 16 ἀλλὰ διὰ τοῦτο ἠλεήθην, ἵνα ἐν ἐμοὶ πρώτῳ ἐνδείξηται Χριστὸς Ἰησοῦς τὴν ἅπασαν μακροθυμίαν πρὸς ὑποτύπωσιν τῶν μελλόντων πιστεύειν ἐπ' αὐτῷ εἰς ζωὴν αἰώνιον.

This saying is trustworthy and deserving of full acceptance: "Christ Jesus came into the world to save sinners"—and I am the worst of them. 16 But I received mercy for this reason, so that in me, the worst of them, **Christ Jesus might demonstrate his extraordinary patience as an example to those who would believe in him for eternal life***.*

Paul presents himself as *an example* (ὑποτύπωσις) of Christ's *extraordinary patience*, since he is *the worst* of sinners, and yet has received mercy. If even Paul, the worst of sinners, can receive Christ's mercy, then others *who would believe in him for eternal life* are not beyond the reach of it either (1:16). Though

---

7. Shogren, *1 & 2 Thessalonians*, 211.

it is not his focus here, Paul makes the connection between believing in Christ and eternal life (v. 16).[8] Belief in Christ (ἐπ αὐτῷ) is presented as the means *for eternal life* (εἰς ζωὴν αἰώνιον), while eternal life is understood as the proof of Christ's mercy and extraordinary patience. These two elements together indicate that eternal life is not something to be achieved or awarded. It is a product of the mercy of Christ, given to those who would believe in him.

1 Tim 6:11–12 Σὺ δέ, ὦ ἄνθρωπε θεοῦ, ταῦτα φεῦγε· δίωκε δὲ δικαιοσύνην εὐσέβειαν πίστιν, ἀγάπην ὑπομονὴν πραϋπαθίαν. 12 ἀγωνίζου τὸν καλὸν ἀγῶνα τῆς πίστεως, **ἐπιλαβοῦ τῆς αἰωνίου ζωῆς, εἰς ἣν ἐκλήθης** καὶ ὡμολόγησας τὴν καλὴν ὁμολογίαν ἐνώπιον πολλῶν μαρτύρων.

But you, man of God, flee from these things, and pursue righteousness, godliness, faith, love, endurance, and gentleness. 12 Fight the good fight of the faith. **Take hold of eternal life to which you were called** *and about which you have made a good confession in the presence of many witnesses.*

Timothy is to flee those things that may destroy his faith (6:9–10) and pursue righteousness and related characteristics (v. 11). This is what it means to fight the good fight of faith (v. 12), as he chooses righteousness over unrighteousness. It seems that a component of that good fight of the faith involves taking hold of eternal life.[9] To "take hold" (ἐπιλαμβάνομαι) of eternal life is a curious notion, since the action of taking hold of something is normally associated with a tangible object, but eternal life is not tangible. According to BDAG this is a figurative use of the verb that conveys the idea of taking hold of something (nontangible, in this case) in order to make it one's own.[10] In other words, Timothy is to "own" the eternal life to which he was called.

This implies that "owning" his eternal life involves a moral component as Timothy fights the good fight and pursues righteousness in his life. Since he was *called* to this eternal life, however, the moral component does not suggest that eternal life is contingent on his performance. His calling precedes his performance. Nevertheless, Timothy is to live in accordance with the life to which he has been called. He is to "own" it by living consistently with it.

This then reveals that eternal life has a moral shape—it is characterized by righteousness, godliness, faith, love, endurance, and gentleness. Obviously,

---

8. Towner, *1–2 Timothy & Titus*, 56.
9. Bernhard Mutschler, "Eschatology in the Pastoral Epistles," in van der Watt, *Eschatology of the New Testament*, 397.
10. BDAG 374, §4.

then, eternal life cannot be understood simply as life without end. It is a *kind* of life; it is a morally informed and shaped life.

2 Tim 2:10–13 διὰ τοῦτο πάντα ὑπομένω διὰ τοὺς ἐκλεκτούς, ἵνα καὶ αὐτοὶ σωτηρίας τύχωσιν τῆς ἐν Χριστῷ Ἰησοῦ μετὰ δόξης αἰωνίου. 11 πιστὸς ὁ λόγος·

> εἰ γὰρ συναπεθάνομεν,
> καὶ συζήσομεν·
> 12 εἰ ὑπομένομεν,
> καὶ συμβασιλεύσομεν·
> εἰ ἀρνησόμεθα,
> κἀκεῖνος ἀρνήσεται ἡμᾶς·
> 13 εἰ ἀπιστοῦμεν,
> ἐκεῖνος πιστὸς μένει,
> ἀρνήσασθαι γὰρ ἑαυτὸν οὐ δύναται.

This is why I endure all things for the elect: so that they also may obtain salvation, which is in Christ Jesus, with eternal glory. 11 This saying is trustworthy:

> **For if we died with him,**
> **we will also live with him;**
> 12 *if we endure,*
> *we will also reign with him;*
> *if we deny him,*
> *he will also deny us;*
> 13 *if we are faithless,*
> *he remains faithful,*
> *for he cannot deny himself.*

This passage has already been discussed at length (see §6.2 above). Here we simply note that to *live with him* (συζήσομεν; 1:11c) is correlated with *salvation* and *eternal glory* (v. 10). Eternal life is in view, as the eschatological nature of the following verses confirm (vv. 12–13).

Again, we observe that eternal life is presented as life *with him* (v. 11c). It is characterized by relationship and fellowship with Christ. Moreover, it is contingent upon dying with Christ. As noted above (see §6.2 above), it is possible that having *died with him* (συναπεθάνομεν) here refers to physical death—that is, dying as a Christian. But Paul elsewhere speaks of dying with Christ in a spiritual manner (e.g., Rom 6:5–8). And if physical death were meant, he would not likely have used the aorist tense-form (συναπεθάνομεν).[11] So, Paul's point is that the person who has spiritually died with Christ in this life will live with him in the life to come.

Thus, eternal life with Christ is one of eternal glory, and it is a product of salvation. But it is also contingent upon a life lived in participation with the death of Christ. If the believer dies with Christ, she will also live with him in eternal glory. But if the believer does not die with Christ, there can be no life with him.

> Titus 3:6–7 οὗ ἐξέχεεν ἐφ' ἡμᾶς πλουσίως
> διὰ Ἰησοῦ Χριστοῦ τοῦ σωτῆρος ἡμῶν,
> 7 ἵνα δικαιωθέντες τῇ ἐκείνου χάριτι
> κληρονόμοι γενηθῶμεν κατ' ἐλπίδα ζωῆς αἰωνίου.

He poured out his Spirit on us abundantly through Jesus Christ our Savior 7 so that, **having been justified by his grace, we may become heirs with the hope of eternal life.**

The pouring out of the Spirit is directly linked here to *eternal life*. Specifically, the Spirit seems to enable believers to share in the inheritance of God: *He poured out his Spirit . . . so that . . . we may become heirs* (3:6–7). This resonates with Paul's notion that the Spirit is the *Spirit of adoption* (Rom 8:15), and *the down payment of our inheritance* (Eph 1:14). For Paul, clearly a connection exists between the Spirit and the inheritance to come. But what is this connection? Romans 8:14–17 offers the clearest insight into this question:

> For all those led by God's Spirit are God's sons. 15 You did not receive a spirit of slavery to fall back into fear. Instead, you received the Spirit of adoption, by whom we cry out, "Abba, Father!" 16 The Spirit himself testifies together with our spirit that we are God's children, 17 and if children, also heirs—heirs of God and coheirs with Christ—if indeed we suffer with him so that we may also be glorified with him.

The Spirit marks those who are God's sons (Rom 8:14). He is the Spirit of adoption, enabling believers to cry out "Abba, Father!" (v. 15). The Spirit

---

11. Köstenberger, *1–2 Timothy & Titus*, 237.

also confirms within believers *that we are God's children* (v. 16). The key point follows: *and if children, also heirs—heirs of God and coheirs with Christ* (v. 17). Thus, the Spirit's role in making believers the adopted children of God secures his connection to inheritance, since the children of God are his heirs. Returning to Titus 3:6–7, it is now clear how the outpouring of the Spirit enables believers to become heirs. The Spirit is the Spirit of adoption, making believers the adopted children of God, who are therefore also heirs of God.

These children are heirs according to *the hope of eternal life* (κατ' ἐλπίδα ζωῆς αἰωνίου; Titus 3:7b). This unusual expression is difficult to parse. The use of κατ' ἐλπίδα ζωῆς αἰωνίου seems to qualify *heirs* (though it could also modify the verb γενηθῶμεν, translated *we may become*).[12] Either way, the hope of eternal life somehow modifies the status of being an heir. Perhaps eternal life *is* the inheritance anticipated for the heirs of God. Or perhaps the inheritance (whatever it is) will be enjoyed within the context of eternal life. Either way, the status of being heirs of God appears to be inextricably tied to eternal life. The inheritance awaiting God's children will be enjoyed for all eternity.

8.3 SUMMARY

Eternal life is the inheritance promised to believers who are made heirs through the grace of God. Through faith in Christ, believers suffer now with him but will live with him in resurrected bodies when he comes. While the reign of sin results in death, so the coming reign of righteousness will result in eternal life through Christ (Rom 5:19–21; 6:21–23). Eternal life requires the resurrection of formerly mortal bodies, whose deeds must be put to death in order to live (Rom 8:10–13). It is reaped from sowing according to the Spirit (Gal 6:7–8), and through faith in Christ (1 Tim 1:16).

Eternal life is not seen as an impersonal, private existence but as life with Christ (1 Thess 5:9–10), informed by righteousness (1 Tim 6:11–12). Living with Christ is the positive counterpart of suffering with him (2 Tim 2:11) and is the hope of heirs who have been justified by the grace of Christ (Titus 3:6–7). Eternal life is thus a relational mode of being, lived in bodies that are no longer subject to death and decay. Believers anticipate living under the reign of righteousness, free from sin, and in eternal peace with Christ.

---

12. Mounce, *Pastoral Epistles*, 451.

CHAPTER 9

INHERITANCE

9.1 Introduction

This chapter explores the concept of inheritance—that which is promised to believers for the age to come. For Paul it begins by understanding the inheritance promised to Abraham—that he and his descendants would inherit the world. Believers, both Jew and gentile, are the true descendants of Abraham, since they share his faith in God, and are therefore made the children of God. As children, they are heirs, and have become co-sharers in the promise to Abraham.

The children of God receive his Spirit as a deposit guaranteeing their inheritance, and they are led by the Spirit. When the time comes, they will be resurrected to immortal bodies that will enable them to inherit the kingdom of God, since it is impossible for flesh and blood to inherit it.

9.2 Inheritance Texts

Rom 4:13–15 Οὐ γὰρ διὰ νόμου ἡ ἐπαγγελία τῷ Ἀβραὰμ ἢ τῷ σπέρματι αὐτοῦ, τὸ κληρονόμον αὐτὸν εἶναι κόσμου, ἀλλὰ διὰ δικαιοσύνης πίστεως. 14 εἰ γὰρ οἱ ἐκ νόμου κληρονόμοι, κεκένωται ἡ πίστις καὶ κατήργηται ἡ ἐπαγγελία· 15 ὁ γὰρ νόμος ὀργὴν κατεργάζεται· οὗ δὲ οὐκ ἔστιν νόμος οὐδὲ παράβασις.

> *For the promise to Abraham or to his descendants that **he would inherit the world** was not through the law, but through the righteousness that comes by faith. 14 **If those who are of the law are heirs, faith is made empty and the promise nullified** 15 because the law produces wrath. And where there is no law, there is no transgression.*

In the context of Paul's extended defense of his doctrine of justification by faith in Romans 4, he considers how Abraham would become the heir (κληρονόμος) of the world (4:13). He states that this could not happen *through the law* (διὰ νόμου), *but through the righteousness that comes by faith* (ἀλλὰ διὰ δικαιοσύνης πίστεως; v. 13b).

The primary reason why those of the law cannot be made heirs is *because the law produces wrath* (v. 15a). Obviously, then, recipients of wrath cannot also be heirs. But the reason why inheriting the world must be *through the righteousness that comes by faith* (v. 13) is less obvious. The clue is in the relationship between *faith* and *the promise*: *If those who are of the law are heirs, faith is made empty and the promise nullified* (v. 14). The significance of faith is that it relies on the promise made by God. Abraham did not have to do anything (such as keep the law) in order to benefit from the promise. He only needed to trust in God's promise to him. If the inheritance were to come through the law, then the promise would mean nothing, nor would the faith that simply trusted in the promise.

Because Abraham believed God, it was credited to him as righteousness (see Gen 15:6). It is from this statement that Paul coined his own—*the righteousness that comes by faith* (Rom 4:13b; cf. also Hab 2:4). And because it was God's promise to him that Abraham believed, which in turn resulted in his being credited with righteousness, so Paul is able to say that the promise to inherit the world came through the righteousness of faith.

But what is this inheritance of the world? Paul does not explain it, and the promises to Abraham in Genesis 12, 15, and 17 do not explicitly refer to it. The physical world is not promised to Abraham, but only the land of Canaan (Gen 12:1; 17:8). Paul must refer, instead, to the promise of Abraham's descendants, who will be as numerous as the stars in the sky (Gen 15:5), and who will form the nations of the earth (Gen 17:6, 16). By becoming the father of many nations (Gen 17:4), Abraham becomes the inheritor of the world.[1] And this inheritance comes by the promise of God, received by faith.

Rom 8:14–22 ὅσοι γὰρ πνεύματι θεοῦ ἄγονται, οὗτοι υἱοὶ θεοῦ εἰσιν. 15 οὐ γὰρ ἐλάβετε πνεῦμα δουλείας πάλιν εἰς φόβον ἀλλὰ ἐλάβετε πνεῦμα υἱοθεσίας ἐν ᾧ κράζομεν· Αββα ὁ πατήρ. 16 **αὐτὸ τὸ πνεῦμα συμμαρτυρεῖ τῷ πνεύματι ἡμῶν ὅτι ἐσμὲν τέκνα θεοῦ. 17 εἰ δὲ τέκνα, καὶ κληρονόμοι· κληρονόμοι μὲν θεοῦ, συγκληρονόμοι δὲ Χριστοῦ, εἴπερ συμπάσχομεν ἵνα καὶ συνδοξασθῶμεν.**

18 Λογίζομαι γὰρ ὅτι οὐκ ἄξια τὰ παθήματα τοῦ νῦν καιροῦ πρὸς τὴν μέλλουσαν δόξαν ἀποκαλυφθῆναι εἰς ἡμᾶς. 19 ἡ γὰρ ἀποκαραδοκία

---

1. "God will rule the world, and will do so through Jesus the Jewish Messiah, in such a way as to bring all nations equally into God's family" (Wright, "Romans," 496).

τῆς κτίσεως τὴν ἀποκάλυψιν τῶν υἱῶν τοῦ θεοῦ ἀπεκδέχεται. 20 τῇ γὰρ ματαιότητι ἡ κτίσις ὑπετάγη, οὐχ ἑκοῦσα ἀλλὰ διὰ τὸν ὑποτάξαντα, ἐφ᾽ ἑλπίδι 21 ὅτι καὶ αὐτὴ ἡ κτίσις ἐλευθερωθήσεται ἀπὸ τῆς δουλείας τῆς φθορᾶς εἰς τὴν ἐλευθερίαν τῆς δόξης τῶν τέκνων τοῦ θεοῦ. 22 οἴδαμεν γὰρ ὅτι πᾶσα ἡ κτίσις συστενάζει καὶ συνωδίνει ἄχρι τοῦ νῦν

For all those led by God's Spirit are God's sons. 15 You did not receive a spirit of slavery to fall back into fear. Instead, you received the Spirit of adoption, by whom we cry out, "Abba, Father!" 16 **The Spirit himself testifies together with our spirit that we are God's children, 17 and if children, also heirs—heirs of God and coheirs with Christ—if indeed we suffer with him so that we may also be glorified with him**. *18 For I consider that the sufferings of this present time are not worth comparing with the glory that is going to be revealed to us. 19 For the creation eagerly waits with anticipation for God's sons to be revealed. 20 For the creation was subjected to futility—not willingly, but because of him who subjected it—in the hope 21 that the creation itself will also be set free from the bondage to decay into the glorious freedom of God's children. 22 For we know that the whole creation has been groaning together with labor pains until now.*

As noted in the discussion on Titus 3:6–7 above (see §8.2), the Spirit marks those who are God's sons (Rom 8:14). He is the Spirit of adoption, enabling believers to cry out "Abba, Father!" (v. 15). The Spirit also confirms within believers *that we are God's children* (v. 16). The key point follows: *And if children, also heirs—heirs of God and coheirs with Christ* (v. 17). Thus, the Spirit's role in making believers the adopted children of God secures his connection to inheritance, since the children of God are God's heirs.

To be heirs of God is to be coheirs with Christ (v. 17a). This means that the inheritance that the Son of God enjoys will be shared with his adopted brothers and sisters. But a prerequisite for sharing his status as heir of God is to *suffer with him* [συμπάσχομεν] *so that we may also be glorified with him* (συνδοξασθῶμεν; v. 17b). Suffering with Christ is not regarded as a "work" that achieves co-status with Christ. Rather, it is an expression of participation with him. As Schweitzer comments, "The thought of following Christ in the path of suffering hardly occurs apart from that of fellowship with Christ in suffering."[2] Indeed, as I have commented elsewhere, "believers share in the ongoing force of Christ's death and the power of his resurrection, and one consequence of this

---

2. Schweitzer, *Mysticism*, 144.

is that believers will undergo suffering."³ Those who are in Christ will suffer with Christ and will also share with him in his inheritance. Suffering with Christ is simply a mark of genuine participation with Christ and will result in being glorified with him.

Suffering is *not worth comparing with the glory that is going to be revealed* in believers (v. 18). In order to underscore the glory to come, Paul draws on the arena of creation in the following verses (vv. 19–22). The creation *was subjected to futility* (v. 20), and *bondage to decay* (v. 21), all the while *groaning together with labor pains until now* (v. 22). But creation was subjected in hope that it *will also be set free from the bondage to decay into the glorious freedom of God's children* (v. 21). Creation is imagined as a mother suffering in labor, about to give birth to God's children (vv. 21–22).

This depiction of creation demonstrates an inextricable connection between it and the children of God. Just as creation suffered the consequences of humanity's fall into sin (Gen 3), so creation will experience liberation and renewal when the sons of God are revealed.

Creation is understood as the arena in which the coheirs with Christ will experience glory. Glory is coming for those who suffer with Christ (Rom 8:18), and the creation will escape its bondage to decay *into the glorious freedom of God's children* (v. 21). The phrase *the glorious freedom of God's children* is better translated *the freedom of glory* (τὴν ἐλευθερίαν τῆς δόξης), since it is contrasted in parallel to *the bondage to decay* (τῆς δουλείας τῆς φθορᾶς). This seems to mean that rather than being subject to decay, creation will become subject to freedom. And this freedom is a glorious one, pertaining to the children of God (τὴν ἐλευθερίαν τῆς δόξης τῶν τέκνων τοῦ θεοῦ).

Though Paul does not explicitly say so, all of this implies that the inheritance coming to the heirs of God and coheirs with Christ is the renewed creation itself. Once the creation gives birth to the anticipated children of God, she will be liberated from bondage into freedom, and will become the arena for the glory of the children of God. They will inherit the earth—and all of creation.

1 Cor 6:9–11 ἢ οὐκ οἴδατε ὅτι **ἄδικοι θεοῦ βασιλείαν οὐ κληρονομήσουσιν**; μὴ πλανᾶσθε· οὔτε πόρνοι οὔτε εἰδωλολάτραι οὔτε μοιχοὶ οὔτε μαλακοὶ οὔτε ἀρσενοκοῖται 10 οὔτε κλέπται οὔτε πλεονέκται, οὐ μέθυσοι, οὐ λοίδοροι, οὐχ ἅρπαγες **βασιλείαν θεοῦ κληρονομήσουσιν**. 11 καὶ ταῦτά τινες ἦτε· ἀλλὰ ἀπελούσασθε, ἀλλὰ ἡγιάσθητε, ἀλλὰ ἐδικαιώθητε ἐν τῷ ὀνόματι τοῦ κυρίου Ἰησοῦ Χριστοῦ καὶ ἐν τῷ πνεύματι τοῦ θεοῦ ἡμῶν.

---

3. Campbell, *Paul and Union with Christ*, 381.

> *Don't you know that **the unrighteous will not inherit God's kingdom?** Do not be deceived: No sexually immoral people, idolaters, adulterers, or males who have sex with males, 10 no thieves, greedy people, drunkards, verbally abusive people, or swindlers **will inherit God's kingdom**. 11 And some of you used to be like this. But you were washed, you were sanctified, you were justified in the name of the Lord Jesus Christ and by the Spirit of our God.*

In a context concerning legal disputes between believers, Paul asserts that *the saints will judge the world* and are therefore able to judge trivial matters (6:2). A believer should not take his fellow believer to court for arbitration by unbelievers (v. 6). Paul then asserts that *the unrighteous will not inherit God's kingdom* (v. 9a). The vice list that characterizes the unrighteous (vv. 9b–10) is used by Paul to remind the Corinthians that *some of you used to be like this* (v. 11a). But such is no longer the case, since *you were washed, you were sanctified, you were justified in the name of the Lord Jesus Christ and by the Spirit of our God* (v. 11b).

Since the Corinthians were once *like this* (ταῦτά τινες ἦτε), the vice list cannot be understood to mean that anyone who commits any of these offenses is forever prohibited from inheriting the kingdom of God. Otherwise the Corinthians too would be lost. Rather, just as the Corinthians had been washed, sanctified, and justified, so the unrighteous can be washed, sanctified, and justified through Christ and the Spirit. It is therefore a settled, unrepentant, unrighteous lifestyle "of open rebellion against God"[4] that is described by the vice list. Such people, who do not come to Christ for cleansing and justification, cannot inherit the kingdom of God. By the same token, only those who enjoy righteous standing before God, having been justified in the name of Christ, are qualified to inherit God's kingdom.

> 1 Cor 15:45–53 οὕτως καὶ γέγραπται, Ἐγένετο ὁ πρῶτος ἄνθρωπος Ἀδὰμ εἰς ψυχὴν ζῶσαν, ὁ ἔσχατος Ἀδὰμ εἰς πνεῦμα ζῳοποιοῦν. 46 ἀλλ᾽ οὐ πρῶτον τὸ πνευματικὸν ἀλλὰ τὸ ψυχικόν, ἔπειτα τὸ πνευματικόν. 47 ὁ πρῶτος ἄνθρωπος ἐκ γῆς χοϊκός, ὁ δεύτερος ἄνθρωπος ἐξ οὐρανοῦ. 48 οἷος ὁ χοϊκός, τοιοῦτοι καὶ οἱ χοϊκοί, καὶ οἷος ὁ ἐπουράνιος, τοιοῦτοι καὶ οἱ ἐπουράνιοι· 49 καὶ καθὼς ἐφορέσαμεν τὴν εἰκόνα τοῦ χοϊκοῦ, φορέσομεν καὶ τὴν εἰκόνα τοῦ ἐπουρανίου.
> 50 Τοῦτο δέ φημι, ἀδελφοί, ὅτι **σὰρξ καὶ αἷμα βασιλείαν θεοῦ κληρονομῆσαι οὐ δύναται οὐδὲ ἡ φθορὰ τὴν ἀφθαρσίαν κληρονομεῖ**. 51 ἰδοὺ μυστήριον ὑμῖν λέγω· πάντες οὐ κοιμηθησόμεθα, πάντες δὲ

---

4. Garland, *1 Corinthians*, 211.

ἀλλαγησόμεθα, 52 ἐν ἀτόμῳ, ἐν ῥιπῇ ὀφθαλμοῦ, ἐν τῇ ἐσχάτῃ σάλπιγγι·
σαλπίσει γὰρ καὶ οἱ νεκροὶ ἐγερθήσονται ἄφθαρτοι καὶ ἡμεῖς ἀλλαγησόμεθα.
53 δεῖ γὰρ τὸ φθαρτὸν τοῦτο ἐνδύσασθαι ἀφθαρσίαν καὶ τὸ θνητὸν τοῦτο
ἐνδύσασθαι ἀθανασίαν.

So it is written, The first man Adam became a living being; the last Adam became a life-giving spirit. 46 However, the spiritual is not first, but the natural, then the spiritual. 47 The first man was from the earth, a man of dust; the second man is from heaven. 48 Like the man of dust, so are those who are of the dust; like the man of heaven, so are those who are of heaven. 49 And just as we have borne the image of the man of dust, we will also bear the image of the man of heaven. 50 What I am saying, brothers and sisters, is this: **Flesh and blood cannot inherit the kingdom of God, nor can corruption inherit incorruption**. *51 Listen, I am telling you a mystery: We will not all fall asleep, but we will all be changed, 52 in a moment, in the twinkling of an eye, at the last trumpet. For the trumpet will sound, and the dead will be raised incorruptible, and we will be changed. 53 For this corruptible body must be clothed with incorruptibility, and this mortal body must be clothed with immortality.*

While 1 Corinthians 15:35–50 and 15:51–58 have already been discussed at length concerning the resurrection of the dead (see §7.2 above), our current interest in the notion of inheritance means we will focus our attention on v. 50b—*Flesh and blood cannot inherit the kingdom of God, nor can corruption inherit incorruption*. This verse functions as a pivot between 15:35–49 and 15:51–58. Its role in relation to the prior section is to provide the conclusion that Paul has been driving at throughout. It is flagged by the *meta-comment, What I am saying . . .* (v. 50a).[5] The important proposition following the meta-comment is that *flesh and blood cannot inherit the kingdom of God, nor can corruption inherit incorruption* (v. 50b). The natural, flesh and blood, corruptible body is not fit for the kingdom of God.[6] Anyone who would inherit the kingdom must therefore be resurrected with a spiritual, incorruptible body like that of Christ.

The notion of *inheritance* also connects to the *image* language of the previous

---

5. A *meta-comment* is "when a speaker stops saying what they are saying in order to comment on what is *going* to be said, speaking abstractly about it, e.g. '*I want you to know that . . .*', 'Don't you know that . . .'" The effect of the meta-comment "is to slow down the flow of the text, and to attract the reader's attention to some important proposition that follows" (Runge, *Lexham Discourse Greek New Testament*, n.p.).

6. As Gardner notes, "Believers cannot inherit all the wondrous covenant promises summarized in the final rule of God in a kingdom of peace and righteousness if they are not appropriately clothed. 'Flesh and blood' is inappropriate because it is frail and decaying in its propensity to sin, and it is not righteous and glorious" (Gardner, *1 Corinthians*, 722).

verse (εἰκών; v. 49). Conformity to the *image* of Christ enables membership in the divine family (see the previous discussion of this text at §7.2 above), and *inheritance* is inherently a familial concept. Thus, anyone who would wish to inherit the kingdom of God must bear the image of the man of heaven (v. 49). Without that token of familial membership, no one is able to receive the heavenly inheritance.

First Corinthians 15:50 pivots to the next section (vv. 51–58), which concerns how corruptible flesh and blood will be changed to an incorruptible resurrection body. Since v. 50 has established that *flesh and blood cannot inherit the kingdom of God*, so vv. 51–54 offers images of the transformation from one to the other. All will be changed in the twinkling of an eye at the last trumpet, and the corruptible, mortal body will be clothed with incorruptibility and immortality (vv. 51–53). Thus, with the resurrection of the body, believers become able to inherit the kingdom of God, which was otherwise barred from access.

> Gal 3:14–18 ἵνα εἰς τὰ ἔθνη ἡ εὐλογία τοῦ Ἀβραὰμ γένηται ἐν Χριστῷ Ἰησοῦ, ἵνα τὴν ἐπαγγελίαν τοῦ πνεύματος λάβωμεν διὰ τῆς πίστεως. 15 Ἀδελφοί, κατὰ ἄνθρωπον λέγω· ὅμως ἀνθρώπου κεκυρωμένην διαθήκην οὐδεὶς ἀθετεῖ ἢ ἐπιδιατάσσεται. 16 τῷ δὲ Ἀβραὰμ ἐρρέθησαν αἱ ἐπαγγελίαι καὶ τῷ σπέρματι αὐτοῦ. οὐ λέγει, Καὶ τοῖς σπέρμασιν, ὡς ἐπὶ πολλῶν ἀλλ' ὡς ἐφ' ἑνός, Καὶ τῷ σπέρματί σου, ὅς ἐστιν Χριστός. 17 τοῦτο δὲ λέγω· διαθήκην προκεκυρωμένην ὑπὸ τοῦ θεοῦ ὁ μετὰ τετρακόσια καὶ τριάκοντα ἔτη γεγονὼς νόμος οὐκ ἀκυροῖ εἰς τὸ καταργῆσαι τὴν ἐπαγγελίαν. 18 **εἰ γὰρ ἐκ νόμου ἡ κληρονομία, οὐκέτι ἐξ ἐπαγγελίας· τῷ δὲ Ἀβραὰμ δι' ἐπαγγελίας κεχάρισται ὁ θεός.**
>
> *The purpose was that the blessing of Abraham would come to the Gentiles by Christ Jesus, so that we could receive the promised Spirit through faith. 15 Brothers and sisters, I'm using a human illustration. No one sets aside or makes additions to a validated human will. 16 Now the promises were spoken to Abraham and to his seed. He does not say "and to seeds," as though referring to many, but referring to one, and to your seed, who is Christ. 17 My point is this: The law, which came 430 years later, does not invalidate a covenant previously established by God and thus cancel the promise. 18* **For if the inheritance is based on the law, it is no longer based on the promise; but God has graciously given it to Abraham through the promise.**

The text parallels the very similar text of Romans 4:13–15 (discussed in this section, above), though the point is arguably a little clearer here. Paul sees

Christ as the true seed of Abraham, and therefore as the fulfillment of the promises spoken to Abraham (Gal 3:15). The law, which came centuries after the promises to Abraham, *does not invalidate a covenant previously established by God and thus cancel the promise* (v. 17; cf. also v. 15). Then follows the key point: *For if the inheritance is based on the law, it is no longer based on the promise* (v. 18a). Paul's argument depends on the previous point—that the giving of the law does not nullify the promises to Abraham—and therefore *promise* remains the way in which God will grant the inheritance of Abraham.

The significance of this point is that the inheritance may be shared by gentiles, who do not have the law. We see the gentile issue raised at the beginning of our text—*the purpose was that the blessing of Abraham would come to the Gentiles by Christ Jesus, so that we could receive the promised Spirit through faith* (v. 14). They can access the promise through faith in Christ, who fulfills the promises to Abraham, and in this way they may be included in the blessings of Abraham even though they do not belong to Israel and are not living under the law.[7]

One final point warrants attention. While our focus has been on the reception of the *inheritance* through the promise of God (3:18), in 3:14 Paul refers to the reception of the *Spirit* through the promise. Does this mean that the Spirit *is* the inheritance? Probably not, though there is clearly a connection. But Paul does not help us resolve the question in this text, or in its larger, surrounding context. If, however, we are permitted to borrow an insight from the later letter to the Ephesians, we see Paul refer to the Spirit as the deposit of the inheritance to come: *The Holy Spirit is the down payment of our inheritance, until the redemption of the possession, to the praise of his glory* (Eph 1:14). If the promised Spirit is a down payment of the inheritance, then Galatians 3:14 and 3:18 can easily be reconciled. Receiving the Spirit through the promise is part and parcel of receiving the inheritance through the Spirit. And they together may be accessed by faith by both Jew and gentile.

Gal 3:26–4:7 Πάντες γὰρ υἱοὶ θεοῦ ἐστε διὰ τῆς πίστεως ἐν Χριστῷ Ἰησοῦ· 27 ὅσοι γὰρ εἰς Χριστὸν ἐβαπτίσθητε, Χριστὸν ἐνεδύσασθε. 28 οὐκ ἔνι Ἰουδαῖος οὐδὲ Ἕλλην, οὐκ ἔνι δοῦλος οὐδὲ ἐλεύθερος, οὐκ ἔνι ἄρσεν καὶ θῆλυ· πάντες γὰρ ὑμεῖς εἷς ἐστε ἐν Χριστῷ Ἰησοῦ. 29 εἰ δὲ ὑμεῖς Χριστοῦ, ἄρα τοῦ Ἀβραὰμ σπέρμα ἐστέ, κατ᾽ ἐπαγγελίαν κληρονόμοι. 4:1 Λέγω δέ, ἐφ᾽ ὅσον χρόνον ὁ κληρονόμος νήπιός ἐστιν, οὐδὲν διαφέρει δούλου κύριος πάντων ὤν, 2 ἀλλὰ ὑπὸ ἐπιτρόπους ἐστὶν καὶ οἰκονόμους ἄχρι

---

7. "For Paul . . . any mingling of faith and law, even if it is claimed that this has only to do with a proper lifestyle and not justification, is a discrediting of the Abrahamic covenant, the work of Christ, the ministry of the Spirit, and the principle of faith" (Richard N. Longenecker, *Galatians*, WBC 41 [Dallas: Word, 1990], 135).

τῆς προθεσμίας τοῦ πατρός. 3 οὕτως καὶ ἡμεῖς, ὅτε ἦμεν νήπιοι, ὑπὸ τὰ στοιχεῖα τοῦ κόσμου ἤμεθα δεδουλωμένοι· 4 ὅτε δὲ ἦλθεν τὸ πλήρωμα τοῦ χρόνου, ἐξαπέστειλεν ὁ θεὸς τὸν υἱὸν αὐτοῦ, γενόμενον ἐκ γυναικός, γενόμενον ὑπὸ νόμον, 5 ἵνα τοὺς ὑπὸ νόμον ἐξαγοράσῃ, ἵνα τὴν υἱοθεσίαν ἀπολάβωμεν. 6 Ὅτι δέ ἐστε υἱοί, ἐξαπέστειλεν ὁ θεὸς τὸ πνεῦμα τοῦ υἱοῦ αὐτοῦ εἰς τὰς καρδίας ἡμῶν κρᾶζον, Αββα ὁ πατήρ. 7 **ὥστε οὐκέτι εἶ δοῦλος ἀλλὰ υἱός· εἰ δὲ υἱός, καὶ κληρονόμος διὰ θεοῦ**.

For through faith you are all sons of God in Christ Jesus. 27 For those of you who were baptized into Christ have been clothed with Christ. 28 There is no Jew or Greek, slave or free, male and female; since you are all one in Christ Jesus. 29 And if you belong to Christ, then you are Abraham's seed, heirs according to the promise. 4:1 Now I say that as long as the heir is a child, he differs in no way from a slave, though he is the owner of everything. 2 Instead, he is under guardians and trustees until the time set by his father. 3 In the same way we also, when we were children, were in slavery under the elements of the world. 4 When the time came to completion, God sent his Son, born of a woman, born under the law, 5 to redeem those under the law, so that we might receive adoption as sons. 6 And because you are sons, God sent the Spirit of his Son into our hearts, crying, "Abba, Father!" 7 **So you are no longer a slave but a son, and if a son, then God has made you an heir.**

Paul's discussion of the purpose of the law (3:19–25) presents it as a guardian (παιδαγωγός) until Christ came. Such a guardian cares for underage children, not fully grown adults. Paul draws on this idea to segue to the notion that believers are *sons of God* (v. 26). The sonship of believers *in Christ Jesus* (v. 26) results from having been *baptized into Christ* and *clothed with Christ* (v. 27). Consequently, *there is no Jew or Greek, slave or free, male and female; since you are all one in Christ Jesus* (v. 28). The point is that sonship removes all other status distinctions, such as race, social standing, and gender. Indeed, those who *belong to Christ* are *Abraham's seed, heirs according to the promise* (v. 29). The discussion of sonship leads naturally to the matter of heirship.

The rest of the text unfolds the implications of being heirs (4:1–7). As a child, an heir is like a slave, since *he is under guardians and trustees until the time set by his father* (vv. 1–2). Just as a slave is under authority, so a child heir is subject to the elements placed over him (v. 3). But at *the time of completion, God sent his Son . . . to redeem those under the law, so that we might receive adoption as sons* (vv. 4–5). The fullness of time indicates a moment in salvation history (the coming of Christ) and represents the moment of maturity for the heirs.

They are no longer regarded as children, but as sons. As sons, *God sent the Spirit of his Son into our hearts, crying, "Abba, Father!"* (v. 6). The Spirit of God's Son causes the adopted sons of God to call on God as Father, thus making the legal status of adoption affective as well as effective.[8] Finally, those that used to be children and slaves *are no longer* slaves but sons, *and if a son, then God has made you an heir* (v. 7).

The logic of this passage intertwines adoption, inheritance, and sonship around union with Christ. Believers are sons of God *in Christ Jesus* (3:26); they are *baptized into Christ* and *clothed with Christ* (3:27). Christ redeems those born under the law (4:4–5), and the Spirit of the Son of God inclines the hearts of God's adopted children to likewise call on God as Father (4:6). Since believers have been made genuine sons of God alongside *the* Son of God, they are also heirs along with him. And they are heirs specifically of the promise made to Abraham (3:29).

Gal 4:28–31 ὑμεῖς δέ, ἀδελφοί, κατὰ Ἰσαὰκ ἐπαγγελίας τέκνα ἐστέ. 29 ἀλλ᾽ ὥσπερ τότε ὁ κατὰ σάρκα γεννηθεὶς ἐδίωκεν τὸν κατὰ πνεῦμα, οὕτως καὶ νῦν. 30 ἀλλὰ τί λέγει ἡ γραφή; ἔκβαλε τὴν παιδίσκην καὶ τὸν υἱὸν αὐτῆς· οὐ γὰρ μὴ κληρονομήσει ὁ υἱὸς τῆς παιδίσκης μετὰ τοῦ υἱοῦ τῆς ἐλευθέρας. 31 διό, ἀδελφοί, οὐκ ἐσμὲν παιδίσκης τέκνα ἀλλὰ τῆς ἐλευθέρας.

Now you too, brothers and sisters, like Isaac, are children of promise. 29 But just as then the child born as a result of the flesh persecuted the one born as a result of the Spirit, so also now. 30 But what does the Scripture say? "Drive out the slave and her son, **for the son of the slave will never be a coheir with the son of the free woman.**" *31 Therefore, brothers and sisters, we are not children of a slave but of the free woman.*

Forming the conclusion to the section concerning the contrast between the two sons of Abraham and their respective mothers (4:21–31), Paul connects his readers to Isaac, being *children of promise* (v. 28). As with the relationship between Isaac and Ishmael, Paul predicts the children *of the flesh* will persecute *the one born as a result of the Spirit* (v. 29). However, Paul employs Genesis 21:10 to affirm that *the son of the slave will never be a coheir with the son of the free*

---

8. "Almost certainly Paul had in mind the legal act of *adoptio*, by which a Roman citizen entered another family and came under the *patria potestas* of its head. . . . Presumably also included in Paul's use of the analogy [of adoption] was the fact that the adopted person was for all legal purposes in the same position as the natural son, with the same rights of succession—so that 'adoption' is fully equivalent to 'sonship'" (James D. G. Dunn, *The Epistle to the Galatians*, BNTC [Grand Rapids: Baker Academic, 1993], 217).

woman (Gal 4:30). This is the chief point of the section—the correspondence of Hagar, Mount Sinai, and the law with the "children of Hagar" under the law (vv. 21–25) means that those under the law cannot be regarded the true heirs of Abraham. But the children of Sarah, of the Jerusalem above, and of the promise (vv. 26–28) are the true heirs and inheritors of Abraham.

The conclusion, that *we are not children of a slave but of the free woman* (v. 31), underscores the point that heirs are children of promise, of freedom, and of the family of Abraham.[9] Those who remain under law are slaves and not true members of the Abrahamic family. They cannot be his heirs.

Gal 5:19–21 φανερὰ δέ ἐστιν τὰ ἔργα τῆς σαρκός, ἅτινά ἐστιν πορνεία, ἀκαθαρσία, ἀσέλγεια, 20 εἰδωλολατρία, φαρμακεία, ἔχθραι, ἔρις, ζῆλος, θυμοί, ἐριθεῖαι, διχοστασίαι, αἱρέσεις, 21 φθόνοι, μέθαι, κῶμοι καὶ τὰ ὅμοια τούτοις, ἃ προλέγω ὑμῖν καθὼς προεῖπον ὅτι οἱ **τὰ τοιαῦτα πράσσοντες βασιλείαν θεοῦ οὐ κληρονομήσουσιν**.

*Now the works of the flesh are obvious: sexual immorality, moral impurity, promiscuity, 20 idolatry, sorcery, hatreds, strife, jealousy, outbursts of anger, selfish ambitions, dissensions, factions, 21 envy, drunkenness, carousing, and anything similar. I am warning you about these things—as I warned you before—**that those who practice such things will not inherit the kingdom of God**.*

While this vice list appears to present features that will disqualify someone from inheriting the kingdom of God, the deeper point is that those whose allegiance is to the flesh will not inherit the kingdom of God. This is made clear by the wider context, in which Paul contrasts the Spirit and the flesh as competing allegiances (5:16–18, 22–26; 6:7–8). The vice list is therefore representative of *the works of the flesh* (v. 19), and if practiced (πράσσω) they will disqualify their practitioners from the inheritance. Given that the deeper point is about allegiance, it follows that the *practice of such things* (v. 21) has more to do with an unrepentant lifestyle that is characterized by such vices rather than incidental—and consequently repented of—actions that believers might fall into on occasion.[10]

---

9. "Since the Galatians were born of the Spirit instead of the flesh, they were children of the Jerusalem above rather than of Hagar and were thereby children of the promise. Therefore, they are children of the free woman, belonging to the heavenly rather than the earthly Jerusalem" (Thomas R. Schreiner, *Galatians*, ZECNT [Grand Rapids: Zondervan, 2010], 306).

10. Since "God's reign or rule is moral in nature . . . those who consistently behave in ways that are opposed to God's nature (cf. 1 Cor 6:9f) show thereby that they have not accepted God's rule through Christ in their lives" (Ronald Y. K. Fung, *The Epistle to the Galatians*, NICNT [Grand Rapids: Eerdmans, 1998], 261–62).

Eph 1:11–14 ἐν ᾧ καὶ **ἐκληρώθημεν** προορισθέντες κατὰ πρόθεσιν τοῦ τὰ πάντα ἐνεργοῦντος κατὰ τὴν βουλὴν τοῦ θελήματος αὐτοῦ 12 εἰς τὸ εἶναι ἡμᾶς εἰς ἔπαινον δόξης αὐτοῦ τοὺς προηλπικότας ἐν τῷ Χριστῷ. 13 ἐν ᾧ καὶ ὑμεῖς ἀκούσαντες τὸν λόγον τῆς ἀληθείας, τὸ εὐαγγέλιον τῆς σωτηρίας ὑμῶν, ἐν ᾧ καὶ πιστεύσαντες ἐσφραγίσθητε τῷ πνεύματι τῆς ἐπαγγελίας τῷ ἁγίῳ, 14 **ὅ ἐστιν ἀρραβὼν τῆς κληρονομίας ἡμῶν,** εἰς ἀπολύτρωσιν τῆς περιποιήσεως, εἰς ἔπαινον τῆς δόξης αὐτοῦ.

*In him **we have** also **received an inheritance**, because we were predestined according to the plan of the one who works out everything in agreement with the purpose of his will, 12 so that we who had already put our hope in Christ might bring praise to his glory. 13 In him you also were sealed with the promised Holy Spirit when you heard the word of truth, the gospel of your salvation, and when you believed. 14* **The Holy Spirit is the down payment of our inheritance,** *until the redemption of the possession, to the praise of his glory.*

In Christ, believers receive an *inheritance*, having been predestined by God to hope in him (1:11–12). Upon belief in the gospel, believers are *sealed with the promised Holy Spirit* (v. 13), who is *the down payment of our inheritance* (v. 14a). The Spirit is therefore regarded as a sign of the future—as an installment of the future inheritance to come to believers. The nature of this inheritance is not specified, except that it seems to be equated with *the possession* that will be redeemed to the praise of his glory (v. 14b).

Both *inheritance* and *possession* terms evoke the promised land of Israel's history (e.g., Exod 32:13; Lev 20:24). While it is not developed here, no doubt this possession has been transfigured to refer to an eschatological, heavenly reality.[11] This expectation comes from the spiritual nature of the down payment of the inheritance—the Spirit himself. If the Spirit is the sign of future expectation, it follows that the inheritance is of a spiritual nature.

That point does not in itself preclude any physical component to the inheritance to come—after all, Paul hopes in the resurrection of the dead—but it will have a spiritual character. Indeed, the resurrection will hold the physical and spiritual together, as Paul elsewhere describes the resurrection body as a spiritual body (1 Cor 15:44).

---

11. Liefeld is correct to note that the inheritance and possession could also refer to believers themselves—they are God's inheritance and possession (Walter L. Liefeld, *Ephesians*, IVPNTC [Downers Grove, IL: InterVarsity Press, 1997], 47–48). Indeed, both concepts are found in the Hebrew Bible—Israel is regarded as God's inheritance (Deut 9:29; 32:9), and the promised land is given to Israel as an inheritance (Exod 32:13; Lev 20:24).

Eph 1:17–18 ἵνα ὁ θεὸς τοῦ κυρίου ἡμῶν Ἰησοῦ Χριστοῦ, ὁ πατὴρ τῆς δόξης, δώῃ ὑμῖν πνεῦμα σοφίας καὶ ἀποκαλύψεως ἐν ἐπιγνώσει αὐτοῦ, 18 πεφωτισμένους τοὺς ὀφθαλμοὺς τῆς καρδίας ὑμῶν εἰς τὸ εἰδέναι ὑμᾶς τίς ἐστιν ἡ ἐλπὶς τῆς κλήσεως αὐτοῦ, τίς **ὁ πλοῦτος τῆς δόξης τῆς κληρονομίας αὐτοῦ ἐν τοῖς ἁγίοις**

I pray that the God of our Lord Jesus Christ, the glorious Father, would give you the Spirit of wisdom and revelation in the knowledge of him. 18 I pray that the eyes of your heart may be enlightened so that you may know what is the hope of his calling, the **wealth of his glorious inheritance in the saints**

Having prayed that his readers would receive the Spirit of wisdom and revelation in the knowledge of God (1:17), Paul adds that they would know *what is the hope of his calling, what is the wealth of his glorious inheritance in the saints* (v. 18).

Again (cf. v. 14 above), the nature of this inheritance is not specified, except that it is *glorious* (τῆς δόξης) and it is *in the saints* (ἐν τοῖς ἁγίοις; v. 18). It is possible, however, to reread the phrase translated *the wealth of his glorious inheritance* as *the wealth of glory—his inheritance* (ὁ πλοῦτος τῆς δόξης τῆς κληρονομίας αὐτοῦ). Such a reading understands the genitives τῆς δόξης τῆς κληρονομίας in a different light, so that τῆς δόξης is taken as a genitive of content, thus describing the *wealth* ("the wealth that consists of glory").[12] Moreover, τῆς κληρονομίας would then be understood as appositional, so that it recounts this wealth of glory as *his inheritance*. If the text is understood this way, we gain more insight into the nature of his inheritance. It is, in a word, *glory*.

However, Greek genitives are notoriously slippery, and in this case there is no compelling reason to accept one reading over the other, except that the reading here proposed sheds more light on our subject of inquiry. But that alone does not add legitimate weight to the reading, and we must be open to accept the reading that is reflected in leading modern translations (e.g., CSB, ESV, NIV), taking τῆς δόξης as attributive, describing the inheritance (*his glorious inheritance*).[13]

Either way, we observe a connection between inheritance and glory. Either the inheritance *is* glory (as our suggested rendering would be understood), or the inheritance is *glorious*. The difference is one of *content* versus *quality*.

---

12. Larkin reads it as an attributed genitive, "rich glory" (William J. Larkin, *Ephesians: A Handbook on the Greek Text*, BHGNT [Waco, TX: Baylor University Press, 2009], 22).

13. So Benjamin L. Merkle, *Ephesians*, EGGNT (Nashville: B&H, 2016), 43.

Eph 3:4–6 πρὸς ὃ δύνασθε ἀναγινώσκοντες νοῆσαι τὴν σύνεσίν μου ἐν τῷ μυστηρίῳ τοῦ Χριστοῦ, 5 ὃ ἑτέραις γενεαῖς οὐκ ἐγνωρίσθη τοῖς υἱοῖς τῶν ἀνθρώπων ὡς νῦν ἀπεκαλύφθη τοῖς ἁγίοις ἀποστόλοις αὐτοῦ καὶ προφήταις ἐν πνεύματι, 6 εἶναι τὰ ἔθνη **συγκληρονόμα καὶ σύσσωμα καὶ συμμέτοχα τῆς ἐπαγγελίας ἐν Χριστῷ Ἰησοῦ διὰ τοῦ εὐαγγελίου**

By reading this you are able to understand my insight into the mystery of Christ. 5 This was not made known to people in other generations as it is now revealed to his holy apostles and prophets by the Spirit: 6 ***The Gentiles are coheirs, members of the same body, and partners in the promise in Christ Jesus through the gospel.***

Though hidden for generations, the mystery of Christ has now been revealed to the apostles and prophets by the Spirit (3:5)—the gentiles are coheirs with the Jews in the promise of the gospel of Christ (v. 6). The promise is *in Christ Jesus* (ἐν Χριστῷ Ἰησοῦ) and comes *through the gospel* (διὰ τοῦ εὐαγγελίου).

The promise is not articulated, but the language of *coheirs* provides the needed clue. If the Jews were regarded as heirs, it was the promise to Abraham that they inherited. By including gentiles as the inheritors of Abraham (cf. Rom 4:13),[14] the people of God are redefined so that the recipients of the promise are also the object of the promise. That is, part of the promise to Abraham was that he would become a blessing to many nations. By the gentiles coming into his family, they have become blessed and so fulfill the promise while also inheriting it.

This of course can only occur *in Christ*, since faith in Christ equalizes the entry requirements—both Jews and gentiles who believe become partners together in the promise through the gospel.

Eph 5:1–6 γίνεσθε οὖν μιμηταὶ τοῦ θεοῦ ὡς τέκνα ἀγαπητὰ 2 καὶ περιπατεῖτε ἐν ἀγάπῃ, καθὼς καὶ ὁ Χριστὸς ἠγάπησεν ἡμᾶς καὶ παρέδωκεν ἑαυτὸν ὑπὲρ ἡμῶν προσφορὰν καὶ θυσίαν τῷ θεῷ εἰς ὀσμὴν εὐωδίας. 3 πορνεία δὲ καὶ ἀκαθαρσία πᾶσα ἢ πλεονεξία μηδὲ ὀνομαζέσθω ἐν ὑμῖν, καθὼς πρέπει ἁγίοις, 4 καὶ αἰσχρότης καὶ μωρολογία ἢ εὐτραπελία, ἃ οὐκ ἀνῆκεν, ἀλλὰ μᾶλλον εὐχαριστία. 5 τοῦτο γὰρ ἴστε γινώσκοντες, ὅτι **πᾶς πόρνος ἢ ἀκάθαρτος ἢ πλεονέκτης, ὅ ἐστιν εἰδωλολάτρης, οὐκ ἔχει κληρονομίαν ἐν τῇ βασιλείᾳ τοῦ Χριστοῦ καὶ θεοῦ.** 6 Μηδεὶς ὑμᾶς ἀπατάτω κενοῖς λόγοις· διὰ ταῦτα γὰρ ἔρχεται ἡ ὀργὴ τοῦ θεοῦ ἐπὶ τοὺς υἱοὺς τῆς ἀπειθείας.

---

14. John Muddiman, *The Epistle to the Ephesians*, BNTC (Peabody, MA: Hendrickson, 2004), 155.

> *Therefore, be imitators of God, as dearly loved children, 2 and walk in love, as Christ also loved us and gave himself for us, a sacrificial and fragrant offering to God. 3 But sexual immorality and any impurity or greed should not even be heard of among you, as is proper for saints. 4 Obscene and foolish talking or crude joking are not suitable, but rather giving thanks. 5 For know and recognize this:* **Every sexually immoral or impure or greedy person, who is an idolater, does not have an inheritance in the kingdom of Christ and of God.** *6 Let no one deceive you with empty arguments, for God's wrath is coming on the disobedient because of these things.*

The text begins with exhortation grounded in a *family* ethic—the *dearly loved children* are to be imitators of God, their heavenly Father (5:1). This is followed by further imitation—this time of Christ's example of sacrificial love (v. 2). Then comes exhortations against sexual immorality, impurity, greed, and obscene, foolish, and crude talk (5:3–4). This is followed by the warning that *every sexually immoral or impure or greedy person . . . does not have an inheritance in the kingdom of Christ and of God* (v. 5). God's wrath is coming *because of these things* (v. 6).

The language of inheritance relates back to the beginning of the passage, where believers are addressed as God's children. As God's children, they are expected to live a certain way. If they do not, Paul implies, they do not really belong to the family of God.[15] This is why they will not share in an inheritance in the kingdom. Only legitimate children are heirs.

This reading is further underscored by the phrase translated *God's wrath is coming on the disobedient because of these things* (v. 6). Literally, God's wrath is coming *on the sons of disobedience* (see CSB footnote; τοὺς υἱοὺς τῆς ἀπειθείας). Such phrasing is not incidental. The heart of the issue is to whom do these children belong? Are they God's beloved children, or are they *sons of disobedience*? The children (τέκνα) and sons (υἱούς) language reveals that the real question is one of allegiance. And one's ultimate allegiance will be expressed by a person's conduct and behavior.

> Col 1:10–14 περιπατῆσαι ἀξίως τοῦ κυρίου εἰς πᾶσαν ἀρεσκείαν, ἐν παντὶ ἔργῳ ἀγαθῷ καρποφοροῦντες καὶ αὐξανόμενοι τῇ ἐπιγνώσει τοῦ θεοῦ, 11 ἐν πάσῃ δυνάμει δυναμούμενοι κατὰ τὸ κράτος τῆς δόξης αὐτοῦ εἰς πᾶσαν ὑπομονὴν καὶ μακροθυμίαν. μετὰ χαρᾶς 12 **εὐχαριστοῦντες τῷ πατρὶ τῷ ἱκανώσαντι ὑμᾶς εἰς τὴν μερίδα τοῦ κλήρου τῶν ἁγίων ἐν τῷ φωτί·**

---

15. John Paul Heil, *Ephesians: Empowerment to Walk in Love for the Unity of All in Christ* (Atlanta: SBL Press, 2007), 213.

13 ὃς ἐρρύσατο ἡμᾶς ἐκ τῆς ἐξουσίας τοῦ σκότους καὶ μετέστησεν εἰς τὴν βασιλείαν τοῦ υἱοῦ τῆς ἀγάπης αὐτοῦ, 14 ἐν ᾧ ἔχομεν τὴν ἀπολύτρωσιν, τὴν ἄφεσιν τῶν ἁμαρτιῶν·

... so that you may walk worthy of the Lord, fully pleasing to him: bearing fruit in every good work and growing in the knowledge of God, 11 being strengthened with all power, according to his glorious might, so that you may have great endurance and patience, joyfully 12 **giving thanks to the Father, who has enabled you to share in the saints' inheritance in the light**. *13 He has rescued us from the domain of darkness and transferred us into the kingdom of the Son he loves. 14 In him we have redemption, the forgiveness of sins.*

Paul prays that the Colossians might be filled with the knowledge of God's will (v. 9) so that they might walk in a manner worthy of the Lord (v. 10). This walking involves endurance and patience (v. 11) and joyfully giving thanks to the Father (v. 12). The thanksgiving is specifically tied to the Father's enabling believers *to share in the saint's inheritance in the light* (v. 12).

The inheritance in the light is contrasted with *the domain of darkness*, from which God has rescued believers (v. 13a). This domain of darkness is in turn contrasted with *the kingdom of the Son* into which they have been transferred (v. 13b). This series of contrasts sheds some light (so to speak) on the *inheritance in the light*. As I have indicated elsewhere, "Realm transfer is clearly in view here, with believers transferred from the domain of darkness into Christ's kingdom."[16] The notion of realm transfer is further underscored by the reference to *redemption* in v. 14, which indicates liberation from imprisonment into freedom.

Realm transfer is, for Paul, a spiritual reality concerning allegiance and authority. These competing realms do not have physical borders or locations; they are determined by who and what exercise authority over others. Obviously, then, the term *the domain of darkness* uses *darkness* as a metaphorical adjective rather than naming the person or thing of authority. In other words, *darkness* is not literally the ruling power in this domain. Rather, this domain is characterized by spiritual darkness, being ruled by evil powers set against Christ.[17] *The kingdom of the Son*, however, indicates directly the ruler who has authority over this domain—the Son of God. Whoever sits under his authority is located in his realm.

This leaves remaining the question of the most likely reading of *the inheritance in the light* (v. 12). Given the understanding of *the domain of darkness* outlined

---

16. Campbell, *Paul and Union with Christ*, 195.
17. McKnight, *Colossians*, 126.

above, it is natural to understand *in the light* in a similar, metaphorical, and adjectival way. The light is "spiritual" rather than physical, as is the darkness. Given the strong parallel between light and darkness, we are forced to ask whether *the inheritance* is to be understood against *the domain (of darkness)* too. That is, does the term *the inheritance* indicate a domain, opposite to *the domain of darkness*?

This does indeed seem to offer the most likely reading. *The saints' inheritance in the light* is a domain of light set in opposition to *the domain of darkness*. If this is correct, it is therefore equivalent to *the kingdom of the Son* (v. 13b). The inheritance is the kingdom of the Son of God.

One element has so far been ignored. This is the language of *the saints* (v. 12). Does this modifier (τῶν ἁγίων) affect our understanding of the inheritance? It ought to, yes. Whether τῶν ἁγίων refers to Jewish believers (as some have suggested),[18] or to Jewish and gentile believers, the heritage of the term no doubt is rooted in Israel's identity as a people set apart and holy for the Lord. This then reminds us of the same heritage of the *inheritance* term, which originally referred to the promised land of Canaan promised to Abraham.

Putting these two things together, then, we see that *the saints' inheritance in the light* is a new-covenant parallel to the promised land of Canaan.[19] But it is not a physical, geographical entity (as argued above); instead, this inheritance is a spiritual domain and realm that is now regarded as the new "promised land." And participation in this inheritance of the saints is made possible by *the Father, who has enabled you* (τῷ πατρὶ τῷ ἱκανώσαντι ὑμᾶς) to share in it (v. 12).

Col 3:22–25 Οἱ δοῦλοι, ὑπακούετε κατὰ πάντα τοῖς κατὰ σάρκα κυρίοις, μὴ ἐν ὀφθαλμοδουλίᾳ ὡς ἀνθρωπάρεσκοι, ἀλλ᾽ ἐν ἁπλότητι καρδίας φοβούμενοι τὸν κύριον. 23 ὃ ἐὰν ποιῆτε, ἐκ ψυχῆς ἐργάζεσθε ὡς τῷ κυρίῳ καὶ οὐκ ἀνθρώποις, 24 εἰδότες ὅτι **ἀπὸ κυρίου ἀπολήμψεσθε τὴν ἀνταπόδοσιν τῆς κληρονομίας**. τῷ κυρίῳ Χριστῷ δουλεύετε· 25 ὁ γὰρ ἀδικῶν κομίσεται ὃ ἠδίκησεν, καὶ οὐκ ἔστιν προσωπολημψία.

*Slaves, obey your human masters in everything. Don't work only while being watched, as people-pleasers, but work wholeheartedly, fearing the Lord. 23 Whatever you do, do it from the heart, as something done for the Lord and not for people, 24 knowing that **you will receive the reward of an inheritance***

---

18. D. W. B. Robinson, "Who Were 'The Saints'?," in *Donald Robinson: Selected Works, Volume I—Assembling God's People*, ed. Peter G. Bolt and Mark D. Thompson (Camperdown: Australian Church Record, 2008), 160–69.

19. John Woodhouse, *Colossians and Philemon: So Walk in Him*, FBC (Fearn: Christian Focus, 2011), 48–49.

from the Lord. *You serve the Lord Christ. 25 For the wrongdoer will be paid back for whatever wrong he has done, and there is no favoritism.*

Since the household code of Colossians 3:18–4:1 is quite truncated compared to its more expansive sister, Ephesians 5:22–6:9, it is striking how much space is given to address slaves. And it is even more striking that, of all parties addressed in the household code, it is only with reference to slaves that *an inheritance from the Lord* is mentioned (Col 3:24).

Both features are probably best explained by the fact that slaves have the worst deal in the household code. They are required to obey their human masters in everything (v. 22a), whether being watched or not, and wholeheartedly out of fear of the Lord (v. 22b). They were not paid, they could not inherit property,[20] they were not free, and they were often mistreated—though Paul seeks their protection in at least that respect when he instructs masters to *deal with your slaves justly and fairly* (4:1).

Since slaves by definition were not remunerated, it is no accident that they alone are encouraged by the promise that they *will receive the reward of an inheritance from the Lord* (3:24a). Since they *serve the Lord Christ* (v. 24b), working *for the Lord and not for people* (v. 23), it is appropriate that slaves are "remunerated" by him. Their future inheritance from the Lord is the "payment" that slaves may joyfully anticipate.

Another element of the inheritance language is striking here. Inheritances are family matters. And though slaves are members of the household, they are not family. Indeed, household slaves exist to *serve* the family. It is thus especially striking that they alone are encouraged by the promise of an inheritance from the Lord. As inheritors, they are regarded as members of the family of Christ.

Titus 3:4–7 ὅτε δὲ ἡ χρηστότης καὶ ἡ φιλανθρωπία ἐπεφάνη
τοῦ σωτῆρος ἡμῶν θεοῦ,
5 οὐκ ἐξ ἔργων τῶν ἐν δικαιοσύνῃ
ἃ ἐποιήσαμεν ἡμεῖς
ἀλλὰ κατὰ τὸ αὐτοῦ ἔλεος
ἔσωσεν ἡμᾶς διὰ λουτροῦ παλιγγενεσίας
καὶ ἀνακαινώσεως πνεύματος ἁγίου,
6 οὗ ἐξέχεεν ἐφ' ἡμᾶς πλουσίως
διὰ Ἰησοῦ Χριστοῦ τοῦ σωτῆρος ἡμῶν,

---

20. N. T. Wright, *The Epistles of Paul to the Colossians and to Philemon*, TNTC (Leicester: Inter-Varsity Press, 1986), 150.

> 7 ἵνα δικαιωθέντες τῇ ἐκείνου χάριτι
> κληρονόμοι γενηθῶμεν κατ' ἐλπίδα ζωῆς αἰωνίου.

*But when the kindness of God our Savior and his love for mankind appeared, 5 he saved us— not by works of righteousness that we had done, but according to his mercy—through the washing of regeneration and renewal by the Holy Spirit. 6 He poured out his Spirit on us abundantly through Jesus Christ our Savior 7 so that, **having been justified by his grace, we may become heirs with the hope of eternal life**.*

Having established that salvation is accomplished not by human works but through the regeneration and renewal of the Spirit (παλιγγενεσίας καὶ ἀνακαινώσεως πνεύματος ἁγίου; 3:4–5), Paul focuses on the gift of the Spirit in the next two verses (vv. 6–7): the Spirit has been poured out through Christ *so that . . . we may become heirs with the hope of eternal life.*

The Spirit works in concert with the grace of God to secure the status of heir for believers. They have *been justified by his grace* (δικαιωθέντες τῇ ἐκείνου χάριτι; v. 7a), which appears to pave the way for the Spirit's pouring out. And it is the pouring out of the Spirit that is explicitly connected to the status of the believer as an heir. God poured out his Spirit through Christ so that believers may become heirs.

If we are to ask exactly how the Spirit enables believers to become heirs, the answer is probably found in 3:5—*through the washing of regeneration and renewal by the Holy Spirit*. While this is directly connected to the salvation wrought by *God our Savior* (3:4–5), there is also an implicit connection with the function of the Spirit to enable heir-status. Indeed, for Paul salvation and inheritance are no doubt two sides of the same coin; the former is rescue from a treacherous situation, while the latter is blessing conferred upon those who are saved. The regeneration wrought by the Spirit is the means by which believers are both saved and conferred with heir-status.

Heir-status is qualified by the phrase translated *with the hope of eternal life*. Literally, the text says *that we might become heirs according to the hope of eternal life* (κληρονόμοι γενηθῶμεν κατ' ἐλπίδα ζωῆς αἰωνίου; 3:7). Heir-status is *according* to this hope. What exactly *according to* (κατά) means here is uncertain. Most likely, its use is best captured by the category listed by BDAG: "Denoting relationship to someth., *with respect to, in relation to*,"[21] though this is not the only possibility. In any case, understood this way, the phrase means something

---

21. BDAG 513, §6.

like, *that we may become heirs with respect to the hope of eternal life*. That is, the inheritance to which heirs are entitled is nothing less than the hope of eternal life.

9.3 Summary

Paul's understanding of inheritance begins with Abraham's inheritance, who is promised that he and his descendants would inherit the world (Rom 4:13–15; Gal 3:14–18). Paul argues that Abraham's true descendants are those who share his faith in God, whether Jew or gentile (Eph 3:6). Those with the faith of Abraham become God's children, and as children they are heirs of God and coheirs with Christ (Rom 8:14–17; Gal 3:26–4:7). The Spirit serves as the down payment of believers' inheritance (Eph 1:13–14).

While the children of God are led by God's Spirit (Rom 8:14; Gal 4:6), the unrighteous will not inherit God's kingdom unless they are washed, sanctified, and justified in the name of Christ (1 Cor 6:9–11; Gal 5:19–21; Eph 5:5; Titus 3:7). Additionally, flesh and blood cannot inherit the kingdom of God, which means that reception of the inheritance depends on the resurrection of believers to incorruptible, glorious, and immortal bodies (1 Cor 15:50–53).

The anticipation of sharing in the inheritance of Abraham enables believers to reframe their activities in this life, especially in relation to work. Slaves, who by definition receive no remuneration for their work, may take comfort in their share in the inheritance from the Lord since they ultimately serve the Lord Christ (Col 3:22–24).

It is not entirely clear what the promised inheritance actually *is*. On the one hand, it seems to be the *world*, since that is what was promised to Abraham (cf. Rom 4:13). But on the other hand, it seems to be the kingdom of God. Perhaps the answer is that the world will one day *be* the kingdom of God.

CHAPTER 10

NEW CREATION

10.1 INTRODUCTION

This chapter explores the role and fate of creation in the eschaton. Paul's eschatological vision includes the full sweep of creation, as all things in heaven and on earth will be renewed and centered around Christ. There is an inextricable link between the fate of humanity and that of creation, with the latter being subjected to decay because of the former, and it will only be released from its bondage once humanity has been restored.

It is clear that, while creation is the arena in which God works for the salvation and glorification of humanity, it is not merely the arena for such activity—it is, in fact, the object of it, as God will restore, renew, and re-center the creation in concert with humanity.

10.2 NEW-CREATION TEXTS

Rom 8:18–25 Λογίζομαι γὰρ ὅτι οὐκ ἄξια τὰ παθήματα τοῦ νῦν καιροῦ πρὸς τὴν μέλλουσαν δόξαν ἀποκαλυφθῆναι εἰς ἡμᾶς. 19 **ἡ γὰρ ἀποκαραδοκία τῆς κτίσεως τὴν ἀποκάλυψιν τῶν υἱῶν τοῦ θεοῦ ἀπεκδέχεται.** 20 τῇ γὰρ ματαιότητι ἡ κτίσις ὑπετάγη, οὐχ ἑκοῦσα ἀλλὰ διὰ τὸν ὑποτάξαντα, ἐφ᾽ ἐλπίδι 21 ὅτι καὶ αὐτὴ **ἡ κτίσις ἐλευθερωθήσεται ἀπὸ τῆς δουλείας τῆς φθορᾶς εἰς τὴν ἐλευθερίαν τῆς δόξης τῶν τέκνων τοῦ θεοῦ.** 22 οἴδαμεν γὰρ ὅτι **πᾶσα ἡ κτίσις συστενάζει καὶ συνωδίνει ἄχρι τοῦ νῦν·** 23 οὐ μόνον δέ, ἀλλὰ καὶ αὐτοὶ τὴν ἀπαρχὴν τοῦ πνεύματος ἔχοντες, ἡμεῖς καὶ αὐτοὶ ἐν ἑαυτοῖς στενάζομεν υἱοθεσίαν ἀπεκδεχόμενοι, τὴν ἀπολύτρωσιν τοῦ σώματος ἡμῶν. 24 τῇ γὰρ ἐλπίδι ἐσώθημεν· ἐλπὶς δὲ βλεπομένη οὐκ ἔστιν ἐλπίς· ὃ γὰρ βλέπει τίς ἐλπίζει; 25 εἰ δὲ ὃ οὐ βλέπομεν ἐλπίζομεν, δι᾽ ὑπομονῆς ἀπεκδεχόμεθα.

For I consider that the sufferings of this present time are not worth comparing with the glory that is going to be revealed to us. 19 **For the creation eagerly waits with anticipation for God's sons to be revealed.** *20 For the creation* *was subjected to futility—not willingly, but because of him who subjected it—in the hope 21 that **the creation itself will also be set free from the bondage to decay into the glorious freedom of God's children**. 22 For we know that **the whole creation has been groaning together with labor pains until now**. 23 Not only that, but we ourselves who have the Spirit as the firstfruits—we also groan within ourselves, eagerly waiting for adoption, the redemption of our bodies. 24 Now in this hope we were saved, but hope that is seen is not hope, because who hopes for what he sees? 25 Now if we hope for what we do not see, we eagerly wait for it with patience.*

This is an extremely important text for understanding Paul's view of creation and new creation—or, perhaps better, the renewal of creation.[1] He begins by discussing *glory* in 8:18, which is going *to be revealed to us* (on this, see §12.2 below). The glorious destiny of human beings is tied to the rest of creation, which *waits with anticipation for God's sons to be revealed* (v. 19). Because of the fall of humanity, creation *was subjected to futility* (v. 20) in the hope that it would *be set free from the bondage to decay* in relation to *the glorious freedom of God's children* (v. 21). That is, creation has been suffering as a result of humanity's fall, and it will be restored from bondage in concert with God's children. In this respect, creation's *groaning* is likened to that of *labor pains* as it eagerly awaits the arrival of the promised children of God.

By implication the renewed creation will be the arena that the promised children of God will inhabit with their redeemed bodies. It seems that resurrected human beings will require a renewed creation in which to live. Whatever part of creation Paul envisages here (e.g., the earth, the heavens), it seems clear that resurrected people will remain in the arena of creation. They will not somehow supersede the created realm. Instead, their renewed creaturely status will be matched by the renewed creation.

There is no hint here that Paul imagines that the "old" creation will pass away in favor of a "new" creation. The passage clearly depicts a "single" creation that is currently subjected to futility but that will be set free from bondage in the future.

2 Cor 5:16–17 Ὥστε ἡμεῖς ἀπὸ τοῦ νῦν οὐδένα οἴδαμεν κατὰ σάρκα· εἰ καὶ ἐγνώκαμεν κατὰ σάρκα Χριστόν, ἀλλὰ νῦν οὐκέτι γινώσκομεν. 17 **ὥστε εἴ τις ἐν Χριστῷ, καινὴ κτίσις**· τὰ ἀρχαῖα παρῆλθεν, ἰδοὺ γέγονεν καινά.

---

1. According to Cranfield, "creation" (κτίσις) here most likely refers "to the sum-total of sub-human nature both animate and inanimate" (Cranfield, *Romans*, 1:411–12). See also Richard N. Longenecker, *The Epistle to the Romans: A Commentary on the Greek Text*, NIGTC (Grand Rapids: Eerdmans, 2016), 719–23, for a summary of the key interpretations of κτίσις and his ultimate agreement with Cranfield.

> *From now on, then, we do not know anyone from a worldly perspective. Even if we have known Christ from a worldly perspective, yet now we no longer know him in this way. 17* **Therefore, if anyone is in Christ, he is a new creation; the old has passed away, and see, the new has come!**

The new creation here is, of course, the person *in Christ*—not the whole created realm, but a member within it.² Rather than regard *anyone from a worldly perspective* (5:16a), Paul sees anyone who is *in Christ* (ἐν Χριστῷ) as *a new creation* (v. 17a). This apparently means that *the old has passed away*, while *the new has come* (v. 17b).

The language of *new creation* evokes the sense of a contrast of realms, in that the person in Christ now belongs under the realm of Christ.³ This is how they are regarded as a new creation—being under the realm of Christ changes who they are, their allegiances, and their purpose for living.

Gal 6:14–16 ἐμοὶ δὲ μὴ γένοιτο καυχᾶσθαι εἰ μὴ ἐν τῷ σταυρῷ τοῦ κυρίου ἡμῶν Ἰησοῦ Χριστοῦ, δι' οὗ ἐμοὶ κόσμος ἐσταύρωται κἀγὼ κόσμῳ. 15 **οὔτε γὰρ περιτομή τί ἐστιν οὔτε ἀκροβυστία ἀλλὰ καινὴ κτίσις.** 16 καὶ ὅσοι τῷ κανόνι τούτῳ στοιχήσουσιν, εἰρήνη ἐπ' αὐτοὺς καὶ ἔλεος καὶ ἐπὶ τὸν Ἰσραὴλ τοῦ θεοῦ.

> *But as for me, I will never boast about anything except the cross of our Lord Jesus Christ. The world has been crucified to me through the cross, and I to the world. 15* **For both circumcision and uncircumcision mean nothing; what matters instead is a new creation.** *16 May peace come to all those who follow this standard, and mercy even to the Israel of God!*

Regarding the issue of circumcision and uncircumcision, neither status means anything in light of the cross of Christ. Paul will certainly *never boast about anything* apart from the cross (6:14) because any fleshly boast or status is made irrelevant by it. What matters instead *is a new creation* (v. 15). This is the *standard* that is to be followed by all who desire peace, even for *the Israel of God* (v. 16). Paul does not elaborate on the meaning of this *new creation*,⁴

---

2. For more on Paul's *new creation* language, and especially its connection to Second Temple literature, see §16.17.1 below.

3. Campbell, *Paul and Union with Christ*, 117.

4. Cole notes that "the word is probably to be translated 'creature' (as in AV), rather than 'creation'. That is to say, the reference is to the regenerating work of God in the individual Christian rather than to the total cosmic result thus secured" (R. Alan Cole, *The Letter of Paul to the Galatians*, rev. ed., TNTC [Leicester: Inter-Varsity Press, 1989], 235). Cole is correct about this translational possibility and to point to the regenerating

but he clearly refers to the person who, like him, has been crucified to the world (v. 14). The notion of being raised with Christ is not mentioned here, but such a concept is more or less implied by the new-creation language. The old has been crucified with Christ already. The person who is raised with Christ is therefore a new person and a new entity. Or, as Paul puts it, *a new creation*.

Eph 1:9–12 γνωρίσας ἡμῖν τὸ μυστήριον τοῦ θελήματος αὐτοῦ, κατὰ τὴν εὐδοκίαν αὐτοῦ ἣν προέθετο ἐν αὐτῷ 10 εἰς οἰκονομίαν τοῦ πληρώματος τῶν καιρῶν, **ἀνακεφαλαιώσασθαι τὰ πάντα ἐν τῷ Χριστῷ, τὰ ἐπὶ τοῖς οὐρανοῖς καὶ τὰ ἐπὶ τῆς γῆς ἐν αὐτῷ**. 11 ἐν ᾧ καὶ ἐκληρώθημεν προορισθέντες κατὰ πρόθεσιν τοῦ τὰ πάντα ἐνεργοῦντος κατὰ τὴν βουλὴν τοῦ θελήματος αὐτοῦ 12 εἰς τὸ εἶναι ἡμᾶς εἰς ἔπαινον δόξης αὐτοῦ τοὺς προηλπικότας ἐν τῷ Χριστῷ.

*He made known to us the mystery of his will, according to his good pleasure that he purposed in Christ 10 as a plan for the right time—***to bring everything together in Christ, both things in heaven and things on earth in him***. 11 In him we have also received an inheritance, because we were predestined according to the plan of the one who works out everything in agreement with the purpose of his will, 12 so that we who had already put our hope in Christ might bring praise to his glory.*

While the language of new creation is not found in this text, the created realm is in view as everything is brought together in Christ, *both things in heaven and things on earth* (1:10). We do not observe a replacement of an "old" creation with a new one but rather the existing creation is unified, or "summed up" (ἀνακεφαλαιόω) in Christ.[5] In this sense, the creation is renewed by virtue of its realignment to Christ.

It is within the context of this renewed, united creation that those predestined according to God's purpose will enjoy their inheritance (1:11). And this in turn leads those who hope in Christ to *bring praise to his glory* (v. 12; on this, see §12.2 below). Thus we see that the eschatological blessings of inheritance and the eschatological goal of glory are set in the arena of the united creation that finds its recapitulation in Christ.

---

work of God in the individual. However, "creation" is nevertheless preferred because it relates the individual to the wider cosmic regenerative work of God. See further on this at §16.17.1 below.

5. For Schnackenburg, this involves the unification of heavenly and earthly spheres: "When the author speaks in 1.10 instead about the 'unification' in Christ of a universe till now strife-torn, he elevates the idea to a cosmic level; in the view of Eph. the supernatural, spiritual 'principalities and powers' which live and work 'in the heavenliness' (cf. 3.10; 6.12) are also part of the universe" (Rudolph Schnackenburg, *Ephesians: A Commentary*, trans. Helen Heron [Edinburgh: T&T Clark, 1991], 60).

Eph 2:1–10 Καὶ ὑμᾶς ὄντας νεκροὺς τοῖς παραπτώμασιν καὶ ταῖς ἁμαρτίαις ὑμῶν, 2 ἐν αἷς ποτε περιεπατήσατε κατὰ τὸν αἰῶνα τοῦ κόσμου τούτου, κατὰ τὸν ἄρχοντα τῆς ἐξουσίας τοῦ ἀέρος, τοῦ πνεύματος τοῦ νῦν ἐνεργοῦντος ἐν τοῖς υἱοῖς τῆς ἀπειθείας· 3 ἐν οἷς καὶ ἡμεῖς πάντες ἀνεστράφημέν ποτε ἐν ταῖς ἐπιθυμίαις τῆς σαρκὸς ἡμῶν ποιοῦντες τὰ θελήματα τῆς σαρκὸς καὶ τῶν διανοιῶν, καὶ ἤμεθα τέκνα φύσει ὀργῆς ὡς καὶ οἱ λοιποί· 4 ὁ δὲ θεὸς πλούσιος ὢν ἐν ἐλέει, διὰ τὴν πολλὴν ἀγάπην αὐτοῦ ἣν ἠγάπησεν ἡμᾶς, 5 καὶ ὄντας ἡμᾶς νεκροὺς τοῖς παραπτώμασιν συνεζωοποίησεν τῷ Χριστῷ,–χάριτί ἐστε σεσῳσμένοι– 6 καὶ συνήγειρεν καὶ συνεκάθισεν ἐν τοῖς ἐπουρανίοις ἐν Χριστῷ Ἰησοῦ, 7 ἵνα ἐνδείξηται ἐν τοῖς αἰῶσιν τοῖς ἐπερχομένοις τὸ ὑπερβάλλον πλοῦτος τῆς χάριτος αὐτοῦ ἐν χρηστότητι ἐφ' ἡμᾶς ἐν Χριστῷ Ἰησοῦ. 8 τῇ γὰρ χάριτί ἐστε σεσῳσμένοι διὰ πίστεως· καὶ τοῦτο οὐκ ἐξ ὑμῶν, θεοῦ τὸ δῶρον· 9 οὐκ ἐξ ἔργων, ἵνα μή τις καυχήσηται. 10 **αὐτοῦ γάρ ἐσμεν ποίημα, κτισθέντες ἐν Χριστῷ Ἰησοῦ ἐπὶ ἔργοις ἀγαθοῖς οἷς προητοίμασεν ὁ θεός**, ἵνα ἐν αὐτοῖς περιπατήσωμεν.

And you were dead in your trespasses and sins 2 in which you previously lived according to the ways of this world, according to the ruler of the power of the air, the spirit now working in the disobedient. 3 We too all previously lived among them in our fleshly desires, carrying out the inclinations of our flesh and thoughts, and we were by nature children under wrath as the others were also. 4 But God, who is rich in mercy, because of his great love that he had for us, 5 made us alive with Christ even though we were dead in trespasses. You are saved by grace! 6 He also raised us up with him and seated us with him in the heavens in Christ Jesus, 7 so that in the coming ages he might display the immeasurable riches of his grace through his kindness to us in Christ Jesus. 8 For you are saved by grace through faith, and this is not from yourselves; it is God's gift—9 not from works, so that no one can boast. 10 ***For we are his workmanship, created in Christ Jesus for good works****, which God prepared ahead of time for us to do.*

The element of new creation in this text is found at its end, referring to those who have been saved by grace through faith—*we are his workmanship, created in Christ Jesus for good works* (2:10a). People who have been saved by grace through faith are regarded as God's *workmanship*, or his "product" (ποίημα), having been *created in Christ Jesus.*

But the notion of new creation has been brewing since the beginning of the passage, where Paul describes people as *dead in your trespasses and sins* (2:1). These humans were spiritually dead, but God *made us alive with Christ* (v. 5).

Thus, the transformation in view is not one of reformation but of spiritual resurrection. In this sense, the old person who was dead has been given new life, but no longer as that old person. Instead he or she is a new creation in Christ.

Moreover, such a new creation is brought about by God's work. This is plainly stated—*we are his workmanship* (v. 10a)—but it is also woven throughout the passage. It is God who gives life to the spiritually dead (v. 5); he raised them up with Christ (v. 6a) and seated them in the heavens with him (v. 6b). Because of these actions, Paul must insist that *you are saved by grace through faith, and this is not from yourselves; it is God's gift* (v. 8). The argument of the whole passage leads inexorably to such a conclusion, since the spiritually dead are not able to save themselves. Only God has acted to bring about their spiritual resurrection.

All of this underscores the nature of the new creation: it is achieved by God's grace and crafted by his workmanship. But those who have been created in Christ Jesus have been fashioned *for good works* (v.10a). Though Paul carefully avoids the notion that their works might contribute to their salvation (vv. 8–9), he then insists on the right place for works in the life of the new creation.[6] Good works have been prepared by God *for us to do* (v. 10b)—or, literally, "for us to walk in" (ἵνα ἐν αὐτοῖς περιπατήσωμεν).

This walking imagery parallels the beginning of the passage in which the spiritually dead *lived* [lit., "walked"] *according to the ways of this world* (περιεπατήσατε κατὰ τὸν αἰῶνα τοῦ κόσμου τούτου). The rhetorical effect of this parallelism is to show that the "walking dead" have been re-created to be the "walking living," no longer slavishly following the ways of the world but now walking in the good deeds that God has prepared. This also underscores the nature of the new creation: while it is achieved by God's grace and crafted by his workmanship, it is oriented to a new way of living and serving.

This new creation is also oriented toward the future, as revealed in 2:7: *So that in the coming ages he might display the immeasurable riches of his grace through his kindness to us in Christ Jesus.* While this verse is sometimes passed over as less significant for the overall argument of the passage, it could be argued that it is, in fact, its high point. Being saved by grace is not the ultimate good here, nor is walking according to good deeds. Rather, being fit to participate *in the coming ages*, and witnessing *the immeasurable riches* of God's grace, is the ultimate good. This is the true high point of the passage and the ultimate end to which all those who have been saved by grace are destined.

---

6. "While still living in the present evil age (1:21) and enduring evil days (5:16; 6:13), in the midst of ravaging powers (2:2, 7; 6:12), they are yet made a shining light to signal the dawn of a new heaven and a new earth" (Markus Barth, *Ephesians: Introduction, Translation, and Commentary on Chapters 1–3*, AB [Garden City, NJ: Doubleday, 1974], 243).

Col 1:15–20 ὅς ἐστιν εἰκὼν τοῦ θεοῦ τοῦ ἀοράτου,
πρωτότοκος πάσης κτίσεως,
16 ὅτι ἐν αὐτῷ ἐκτίσθη τὰ πάντα
ἐν τοῖς οὐρανοῖς καὶ ἐπὶ τῆς γῆς,
τὰ ὁρατὰ καὶ τὰ ἀόρατα,
εἴτε θρόνοι εἴτε κυριότητες
εἴτε ἀρχαὶ εἴτε ἐξουσίαι·
τὰ πάντα δι' αὐτοῦ καὶ εἰς αὐτὸν ἔκτισται·
17 καὶ αὐτός ἐστιν πρὸ πάντων
καὶ τὰ πάντα ἐν αὐτῷ συνέστηκεν,
18 καὶ αὐτός ἐστιν ἡ κεφαλὴ τοῦ σώματος τῆς ἐκκλησίας·
ὅς ἐστιν ἀρχή,
πρωτότοκος ἐκ τῶν νεκρῶν,
ἵνα γένηται ἐν πᾶσιν αὐτὸς πρωτεύων,
19 ὅτι ἐν αὐτῷ εὐδόκησεν πᾶν τὸ πλήρωμα κατοικῆσαι
20 καὶ δι' αὐτοῦ ἀποκαταλλάξαι τὰ πάντα εἰς αὐτόν,
εἰρηνοποιήσας διὰ τοῦ αἵματος τοῦ σταυροῦ αὐτοῦ,
εἴτε τὰ ἐπὶ τῆς γῆς
εἴτε τὰ ἐν τοῖς οὐρανοῖς.

He is the image of the invisible God,
the firstborn over all creation.
16 For everything was created by him,
in heaven and on earth,
the visible and the invisible,
whether thrones or dominions
or rulers or authorities—
all things have been created through him and for him.
17 He is before all things,
and by him all things hold together.
18 He is also the head of the body, the church;
he is the beginning,
the firstborn from the dead,
so that he might come to have
first place in everything.
19 For God was pleased to have
all his fullness dwell in him,
20 and through him to reconcile
everything to himself,

> *whether things on earth or things in heaven,*
> *by making peace*
> *through his blood, shed on the cross.*

A key passage regarding the relationship of Christ to the created order, we observe his preeminence over it as its creator (1:16), sustainer (v. 17), and as its *telos* (v. 16). There is clearly an intimate and intricate connection between creator and creation that characterizes the nature of creation from its beginning into the future.

Here we do not see two created orders—an "old" creation waiting to be replaced by a superior, new creation—but rather a renewed creation is envisaged through the lens of reconciliation. Everything was created by him (v. 16), and everything is reconciled through him—*whether things on earth or things in heaven* (v. 20). The renewal of the created order is, then, one of reunification, reconciliation, and peace-making through the blood of Christ shed on the cross. Thus the "new" created order is a better version of the old, but it is not discontinuous from it. There is no sense in which one is scrapped and replaced with the other.

10.3 SUMMARY

There is an intimate connection between the fate of humanity and that of the entire creation. The latter was subjected to decay because of the fall of humanity, and it will only be released from its futility when the children of God are revealed (Rom 8:19–22). This restoration of creation will be characterized by unification around Christ, since God has planned to bring everything together in Christ, things in heaven and on earth (Eph 1:9–10; Col 1:20). Each believer is already regarded as a new creation in Christ (2 Cor 5:17; Eph 2:10), and this is what really matters in comparison to trivial issues such as circumcision (Gal 6:15).

The sweep of Paul's eschatology includes the entirety of creation. Creation is not simply the canvas upon which the salvation of humanity is painted, nor is it simply the arena in which God acts. Creation is *itself* the painting. It is the arena *and object* of God's restorative work. All things in heaven and earth will be transformed through renewal and unification around Christ.

CHAPTER 11

ISRAEL

11.1 INTRODUCTION

The place of Israel in Paul's thought is complex and regularly debated. Since our interest is his eschatology, we need only be concerned with the role of Israel in Paul's eschatological expectation. Romans 9–11 is the key text for such a discussion.

The central issues revolve around whether Paul expects an eschatological conversion of Israel. That is, will ethnic Israel repent and turn to Christ before Christ returns? Certainly Romans 9–11 has been read in such a way. But there are two important factors that bear directly on the question. First, what does Paul mean by "Israel"? Second, does he really say that "Israel" will be saved, as is commonly supposed?

What follows represents an attempt at a careful reading of the salient portions of Romans 9–11 (with Gal 6:15–16 included because of its mention of Israel). It will become clear that Paul's primary purpose through this section is to defend the sovereignty and faithfulness of God despite the appearance that "Israel" has rejected Christ and the new covenant he has established. Paul sees a faithful remnant as representing Israel, who therefore constitutes the recipients of the promises of God. Unbelieving Israel has been hardened for the sake of the gentile mission, but is not beyond recovery.

11.2 ISRAEL TEXTS

Rom 9:6–9 Οὐχ οἷον δὲ ὅτι ἐκπέπτωκεν ὁ λόγος τοῦ θεοῦ. **οὐ γὰρ πάντες οἱ ἐξ Ἰσραὴλ οὗτοι Ἰσραήλ·** 7 οὐδ' ὅτι εἰσὶν σπέρμα Ἀβραὰμ πάντες τέκνα, ἀλλ', Ἐν Ἰσαὰκ κληθήσεταί σοι σπέρμα. 8 τοῦτ' ἔστιν, οὐ τὰ τέκνα τῆς σαρκὸς ταῦτα τέκνα τοῦ θεοῦ ἀλλὰ τὰ τέκνα τῆς ἐπαγγελίας λογίζεται εἰς σπέρμα. 9 ἐπαγγελίας γὰρ ὁ λόγος οὗτος, Κατὰ τὸν καιρὸν τοῦτον ἐλεύσομαι καὶ ἔσται τῇ Σάρρᾳ υἱός.

Now it is not as though the word of God has failed, **because not all who are descended from Israel are Israel.** *7 Neither are all of Abraham's children*

his descendants. *On the contrary, your offspring will be traced through Isaac. 8 That is, it is not the children by physical descent who are God's children, but the children of the promise are considered to be the offspring. 9 For this is the statement of the promise: At this time I will come, and Sarah will have a son.*

This text serves as an interpretative key for the whole of Romans 9–11 and Paul's detailed discussion of Israel. The central issue here is one of definition: When Paul speaks of Israel, who, exactly, does he mean? In defense of the veracity of God's word (*it is not as though the word of God has failed*; 9:6a),[1] Paul claims that *not all who are descended from Israel are Israel* (v. 6b). While the wording is literally *not all who are out of Israel, these (are) Israel* (οὐ γὰρ πάντες οἱ ἐξ Ἰσραὴλ οὗτοι Ἰσραήλ), the hereditary intent of *out of Israel* (ἐξ Ἰσραήλ) is confirmed in the following phrase—*neither are all of Abraham's children his descendants* (v. 7a; οὐδ᾽ ὅτι εἰσὶν σπέρμα Ἀβραὰμ πάντες τέκνα). This is enough to establish the point that when Paul discusses "Israel" he does not necessarily mean "Israel" as defined by hereditary descent; not all of Abraham's descendants are his children (pointing to a believing "remnant" within hereditary Israel; cf. 11:5), or not all of Abraham's children are his descendants (pointing to the inclusion of gentiles; cf. 9:30).[2] Paul is beginning to redefine the meaning and extent of "Israel."

This redefinition is along the lines of promise.[3] Quoting Genesis 21:12, *your offspring will be traced through Isaac* (Rom 9:7), Paul explains that *it is not the*

---

1. Cranfield regards the half-verse of 9:6a as "the sign and theme of the whole of chapters 9–11" (Cranfield, *Romans*, 2:473).

2. Fitzmyer acknowledges both possibilities, since "the Israel of God" in Gal 6:16 includes gentile Christians and might mean so here. But he prefers to read the second "Israel" reference in 9:6 as referring to Jewish Christians—that is, a believing remnant within hereditary Israel (Fitzmyer, *Romans*, 560). However, it may be unnecessary to choose between the two options, allowing Paul the freedom to set up two points at once—namely that the concept of a believing remnant within hereditary Israel has always been according to promise, and this fact helps to establish the validity of the inclusion of believing gentiles who are also deemed the children of Abraham by promise (and not heritage). In support of this ambiguity, the syntax of οὐδ᾽ ὅτι εἰσὶν σπέρμα Ἀβραὰμ πάντες τέκνα could be taken either way. While it is convoluted by the negation (οὐδ᾽) and by the genitive modifier Ἀβραάμ (which could modify σπέρμα or πάντες τέκνα), this is a subject-predicate construction governed by the equative verb εἰσίν. The equative verb takes two nominatives—σπέρμα and πάντες τέκνα—one of which must be read as the subject of εἰσίν and the other its predicate. But according to the rules of syntax, it is ambiguous as to which should be read as the subject and which is the predicate (see Daniel B. Wallace, *Greek Grammar Beyond the Basics: An Exegetical Syntax of the New Testament* [Grand Rapids: Zondervan, 1996], 42–45). Taken one way, the text would mean *the seed are not all children* (cf. NIV). Taken the other way, it would mean *not all children are the seed* (cf. CSB). The former option would support the notion that not all hereditary Israelites are the true children of Abraham (i.e., pointing to a believing remnant within ethnic Israel). The latter option would support the notion that the true children of Abraham do not consist solely of the hereditary descendants of Abraham (i.e., pointing to the inclusion of believing gentiles). Again, this syntactical ambiguity may actually serve Paul's purpose here in setting up *both* points, namely, that only a believing remnant within hereditary Israel can be true children of Abraham *and* that the true children of Abraham will include believing gentiles.

3. Thus Bird prefers the distinction between "ethnic Israel" and "promissory Israel" (Bird, *Romans*, 325–26).

children by physical descent who are God's children, but the children of the promise are considered to be the offspring (v. 8). By referencing Genesis 21:12, Paul is able to defend his redefinition of Israel along the lines of promise since it has always been defined that way. The descendants of Ishmael (Abraham's other son) are not Israel, but only those who descended through Isaac—the son given to Abraham by the promise of God rather than through Abraham's own volition. This is further ratified by Paul's quotation of the promise itself—*At this time I will come, and Sarah will have a son* (v. 9; Gen 18:10, 14).

As the discussion about Israel unfolds in Romans 9–11, this text must be understood as the key for interpreting what is meant by "Israel," though admittedly the discussion nevertheless remains convoluted, as we will see as we move further into the argument.

Rom 11:1–6 Λέγω οὖν, μὴ ἀπώσατο ὁ θεὸς τὸν λαὸν αὐτοῦ; μὴ γένοιτο· **καὶ γὰρ ἐγὼ Ἰσραηλίτης εἰμί, ἐκ σπέρματος Ἀβραάμ, φυλῆς Βενιαμίν.** 2 οὐκ ἀπώσατο ὁ θεὸς τὸν λαὸν αὐτοῦ ὃν προέγνω. **ἢ οὐκ οἴδατε ἐν Ἠλίᾳ τί λέγει ἡ γραφή, ὡς ἐντυγχάνει τῷ θεῷ κατὰ τοῦ Ἰσραήλ;** 3 Κύριε, τοὺς προφήτας σου ἀπέκτειναν, τὰ θυσιαστήριά σου κατέσκαψαν, κἀγὼ ὑπελείφθην μόνος καὶ ζητοῦσιν τὴν ψυχήν μου. 4 ἀλλὰ τί λέγει αὐτῷ ὁ χρηματισμός; Κατέλιπον ἐμαυτῷ ἑπτακισχιλίους ἄνδρας, οἵτινες οὐκ ἔκαμψαν γόνυ τῇ Βάαλ. 5 οὕτως οὖν καὶ ἐν τῷ νῦν καιρῷ λεῖμμα κατ' ἐκλογὴν χάριτος γέγονεν· 6 εἰ δὲ χάριτι, οὐκέτι ἐξ ἔργων, ἐπεὶ ἡ χάρις οὐκέτι γίνεται χάρις.

I ask, then, has God rejected his people? Absolutely not! **For I too am an Israelite, a descendant of Abraham, from the tribe of Benjamin.** *2 God has not rejected his people whom he foreknew.* **Or don't you know what the Scripture says in the passage about Elijah—how he pleads with God against Israel?** *3 Lord, they have killed your prophets and torn down your altars. I am the only one left, and they are trying to take my life! 4 But what was God's answer to him?* I *have left seven thousand for myself who have not bowed down to Baal. 5 In the same way, then, there is also at the present time a remnant chosen by grace. 6 Now if by grace, then it is not by works; otherwise grace ceases to be grace.*

A central issue that Paul addresses in Romans 9–11 is the question of whether God has rejected his people—the very question asked explicitly here in 11:1. Paul's short answer is to the point—*Absolutely not!* (μὴ γένοιτο). The longer answer involves two parts: the argument from Paul's own Abrahamic heritage, and the example of Elijah and the remnant who have not worshiped Baal.

As for the first part, Paul's argument is simple—*I too am an Israelite, a descendent of Abraham, from the tribe of Benjamin* (11:1). Paul's experience of God's grace confirms that God has not rejected his people, since Paul represents the epitome of an Israelite. God's inclusion of Paul among the people of Christ demonstrates that not *all* Israelites are found to be outside the parameters of the new covenant.[4]

Paul then apparently anticipates the obvious objection to this argument. The objection is that Paul does not represent the majority of Israelites—what about the multitude that have rejected Christ? Perhaps a few individual Israelites here or there have accepted Christ, but that hardly satisfies the question of whether God has rejected his people. And so Paul turns to discuss the concept of a *remnant*.

God has not, in fact, *rejected his people whom he foreknew* (v. 2a). But it becomes clear that when Paul refers to *his people whom he foreknew*, he does not simply mean the entirety of the nation of Israel. The story of Elijah from 1 Kings 19 is used to make the case that God has long operated with the notion of a remnant within Israel. When Elijah pleaded with God about the murderous Israelites (v. 3; 1 Kgs 19:10), his response is that *I have left seven thousand for myself who have not bowed down to Baal* (Rom 11:4; 1 Kgs 19:18). Though the nation as a whole has rejected God, there remains a remnant to whom God will continue to show his covenant faithfulness.

Paul immediately pounces on this point to assert that *in the same way, then, there is also at the present time a remnant chosen by grace* (Rom 11:5). In this current situation in which the majority of Israelites have rejected Christ, Paul's point is that there is now *a remnant* within Israel who have accepted him. Just as in Elijah's day when the majority was found to be wrong and, indeed, idolatrous, so Paul can effectively claim the same now. The majority is wrong to reject Christ. But the minority who have embraced him are the recipients of God's grace.

Paul concludes this section by reflecting on the nature of grace—*now if by grace, then it is not by works; otherwise grace ceases to be grace* (v. 6). By definition, grace cannot depend on human effort, performance, or credential of any kind. Even Abrahamic heritage is not a credential to be relied on when it comes to God's election. If it were so, grace would not be grace, since it is the unmerited favor of God.

The argument of this text needs to be correlated with that of Romans 9:6–9 (see above), which argues that not all Israel is Israel. While that passage defines

---

4. Keener, *Romans*, 130.

"true" Israel in terms of the promise of God, here it is defined by its remnant status. The remnant *is* "true" Israel. And this means that the children of the promise (9:8) constitute the remnant chosen by grace (11:5).

Rom 11:11–24 Λέγω οὖν, μὴ ἔπταισαν ἵνα πέσωσιν; μὴ γένοιτο· ἀλλὰ τῷ αὐτῶν παραπτώματι **ἡ σωτηρία τοῖς ἔθνεσιν εἰς τὸ παραζηλῶσαι αὐτούς**. 12 εἰ δὲ τὸ παράπτωμα αὐτῶν πλοῦτος κόσμου καὶ τὸ ἥττημα αὐτῶν πλοῦτος ἐθνῶν, πόσῳ μᾶλλον τὸ πλήρωμα αὐτῶν. 13 Ὑμῖν δὲ λέγω τοῖς ἔθνεσιν· ἐφ' ὅσον μὲν οὖν εἰμι ἐγὼ ἐθνῶν ἀπόστολος, τὴν διακονίαν μου δοξάζω, 14 εἴ πως παραζηλώσω μου τὴν σάρκα καὶ σώσω τινὰς ἐξ αὐτῶν. 15 εἰ γὰρ ἡ ἀποβολὴ αὐτῶν καταλλαγὴ κόσμου, τίς ἡ πρόσλημψις εἰ μὴ ζωὴ ἐκ νεκρῶν; 16 εἰ δὲ ἡ ἀπαρχὴ ἁγία, καὶ τὸ φύραμα· καὶ εἰ ἡ ῥίζα ἁγία, καὶ οἱ κλάδοι. 17 Εἰ δέ τινες τῶν κλάδων ἐξεκλάσθησαν, σὺ δὲ ἀγριέλαιος ὢν ἐνεκεντρίσθης ἐν αὐτοῖς καὶ συγκοινωνὸς τῆς ῥίζης τῆς πιότητος τῆς ἐλαίας ἐγένου, 18 μὴ κατακαυχῶ τῶν κλάδων· εἰ δὲ κατακαυχᾶσαι οὐ σὺ τὴν ῥίζαν βαστάζεις ἀλλ' ἡ ῥίζα σέ. 19 ἐρεῖς οὖν· ἐξεκλάσθησαν κλάδοι ἵνα ἐγὼ ἐγκεντρισθῶ. 20 καλῶς· τῇ ἀπιστίᾳ ἐξεκλάσθησαν, σὺ δὲ τῇ πίστει ἕστηκας. μὴ ὑψηλὰ φρόνει ἀλλὰ φοβοῦ· 21 εἰ γὰρ ὁ θεὸς τῶν κατὰ φύσιν κλάδων οὐκ ἐφείσατο, οὐδὲ σοῦ φείσεται. 22 ἴδε οὖν χρηστότητα καὶ ἀποτομίαν θεοῦ· ἐπὶ μὲν τοὺς πεσόντας ἀποτομία, ἐπὶ δὲ σὲ χρηστότης θεοῦ, ἐὰν ἐπιμένῃς τῇ χρηστότητι, ἐπεὶ καὶ σὺ ἐκκοπήσῃ. 23 κἀκεῖνοι δέ, ἐὰν μὴ ἐπιμένωσιν τῇ ἀπιστίᾳ, ἐγκεντρισθήσονται· δυνατὸς γάρ ἐστιν ὁ θεὸς πάλιν ἐγκεντρίσαι αὐτούς. 24 εἰ γὰρ σὺ ἐκ τῆς κατὰ φύσιν ἐξεκόπης ἀγριελαίου καὶ παρὰ φύσιν ἐνεκεντρίσθης εἰς καλλιέλαιον, πόσῳ μᾶλλον οὗτοι οἱ κατὰ φύσιν ἐγκεντρισθήσονται τῇ ἰδίᾳ ἐλαίᾳ.

I ask, then, have they stumbled so as to fall? Absolutely not! On the contrary, by their transgression, **salvation has come to the Gentiles to make Israel jealous**. *12 Now if their transgression brings riches for the world, and their failure riches for the Gentiles, how much more will their fullness bring! 13 Now I am speaking to you Gentiles. Insofar as I am an apostle to the Gentiles, I magnify my ministry, 14 if I might somehow make my own people jealous and save some of them. 15 For if their rejection brings reconciliation to the world, what will their acceptance mean but life from the dead? 16 Now if the firstfruits are holy, so is the whole batch. And if the root is holy, so are the branches. 17 Now if some of the branches were broken off, and you, though a wild olive branch, were grafted in among them and have come to share in the rich root of the cultivated olive tree, 18 do not boast that you are better than those branches. But if you do boast—you do not sustain the root, but the root sustains you. 19 Then you will* say, *"Branches were broken off so that I might be grafted in." 20 True enough; they were broken off because of unbelief, but you stand by faith. Do not be arrogant, but beware, 21 because if God did not spare the natural branches, he will not spare you either. 22 Therefore, consider God's kindness and severity: severity toward those who have fallen but God's kindness toward you—if you remain in his kindness. Otherwise you too will be cut off. 23 And even they, if they do not remain in unbelief, will be grafted in, because God has the power to graft them in again. 24 For if you were cut off from your native wild olive tree and against nature were grafted into a cultivated olive tree, how much more will these—the natural branches—be grafted into their own olive tree?*

Now that Paul has explained how it is possible that the majority of Israelites have rejected Christ and yet God has not forsaken his people, he turns now to address the issues of gentile inclusion and the potential repentance of unbelieving Israelites.

He begins with the latter, asking, *have they stumbled so as to fall?* (11:11a). Again, the short answer is *absolutely not!* (v. 11b; μὴ γένοιτο). This then segues to the former issue of gentile inclusion as Paul states that by Israelite transgression *salvation has come to the Gentiles to make Israel jealous* (v. 11c). Paul apparently imagines that gentile worship of the Jewish messiah will eventually lead to Israelite envy. He then applies a *qal wahomer* ("lesser to greater") argument, stating that if Israelite failure brings *riches for the Gentiles, how much more will their fullness bring!* (v. 12). The point here is that Israelite belief in Christ will benefit everyone and is an outcome to be desired.

Paul then explicitly turns to address his gentile readers (*Now I am speaking to you Gentiles*; v. 13) and imagines that his own role as apostle to the gentiles would be magnified if his ministry to the gentiles *might somehow make my own people jealous and save some of them* (vv. 13–14).

But his message to the gentiles consists of more than persuading them of the value of Israelite repentance. Paul also wants them to know their place in the context of salvation history.[5] They are like *a wild olive branch* that has been *grafted in* to the *cultivated olive tree* (v. 17). As such, they are no better than the branches that were broken off because of unbelief (unbelieving Israelites; vv. 17–20). Their recognition of this carries an implicit warning that Paul then makes explicit—*if God did not spare the natural branches, he will not spare you either* (v. 21). Should the gentiles also turn to unbelief, they too will be cut out of the olive tree (v. 22).

---

5. Thielman, *Romans*, 536.

By the same token, if the Israelites turn from their unbelief, they *will be grafted in, because God has the power to graft them in again* (v. 23). Indeed, pressing the horticultural image further, Paul adds that if a wild gentile branch can be grafted into a cultivated olive tree *against nature*, how much more will the natural branches *be grafted into their own olive tree?* (v. 24).[6]

Nowhere in this text does Paul indicate that Israelite repentance is certain to happen. The most he says is that they have not stumbled as to fall. That is, their rejection of Christ is not *necessarily* permanent. Even Paul's imagined Israelite jealousy at gentile inclusion is not expressed with any kind of definitive expectation. The conditionality throughout the text is easily observed by its frequent use of conditional sentences (11:12, 14, 15, 16, 17, 18, 21, 22, 23, 24). Admittedly, not all of these refer to Israelite repentance (e.g., 11:18, 22), and not all express a hypothetical conditionality (e.g., 11:16, 17). Nevertheless, the preponderance of conditional sentences in this relatively brief passage lends a strongly hypothetical mood to the whole.

Paul's intent, therefore, is *not* to indicate his expectation of Israelite repentance and embrace of Christ. Rather, he wishes to inform (and perhaps correct) gentile thinking with respect to unbelieving Israel, and to shape their attitude (as wild branches) toward the established root of the cultivated olive tree.

Rom 11:25–32 Οὐ γὰρ θέλω ὑμᾶς ἀγνοεῖν, ἀδελφοί, τὸ μυστήριον τοῦτο, ἵνα μὴ ἦτε ἑαυτοῖς φρόνιμοι, ὅτι **πώρωσις ἀπὸ μέρους τῷ Ἰσραὴλ γέγονεν ἄχρι οὗ τὸ πλήρωμα τῶν ἐθνῶν εἰσέλθῃ** 26 **καὶ οὕτως πᾶς Ἰσραὴλ σωθήσεται**, καθὼς γέγραπται,

ἥξει ἐκ Σιὼν ὁ ῥυόμενος,
ἀποστρέψει ἀσεβείας ἀπὸ Ἰακώβ.
27 καὶ αὕτη αὐτοῖς ἡ παρ' ἐμοῦ διαθήκη,
ὅταν ἀφέλωμαι τὰς ἁμαρτίας αὐτῶν.

28 κατὰ μὲν τὸ εὐαγγέλιον ἐχθροὶ δι' ὑμᾶς, κατὰ δὲ τὴν ἐκλογὴν ἀγαπητοὶ διὰ τοὺς πατέρας· 29 ἀμεταμέλητα γὰρ τὰ χαρίσματα καὶ ἡ κλῆσις τοῦ θεοῦ. 30 ὥσπερ γὰρ ὑμεῖς ποτε ἠπειθήσατε τῷ θεῷ, νῦν δὲ ἠλεήθητε τῇ τούτων ἀπειθείᾳ, 31 οὕτως καὶ οὗτοι νῦν ἠπείθησαν τῷ ὑμετέρῳ ἐλέει, ἵνα καὶ αὐτοὶ

---

6. In his excursus on Paul's olive-tree analogy, Kruse points out that the idea of grafting a wild olive shoot into a good olive tree is contrary to normal oleicultural practice in which cultivated branches were grafted into wild olive trees. The point of this deliberate subversion of a known practice would be that God's inclusion of the gentiles does not rest in their desirability but instead expresses his tendency to choose the undesirable (Kruse, *Romans*, 439–41).

νῦν ἐλεηθῶσιν. 32 συνέκλεισεν γὰρ ὁ θεὸς τοὺς πάντας εἰς ἀπείθειαν, ἵνα τοὺς πάντας ἐλεήσῃ.

I don't want you to be ignorant of this mystery, brothers and sisters, so that you will not be conceited: **A partial hardening has come upon Israel until the fullness of the Gentiles has come in. 26 And in this way all Israel will be saved,** *as it is written,*

> *The Deliverer will come from Zion;*
> *he will turn godlessness away from Jacob.*
> *27 And this will be my covenant with them*
> *when I take away their sins.*

28 Regarding the gospel, they are enemies for your advantage, but regarding election, they are loved because of the patriarchs, 29 since God's gracious gifts and calling are irrevocable. 30 As you once disobeyed God but now have received mercy through their disobedience, 31 so they too have now disobeyed, resulting in mercy to you, so that they also may now receive mercy. 32 For God has imprisoned all in disobedience so that he may have mercy on all.

Paul here develops the theme begun in the previous section (11:11–24), concerning the benefit to gentiles of Israelite rejection of Christ. Israel has been partially hardened *until the fullness of the Gentiles has come in* (v. 25); *they are enemies for your advantage* (v. 28); their disobedience results in mercy on the gentiles (v. 31).

The benefit of Israelite unbelief serves as an apologetic that continues to answer the question asked in 11:1: *Has God rejected his people?* By asserting that their disobedience is all part of God's plan, Paul is able to answer the question negatively: no, God has not rejected his people; their lack of faith is part of his design for the sake of the gentiles.

Moreover, the benefit to gentiles of Israelite unbelief also serves to underpin the expectation that Israel's hardening will be temporary. While this notion was explored previously in vv. 11–24, it was not asserted definitively; it was put tentatively and hypothetically (see on vv. 11–24 above). But here Paul's stance apparently becomes more definitive—*a partial hardening has come upon Israel until the fullness of the Gentiles has come in* (v. 25b).

The extent of the word *until* (ἄχρι) can be debated. In English, it is natural to understand it as referring to a point after which Israel will no longer be hardened. Once the gentiles come in, the partial hardening of Israel will come to an end. But the Greek preposition ἄχρι does not necessarily imply that after the gentiles come, Israel will cease to be hardened. The word is "used to indicate an interval between two points";[7] it can simply look toward that second point without implying any subsequent eventuation. What will happen after the gentiles come in cannot be implied by the word *until*.

While the wider context might be pressed more strongly to support the notion of Israel's *un*-hardening, this too must be scrutinized carefully. Paul follows the "until" statement of v. 25 with the strong claim, *and in this way all Israel will be saved* (v. 26a). The phrase *in this way* (οὕτως) links the two statements so that the *partial* hardening *until* the gentiles come in (v. 25) is interpreted in light of the phrase *all Israel* in v. 26. For most interpreters, this will mean that after the fullness of the gentiles has come in, the remainder of Israel will be saved. Unbelieving Israel will repent once the gentiles have all come to faith.

But this reading is likely mistaken. Paul has already established what is meant by the term *Israel* in 9:6–9—not all descended from Israel are Israel (see on this passage, above). If "Israel" refers to the believing remnant (see also on 11:1–6 above), then *all Israel* must be understood in that light. The remnant is true Israel, and is therefore now "all" Israel.[8] This is still to be correlated with the previous statement of 11:25—*a partial hardening has come upon Israel until the fullness of the Gentiles has come in*—but the connection point is not the *until*; it is, rather the *partial hardening*. If Israel's hardening is only partial, then part of Israel has not been hardened—this is of course the remnant upon which Paul has already expounded. When Paul then says *in this way all Israel will be saved*, he means that the part of Israel that has not been hardened—the believing remnant—will be saved. He does not mean that all members of ethnic, national Israel will be saved at some miraculous point in the future.

God's love for "Israel" (*they are loved because of the patriarchs*; v. 28b) and his irreversible calling of them (*God's gracious gifts and calling are irrevocable*; v. 29) do not undermine the argument presented above. Once Israel has been defined as "believing Israel," or as the remnant, these statements remain in full force without implying that every Israelite descendent of Abraham will some day come to faith in Christ.

Admittedly, however, the categories become rather more blurred in the following three verses (vv. 30–32). The reference to *their disobedience* (v. 30) refers

---

7. BDAG 160.
8. "The 'all' in 'all Israel' here is in my judgment best understood as a typically Pauline (and characteristically cryptic) note of redefinition, in line with the other such points elsewhere, not least Galatians 6.16" (Wright, *Paul and the Faithfulness of God*, 1244).

to unbelieving Israel, while *they too have now disobeyed . . . so that they also may receive mercy* (v. 31) refers again to the believing remnant. All the while, however, the term "Israel" does not appear. Most likely this blurring of categories is due to the recapitulating purpose of these verses—Paul is restating in short form what he has already laid out in longer form. As a result, the two "Israels" blend into each other a little, which may be why he does not even use the term.

The overarching point, however, is clear: from the perspective of salvation history, "Israel's" disobedience and obedience is part of God's sovereign plan. Their disobedience facilitates gentile inclusion, while their obedience constitutes a faithful remnant. Through the believing remnant, God keeps his promises to "Israel" even while most Israelites exclude themselves from the new covenant. And through the disbelieving majority, God keeps his promise to Abraham that the nations would be blessed through him, since his descendants have unwittingly opened the door to the gentiles.

While this passage comes closest in Romans 9–11 to indicating an expectation that one day ethnic and national Israel will turn to Christ, it cannot be substantiated that the passage truly supports such a view. A close reading of the text reveals that Paul's central concern is to defend the sovereignty and faithfulness of God, while demonstrating how Israelite unbelief serves God's purposes in bringing about gentile repentance. He affirms the salvation of a believing remnant, while the partial hardening of Israel serves his gentile mission.

> Gal 6:14–16 ἐμοὶ δὲ μὴ γένοιτο καυχᾶσθαι εἰ μὴ ἐν τῷ σταυρῷ τοῦ κυρίου ἡμῶν Ἰησοῦ Χριστοῦ, δι' οὗ ἐμοὶ κόσμος ἐσταύρωται κἀγὼ κόσμῳ. 15 οὔτε γὰρ περιτομή τί ἐστιν οὔτε ἀκροβυστία ἀλλὰ καινὴ κτίσις. 16 καὶ ὅσοι τῷ κανόνι τούτῳ στοιχήσουσιν, εἰρήνη ἐπ' αὐτοὺς καὶ ἔλεος καὶ ἐπὶ τὸν **Ἰσραὴλ τοῦ θεοῦ**.

> *But as for me, I will never boast about anything except the cross of our Lord Jesus Christ. The world has been crucified to me through the cross, and I to the world. 15 For both circumcision and uncircumcision mean nothing; what matters instead is a new creation. 16 May peace come to all those who follow this standard, and mercy even to **the Israel of God**!*

As already noted on this passage (see §10.2 above), neither circumcision nor uncircumcision mean anything in light of the cross of Christ. Rather, *what matters instead is a new creation* (6:15), by which Paul means the person who has been crucified with Christ, as he has. This then leads to Paul's wish—*May peace come to all those who follow this standard, and mercy even to the Israel of God!*

(v. 16). The key question is to whom does he refer by the term *the Israel of God*? On the one hand, the immediate context includes discussion of circumcision and uncircumcision (as does the wider context, of course), which suggests that "Israel" refers to ethnic, religious Israel. On the other hand, he has just stated that neither circumcision nor uncircumcision mean anything, which suggests that "Israel" may *not* refer to the people defined by such religious symbolism. That is, *the Israel of God* would refer to a reconstituted "Israel" that is defined by allegiance to Christ rather than by circumcision.

The former option is most likely here—*the Israel of God* refers to ethnic, religious Israel. The primary reason for this adjudication is that Paul's wish is that peace might come *to all who follow this standard* (v. 16a; ὅσοι τῷ κανόνι τούτῳ στοιχήσουσιν)—*this standard* referring to the standard of the new creation, concerning which circumcision and uncircumcision mean nothing. When he then adds to his wish *mercy even to the Israel of God* (v. 16b), Paul seems to be wishing that even Israel might come to recognize and accept this standard also. If that is the case, then *the Israel of God* must refer to the ethnic and religious entity that does not currently accept Paul's standard of the new creation, which is above and beyond the distinction between circumcision and uncircumcision.[9]

In short, Galatians 6:16 constitutes a wish for peace to those who currently follow the standard of the new creation (i.e., those already in Christ), and a wish for mercy toward Israelites who do not yet accept that standard.

11.3 Summary

The question of Israel in Paul's writings remains a convoluted and controversial notion. Of first importance is to grasp his definition of Israel, since not all "Israel" is Israel. This means that not all of Abraham's children are regarded as his descendants (Rom 9:6–9). Paul's firm conviction is that God has not rejected his people, Israel. As the epitome of an Israelite, Paul's acceptance of Christ demonstrates that not all Israelites are outside the new covenant.[10] Instead, a remnant represents believing Israel, which is a concept found elsewhere in Israel's history (Rom 11:1–6). It is this remnant of Israel that Paul regards as "Israel."[11]

---

9. So F. F. Bruce, *The Epistle to the Galatians*, NIGTC (Grand Rapids: Eerdmans, 1982), 273–75.

10. As Dunn states, "Paul, himself an Israelite (Rom 11:1) seeks to understand his heritage as an Israelite and to claim a place for Gentiles within that heritage" (Dunn, *Theology of Paul the Apostle*, 508).

11. Shayna Sheinfeld, "Who is the Righteous Remnant in Romans 9–11? The Concept of Remnant in the Hebrew Bible, Early Jewish Literature and Paul's Letter to the Romans," in *Paul the Jew: Rereading the Apostle as a Figure of Second Temple Judaism*, ed. Gabriele Boccaccini and Carlos A. Segovia (Minneapolis: Fortress, 2016), 47.

Though only a remnant of Israel believes in Christ, Paul asserts that the rest have not stumbled beyond recovery. Salvation has come to the gentiles in order to make Israel jealous. And yet gentile believers should not become arrogant, but rather should appreciate their place in salvation history as the engrafted branches, while Israel is the olive tree (Rom 11:11–24). A partial hardening has come to Israel until all the gentiles come in (11:25–32).

While it remains a controversial issue within scholarship, it is not clear that Paul expects widescale Israelite repentance before Christ returns. Romans 9–11 defends the sovereignty and faithfulness of God, and Israelite unbelief does not undermine this. Paul holds out hope that national Israel's unbelief might not be permanent, but this cannot be pressed into the service of an eschatological expectation that all Israel will believe before the end. The only thing Paul says for sure is that "Israel," meaning the believing remnant of Israel, will be saved. With Wright,

> He is not going to make any predictions about whether God will save a myriad of his presently unbelieving fellow Israelites, or somewhat less; only (a) that he will save 'some', in other words considerably more than at present, (b) that this will count as a 'fullness' (*pleroma*), and (c) that this will be the full extension of the small but growing 'remnant' of which he, Paul, is himself a part.[12]

---

12. Wright, *Paul and the Faithfulness of God*, 1209.

CHAPTER 12

GLORY

12.1 INTRODUCTION

This chapter explores the subtheme of glory as it relates to Paul's eschatological vision. Glory appears to be the ultimate end of all things as far as Paul is concerned. The glory of God is the highest purpose of humanity and of creation in general. It is the greatest motivation for serving Christ, and it is the highest hope to which believers aspire.

Glory is ascribed to God's person as well as to his deeds—especially those involving creation, resurrection, and re-creation. The glory of God is already a present reality—though it can only be glimpsed partially now—and it is a future reality that will be apprehended by all people one day.

The work and gifts of God in Christ are intended to inspire praise to his glory; they are not ends in themselves but ought to lead to the appropriate ascription of glory to God and Christ. Not only should glory shape believers' responses to the deeds and person of God, but those in Christ will personally share in the glory of Christ. Those who suffer with him will be glorified with him with a glory that will resonate throughout creation itself.

12.2 GLORY TEXTS

Rom 5:1–2 Δικαιωθέντες οὖν ἐκ πίστεως εἰρήνην ἔχομεν πρὸς τὸν θεὸν διὰ τοῦ κυρίου ἡμῶν Ἰησοῦ Χριστοῦ 2 δι' οὗ καὶ τὴν προσαγωγὴν ἐσχήκαμεν τῇ πίστει εἰς τὴν χάριν ταύτην ἐν ᾗ ἑστήκαμεν καὶ **καυχώμεθα ἐπ' ἐλπίδι τῆς δόξης τοῦ θεοῦ.**

*Therefore, since we have been declared righteous by faith, we have peace with God through our Lord Jesus Christ. 2 We have also obtained access through him by faith into this grace in which we stand, and **we rejoice in the hope of the glory of God.***

With the declaration of righteousness and peace with God through Christ (5:1), believers have access *into this grace in which we stand* (v. 2a). All of this describes the status enjoyed by believers—righteousness, peace, and the standing of grace. But the final phrase describes the response of grateful believers to whom so much has been granted—*we rejoice in the hope of the glory of God* (v. 2b).

Literally, believers *boast* in this hope (καυκάομαι), indicating that Paul imagines a response that is less about celebrating (though there is no reason why it should exclude celebration), and more about expressing the object of one's confidence. Believers who have received righteousness, peace, and grace through Christ by faith have no boast or confidence of their own. It is entirely cast upon the hope that arises from their granted status. Additionally, the form καυχώμεθα could be indicative or subjunctive in mood, with most interpreters preferring the former.[1] But with Jewett, the (hortatory) subjunctive seems more appropriate, so that Paul is advocating a "new form of boasting to replace the claims of honourable status and performance that mark traditional religion in the Greco-Roman world."[2] The phrase in 5:2b could then be translated, *let us rejoice in the hope of the glory of God*.

But what is *the hope of the glory of God*? Surely Paul does not hope that God will be glorious, since he already affirms the uncontested glory of God. His glory is not a merely future eventuality; it can be seen now, notwithstanding the choice of many to reject or ignore it (e.g., Rom 1:18–21). Rather, Paul imagines a future glory of God that is in some sense the object of current hope.

Since this glory of God is the object of hope, Paul may mean that believers will share in the glory of God in the eschaton. God is already glorious, to be sure, but in the future his glory will be unveiled for all to acknowledge. Moreover, believers will be caught up in his glory. To share in the glory of God at the eschaton must rank among the greatest of all privileges for those whose hope is in Christ. It thus constitutes the boast arising out of the status received through Christ.

Having been declared righteous, having peace with God, and having the standing of grace leads Paul to boast in the future hope of sharing in the glory of God at the eschaton. He cannot boast of his own glory; nor can any believer. But he looks forward to a glorious future nonetheless, since the glory of God will be shared with him and all who share his hope.

---

1. Longenecker makes an unfortunate argument for the indicative by claiming that as a deponent verb καυχώμεθα should be understood as active in meaning and indicative in mood (Longenecker, *Romans*, 559). But there are two significant problems with this argument. First, deponency is no longer regarded a legitimate category through which to understand "middle-only" Greek lexemes; see Constantine R. Campbell, *Advances in the Study of Greek: New Insights for Reading the New Testament* (Grand Rapids: Zondervan, 2015), ch. 4. Second, as a category pertaining to *voice*, there is no reason that a so-called deponent verb should also be regarded indicative rather than subjunctive in *mood*.

2. Jewett, *Romans*, 351.

Rom 6:3–4 ἢ ἀγνοεῖτε ὅτι, ὅσοι ἐβαπτίσθημεν εἰς Χριστὸν Ἰησοῦν, εἰς τὸν θάνατον αὐτοῦ ἐβαπτίσθημεν; 4 συνετάφημεν οὖν αὐτῷ διὰ τοῦ βαπτίσματος εἰς τὸν θάνατον, ἵνα **ὥσπερ ἠγέρθη Χριστὸς ἐκ νεκρῶν διὰ τῆς δόξης τοῦ πατρός, οὕτως καὶ ἡμεῖς ἐν καινότητι ζωῆς περιπατήσωμεν**.

Or are you unaware that all of us who were baptized into Christ Jesus were baptized into his death? 4 Therefore we were buried with him by baptism into death, in order that, ***just as Christ was raised from the dead by the glory of the Father, so we too may walk in newness of life***.

This is an interesting case in which *the glory of the Father* is said to be the power (or instrument; διά) with which Christ was raised from the dead. It is difficult to know whether Paul imagines *the glory of the Father* as an actualized force, like strength, or whether it is more of a rhetorical flourish. If the former, this would be the only occurrence in which glory is spoken of in such a way. Glory is an operative instrument at the disposal of the Father's agency.

If the latter, Paul's rhetorical flourish has "instrumentalized" glory in a similar manner to the way that personification personifies a nonpersonal entity. A personified entity is not actually personal but is spoken of in such a way for rhetorical effect. In the same way, the glory of the Father is not actually an instrument but is spoken of in such a way for rhetorical effect.

Most likely the latter option does best justice to Paul's expression. The glory of the Father is imagined instrumentally, when in fact it is a quality pertaining to his person. Just as the quality of, say, humility describes a person and not an action, when actions are performed "out of humility," they are understood to be executed in a way that is consistent with a person's humble character. So too the raising of Christ by the glory of the Father is an action that has come "out of the Father's glory." That is, his glorious nature, power, and majesty have effected the resurrection of Christ.[3] In this way, Paul can say that *Christ was raised from the dead by the glory of the Father*.

A direct parallel is drawn between Christ's resurrection and the *newness of life* in which believers may walk (6:4b). Just as believers *were buried with him by baptism into death*, so too they participate in the resurrection of Christ. Until the resurrection of their physical bodies, such participation is spiritual in nature—believers are spiritually raised from the dead. As spiritually risen people, they are to walk in a new way of life.

---

3. "God's use of His power is always glorious, and His use of it to raise the dead is a specially clear manifestation of His glory" (Cranfield, *Romans*, 1:304).

Though not stated, we can safely understand that *the glory of the Father* that saw Christ raised from the dead is the same "power" operating in the spiritual resurrection of believers. They too are raised by the glory of the Father. Moreover, the eschatological implications are also not stated but may be assumed. The resurrection of the dead will occur by the glory of the Father. Just as the Father raised Christ out of his glorious might, so he will raise the dead in Christ.

Rom 8:16–21 αὐτὸ τὸ πνεῦμα συμμαρτυρεῖ τῷ πνεύματι ἡμῶν ὅτι ἐσμὲν τέκνα θεοῦ. 17 εἰ δὲ τέκνα, καὶ κληρονόμοι· κληρονόμοι μὲν θεοῦ, συγκληρονόμοι δὲ Χριστοῦ, εἴπερ συμπάσχομεν **ἵνα καὶ συνδοξασθῶμεν**. 18 Λογίζομαι γὰρ ὅτι οὐκ ἄξια τὰ παθήματα τοῦ νῦν καιροῦ πρὸς **τὴν μέλλουσαν δόξαν ἀποκαλυφθῆναι εἰς ἡμᾶς**. 19 ἡ γὰρ ἀποκαραδοκία τῆς κτίσεως τὴν ἀποκάλυψιν τῶν υἱῶν τοῦ θεοῦ ἀπεκδέχεται. 20 τῇ γὰρ ματαιότητι ἡ κτίσις ὑπετάγη, οὐχ ἑκοῦσα ἀλλὰ διὰ τὸν ὑποτάξαντα, ἐφ' ἐλπίδι 21 ὅτι καὶ αὐτὴ ἡ κτίσις ἐλευθερωθήσεται ἀπὸ τῆς δουλείας τῆς φθορᾶς εἰς **τὴν ἐλευθερίαν τῆς δόξης τῶν τέκνων τοῦ θεοῦ**.

*The Spirit himself testifies together with our spirit that we are God's children, 17 and if children, also heirs—heirs of God and coheirs with Christ—if indeed we suffer with him so **that we may also be glorified with him**. 18 For I consider that the sufferings of this present time are not worth comparing with **the glory that is going to be revealed to us**. 19 For the creation eagerly waits with anticipation for God's sons to be revealed. 20 For the creation was subjected to futility—not willingly, but because of him who subjected it—in the hope 21 that the creation itself will also be set free from the bondage to decay into **the glorious freedom of God's children**.*

As explored previously (see §9.2 above), this passage intertwines the themes of sons and heirs of God, coheirs of Christ, and suffering and glory. The Spirit assures believers that they are God's children, who are also heirs of God with Christ (8:16–17). The coheirs of Christ affirm their participation with him in suffering, which in turn results in glorification with him (v. 17).

For Paul, suffering is the mode of experience for this earthly life. Glory belongs to the next life, being oriented toward the future, as indicated by the following verses: such glory *is going to be revealed* (v. 18) when the creation will *be set free from the bondage to decay into the glorious freedom of God's children* (v. 21).

Specifically, this passage offers three insights about future glory. First, believers participate in the glory of Christ, just as they have participated in his sufferings. Glory is shared with Christ as his coheirs.

Second, current suffering is not comparable *with the glory that is going to be revealed to us* (v. 18). The comparison between suffering and glory is of course Paul's interest here, but we are also interested in what the phrase *revealed to us* means (ἀποκαλυφθῆναι εἰς ἡμᾶς). If the prepositional phrase εἰς ἡμᾶς is understood in the way it is here translated (*to us*; so also ESV), then Paul seems simply to be saying that believers will witness and behold the glory of Christ to come. If, however, the prepositional phrase is understood as *in us*—as in the NIV, *the glory that will be revealed in us*—then we have something different. Certainly the preposition εἰς is capable of such a rendering, especially in uses that overlap with the preposition ἐν (*in*).[4]

If this is a better way to understand εἰς ἡμᾶς, what would it mean? Rather than mere spectators of glory, this reading would indicate that believers will be the focal point of glory in some sense. Believers will be seen to share in the glory of Christ and will in that sense become the locality of glory.[5]

Glory revealed *in us* is probably a better reading than glory revealed *to us* because of the surrounding context. Paul has already said that believers will be glorified with Christ (v. 17). The creation waits for God's sons to be revealed (v. 19)—note the coincidence of the language of revelation in v. 18 (ἀποκαλύπτω) and v. 19 (ἀποκάλυψις)—glory will be *revealed* in us (v. 18), and creation waits for God's sons to be *revealed* (v. 19). In other words, when the sons of God are revealed they will be revealed in glory.

Furthermore, *the creation will be also be set free from the bondage to decay into the glorious freedom of God's children* (v. 21). I have already argued (see §9.2 above) that the phrase *the glorious freedom of God's children* is better translated "the freedom of glory" (τὴν ἐλευθερίαν τῆς δόξης), since it is contrasted in parallel to *the bondage to decay* (τῆς δουλείας τῆς φθορᾶς). This seems to mean that rather than being subject to decay, creation will become subject to freedom. And this freedom is a glorious one, pertaining to the children of God (τὴν ἐλευθερίαν τῆς δόξης τῶν τέκνων τοῦ θεοῦ).

The three insights concerning glory in this passage connect to each other in an unfolding manner. It begins with participation with Christ—the coheirs of Christ will be glorified with him. When the sons of God are revealed, the glory of Christ will be revealed in them. And the whole creation will be set free from bondage into the freedom of the glory of the children of God. The glory revealed in believers will shine throughout the created realm alongside the glory of Christ.

---

4. BDAG 289, §1.a.δ.
5. So Wright: "The future revelation will bestow glory upon us, from above, as a gift" (Wright, "Romans," 595).

Rom 8:28–30 οἴδαμεν δὲ ὅτι τοῖς ἀγαπῶσιν τὸν θεὸν πάντα συνεργεῖ εἰς ἀγαθόν, τοῖς κατὰ πρόθεσιν κλητοῖς οὖσιν. 29 ὅτι οὓς προέγνω, καὶ προώρισεν συμμόρφους τῆς εἰκόνος τοῦ υἱοῦ αὐτοῦ, εἰς τὸ εἶναι αὐτὸν πρωτότοκον ἐν πολλοῖς ἀδελφοῖς· 30 οὓς δὲ προώρισεν, τούτους καὶ ἐκάλεσεν· καὶ οὓς ἐκάλεσεν, τούτους καὶ ἐδικαίωσεν· **οὓς δὲ ἐδικαίωσεν, τούτους καὶ ἐδόξασεν.**

We know that all things work together for the good of those who love God, who are called according to his purpose. 29 For those he foreknew he also predestined to be conformed to the image of his Son, so that he would be the firstborn among many brothers and sisters. 30 And those he predestined, he also called; and those he called, he also justified; ***and those he justified, he also glorified.***

Paul enumerates a chain of actions bestowed on believers by God, culminating in glorification. Before looking more closely, we must ask how the string of aorist indicative tense-forms is operating here. God *foreknew* (προέγνω), *predestined* (προώρισεν), *called* (ἐκάλεσεν), *justified* (ἐδικαίωσεν), and *glorified* (ἐδόξασεν) believers. While most translations render all these aorists as past referring, since that is the default understanding of aorist indicatives, the final item *glorified* (ἐδόξασεν) proves difficult to render this way, since it is clearly a future event. Moreover, it can be argued that *justified* (ἐδικαίωσεν) is also future referring, but Paul does speak of justification as a present reality as well as occurring in the future, so it is not necessary to understand it as future referring here.

In any case, *glorified* (ἐδόξασεν) can only be understood as a future activity of God, since Paul expects such to occur at the parousia and eschaton, not in this current age. Exegetes who retain a rigid temporal-based understanding of the Greek verb are forced to explain why a "past tense" is used to refer to the future event of glorification. Most often, they attempt to explain it as a way of stressing Paul's certainty of the future—he is *so* certain of future glorification that he uses a past tense; it has already "been done" from God's perspective.[6]

However, this explanation is forced upon interpreters by an outdated understanding of Greek verbs. It raises the question, why use the aorist for *this* future event of which Paul is certain, and not others? It is odd that the plethora of future events that Paul hopes in are not also portrayed through the "past tense."

---

6. As Moo summarizes, "Most interpreters conclude, probably rightly, that Paul is looking at the believer's glorification from the standpoint of God, who has already decreed that it should take place" (Moo, *Romans*, 536). However, Moo also acknowledges the risk of "making temporal categories too important in interpreting the Greek tenses, and it may be that Paul uses the aorist simply to state the 'completion' of the action without regard to time" (Moo, *Romans*, 536n.165).

Is it because Paul is not as "certain" of those other future events? Why is this event alone singled out—in the entire Pauline corpus—as requiring special verbal treatment to underscore Paul's certainty of the future?

As several Greek scholars—myself included—have argued, the temporal reference of Greek verbs is not their primary meaning (or it is not a built-in meaning at all). Rather, verbs express *aspect*, and the aorist conveys *perfective aspect* specifically. This means that the aorist portrays an event as an undefined whole, from an *external viewpoint*.[7] Because of the nature of perfective aspect, it is often used of events that occurred in the past. But this is not an essential element of the aorist. Indeed, approximately 15 percent of aorist indicatives in the New Testament do *not* refer to the past (e.g., Mark 1:11). Indeed, when the context strongly suggests a *non*-past rendering of an aorist, we should not be straightjacketed by traditional convention, nor by the tradition of translations. Since *glorification* is a future event in Paul's mind, we should not hesitate to understand the aorist verb ἐδόξασεν as non-past referring.

But rather than treat the final aorist indicative differently from the previous aorist verbs in the string, it is better to regard the latter half of the string as functioning in the same way. In terms of the possible functions for aorist indicatives, a *gnomic* understanding is the best candidate for treating the last five aorists in the string (ἐκάλεσεν, ἐκάλεσεν, ἐδικαίωσεν, ἐδικαίωσεν, ἐδόξασεν) the same way, and to allow them to make sense in the context. The gnomic *Aktionsart* is an aorist function that conveys an action in a timeless manner. It still presents the action as an undefined whole, from an external viewpoint (as do all aorists), but rather than limiting the action to the past, it pertains to "all time."[8]

Before contemplating the difference this reading would make to the text, it is worth noting that the first three aorists (προέγνω, προώρισεν, προώρισεν) should continue to be understood as past referring because of the lexemes involved. The προ- prefix ("before") indicates temporal anteriority. While a gnomic reading remains nonetheless possible for these aorists, it would be forced. The lexemes naturally lend themselves to past temporal reference.

If we understand the first three aorists of Romans 8:29–30 as expressing past temporal reference, and the last five aorists as gnomic in *Aktionsart*, the verses could be translated as follows: *For those he foreknew he also predestined to be conformed to the image of his Son, so that he would be the firstborn among many brothers and sisters. And those he predestined, he also calls; and those he calls, he also justifies; and those he justifies, he also glorifies.*

---

7. See Campbell, *Advances in the Study of Greek*, ch. 5.
8. Campbell, *Basics of Verbal Aspect*, 88–89.

Admittedly, this reading of the aorists does significantly alter how Romans 8:29–30 is understood. Rather than detailing the past actions of God toward believers in a purely historical fashion, it indicates the ongoing actions of God that are predicated on his past actions. His foreknowing and predestining are firmly rooted in the past. But his calling and justifying are activities that continue to happen to this day, as God mercifully calls and declares righteous those he already foreknew and predestined. And God's glorification of those who have been called and justified is a future reality. But the gnomic understanding of calling, justifying, and glorifying does not limit these actions to a single temporal frame. These are the things that God simply "does," irrespective of when he does them.

Now we turn to consider the other elements of this text. *All things work together for the good of those who love God* (v. 28), and *all things* and *the good* should be understood in light of what follows in 8:29–30. If the aorist string details the saving activity of God that operates from before the creation of the world (foreknowledge, predestination) through to the ultimate future (glorification), then *all things* are bound up in that schema. There is nothing that can happen in this life that does not fall under the umbrella of this inauguration-to-consummation schema.

By the same token, all things work together *for the good of those who love God* because we know how the schema of salvation ends—all believers are glorified. Again, no matter what may happen in the interim, the final outcome is assured—glorification.

The foreknowledge and predestination of believers is for the purpose of being *conformed* (συμμόρφους) *to the image of* God's Son (v. 29a). We need not be distracted at this juncture by the scope of God's foreknowing and predestining—whether it pertains to all believers individually or as a corporate whole. Many other conversations have been taken up with such questions, but they often leave the other elements of the text underexamined. The main point ought to be understood that believers (individually or corporately, or both) are preordained to be conformed to Christ. And this results in the birth of a family of siblings—*so that he would be the firstborn among many brothers and sisters* (v. 29b). In other words, believers are foreknown and predestined for the purpose of becoming the family of God and the brothers and sisters of Christ.

On the basis of predestination, believers are called, justified, and glorified. Arguably this reflects a type of *ordo salutis* in which there is a logical progression from predestination, to calling, to justifying, to glorifying. There is also arguably a progression in the proximity of relationship through the sequence. People predestined are foreknown by God, but they do not yet know him.

But once called, they come into a relationship with him through Christ. And once in Christ, they are justified and set right with God without any barrier of sin or shame. And because they are justified, they will be glorified on the last day—which, as we have seen on several occasions, will involve *sharing* in the glory of Christ. This participation in the glorification of Christ is a relationally intimate, shared experience of glory. Unlike other elements of participation with Christ—dying with Christ, burial with Christ, rising with Christ, suffering with Christ—glorification with Christ will occur *in his physical presence*.

The significance of this should not be underestimated. To share in Christ's sufferings is no doubt an intimate experience, but it is nonetheless experienced in his "absence" (physical absence, at least). But glorification with Christ is fundamentally a different type of experience because of the physical proximity with him. In this way, glorification with Christ is not only the end point of the chain of God-ordained events leading to *the good* of *all things*, but it is the relational pinnacle of it all too. Glorification will be, in a word, glorious, because of the presence of the person to whom believers have been conformed.

> Rom 11:35–36 ἢ τίς προέδωκεν αὐτῷ,
> καὶ ἀνταποδοθήσεται αὐτῷ;
> 36 ὅτι ἐξ αὐτοῦ καὶ δι' αὐτοῦ καὶ εἰς αὐτὸν τὰ πάντα·
> **αὐτῷ ἡ δόξα εἰς τοὺς αἰῶνας, ἀμήν.**
>
> And who has ever given to God,
> that he should be repaid?
> 36 For from him and through him
> and to him are all things.
> **To him be the glory forever**. Amen.

This is the end of a brief doxology (11:33–36) that ascribes eternal glory to God. Of course, doxologies are named such because of the notion of glory, derived from the word δόξα (*glory*). While *all things* are *from him and through him and to him* (v. 36), *glory* is singled out and predicated to God. Since the final Greek clause lacks a verb, English translations supply the verb *to be*, assuming an optative expression—*to him be the glory*. The expression both ascribes and wishes glory to God.

While it is most likely correct to understand the familiar Greek idiom as optative in expression, it is not the only way the phrase can be understood. The Greek simply says *to him the glory forever* (αὐτῷ ἡ δόξα εἰς τοὺς αἰῶνας). The personal pronoun αὐτῷ could easily be understood to mean *with him* rather than *to him*. And the supplied verb *to be* could take on an indicative rather than optative sense, as we see in the previous (also verbless) clause—*for from him and through him and to him are all things* (ὅτι ἐξ αὐτοῦ καὶ δι' αὐτοῦ καὶ εἰς αὐτὸν τὰ πάντα). This would then cause the phrase to read, *with him is the glory forever.* Such a reading still ascribes eternal glory to God, but it removes the "wish" element that pertains to the optative mood.

While the optative "wish" element is probably intended, both ways of understanding the phrase ascribe eternal glory to God. And this glory is alone singled out in the context of the doxology. It seems, then, that the ascription of glory occupies a special place in Paul's vision of the eternal God. Above all else, he is glorious.

Rom 16:25–27 Τῷ δὲ δυναμένῳ ὑμᾶς στηρίξαι κατὰ τὸ εὐαγγέλιόν μου καὶ τὸ κήρυγμα Ἰησοῦ Χριστοῦ, κατὰ ἀποκάλυψιν μυστηρίου χρόνοις αἰωνίοις σεσιγημένου, 26 φανερωθέντος δὲ νῦν διά τε γραφῶν προφητικῶν κατ' ἐπιταγὴν τοῦ αἰωνίου θεοῦ εἰς ὑπακοὴν πίστεως εἰς πάντα τὰ ἔθνη γνωρισθέντος, 27 **μόνῳ σοφῷ θεῷ, διὰ Ἰησοῦ Χριστοῦ, ᾧ ἡ δόξα εἰς τοὺς αἰῶνας,** ἀμήν.

Now to him who is able to strengthen you according to my gospel and the proclamation about Jesus Christ, according to the revelation of the mystery kept silent for long ages 26 but now revealed and made known through the prophetic Scriptures, according to the command of the eternal God to advance the obedience of faith among all the Gentiles—27 **to the only wise God, through Jesus Christ—to him be the glory forever!** *Amen.*

The wording of the final clause of this doxology (16:27b) almost exactly matches that of 11:36—the only difference is that here the relative pronoun ᾧ is used instead of the personal pronoun αὐτῷ. The remaining ἡ δόξα εἰς τοὺς αἰῶνας, ἀμήν is identical in both texts.

This again raises, therefore, the question of the intended supplied verb—should it be understood as an optative or indicative *to be*? Compared to 11:36, in this instance the optative is the clear favorite. This is because of the way the doxology begins—*Now to him who is able to strengthen you . . .* (τῷ δὲ δυναμένῳ ὑμᾶς στηρίξαι; 16:25). From the beginning, the doxology is "wishing" toward God. It begins with *to him* in 16:25 and then finally gets to the glory wished upon God in v. 27—*To him . . . to him be the glory forever.* Thus, we should supply the optative verb *to be* in v. 27 and understand that Paul is wishing, as well as ascribing, eternal glory to God.

1 Cor 2:6–8 Σοφίαν δὲ λαλοῦμεν ἐν τοῖς τελείοις, σοφίαν δὲ οὐ τοῦ αἰῶνος τούτου οὐδὲ τῶν ἀρχόντων τοῦ αἰῶνος τούτου τῶν καταργουμένων· 7 ἀλλὰ λαλοῦμεν θεοῦ σοφίαν ἐν μυστηρίῳ τὴν ἀποκεκρυμμένην, ἣν προώρισεν ὁ θεὸς πρὸ τῶν αἰώνων εἰς **δόξαν** ἡμῶν, 8 **ἣν οὐδεὶς τῶν ἀρχόντων τοῦ αἰῶνος τούτου ἔγνωκεν· εἰ γὰρ ἔγνωσαν, οὐκ ἂν τὸν κύριον τῆς δόξης ἐσταύρωσαν.**

We do, however, speak a wisdom among the mature, but not a wisdom of this age, or of the rulers of this age, who are coming to nothing. 7 On the contrary, we speak God's hidden wisdom in a mystery, a wisdom God predestined before the ages for our **glory**. 8 ***None of the rulers of this age knew this wisdom, because if they had known it, they would not have crucified the Lord of glory***.

The chief concern in the wider context of this passage is Paul's exposition of the wisdom of God seen in the crucifixion of Christ. The subtheme of glory could easily be missed but is intriguingly woven in with respect to believers and with respect to Christ.

God's wisdom was hidden in a mystery, and it was *a wisdom God predestined before the ages for our glory* (2:7). Thus we see the connection between wisdom, predestining, and glory. The glory appears to be the endpoint and goal of such predestined wisdom, and it is clearly the glory of believers that Paul imagines. But we are not given any clues as to whether this is glory to be experienced in the pre-resurrected state or only post-resurrection. Either way, it is striking that the glorification of believers was predestined by God *before the ages* (v. 7). Their glory has been part of God's design from the very beginning.

The second reference to glory relates to Christ, who is described as *the Lord of glory* (v. 8).[9] There is an intentional irony in the use of this description, since Paul combines it with the crucifixion of Christ. Crucifixion was, of course, deeply dishonorable—which is its offense to the wisdom of the world—so it jars strongly against the description of Christ as *the Lord of glory*.

But such jarring plays into Paul's agenda throughout the wider context, in which he argues that the wisdom and power of God are revealed in the foolishness and weakness of the cross (cf. 1:18–31). It is a reversal of human expectation that puts crucifixion and the Lord of glory together, and such matching bespeaks of the hidden wisdom and mystery of God. The Lord of

---

9. The expression is unique for Paul but common in 1 Enoch (22.14; 25.3, 7; 27.3, 4; 66.2; 75.3); Barrett, *First Epistle to the Corinthians*, 72.

glory would not have been crucified if *the rulers of this age knew this wisdom* or who he was (2:8).

Because Paul describes Christ as *the Lord of glory* in connection with his crucifixion, and he says that *the rulers of this age* would not have crucified him had they known God's wisdom, we may safely assume that Paul sees Christ as glorious in his pre-resurrected state—indeed, even as he hung on the cross. He was the Lord of glory at the time of his crucifixion, not only after it. Given this, we may also safely assume that Paul regards the glory of Christ as *hidden* at that time. The hiddenness of his glory conveys apocalyptic overtones, in that the reality of the situation was not at the time revealed, though it would be later.

If this reading is correct, then it may feed back to the earlier question of whether the glory of believers (2:7) is to be understood as a type of present glory, or a future, post-resurrection glory. The apocalyptic overtones detected in 2:8, with the hidden glory of the crucified Christ, suggest that the same kind of glory is envisaged in 2:7. That is, the glory of believers that results from the predestined wisdom of God is a current, pre-resurrection glory. It is now hidden from the world in the same way that the glory of Christ, the Lord of glory, was once hidden.

> 1 Cor 15:42–44 Οὕτως καὶ ἡ ἀνάστασις τῶν νεκρῶν. σπείρεται ἐν φθορᾷ, ἐγείρεται ἐν ἀφθαρσίᾳ· 43 **σπείρεται ἐν ἀτιμίᾳ, ἐγείρεται ἐν δόξῃ·** σπείρεται ἐν ἀσθενείᾳ, ἐγείρεται ἐν δυνάμει· 44 σπείρεται σῶμα ψυχικόν, ἐγείρεται σῶμα πνευματικόν. εἰ ἔστιν σῶμα ψυχικόν, ἔστιν καὶ πνευματικόν.
>
> *So it is with the resurrection of the dead: Sown in corruption, raised in incorruption; 43* ***sown in dishonor, raised in glory****; sown in weakness, raised in power; 44 sown a natural body, raised a spiritual body. If there is a natural body, there is also a spiritual body.*

Paul draws on the seed imagery introduced at 15:36–37—*You fool! What you sow does not come to life unless it dies. And as for what you sow—you are not sowing the body that will be, but only a seed, perhaps of wheat or another grain.* Just as a seed must die in order to become something else—something greater—*so it is with the resurrection of the dead* (v. 42a). The body is *sown in corruption, raised in incorruption; sown in dishonor, raised in glory* (vv. 42b–43a). This means that at the point of death, the body is corrupted and dishonorable, but in the resurrection it is raised incorruptible and glorious.

It is clear, then, that *glory* is a quality bestowed on believers in the future, at the moment of resurrection. It must have some sort of physicality to it, since it pertains to the raised body. The body will be *in glory*—it will be glorious and will be fit for glory. Moreover, glory is part of what it means to have a *spiritual body*. Whatever else distinguishes it from a *natural body*, glory is a key distinction.

> 2 Cor 3:12–18 Ἔχοντες οὖν τοιαύτην ἐλπίδα πολλῇ παρρησίᾳ χρώμεθα 13 καὶ οὐ καθάπερ Μωϋσῆς ἐτίθει κάλυμμα ἐπὶ τὸ πρόσωπον αὐτοῦ πρὸς τὸ μὴ ἀτενίσαι τοὺς υἱοὺς Ἰσραὴλ εἰς τὸ τέλος τοῦ καταργουμένου. 14 ἀλλὰ ἐπωρώθη τὰ νοήματα αὐτῶν. ἄχρι γὰρ τῆς σήμερον ἡμέρας τὸ αὐτὸ κάλυμμα ἐπὶ τῇ ἀναγνώσει τῆς παλαιᾶς διαθήκης μένει, μὴ ἀνακαλυπτόμενον ὅτι ἐν Χριστῷ καταργεῖται· 15 ἀλλ᾽ ἕως σήμερον ἡνίκα ἂν ἀναγινώσκηται Μωϋσῆς, κάλυμμα ἐπὶ τὴν καρδίαν αὐτῶν κεῖται· 16 ἡνίκα δὲ ἐὰν ἐπιστρέψῃ πρὸς κύριον, περιαιρεῖται τὸ κάλυμμα. 17 ὁ δὲ κύριος τὸ πνεῦμά ἐστιν· οὗ δὲ τὸ πνεῦμα κυρίου, ἐλευθερία. 18 **ἡμεῖς δὲ πάντες ἀνακεκαλυμμένῳ προσώπῳ τὴν δόξαν κυρίου κατοπτριζόμενοι τὴν αὐτὴν εἰκόνα μεταμορφούμεθα ἀπὸ δόξης εἰς δόξαν** καθάπερ ἀπὸ κυρίου πνεύματος.

> *Since, then, we have such a hope, we act with great boldness. 13 We are not like Moses, who used to put a veil over his face to prevent the Israelites from gazing steadily until the end of the glory of what was being set aside, 14 but their minds were hardened. For to this day, at the reading of the old covenant, the same veil remains; it is not lifted, because it is set aside only in Christ. 15 Yet still today, whenever Moses is read, a veil lies over their hearts, 16 but whenever a person turns to the Lord, the veil is removed. 17 Now the Lord is the Spirit, and where the Spirit of the Lord is, there is freedom. 18* **We all, with unveiled faces, are looking as in a mirror at the glory of the Lord and are being transformed into the same image from glory to glory;** *this is from the Lord who is the Spirit.*

Hope-inspired boldness allows Paul and his fellow ministers to act differently from Moses, who covered his face with a veil to prevent the people from beholding the temporary glory of the old covenant (3:12–13). The same veil covers the hearts of those today who remain under that covenant (vv. 14–15). When a Jew turns to Christ, however, the veil is removed, bringing freedom (vv. 16–17). Unlike Moses and those who read Moses in Paul's day, he and all those under the new covenant have unveiled faces and hearts and look directly *at the glory of the Lord* (v. 18a). The contrast here concerns the nature of the two covenants—one has a fading glory; the other an everlasting glory (v. 13b). For one, it is appropriate not to look at its glory directly (vv. 13, 15); for the other, it is appropriate to look and even to be transformed by its glory (v. 18).

The reference to looking *as in a mirror at the glory of the Lord* (v. 18) could be understood to mean that Paul supposes that new-covenant believers see the glory of the Lord reflected in themselves. In the phrase it translates (τὴν δόξαν κυρίου κατοπτριζόμενοι), the verb (κατοπτρίζω) can be understood in such a way,[10] though it can also be understood as "to contemplate something."[11] These two options put the focus on different things. With the former, the focus is on the transformation that the Lord's glory brings to his people such that they reflect his glory in themselves. With the latter, the focus is simply on the Lord's glory. While at first blush the latter reading might seem more appropriate (to focus on the Lord's glory),[12] on balance the former is more likely correct. This is because, first, v. 18b refers to the transformation of believers. Second, this transformation is *into the same image* (τὴν αὐτὴν εἰκόνα; likely referring to the image of the Lord). The *image* language may involve a wordplay with the notion of a mirror's reflection, so that looking into a mirror one sees oneself becoming the image of the Lord—one's own reflection is *the same image* as the Lord. Third, this transformation into the same image occurs *from glory to glory* (ἀπὸ δόξης εἰς δόξαν). While this expression is delightfully vague, it *may* be shorthand for what the whole verse so far has been getting at, namely, that believers are transformed into the Lord's image *from his glory* into *our glory*. Fourth, the final phrase of v. 18 says that *this is from the Lord who is the Spirit* (καθάπερ ἀπὸ κυρίου πνεύματος), which is similar to *the Lord is the Spirit* in v. 17a (ὁ δὲ κύριος τὸ πνεῦμά ἐστιν)—clearly also used in a transformative context (vv. 16–17). The Lord who removes the veil and brings freedom is the Spirit, and the Lord who effects transformation of believers into the image of the Lord is the Spirit. Thus, the whole thrust of v. 18 is concerned with transformation.

Putting all this together, we see that glory is at the heart of new-covenant faith and involves both the glory of the Lord and the glory that he shares with his people. Through contemplating his glory, believers begin to look as in a mirror, seeing the Lord's glory in themselves as he transforms them with his glory. This means that the Lord's glory is transformative and changes believers now. Glory is not only a feature of the future; it is powerful and active in this present age.

2 Cor 4:16–18 Διὸ οὐκ ἐγκακοῦμεν, ἀλλ' εἰ καὶ ὁ ἔξω ἡμῶν ἄνθρωπος διαφθείρεται, ἀλλ' ὁ ἔσω ἡμῶν ἀνακαινοῦται ἡμέρᾳ καὶ ἡμέρᾳ. 17 τὸ γὰρ

---

10. BDAG 535: "Look at someth. as in a mirror." See also Fredrick J. Long, *2 Corinthians: A Handbook on the Greek Text*, BHGNT (Waco, TX: Baylor University Press, 2015), 73–74.
11. BDAG 535.
12. See Seifrid for a defense of this reading (*Second Letter to the Corinthians*, 180n.293).

παραυτίκα ἐλαφρὸν τῆς θλίψεως ἡμῶν καθ' ὑπερβολὴν εἰς ὑπερβολὴν αἰώνιον βάρος δόξης κατεργάζεται ἡμῖν, 18 μὴ σκοπούντων ἡμῶν τὰ βλεπόμενα ἀλλὰ τὰ μὴ βλεπόμενα· τὰ γὰρ βλεπόμενα πρόσκαιρα, τὰ δὲ μὴ βλεπόμενα αἰώνια.

*Therefore we do not give up. Even though our outer person is being destroyed, our inner person is being renewed day by day. 17 **For our momentary light affliction is producing for us an absolutely incomparable eternal weight of glory**. 18 So we do not focus on what is seen, but on what is unseen. For what is seen is temporary, but what is unseen is eternal.*

Though the *outer person*—the pre-resurrected physical body—*is being destroyed* (4:16a), the *inner person is being renewed day by day* (v. 16b). Paul does not explain what exactly is meant by the *inner person*, but it appears to be related to *glory* (v. 17), and it is *unseen* and *eternal* (v. 18). Thus the *inner person* most likely represents the person irrespective of the body. In the following passage Paul develops this notion further by discussing the clothing of our eternal and heavenly dwelling, which is juxtaposed with our earthly tent (5:1–4). This exchange from earthly tent to heavenly dwelling implies that the same inner person will dwell in each—it is the "outer" shelter that will change.

All of this seems to mean that, while the pre-resurrected body is subjected to decay and will be replaced—or perhaps better, upgraded—the inner person is even now being refreshed. This is what is meant by the *inner person is being renewed day by day* (4:16). The renewal of the inner person implies that, by the presence of the Spirit, the inner person is already being prepared for eternal glory. Indeed, this is what the following verse means—*For our momentary light affliction is producing for us an absolutely incomparable eternal weight of glory* (v. 17). The present experiences of suffering, described by Paul as *momentary* and *light*, are already producing (κατεργάζεται) something of enduring value within believers.

While this production of glory could be understood to refer to a result only to be experienced and enjoyed after bodily resurrection, the context leans toward it referring to something unfolding even now in this present life. Indeed, it may be better to understand ἡμῖν to mean "in us" rather than "for us," which is a perfectly natural (and preferable) rendering of the dative.[13] That is, the eternal

---

13. Admittedly, most commentators and translations (e.g., CSB, NIV, ESV) go the other way, taking ἡμῖν as a dative of advantage (e.g., Guthrie, *2 Corinthians*, 272; Martin, *2 Corinthians*, 238; Long, *2 Corinthians*, 90). But this is asserted, not argued. While the dative can indicate advantage ("for us") or location ("in us"), the focus on the "inner person" and its renewal in 4:16 strongly supports the locative reading. Paul's interest

weight of glory is being produced *in us*. Yes, this glory is eternal (αἰώνιον), but that does not mean it must therefore only begin *after* the temporary is dispensed with. Indeed, *what is unseen is eternal* (v. 18), which most likely refers to the inner person already in view. Thus, the inner person is eternal. It is the "outer dwelling" that will be changed at the point of bodily resurrection, but the inner person housed within both old and new dwellings will experience continuity.

All of this means that the *incomparable eternal weight of glory* is something that is now being produced within believers. The inner person is already moving toward glory. Taking other passages into account, this is not the fullness of glory that is to come, since glory does not yet pertain to the body. The future resurrected body will be one of glory, in comparison to the current inglorious body (see on 1 Cor 15:42–44 above). Thus, glory will not be seen in its fullness until it can be predicated of the outer person as well as the inner person. In the resurrection, both "glories" will be united in each raised person.

Gal 1:3–5 χάρις ὑμῖν καὶ εἰρήνη ἀπὸ θεοῦ πατρὸς ἡμῶν καὶ κυρίου Ἰησοῦ Χριστοῦ 4 τοῦ δόντος ἑαυτὸν ὑπὲρ τῶν ἁμαρτιῶν ἡμῶν, ὅπως ἐξέληται ἡμᾶς ἐκ τοῦ αἰῶνος τοῦ ἐνεστῶτος πονηροῦ κατὰ τὸ θέλημα τοῦ θεοῦ καὶ πατρὸς ἡμῶν, 5 ᾧ ἡ **δόξα εἰς τοὺς αἰῶνας τῶν αἰώνων**, ἀμήν.

Grace to you and peace from God the Father and our Lord Jesus Christ, 4 who gave himself for our sins to rescue us from this present evil age, according to the will of our God and Father. 5 **To him be the glory forever and ever.** *Amen.*

This brief doxological note at the tail of Paul's greeting to the Galatians (1:5) is again similar to those observed thus far (cf. Rom 11:36; 16:27). Indeed, the wording is exactly the same as Romans 16:27 except that here an extra τῶν αἰώνων is added to εἰς τοὺς αἰῶνας (*forever and ever*). As such the same issue detected in the previous two doxologies also pertains to this one—how to understand the supplied verb *to be*. As with the previous two doxologies, the optative understanding is most likely. Paul is "wishing" and ascribing eternal glory to the God and Father of our Lord Jesus Christ.

Eph 1:5–6 προορίσας ἡμᾶς εἰς υἱοθεσίαν διὰ Ἰησοῦ Χριστοῦ εἰς αὐτόν, κατὰ τὴν εὐδοκίαν τοῦ θελήματος αὐτοῦ, 6 εἰς **ἔπαινον δόξης τῆς χάριτος αὐτοῦ** ἧς ἐχαρίτωσεν ἡμᾶς ἐν τῷ ἠγαπημένῳ.

---

is to describe what is happening "within"—the inner person is renewed through the production "in us" of an eternal glory.

*He predestined us to be adopted as sons through Jesus Christ for himself, according to the good pleasure of his will, 6 **to the praise of his glorious grace** that he lavished on us in the Beloved One.*

While this example may appear to be doxological in a manner similar to Romans 11:36, 16:27, and Galatians 1:5, it differs in two important respects. First, glory is not treated as the central entity of the expression. In the doxologies previously examined, glory is the substantive entity that is wished and ascribed to God. Here, the genitive noun δόξης ("glory") is attributed (*glorious*)—a regular function of genitive nouns—modifying *his grace* (τῆς χάριτος αὐτοῦ).[14] Grace is thus the central concept in view, rather than glory. But this grace is *glorious*.[15]

Second, glory (or *glorious*) is found within a purpose clause—*the praise for his glorious grace* (εἰς ἔπαινον δόξης τῆς χάριτος αὐτοῦ; Eph 1:6). This is not doxological in the usual sense of wishing or ascribing eternal glory to God but rather indicates the end point and goal of God's predestining and adopting activity. These are *according to the good pleasure of his will* (v. 5), and lead to the praise of his glorious grace. The praise of God's glorious grace is thus the ultimate *telos* of God's redeeming work. Thus, Paul is not in pure doxological mode but in a kind of doxo-theological frame. He is stating that praise has come, and will come, aimed at God's glorious grace, as predestined and adopted believers in Christ realize all that God has done for them.

Eph 1:11–14 ἐν ᾧ καὶ ἐκληρώθημεν προορισθέντες κατὰ πρόθεσιν τοῦ τὰ πάντα ἐνεργοῦντος κατὰ τὴν βουλὴν τοῦ θελήματος αὐτοῦ 12 εἰς τὸ εἶναι ἡμᾶς εἰς ἔπαινον **δόξης αὐτοῦ** τοὺς προηλπικότας ἐν τῷ Χριστῷ. 13 ἐν ᾧ καὶ ὑμεῖς ἀκούσαντες τὸν λόγον τῆς ἀληθείας, τὸ εὐαγγέλιον τῆς σωτηρίας ὑμῶν, ἐν ᾧ καὶ πιστεύσαντες ἐσφραγίσθητε τῷ πνεύματι τῆς ἐπαγγελίας τῷ ἁγίῳ, 14 ὅ ἐστιν ἀρραβὼν τῆς κληρονομίας ἡμῶν, εἰς ἀπολύτρωσιν τῆς περιποιήσεως, **εἰς ἔπαινον τῆς δόξης αὐτοῦ**.

In him we have also received an inheritance, because we were predestined according to the plan of the one who works out everything in agreement with the purpose of his will, 12 so that we who had already put our hope in Christ might

---

14. Merkle, *Ephesians*, 21–22.
15. Since the expression δόξης τῆς χάριτος αὐτοῦ contains *two* genitive nouns, one may wonder whether χάριτος (*grace*) ought to be understood as the adjectival genitive, rather than δόξης (*glorious*). But this is unlikely for two reasons. First, τῆς χάριτος has the article, while δόξης does not. This alone pushes toward accepting δόξης as the adjectival genitive. Second, τῆς χάριτος is modified by the personal pronoun αὐτοῦ, which also points to it being the main noun.

*bring **praise to his glory**. 13 In him you also were sealed with the promised Holy Spirit when you heard the word of truth, the gospel of your salvation, and when you believed. 14 The Holy Spirit is the down payment of our inheritance, until the redemption of the possession, **to the praise of his glory**.*

The two references to *glory* here (1:12, 14) are very similar to that found in 1:6. The similarities include the fact that all three instances occur within purpose clauses indicating the end point and goal of God's gracious activity toward human beings—that believers *might bring praise to his glory* (εἰς τὸ εἶναι ἡμᾶς εἰς ἔπαινον δόξης αὐτοῦ; v. 12); *to the praise of his glory* (εἰς ἔπαινον τῆς δόξης αὐτοῦ; v. 14). The end point and goal of all God's saving activity is that praise will be issued from redeemed humanity.

The significant difference, however, between these two instances and that found in 1:6 is that here *glory* is the central concept and the object of praise. While 1:6 saw δόξης (translated *glorious*) function as an attributed genitive modifying τῆς χάριτος αὐτοῦ (*his grace*), *glory* stands alone in 1:12 and 1:14, so there is no possible confusion as to which of the two genitives is the object of praise and which functions adjectivally. More importantly, this means that glory itself is treated independently as the object of praise rather than grace.[16]

Similar to 1:6, however, these statements are only partly doxological, since Paul is not in doxological mode but is theologizing *about* glory and its reception of praise flowing forth from the redeemed people of God. As with 1:6, the praise of God's glory is the purpose of God's predestining work—*we were predestined . . . so that we who had already put our hope in Christ might bring praise to his glory* (vv. 11–12). Alongside this Paul adds that the Holy Spirit secures our inheritance *until the redemption of the possession, to the praise of his glory* (v. 14). Believers' reception of the possession—likely a synonym for the inheritance—also has the end point and goal of *the praise of his glory*. Thus, when the magnificent and eternal inheritance is finally possessed by the people of God, it will all work toward the praise of his glory, as they recognize and appreciate all that God is and all that he has done.

Eph 1:17–18 ἵνα ὁ θεὸς τοῦ κυρίου ἡμῶν Ἰησοῦ Χριστοῦ, ὁ πατὴρ **τῆς δόξης**, δώῃ ὑμῖν πνεῦμα σοφίας καὶ ἀποκαλύψεως ἐν ἐπιγνώσει αὐτοῦ, 18 πεφωτισμένους τοὺς ὀφθαλμοὺς τῆς καρδίας ὑμῶν εἰς τὸ εἰδέναι ὑμᾶς τίς ἐστιν ἡ ἐλπὶς τῆς κλήσεως αὐτοῦ, **τίς ὁ πλοῦτος τῆς δόξης τῆς κληρονομίας αὐτοῦ ἐν τοῖς ἁγίοις**

---

16. Larkin, *Ephesians*, 14.

*I pray that the God of our Lord Jesus Christ, **the glorious** Father, would give you the Spirit of wisdom and revelation in the knowledge of him. 18 I pray that the eyes of your heart may be enlightened so that you may know what is the hope of his calling, **what is the wealth of his glorious inheritance in the saints***

The God to whom Paul prays is described as *glorious*, with the genitive τῆς δόξης clearly functioning as an attributive genitive.[17] In this prayer for his readers, Paul hopes that *the eyes of* their *heart may be enlightened* so that they would know *the wealth of his glorious inheritance in the saints* (1:18). As an attributive use of the genitive noun, δόξης modifies *his inheritance* (τῆς κληρονομίας αὐτοῦ).[18] The inheritance of the saints is a future reality that will one day be received by believers, as 1:14 indicates—*The Holy Spirit is the down payment of our inheritance, until the redemption of the possession, to the praise of his glory.* The language of *down payment* and *until the redemption of the possession* demonstrates that the full reception of the inheritance is yet to be realized. The Spirit guarantees the obtainment of believers' future inheritance. This future inheritance is glorious in nature; indeed, Paul wants them to grasp the *wealth* of this glorious inheritance.

Eph 3:12–13 ἐν ᾧ ἔχομεν τὴν παρρησίαν καὶ προσαγωγὴν ἐν πεποιθήσει διὰ τῆς πίστεως αὐτοῦ. 13 διὸ αἰτοῦμαι μὴ ἐγκακεῖν ἐν ταῖς θλίψεσίν μου ὑπὲρ ὑμῶν, **ἥτις ἐστὶν δόξα ὑμῶν.**

*In him we have boldness and confident access through faith in him. 13 So then I ask you not to be discouraged over my afflictions on your behalf, **for they are your glory.***

Paul does not want his readers to be discouraged over his afflictions on their behalf. He sees himself as a suffering servant whose suffering is not incidental or without meaning; rather, he suffers for them. Moreover, Paul regards his suffering as being their glory (ἥτις ἐστὶν δόξα ὑμῶν; 3:13). This pregnant expression seems to mean that his afflictions contribute to their standing in Christ, which in turns secures for them eternal glory.[19]

This reading would seem to be supported by the previous verse, in which Paul gives expression to the bold and confident access to God that believers

---

17. Merkle, *Ephesians*, 41.
18. Merkle, *Ephesians*, 43; contra Larkin, *Ephesians*, 21–22, who takes τῆς δόξης as an attributed genitive modifying ὁ πλοῦτος ("rich glory") rather than τῆς κληρονομίας αὐτοῦ.
19. Mark D. Roberts, *Ephesians*, SGBC (Grand Rapids: Zondervan, 2016), 99.

have through faith in Christ (v. 12). Since Paul proclaims Christ, it is his work that enables others to come to faith in him and thereby enjoy the glory of God through confident access. This is the connection between Paul's afflictions and believers' glory—the proclamation of the gospel, which brings suffering to Paul, also brings salvation and glorification of those who come to Christ.

Eph 3:20–21 Τῷ δὲ δυναμένῳ ὑπὲρ πάντα ποιῆσαι ὑπερεκπερισσοῦ ὧν αἰτούμεθα ἢ νοοῦμεν κατὰ τὴν δύναμιν τὴν ἐνεργουμένην ἐν ἡμῖν, 21 **αὐτῷ ἡ δόξα ἐν τῇ ἐκκλησίᾳ καὶ ἐν Χριστῷ Ἰησοῦ εἰς πάσας τὰς γενεὰς** τοῦ αἰῶνος τῶν αἰώνων, ἀμήν.

Now to him who is able to do above and beyond all that we ask or think according to the power that works in us—21 **to him be glory in the church and in Christ Jesus to all generations**, *forever and ever. Amen.*

This doxology contains elements we have seen before, along with some new features. As with Romans 16:25–27, the doxology begins, *Now to him who is able* . . . (τῷ δὲ δυναμένῳ; Eph 3:20). And as with that passage and Romans 11:35–36, the doxology ends with a verbless clause wishing and ascribing eternal glory to God.

What is unusual about this doxology, however, is the inclusion of two "arenas" for the eternal glory of God. This glory is to be *in the church and in Christ Jesus to all generations* (Eph 3:21). These are described as "arenas" because Paul seems to view the church and Christ as "locations" in which the glory of God will be displayed.

The redeemed and sanctified collection of God's people in Christ will reflect and "house" the glory of God, so that when the cosmos sees the church, it testifies to that glory.[20] Likewise, the eternal glory of God is reflected and housed in Christ Jesus himself. As the Lord over all creation and all rulers and authorities (1:20–23), and as the Savior and husband of the church (5:23–27), he will be preeminently glorious. But the point here is that he will display the glory of God.

An additional novelty here is the way in which the glory of God is to be displayed in the two arenas of the church and of Christ *to all generations* (3:21). Doubtless this ascription is meant to complement the eternal duration of the glory of God—it will not only endure *forever and ever* but will be *to all generations*. More specifically, it focuses on people rather than timespan. The point is that the eternal glory of God will be displayed in the church and

---

20. "The church makes God's glory known because its very existence as a multiethnic community that is reconciled to God testifies to God's beautifully complex wisdom (3:10; cf. 2:11–22)" (Thielman, *Ephesians*, 243).

in Christ for all to see. It will be witnessed by every generation of humanity, past, present, and future.

> Phil 2:9–11 διὸ καὶ ὁ θεὸς αὐτὸν ὑπερύψωσεν
> καὶ ἐχαρίσατο αὐτῷ τὸ ὄνομα
> τὸ ὑπὲρ πᾶν ὄνομα,
> 10 ἵνα ἐν τῷ ὀνόματι Ἰησοῦ
> πᾶν γόνυ κάμψῃ
> ἐπουρανίων καὶ ἐπιγείων καὶ καταχθονίων
> 11 καὶ πᾶσα γλῶσσα ἐξομολογήσηται ὅτι
> κύριος Ἰησοῦς Χριστὸς
> εἰς δόξαν θεοῦ πατρός.

> *For this reason God highly exalted him*
> *and gave him the name*
> *that is above every name,*
> *10 so that at the name of Jesus*
> *every knee will bow—*
> *in heaven and on earth*
> *and under the earth—*
> *11 and **every tongue will confess***
> ***that Jesus Christ is Lord,***
> ***to the glory of God the Father.***

The second half of the "Christ hymn" of Philippians 2:6–11 ends on the note of the glory of God (v. 11b). This follows the exaltation of Christ, with its bestowal of his name above all names (v. 9), the acknowledgement and submission of all *in heaven and on earth and under the earth* (v. 10), and the universal confession *that Jesus Christ is Lord* (2:11a).

This vivid and extensive description of the exaltation of Christ serves to underscore the grandeur and splendor of the glory of God the Father. The final clause of the Christ hymn (v. 11b) ought not be ignored as a side note or mere embellishment. It is more likely intended to be the climax of the whole thing—in the end, after all has been accomplished, after Christ has received full acknowledgement of his exaltation, the final and climactic element of it all is the glory of God the Father.[21]

---

21. For Fowl, "the acclamation of Jesus as 'Lord' serves to enhance rather than compete with the glory of the God who says, 'I am the Lord, that is my name; my glory I give to none other'" (Isa 42:8). Just as 2:6 identifies Christ with God in terms of 'appearance' and 'equality,' 2:11 identifies Christ with God in that the

This point demonstrates how significant the glory of God is for Paul. If this reading of the Christ hymn is correct, the glory of God should be seen as the greatest possible outcome of all things. It is the chief end, *telos*, and greatest good of the cosmos.

Phil 3:18–21 πολλοὶ γὰρ περιπατοῦσιν οὓς πολλάκις ἔλεγον ὑμῖν, νῦν δὲ καὶ κλαίων λέγω, τοὺς ἐχθροὺς τοῦ σταυροῦ τοῦ Χριστοῦ, 19 ὧν τὸ τέλος ἀπώλεια, ὧν ὁ θεὸς ἡ κοιλία καὶ **ἡ δόξα ἐν τῇ αἰσχύνῃ αὐτῶν**, οἱ τὰ ἐπίγεια φρονοῦντες. 20 ἡμῶν γὰρ τὸ πολίτευμα ἐν οὐρανοῖς ὑπάρχει, ἐξ οὗ καὶ σωτῆρα ἀπεκδεχόμεθα κύριον Ἰησοῦν Χριστόν, 21 **ὃς μετασχηματίσει τὸ σῶμα τῆς ταπεινώσεως ἡμῶν σύμμορφον τῷ σώματι τῆς δόξης αὐτοῦ** κατὰ τὴν ἐνέργειαν τοῦ δύνασθαι αὐτὸν καὶ ὑποτάξαι αὐτῷ τὰ πάντα.

For I have often told you, and now say again with tears, that many live as enemies of the cross of Christ. 19 Their end is destruction; their god is their stomach; ***their glory is in their shame****. They are focused on earthly things, 20 but our citizenship is in heaven, and we eagerly wait for a Savior from there, the Lord Jesus Christ. 21* ***He will transform the body of our humble condition into the likeness of his glorious body****, by the power that enables him to subject everything to himself.*

The *enemies of the cross of Christ* have a type of glory, meant ironically by Paul of course, which is found in their shame (3:19a). This is a worldly "glory" as *they are focused on earthly things* (v. 19b). In contrast, believers' *citizenship is in heaven*, meaning that their focus is not on earthly things. Rather than being consumed by their "stomach" and various shameful behaviors, believers await their Savior from heaven (v. 20).

Not only are believers heavenly minded, but they will also become heavenly *bodied* when *the body of* their *humble condition* is transformed *into the likeness of his glorious body* (v. 21a). In keeping with their heavenly mindedness and heavenly expectation of the coming of Christ, the glory that believers will enjoy is by way of their heavenly body. It will be a glorious body, like that of Christ. This then provides further contrast with the enemies of Christ, whose glory is in their shame. Their "glory" is temporal and this worldly, while also being an "anti-glory" from a heavenly perspective. In contrast, believers partake in a future, heavenly glory that is facilitated by the transformation of their bodies.[22]

---

worship reserved for Yawheh alone is directed to Christ, without diminishing or competing with the glory of God the Father" (Stephen E. Fowl, *Philippians*, THNTC [Grand Rapids: Eerdmans, 2005], 104).

22. "From bodies of humiliation ... Christ will transfigure them into bodies like his own glorious

Christ is empowered to effect this transformation *by the power that enables him to subject everything to himself* (v. 21b). While this *power* is not specified, we may assume that Paul refers to an authority delegated to him by the Father, the one who raised Christ from the dead.

Phil 4:18–20 ἀπέχω δὲ πάντα καὶ περισσεύω· πεπλήρωμαι δεξάμενος παρὰ Ἐπαφροδίτου τὰ παρ' ὑμῶν, ὀσμὴν εὐωδίας, θυσίαν δεκτήν, εὐάρεστον τῷ θεῷ. 19 ὁ δὲ θεός μου πληρώσει πᾶσαν χρείαν ὑμῶν κατὰ τὸ πλοῦτος αὐτοῦ ἐν δόξῃ ἐν Χριστῷ Ἰησοῦ. 20 τῷ δὲ θεῷ καὶ πατρὶ ἡμῶν ἡ δόξα εἰς τοὺς αἰῶνας τῶν αἰώνων, ἀμήν.

But I have received everything in full, and I have an abundance. I am fully supplied, having received from Epaphroditus what you provided—a fragrant offering, an acceptable sacrifice, pleasing to God. **19 And my God will supply all your needs according to his riches in glory in Christ Jesus.** **20 Now to our God and Father be glory forever and ever.** *Amen.*

Through Epaphroditus, the Philippians have given generously in support of Paul (1:18). Having given sacrificially of their resources, Paul affirms that their needs will be met, as *God will supply all your needs according to his riches in glory in Christ Jesus* (v. 19). The meaning of this statement, apart from the obvious (that God will supply their needs), requires some teasing out. The basic idea appears to be that God's provision of the Philippians' needs will come from *his riches* (τὸ πλοῦτος αὐτοῦ).

But we then see that these are *his riches in glory in Christ Jesus*. And therein lies the confusion. Paul has been discussing the Philippians' material needs, which he says will be supplied by God out of his riches. After all, the earth and everything in it belongs to the Lord. But the discussion of material need is then transposed to something else when Paul adds *in glory in Christ Jesus*. God will supply their needs out of his riches in glory. Since it is not normal to regard *glory* as a material substance, there is a cognitive dissonance created when Paul assures the Philippians that their material needs will be supplied by immaterial glory. It is a little like saying that one's hunger will be resolved with love and kindness.

Perhaps, however, there is no cognitive dissonance for Paul. Whatever class of substance we might assign to *glory*, it is not without consequence in the material

---

resurrected body, that is, bodies infused with a new determining force of the Spirit that is heavenly and divine, bodies that are imperishable and immortal, models of glory and power" (Gerald F. Hawthorne, *Philippians*, WBC 43 [Waco, TX: Word, 1983], 174).

world. Paul seems to believe that the immaterial glory of God can effect and empower change within the material world. Thus, God's riches in glory *do* constitute the treasure-store out of which material needs of human beings may be met. The glory of God transcends the material-immaterial distinction, just as God (who is spirit) does also. If he is able to act and effect his will within the material world, while being nonmaterial himself, then the riches of his glory can supply the material needs facing the Philippians.[23]

Finally, before concluding the letter with greetings (4:21–23), Paul offers a brief doxology, wishing and ascribing eternal glory to God (4:20).

Col 1:24–27 Νῦν χαίρω ἐν τοῖς παθήμασιν ὑπὲρ ὑμῶν καὶ ἀνταναπληρῶ τὰ ὑστερήματα τῶν θλίψεων τοῦ Χριστοῦ ἐν τῇ σαρκί μου ὑπὲρ τοῦ σώματος αὐτοῦ, ὅ ἐστιν ἡ ἐκκλησία, 25 ἧς ἐγενόμην ἐγὼ διάκονος κατὰ τὴν οἰκονομίαν τοῦ θεοῦ τὴν δοθεῖσάν μοι εἰς ὑμᾶς πληρῶσαι τὸν λόγον τοῦ θεοῦ, 26 τὸ μυστήριον τὸ ἀποκεκρυμμένον ἀπὸ τῶν αἰώνων καὶ ἀπὸ τῶν γενεῶν – νῦν δὲ ἐφανερώθη τοῖς ἁγίοις αὐτοῦ, 27 **οἷς ἠθέλησεν ὁ θεὸς γνωρίσαι τί τὸ πλοῦτος τῆς δόξης τοῦ μυστηρίου τούτου ἐν τοῖς ἔθνεσιν, ὅ ἐστιν Χριστὸς ἐν ὑμῖν, ἡ ἐλπὶς τῆς δόξης**

Now I rejoice in my sufferings for you, and I am completing in my flesh what is lacking in Christ's afflictions for his body, that is, the church. 25 I have become its servant, according to God's commission that was given to me for you, to make the word of God fully known, 26 the mystery hidden for ages and generations but now revealed to his saints. 27 ***God wanted to make known among the Gentiles the glorious wealth of this mystery, which is Christ in you, the hope of glory.***

Paul is the servant of the church *to make the word of God fully known* (1:25), which he explains is bound up with *the mystery hidden for ages and generations but now revealed to his saints* (v. 26). In particular, as the apostle to the gentiles, he plays a central role in God's desire *to make known among the Gentiles the glorious wealth of this mystery* (v. 27a). The content of the mystery *is Christ in you, the hope of glory* (v. 27b). The fact that Christ lives among the gentiles (by his Spirit) is the solution to the riddle that has been kept hidden until the proper time: How would God bless the nations through Abraham? The answer is found in Christ.

---

23. "The beauty, power, and majesty of the cosmos and the subatomic particle—and all in between—belong to our God" (Lynn H. Cohick, *Philippians*, SGBC [Grand Rapids: Zondervan, 2013], 254).

According to Paul, God wanted the gentiles to know *the glorious wealth of this mystery* (τὸ πλοῦτος τῆς δόξης τοῦ μυστηρίου τούτου). In this translation, τῆς δόξης is understood as an attributive genitive (*glorious*), modifying the *wealth* or riches (τὸ πλοῦτος)—*the glorious wealth*. But it could also be understood as a genitive of content—*the wealth of glory*.[24] That is, the wealth or riches are composed of glory. The latter reading is preferable, as it puts emphasis on the glory of the mystery rather than the riches of the mystery. Read this way, Paul is saying that God wanted to make known among the Gentiles the riches of glory of this mystery. The mystery is one of glory; a wealth of glory no less.

This reading gains support from the final clause, stating that this mystery is *Christ in you, the hope of glory* (v. 27b). Glory seems to be the endpoint, the *telos*, since Christ is the hope that secures glory for the gentiles. Because of this, it makes better sense to see glory as the content of the riches rather than modifying the riches adjectivally, since it is all heading toward glory in the end.

As the hope of glory, Christ represents the source and means through which glory may be accessed. Again, it appears that the glory that Christ facilitates for gentiles (and Jews) stands as the endpoint and *telos* of the mystery that was hidden for ages and generations but now revealed to God's people.

As such, Paul is ultimately a servant not only of the church but of glory itself. Through making known the word of God and the mystery once hidden, Paul leads gentiles to Christ, who in turn leads them to glory. Though a servant of glory, Paul suffers afflictions and rejoices in doing so. In anticipation of glory, it is little wonder why.

Col 3:1–4 Εἰ οὖν συνηγέρθητε τῷ Χριστῷ, τὰ ἄνω ζητεῖτε, οὗ ὁ Χριστός ἐστιν ἐν δεξιᾷ τοῦ θεοῦ καθήμενος· 2 τὰ ἄνω φρονεῖτε, μὴ τὰ ἐπὶ τῆς γῆς. 3 ἀπεθάνετε γὰρ καὶ ἡ ζωὴ ὑμῶν κέκρυπται σὺν τῷ Χριστῷ ἐν τῷ θεῷ· 4 ὅταν ὁ Χριστὸς φανερωθῇ, ἡ ζωὴ ὑμῶν, τότε καὶ ὑμεῖς σὺν αὐτῷ φανερωθήσεσθε ἐν δόξῃ.

So if you have been raised with Christ, seek the things above, where Christ is, seated at the right hand of God. 2 Set your minds on things above, not on earthly things. 3 For you died, and your life is hidden with Christ in God. 4 **When Christ, who is your life, appears, then you also will appear with him in glory.**

---

24. A genitive of content need not indicate physical content only but can also refer to communicative or figural content (Köstenberger, Merkle, and Plummer, *Going Deeper with New Testament Greek*, 94–95).

As a consequence of having been raised with Christ, believers are to set their minds *on things above*, where Christ is, rather than *on earthly things* (3:1–2). Participation in the resurrection of Christ changes the orientation of believers, reorienting their minds toward the heavenly realm.[25]

Moreover, participation in the death of Christ means that believers' new lives are *hidden with Christ in God* (v. 3). This phrase "denotes the present, hidden, eschatological being of Christians."[26] It is a *hidden* being because of believers' union with Christ, who is himself hidden in God. The true status of Christ (and believers in him) is not something that can be observed in the present world. As Christ is hidden in God, so believers are hidden with him.[27]

But in the following verse, we see that *Christ, who is your life,* will appear, and at that point believers *will appear with him in glory* (v. 4). This of course refers to the revelation of Christ at the parousia, at which point Paul envisages the revelation of believers alongside him. The idea is that those in Christ, who are hidden in God along with Christ, will on that day be revealed as belonging to God in Christ—a reality that is currently hidden.

The key point of interest here is that this revelation of believers alongside Christ will be *in glory* (ἐν δόξῃ). In this context, *glory* appears to be part of the opposite counterpart of hiddenness. Christ and those hidden with him will not only be revealed but will be revealed in glory. What is now the hidden status of believers in Christ will then be seen in glory, so that glory is understood as an element of the visible manifestation of believers' union with Christ.

Consequently, we observe that participation with Christ pertains to believers' current existence *and* to their future existence alongside Christ. Being with Christ does not change. What changes is the "visibility" of that relationship. Believers will be seen to be with Christ, and just as he will appear in glory so too will those with him.

It is possible that glory exists for believers now and is part of the current hiddenness. In that case, all that will change at the parousia is the visibility of that glory, when Christ is revealed along with his people. The context, however, favors viewing this glory as entirely future oriented. The collocation of *glory* and *appearing* pushes us in that direction; as noted above, glory is understood as an element of the visible manifestation of believers' union with Christ. When revelation occurs, so too will glorification.

---

25. Campbell, *Paul and Union with Christ*, 235–36.
26. Walter Grundmann, "σύν-μετά," *TDNT* 7:785–86. See also Campbell, *Paul and Union with Christ*, 219.
27. Campbell, *Paul and Union with Christ*, 222.

1 Thess 2:11–12 καθάπερ οἴδατε, ὡς ἕνα ἕκαστον ὑμῶν ὡς πατὴρ τέκνα ἑαυτοῦ 12 παρακαλοῦντες ὑμᾶς καὶ παραμυθούμενοι καὶ μαρτυρόμενοι εἰς τὸ περιπατεῖν ὑμᾶς ἀξίως τοῦ θεοῦ τοῦ καλοῦντος ὑμᾶς εἰς τὴν ἑαυτοῦ βασιλείαν καὶ δόξαν.

As you know, like a father with his own children, 12 we encouraged, comforted, and implored each one of you **to live worthy of God, who calls you into his own kingdom and glory.**

This is an extraordinary little passage that succinctly expresses what believers are called into—God's *own kingdom and glory* (2:12). It is hardly surprising to find language of God's calling into his kingdom. But calling into his *glory* is striking. On the one hand, it could be that God's kingdom and his glory are meant synonymously. But there is no evidence for this more broadly; nowhere do we see the kingdom of God equated with his glory, though it is natural to understand them as related to each other. Most likely, then, these are two entities in which believers have been called.

As we have observed elsewhere, glory appears to have a kind of ultimate existence. Alongside membership in the kingdom of God, the purpose of God's calling is to enable believers to share his glory. They "will reflect what their Spirit-empowered life together has been in the process of becoming, that is, a visible, public display of the very character and holiness of the Lord they meet."[28] Glory is the endpoint and *telos* of the call of God, and its significance therefore can hardly be overstated.

2 Thess 1:9–12 οἵτινες δίκην τίσουσιν ὄλεθρον αἰώνιον ἀπὸ προσώπου τοῦ κυρίου καὶ ἀπὸ τῆς δόξης τῆς ἰσχύος αὐτοῦ, 10 ὅταν ἔλθῃ ἐνδοξασθῆναι ἐν τοῖς ἁγίοις αὐτοῦ καὶ θαυμασθῆναι ἐν πᾶσιν τοῖς πιστεύσασιν, ὅτι ἐπιστεύθη τὸ μαρτύριον ἡμῶν ἐφ' ὑμᾶς, ἐν τῇ ἡμέρᾳ ἐκείνῃ. 11 εἰς ὃ καὶ προσευχόμεθα πάντοτε περὶ ὑμῶν, ἵνα ὑμᾶς ἀξιώσῃ τῆς κλήσεως ὁ θεὸς ἡμῶν καὶ πληρώσῃ πᾶσαν εὐδοκίαν ἀγαθωσύνης καὶ ἔργον πίστεως ἐν δυνάμει, 12 ὅπως ἐνδοξασθῇ τὸ ὄνομα τοῦ κυρίου ἡμῶν Ἰησοῦ ἐν ὑμῖν, καὶ ὑμεῖς ἐν αὐτῷ, κατὰ τὴν χάριν τοῦ θεοῦ ἡμῶν καὶ κυρίου Ἰησοῦ Χριστοῦ.

***They will pay the penalty of eternal destruction from the Lord's presence and from his glorious strength** 10 **on that day when he comes to be glorified by his saints** and to be marveled at by all those who have believed,*

---

28. Johnson, *1 & 2 Thessalonians*, 72.

*because our testimony among you was believed. 11 In view of this, we always pray for you that our God will make you worthy of his calling, and by his power fulfill your every desire to do good and your work produced by faith, 12 **so that the name of our Lord Jesus will be glorified by you**, and you by him, according to the grace of our God and the Lord Jesus Christ.*

This passage is striking in that the glory of God is displayed both through the eternal destruction of unbelievers, but also through the marveling of the saints and through their good deeds in the name of Christ. First, we see that those who don't know God or obey the gospel of Christ (1:8) will *pay the penalty of eternal destruction* that will proceed *from the Lord's presence and from his glorious strength* (v. 9). This punishment is executed through the Lord's active presence (as argued above in §6.2). The genitive τῆς δόξης is here understood as functioning attributively, modifying God's strength (*his glorious strength*).[29] While representing only a subtle difference, the meaning is altered a little if τῆς δόξης is understood independently rather than attributively. In this case, it would be translated *from the glory of his strength*. This rendering still conveys a glory that emanates from the Lord's strength, just as *his glorious strength* does, but it also treats glory as an independent quality coming from his strength rather than just a descriptor that modifies the strength itself. In other words, the Lord's strength emanates glory. It is glorious, yes, but it also issues its own glory. Either way, it is striking that the glory of the Lord's strength is the means of executing the penalty of eternal destruction.

2 Thess 2:13–14 Ἡμεῖς δὲ ὀφείλομεν εὐχαριστεῖν τῷ θεῷ πάντοτε περὶ ὑμῶν, ἀδελφοὶ ἠγαπημένοι ὑπὸ κυρίου, ὅτι εἵλατο ὑμᾶς ὁ θεὸς ἀπαρχὴν εἰς σωτηρίαν ἐν ἁγιασμῷ πνεύματος καὶ πίστει ἀληθείας, 14 εἰς ὃ καὶ **ἐκάλεσεν ὑμᾶς διὰ τοῦ εὐαγγελίου ἡμῶν εἰς περιποίησιν δόξης τοῦ κυρίου ἡμῶν Ἰησοῦ Χριστοῦ**.

*But we ought to thank God always for you, brothers and sisters loved by the Lord, because from the beginning God has chosen you for salvation through sanctification by the Spirit and through belief in the truth. 14 **He called you to this through our gospel, so that you might obtain the glory of our Lord Jesus Christ**.*

In what could be described as a type of *ordo salutis*, Paul indicates a chain of events leading to the obtainment of glory. God has chosen the Thessalonians

---

29. Köstenberger, Merkle, and Plummer, *Going Deeper with New Testament Greek*, 90–91.

for salvation, which has apparently come *through sanctification by the Spirit and belief in the truth* (2:13). While the ἐν (*in*) of ἐν ἁγιασμῷ πνεύματος καὶ πίστει ἀληθείας (*by the Spirit and through belief in the truth*) can be understood in other ways, the instrumental rendering here seems most likely. Salvation is thus mediated by sanctification and belief.

Furthermore, God called these believers *through our gospel*, which indicates another step in the so-called *ordo salutis* (v. 14a). However, this step seems to overlap somewhat with the first, since the aforementioned sanctification and belief in the truth are no doubt also caught up in the gospel. Most likely it is through belief in the truth of the gospel that the Spirit has wrought their sanctification and hence salvation.

In any case, the call of God through the gospel has an endpoint—*so that you might obtain the glory of our Lord Jesus Christ* (v. 14b). The purpose of God's calling is indicated by εἰς (*so that*), and its object is the obtainment (περιποίησιν) of glory. This glory is described as being *of our Lord Jesus Christ* (τοῦ κυρίου ἡμῶν Ἰησοῦ Χριστοῦ). The genitive could indicate possession—it is the glory *belonging to* Christ. Or it could indicate source—the glory *from* Christ. Or the genitive could be either attributive or attributed—that is, the glory is an attribute of Christ, or Christ is an attribute of the glory. Such genitive phrases are often open to multiple interpretations, this one being open to any of the aforementioned options. Whichever way it is understood here—my preference being possessive—it[30] is clear that glory is associated with, and connected to, Christ.

This means that the goal and endpoint of being called by God through the gospel, and being chosen for salvation through sanctification and belief, is that believers might share in the glory of Christ. It is rightly *his* glory, but we see that sharing it with his people is the ultimate end of their salvation.

1 Tim 1:17 τῷ δὲ βασιλεῖ τῶν αἰώνων, ἀφθάρτῳ ἀοράτῳ μόνῳ θεῷ, τιμὴ καὶ **δόξα εἰς τοὺς αἰῶνας τῶν αἰώνων**, ἀμήν.

*Now to the King eternal, immortal, invisible, the only God, be honor and **glory forever and ever**. Amen.*

As with other doxologies observed thus far, this brief one wishes and ascribes glory to God. Alongside *honor*, this glory is ascribed *forever and ever* (εἰς τοὺς αἰῶνας τῶν αἰώνων).

---

30. So Weima, *1–2 Thessalonians*, 555.

1 Tim 3:16 καὶ ὁμολογουμένως μέγα ἐστὶν τὸ τῆς εὐσεβείας μυστήριον·

ὃς ἐφανερώθη ἐν σαρκί,
    ἐδικαιώθη ἐν πνεύματι,
ὤφθη ἀγγέλοις,
    ἐκηρύχθη ἐν ἔθνεσιν,
ἐπιστεύθη ἐν κόσμῳ,
    ἀνελήμφθη ἐν δόξῃ.

And most certainly, the mystery of godliness is great:

He was manifested in the flesh,
vindicated in the Spirit,
seen by angels,
preached among the nations,
believed on in the world,
taken up in glory.

This possibly preformed hymnic statement offers a brief summary of the life and impact of Christ. It begins with his birth (*manifested in the flesh*), and moves through his resurrection (*vindicated in the Spirit*), post-resurrection appearances (*seen by angels*), the apostolic witness to Christ among Jews and gentiles (*preached among the nations*), the formation of Christ-centered churches (*believed on in the world*), and—apparently out of sequence—the ascension of Christ (*taken up in glory*).[31]

While the ascension of Christ is apparently out of sequence—following the formation of believing churches throughout the world—it seems to fit the poetic shape of the hymn. Each couplet contrasts the two elements found at the end of each line: *flesh* vs *Spirit*; *angels* vs *nations* (i.e., people, or people groups); and *world* vs *glory*. The effect of this parallelism is not to pit each item against its partner. Rather, the pairs draw the scope of Christ's significance; in both material and spiritual realms, angelic and human, worldly and heavenly, Christ is known.

The last of these realms is that of *glory*. The effect of its placement at the end of the hymnic statement—though technically out of sequence—is to heighten its significance. That Jesus was *taken up in glory* is presented as the high point of the series, giving heightened significance both to Christ's ascension and to glory. Glory is thus understood as the ultimate and climactic reality in which Christ dwells.

---

31. Knight, *Pastoral Epistles*, 186.

2 Tim 2:8–10 Μνημόνευε Ἰησοῦν Χριστὸν ἐγηγερμένον ἐκ νεκρῶν, ἐκ σπέρματος Δαυίδ, κατὰ τὸ εὐαγγέλιόν μου, 9 ἐν ᾧ κακοπαθῶ μέχρι δεσμῶν ὡς κακοῦργος, ἀλλὰ ὁ λόγος τοῦ θεοῦ οὐ δέδεται· 10 **διὰ τοῦτο πάντα ὑπομένω διὰ τοὺς ἐκλεκτούς, ἵνα καὶ αὐτοὶ σωτηρίας τύχωσιν τῆς ἐν Χριστῷ Ἰησοῦ μετὰ δόξης αἰωνίου.**

Remember Jesus Christ, risen from the dead and descended from David, according to my gospel, 9 for which I suffer to the point of being bound like a criminal. But the word of God is not bound. 10 ***This is why I endure all things for the elect: so that they also may obtain salvation, which is in Christ Jesus, with eternal glory.***

Paul suffers for the gospel he preaches, even *to the point of being bound like a criminal* (2:9). But he endures all such suffering for the salvation of the elect, *which is in Christ Jesus, with eternal glory* (v. 10). "Salvation is conditioned by Christ, such that ἐν Χριστῷ marks out 'the specifically Christian character of the salvation to be obtained.'"[32] But what of the *eternal glory*?

The preposition *with* (μετά) implies that salvation in Christ Jesus will be accompanied by *eternal glory* (v. 10). This means that salvation will not only consist of the remission of sins and rescue from condemnation but will be characterized by *glory*. The elect are chosen not simply to experience God's mercy in judgment but also to share in the eternal glory of Christ.

2 Tim 4:18 ῥύσεταί με ὁ κύριος ἀπὸ παντὸς ἔργου πονηροῦ καὶ σώσει εἰς τὴν βασιλείαν αὐτοῦ τὴν ἐπουράνιον· **ᾧ ἡ δόξα εἰς τοὺς αἰῶνας τῶν αἰώνων,** ἀμήν.

The Lord will rescue me from every evil work and will bring me safely into his heavenly kingdom. ***To him be the glory forever and ever!*** *Amen.*

This very brief doxology wishes and ascribes glory to God, in keeping with the other doxologies observed thus far.

Titus 2:11–13 Ἐπεφάνη γὰρ ἡ χάρις τοῦ θεοῦ σωτήριος πᾶσιν ἀνθρώποις 12 παιδεύουσα ἡμᾶς, ἵνα ἀρνησάμενοι τὴν ἀσέβειαν καὶ τὰς κοσμικὰς ἐπιθυμίας σωφρόνως καὶ δικαίως καὶ εὐσεβῶς ζήσωμεν ἐν τῷ νῦν αἰῶνι,

---

32. Campbell, *Paul and Union with Christ*, 94, citing Guthrie, *Pastoral Epistles*, 156.

13 προσδεχόμενοι τὴν μακαρίαν ἐλπίδα καὶ ἐπιφάνειαν τῆς δόξης τοῦ μεγάλου θεοῦ καὶ σωτῆρος ἡμῶν Ἰησοῦ Χριστοῦ

For the grace of God has appeared, bringing salvation for all people, 12 instructing us to deny godlessness and worldly lusts and to live in a sensible, righteous, and godly way in the present age, 13 while **we wait for the blessed hope, the appearing of the glory of our great God and Savior, Jesus Christ***.*

The *appearing of the glory of our great God and Savior, Jesus Christ*, also described as *the blessed hope* (2:13), is held out as the object of believers' patient waiting. The mode in which believers are to deny godlessness and live in a godly way is one of waiting (v. 12). In other words, believers are to live in a *godly way in the present age* while waiting for the glory of Christ.

The passage presents the glory of Christ as the end point of the Christian life—its goal and telos. Until his glory comes, believers are to wait and avoid the trappings of this current age.

12.3 SUMMARY

The outcome of having been declared righteous by faith, having peace with God, and obtaining access to God's grace is to rejoice in the hope of the glory of God (Rom 5:1–2; Col 1:26–27). It is the glory of the Father that raised Christ from the dead (Rom 6:4; 1 Tim 3:16), and believers will be raised in glory (1 Cor 15:42–44; Phil 3:21; Col 3:3–4) once the glory of Christ appears (Titus 2:11–13).

Believers can be confident that if they suffer with Christ, they will also be glorified with him with a glory that will resonate throughout creation itself (Rom 8:16–21; 1 Thess 2:12), and even now the glory of the Lord transforms believers into his glorious image (2 Cor 3:18). Their momentary, light affliction is producing an incomparable, eternal weight of glory (2 Cor 4:16–18), sharing in the glory of Christ (2 Thess 2:13–14; 2 Tim 2:10). God predestined this glory before the ages (1 Cor 2:7–8).

All that God has done for believers in Christ ought to issue in praise to his glorious grace (Eph 1:5–6, 12, 14; Phil 2:11) and the glorification of the name of Christ (2 Thess 1:10, 12). Unsurprisingly, the ascription of the glory of God is the "wish" of several doxologies, such that it is clear that glory occupies a special place in Paul's vision of the eternal God (Rom 11:35–36; 16:25–27; Gal 1:5; Eph 3:20–21; Phil 4:20; 1 Tim 1:17; 2 Tim 4:18).

It is difficult to explain what, exactly, glory *is* for Paul. He never articulates its attributes, apart from its eternal and incomparable nature. But what is clear is that it pertains to God's nature as well as to his deeds. God is, in and of himself, glorious. And his life-giving, resurrecting, and re-creating deeds are glorious in character.

Glory is ascribed to Christ and will be shared with those in Christ, as planned by God before time. While glory can be glimpsed now through reflection on the work of Christ and the glory to come as well as through the experience of its transformative power, it will only be fully apprehended in the eschaton.

There is something all-consuming about the glory of God in the eschaton. It seems to be the ultimate end of everything from Paul's perspective. The highest goal of life, of humanity, and of creation is the glory of God in Christ. It is true to say that everything exists to serve this eternal glory in the end.

CHAPTER 13

HOPE

13.1 INTRODUCTION

This chapter explores Paul's hope for the future. As will become clear from the volume of references, Paul regards hope as of central significance for those in Christ. It is not wishful thinking nor mere optimism; hope rather is the certain expectation of what God will do based on his promises and his past faithfulness. Believers share in the hope of eternal life, based on the justifying work of God's grace. In the eschaton they will share in the glory of God, and their hope to this end is produced through affliction, endurance, and character. They rejoice in this hope.

Without a certain hope for the future, believers are pitiable because they suffer all things in this present life without any sure comfort to follow. By the same token, unbelievers do not have hope in the face of death and grief. The hope of heaven, on the other hand, produces other attributes in the believer's life, such as faith and love. It produces praise to the glory of Christ.

With the theme of hope, we see how Paul's eschatological expectation profoundly shapes the life of the believer. Without hope, the Christian life is nothing. But properly understood, hope empowers believers to stand against all trials, persecutions, and sufferings in this present age.

13.2 HOPE TEXTS

Rom 4:17–21 καθὼς γέγραπται ὅτι *Πατέρα πολλῶν ἐθνῶν τέθεικά σε*, κατέναντι οὗ ἐπίστευσεν θεοῦ τοῦ ζῳοποιοῦντος τοὺς νεκροὺς καὶ καλοῦντος τὰ μὴ ὄντα ὡς ὄντα. 18 **ὃς παρ' ἐλπίδα ἐπ' ἐλπίδι ἐπίστευσεν** εἰς τὸ γενέσθαι αὐτὸν *πατέρα πολλῶν ἐθνῶν* κατὰ τὸ εἰρημένον, *Οὕτως ἔσται τὸ σπέρμα σου,* 19 καὶ μὴ ἀσθενήσας τῇ πίστει κατενόησεν τὸ ἑαυτοῦ σῶμα νενεκρωμένον, ἑκατονταετής που ὑπάρχων, καὶ τὴν νέκρωσιν τῆς μήτρας Σάρρας· 20 εἰς δὲ τὴν ἐπαγγελίαν τοῦ θεοῦ οὐ διεκρίθη τῇ ἀπιστίᾳ ἀλλ' ἐνεδυναμώθη τῇ πίστει, δοὺς δόξαν τῷ θεῷ 21 καὶ πληροφορηθεὶς ὅτι ὃ ἐπήγγελται δυνατός ἐστιν καὶ ποιῆσαι.

As it is written: I have made you the father of many nations. He is our father in God's sight, in whom Abraham believed—the God who gives life to the dead and calls things into existence that do not exist. 18 **He believed, hoping against hope**, *so that he became the father of many nations according to what had been spoken: So will your descendants be. 19 He did not weaken in faith when he considered his own body to be already dead (since he was about a hundred years old) and also the deadness of Sarah's womb. 20 He did not waver in unbelief at God's promise but was strengthened in his faith and gave glory to God, 21 because he was fully convinced that what God had promised, he was also able to do.*

The hope of Abraham is grounded in the promise of God that he would become the father of many nations. Though his own body was as good as dead and his wife was barren (4:19), Abraham believed that the God *who gives life to the dead* (v. 17) was able to do what he had promised (v. 21).

Abraham's hope is described as *hope against hope*, rendering the ambiguous παρ' ἐλπίδα ἐπ' ἐλπίδι (v. 18). BDAG regards this use of παρά as a "marker of that which does not correspond to what is expected, *against, contrary to*."[1] Furthermore, BDAG regards παρ' ἐλπίδα as part of a wordplay with ἐπ' ἐλπίδι. The expression seems to mean, therefore, that Abraham believed *against hope upon hope*. That is, against the expectation of hopelessness, Abraham rested his trust in hope.[2]

Abraham's faithful hoping was credited as righteousness (v. 22), which in turn is held out as an example for believers (vv. 23–24). This speaks to the role of hope in salvation-historical terms, since Abraham's hope was that God would produce descendants from many nations. But it is also transfigured to eschatological hope by Paul's application to believers in Christ. Just as Abraham was credited with righteousness, so believers will be justified on the day of judgment by their hope and faith in the one who raised Christ from the dead (v. 24).

Rom 5:1–5 Δικαιωθέντες οὖν ἐκ πίστεως εἰρήνην ἔχομεν πρὸς τὸν θεὸν διὰ τοῦ κυρίου ἡμῶν Ἰησοῦ Χριστοῦ 2 δι' οὗ καὶ τὴν προσαγωγὴν ἐσχήκαμεν τῇ πίστει εἰς τὴν χάριν ταύτην ἐν ᾗ ἑστήκαμεν καὶ **καυχώμεθα ἐπ' ἐλπίδι τῆς δόξης τοῦ θεοῦ**. 3 οὐ μόνον δέ, ἀλλὰ καὶ καυχώμεθα ἐν ταῖς θλίψεσιν, εἰδότες ὅτι ἡ θλῖψις ὑπομονὴν κατεργάζεται, 4 ἡ δὲ ὑπομονὴ δοκιμήν,

---

1. BDAG 758, §6.
2. Peterson, *Romans*, 222.

ἡ δὲ δοκιμὴ ἐλπίδα. 5 ἡ δὲ ἐλπὶς οὐ καταισχύνει, ὅτι ἡ ἀγάπη τοῦ θεοῦ ἐκκέχυται ἐν ταῖς καρδίαις ἡμῶν διὰ πνεύματος ἁγίου τοῦ δοθέντος ἡμῖν.

Therefore, since we have been declared righteous by faith, we have peace with God through our Lord Jesus Christ. 2 We have also obtained access through him by faith into this grace in which we stand, and **we rejoice in the hope of the glory of God.** *3 And not only that, but we also rejoice in our afflictions, because we know that affliction produces endurance, 4 endurance produces proven character, and* **proven character produces hope.** *5* **This hope will not disappoint us**, *because God's love has been poured out in our hearts through the Holy Spirit who was given to us.*

As noted above (see §12.2), with the declaration of righteousness and peace with God through Christ (5:1), believers have access *into this grace in which we stand* (v. 2a). All of this describes the status enjoyed by believers—righteousness, peace, and the standing of grace. But the next phrase describes the response of grateful believers to whom so much has been granted—*we rejoice in the hope of the glory of God* (v. 2b).

Again, as already noted in §12.2, believers literally *boast* in this hope (καυχάομαι), as Paul imagines a response that is less about celebrating and more about expressing the object of one's confidence. Believers who have received righteousness, peace, and grace through Christ by faith have no boast or confidence of their own. It is entirely cast upon the hope that arises from their granted status. As argued in §12.2, *the hope of the glory of God* is the hope that believers will be caught up in the glory of God in the eschaton, which must rank among the greatest of all privileges for those whose hope is in Christ.[3]

This hope of sharing in the glory of God shapes Paul's view of suffering in this life. He also boasts in afflictions because they produce endurance, which in turn produces proven character, which produces hope (vv. 3–4). And this hope is not wishful thinking *because God's love has been poured out in our hearts through the Holy Spirit who was given to us* (v. 5).

The connection between God's love and the hope that is produced through affliction, endurance, and proven character appears to be one of verification and confirmation. It is not an empty hope because God's love is its guarantor. The fact of God's love, which is experienced subjectively in believers' hearts

---

3. As Schreiner notes, "Exulting in the hope of God's glory introduces the major motif of the paragraph. Those who scorned God's glory (Rom 1:21–23) and have fallen short of it (3:23) are now promised a future share in it" (Schreiner, *Romans*, 254).

through the Spirit, has been demonstrated objectively in the giving of his Son for sinners (vv. 6–8).

So, with the surety given by God's love, believers hope to share in the eschatological glory of God. This hope is reason for boasting, and it is the high point of Christian living while believers continue to suffer through this life with its various afflictions and trials.

Rom 8:20–25 τῇ γὰρ ματαιότητι ἡ κτίσις ὑπετάγη, οὐχ ἑκοῦσα ἀλλὰ διὰ τὸν ὑποτάξαντα, **ἐφ' ἐλπίδι 21 ὅτι καὶ αὐτὴ ἡ κτίσις ἐλευθερωθήσεται ἀπὸ τῆς δουλείας τῆς φθορᾶς εἰς τὴν ἐλευθερίαν τῆς δόξης τῶν τέκνων τοῦ θεοῦ.** 22 οἴδαμεν γὰρ ὅτι πᾶσα ἡ κτίσις συστενάζει καὶ συνωδίνει ἄχρι τοῦ νῦν· 23 οὐ μόνον δέ, ἀλλὰ καὶ αὐτοὶ τὴν ἀπαρχὴν τοῦ πνεύματος ἔχοντες, ἡμεῖς καὶ αὐτοὶ ἐν ἑαυτοῖς στενάζομεν υἱοθεσίαν ἀπεκδεχόμενοι, τὴν ἀπολύτρωσιν τοῦ σώματος ἡμῶν. **24 τῇ γὰρ ἐλπίδι ἐσώθημεν· ἐλπὶς δὲ βλεπομένη οὐκ ἔστιν ἐλπίς· ὃ γὰρ βλέπει τίς ἐλπίζει; 25 εἰ δὲ ὃ οὐ βλέπομεν ἐλπίζομεν, δι' ὑπομονῆς ἀπεκδεχόμεθα.**

*For the creation was subjected to futility—not willingly, but because of him who subjected it—**in the hope 21 that the creation itself will also be set free** from the bondage to decay into the glorious freedom of God's children. 22 For we know that the whole creation has been groaning together with labor pains until now. 23 Not only that, but we ourselves who have the Spirit as the firstfruits—we also groan within ourselves, eagerly waiting for adoption, the redemption of our bodies. **24 Now in this hope we were saved, but hope that is seen is not hope, because who hopes for what he sees? 25 Now if we hope for what we do not see, we eagerly wait for it with patience**.*

In this text, hope is related both to the redemption of creation (8:20–21) and *the redemption of our bodies* (v. 23). Moreover, the subject of the former hope is God himself, while the latter hope is held by believers. God's hope is reflected in 8:20–21: *For the creation was subjected to futility—not willingly, but because of him who subjected it—in the hope that creation itself will also be set free from the bondage to decay into the glorious freedom of God's children.* It is striking that hope is predicated of God, since Paul regards God as exercising sovereign power over all creation. But this demonstrates that the hope of which he speaks does not carry the connotation of insecurity that is inherent in the English word. God does not "hope" things will work out the way he intends. Rather he looks ahead to the certain fulfillment of his plans and purposes. This is what *hope* means here. Nevertheless, God's *hope*—his certain expectation—is that creation will one day be liberated from its bondage to decay into glorious freedom.

This then helps us to understand Paul's following comments about human hope in vv. 24–25. When he says that *in this hope we were saved* (v. 24), he is referring to the aforementioned expectation of resurrection—*eagerly waiting for adoption, the redemption of our bodies* (v. 23). The eager waiting is the hope in which believers are saved. Again, then, it is clear that *hope* is not insecure wishful thinking but an eager expectation of something certain to come. This is further underscored by the following comments—*But hope that is seen is not hope, because who hopes for what he sees? Now if we hope for what we do not see, we eagerly wait for it with patience* (vv. 24–25). Presumably the point of these comments about hoping for what is not seen is not that the object of hope must be *invisible*. The point, rather, is that the object of hope has not yet *arrived* (and therefore is not seen).[4] Once the object has come, hope has no further role, since hope is about the expectation of what is to come. Thus Paul adds that *if we hope for what we do not see* (that is, what has not yet come), *we eagerly wait for it with patience* (v. 25). Again, we see that hope involves eager waiting.

This passage, perhaps to a greater extent than any other, demonstrates what Paul means by *hope*. Far from an insecure form of wishful thinking, hope involves eager expectation. God's hope is the expectation that his design for creation will meet its fulfillment in concert with the glorious freedom of God's children. Paul's hope is the expectation of the redemption of the body, and it is this hope in which believers are saved.

Rom 12:12 τῇ ἐλπίδι χαίροντες, τῇ θλίψει ὑπομένοντες, τῇ προσευχῇ προσκαρτεροῦντες

Rejoice in hope; *be patient in affliction; be persistent in prayer.*

This simple instruction to *rejoice in hope* is not accidentally grouped with the other two exhortations in this verse. Hope is the eager expectation of the future action of God (especially the redemption of the body; see above on 8:20–25). To rejoice in that expectation is to take joy in the prospect of God's certain future blessings. This expectation of the certain future blessings of God is to be set against the difficulties currently experienced in this life. Thus, believers are to

---

4. "We exercise hope in relation to that which lies ahead of us, in the still invisible future. Paul the Christian will not allow his attention to become wholly absorbed in the present, whether its responsibilities or its frustrations. His gaze repeatedly fits to the far horizon, and the hope of what lies beyond it is what sustains his faith despite the contradictions of the present" (Dunn, *Romans 1–8*, 491).

be patient in affliction. Suffering and affliction mark the experience of believers in their current reality, but their hope points forward to a better reality to come. In the meantime, they are to exercise patience. They are likewise expected to be persistent in prayer, which is the expression of their dependence on God for his provision, protection, and future blessing. Overarching their patience and prayerfulness is the rejoicing that comes from the certain expectation of the future blessings of God.

Rom 15:1–4 Ὀφείλομεν δὲ ἡμεῖς οἱ δυνατοὶ τὰ ἀσθενήματα τῶν ἀδυνάτων βαστάζειν καὶ μὴ ἑαυτοῖς ἀρέσκειν. 2 ἕκαστος ἡμῶν τῷ πλησίον ἀρεσκέτω εἰς τὸ ἀγαθὸν πρὸς οἰκοδομήν· καὶ γὰρ ὁ Χριστὸς οὐχ ἑαυτῷ ἤρεσεν·, ἀλλὰ καθὼς γέγραπται, Οἱ ὀνειδισμοὶ τῶν ὀνειδιζόντων σε ἐπέπεσαν ἐπ' ἐμέ. 4 ὅσα γὰρ προεγράφη, εἰς τὴν ἡμετέραν διδασκαλίαν ἐγράφη, ἵνα διὰ τῆς ὑπομονῆς καὶ διὰ τῆς παρακλήσεως τῶν γραφῶν τὴν ἐλπίδα ἔχωμεν.

Now we who are strong have an obligation to bear the weaknesses of those without strength, and not to please ourselves. 2 Each one of us is to please his neighbor for his good, to build him up. For even Christ did not please himself. On the contrary, as it is written, The insults of those who insult you have fallen on me. 4 For whatever was written in the past was written for our instruction, **so that we may have hope through endurance and through the encouragement from the Scriptures.**

Paul appeals to the example of Christ as he addresses the weak and the strong. The *strong have an obligation to bear the weaknesses of those without strength, and not to please ourselves* (15:1). The exhortation that each one should *please his neighbor for his good* is grounded in Christ's service—*For even Christ did not please himself* (v. 2). And Christ's example is likewise supported by Paul's citation of Psalm 69:9—*The insults of those who insult you have fallen on me* (v. 3). While the psalmist refers to his personal bearing of insults directed at God, Paul is able to draw on the principle of bearing another's burden and applying it to Christ's service.[5] Christ did not please himself but chose to bear the burdens of others in a somewhat similar fashion as the psalmist.

Having cited the psalm, Paul then reflects on the hope that is garnered from the Scriptures. The writings of the past were *written for our instruction, so that we may have hope through endurance and through the encouragement from*

---

5. "Paul cites Ps 69:9 from a psalm of a righteous sufferer, applied *par excellence* to Jesus" (Keener, *Romans*, 171).

the Scriptures (v. 4). The encouragement that comes from the Scriptures may refer to the way in which the Scriptures record the promises and plans of God, alongside their fulfillment in various ways, as well as their pointing forward to their ultimate fulfillment in Christ. In other words, the Scriptures offer hope because of the way they record God's faithfulness to do what he says he will do. In this way, they attest to the reliability of God's promises. Since hope is the expectation that God will do what he has said he will do, the Scriptures thus offer plenty of support for such hope. God has always acted according to his promises, and the promises yet to be fulfilled will be no different.

The hope of believers is thus fueled by the encouragement of the Scriptures. And this hope will operate *through endurance*, since it sustains believers amid the various difficult scenarios and experiences of this life.

Rom 15:12–13 καὶ πάλιν Ἡσαΐας λέγει,

ἔσται ἡ ῥίζα τοῦ Ἰεσσαὶ
 καὶ ὁ ἀνιστάμενος ἄρχειν ἐθνῶν,
ἐπ' αὐτῷ ἔθνη ἐλπιοῦσιν.

13 ὁ δὲ θεὸς τῆς ἐλπίδος πληρῶσαι ὑμᾶς πάσης χαρᾶς καὶ εἰρήνης ἐν τῷ πιστεύειν, εἰς τὸ περισσεύειν ὑμᾶς ἐν τῇ ἐλπίδι ἐν δυνάμει πνεύματος ἁγίου.

And again, Isaiah says,

The root of Jesse will appear,
the one who rises to rule the Gentiles;
the Gentiles will hope in him.

13 Now may the God of hope fill you with all joy and peace as you believe **so that you may overflow with hope by the power of the Holy Spirit**.

This citation of Isaiah 11:10 is the fourth of four Old Testament quotations in Romans 15:9–12 that Paul uses in support of his gentile mission, *so that Gentiles may glorify God for his mercy* (Rom 15:9). Here we see Isaiah's expectation that *the Gentiles will hope in* the one described as *the root of Jesse; the one who rises to rule the Gentiles* (v. 12). The *root of Jesse* is Isaiah's way of referring to David, and this prophecy is of course understood by the New Testament authors as pointing to Christ, the son of David. Paul's mission to the gentiles is fueled by the prophetic expectation that their hope in Christ is part of the sovereign plan of God.

This then segues into the prayer uttered in v. 13—*Now may the God of hope fill you with all joy and peace as you believe so that you may overflow with hope by the power of the Holy Spirit.* God is described as *the God of hope* since he fulfills his promises—those who believe in him are able to share in hope because God can be trusted to do what he has said he will do.[6] This point is implicitly supported by the catena of Old Testament prophecies (vv. 9–12) that have all been fulfilled in Christ. God is the God of hope because he sets future expectations and then meets them.

Paul wants God to fill his readers with *all joy and peace* as they believe, but these seem to be overshadowed by a third quality—*so that you may overflow with hope* (v. 13). This overflow of hope is powered by the Holy Spirit. As already discussed, hope is understood to consist of certain expectation (see on Rom 8:20–25 above). And here hope has a double object—the gentiles will hope in Christ, and God is the God of hope. Of course, in the end these two objects of hope are one and the same, since to hope in Christ is to hope in the one whom God has exalted. To set one's expectations on Christ is to express hope in God.

> Rom 15:23–24 νυνὶ δὲ μηκέτι τόπον ἔχων ἐν τοῖς κλίμασι τούτοις, ἐπιποθίαν δὲ ἔχων τοῦ ἐλθεῖν πρὸς ὑμᾶς ἀπὸ πολλῶν ἐτῶν, 24 ὡς ἂν πορεύωμαι εἰς τὴν Σπανίαν· **ἐλπίζω γὰρ διαπορευόμενος θεάσασθαι ὑμᾶς** καὶ ὑφ' ὑμῶν προπεμφθῆναι ἐκεῖ ἐὰν ὑμῶν πρῶτον ἀπὸ μέρους ἐμπλησθῶ.

> But now I no longer have any work to do in these regions, and I have strongly desired for many years to come to you 24 whenever I travel to Spain. **For I hope to see you when I pass through** and to be assisted by you for my journey there, once I have first enjoyed your company for a while.

Since this example is clearly not related to eschatological hope, it requires no further comment.

1 Cor 9:9–11 ἐν γὰρ τῷ Μωϋσέως νόμῳ γέγραπται, οὐ κημώσεις βοῦν ἀλοῶντα. μὴ τῶν βοῶν μέλει τῷ θεῷ 10 ἢ δι' ἡμᾶς πάντως λέγει; δι' ἡμᾶς γὰρ ἐγράφη ὅτι **ὀφείλει ἐπ' ἐλπίδι ὁ ἀροτριῶν ἀροτριᾶν καὶ ὁ ἀλοῶν ἐπ'**

---

6. Kruse notes that the description "the God of hope" is found nowhere else in the New Testament or the Septuagint. He rightly notes, "Seeing that Paul in this verse prays that the believers may 'overflow with hope,' the expression 'the God of hope' probably means the God who inspires hope in his people" (Kruse, *Romans*, 534).

ἐλπίδι τοῦ μετέχειν. 11 εἰ ἡμεῖς ὑμῖν τὰ πνευματικὰ ἐσπείραμεν, μέγα εἰ ἡμεῖς ὑμῶν τὰ σαρκικὰ θερίσομεν;

For it is written in the law of Moses, Do not muzzle an ox while it treads out grain. Is God really concerned about oxen? 10 Isn't he really saying it for our sake? Yes, this is written for our sake, because **he who plows ought to plow in hope, and he who threshes should thresh in hope of sharing the crop**. *11 If we have sown spiritual things for you, is it too much if we reap material benefits from you?*

While this text does not directly address eschatological hope, it nevertheless helps to shed some light on Paul's use of the word ἐλπίς. As observed elsewhere (see, especially Rom 8:20–25 above), hope has to do with *expectation* rather than insecure, wishful thinking. When Paul says that *he who plows ought to plow in hope* (1 Cor 9:10), he does not mean that the farmer should only entertain a glimmer of wishful thinking with respect to *sharing* (or "partaking"; τοῦ μετέχειν) in the crop. Rather, the farmer plows and threshes with the *expectation* that there will be a crop in which to partake. Of course, it is possible that something may happen to his crop, given the vicissitudes of agricultural life, but that is simply a limitation of the analogy. The point remains clear: farmers plow, plant, water, and thresh crops because crops yield a harvest. All things being equal, this is a perfectly sensible and well-attested expectation.

Paul applies this logic to his relationship with the Corinthians in that he has *sown spiritual things for you* (or "among you"; ὑμῖν) and expects to reap some material benefit from them (v. 11). Again, this is not an eschatological expectation, but it reflects the fact that for Paul *hope* is about a logical and sensible expectation.

1 Cor 13:6–7 οὐ χαίρει ἐπὶ τῇ ἀδικίᾳ, συγχαίρει δὲ τῇ ἀληθείᾳ· 7 πάντα στέγει, πάντα πιστεύει, **πάντα ἐλπίζει**, πάντα ὑπομένει.

Love finds no joy in unrighteousness but rejoices in the truth. 7 It bears all things, believes all things, **hopes all things**, *endures all things.*

It is not immediately clear what this truncated statement really means, that love *hopes all things* (13:7). Clearly the *all* is part of the rhetoric of the verse (love *bears all things, believes all things, hopes all things, endures all things*), but in what sense does love hope all things? Probably Paul means that love causes people to trust their loved one(s) with cheerful expectancy rather than to settle into a doubtful mood of distrust—"Love will never stop having faith and will never lose hope."[7] In other words, love offers the benefit of the doubt and chooses to hope rather than to resort to hopelessness.

> 1 Cor 13:13 νυνὶ δὲ μένει πίστις, ἐλπίς, ἀγάπη, τὰ τρία ταῦτα· μείζων δὲ τούτων ἡ ἀγάπη.
>
> *Now these three remain: faith, **hope**, and love—but the greatest of these is love.*

This classic formulation puts love above hope, but it should be remembered that faith and hope are also in the top three.

> 1 Cor 15:17–19 εἰ δὲ Χριστὸς οὐκ ἐγήγερται, ματαία ἡ πίστις ὑμῶν, ἔτι ἐστὲ ἐν ταῖς ἁμαρτίαις ὑμῶν, 18 ἄρα καὶ οἱ κοιμηθέντες ἐν Χριστῷ ἀπώλοντο. 19 εἰ ἐν τῇ ζωῇ ταύτῃ ἐν Χριστῷ ἠλπικότες ἐσμὲν μόνον, ἐλεεινότεροι πάντων ἀνθρώπων ἐσμέν.
>
> *And if Christ has not been raised, your faith is worthless; you are still in your sins. 18 Those, then, who have fallen asleep in Christ have also perished. 19 **If we have put our hope in Christ for this life only, we should be pitied more than anyone.***

Without the resurrection of Christ, faith accomplishes nothing, and believers remain in their sins (15:17). This means that those who have already died are gone forever, since there will be no resurrection for them either (v. 18). And without resurrection, hope in Christ must therefore be *for this life only* (v. 19). This would be a pitiable situation in which our hope "is nothing more than whistling in the dark."[8]

But if we reverse these statements in light of Paul's conviction that Christ *has* been raised from the dead, we see that believers are *not* still in their sins; those who have already died have *not* perished forever; believers have put their hope in Christ for this life *and* the next; and they should *not* be pitied. This, of course, is the true state of affairs according to Paul, which means that *hope in Christ* involves an expectation of resurrection in the life to come. As is clear throughout the wider context, this expectation of resurrection in the life to come is not without basis. It is, rather, based on the firm belief that Christ has

---

7. Gardner, *1 Corinthians*, 573.
8. Garland, *1 Corinthians*, 703.

been raised from the dead. His resurrection guarantees the resurrection of all who trust in him, since he is *the firstfruits of those who have fallen asleep* (v. 20).

As observed elsewhere, hope in Christ for resurrection in the life to come consists of a reasonable expectation based on an established warrant. Christ has been raised from the dead, as a plethora of witnesses have attested (vv. 3–8), and as such Paul has confidence in the coming resurrection of all those who are in Christ.

1 Cor 16:7–9 οὐ θέλω γὰρ ὑμᾶς ἄρτι ἐν παρόδῳ ἰδεῖν, **ἐλπίζω γὰρ χρόνον τινὰ ἐπιμεῖναι πρὸς ὑμᾶς** ἐὰν ὁ κύριος ἐπιτρέψῃ. 8 ἐπιμενῶ δὲ ἐν Ἐφέσῳ ἕως τῆς πεντηκοστῆς· 9 θύρα γάρ μοι ἀνέῳγεν μεγάλη καὶ ἐνεργής, καὶ ἀντικείμενοι πολλοί.

*I don't want to see you now just in passing, **since I hope to spend some time with you**, if the Lord allows. 8 But I will stay in Ephesus until Pentecost, 9 because a wide door for effective ministry has opened for me—yet many oppose me.*

Since this instance does not express eschatological hope, no further comment is required.

2 Cor 1:6–7 εἴτε δὲ θλιβόμεθα, ὑπὲρ τῆς ὑμῶν παρακλήσεως καὶ σωτηρίας· εἴτε παρακαλούμεθα, ὑπὲρ τῆς ὑμῶν παρακλήσεως τῆς ἐνεργουμένης ἐν ὑπομονῇ τῶν αὐτῶν παθημάτων ὧν καὶ ἡμεῖς πάσχομεν. 7 καὶ **ἡ ἐλπὶς ἡμῶν βεβαία ὑπὲρ ὑμῶν** εἰδότες ὅτι ὡς κοινωνοί ἐστε τῶν παθημάτων, οὕτως καὶ τῆς παρακλήσεως.

*If we are afflicted, it is for your comfort and salvation. If we are comforted, it is for your comfort, which produces in you patient endurance of the same sufferings that we suffer. 7 And **our hope for you is firm**, because we know that as you share in the sufferings, so you will also share in the comfort.*

While this example does not address eschatological hope directly, it is nevertheless valuable for assessing Paul's notion of hope. His affliction and comfort are directed toward the Corinthians' comfort, salvation, and patient endurance. They are to endure *the same sufferings that we suffer* (1:6). Paul's hope for the Corinthians is therefore firm, because he knows that their sharing in suffering means that they will also share in comfort (v. 7).

Paul's confidence that the Corinthians will share in comfort because they share in sufferings is grounded in his earlier statement that God *comforts us in all our affliction, so that we may be able to comfort those who are in any kind of affliction, through the comfort we ourselves receive from God* (v. 4). This statement demonstrates the link between suffering and comfort—God will comfort those suffering affliction. As such, the Corinthians will experience the comfort of God because they are experiencing suffering. It is because of this reasoning that Paul's hope for the Corinthians is *firm* (βεβαία)—he has a certain expectation that they will receive comfort from God, because they share in sufferings, and Paul believes that God will comfort those enduring any kind of affliction.

2 Cor 1:8–11 Οὐ γὰρ θέλομεν ὑμᾶς ἀγνοεῖν, ἀδελφοί, ὑπὲρ τῆς θλίψεως ἡμῶν τῆς γενομένης ἐν τῇ Ἀσίᾳ, ὅτι καθ᾽ ὑπερβολὴν ὑπὲρ δύναμιν ἐβαρήθημεν ὥστε ἐξαπορηθῆναι ἡμᾶς καὶ τοῦ ζῆν· 9 ἀλλ᾽ αὐτοὶ ἐν ἑαυτοῖς τὸ ἀπόκριμα τοῦ θανάτου ἐσχήκαμεν, ἵνα μὴ πεποιθότες ὦμεν ἐφ᾽ ἑαυτοῖς ἀλλ᾽ ἐπὶ τῷ θεῷ τῷ ἐγείροντι τοὺς νεκρούς· 10 ὃς ἐκ τηλικούτου θανάτου ἐρρύσατο ἡμᾶς καὶ ῥύσεται, **εἰς ὃν ἠλπίκαμεν ὅτι καὶ ἔτι ῥύσεται**, 11 συνυπουργούντων καὶ ὑμῶν ὑπὲρ ἡμῶν τῇ δεήσει, ἵνα ἐκ πολλῶν προσώπων τὸ εἰς ἡμᾶς χάρισμα διὰ πολλῶν εὐχαριστηθῇ ὑπὲρ ἡμῶν.

We don't want you to be unaware, brothers and sisters, of our affliction that took place in Asia. We were completely overwhelmed—beyond our strength—so that we even despaired of life itself. 9 Indeed, we felt that we had received the sentence of death, so that we would not trust in ourselves but in God who raises the dead. 10 He has delivered us from such a terrible death, and he will deliver us. **We have put our hope in him that he will deliver us again** *11 while you join in helping us by your prayers. Then many will give thanks on our behalf for the gift that came to us through the prayers of many.*

While this example also does not address eschatological hope directly, again we may glimpse what the notion of hope means for Paul. The affliction he experienced in Asia was overwhelming, leading to his despairing of life itself (1:8). Preparing to face death, he could trust only *in God who raises the dead*, thus expressing his only hope in the face of death—resurrection wrought by God (v. 9). But God *delivered us from such a terrible death, and he will deliver us* (v. 10a). The fact that God rescued Paul and his companions from certain death in Asia gives Paul confidence that he will continue to deliver them. As such, *we have put our hope in him that he will deliver us again* (v. 10b).

As we have observed several times now, Paul's hope is not insecure, wishful thinking. It is, rather, an expectation based on God's faithfulness seen in previous acts and events. In this case, God's deliverance of Paul from certain death in Asia grounds his expectation that he will deliver him again. It might be objected, however, that no one can have certainty of God's deliverance based on the experience of a past deliverance. Who can know the will of God in such situations? Maybe the next violent encounter will be the end. After all, in the end even Paul was not spared from the sword of Nero.[9]

To this objection, two responses may be offered. First, even if there *is* a logical misstep on Paul's part here, it does not undermine the point that his hope is an expectation based on God's previous faithfulness. We are still able to observe what hope means for Paul, even if some may conclude that his hope is less secure than he thinks it is. Second, there may be more to Paul's expectation than he has revealed here. There are several instances recorded in Acts and in Paul's letters that indicate his sense of mission and of what God has designed for him to do, including one day appearing before Caesar in Rome (e.g., Acts 27:21–26). It may well be that one such divinely revealed expectation lies in the background here. Paul's deliverance from death in Asia was according to the plan of God, and Paul likewise knows that God will continue to deliver him from danger until his mission is complete.

In any case, we observe in this text yet another example of Paul's hope constituting an expectation based on the evidence of God's prior action and faithfulness.

2 Cor 1:13–14 οὐ γὰρ ἄλλα γράφομεν ὑμῖν ἀλλ' ἢ ἃ ἀναγινώσκετε ἢ καὶ ἐπιγινώσκετε· **ἐλπίζω δὲ ὅτι ἕως τέλους ἐπιγνώσεσθε**, 14 καθὼς καὶ ἐπέγνωτε ἡμᾶς ἀπὸ μέρους, ὅτι καύχημα ὑμῶν ἐσμεν καθάπερ καὶ ὑμεῖς ἡμῶν ἐν τῇ ἡμέρᾳ τοῦ κυρίου Ἰησοῦ.

For we are writing nothing to you other than what you can read and also understand. ***I hope you will understand completely****—14 just as you have partially understood us—that we are your reason for pride, just as you also are ours in the day of our Lord Jesus.*

As this instance does not express eschatological hope, it requires no further comment.

2 Cor 3:9–12 εἰ γὰρ τῇ διακονίᾳ τῆς κατακρίσεως δόξα, πολλῷ μᾶλλον περισσεύει ἡ διακονία τῆς δικαιοσύνης δόξῃ. 10 καὶ γὰρ οὐ δεδόξασται τὸ δεδοξασμένον ἐν τούτῳ τῷ μέρει εἵνεκεν τῆς ὑπερβαλλούσης δόξης.

---

9. "God's 'deliverances' in this life are always partial" (Barnett, *2 Corinthians*, 34).

11 εἰ γὰρ τὸ καταργούμενον διὰ δόξης, πολλῷ μᾶλλον τὸ μένον ἐν δόξῃ.
12 Ἔχοντες οὖν τοιαύτην ἐλπίδα πολλῇ παρρησίᾳ χρώμεθα

*For if the ministry that brought condemnation had glory, the ministry that brings righteousness overflows with even more glory. 10 In fact, what had been glorious is not glorious now by comparison because of the glory that surpasses it. 11 For if what was set aside was glorious, what endures will be even more glorious. 12 **Since, then, we have such a hope, we act with great boldness.***

Paul contrasts the ministry of Moses, which had glory though it brought condemnation, with the ministry of the new covenant that brings righteousness, and so *overflows with even more glory* in comparison (3:9). Indeed, the former is so superseded by the latter that it is no longer considered glorious (v. 10). Paul then engages a *qal wahomer* ("lesser to greater") argument to further underscore the glory of new-covenant ministry—*For if what was set aside was glorious, what endures will be even more glorious* (v. 11). The fact that the old covenant has been set aside, while the new covenant will endure, means that it *will be even more glorious*.

This then grounds the hope that enables Paul to act with great boldness (v. 12). His hope is based on the surpassing glory of new-covenant ministry and the fact that it will not be laid aside like the ministry of Moses, as glorious as it was in its day.[10] The ministry of the new covenant is more glorious and will endure rather than be superseded. The surety of this reality provides the firm foundation for hope that inspires Paul's boldness.

2 Cor 5:11 Εἰδότες οὖν τὸν φόβον τοῦ κυρίου ἀνθρώπους πείθομεν, θεῷ δὲ πεφανερώμεθα· ἐλπίζω δὲ καὶ ἐν ταῖς συνειδήσεσιν ὑμῶν πεφανερῶσθαι.

*Therefore, since we know the fear of the Lord, we try to persuade people. What we are is plain to God, **and I hope it is also plain to your consciences**.*

As this instance does not concern eschatological hope, it requires no further comment.

2 Cor 8:3–5 ὅτι κατὰ δύναμιν, μαρτυρῶ, καὶ παρὰ δύναμιν, αὐθαίρετοι 4 μετὰ πολλῆς παρακλήσεως δεόμενοι ἡμῶν τὴν χάριν καὶ τὴν κοινωνίαν τῆς διακονίας τῆς εἰς τοὺς ἁγίους, 5 **καὶ οὐ καθὼς ἠλπίσαμεν** ἀλλ' ἑαυτοὺς ἔδωκαν πρῶτον τῷ κυρίῳ καὶ ἡμῖν διὰ θελήματος θεοῦ

---

10. Belleville, *2 Corinthians*, 102.

I can testify that, according to their ability and even beyond their ability, of their own accord, 4 they begged us earnestly for the privilege of sharing in the ministry to the saints, 5 **and not just as we had hoped***. Instead, they gave themselves first to the Lord and then to us by God's will.*

Likewise, here Paul's hope is not of an eschatological nature, so requires no further comment.

2 Cor 10:15 οὐκ εἰς τὰ ἄμετρα καυχώμενοι ἐν ἀλλοτρίοις κόποις, **ἐλπίδα δὲ ἔχοντες αὐξανομένης τῆς πίστεως ὑμῶν** ἐν ὑμῖν μεγαλυνθῆναι κατὰ τὸν κανόνα ἡμῶν εἰς περισσείαν

We are not boasting beyond measure about other people's labors. **On the contrary, we have the hope that as your faith increases,** *our area of ministry will be greatly enlarged*

This reference to hope is not eschatological in nature and requires no further comment.

2 Cor 13:5–6 Ἑαυτοὺς πειράζετε εἰ ἐστὲ ἐν τῇ πίστει, ἑαυτοὺς δοκιμάζετε· ἢ οὐκ ἐπιγινώσκετε ἑαυτοὺς ὅτι Χριστὸς Ἰησοῦς ἐν ὑμῖν; εἰ μήτι ἀδόκιμοί ἐστε. 6 ἐλπίζω δὲ ὅτι γνώσεσθε ὅτι ἡμεῖς οὐκ ἐσμὲν ἀδόκιμοι.

Test yourselves to see if you are in the faith. Examine yourselves. Or do you yourselves not recognize that Jesus Christ is in you?—unless you fail the test. 6 **And I hope you will recognize that we ourselves do not fail the test.**

This reference to hope is not eschatological in nature and requires no further comment.

Gal 5:4–6 κατηργήθητε ἀπὸ Χριστοῦ, οἵτινες ἐν νόμῳ δικαιοῦσθε, τῆς χάριτος ἐξεπέσατε. 5 ἡμεῖς γὰρ **πνεύματι ἐκ πίστεως ἐλπίδα δικαιοσύνης ἀπεκδεχόμεθα.** 6 ἐν γὰρ Χριστῷ Ἰησοῦ οὔτε περιτομή τι ἰσχύει οὔτε ἀκροβυστία ἀλλὰ πίστις δι' ἀγάπης ἐνεργουμένη.

You who are trying to be justified by the law are alienated from Christ; you have fallen from grace. 5 **For we eagerly await through the Spirit, by faith, the hope of righteousness.** *6 For in Christ Jesus neither circumcision nor uncircumcision accomplishes anything; what matters is faith working through love.*

In broad outline, Paul contrasts justification by the law with awaiting the hope of righteousness, but there are in fact several elements of contrast embedded in 5:4–5. First is the contrast between law and faith, which Paul pursues throughout the letter. Justification comes by faith in Christ, not by the law of Moses. Second, the agency is contrasted in that he says *you who are trying to be justified by the law* (v. 4; οἵτινες ἐν νόμῳ δικαιοῦσθε)—in which the middle voice of δικαιοῦσθε indicates *subject affectedness*,[11] most likely with a reflexive function (i.e., *justify yourselves*)—while justification by faith occurs *through the Spirit* (v. 5). Third, justification by the law is a *present* attempt to receive righteousness, while justification by faith is synonymous with *the hope of righteousness* or *the hope* for *righteousness* (v. 6). That is, righteousness is awaited because it is received in the future.[12]

Given the shape of the argument presented in Galatians, *the hope of righteousness* cannot be understood as insecure, wishful thinking. It is clearly an expectation based on the work of Christ and the covenant of God. Moreover, Paul says that *we eagerly await* (ἀπεκδεχόμεθα) for the fulfillment of this expectation (v. 5). The reception of righteousness through faith is a certain expectation that Paul awaits based on the work of Christ.

Eph 1:11–12 ἐν ᾧ καὶ ἐκληρώθημεν προορισθέντες κατὰ πρόθεσιν τοῦ τὰ πάντα ἐνεργοῦντος κατὰ τὴν βουλὴν τοῦ θελήματος αὐτοῦ 12 εἰς τὸ εἶναι ἡμᾶς εἰς ἔπαινον δόξης αὐτοῦ τοὺς προηλπικότας ἐν τῷ Χριστῷ.

In him we have also received an inheritance, because we were predestined according to the plan of the one who works out everything in agreement with the purpose of his will, 12 ***so that we who had already put our hope in Christ might bring praise to his glory***.

The eschatological shape of this text is found through reference to *an inheritance*, predestination, God's working out everything according to his purpose, and the praise of God's glory. While this *praise to his glory* might refer

---

11. See Campbell, *Advances in the Study of Greek*, ch. 4.

12. There is considerable discussion about the meaning of the phrase *the hope of righteousness* (ἐλπίδα δικαιοσύνης). Fung offers a helpful summary of views and concludes that it communicates the sense of "the realization of the hoped-for things pertaining to the state of righteousness conferred in justification" or, more simply, "the hope to which the justification of believers points them forward" (Fung, *Epistle to the Galatians*, 224–26 [226]). While this is certainly possible, our reading of the phrase seems more likely. The hope *for* righteousness correlates with waiting through the Spirit by faith for it (5:5), rather than trying to be justified (= made righteous) by the law (5:4). Law-based human effort to achieve righteousness is contrasted with Spirit- and faith-based hope, or expectation, of righteousness (as we know, Paul can speak of righteousness received *now* or in the *future*).

to a current actuality, it most likely points to a future event of praise due to the elements already identified that indicate the eschatological shape of these two verses.

The phrase *we who had already put our hope in Christ* (τοὺς προηλπικότας ἐν τῷ Χριστῷ) seems to point to prior Christian experience—before others have come to similar hope. Muddiman writes, "Since hope inevitably precedes its realisation, the prefix (of προηλπικότας) cannot simply mean 'we hoped before we experienced' but must mean 'we hoped before others did.'"[13] This prior hope might refer to Israel's messianic expectation, or to Paul and the first generation of believers as "spiritual predecessors" of his readers.

Given the reception of an inheritance, predestination, and the confidence that God works out all things in accordance to his will, the current experience of hope must be understood as the expectation of what God has already determined to do. Thus, hope is yet again observed as an expectation grounded in the work and character of God.

> Eph 1:18–19 πεφωτισμένους τοὺς ὀφθαλμοὺς τῆς καρδίας ὑμῶν εἰς τὸ εἰδέναι ὑμᾶς τίς ἐστιν **ἡ ἐλπὶς τῆς κλήσεως αὐτοῦ**, τίς ὁ πλοῦτος τῆς δόξης τῆς κληρονομίας αὐτοῦ ἐν τοῖς ἁγίοις, 19 καὶ τί τὸ ὑπερβάλλον μέγεθος τῆς δυνάμεως αὐτοῦ εἰς ἡμᾶς τοὺς πιστεύοντας κατὰ τὴν ἐνέργειαν τοῦ κράτους τῆς ἰσχύος αὐτοῦ.

> *I pray that the eyes of your heart may be enlightened so that you may know what is **the hope of his calling**, what is the wealth of his glorious inheritance in the saints, 19 and what is the immeasurable greatness of his power toward us who believe, according to the mighty working of his strength.*

Here *the hope of his calling* is parallel to *the wealth of his glorious inheritance* and *the immeasurable greatness of his power*. Just as *wealth* (*of his glorious inheritance*) and *immeasurable greatness* (*of his power*) modify their objects adjectivally, so *hope* ought to be understood as modifying *his calling*. The three-way parallel helps to understand the nature of the genitive relationship of *the hope of his calling* (ἡ ἐλπὶς τῆς κλήσεως αὐτοῦ). This is not likely a hope *for* his calling (i.e., believers hope to receive his call), but is descriptive of the calling, just as *wealth* and *immeasurable greatness* describe the glorious inheritance and God's power. Thus, *the hope of his calling* refers to an expectancy that accompanies, or modifies, the call of God. When people are called by God, their calling comes with an expectation.

---

13. Muddiman, *Ephesians*, 77.

This reading is exactly reverse of that which understands the genitive relationship to mean "the hope for his calling." According to such a reading, the calling is not in hand but is awaited. According to our reading, however, the calling is secure and produces a hope associated with it. This is then a secure hope and an expectation that comes from the calling that is already received.

This then explains what is meant by Paul's prayer *that the eyes of your heart may be enlightened so that you may know what is the hope of his calling* (v. 18). Paul prays that believers would see and know the hope that accompanies their calling. They have been called to belong to God, and this calling produces a certain expectation in keeping with his call. The Ephesians ought to know the implications of their calling; they ought to know the expectation that is grounded in the call of God, some of which is mentioned forthwith—*the wealth of his glorious inheritance in the saints* and *the immeasurable greatness of his power toward us who believe.*

Eph 2:11–12 Διὸ μνημονεύετε ὅτι ποτὲ ὑμεῖς τὰ ἔθνη ἐν σαρκί, οἱ λεγόμενοι ἀκροβυστία ὑπὸ τῆς λεγομένης περιτομῆς ἐν σαρκὶ χειροποιήτου, 12 ὅτι ἦτε τῷ καιρῷ ἐκείνῳ χωρὶς Χριστοῦ, ἀπηλλοτριωμένοι τῆς πολιτείας τοῦ Ἰσραὴλ καὶ ξένοι τῶν διαθηκῶν τῆς ἐπαγγελίας, **ἐλπίδα μὴ ἔχοντες** καὶ ἄθεοι ἐν τῷ κόσμῳ.

So then, remember that at one time you were Gentiles in the flesh—called "the uncircumcised" by those called "the circumcised," which is done in the flesh by human hands. 12 At that time you were without Christ, excluded from the citizenship of Israel, and foreigners to the covenants of promise, **without hope** *and without God in the world.*

The description of gentiles being *without Christ, excluded from the citizenship of Israel, and foreigners to the covenants of promise* (2:12) is the ground upon which their lack of hope is established. Or, to put it another way, without Christ, without membership in Israel, and without participation in the covenants, there are no grounds for hope. Implicitly, then, we see that hope must be grounded in something. It is the expectation that arises from some other established reality. Without such establishment, there are no grounds for hope.

Eph 4:4–6 ἓν σῶμα καὶ ἓν πνεῦμα, καθὼς καὶ **ἐκλήθητε ἐν μιᾷ ἐλπίδι τῆς κλήσεως ὑμῶν·** 5 εἷς κύριος, μία πίστις, ἓν βάπτισμα, 6 εἷς θεὸς καὶ πατὴρ πάντων, ὁ ἐπὶ πάντων καὶ διὰ πάντων καὶ ἐν πᾶσιν.

*There is one body and one Spirit—just as **you were called to one hope at your calling**—5 one Lord, one faith, one baptism, 6 one God and Father of all, who is above all and through all and in all.*

The fact that Paul refers to *one hope* indicates that he is not referring to a subjective sensation. Just as there is *one body and one Spirit*, so there is *one hope*, which refers to an expectation to which believers are called. The *one God and Father of all* has called believers into *one body* by *one Spirit* to *one Lord*, *one faith*, and *one baptism*. These things constitute the ground for hopeful expectation.[14]

Phil 1:16–20 οἱ μὲν ἐξ ἀγάπης, εἰδότες ὅτι εἰς ἀπολογίαν τοῦ εὐαγγελίου κεῖμαι, 17 οἱ δὲ ἐξ ἐριθείας τὸν Χριστὸν καταγγέλλουσιν, οὐχ ἁγνῶς, οἰόμενοι θλῖψιν ἐγείρειν τοῖς δεσμοῖς μου. 18 τί γάρ; πλὴν ὅτι παντὶ τρόπῳ, εἴτε προφάσει εἴτε ἀληθείᾳ, Χριστὸς καταγγέλλεται, καὶ ἐν τούτῳ χαίρω. ἀλλὰ καὶ χαρήσομαι, 19 οἶδα γὰρ ὅτι τοῦτό μοι ἀποβήσεται εἰς σωτηρίαν διὰ τῆς ὑμῶν δεήσεως καὶ ἐπιχορηγίας τοῦ πνεύματος Ἰησοῦ Χριστοῦ 20 κατὰ **τὴν ἀποκαραδοκίαν καὶ ἐλπίδα μου, ὅτι ἐν οὐδενὶ αἰσχυνθήσομαι** ἀλλ᾽ ἐν πάσῃ παρρησίᾳ ὡς πάντοτε καὶ νῦν μεγαλυνθήσεται Χριστὸς ἐν τῷ σώματί μου, εἴτε διὰ ζωῆς εἴτε διὰ θανάτου.

*These preach out of love, knowing that I am appointed for the defense of the gospel; 17 the others proclaim Christ out of selfish ambition, not sincerely, thinking that they will cause me trouble in my imprisonment. 18 What does it matter? Only that in every way, whether from false motives or true, Christ is proclaimed, and in this I rejoice. Yes, and I will continue to rejoice 19 because I know this will lead to my salvation through your prayers and help from the Spirit of Jesus Christ. 20 **My eager expectation and hope is that I will not be ashamed about anything**, but that now as always, with all courage, Christ will be highly honored in my body, whether by life or by death.*

This reference to Paul's hope is set in the context of opposition from those who *proclaim Christ out of selfish ambition*, hoping to cause him trouble (1:17). Paul rejoices that Christ is preached in any case (v. 18), and will continue to rejoice despite his afflictions and opposition because he believes *this will lead to my salvation* or deliverance or vindication (v. 19; σωτηρία).

It is unclear what exactly Paul refers to by his salvation here (v. 19; σωτηρία). On the one hand, he may simply mean that he will be delivered from all worldly

---

14. Arnold, *Ephesians*, 233–34.

opposition *through your prayers and help from the Spirit of Jesus Christ* (v. 19). This would explain why he sees the Philippians' prayers as instrumental (along with the Spirit)—their intercession for Paul will help to secure his deliverance from his trials. If, however, Paul is referring to his eschatological salvation, it is unclear why he sees their prayers as instrumental. After all, Paul is already secure in his saved status, and this is by his faith in Christ, not by the prayers of others.

In favor of eschatological salvation, however, Paul goes on to say that he expects *not to be ashamed about anything* (v. 20a), which sounds very much like he is referring to eschatological judgment. Yet then he adds *but that now as always, with all courage, Christ will be highly honored in my body, whether by life or by death* (v. 20b), which sounds like he might be referring to his current situation after all.

The solution is probably both-and, and not either-or. Paul refers to *now* and to *always*, which can be understood to refer to his current experience as well as to any future reality (including the eschaton). He also hopes that Christ will be highly honored in his body, *whether by life or by death*. *Life* and *death* are apt ways to indicate current experience and the future eschatological experience to come. Thus, Paul appears to refer to the entirety of his existence—inclusive of his life lived before and after death.

As such, Paul's *eager expectation and hope* (τὴν ἀποκαραδοκίαν καὶ ἐλπίδα μου) that he will not be ashamed about anything pertains to his current pre-death existence *and* his post-death existence. His expectation is grounded in his confidence that he has nothing to be ashamed about.[15] His conscience is clear with respect to his motivation for proclamation (contra those who oppose him) and in his endurance of such opposition. Through the intercession of others and with the help of the Spirit, Paul's conduct gives him no reason to fear shame either in this age or the age to come.

Phil 2:23 τοῦτον μὲν οὖν ἐλπίζω πέμψαι ὡς ἂν ἀφίδω τὰ περὶ ἐμὲ ἐξαυτῆς

Therefore, **I hope to send him** *as soon as I see how things go with me.*

As this example does not express eschatological hope, it requires no further comment.

Col 1:3–6 Εὐχαριστοῦμεν τῷ θεῷ πατρὶ τοῦ κυρίου ἡμῶν Ἰησοῦ Χριστοῦ πάντοτε περὶ ὑμῶν προσευχόμενοι, 4 ἀκούσαντες τὴν πίστιν ὑμῶν ἐν

---

15. Gordon D. Fee, *Paul's Letter to the Philippians*, NICNT (Grand Rapids: Eerdmans, 1995), 135.

Χριστῷ Ἰησοῦ καὶ τὴν ἀγάπην ἣν ἔχετε εἰς πάντας τοὺς ἁγίους 5 διὰ τὴν ἐλπίδα τὴν ἀποκειμένην ὑμῖν ἐν τοῖς οὐρανοῖς, ἣν προηκούσατε ἐν τῷ λόγῳ τῆς ἀληθείας τοῦ εὐαγγελίου 6 τοῦ παρόντος εἰς ὑμᾶς, καθὼς καὶ ἐν παντὶ τῷ κόσμῳ ἐστὶν καρποφορούμενον καὶ αὐξανόμενον καθὼς καὶ ἐν ὑμῖν, ἀφ' ἧς ἡμέρας ἠκούσατε καὶ ἐπέγνωτε τὴν χάριν τοῦ θεοῦ ἐν ἀληθείᾳ

We always thank God, the Father of our Lord Jesus Christ, when we pray for you, 4 for we have heard of your faith in Christ Jesus and of the love you have for all the saints 5 because of **the hope reserved for you in heaven. You have already heard about this hope in the word of truth, the gospel** *6 that has come to you. It is bearing fruit and growing all over the world, just as it has among you since the day you heard it and came to truly appreciate God's grace.*

Paul thanks God for the Colossians' faith in Christ and their love for the saints (1:3–4). The latter of these, or perhaps both, has arisen *because of the hope reserved for you in heaven* (v. 5a). Clearly, then, Paul sees the Colossians' hope as the grounds for their love (and possibly their faith also). Apparently their hope enables them to demonstrate love to others; their secure expectation enables them to be open to others' needs and concerns.

It is striking that this hope is *reserved* for them in heaven (τὴν ἐλπίδα τὴν ἀποκειμένην ὑμῖν ἐν τοῖς οὐρανοῖς)—Paul speaks of it as though it is a commodity or object rather than a subjective disposition or attitude. First, it is *reserved* for them—it is not experiential; second, it is *in heaven*—it is not "in" them. What exactly is this hope? Paul says that the Colossians *heard about this hope in the word of truth, the gospel* (v. 5b). This gospel is *bearing fruit and growing all over the world* and has been doing so among the Colossians since the day they heard it *and came to truly appreciate God's grace* (v. 6). Thus we see that the gospel reveals both God's grace and the hope that is reserved in heaven. It is reasonable to suppose, then, that the hope reserved in heaven is a product of God's grace—it is a heavenly inheritance given by God.[16] Indeed, this notion is supported by v. 12 a little further into the introduction to the letter—*the Father . . . has enabled you to share in the saints' inheritance in the light*.

Putting this together, then, we observe that Paul regards the Colossians' hope as a heavenly inheritance granted to them by God through the gospel. Their hope is not a subjective disposition or attitude but is the confident expectation of what will be theirs based on the promise of God in the gospel. Moreover,

---

16. Marianne Meye Thompson, *Colossians and Philemon*, THNTC (Grand Rapids: Eerdmans, 2005), 20.

their hope constitutes the basis from which the Colossians are able to demonstrate love to others.

> Col 1:22–23 νυνὶ δὲ ἀποκατήλλαξεν ἐν τῷ σώματι τῆς σαρκὸς αὐτοῦ διὰ τοῦ θανάτου παραστῆσαι ὑμᾶς ἁγίους καὶ ἀμώμους καὶ ἀνεγκλήτους κατενώπιον αὐτοῦ, 23 εἴ γε ἐπιμένετε τῇ πίστει τεθεμελιωμένοι καὶ ἑδραῖοι καὶ μὴ μετακινούμενοι ἀπὸ τῆς ἐλπίδος τοῦ εὐαγγελίου οὗ ἠκούσατε, τοῦ κηρυχθέντος ἐν πάσῃ κτίσει τῇ ὑπὸ τὸν οὐρανόν, οὗ ἐγενόμην ἐγὼ Παῦλος διάκονος.
>
> *But now he has reconciled you by his physical body through his death, to present you holy, faultless, and blameless before him—* **23 *if indeed you remain grounded and steadfast in the faith and are not shifted away from the hope of the gospel that you heard*.** *This gospel has been proclaimed in all creation under heaven, and I, Paul, have become a servant of it.*

The *hope of the gospel* (1:23) no doubt refers to the reconciliation of believers through Christ's death *to present you holy, faultless, and blameless before him* (v. 22). This presentation *before him* refers to a forensic scenario—it is a picture of judgment in light of reconciliation.[17] The blamelessness of believers in judgment is therefore a result of their reconciliation with God through Christ.

But this positive standing in judgment is conditional on remaining *grounded and steadfast in the faith* and not being *shifted away from the hope of the gospel* that they heard (v. 23). From this formulation it is clear that *the faith* and *the hope of the gospel* are both regarded as objective, rather than subjective, entities. This is seen by the fact that Paul refers to being *grounded and steadfast* in the faith and not shifting away from the hope of the gospel; they are entities on which believers may be grounded, and away from which they may stray. Rather than focusing on an individual's experience of faith or hope—which are internal, subjective experiences—Paul refers to them like a foundation stone (*faith*) and a beacon (*hope*) to which believers must remain oriented if they are to benefit from the gospel that they heard.

Thus it is clear that the Colossians' assurance in the face of judgment is not dependent on their own subjective feelings and experiences but on the objective entities of *the faith* and *hope* of the gospel. Paul is a servant of this gospel (v. 23c) because *it* carries the hope of reconciliation through Christ.

---

17. See Campbell, *Paul and Union with Christ*, 107–8.

Col 1:27 οἷς ἠθέλησεν ὁ θεὸς γνωρίσαι τί τὸ πλοῦτος τῆς δόξης τοῦ μυστηρίου τούτου ἐν τοῖς ἔθνεσιν, ὅ ἐστιν **Χριστὸς ἐν ὑμῖν, ἡ ἐλπὶς τῆς δόξης**

*God wanted to make known among the Gentiles the glorious wealth of this mystery, which is **Christ in you, the hope of glory**.*

Reflecting on his own role in the proclamation of the word of God to the gentiles (1:24–29), Paul refers to God's intention for the apostle's service—*God wanted to make known among the Gentiles the glorious wealth of this mystery, which is Christ in you, the hope of glory* (v. 27). This mystery was *hidden for ages and generations but* is *now revealed to his saints* (v. 26), meaning that it was a riddle for a time, but now has been solved. He calls it a mystery (μυστήριον, perhaps better translated "secret"),[18] but it is no longer mysterious or secret.

But what exactly is this mystery? It is nothing less than *Christ in you*. The fact that Christ, the king of the Jews, is *in* or *among* the gentiles is the solution of this formerly unsolved riddle. It fulfills the promises made to Abraham that all the peoples on earth will be blessed through him (Gen 12:1–3). Until Christ, it was not clear through Israel's history how this promise would be fulfilled. But now that Christ has come, the promise to bless the peoples of the earth through Abraham has been fulfilled—one of his descendants would be the Christ, whose reign and salvation would not be restricted to Abraham's physical descendants but would be available to all who trusted in him.

Paul qualifies *Christ in you* as *the hope of glory*. But it is unclear whether *Christ* (alone) is to be understood as *the hope of glory*, or if *Christ in you* is this hope. That is, is *Christ* the hope, or is his presence in and among the gentiles the hope? While it is difficult to answer this question with certainty, it seems most likely that the former of the two options is correct. Otherwise, Christ as the hope of glory would be limited to his presence among the gentiles instead of being the hope of glory for all people, Jew and gentile alike. Just because the *mystery* is Christ among the gentiles does not mean that *the hope of glory* need be limited to the gentiles in the same way.

Thus, Christ is *the hope of glory*. Hope is connected to glory, with glory assuming its position as the ultimate good of all things. But what is the nature of the connection? What is the intended meaning of the genitive construction, ἡ ἐλπὶς τῆς δόξης? If the genitive τῆς δόξης is an *attributive* genitive, then the hope is a hope defined by glory. It is a glorious hope. But if the genitive is an

---

18. BDAG 662.

attributed genitive, then hope defines glory—*the hopeful glory* (or something like that). There are other possibilities too, such as the genitive of content (glory is the content of hope), the epexegetical genitive (glory is a particular subset of hope), and the genitive of product (hope produces glory).[19]

But most likely is the somewhat rare category, the genitive of destination or purpose. According to Wallace, this genitive "indicates where the head noun is going (or the direction it is 'moving' in) or the purpose of its existence."[20] The sense is that the destination or purpose of hope is glory. Glory is where hope is pointed, and glory is where hope is going.

This makes most sense of the idea that Christ himself is the hope of glory. He is, in his person, the hope that points to glory and the hope that is headed to glory. For Paul, this is no doubt because of his resurrection to an immortal and eternal body. His resurrection from the dead is the hope for all human beings who long to face death with the confidence of resurrected glory. As the firstfruits of the resurrection (1 Cor 15:20, 23), Christ paves the way to glory for all who are in him.

Putting all this together, we see that God's glorious mystery or secret has been made known among the gentiles, and it declares that Christ is in and among them. This is eminently good news for the gentiles, since Christ is the hope whose destination is resurrected, eternal glory.

1 Thess 1:2–3 Εὐχαριστοῦμεν τῷ θεῷ πάντοτε περὶ πάντων ὑμῶν μνείαν ποιούμενοι ἐπὶ τῶν προσευχῶν ἡμῶν, ἀδιαλείπτως 3 μνημονεύοντες ὑμῶν τοῦ ἔργου τῆς πίστεως καὶ τοῦ κόπου τῆς ἀγάπης καὶ **τῆς ὑπομονῆς τῆς ἐλπίδος τοῦ κυρίου ἡμῶν Ἰησοῦ Χριστοῦ** ἔμπροσθεν τοῦ θεοῦ καὶ πατρὸς ἡμῶν

*We always thank God for all of you, making mention of you constantly in our prayers. 3 We recall, in the presence of our God and Father, your work produced by faith, your labor motivated by love, and **your endurance inspired by hope in our Lord Jesus Christ**.*

This reference to hope is found in a genitive chain in which the head nouns (*work, labor,* and *endurance*) are genitives (τοῦ ἔργου, τοῦ κόπου, τῆς ἀγάπης) as are their genitive modifiers (*faith*, τῆς πίστεως; *love*, τῆς ἀγάπης; *hope*, τῆς ἐλπίδος). The head nouns are in the genitive case because they follow the participle μνημονεύοντες (*recall*), which often takes genitive objects.[21]

---

19. See Wallace, *Greek Grammar Beyond the Basics*, 86–100.
20. Wallace, *Greek Grammar Beyond the Basics*, 100–101.
21. BDAG 655, §1.a.

In the translation above (CSB), the genitive modifiers are correctly understood as genitives of production,[22] so that the head nouns are produced by them. That is, the Thessalonians' work is produced by faith (τοῦ ἔργου τῆς πίστεως), their labor is produced by love (τοῦ κόπου τῆς ἀγάπης), and their endurance is produced by hope (τῆς ὑπομονῆς τῆς ἐλπίδος). Thus, it is true to say that faith, hope, and love are the marks of the Christian life (cf. 1 Cor 13:13) as they produce the characteristics and actions consistent with faith in Christ.

The hope that produces endurance is *hope in our Lord Jesus Christ* (τῆς ἐλπίδος τοῦ κυρίου ἡμῶν Ἰησοῦ Χριστοῦ). While *in our Lord Jesus Christ* renders yet another genitival expression (τοῦ κυρίου ἡμῶν Ἰησοῦ Χριστοῦ), there is no reason to doubt the objective-genitive reading advanced in the translation here (*in our Lord Jesus Christ*). This hope is grounded in the person of Christ. There is no specific attribute or action of Christ mentioned, so this is likely a summary expression that encapsulates all of who Christ is and all that he has done, is doing, and will do. Such hope is not wishful thinking but is founded on all that Christ represents. It is a secure hope, therefore, since on Christ rests the entirety of Christian expectation.

1 Thess 2:19–20 τίς γὰρ **ἡμῶν ἐλπὶς** ἢ χαρὰ ἢ στέφανος καυχήσεως – ἢ οὐχὶ καὶ ὑμεῖς – ἔμπροσθεν τοῦ κυρίου ἡμῶν Ἰησοῦ ἐν τῇ αὐτοῦ παρουσίᾳ; 20 ὑμεῖς γάρ ἐστε ἡ δόξα ἡμῶν καὶ ἡ χαρά.

*For who is **our hope** or joy or crown of boasting in the presence of our Lord Jesus at his coming? Is it not you? 20 Indeed you are our glory and joy!*

This is quite an extraordinary statement for Paul to make, since he locates his hope with the Thessalonians. Elsewhere his hope has been squarely fixed on Christ rather than on any earthly or human factor. Here Paul's expectation is that the Thessalonians will be the ground for his hope, joy, and crown of boasting when the Lord Jesus comes (2:19). He even adds that they are *our glory and joy!* (v. 20).

Strange as it is, this text demonstrates that Paul's hope is not individualistic in nature. His expectation is not limited to his own deliverance at the coming of Christ, his own crown of boasting, or his own glory and joy. He expects to share these things with others. In particular, he expects to share it with those to whom he has ministered and loved. The Thessalonians' participation in joy and glory in the presence of the Lord Jesus is Paul's joyful hope and expectation.

---

22. Wallace, *Greek Grammar Beyond the Basics*, 106.

1 Thess 4:13–14 Οὐ θέλομεν δὲ ὑμᾶς ἀγνοεῖν, ἀδελφοί, περὶ τῶν κοιμωμένων, ἵνα μὴ λυπῆσθε καθὼς καὶ οἱ λοιποὶ οἱ μὴ ἔχοντες ἐλπίδα. 14 εἰ γὰρ πιστεύομεν ὅτι Ἰησοῦς ἀπέθανεν καὶ ἀνέστη, οὕτως καὶ ὁ θεὸς τοὺς κοιμηθέντας διὰ τοῦ Ἰησοῦ ἄξει σὺν αὐτῷ.

*We do not want you to be uninformed, brothers and sisters, concerning those who are asleep, so that **you will not grieve like the rest, who have no hope**. 14 For if we believe that Jesus died and rose again, in the same way, through Jesus, God will bring with him those who have fallen asleep.*

The grief experienced by believers is not like the grief experienced by those *who have no hope* (4:13). Unbelievers' lack of hope could be understood as a subjective, personal experience—they do not feel hopeful in the face of losing loved ones. Or, the hope they do not have could be understood in a more objective sense—there are no grounds for anything positive to follow death.

The following verse sheds some light on the issue, as Paul reminds the Thessalonians of the ground of their hope in the face of death—*if we believe that Jesus died and rose again, in the same way, through Jesus, God will bring with him those who have fallen asleep* (v. 14). The hopeful expectation that believers enjoy is that God will bring with Jesus those who have died in Christ. That is why the Thessalonians can grieve with hope—their hope is the resurrection of the dead.

And this hope is grounded in the belief *that Jesus died and rose again* (v. 14a). These events are the security for believers' hope. If they are accepted, then the hope of resurrection can be regarded as secure. Theirs is not wishful thinking in the face of death, without any objective grounds for hope. Their expectation of resurrection is due to the death and resurrection of Christ.

1 Thess 5:7–10 Οἱ γὰρ καθεύδοντες νυκτὸς καθεύδουσιν καὶ οἱ μεθυσκόμενοι νυκτὸς μεθύουσιν· 8 ἡμεῖς δὲ ἡμέρας ὄντες νήφωμεν ἐνδυσάμενοι θώρακα πίστεως καὶ ἀγάπης καὶ **περικεφαλαίαν ἐλπίδα σωτηρίας**· 9 ὅτι οὐκ ἔθετο ἡμᾶς ὁ θεὸς εἰς ὀργὴν ἀλλὰ εἰς περιποίησιν σωτηρίας διὰ τοῦ κυρίου ἡμῶν Ἰησοῦ Χριστοῦ 10 τοῦ ἀποθανόντος ὑπὲρ ἡμῶν, ἵνα εἴτε γρηγορῶμεν εἴτε καθεύδωμεν ἅμα σὺν αὐτῷ ζήσωμεν.

*For those who sleep, sleep at night, and those who get drunk, get drunk at night. 8 But since we belong to the day, let us be self-controlled and put on the armor of faith and love, and **a helmet of the hope of salvation**. 9 For God did not appoint us to wrath, but to obtain salvation through our Lord Jesus Christ, 10 who died for us, so that whether we are awake or asleep, we may live together with him.*

Faith, hope, and love are again seen as the marks of the Christian life (cf. 1:2–3; 1 Cor 13:13), and this time they are depicted metaphorically as *the armor of faith and love* and *a helmet of the hope of salvation* (1 Thess 5:8). Faith, hope, and love, then, constitute the "equipment" that believers require in order to live self-controlled lives in this time of spiritual warfare (cf. Eph 6:10–17).

As a *helmet*, the hope of salvation refers to the confident expectation of salvation in the face of judgment. This is seen in the following two verses—*For God did not appoint us to wrath, but to obtain salvation through our Lord Jesus Christ, who died for us, so that whether we are awake or asleep, we may live together with him* (1 Thess 5:9–10). The outcome of salvation is already assured by the appointment of God and through the death of Christ. Because of these twin factors, believers will *live together with him*.

This expectation of resurrection life together with Christ is the content of the hope of salvation. Hope functions as the metaphorical helmet in the believer's battle against evil and is grounded in the decision of God and the sacrificial work of Christ.[23]

2 Thess 2:16–17 Αὐτὸς δὲ ὁ κύριος ἡμῶν Ἰησοῦς Χριστὸς καὶ ὁ θεὸς ὁ πατὴρ ἡμῶν ὁ ἀγαπήσας ἡμᾶς καὶ δοὺς παράκλησιν αἰωνίαν καὶ ἐλπίδα ἀγαθὴν ἐν χάριτι, 17 παρακαλέσαι ὑμῶν τὰς καρδίας καὶ στηρίξαι ἐν παντὶ ἔργῳ καὶ λόγῳ ἀγαθῷ.

May our Lord Jesus Christ himself and God our Father, who has loved us and given us eternal encouragement and good hope by grace, 17 encourage your hearts and strengthen you in every good work and word.

Eternal encouragement and good hope have been granted to believers by God, who has shown them love (2:16). This *eternal encouragement and good hope* has been given *by grace* (or, "in grace"; ἐν χάριτι). There is certainly a subjective element to hope in this context, since it—along with the *eternal encouragement*—is to encourage the Thessalonians' hearts and strengthen them *in every good work and word* (v. 17). Eternal encouragement and hope—these encourage their *hearts*. But there is also an objective element to this good hope, since it is given to believers by God's grace. They are not simply feelings that are generated for arbitrary reasons—they have been established by God himself.

Moreover, it is striking that the encouragement given by God is *eternal*

---

23. Green, *Letters to the Thessalonians*, 241.

encouragement. Does this mean that the encouragement will endure for eternity, or that it is encouragement that is directed toward and points to eternity? The latter is most likely, since encouragement functions to help believers to persevere unto the end. Once the goal has been reached, encouragement has done its job; it does not need to endure eternally (such is the same for subjective hope; cf. Rom 8:24). So, *eternal encouragement* is exhortation and comfort that points to the eternal life to come.

In the same way, it follows that *good hope* is likewise oriented toward the future realities to come.[24] The eternal realities of resurrection, salvation, and peace with God are secured by the grace of God. They are not the dreams of wishful thinking but the objects of a secure hope and expectation based on the grace and love of God.

1 Tim 1:1 Παῦλος ἀπόστολος Χριστοῦ Ἰησοῦ κατ' ἐπιταγὴν θεοῦ σωτῆρος ἡμῶν καὶ **Χριστοῦ Ἰησοῦ τῆς ἐλπίδος ἡμῶν**

Paul, an apostle of Christ Jesus by the command of God our Savior and of **Christ Jesus our hope**

In this very truncated reference, *Christ Jesus* himself is described as *our hope* without qualification or specification. Similar to 1 Thessalonians 1:3, in which hope is simply placed in the person of Christ (*hope in our Lord Jesus Christ*), this reference goes a step further. Hope is not *in* Christ Jesus; rather, hope is personified *as* Christ Jesus.[25] This is a way of summarizing the various ways in which Christ constitutes the grounds for hope. Elsewhere Paul refers to his death and resurrection as the source of hope, but such particulars are unnecessary here. It is enough to remind Timothy who it is that grounds their common faith. Their hope and future expectation are secured by Christ himself.

1 Tim 3:14 Ταῦτά σοι γράφω **ἐλπίζων ἐλθεῖν πρὸς σὲ ἐν τάχει**·

I write these things to you, **hoping to come to you soon**.

Since this example does not express eschatological hope, no further comment is required.

---

24. Best, *First and Second Epistles to the Thessalonians*, 321.
25. Marshall, *Pastoral Epistles*, 355.

1 Tim 4:10 εἰς τοῦτο γὰρ κοπιῶμεν καὶ ἀγωνιζόμεθα, ὅτι **ἠλπίκαμεν ἐπὶ θεῷ ζῶντι**, ὅς ἐστιν σωτὴρ πάντων ἀνθρώπων μάλιστα πιστῶν.

*For this reason we labor and strive, because **we have put our hope in the living God**, who is the Savior of all people, especially of those who believe.*

Discussion of this verse is plagued by two debates. First is the question of whether *the living God, who is the Savior of all people* refers to Christ or to the Father, since the term *Savior* is normally reserved for the former in Paul's writings. If the former, then we observe an explicit reference to Paul's belief in the deity of Christ, since he directly calls him *the living God*. But most likely he refers to the Father as the living God and Savior of all people. Second, the phrases *the Savior of all people, especially of those who believe* are often cited within debates about universalism, since they seem to affirm salvation for all people, only with special emphasis on those who believe. This is a complicated discussion that does not bear on the question at hand.[26]

Paul labors and strives *because we have put our hope in the living God*. His hope is in God, and this forms the platform for his striving labor. If God can be trusted at all, hope in him will be secure. This is underscored by the fact that God is already the Savior of all people (or of those who believe); Paul's hope is placed in a saving God who will deliver his people as promised.

1 Tim 5:5–6 ἡ δὲ ὄντως χήρα καὶ μεμονωμένη **ἤλπικεν ἐπὶ θεὸν** καὶ προσμένει ταῖς δεήσεσιν καὶ ταῖς προσευχαῖς νυκτὸς καὶ ἡμέρας, 6 ἡ δὲ σπαταλῶσα ζῶσα τέθνηκεν.

*The widow who is truly in need and left all alone **has put her hope in God** and continues night and day in her petitions and prayers; 6 however, she who is self-indulgent is dead even while she lives.*

Paul makes it clear that the godly widow without anything or anyone has no recourse but to hope in God. Without the possibility of investing her hope in earthly things or people, she looks to God for her needs. Her petitions and prayers offered night and day express her hope in God. Her hope that God will provide her needs fuels her devotion.

However, the woman *who is self-indulgent* does not hope in God but indulges herself with earthly delights. This reflects a lack of hope in God, which is why

---

26. But see the discussion of universalism at §16.16.2 below, and Mounce, *Pastoral Epistles*, 256–57.

Paul declares that she *is dead even while she lives*. Without hope in God, the widow is spiritually lifeless.

> 1 Tim 6:17–19 Τοῖς πλουσίοις ἐν τῷ νῦν αἰῶνι παράγγελλε μὴ ὑψηλοφρονεῖν μηδὲ ἠλπικέναι ἐπὶ **πλούτου ἀδηλότητι** ἀλλ' ἐπὶ θεῷ τῷ παρέχοντι ἡμῖν πάντα πλουσίως εἰς ἀπόλαυσιν, 18 ἀγαθοεργεῖν, πλουτεῖν ἐν ἔργοις καλοῖς, εὐμεταδότους εἶναι, κοινωνικούς, 19 ἀποθησαυρίζοντας ἑαυτοῖς θεμέλιον καλὸν εἰς τὸ μέλλον, ἵνα ἐπιλάβωνται τῆς ὄντως ζωῆς.
>
> *Instruct those who are rich in the present age not to be arrogant or* **to set their hope on the uncertainty of wealth**, *but on God, who richly provides us with all things to enjoy. 18 Instruct them to do what is good, to be rich in good works, to be generous and willing to share, 19 storing up treasure for themselves as a good foundation for the coming age, so that they may take hold of what is truly life.*

The wealthy are *rich in the present age* (6:17a), implying that their wealth is good only for this age and not for the age to come. Wealth is not to be relied on, both because it is only good for this world and because of its uncertainty even in this world (v. 17:b)—wealth can come and go. On the other hand, they should set their hope on God rather than on wealth. He *richly* [pun intended] *provides us with all things to enjoy* (v. 17).

The contrast between wealth and God as the object of hope is instructive. It demonstrates that hope is intended to be placed in some objective reality—wealth, for example, is a *real*, not imagined, commodity. It may disappoint those who hope in it, but it is a tangible object of hope. In the same way, Paul regards God as a tangible entity on whom to set one's hope. He is likewise a *real*, not imagined, object of hope. This implies that hope is meant to be secured to something tangible and outside oneself rather than constituting a subjective, internal experience. Moreover, God, though invisible, is a more secure object for hope. The *uncertainty of wealth* contrasts the reliability and goodness of God.

Furthermore, the wealthy are to express their hope in God by being *rich in good works* [again, pun intended], and *to be generous and willing to share* (v. 18). Their hope in God enables them to hold their wealth loosely since they do not rely on it. They can share it generously with others.[27] By so doing, they will store up for themselves a treasure (pun yet again intended) in the age to come (v. 19a). This more or less states that their good deeds and generosity will be rewarded in the future. And such is put in more explicit terms in the final

---

27. Köstenberger, *1–2 Timothy & Titus*, 197.

clause—*so that they may take hold of what is truly life* (v. 19b). *What is truly life* implicitly contrasts the false life offered by wealth in this present age. And it seems to be the content of their next-age treasure.

While this passage seems to endorse a works/rewards soteriology, the key exhortation is that the wealthy should set their hope on God. The good works that are to accompany their hope *follow* from it. Thus, their good works are indicative of the reality of their hope. They are the evidence that their hope really does rest in God, and so they will *take hold of what is truly life*, which is nothing less than life with God in the age to come.

> Titus 1:1–2 Παῦλος δοῦλος θεοῦ, ἀπόστολος δὲ Ἰησοῦ Χριστοῦ κατὰ πίστιν ἐκλεκτῶν θεοῦ καὶ ἐπίγνωσιν ἀληθείας τῆς κατ᾽ εὐσέβειαν 2 ἐπ᾽ ἐλπίδι ζωῆς αἰωνίου, ἣν ἐπηγγείλατο ὁ ἀψευδὴς θεὸς πρὸ χρόνων αἰωνίων
>
> *Paul, a servant of God and an apostle of Jesus Christ, for the faith of God's elect and their knowledge of the truth that leads to godliness, 2 in **the hope of eternal life that God, who cannot lie, promised before time began**.*

Paul describes his apostleship as being *for* (or "according to"; κατά) *the faith of God's elect*—his apostolic purpose is to see those chosen by God to come to faith in him (1:1b). In addition to faith, the elect are to come to a *knowledge of the truth that leads to godliness, in the hope of eternal life* (1:1c–2a). If the faith of the elect can be described as their disposition toward God, and their knowledge of the truth describes the content of their confession, then their hope of eternal life is the mode of their existence. It characterizes and shapes all else—their faith, their knowledge, and their godliness.

Hope is qualified by the genitive expression *of eternal life* (ἐλπίδι ζωῆς αἰωνίου), which most likely is to be understood as a genitive of destination or purpose. Wallace describes this as indicating "where the head noun is going (or the direction it is 'moving' in) or the purpose of its existence."[28] Though a rare category of genitival usage, it fits well here. Hope is heading in the direction of eternal life; the purpose of hope is to lead to eternal life.

As usual, such hope is not mere wishful thinking. The hope of eternal life was promised by God, *who cannot lie*, and it was *promised before time began* (v. 2b). This extraordinary claim underscores the certainty of Paul's expectation of eternal life. It was *promised* by God; if the promise of God cannot be trusted, what can be? He adds that this God *cannot lie*, which further strengthens the

---

28. Wallace, *Greek Grammar Beyond the Basics*, 100.

force of the previous point. Paul then finally says that this promise was made by God *before time began*, indicating its significance in the eternal plan of God. Granting eternal life to the elect is no afterthought; it is part of the divine design that predates all of creation.

Hope is thus the mode that characterizes the faith and knowledge of the elect, and the destination to which hope points is eternal life. This hope of eternal life is secured by the trustworthiness of the preordained promise of God. And to see people shaped by such a hope is part of Paul's apostolic calling.

> Titus 2:11–13 Ἐπεφάνη γὰρ ἡ χάρις τοῦ θεοῦ σωτήριος πᾶσιν ἀνθρώποις 12 παιδεύουσα ἡμᾶς, ἵνα ἀρνησάμενοι τὴν ἀσέβειαν καὶ τὰς κοσμικὰς ἐπιθυμίας σωφρόνως καὶ δικαίως καὶ εὐσεβῶς ζήσωμεν ἐν τῷ νῦν αἰῶνι, 13 **προσδεχόμενοι τὴν μακαρίαν ἐλπίδα καὶ ἐπιφάνειαν τῆς δόξης τοῦ μεγάλου θεοῦ καὶ σωτῆρος ἡμῶν Ἰησοῦ Χριστοῦ**

> *For the grace of God has appeared, bringing salvation for all people, 12 instructing us to deny godlessness and worldly lusts and to live in a sensible, righteous, and godly way in the present age, 13* ***while we wait for the blessed hope, the appearing of the glory of our great God and Savior, Jesus Christ.***

The blessed hope, also described as *the appearing of the glory of our God and Savior, Jesus Christ* (2:13),[29] is held out as the object of believers' patient waiting. The mode in which believers are to deny godlessness and live in a godly way is one of waiting. In other words, believers are to live in a *godly way in the present age* while waiting for the blessed hope—the glory of Christ.

This instance is a little unusual when compared to other expressions of hope, since hope is itself the object of waiting. Normally hope is regarded as the mode of waiting itself. That is, hope is what one has while waiting for its fulfillment. But here, waiting anticipates *the blessed hope*. Hope is not the mode of waiting but the object that is awaited.

This unusual use of hope is explained by the way it relates to the following phrase—*the appearing of the glory of our great God and Savior, Jesus Christ* (v. 13b). This phrase stands in apposition to *the blessed hope*, giving it definition. That is, the blessed hope *is* the appearing of the glory of Christ. The blessed hope, then, is not a subjective experience. It is the appearance of the glory of

---

29. While the apparently high Christology of this expression is not our interest here, the phrase τοῦ μεγάλου θεοῦ καὶ σωτῆρος ἡμῶν Ἰησοῦ Χριστοῦ is an example of Granville Sharp's rule, which if accepted means that Paul identifies Jesus Christ as "God" (see Wallace, *Greek Grammar Beyond the Basics*, 276–77).

Christ. This is the hope for which believers wait while they live godly lives in the present age.

> Titus 3:6–7 οὗ ἐξέχεεν ἐφ' ἡμᾶς πλουσίως
> διὰ Ἰησοῦ Χριστοῦ τοῦ σωτῆρος ἡμῶν,
> 7 ἵνα δικαιωθέντες τῇ ἐκείνου χάριτι
> κληρονόμοι γενηθῶμεν κατ' ἐλπίδα ζωῆς αἰωνίου.

He poured out his Spirit on us abundantly through Jesus Christ our Savior 7 so that, **having been justified by his grace, we may become heirs with the hope of eternal life.**

The outpouring of the Spirit through Christ the Savior confers on believers the status of heirs, *having been justified by his grace* (3:6–7). These heirs are characterized by *the hope of eternal life*. As seen elsewhere, the genitive construction (ἐλπίδα ζωῆς αἰωνίου) most likely conveys the sense of destination or purpose of the head noun,[30] such that hope leads in the direction, and has the purpose of, eternal life.

As heirs, believers have a confident expectation. Heirs need not resort to wishful thinking since their inheritance is legally guaranteed. Thus their hope is a confident expectation of eternal life. Moreover, believers are made heirs through their justification by grace—their status as heirs is assured by the gift of God. Furthermore, God has poured out on them his Spirit through Jesus Christ the Savior—the same Spirit who is elsewhere described as the deposit guaranteeing the heirs' inheritance (Eph 1:14). All of this demonstrates the solid expectation that constitutes the hope that believers enjoy as the Spirit-endowed, justified, heirs of eternal life.

> Phlm 22 ἅμα δὲ καὶ ἑτοίμαζέ μοι ξενίαν· ἐλπίζω γὰρ ὅτι διὰ τῶν προσευχῶν ὑμῶν χαρισθήσομαι ὑμῖν.

Meanwhile, also prepare a guest room for me, **since I hope that through your prayers I will be restored to you.**

As this instance does not convey eschatological hope, it requires no further comment.

---

30. Wallace, *Greek Grammar Beyond the Basics*, 100.

13.3 Summary

Hope is not merely a subjective, experiential factor in the lives of believers, according to Paul. While it certainly does shape the experience of believers (Rom 15:13; 2 Thess 2:16–17), hope is regarded more as a pillar of theological expectation. It reflects a confident anticipation of what God will do based on his promises and his past faithfulness in doing what he says he will do (Titus 1:1–2). It is the belief that, having been justified by God's grace, believers will inherit eternal life (Titus 3:7).

Paul's theology of hope begins with the hope of Abraham, who hoped against hope, and it was credited to him as righteousness. The hope of Abraham established him as the father of many nations, and he stands now as an example for all believers to hope in the God who does what he promises (Rom 4:17–21; Gal 5:5).

Believers hope in the glory of God, which is to say they expect to be caught up in the glory of God in the eschaton. This hope arises as a characteristic of those who know affliction and endurance, since these experiences produce character, which in turn produces hope (Rom 5:1–5; 15:4). Such hope is cause for rejoicing (12:12).

The certain expectation of *hope* is reflected in Paul's statement that God himself subjected the creation to frustration in the hope that it will also be set free from bondage to decay. That is, this hope is not an insecure longing but a certain expectation of the fulfillment of God's plans and intentions. Believers' hope is predicated on the "hope" of God to redeem creation. Since God can be trusted to carry out his purposes for creation, he can be trusted with the redemption of our bodies, which are, after all, a subset of the creation. This hope to come is to be awaited with patience (Rom 8:20–25).

Without a future-oriented hope in Christ, believers should be pitied more than anyone (1 Cor 15:17–19), while unbelievers have no hope at all (Eph 2:12; 1 Thess 4:13). But there are also several examples of non-eschatologically oriented hope to be seen, such as Paul's hope to spend time with the Corinthians (1 Cor 16:7–9), to visit the Romans on his way to Spain (Rom 15:24), to come to Timothy (1 Tim 3:14), and that God will deliver him again from a terrible death (2 Cor 1:10). Only these noneschatological references to hope exhibit something less than the certain expectation witnessed in the eschatological examples.

Hope in the new covenant affects life in the present, so that believers will act with great boldness, knowing what lies ahead (2 Cor 3:9–12). Paul holds present and future hope that he will not need to be ashamed about anything as he seeks to honor Christ in his body (Phil 1:16–20). The Colossians' faith in

Christ and love for the saints is driven by the hope reserved for them in heaven (Col 1:4–5), the hope of the gospel (v. 23), while the Thessalonians' endurance is inspired by their hope in Christ (1 Thess 1:3). On the other hand, the rich are not to set their hope on the uncertainty of wealth (1 Tim 6:17). Hope in Christ, who is himself the hope of glory (Col 1:27; 1 Tim 1:1; Titus 2:13), is also expected to issue praise to his glory (Eph 1:11–12).

Through his multitudinous references to hope it is clear that it is the central way in which eschatology shapes Paul's vision of the Christian life. Whatever else it may mean to live in Christ, genuine Christian living is nothing without hope for the future. It is the future eschaton, with its redemption of creation and resurrection of the body, with its shared glory and eternal life, that makes following Christ overwhelmingly positive even in the face of the overwhelming negativity and evil of this present age.

Part 3

Theological Study

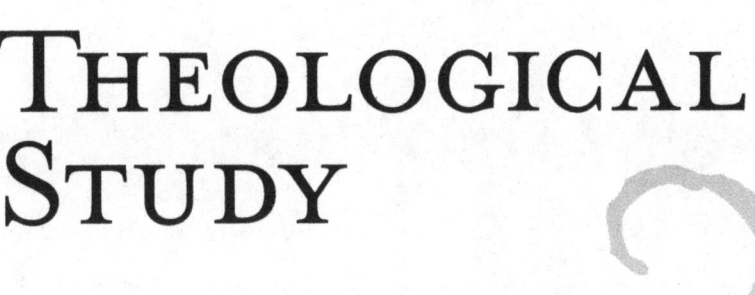

CHAPTER 14

CHRISTOCENTRIC ESCHATOLOGY

14.1 INTRODUCTION

In this chapter we explore the irreducibly Christocentric nature of Paul's eschatology. That Paul's eschatological vision is Christocentric is self-evident. What is perhaps less so are the ways in which Paul ties each element of his eschatological thought together in Christ. Paul's eschatology is shaped by Christ because it is formed through his reflection on the meaning and significance of Christ's death, resurrection, and ascension. Once these past events have properly been thought through, the rest of Paul's eschatology takes shape. It is no exaggeration to claim that the Christ-shaped future of the universe is created by the Christ-events of two thousand years ago. The death, resurrection, and ascension of Christ set the table for what is to come at the eschaton. And when the eschaton comes with Christ, it will represent the fulfillment of all that was entailed in those past events in embryonic form.

The chapter will first review the relevant exegetical material found in part 2 of the book, focusing on the christological import of the topics addressed in those chapters, such as the two realms (ch. 3), judgment (ch. 6), and eternal life (ch. 8). This will culminate in a synthesis of the christological insights gleaned from that material, which will lead to the major discussion of the chapter—the eschatological nature of the death, resurrection, and ascension of Christ. Each of these eschatological events will be treated in turn, concluding with some reflections on believers' participation in those events. Finally, the chapter will address the roles of Christ in the eschaton. It will be demonstrated that these roles have already been determined by the Christ-events of two thousand years ago.

14.2 CHRIST AS LORD OF THE NEW REALM

In chapter 3, addressing the themes of two realms and two ages, we observe the work of Christ explicitly related to them in the following ways. By virtue of his death on the cross, Christ has disarmed competing rulers, disgracing and triumphing over them (Col 2:14–15). By virtue of his resurrection and ascension, Christ has been positioned above all rulers and authorities in this age and the one to come (Eph 1:20–23), the same authorities created by and for Christ (Col 1:16). Though the enemies of Christ have been put under his feet by way of appointment and position, Christ's reign is not yet fully realized. But when the last enemy, death, is destroyed, then Christ will hand his kingdom over to the Father (1 Cor 15:23–28).

Believers have been rescued from the domain of darkness and have been transferred into the kingdom of the Son by virtue of redemption, the forgiveness of their sins (Col 1:13–14). It is through their membership in the realm of Christ that believers are ruled by grace and righteousness, resulting in eternal life (Rom 5:19–21), while competing powers and rulers are powerless to separate them from the love of God that is in Christ Jesus (Rom 8:38–39). Indeed, believers are filled by Christ, who is head over every ruler and authority (Col 2:8–10). Believers have died with Christ to the elements of the world and ought not follow human-made religion (Col 2:20–23). As a further expression of their allegiance to the realm of Christ, believers are to put on the armor of light, which is also to put on Christ himself (Rom 13:11–14). Godly living in the present age consists of waiting for the appearing of Christ and to live according to the values of the age to come (Titus 2:11–13).

The disobedient, on the other hand, do not belong to the realm of Christ, but his authority over them nevertheless remains since they will face his judgment in the end (Eph 5:5–6).

14.3 Christ and His Parousia

In chapter 4, we examined the theme of Christ's parousia. There we observed that at his arrival Christ will make alive those who belong to him (1 Cor 15:20–26). He will descend from heaven with a shout, with the archangel's voice, and with the trumpet of God, and the dead in Christ will rise first, then those alive at his arrival will meet him in the air (1 Thess 4:15–18).

The arrival of Christ will mark a day of judgment, in anticipation of which Christ will strengthen believers in order that they would be found blameless on that day (1 Cor 1:6–8; 1 Thess 3:13). His parousia will reveal the secrets of people's hearts, leading to judgment and to praise (1 Cor 4:4–5), but he will rescue believers from the coming wrath (1 Thess 1:9–10). The presence of Christ will bring vengeance on his enemies and relief for the afflicted, and he will be glorified by his saints (2 Thess 1:5–10). The lawless one will be destroyed at Christ's coming by the breath of his mouth (2 Thess 2:8).

In the interim period before he arrives, believers eagerly await the appearing of Christ (1 Cor 1:6–8; Phil 3:18–21; 1 Thess 1:9–10; Titus 2:11–13), when they will appear with him in glory (Col 3:1). Timothy is to keep Paul's command to him until the appearing of Christ (1 Tim 6:13–14; 2 Tim 4:1–2), and when Christ comes Paul anticipates that the recipients of his ministry will become a crown of boasting (1 Thess 2:19–20) and that Christ will award him the crown of righteousness along with all who have loved his appearing (2 Tim 4:6–8). But believers are to be wary of the predictions of false teachers regarding the timing of that day (2 Thess 2:1–2).

14.4 Christ at the Eschaton

In chapter 5, we addressed the last day, the eschaton. There we saw that on that day God will judge people's secrets according to the gospel through Christ (Rom 2:14–16). When the end comes, Christ will hand the kingdom over to the Father, having abolished every rule and authority (1 Cor 15:23–28). On that day Christ will be glorified by his saints (2 Thess 1:5–10), while all who love his appearing will receive from him the crown of righteousness (2 Tim 4:6–8).

14.5 Christ the Judge

Chapter 6 explored the theme of judgment. There we observed that judgment day is called the day of Christ (1 Cor 1:6–8), when all must appear before the judgment seat of Christ (2 Cor 5:8–10). He will bring to light what is hidden in people's hearts (1 Cor 4:3–5) and will judge the living and the dead (2 Tim 4:1–2).

Though Christ is himself the judge, he is also the one who saves his people from the coming wrath (Rom 5:8–10; 1 Thess 1:9–10; 5:9–10). Indeed, salvation is in Christ with eternal glory (2 Tim 2:10–13). As the righteous judge, Christ will also give the crown of righteousness to those who love his appearing (2 Tim 4:8).

14.6 The Resurrection of Christ and Believers

Chapter 7 investigated the resurrection of the dead. There we observed several connections with the work of Christ—his own resurrection being of central significance. Those who die with Christ will rise with him (Rom 6:4–11). The Spirit who raised Christ will also raise believers (Rom 8:11) by the power of God (1 Cor 6:14; 2 Cor 4:11–14).

If there is no resurrection of the dead, then not even Christ has been raised (1 Cor 15:12–19), in which case there is no hope in the face of death (1 Cor

15:29–34). But, of course, he has been raised and is the firstfruits of those who will be made alive in him (1 Cor 15:20–23). Following Christ the firstfruits—the firstborn from the dead (Col 1:18)—believers' bodies will be transformed at the resurrection, being raised incorruptible, in glory, in power, in a spiritual body in the image of the man from heaven (1 Cor 15:35–50), and in the likeness of his glorious body (Phil 3:18–21). In the end, death will be swallowed up in the victory that comes through Christ (1 Cor 15:51–58).

Believers have already been made alive with Christ in a spiritual sense (Eph 2:4–6; Col 2:11–13). Having been raised with Christ, they are to think of things above, where Christ is at God's right hand (Col 3:1), with the goal to know Christ and the power of his resurrection, seeking to reach the physical resurrection from the dead (Phil 3:10–11).

The belief that Jesus died and rose again gives hope for the resurrection of those who have already died, and the dead in Christ will rise first at the resurrection (1 Thess 4:13–18). Christ has abolished death and brought life and immortality to light through the gospel (2 Tim 1:9–10).

14.7 CHRIST AND ETERNAL LIFE

Chapter 8 addressed the theme of eternal life. There we saw the work of Christ intersect with it in the following ways. Eternal life is the gift of God in Christ (Rom 6:21–23), since Christ died for us so that we may live together with him (1 Thess 5:9–10). Believing in him results in eternal life (1 Tim 1:15–16), and those who die with Christ will live with him (2 Tim 2:10–13). While sin reigned in death, grace will reign through righteousness, resulting in eternal life through Christ (Rom 5:19–21). Having been justified by Christ's grace, believers may become heirs with the hope of eternal life (Titus 3:6–7). The Spirit of God who raised Jesus will bring mortal bodies to life too (Rom 8:10–13).

14.8 CHRIST AND INHERITANCE

As seen in chapter 9, the centrality of Christ for the concept of a future inheritance is evident by the notion that believers are coheirs with Christ (Rom 8:14–22). But this status is qualified by the essential participation in Christ's suffering and, later, his glorification (vv. 17–18). It also depends on baptism into Christ and being clothed with Christ (Gal 3:27).

Alongside such participation in Christ, Christocentric justification is the means by which otherwise unfit people become fit for the inheritance to come, having been justified in the name of the Lord Jesus Christ (1 Cor 6:9–11; Titus 3:6–7; cf. Gal 5:19–21; Eph 5:5). Through Christ, God has enabled believers to share in the saints' inheritance in the light (Col 1:12), by rescuing them from the domain of darkness and transferring them into the kingdom of the Son he loves (v. 13). In the realm of Christ, we have redemption, the forgiveness of sins (v. 14) and are thus qualified to share in the future inheritance of the saints.

A third prerequisite for the future inheritance is that believers must bear the image of the man of heaven (1 Cor 15:49). Only by being conformed to the image of the resurrected and exalted Christ may believers receive the inheritance to come, since flesh and blood cannot inherit the kingdom of God, nor can corruption inherit incorruption (v. 50). Corruptible bodies must be clothed with immortality, and this only through incorporation into Christ.

Furthermore, all believers—both Jews and gentiles—may access the inheritance promised to Abraham since this promise was made to Abraham and to his seed (Gal 3:16), and the seed of Abraham is Christ himself (v. 17). Believers may share in the promise by becoming one with Christ—the seed of Abraham—and thereby themselves become Abraham's seed by extension (v. 29; Eph 3:6). The Holy Spirit, also known as the Spirit of the Son (Gal 4:6), is the down payment for this inheritance to come (Eph 1:14).

Christ's inheritance will be shared with believers, and more specifically it will be bestowed by him personally, as we see in Paul's encouragement of slaves who will receive the reward of an inheritance from the Lord (Col 3:24). Since it is ultimately Christ whom they are serving, he rewards them with a share of the inheritance.

14.9 CHRIST AND THE NEW CREATION

In chapter 10, we observed that *personal* new creation (i.e., the new creation of an individual rather than the entire created order) occurs by being found *in Christ* (2 Cor 5:17; Gal 6:15; Eph 2:10). But so is *cosmic* new creation, as all things in heaven and earth are brought *together in Christ* (Eph 1:10), having been created by him, through him, and for him (Col 1:16). The renewal of individuals and of the entire created order is centered on, and achieved by, Christ.

14.10 CHRIST AND ISRAEL

The eschatological fate of Israel is discussed in chapter 11. The chief christological concern through Romans 9–11 is the fact that ethnic Israel has rejected her messiah. This is the question at issue throughout Paul's argumentation, as he seeks to vindicate the sovereignty and plan of God in the face of such rejection.

A key element of Paul's argument is that not all of Abraham's children are his true descendants (Rom 9:7), and while he does not develop the christological essence of this argument here, it may be assumed from elsewhere (e.g., Rom 4:13–25; Gal 3:27–4:7). Because Christ is the true seed of Abraham (2:16), those united to him also become his seed, whether Jew or gentile (3:29). This theological reappropriation of Abraham's descendancy informs the rest of Paul's treatment of the future salvation of Israel. Those who accept Israel's messiah by faith—the true descendants of Abraham—will be saved.

14.11 Christ and Glory

As seen in chapter 12, the hope of the glory of God comes through peace with God, which comes through our Lord Jesus Christ (Rom 5:1–2). The hope of glory is especially evident by the presence of Christ among the gentiles—his very presence is this hope (Col 1:27). Believers are called by God to obtain the glory of our Lord Jesus Christ (2 Thess 2:14), which is part and parcel of their salvation (2 Tim 2:10). As children of God and coheirs with Christ, believers will share in his resurrection glory (Rom 8:17; 1 Cor 15:43), which will far outweigh any present suffering (Rom 8:18; 2 Cor 4:17). Indeed, glorification is the inevitable result of justification (Rom 8:30), which for Paul is irreducibly Christocentric in nature.

Moreover, Christ is known as the Lord of glory—a title ironically uttered in the context of his crucifixion (1 Cor 2:8) and realized in his ascension (1 Tim 3:16) and his next appearing (Titus 2:13). By gazing into the mirror image of the glory of the Lord, believers are being transformed into the same image from glory to glory (2 Cor 3:18). But final glorification will come when Christ will transform the body of the believer's humble condition into the likeness of his glorious body (Phil 3:21). When Christ appears, believers will also appear with him in glory (Col 3:4) and will in turn glorify the name of the Lord Jesus (1 Thess 1:12).

Of Paul's characteristic doxological statements, a number of these are directly Christocentric in nature. Eternal glory is ascribed to the only wise God—and this through Jesus Christ (Rom 16:27). God's glory will be seen in the church and in Christ Jesus to all generations, forever and ever (Eph 3:21; Phil 4:19). Praise is bestowed to God's glorious grace, which is lavished on believers in Christ (Eph 1:6). Moreover, believers will bring praise to the glory of God because of their hope in Christ (v. 12). Finally, when every tongue confesses that Jesus Christ is Lord, it will be to the glory of God the Father (Phil 2:11).

14.12 Christ and Hope

Chapter 13 deals with Paul's voluminous references to hope. While all of Paul's hope is christological in nature, the references that explicitly connect hope to Christ include the following. Romans 15:13, citing Isaiah 11:10, points to the hope of the gentiles in *the root of Jesse*, whom Paul regards as fulfilled in Christ. Hope in Christ is not for this life only; indeed, if it is, believers are to be pitied more than anyone (1 Cor 15:19). Instead, those who hope in Christ bring praise to his glory (Eph 1:12).

Those without Christ are *without hope* (2:12). But those who share in the one Lord, one faith, and the one baptism are *called to one hope* (4:4–5). The presence of Christ among believers (especially, in context, the gentiles) is *the hope of glory* (Col 1:27). This hope in Christ inspires endurance for this present life (1 Thess 1:3). The belief *that Jesus died and rose again* enables believers to grieve in light of the hope of the resurrection of the dead (4:13–14). Believers don *a helmet of the hope of salvation*, a salvation obtained *through our Lord Jesus Christ* (5:8–9). Indeed, Christ is the one who bestows *good hope by grace* (2 Thess 2:16). It is his grace that justifies believers, resulting in their becoming *heirs with the hope of eternal life* (Titus 3:7).

In short, Christ Jesus is the believer's hope (1 Tim 1:1). His future appearing is *the blessed hope* for which believers patiently await (Titus 2:12–13).

14.13 SYNTHESIS

Paul's eschatological vision is inherently Christocentric. Each sphere of his eschatological thought centers around Christ, and Paul views Christ as the one through whom each sphere becomes what it is. Christ is the means and location of the new creation, both personal and cosmic. Each person found in Christ becomes a new creation, with attendant new works for him or her to complete. And the entire created order is renewed in, through, and for Christ. Christ has disarmed competing authorities and power structures through his death and resurrection, which have all been placed under his feet. He is the Lord of the new realm into which believers have been transferred.

It is the resurrection of Christ that makes possible the bodily resurrection of believers on the last day as well as their spiritual resurrection now. He is the firstfruits who reveals the harvest to come, and he will transform their mortal bodies into immortal bodies through their union with him. When Christ comes, the dead will be raised in anticipation of judgment, when he will reveal the secrets of hearts and rescue believers from wrath. He will grant eternal life to those in Christ, resulting in life together with him. This eternal life will consist of the promised inheritance enjoyed by all in Christ, as he shares his rightful inheritance as the Son with those grafted into Christ to become Abraham's seed, the spiritual Israel. The highpoint of sharing with Christ, after sharing in his suffering, is to share in his eternal glory. Such sharing is bundled into the salvation achieved by Christ and will be revealed when he comes. Christ will be glorified by his saints on that day when he will hand the kingdom over to his Father.

Christ is the source of Paul's eschatological hope, and he is its goal.

14.14 THE DEATH, RESURRECTION, AND ASCENSION OF CHRIST AS ESCHATOLOGICAL EVENTS

The Christocentric nature of Paul's eschatology is not seen simply with the coming of Christ, his work of final judgment, and his rule over the coming renewed creation. It is also seen in Paul's eschatological understanding of the death, resurrection, and ascension of Christ. These three events in the life of Christ are not regarded as mere historical realities that give birth to Paul's eschatological expectation. No, these historical events are, in themselves, inherently eschatological, and they "signify the ultimate turning point in history."[1]

The three events must be understood together. Paul's eschatological thinking is deeply intertwined, and the whole conception grows out of the death, resurrection, and ascension of Christ in an organic way that defies easy separation of one event out from the other two. However, in order to articulate his eschatological conception, we must attempt to speak of one event at a time—but not in chronological order. In speaking about the eschatological nature of the death, resurrection, and ascension of Christ, we must begin with the resurrection. This is not because the resurrection is "more important" than the other two (as though Paul would ever accept such a facile distinction), but because it reveals more of the eschatological inner workings, which then enable us to look into the death and ascension of Christ with more clarity.

14.14.1 THE RESURRECTION OF CHRIST AS ESCHATOLOGICAL EVENT

While Paul's writings contain many references to the resurrection of Christ (see ch. 7), none can be more important for our topic than 1 Corinthians 15 (but see also Rom 6:5; Phil 3:21). This text has already been discussed at some length, and it is unnecessary to repeat the exegesis offered in §7.2. But some recapitulation of the main observations recorded there will be helpful.

First, the resurrection of Christ must be understood in light of a theology of the general resurrection of the dead. Rebutting the Corinthians' lack of belief in a future resurrection of the dead, Paul claims that *if there is no resurrection of the dead, then not even Christ has been raised* (1 Cor 15:13). But this claim only makes sense if Paul presupposes that Christ's resurrection should be understood as part of the general resurrection of the dead. Without a general resurrection of the dead, Christ cannot have been raised, *for if the dead are not raised, not even*

---

1. Stephan Joubert, "Paul's Apocalyptic Eschatology in 2 Corinthians," in van der Watt, *Eschatology of the New Testament*, 229.

Christ has been raised (v. 16). And the most striking implication of this follows: *if Christ has not been raised, your faith is worthless; you are still in your sins* (v. 17). We will need to return to this point.

Paul then draws out more explicitly the link between the general resurrection of the dead and the resurrection of Christ in vv. 20–23. Christ is depicted as *the firstfruits of those who have fallen asleep* (v. 20; cf. Col 1:18), so that his resurrection reveals the type and quality of the coming resurrection of believers, as well as its certainty (we will return to this concept below). The firstfruits imagery is grounded in Paul's Adam Christology (1 Cor 15:21–22). Through his resurrection, Christ reverses the effect of Adam's fall that released death into human experience (v. 21). This Adam-Christ typology divides humanity into those who belong to the realm of Adam and those who belong to the realm of Christ (v. 22). Those who belong to Christ will be made alive just as Christ, the firstfruits, has been made alive. This will happen at his coming (v. 23).

In the centrally important vv. 35–50, we observe Paul's fullest eschatological treatment of the resurrection of Christ. The section begins with Paul raising the anticipated questions, *"How are the dead raised? What kind of body will they have when they come?"* (v. 35). Drawing on the imagery of a seed, he argues that a seed must die in order to produce a crop, and the crop that comes from the seed is determined by its design (vv. 36–38). So the body is sown in dishonor and is raised in glory; death must precede immortality (vv. 42–44).

This then returns Paul to his Adam Christology, so that Adam represents the seed sown in dishonor, and Christ represents the harvest that results (vv. 45–47; cf. vv. 22–23). Consequently, those who are in the realm of Adam remain consigned to death. But those in the realm of Christ will be made alive as Christ was. They will bear the image of the man of heaven (v. 49), which is necessary since *flesh and blood cannot inherit the kingdom of God* (v. 50b). The future inheritance of the kingdom of God has been Paul's concern all along, and the corrupted, flesh-and-blood body is incapable of inheriting it. Only those who have been resurrected with a spiritual, incorruptible body in the image of Christ are able to receive the inheritance.

In sum, believers must receive a resurrection body like Jesus's resurrected body. If Jesus was not raised, believers cannot receive a body like his and cannot therefore inherit the kingdom of God.

14.14.1.1 *The Firstfruits of the Resurrection*

Much has already been said about Christ as the firstfruits of the resurrection (see §7.2), its meaning, and its role in the argument of 1 Corinthians. Here, however, we pause to consider the deeper eschatological significance of this imagery. By definition, the pre-harvest reality of firstfruits not only indicates what is to come but is properly understood as *belonging to* what is to come. That is, the firstfruits represent the *early* arrival of a portion of the harvest. It is a mistake, therefore, to regard the firstfruits as a detached entity with an integrity of its own. It is, rather, part of the harvest that has simply arrived earlier than the rest. This is of central importance for understanding the eschatological significance of the resurrection of Christ.

The resurrection of Christ is not an isolated historical event with its own integrity. It is not a singularity. Properly understood, the resurrection of Christ belongs to the general resurrection of the dead that is yet to come. As the firstfruits of what is to come, it is simply the *early arrival* of a portion of that harvest. The general resurrection of the dead was anticipated by the Hebrew Scriptures (e.g., Dan 12:1–2; cf. John 11:24) and is an essential component for understanding Paul's eschatology in general, but especially so for his understanding of the resurrection of Christ. As Beker states,

> Resurrection language properly belongs to the domain of the new age to come and is an inherent part of the transformation and the re-creation of all reality in the apocalyptic age. Thus, the resurrection of Christ, the coming reign of God, and the future resurrection of the dead belong together.[2]

So when we consider the significance of the resurrection of Christ, we must recognize that Paul saw it as *the beginning of the end*. Since resurrection was assigned to the last day—to the end of time and the end of this current world—the resurrection of a man *in the middle of ongoing history* (to borrow a phrase from N. T. Wright)[3] must have dramatic eschatological significance. Part of the harvest has arrived early; the rest must soon follow!

This eschatological reading of the resurrection of Christ has several enormously important consequences for Paul's overall eschatological vision. First, it explains why Paul (and the other NT authors) posit an *overlap of the ages*, or *two-realms* framework (see ch. 3). Paul boldly declares that the new age has already arrived in Christ. But this has happened before the old age has been wrapped up once and for all. Hence, there is an overlap between old and new, and there is conflict between the old realm and the realm of Christ. As summarized in chapter 3, the rubric of realm and age gives shape to Paul's

---

2. Beker, *Paul the Apostle*, 153. Beker adds, "Therefore, the resurrection of Christ cannot be asserted apart from the future apocalyptic resurrection, because it derives its meaning from its future referent (cf. Rom. 1:4)" (167).

3. Wright, *Paul and the Faithfulness of God*, 1061.

overall eschatological vision of reality. All reality is shaped by two realms and two ages. The breaking into the present of the age to come has created a realm of righteousness to which believers in Christ now already belong. They have been transferred out of the present evil age and realm and exist under the future (but present) age and realm. This reality has deeply significant consequences for the ways in which believers must conduct themselves. They no longer belong to the realm ruled by sin, death, and the devil, and as such are to show no allegiance to it. Rather, as people who belong to Christ, they are to live according to the values of his realm—according to righteousness, grace, and godliness. The foregoing summary includes within its scope the entirety of the Christian life. All human reality is controlled by these two opposing realms.

This realm structure, or overlap of the ages, is created by the resurrection of a man in the middle of time. By his resurrection from the dead, Christ has pulled the future into the present; the end has come now, and this changes everything for Paul.

14.14.1.2 Resurrection as Eschatological Vindication

One of the dramatic consequences of the eschatological resurrection of Christ is that justification has become a present reality, while also at the same time belonging to the final day of judgment. This is a direct outworking of the overlap of the ages, since according to Second Temple Jewish thought final justification or vindication would happen on the last day, the day of judgment. Since that day has broken into present reality, justification is present and future at the same time. This is why Paul can say that believers are *now* justified and *will be* saved—without contradiction (Rom 5:9). There are *not* two justifications—a present and future one; rather, the *one* final declaration of righteousness has already been sounded and will be fully revealed through the bodily resurrection of believers when Christ comes.

But the eschatological nature of justification hinges even more specifically on the resurrection of Christ than other now-and-not-yet notions, since resurrection is inextricably linked to justification in Jewish thought. The resurrection of the righteous on the day of judgment *is* their vindication. It *is* the declaration of their righteousness. This means that, for Paul, when he is confronted with the resurrection of Christ, he inevitably must join these dots. The resurrection of a man in the middle of time means that the end has come, and his vindication following death *has already happened*. The final judgment of God has already been applied to Christ—he has been vindicated through his resurrection from the dead.

The justification or vindication of Christ in his resurrection directly effects the justification of believers, because they share in his righteousness. By their participation in Christ, and specifically by their participation in his resurrection from the dead,[4] believers are declared righteous *now*. The final end-time declaration of righteousness on the day of judgment has already been applied to believers because it has already been applied to Christ. By participating in his resurrection, believers also participate in his vindication at the final judgment. This is how Paul can declare—quite astonishingly, for a Jew—that believers in Christ are declared righteous now, before the end of time. Because, as we have seen, the end of time has met us in the middle. Christ has been raised, he has been declared righteous, and he has been vindicated. It therefore follows that those in Christ are likewise spiritually raised, declared righteous, and vindicated. This is what Paul means at Romans 4:25b—that Christ was *raised for our justification*.

14.14.1.2.1 ROMANS 4:25B

Though commonly misinterpreted (or at least *under*interpreted), this short phrase packs a lot of eschatological-resurrection-justification punch. Understood correctly, Romans 4:25 compresses into short form all the foregoing concepts—that the resurrection of Christ is essential for the justification of believers because it *is* their justification.[5] Without the resurrection of Christ, there can be no justification, which is why Paul says in 1 Corinthians 15:17 that if Christ has not been raised, believers are still in their sins.

Nevertheless, the (half-)verse has seen much debate, and it is worth taking some of this discussion into account, especially as it relates to the preposition διά.[6] In this verse are two instances of the preposition διά ("delivered up *for* [διά] our trespasses" and "raised *for* [διά] our justification"). Both instances are relevant to this discussion, though the function of the second is our primary interest. It is important first to outline the theological issues surrounding this verse.

There is of course a long history of connecting justification with the *death* of Christ, but also some reluctance to acknowledge a relationship between justification and his *resurrection*. This reluctance has caused a problem for interpreters of Romans 4:25, which seems to draw such a connection quite tightly. According

---

4. Participation in the resurrection of Christ will be addressed directly, alongside participation in his death and ascension (see below).

5. In case it is objected that I am attempting to hang too much on one (half-)verse, in fact my intention is the opposite. My claim is that Romans 4:25 compresses into a short statement some of Paul's wider theological and eschatological convictions. Unpacking and understanding those convictions is the burden of this whole book. But a verse like this can function as a test as to whether one's wider theological reconstruction has explanatory power. If our reconstruction of Paul's wider thought is off the mark, it may struggle to explain such a statement adequately. Thus Romans 4:25, and a few other verses like it, offers an important fulcrum by which our broader understanding may be validated or challenged.

6. The remainder of this section is adapted from my essay, Constantine R. Campbell, "Prepositions and Exegesis: What's in a Word?," in *Getting into the Text: New Testament Essays in Honor of David Alan Black*, ed. Daniel L. Akin and Thomas W. Hudgins (Eugene, OR: Pickwick, 2017), 39–54.

to Fitzmyer, since the Latin Fathers the common solution to this problem has been to treat the final phrase of 4:25 as an appendage, or as "an exemplary confirmation of Jesus's death, which they considered to be the real cause of forgiveness of sins and justification.[7] "While the trend to associate justification with the death of Jesus—and *not* his resurrection—has a long history,[8] this has no doubt been exacerbated by the crucicentrism of the modern evangelical movement, since its awakening in Britain in the 1730s and following.[9] Adding to the traditional reluctance to connect justification to resurrection is current resistance against some exponents of the so-called New Perspective on Paul, N. T. Wright in particular. Since Wright draws a strong connection between resurrection and justification, that very idea can become guilty by association in the minds of those who reject Wright's approach to justification in Paul.

The key issue in understanding the use of διά in Romans 4:25 is whether it is to be regarded as *retrospective* or *prospective*. That is, does it mean "he was raised *because of* our justification" (retrospective) or "he was raised *for* our justification" (prospective). This question must be evaluated with respect to the other use of διά in the previous clause in the same verse: "He was delivered up for our trespasses." It is often assumed that the parallel uses of διά in both clauses of 4:25 indicates that they both must be taken the same way—both are either retrospective or prospective. Michael Bird rejects this assumption and points to the fact that in the two preceding verses, vv. 23–24, the same preposition is also used in parallel: "In v.23 it says 'these things were not written (διά) *because of* him only' (retrospective), and in v.24 it states 'but also (διά) *for* us' (prospective)."[10] Bird therefore makes the case that, grammatically, "the juxtaposition of the retrospective and prospective uses of the preposition διά is continued on in v.25."[11] In other words, interpreters are not incorrect to read the second διά of v. 25 in parallel; it's just that the parallel is usually not comprehensive enough.[12] It is not parallel to the first διά of v. 25, but both

---

7. Fitzmyer, *Romans*, 389. See also Bruce A. Lowe, "Oh διά! How Is Romans 4:25 to Be Understood?," *JTS* 57.1 (2006): 149.

8. For a recent example, see G. K. Beale, "The Eschatology of Paul," in *Studies in the Pauline Epistles: Essays in Honor of Douglas J. Moo*, ed. Matthew S. Harmon and Jay E. Smith (Grand Rapids: Zondervan, 2014), 206–7, whose discussion of Paul's eschatology connects justification to the death of Christ but does not connect it to the resurrection at all.

9. David W. Bebbington, *Evangelicalism in Modern Britain: A History from the 1730s to the 1980s* (London: Routledge, 1989).

10. Michael F. Bird, "Raised for Our Justification: A Fresh Look at Romans 4:25," *Colloquium* 35.1 (2003): 43.

11. Bird, "Raised for Our Justification," 43.

12. "Almost universally, discussion of the meaning of διά in v. 25b has been reduced to a comparison with the διά clause in the first part of the same verse. In spite of the fact that all four prepositional phrases are διά + accusative, the first two (vv. 23–4), are usually overlooked. The emphasis in these two occurrences, however, is highly instructive for the emphasis that should be read in v. 25" (Lowe, "Oh διά!," 150).

uses of διά in v. 25 are parallel to the double use in vv. 23–24. Thus, there is grammatical and rhetorical support for the retrospective-prospective reading of the two instances of διά in 4:25.

Having established the grammatical plausibility of the prospective reading of διά in the phrase *he was raised for our justification* in Romans 4:25, we return now to consider how well this fits Paul's eschatological theology of resurrection and justification. Several scholars have drawn a connection between justification and resurrection in Paul's thought.[13] Jewish eschatology anticipated resurrection for the righteous on the last day, and Paul likely drew on this expectation for his understanding of the theological significance of Christ's resurrection.[14] The resurrection of Christ signals his vindication in God's sight; he has been declared righteous through his resurrection from the dead.[15] As Kirk states, "The resurrection is Jesus's justification."[16]

If the justification of Christ occurs through his resurrection, it can be argued that the justification of believers occurs by their participation with him.[17] Burger writes, "Just as Christ participated in our unrighteousness, we now participate in his vindication and become justified. Our justification is a gracious participation of the ungodly in the vindication of Christ."[18] Believers share in the vindication of Christ's resurrection by dying and rising with him; they are declared righteous by virtue of their participation in these events.[19] Gaffin endorses such logic:

---

13. For instance, J. R. Daniel Kirk, *Unlocking Romans: Resurrection and the Justification of God* (Grand Rapids: Eerdmans, 2008), 14–32; Hans Burger, *Being in Christ: A Biblical and Systematic Investigation in a Reformed Perspective* (Eugene, OR: Wipf & Stock, 2009), 250; Michael F. Bird, *The Saving Righteousness of God: Studies on Paul, Justification and the New Perspective* (Milton Keyes: Paternoster, 2006), 40–59. This is by no means taken for granted, however. Wright laments that "there seems to be something about the joining together of resurrection and justification which some of our Western traditions have failed to grasp" (Tom Wright, *Justification: God's Plan and Paul's Vision* [London: SPCK, 2009], 219).

14. Powers says that while Paul probably developed most of his understanding of believers' eschatological resurrection as a participation in Jesus's resurrection, "one should not too readily dismiss the possibility that Paul borrowed the principal elements of this conception from Jewish tradition. Indeed, in the Assumption of Moses, there are certain eschatological motifs which seem to parallel, and perhaps even underlie, Paul's understanding of the believers' eschatological resurrection as a participation in Jesus's resurrection" (Daniel G. Powers, *Salvation through Participation: An Examination of the Notion of the Believers' Corporate Unity with Christ in Early Christian Soteriology* [Leuven: Peeters, 2001], 215).

15. Powers, *Salvation through Participation*, 82–83; Morna D. Hooker, *From Adam to Christ: Essays on Paul* (Cambridge: Cambridge University Press, 1990; repr., Eugene, OR: Wipf & Stock, 2008), 40.

16. Kirk, *Unlocking Romans*, 78.

17. So Hooker: "Christ's death and resurrection lead to 'justification' for many precisely because he himself is 'justified' by God and acknowledged as righteousness" (Hooker, *From Adam to Christ*, 31).

18. Burger, *Being in Christ*, 248. Bird writes, "Jesus's resurrection is his justification, and believers are justified in so far as they have union with the justified Messiah" (Bird, *Saving Righteousness*, 2). He later writes that "union with Christ is union with the justified Messiah and the now Righteous One. Jesus by fact of his resurrection is the locus of righteousness and redemption, and believers are justified only because they have been united with the justified Messiah" (56).

19. Hooker writes, "To be in Christ is to be identified with what he is. It is not surprising, then, if his resurrection and vindication as the righteous one lead both to the acknowledgement of believers as righteous, and to their resurrection" (Hooker, *From Adam to Christ*, 37).

"In view of the solidarity involved, being raised with Christ has the same significance for believers that his resurrection has for Christ."[20] In fact, Gaffin goes much further; he argues that whenever Paul speaks of the believer's justification, adoption, sanctification, glorification, or any other benefit connected to them, in such instances the underlying consideration is resurrection with Christ.[21]

After his death for sin, the righteousness of Christ is declared by his resurrection, which is the sign of his vindication. Bird writes, "Christ's death constitutes the verdict against sin for justification to proceed, whilst resurrection 'enacts' or 'executes' the verdict both now and in the future."[22] Believers are regarded as having died with Christ, having been raised with him, and likewise therefore as being righteous with him. The justification of believers is the result of their death and resurrection with Christ, just as the righteousness of Christ results from his own death and resurrection.[23] Thus Gorman correctly states that "for Paul justification is an experience of participating in Christ's resurrection life that is effected by co-crucifixion with him."[24]

14.14.2 THE DEATH OF CHRIST AS ESCHATOLOGICAL EVENT

The foregoing discussion of the eschatological nature of the resurrection of Christ enables us to pivot now to consider the eschatological nature of his death. It is perhaps a little ironic that in traditional Protestant theology the resurrection is sometimes treated as an addendum to the death of Christ, since here it is necessary to move in the reverse direction. As noted above, however, this is not because the resurrection is more important than Christ's death. It is, rather, necessary to move from resurrection to death because the former is more obviously eschatological in nature and provides the tools with which we may recognize the equally eschatological nature of Christ's death, which is "at the heart of Paul's inaugurated eschatology."[25]

---

20. Richard B. Gaffin, *The Centrality of the Resurrection: A Study in Paul's Soteriology* (Grand Rapids: Baker, 1978), 129. He adds: "To be more exact, the notion that the believer has been raised with Christ brings into view all that now characterizes him as a result that he has been justified, adopted, sanctified, and glorified with Christ, better, that he has been united with the Christ, who is justified, adopted, sanctified, and glorified, and so by virtue of this (existential) union shares these benefits" (129).

21. Gaffin, *Resurrection*, 129. Cf. Powers: "Paul views reconciliation, justification, and the non-reckoning of sins to the believer as being the result of the mutual participation and identification of Christ with the believer and the believer with Christ" (Powers, *Salvation through Participation*, 83–84).

22. Bird, "Raised for Our Justification," 46.

23. So Gaffin: "For Christians, then, Christ's justification, given with his resurrection, becomes theirs, when united, by faith, to the resurrected Christ, that is, the justified Christ, his righteousness is reckoned as theirs or imputed to them" (Richard B. Gaffin, "Justification and Eschatology," in *Justified in Christ: God's Plan for Us in Justification*, ed. K. Scott Oliphant [Fearn: Mentor, 2007], 6).

24. Michael J. Gorman, *Inhabiting the Cruciform God: Kenosis, Justification, and Theosis in Paul's Narrative Soteriology* (Grand Rapids: Eerdmans, 2009), 40.

25. Wright, *Paul and the Faithfulness of God*, 1071.

As with the resurrection, we must begin in 1 Corinthians 15. Though dominated by the resurrection of Christ and the subsequent resurrection of those in Christ, the chapter offers one very important insight related to the death of Christ that must be probed at some length: *The sting of death is sin, and the power of sin is the law* (v. 56). This verse has already been discussed in §7.2, so the main contours of that discussion will be outlined here.

14.14.2.1 1 Corinthians 15:56

It was argued above (§7.2) that *the sting of death* should be understood in its objective sense, like a bee's *sting*, rather than in a subjective sense ("I feel its *sting*"). Objectively understood, death's sting is death's *stinger* (κέντρον can mean either)—it is the instrument with which death attacks and conquers its prey. Thus, sin is death's instrument; sin is the stinger that death uses to attack and conquer its victims. Once human beings succumb to sin, they succumb to death, since the wages of sin is death (Rom 6:23; cf. Gen 3).

The stinger of death, sin, is powered by the law, as 1 Corinthians 15:56b says—*the power of sin is the law*. As noted above (§7.2), this accords with Paul's argument in Romans 7:7–13 in that sin takes advantage of the law to strengthen its position and power. The law condemns sinners, allowing sin to step in to kill its victims. It empowers sin to do what it does. Thus, sin, together with the law, brings death.

Death, sin, and the law work in concert as a formidable triumvirate that, unchallenged, spells the end of human life. But the death of Christ challenges and overcomes it. First, in reference to the law, Paul says that *Christ redeemed us from the curse of the law by becoming a curse for us, because it is written, "Cursed is everyone who is hung on a tree"* (Gal 3:13). In his death, Christ bore the curse of the law, thus taking the penalty for the transgressions of humanity. He was delivered up for our trespasses (Rom 4:25a). Second, sin is wholly dealt with by the death of Christ: "It announces the negation of the power of sin that controls the world."[26] God *condemned sin in the flesh by sending his own Son in the likeness of sinful flesh as a sin offering* (Rom 8:3b), fulfilling the law's requirement (v. 4). If the demand of the law is fulfilled by Christ's death, sin loses its power and is itself overpowered. Third, by conquering sin, death itself is defeated. Since sin is death's stinger, once sin has been condemned, death consequently loses its grip. Once death loses its stinger, it becomes harmless and, like the bee, will itself inevitably die.

It is usually supposed that it is Christ's resurrection that overcomes death, and so it is in one sense. But in another sense, it is the death of Christ that

---

26. Beker, *Paul the Apostle*, 191.

overcomes death. Christ's law-fulfilling and sin-condemning death is the mechanism by which it is possible to overcome death, because without its other two operatives at work, death loses its power. Thus, the resurrection of Christ is the outcome of the overthrow of death; it is the inevitable consequence of robbing death of its sting. It is the proof that death has indeed been conquered.

In this way, the death of Christ is to be regarded as eschatological in nature. It is the key to unlocking death's grip on humanity, thus opening the way to liberation from the powers of sin and death and ensuring eternal life for those in Christ. As Gieschen remarks, "The past salvific work of Christ's death is the foundation for the certain hope in Christ's future salvific work of end-time resurrection, deliverance from wrath against unbelief, and restored glory."[27] It also effects the transference of realm that believers undergo when they participate in the death and resurrection of Christ (more on this below). According to Beker, therefore, the cross "is the apocalyptic turning point of history. The breaking-in of the new age means the destruction and judgment of the old age."[28] But it is also, as Wright insists, the "paradoxical climax to the long story, the 'covenant' narrative . . . which would radically transform that narrative even as it fulfilled it."[29]

14.14.2.2 Overpowering the Powers

Sin and death are not the only powers that are conquered through the death of Christ. All rulers and authorities were disarmed by it (Col 2:15), such that "the death of Christ marks the defeat of the apocalyptic powers and is thus not merely a moral act but an apocalyptic event."[30] In Colossians 2:14, the law's demand is again seen as dealt with by the cross—*he erased the certificate of debt, with its obligations, that was against us and opposed to us, and has taken it away by nailing it to the cross.* Immediately following this statement, we see that the cross was also the means by which the rulers and authorities were disarmed and triumphed over (v. 15).[31] The phrase *triumphed over* (θριαμβεύσας) refers to a triumphal procession,[32] which denotes a victory march after a great conflict. The Romans, for example, would stage a procession to celebrate their military victory, sometimes with their defeated enemy on display—humiliated, mocked,

---

27. Gieschen, "Christ's Coming and the Church's Mission," 53.
28. Beker, *Paul the Apostle*, 206–7. Cf. Madigan and Levenson: "In Paul's thinking, Christ's death atoned for sin, to be sure. But its main result was to have effected a change in lordships and sonships" (Madigan and Levenson, *Resurrection*, 37).
29. Wright, *Paul and the Faithfulness of God*, 408.
30. Beker, *Paul the Apostle*, 189.
31. The remainder of this paragraph, and the one following, is adapted from Constantine R. Campbell, "With Christ over the Powers," in *Christ's Victory over Evil: Biblical Theology and Pastoral Ministry*, ed. Peter G. Bolt (Nottingham: Apollos, 2009), 150–65. Used with permission.
32. BDAG 459, §1.

despised.[33] Moreover, the word that is translated *disarmed* (ἀπεκδυσάμενος) in v. 15 can be translated *stripped*. This coordinates with *triumphed over* such that the image conveyed is one of enemies stripped naked, put to public shame, and led in a triumphal procession. Paul's point in v. 15 is, of course, that this is the kind of victory that Jesus's cross achieved over the dark powers of evil.

At this point, however, there is a profound irony embedded in Colossians 2:15, since Jesus's defeat of the powers is depicted in a manner that evokes his own experience. Jesus was stripped naked, put to open shame, and paraded in a victory procession to the place of his execution. He was mocked, humiliated, shamed, and defeated. Yet the irony is that through these events the reverse was taking place. By his cross, Jesus's enemies were defeated. They were exposed, humiliated, and conquered. This, indeed, is the paradox of the cross: while Jesus was defeated and shamed, through his death he conquered evil and put the powers to shame. This insight has implications for our forthcoming discussion about the apocalyptic nature of Paul's eschatology (see ch. 15 below).

Though Paul does not spell out the connection, there is an implicit relationship between Colossians 2:14 and 2:15 such that the debt-canceling achievement of the cross relates to its apocalyptic triumph over the rulers and authorities. It is most likely the kind of relationship explored above with respect to 1 Corinthians 15:56—once the demand of the law is met, and sin is condemned, then death is defeated. So here, the cancellation of the law's certificate of debt leads to the disarmament of the rulers and authorities. Without sinners remaining indebted and condemned by their transgressions, the dark powers lose their authority over them. Thus, by Christ's death on the cross they are overpowered.[34]

14.14.3 THE ASCENSION OF CHRIST AS ESCHATOLOGICAL EVENT

The ascension of Christ is an eschatological event in at least three ways. First, it represents the "visible" enthronement of Christ as Lord over all.[35] We are unable to engage issues of cosmology with any depth here, but the ascension of Christ raises obvious cosmological questions. It is enough simply to affirm with Wright that heaven and earth "are not two different locations within the same continuum of space or matter. They are two different dimensions of God's good creation."[36] This means that Christ's physical ascension served as a

---

33. An apt example of this may be seen in the Roman soldiers' treatment of Vitellius, as portrayed in Dio Cassius, *Roman History* 8.20–21.
34. Wright, *Paul and the Faithfulness of God*, 1068.
35. On the entire subject of the kingship of Christ, and how Paul envisages it against ancient kingship discourses, see Joshua W. Jipp, *Christ Is King: Paul's Royal Ideology* (Minneapolis: Fortress, 2015).
36. Wright, *Surprised by Hope*, 110.

spatial metaphor representing his exalted entrance to heaven, which biblically speaking is frequently regarded as "up there" in a phenomenological sense but in reality is an entirely different dimension to our own.

The ascension of Christ is his exaltation, at which point he was given the name above every name, so that in the coming days every knee will bow at the name of Jesus (Phil 2:9–10). Christ is seated at the Father's right hand in the heavens, above every ruler, authority, power, dominion, and every title given—not only in this age but also in the one to come (Eph 1:20–21). While the death and resurrection of Christ represent his victory over opposing powers, Christ's exaltation is this victory's glorious manifestation.

14.14.3 1 Corinthians 15:23–28

But this is not the whole story. As with the death and resurrection of Christ, 1 Corinthians 15 is of utmost importance for grasping the eschatological nature of his ascension. The specific text of vv. 23–28 is addressed above in §4.2. It points to Christ's final subjugation of opposing powers—*he must reign until he puts all his enemies under his feet* (v. 25)—even while God has already *put everything under his feet* (v. 27). The juxtaposition of these two statements speaks to the now-and-not-yet nature of Christ's ascendant rule; he has already been enthroned, but opposing authorities remain extant. Death is the classic example, since death has already been conquered through the death and resurrection of Christ, and yet it remains in full force, taking its victims throughout the world. But the conquering of death, along with all other evil powers, assures their final abolition and destruction.

As discussed in §3.2, Paul's use of Psalm 8:6 (*you put everything under his feet*) helps to address this now-and-not-yet tension. The psalm speaks to the dignified position with which humanity has been bestowed over the rest of creation. While humanity enjoys such an elevated position, this does not mean that we see all of creation subjected to him. Humanity's dominion has been established but is not yet consummated. In the same way, Christ—humanity's ultimate representative—has been granted dominion over all, though his rule is not yet fully consummated. And when that moment comes, Christ will hand over the kingdom to the Father (1 Cor 15:24a).

Thus the ascension of Christ declares his elevation to the highest place. And it announces the imminent subjugation of those who are now, by declaration, under his feet.[37]

Second, the ascension of Christ marks the age of the Spirit. The notion

---

37. According to Harrison, Paul's portrayal of Christ as the eschatological figure of the world and cosmic history "would have registered with Romans imbued with the Augustan eschatology," as well as his Jewish readers (J. R. Harrison, "Paul, Eschatology and the Augustan Age of Grace," *TynBul* 50.1 [1999]: 90).

that the ascended Christ poured out the Spirit is not explicitly found in Paul's writings, though it is arguably implied. The clearest New Testament text that associates the ascension of Christ with the outpouring of the Spirit is Peter's Pentecost sermon in Acts 2—*since he has been exalted to the right hand of God and has received from the Father the promised Holy Spirit, he has poured out what you both see and hear* (Acts 2:33). It is highly likely that Paul would have known of this speech, given his association with Peter and several other early Jerusalem believers, and would no doubt make the same association between the ascension of Christ and the outpouring of the Spirit.

The closest Paul comes to this is in Titus 3:4–7. When God our Savior appeared, he saved believers through water of rebirth and renewal by the Holy Spirit. *He poured out his Spirit on us abundantly through Jesus Christ our Savior* (Titus 3:6). As with several other references, God the Father is the ultimate agent who gives the Spirit, but here we see that his outpouring of the Spirit comes through Christ. It is not difficult to imagine this working in concert with Acts 2:33. Indeed, there Peter says that Christ received the Spirit from his Father and hence poured him out. God working through Christ is Paul's way of saying the same thing.

In any case, for Paul the ascension marks the beginning of the age of the Spirit. The Spirit is the Spirit of the Son (Gal 4:6), and anyone who does not have the Spirit of Christ does not belong to Christ (Rom 8:9). Rather, the Spirit testifies that believers are the children of God and coheirs with Christ (vv. 16–17), and the Spirit is received through faith in Christ (Gal 3:14). The Christian life is defined by walking in step with the Spirit (5:16), who will produce his fruit in anticipation of eternal life (vv. 22–23; 6:8). As the deposit guaranteeing the inheritance promised in Christ (Eph 1:14), the Spirit is the eschatological agent who binds believers to Christ in his absence.[38] Or, perhaps more accurately, the Spirit mediates the presence of Christ in his physical absence. And, of course, the physical absence of Christ began with his ascension and will end with his return.

While Paul may not explicitly connect the ascension to the outpouring of the Spirit, he does connect it to the outpouring of other gifts, as seen in Ephesians 4:7–12:

> Now grace was given to each one of us according to the measure of Christ's gift. 8 For it says:

---

38. As Beale comments, "the Holy Spirit is what causes us to be existentially linked with the new world to come" (Beale, "Eschatology of Paul," 204).

> When he ascended on high,
> he took the captives captive;
> he gave gifts to people.
>
> 9 But what does "he ascended" mean except that he also descended to the lower parts of the earth? 10 The one who descended is also the one who ascended far above all the heavens, to fill all things. 11 And he himself gave some to be apostles, some prophets, some evangelists, some pastors and teachers, 12 equipping the saints for the work of ministry, to build up the body of Christ.

As the one who *descended to the lower parts of the earth*, Christ *is also the one who ascended* (vv. 9–10). And it is from his exalted position *far above all the heavens* (v. 10) that Christ gave gifts to the church in the form of apostles, prophets, evangelists, and pastors and teachers. These gifts are given to equip the saints for service, that they might work together to build up the body of Christ. In other words, the gifts given by the ascended Christ serve the purpose of strengthening the body of Christ during this present eschatological age.

All of this points to the third eschatological dimension of the ascension of Christ. His exaltation to the right hand of the Father marks the elevation of Christ, but it also marks his physical absence from this world. The entirety of life lived in this present age, therefore, is irreducibly defined by the ascension of Christ. It is the age of the Spirit, who keeps believers in Christ, and it is the age of the body of Christ (the church), which must grow and mature until Christ's (personal) body is no longer absent.

The ascension of Christ also creates the expectation of his parousia. His present absence anticipates his future presence. And on the day of Christ, he will come from heaven (Phil 3:20; 1 Thess 3:13), where he has sat at God's right hand since his ascension.

14.14.4 Participation in the Death, Resurrection, and Ascension of Christ

Presupposed throughout the previous sections addressing the eschatological nature of the death, resurrection, and ascension of Christ has been the notion of believers' participation in these events. This is a huge topic by itself, to which my earlier book, *Paul and Union with Christ*, is devoted.[39] At this juncture, it is sufficient to paint with broad brushstrokes rather than rehash detailed

---

39. Campbell, *Paul and Union with Christ*.

argumentation, in order to demonstrate how participation fits into the current discussion. Interested readers may of course follow up with the earlier book for further thoughts.

I have argued that Paul's conception of participation with Christ may be summarized as *union, participation, identification,* and *incorporation*.[40] These are briefly defined as follows.

> *Union* gathers up faith union with Christ, mutual indwelling, trinitarian, and nuptial notions. *Participation* conveys partaking in the events of Christ's narrative. *Identification* refers to believers' location in the realm of Christ and their allegiance to his lordship. *Incorporation* encapsulates the corporate dimensions of membership in Christ's body.[41]

The second term, *participation*, relates most directly to our present discussion, since it is concerned with partaking in the events of Christ's narrative—his death, resurrection, and ascension. For Paul, participation with Christ is inherently eschatological and eschatology is inherently participatory. It is impossible to understand either sphere without reference to the other. We will briefly discuss how participation fits with the eschatological understanding of the death, resurrection, and ascension of Christ, as developed above.

14.14.4.1 Participation in the Eschatological Death of Christ

The key text here is Romans 6:4–11, which is discussed in §7.2. Paul affirms that those who participate in the death of Christ will also participate in his resurrection—*for if we have been united with him in the likeness of his death, we will certainly also be in the likeness of his resurrection* (6:5). The *likeness of his death* refers to being buried with Christ by baptism into death (v. 4), while the *likeness of his resurrection* points forward to the future, bodily resurrection of believers. The point is clear: participation in death guarantees participation in resurrection.

This idea is expanded in the following verses, with reference to the crucifixion of the *old self*, which results in becoming *freed from sin* (vv. 6–7). Then the connection between death and resurrection is again affirmed—*now if we died with Christ, we believe that we will also live with him* (v. 8). Christ's death means that death can no longer rule over him (v. 9b), and it was a death *to sin once for all time*, which means that his new life is lived to God (v. 10).

This, then, means that believers who are in Christ, sharing in his death and

---

40. Campbell, *Paul and Union with Christ*, ch. 12.
41. Campbell, *Paul and Union with Christ*, 413.

resurrection, are to consider themselves *dead to sin and alive to God in Christ Jesus* (v. 11). In other words, the spiritual reality of participation in Christ's death and resurrection has implications for life here and now. Like Christ, believers are now *dead to sin and alive to God*; they are therefore to think of themselves as such and live accordingly.

Christ snapped the stinger of death in his own death (1 Cor 15:56; see above), but believers can only be freed from death's dominion by participating with him in his victory. Without such participation, Christ's conquering of sin would bear no relation to anyone; it would be without effect for anyone other than Christ. Thus, the eschatological nature of Christ's death determines believers' own eschatological status by virtue of their participation in his death. The old self is gone, and the dominion of death is no more. All that remains is resurrection into a new eschatological realm.

14.14.4.2 Participation in the Eschatological Resurrection of Christ

Participation in the resurrection of Christ yields two aspects. First, it causes believers to be made spiritually alive *now*; second, it causes believers to be physically raised from the dead to resurrection life when Christ comes. These will be addressed in turn.

A key text for the former is Ephesians 2:1–7 (see §7.2 above). The first three verses depict a dark picture of spiritual deadness. People were dead in their transgressions and sins in which they walked after the ways of the world, following the evil one (*the ruler of the power of the air*) and gratifying their ungodly desires (vv. 1–3). The spiritually dead *were by nature children under wrath* (v. 3b). This portrayal of spiritual deadness provides the backdrop for the remarkable claim that God, because of his mercy and love, has *made us alive with Christ even though we were dead in trespasses* (vv. 4–5). It is this participation in Christ's resurrection that underpins the entire argument that salvation is by grace (vv. 5b, 8). Since people are naturally children of wrath and spiritually dead, it takes the intervention of God to make them alive.

The idea of spiritual resurrection can easily be correlated with the expectation of a future bodily resurrection—the second aspect of participation in the resurrection of Christ. In Romans 6, the anticipation of future resurrection (v. 5) allows Paul to speak of walking in the newness of life now (v. 4) and being alive to God (v. 11). That is, before physical resurrection has occurred, believers are nonetheless able to live a new life in relation to God because of their union with the resurrected Christ. Such a notion is not far removed from that found in Ephesians 2.

Tannehill helpfully articulates the inner significance of dying and rising with Christ. He writes, "Christ's death and resurrection are not merely events which produce benefits for the believer, but also are events in which the believer himself partakes. The believer's new life is based upon his personal participation in these saving events."[42] In Romans 6, Tannehill observes one central idea emanating from the motif of dying and rising with Christ: "[Paul] is interested in the idea of dying and rising with Christ because it implies death to the old dominion of sin and new life to God."[43] And so the key notion at the heart of participation in Christ's resurrection is a change of lordship, since "the believer dies to the powers of the old aeon and enters into a new life under a new power."[44]

Dying with Christ is necessary to escape the dominion of sin and death, since death is the only way out of their grip. But believers do not remain "dead" and are reborn into the realm of Christ, under his lordship and governed by the principles of righteousness and love. Without participation in Christ, people are unable to escape sin and death and are unable to enter into the realm of Christ. Dying and rising with Christ are therefore essential elements for eschatological salvation.

14.14.4.3 Participation in the Eschatological Ascension of Christ

For Paul, participation in the death and resurrection of Christ are central tenets of eschatological salvation, for they achieve the transfer of realm that liberates believers from the tyranny of sin and death and gives them new life under the rule of Christ. Yet Paul does also imagine participation in the ascension of Christ (at least if Ephesians is regarded as Pauline). Having asserted the spiritual resurrection of believers with Christ, Paul adds that God *also raised us up with him and seated us with him in the heavens in Christ Jesus* (Eph 2:6). If this is understood to be past-referring (as it should), the raising and seating with Christ can only be comprehended in a spiritual way—or at least not in a physical way, since believers have obviously not physically ascended to the heavens.

In the flow of Ephesians 2, ascension with Christ is significant for at least two reasons. First, it represents the complete reversal of being dead in trespasses and sins (2:1). From a Jewish perspective, being dead means being buried (cf. Rom 6:4). Thus, when believers are made alive with Christ (Eph 2:5), their death is reversed. But when they are raised up with Christ (v. 6), their burial under the earth is also reversed so that they are now seated with Christ in the heavens above.

Second, participation in the ascension of Christ has an immediate purpose —*so that in the coming ages he might display the immeasurable riches of his grace*

---

42. Robert C. Tannehill, *Dying and Rising with Christ: A Study in Pauline Theology* (Berlin: Töpelmann, 1967; repr., Eugene, OR: Wipf & Stock, 2006), 1.

43. Tannehill, *Dying and Rising*, 9.

44. Campbell, *Paul and Union with Christ*, 339.

through his kindness to us in Christ Jesus (v. 7). Ascension with Christ apparently enables access to divine revelation that otherwise would remain hidden. The specific revelation in view is the riches of God's grace and kindness. Being seated with Christ in the heavens enables believers to witness the splendor of God's character as it has been extended to humanity.

While this revelation will be seen *in the coming ages* (v. 7), those raised with Christ must in the meantime *seek the things above, where Christ is, seated at the right hand of God* (Col 3:1). Here Paul seems to compress the resurrection and ascension together so that being *raised with Christ* includes both movements. It is the counterpart to dying with Christ (Col 2:20)—hence resurrection with Christ—but it also involves seeking and focusing on heavenly things above (3:1–2)—an outworking of ascension with Christ. Moreover, believers are *hidden with Christ in God* (v. 3) until Christ appears, when they *also will appear with him in glory* (v. 4). Believers are *hidden with Christ* because they have spiritually ascended with him and are spiritually seated with him in the heavens (Eph 2:6).

Participation in the ascension of Christ changes believers' address. Instead of being buried under the earth in a state of spiritual death, they have been raised to the heavens. Thus, from an eschatological perspective, ascension with Christ is another way of articulating the reality of realm transference. The earth is no longer believers' home address; they are now spiritually located in the heavens. From that location they are poised to view the coming revelation of God's goodness in the next eschatological age. And though Christ is physically absent from the earth by virtue of his ascension, believers are not absent from his presence as they are seated in the heavens with him.

All of this may be viewed in tension with one of the implications of Christ's own ascension, namely, his physical absence from believers. As discussed above, his presence is mediated by the Spirit during this age in which he is physically absent. But if he is absent from believers, how can we also say that believers are *seated with him in the heavens*? The answer, most probably, is that the Spirit mediates in both directions. On the one hand, the Spirit makes Christ present to believers in his absence. On the other hand, he makes believers present to Christ in their absence. Rather than a one-sided telephone call in which only one party is represented, the participation between Christ and his people goes both ways, as he is present with them by the Spirit and they are present with him by that same Spirit.

14.14.5 CONCLUSION

The death, resurrection, and ascension of Christ are inherently eschatological events in Paul's mind. Each one makes a distinct contribution to the eschatological landscape, and together they constitute the formidable power of

Christ to conquer the powers of sin and death, to overturn their dominion over humanity, and to triumph over all other authorities that stood opposed to him. The benefits of Christ's eschatological death, resurrection, and ascension are appropriated by believers' participation in each. Believers have died with Christ, been raised with Christ, and have been seated with him in the heavens. By their participation in Christ, believers have been set free from the tyranny of sin and death and have begun a new life with Christ in the realm of Christ. In Christ they are seated with God already, poised to witness the coming revelations of his extraordinary mercy and kindness.

14.15 THE ROLES OF CHRIST IN THE ESCHATON

While Paul regards the death, resurrection, and ascension of Christ as inherently eschatological in nature, by no means do they exhaust his eschatological work. Indeed, the eschatological nature of Christ's death, resurrection, and ascension set the table for what is to come with the coming of Christ. This is anticipated by Barth, who sees the past, present, and future work of Christ as one continuous act unfolding through time.

> As the Resurrected from the dead Jesus Christ is virtually engaged already in the outpouring of the Holy Spirit, and in the outpouring of the Holy Spirit He is engaged in the resurrection of all the dead and the execution of the last judgment. The outpouring of the Holy Spirit obviously takes place in the power of His resurrection from the dead, yet it is already His knocking as the One who comes finally and definitively, and it is active and perceptible as such. Similarly His final coming to resurrection and judgment is only the completion of what He has begun in His own resurrection and continued in the outpouring of the Holy Spirit.[45]

When he comes, Christ will bring judgment, resurrection, eternal life, and the promised inheritance—along with ultimate glory.[46] Each of these topics have already been addressed at length (see chs. 6, 7, 8, 9). It is only necessary here, therefore, to bring together the main contours of thought.

---

45. Barth, *Church Dogmatics*, IV/3.1, 296.
46. The expectation of the coming of a heavenly eschatological agent is attested in four key Jewish writings—the Sibylline Oracles, 4 Ezra, the Similitudes of Enoch (1 Enoch 37–71), and the Apocalypse of Baruch. The tradition reflected in these texts bear resemblance to Paul's expectation of the coming of Christ. However, as Hollman explains, these texts postdate Paul's writings and thus cannot have been used as a source for his parousia expectations. In the absence of parallel ideas in earlier extant texts, "the most one can do seems to be to point to analogous Jewish concepts from a later but not too distant period of time" (Joost Holleman, *Resurrection and Parousia: A Traditio-Historical Study of Paul's Eschatology in 1 Corinthians 15* [Leiden: Brill, 1996], 107–8).

14.15.1 THE PAROUSIA OF CHRIST

As noted above, the ascension of Christ creates the expectation of his return at the end of the age. The culmination of the redemptive plan of God involves Christ's presence with his people, and thus any scenario in which he is absent must be penultimate. The ascension of Christ into the heavens and physically away from humanity therefore necessitates an expectation of his coming again.

The parousia, or "royal appearing,"[47] of Christ functions in four ways for Paul. It is the event of expectation for believers in this current age—they are to live in anticipation of his arrival. It will bring the end of the age, the resurrection of the dead, and his presence among his people. It will inaugurate final judgment when he punishes his enemies and glorifies those who belong to him. Finally, the royal appearing of the Messiah will establish his "rule over the whole world" with "the reign of God's restorative justice and healing peace" brought to it.[48]

This event is cast as his *arrival* or *presence* (ἡ παρουσία),[49] his *revelation* (ἡ ἀποκάλυψις), his *appearing* (φανερόω), and his *descent* (καταβαίνω), all of which signal *the day of our Lord Jesus Christ* (ἡ ἡμέρα τοῦ κυρίου ἡμῶν Ἰησοῦ Χριστοῦ). Paul selectively uses apocalyptic imagery to make his assertions about the parousia.[50] Only through such imagery is a "physical" description of it (for want of a better term) offered: Christ will descend from heaven with a shout, with the archangel's voice, and with the trumpet of God (1 Thess 4:16; cf. 2 Thess 1:7). When he arrives, Christ's rightful rule will finally be revealed for all to see, instead of remaining hidden as it presently is.

Discussion of the parousia of Christ inevitably raises the scholarly question of his apparent "delay." While some earlier scholars such as Schweitzer made much of the delay of the parousia and what it meant for Paul, this question is far less interesting to more recent interpreters.[51] We have already noted that it is

---

47. Wright, *Paul and the Faithfulness of God*, 550.
48. Wright, *Paul and the Faithfulness of God*, 550.
49. As Witherington notes, Paul may have been the first person to use the term *parousia* to refer to the return of Christ. The term itself does not mean "return" or "second" coming; it simply means "arrival" or "presence" (Witherington, *Jesus, Paul, and the End of the World*, 152).
50. Burkeen, "Parousia of Christ," 172.
51. So Burkeen finds that in Schweitzer "there is an over-enthusiasm for the role which eschatological problems played in the development of Paul's thought. It grossly exaggerates the situation to state that the first and most immediate problem of the early Christian community was the temporal separation of the resurrection and the return of Jesus Christ, and that Paul's whole theology is an endeavor to answer this problem" (Burkeen, "Parousia of Christ," 9). For an example of modern dissent, however, see Hays: "Even if one wants to construe Paul's expectation of the nearness of the end relative to the entire length of the exile, the return of Christ has proved to tarry three-times longer than the exile itself did. That's nearly twice the interval between Jesus and the Davidic monarchy. 'Soon' it was not. No amount of appeal to imminence and uncertainty can account for the fact that the delay of Christ proportionally dwarfs the entirety of the exile" (Christopher M. Hays, "Prophecy: A History of Failure?," in *When the Son of Man Didn't Come: A Constructive*

unnecessary to read an imminent expectation of the parousia into Paul's writings (see ch. 4).[52] And, as Bartsch claims, it "is more a modern feeling looking back on almost two thousand years of Christianity" that is the issue, "and we take it for granted that Paul felt the same."[53] Rather, it is inappropriate to speak of Paul's frustrated expectation of the coming of Christ in the immediate future since there is no evidence that Paul himself felt such frustration.[54]

14.15.2 EXECUTING JUDGMENT

The arrival of Christ will inaugurate the day of Christ and all it entails. The day of Christ will be a day of judgment (1 Cor 1:8), when all will stand before the judgment seat of Christ (2 Cor 5:8–10).[55] As judge of the living and the dead (2 Tim 4:1–2), Christ will expose the secrets hidden in their hearts (1 Cor 4:3–5). With Christ as Lord over all creation, judgment is the necessary means of expressing his rule. It is how Christ will exert righteousness and peace over all, by bringing to account all evil and injustice. Yet the judge of all is also the savior of his people, delivering them from the coming wrath (Rom 5:8–10; 1 Thess 1:9–10; 5:9–10). Christ not only delivers but rewards them for their faith and love (2 Tim 4:8). Believers can therefore live in faithful allegiance to Christ, knowing that he will reward their devotion—come what may in their current experiences.

14.15.3 RESURRECTING THE DEAD

Paul nowhere claims that Christ will raise the dead on the day of Christ. This is portrayed as the act of the Father, as we see, for example, in Romans 8:11—*he who raised Christ from the dead will also bring your mortal bodies to life* (cf. 1 Cor 6:14; 2 Cor 4:14). The one possible exception is found in Philippians 3:21—*[Christ] will transform the body of our humble condition into the likeness of his glorious body.* While the language of resurrection is absent here, it is clear that Paul regards the transformation of the body as a feature of bodily resurrection, as seen, for example, in 1 Corinthians 15:52—*for the trumpet will sound, and the dead will be raised incorruptible, and we will be changed* (see the surrounding context for wider verification of this claim).

Proposal on the Delay of the Parousia, ed. Christopher M. Hays in collaboration with Brandon Gallaher, Julia S. Konstantinovsky, Richard J. Ounsworth, and C. A. Strine [Minneapolis: Fortress, 2016], 35).

52. Witherington, *Jesus, Paul, and the End of the World*, 45–48.

53. Hans-Werner Bartsch, "Paul's Eschatology and Its Meaning Today," *Brethren Life and Thought* 12.3 (1967): 5.

54. Bartsch, "Paul's Eschatology," 5.

55. Gordon D. Fee, *Pauline Christology: An Exegetical-Theological Study* (Peabody, MA: Hendrickson, 2007), 568–74.

However, it is clear that the resurrection of believers happens *because of Christ*, *through Christ*, and with the goal of *being with Christ*. The future, bodily resurrection of believers depends entirely on the death and resurrection of Christ (*because of Christ*), since through these events the condemnation of sin and the defeat of death are achieved—as discussed above. Participation in these events enables believers to benefit from them (*through Christ*). And the final goal of bodily resurrection is that *we will always be with the Lord* (1 Thess 4:17; *being with Christ*). So, while Christ might not be the ultimate agent who raises the dead (that privilege is reserved for the Father), Christ is the instrument through whom God will do it by the power of the Spirit (Rom 8:11).[56] This arrangement makes sense of Christ as the firstfruits of the resurrection of the dead (1 Cor 15:20–23). He is not the farmer who reaps the harvest; he is, rather, part of the harvest itself. As the firstfruits of the resurrection, Christ paves the way for the rest of the harvest to follow, but the Father remains the harvester (cf. 1 Cor 3:6).

14.15.4 Eternal Life with Christ

Upon bodily resurrection, believers will enjoy eternal life with Christ. Christ died for us so that we may live together with him (1 Thess 5:9–10). The death of Christ brought about the condemnation of sin, which in turn overturned the power of death. Thus, upon their bodily resurrection, those in Christ can no longer be subject to death. Resurrection life is necessarily eternal. But eternal life is more than just life without end. It is life *with Christ*. The relational element demonstrates the true purpose of overturning human death—it is so that the people of Christ may dwell with him.

14.15.5 Sharing the Promised Inheritance

Christ, the Lord of glory (1 Cor 2:8), will also share his resurrection glory with those in Christ (Rom 8:17). He will himself transform their bodies into the likeness of his glorious body (Phil 3:21). Having been hidden in Christ, believers will appear with him in his parousia glory (Col 3:4). Those in Christ are coheirs with him (Rom 8:14–22), through participation in his suffering and then glorification (9:17–18). The inheritance that believers will share with Christ belongs to the realm of Christ. Because they have been transferred from the domain of darkness into the kingdom of the Son (Col 1:13) they will share their inheritance in the light (v. 12). Thus, being coheirs with Christ is enacted

---

56. The instrumentality of Christ is frequently observed in Paul's articulations of the work of God. See Campbell, *Paul and Union with Christ*, passim.

by membership in the realm of Christ. It is in the first place his inheritance, but he shares it with all who belong to him.

This inheritance appears to be nothing less than the entire created order. All things in heaven and earth are brought together in Christ (Eph 1:10), having been created by him, through him, and for him (Col 1:16). In the eschaton, the *for him* element will finally be witnessed by all, as Christ's ascended position as Lord of the universe will be revealed. In this way, a central role of Christ will be to rule over all things overtly and without competition. His rule will be characterized by unending glory.

14.15.6 CONCLUSION

It is unsurprising that Paul envisages the centrality of Christ in the eschaton. Christ will execute several essential functions that bring the old age to a close, inaugurate the new age, and establish the forthgoing reality that has been promised. When Christ comes, the dead will be raised in anticipation of judgment when he will reveal the secrets of hearts and rescue believers from wrath. He will grant eternal life to those in Christ, resulting in life together with him. This eternal life will consist of the promised inheritance enjoyed by all in Christ, as he shares his rightful inheritance as the Son with those grafted into Christ to become Abraham's seed, the spiritual Israel. The highpoint of sharing with Christ, after sharing in his suffering, is to share in his eternal glory.

Though these future realities are of utmost importance to Paul, he does not elaborate on their details or specifics. Indeed, there is a little ambiguity concerning some of it. For example, it is not entirely clear whether he envisions the resurrection of the dead *before* judgment or *after* judgment. We will return to this issue in a subsequent chapter (see §16.15.1 below). By contrast, there is much more clarity and detail offered with respect to our previous topic—the eschatological death, resurrection, and ascension of Christ. But this should not surprise us, as it is characteristic of the New Testament in general to offer more detail regarding things that have been seen or can be studied directly now, and less clarity on future realities. Paul and the other New Testament authors do not equivocate about the future, but it must be admitted that their bold vision is not replete with the details we might like. Such apparent lack of detail should not be interpreted to mean that the future actions of Christ are relatively less important to Paul than the past actions of Christ. Christ's death, resurrection, and ascension set the table for what is to come at the eschaton. When the eschaton comes, it will be the culmination of all those things have accomplished.

14.16 CHAPTER CONCLUSION

This chapter draws together the exegetical results of part 2 that relate to Paul's Christocentric eschatology. Christ has been positioned above all rulers and authorities in this age and the one to come, and he has established a kingdom to which believers have now been transferred. Christ's coming will inaugurate a day of deliverance and judgment, vindication and condemnation, when the dead in Christ will be raised and transformed into the likeness of his glorious body. Death will be vanquished once and for all, and believers will enjoy eternal fellowship with Christ. Christ will share with them his inheritance of the entire created universe along with his everlasting glory.

The main contribution of this chapter has been to establish the eschatological nature of the death, resurrection, and ascension of Christ. For Paul, these are inherently eschatological events, and each makes an important contribution to his entire eschatological framework. His death achieved the condemnation of sin and therefore the defeat of death. His resurrection as the firstfruits of the resurrection of the dead is his eschatological vindication that makes human justification possible. His ascension to the right hand of the Father is his installment as Lord and Master over all other powers and authorities. By being in Christ, believers participate in each of these achievements and are thereby made secure for the coming eschaton. The roles of Christ in the eschaton are each determined by the eschatological DNA bound up in the past events of his narrative. The design of the eschaton is nothing less than the unfurling of the embryonic promise contained within the death, resurrection, and ascension of Christ.

CHAPTER 15

APOCALYPTIC ESCHATOLOGY

15.1 INTRODUCTION

One of the major topics that has dominated discussions about Paul's eschatology in recent years is to what extent Paul reflects apocalyptic themes in his thinking and writing. Paul did not write apocalyptic *literature*—he wrote epistles, not apocalypses—but is his eschatological perspective "apocalyptic" in shape? The discussion can be approached from two directions. First, there is the consideration of Paul's apocalypticism from the direction of Pauline scholarship. Though this really begins with Albert Schweitzer, its modern impetus stems from Ernst Käsemann and includes scholars such as J. Christiaan Beker, J. Louis Martyn, Martinus de Boer, Beverly Gaventa, and Douglas Campbell. The second direction from which Paul's apocalypticism has been considered is from Jewish apocalyptic studies. This includes scholars such as John J. Collins and J. P. Davies.

The approach of this chapter will be to outline the claims made by the first group, to consider the input of the second group, and then to reflect on some relevant features of Paul's writings before coming to a conclusion. The assessment of the apocalyptic nature of Paul's writings is not an esoteric topic for scholars to debate among themselves. The question has bearing on the way we read and understand Paul and must, therefore, be considered carefully.

15.2 PAUL'S APOCALYPTICISM AND PAULINE STUDIES

Current discussions about Paul's apocalypticism do not operate with a uniform sense of what is meant by *apocalyptic*,[1] since the term has not always

---

1. Benjamin E. Reynolds and Loren T. Stuckenbruck, eds., *The Jewish Apocalyptic Tradition and the Shaping of New Testament Thought* (Minneapolis: Fortress, 2017), 2.

been understood the same way. Käsemann spoke of "apocalyptic to denote the expectation of an imminent Parousia."[2] The disciples' expectation that Jesus's resurrection was "the dawn of the general resurrection and therefore interpreted apocalyptically"[3] shows that for Käsemann, *apocalyptic* means more or less what others mean by *eschatological*.[4] Käsemann wrote at a time when it could not be assumed that Paul was more influenced by Second Temple Judaism than by Hellenistic thought, so his belief that Paul was a Jewish apocalyptic (= eschatological) thinker needed to be argued. Today, this is assumed by most Pauline scholars.

However, Käsemann's contribution goes beyond simply asserting that Paul held to eschatological expectations that matched his Jewish worldview. His treatment of the righteousness of God (δικαιοσύνη θεοῦ; Rom 1:17; 3:21) is more "apocalyptic" than the sense in which the word is typically used today with respect to Paul; "δικαιοσύνη θεοῦ is for Paul God's sovereignty over the world revealing itself eschatologically in Jesus."[5] The righteousness of God is not primarily to be understood in individualistic terms—as God bestowing his righteousness to individuals through their faith in Christ—rather, it demonstrates that "God's power reaches out for the world, and the world's salvation lies in its being recaptured for the sovereignty of God."[6] This approach to the righteousness of God is apocalyptic in the sense that God is seen to dramatically intervene in the world. His righteousness has interrupted the present world order and asserted God's sovereignty over it in Christ. God brings salvation in Christ through this apocalyptic intervention of the righteousness of God. Käsemann's apocalyptic reading of the righteousness of God set the table for the present discussion of Paul's apocalypticism.

Following Käsemann's lead, Beker begins by summarizing Koch's eight-point description of Jewish apocalyptic thought, which is useful to reproduce here:

1. An urgent expectation of the impending overthrow of all earthly conditions in the immediate future.
2. The end appears as a vast cosmic catastrophe.
3. The time of this world is divided into segments.
4. The introduction of an army of angels and demons to explain the course of historical events and the happenings of the end time.

---

2. Käsemann, "Christian Apocalyptic," 109n.1.
3. Käsemann, "Christian Apocalyptic," 114.
4. A more recent example of this is Frederick J. Murphy, *Apocalypticism in the Bible and Its World: A Comprehensive Introduction* (Grand Rapids: Baker, 2012).
5. Käsemann, "Righteousness of God," 180.
6. Käsemann, "Righteousness of God," 181–82.

5. Beyond the catastrophe a new salvation arises, paradisal in character and destined for the faithful remnant.
6. The transition from disaster to final redemption takes place by means of an act issuing from the throne of God, which means the visibility on earth of the kingdom of God.
7. The frequent introduction of a mediator with royal functions.
8. The catchword *glory* is used wherever the final state of affairs is set apart from the present and whenever a final amalgamation of the earthly and heavenly spheres is prophesied.[7]

Beker maintains that the pre-Christian, Pharisaic Paul was an apocalypticist whose apocalyptic structure of thought remained the same both in his pre-Christian and Christian periods of life.[8] Though Paul modifies his apocalyptic expectations in light of Christ, the basic contours remain the same. For Paul, the major apocalyptic forces are "those ontological powers that determine the human situation within the context of God's created order and comprise the 'field' of death, sin, the law, and the flesh."[9] Paul's apocalypticism does not endorse a contempt for this world, but views the Christ-event as negating the old order and initiating the hope for the transformation of the creation with its redemption from decay. Beker writes, "Although the glory of God will break into our fallen world, it will not annihilate the world but only break off its present structure of death, because it aims to transform the cosmos rather than to confirm its ontological nothingness."[10]

Against popular opinion, Beker argues that Paul's two-age eschatological structure is not unique to the Christian gospel and can be seen in Jewish apocalyptic circles like that at Qumran. Beker writes, "The Qumran community knows itself to be alive in the end time and to be 'the new covenant' of the saved, in possession of the eschatological Spirit, so that it already claims the gifts of the end time in its midst."[11] Thus the tension between the new and old ages is not new with Paul. But, according to Beker, "the resurrection of Christ heightens the tension in the Jewish-apocalyptic scheme of the two ages between the 'already' and 'not yet.'"[12]

Martyn's 1997 commentary on Galatians was the first to expound Paul's

---

7. Beker, *Paul the Apostle*, 135–36.
8. Beker, *Paul the Apostle*, 144.
9. Beker, *Paul the Apostle*, 145.
10. Beker, *Paul the Apostle*, 149.
11. Beker, *Paul the Apostle*, 159. See also John J. Collins, *The Apocalyptic Imagination: An Introduction to Jewish Apocalyptic Literature*, 2nd ed. (Grand Rapids: Eerdmans, 1998), 268.
12. Beker, *Paul the Apostle*, 159.

apocalyptic thinking through an entire epistle. He cites four uses either of the noun ἀποκαλύψις or the verb ἀποκαλύπτω in Galatians (1:12, 15–16; 2:2; 3:23) and argues for the significance of "revelation" as a "disjunctive apocalypse" and an "invasion."[13] Martyn says, "The genesis of Paul's apocalyptic—as we see it in Galatians—lies in the apostle's certainty that God has *invaded* the present evil age by sending Christ and his Spirit into it."[14] In contrast to Beker, however, for Martyn this invasion of Christ into the present age is not in keeping with a horizontal, linear history (such as salvation history); rather, "as for all thoroughly apocalyptic thinkers, this liberating redemption does not at all grow out of the present scene. Redemption is a matter of God's invasive movement into that scene."[15]

Here we also summarize some insights from Martyn's recent essay on the human moral dilemma. In keeping with apocalyptic thought, Paul does not view human beings as independent moral agents, but as living "amidst orbs of power."[16] Sin is an enslaving power, but it is also a human act. But the slave-master role of sin is the primary sense, while individual human acts of sin are secondary.[17] Sin thus involves a dual agency: "Held captive by the enslaving power of Sin, human beings commit sin."[18]

But God's invasive act of sending his Son creates a redemptive dual agency, so that "when a human being believes the gospel, that event is one in which God has played—and plays—an active role."[19] Just as sin takes humanity captive and human beings then become complicit with it, so God reclaims people through the preaching of the gospel. Their "faith is *incited* by the power of the gospel (Rom 10:17)."[20]

Martyn's student, Martinus de Boer, has sought to explain this dual agency in terms of a two-track apocalyptic eschatology found within Judaism.[21] He summarizes these two tracks as following.

---

13. Martyn, *Galatians*, 98–99. Martyn helpfully outlines his views in his "Comment #3: Apocalyptic Theology in Galatians," 97–105.
14. Martyn, *Galatians*, 99.
15. Martyn, *Galatians*, 100.
16. J. Louis Martyn, "Afterword: The Human Moral Dilemma," in *Apocalyptic Paul: Cosmos and Anthropos in Romans 5–8*, ed. Beverly Roberts Gaventa (Waco, TX: Baylor University Press, 2013), 162.
17. Martyn, "Human Moral Dilemma," 163.
18. Martyn, "Human Moral Dilemma," 163.
19. Martyn, "Human Moral Dilemma," 165.
20. Martyn, "Human Moral Dilemma," 165.
21. Martinus C. de Boer, "Paul and Jewish Apocalyptic Eschatology," in *Apocalyptic and the New Testament* (Sheffield: JSOT, 1989), 172. De Boer's discernment of these two tracks began in his doctoral dissertation, published as *The Defeat of Death: Apocalyptic Eschatology in 1 Corinthians 15 and Romans 5*, JSNTSup 22 (Sheffield: JSOT, 1988), and has been developed in his subsequent publications, such as "Paul and Apocalyptic Eschatology," in *The Encyclopedia of Apocalypticism*, ed. John J. Collins and Bernard McGinn (New York: Continuum, 2000), 345–83.

Track 1: "'This age' is characterized by the fact that evil angelic powers have, in some primeval time (namely, the time of Noah), come to rule over the world."[22]

Track 2: "'This age' is characterized by the fact that human beings willfully reject or deny the Creator, who is the God of Israel, thereby bringing about death and the perversion and corruption of the world. Adam and/or Eve are the primal ancestors who set the pattern for all subsequent human beings."[23]

According to de Boer, these two tracks can be found "in nearly 'pure' form in *1 Enoch* 1–36 and the apocalypse of *2 Baruch*," but other documents, especially those found among the Dead Sea Scrolls (e.g., 1QS 1–4; 1QM; CD), show that the two tracks can run side by side and overlap in various ways in the one document.[24]

Paul lived at a time when both tracks were prominent within Jewish apocalyptic eschatology, and as a result both can be detected in his writings—Romans offering a prominent example of such. In Romans "1.1–5.11, the elements of forensic apocalyptic eschatology clearly dominate. In Rom. 6.1–8.38, however, the elements of cosmological apocalyptic eschatology are notably prominent (e.g. sin, death, righteousness, flesh, the spirit as cosmological powers)."[25] These two tracks are coordinated so that the forensic elements of salvation are part of the bigger picture of overpowering hostile cosmic powers. As de Boer says, "Christ's death cannot be understood in exclusively forensic terms, since it marks God's triumphant invasion of the world 'under sin' to liberate human beings (the ungodly) from its deadly power."[26]

Käsemann, Beker, and Martyn's influence is also seen in the work of Beverly Gaventa, whose most important contribution to this subject links Paul's frequent references to motherhood with the apocalyptic nature of his theology.[27] Maternal metaphors are drawn out of Paul's apocalyptic framework in the sense that the tribulation of labor pains and the deliverance of new birth are dramatic images that point to world-shattering apocalyptic events. For Gaventa, therefore, Paul's

---

22. De Boer, "Paul and Jewish Apocalyptic Eschatology," 174.
23. De Boer, "Paul and Jewish Apocalyptic Eschatology," 175.
24. De Boer, "Paul and Jewish Apocalyptic Eschatology," 177.
25. De Boer, "Paul and Jewish Apocalyptic Eschatology," 182. See also Martinus C. de Boer, "Paul's Mythologizing Program in Romans 5–8," in Gaventa, *Apocalyptic Paul*, 1–20.
26. De Boer, "Paul and Jewish Apocalyptic Eschatology," 184.
27. Beverly Roberts Gaventa, *Our Mother Saint Paul* (Louisville: Westminster John Knox, 2007), 79. For critique of some of Gaventa's conclusions, see J. P. Davies, "What to Expect When You're Expecting: Maternity, Salvation History, and the 'Apocalyptic Paul,'" *JSNT* 383.3 (2016): 301–15.

soteriology is inherently bound up in this cosmological-apocalyptic worldview, such that "Paul's cosmology is soteriology."[28]

Following Martyn's emphasis on the "vertical" intervention of God into this present world, Douglas Campbell concludes that Paul is not interested in a covenantal, "horizontal" soteriology and he also lacks a forensic theology (or "justification theory"). In such a light, traditional Protestant readings of Paul that emphasize human sin, guilt, and atonement for sin are undermined in favor of a cosmic, power-shattering, intervention of the righteousness of God. Believers are caught up in a cosmic battle with the evil spiritual realm, but the death and resurrection of Christ have brought victory and the deliverance of God. Thus Paul teaches an apocalyptic, liberative, and unconditional paradigm of salvation.[29]

Campbell's apocalyptic reading of Paul addresses the deliverance of God through Christ's assumption of Adamic ontology, which is executed in his death. Believers respond by dying with Christ, who then receive a new "in Christ" ontology, which is communal and participatory. Campbell pits this apocalyptic-participatory gospel against justification, arguing that "Paul's account of sanctification *is* the gospel. His description of deliverance and cleansing 'in Christ,' through the work of the Spirit, at the behest of the Father, the entire process being symbolized by baptism, *is* the good news."[30]

While some of these apocalyptic interpreters of Paul push harder than others, what began as a recognition of Paul's apocalyptic worldview has become an alternate way to read Paul that radically redefines the Paul we thought we knew. As Wright observes,

> We are to choose: either "apocalyptic," in the sense of a "vertical" divine action to liberate the world from enslaving powers, or some mixture of "forensic," "covenantal," or "salvation-historical" thought. *Either* a "vertical" "apocalyptic," *or* a "horizontal" or "covenantal" historical line.[31]

---

28. Beverly Roberts Gaventa, "Neither Height nor Depth: Discerning the Cosmology of Romans," *SJT* 64.3 (2011): 276.

29. Douglas A. Campbell, *The Deliverance of God: An Apocalyptic Rereading of Justification in Paul* (Grand Rapids: Eerdmans, 2009).

30. Campbell, *Deliverance of God*, 934. For an astute review of the issues surrounding apocalyptic interpretation and forensic justification with respect to Campbell's treatment alongside those of Martyn and de Boer, see Hefin J. Jones, "Πίστις, Δικαιόω and the Apocalyptic Paul: Assessing Key Aspects of the Apocalyptic Reading of Galatians" (MTh thesis, Moore Theological College, 2015).

31. N. T. Wright, "A New Perspective on Käsemann? Apocalyptic, Covenant, and the Righteousness of God," in *Studies in the Pauline Epistles: Essays in Honor of Douglas J. Moo*, ed. Matthew S. Harmon and Jay E. Smith (Grand Rapids: Zondervan, 2014), 249. Davies makes the same point: "The 'apocalyptic Paul' movement is characterized in each area by problematic dichotomies, strict dualisms which unnecessarily screen out what Paul's apocalyptic thought affirms" (J. P. Davies, *Paul among the Apocalypses? An Evaluation of the "Apocalyptic Paul" in the Context of Jewish and Christian Apocalyptic Literature*, LNTS 562 [London: Bloomsbury T&T Clark, 2016], 1).

Wright argues that these are a series of false dichotomies that Käsemann, the modern founder of the apocalyptic-Paul school, himself contradicts. By appealing to Käsemann's later lectures, Wright demonstrates that the "horizontal" notion of covenant features prominently in Käsemann's thought. Thus, "any antithesis of 'apocalyptic' and 'covenant' cannot claim Käsemann as its patron."[32] This shrewd move appeals to the father of the (modern) apocalyptic-Paul movement to show that the vertical nature of apocalyptic theology need not be at odds with the horizontal nature of covenant theology; at least not among Pauline scholars. So the question remains: What view do Paul's writings support? If Paul *does* display apocalyptic elements, or an apocalyptic worldview, are covenantal and forensic elements thereby negated?

15.3 Paul's Apocalypticism and Jewish Apocalyptic Studies

The other direction from which to evaluate Paul's supposed apocalypticism is from the perspective of Jewish apocalyptic studies. First, it is important to distinguish between the term *apocalypse* as a literary genre (e.g., Revelation, 1 Enoch, 2 Baruch), *apocalypticism*, which refers to a social ideology, and *apocalyptic eschatology*, which conveys "a set of ideas and motifs that may also be found in other literary genres and social settings."[33]

Second, there are problems in evaluating the evidence used to invoke all three labels. For example, prior to the New Testament book of Revelation, no Jewish apocalypses were labeled as *apocalypsis* (revelation), so that most of the texts that are today regarded as apocalypses are identified by their shared characteristics rather than a literary self-awareness of the genre.[34] Moreover, several works display the features of multiple genres, such as the book of Daniel, and are therefore not full-blown apocalypses, though they share the literary features of an apocalypse in significant portions of the work.

Collins defines apocalypse as

---

32. Wright, "New Perspective on Käsemann?," 253.
33. Collins, *Apocalyptic Imagination*, 2. Bauckham, however, avoids the terms *apocalyptic* and *apocalypticism* to describe eschatology "because it may suggest too much uniformity in worldview and the kind of eschatology to be found in the apocalypses is not what distinguishes them from other literature, and because apocalyptic revelations concern a variety of topics beside eschatology" (Richard Bauckham, *The Fate of the Dead: Studies on the Jewish and Christian Apocalypses*, NovTSup 93 [Leiden: Brill, 1998], 4). Macaskill offers similar caution: "Where we must be cautious is in using the word 'apocalyptic' to denote a worldview or a movement.... A more general problem with such a usage of the adjective is that it can assume a consistency in the worldview that lies behind the genre taken as a whole, a dangerous assumption to make" (Grant Macaskill, *Revealed Wisdom and Inaugurated Eschatology in Ancient Judaism and Early Christianity*, JSJSup 115 [Leiden: Brill, 2007], 19).
34. Collins, *Apocalyptic Imagination*, 3–4.

a genre of revelatory literature with a narrative framework, in which a revelation is mediated by an otherworldly being to a human recipient, disclosing a transcendent reality which is both temporal, insofar as it envisages eschatological salvation, and spatial insofar as it involves another, supernatural world.[35]

This definition applies to sections of 1 Enoch, Daniel, 4 Ezra, 2 Baruch, Apocalypse of Abraham, 3 Baruch, 2 Enoch, Testament of Levi 2–5, Apocalypse of Zephaniah, and (with qualification) to Jubilees and the Testament of Abraham.[36]

The other two terms, *apocalypticism* and *apocalyptic eschatology*, are derived from features observed in the literary works labeled apocalypses. The first term may be applied to a community, such as that in Qumran, since they espoused "a worldview in which supernatural revelation, the heavenly world, and eschatological judgment played essential parts."[37] The second term may be applied to literature that espouses "a transcendent eschatology that looks for retribution beyond the bounds of history."[38] These descriptions are sufficiently broad to account for the variations within the known apocalypses.

Given this background, Collins regards the writings of Paul to be "colored by an apocalyptic worldview to a significant degree."[39] Davies likewise concludes that "we must approach Paul's letters with recognition of his 'apocalyptic' way of thinking if the apostle is properly to be understood."[40] Though Paul writes no apocalypses, his revelation is declared to be a *mystery*; Paul is a steward of the mysteries (1 Cor 4:1), which embrace the full plan of God that previously had remained hidden. Moreover, the coming of the Son of Man is imminent, and Paul urges readers to be watchful and alert, aware that this world was passing away.[41] Furthermore, "the death of Jesus showed that salvation must be sought beyond this life in resurrection."[42] Paul demonstrates apocalyptic motifs such as "an epistemology of revealed knowledge, the eschatological doctrine of 'two ages,' a cosmology characterized by two realms, and a soteriology which

---

35. Collins, *Apocalyptic Imagination*, 4–5. Bauckham's description is similar: "The ancient apocalypses are a literature of revelation. In visions, auditions, and cosmic and otherworldly journeys, the seers to whom they are attributed receive, by heavenly agency, revelations of the mysteries of creation and the cosmos, history and eschatology. The kinds of secrets that are disclosed are quite wide-ranging and vary from one apocalypse to another, but prominent among them is the fate of the dead" (Bauckham, *Fate of the Dead*, 1).

36. Collins, *Apocalyptic Imagination*, 5. The definition can also be applied to a broad collection of Christian and gnostic literature, and to some Persian and Greco-Roman writings (5).

37. Collins, *Apocalyptic Imagination*, 13.

38. Collins, *Apocalyptic Imagination*, 12.

39. Collins, *Apocalyptic Imagination*, 256. See also Christopher Rowland, "Paul as an Apocalyptist," in Reynolds and Stuckenbruck, *Jewish Apocalyptic Tradition*, 131–53.

40. Davies, *Paul among the Apocalypses?*, 1. See also James H. Charlesworth, "Paul, the Jewish Apocalypses, and Apocalyptic Eschatology," in Boccaccini and Segovia, *Paul the Jew*, 83–105.

41. Collins, *Apocalyptic Imagination*, 264–67.

42. Collins, *Apocalyptic Imagination*, 267.

emphasizes divine victory."[43] In the end, Collins concludes that the chief distinction between Jewish and Christian apocalypticism in the first century was that the Christians believed that the messiah had come and that the firstfruits of the resurrection had already taken place.[44]

However, as Wright points out (above), and as Davies develops further, the apocalyptic-Paul school of thought tends to deny certain themes that are perceived to be negated by the apocalyptic ones. As Davies summarizes, it promotes "revelatory epistemology *therefore not* human wisdom; 'apocalyptic' eschatology *therefore not* salvation history; a cosmology of invasion *therefore not* the unveiling of God's abiding presence; a soteriology of deliverance *therefore not* forensic justification."[45]

15.4 Evaluation of Paul's Apocalypticism from the Perspective of Jewish Apocalyptic Studies

Given that the impetus for this discussion is the claim of Pauline studies that Paul is an apocalypticist, it makes sense to begin our evaluation from the other direction—from the perspective of Jewish apocalyptic studies—before circling back to evaluate the claims of Pauline studies.

As indicated above, Collins defines three terms—*apocalypse*, *apocalypticism*, and *apocalyptic eschatology*. The first is quickly dismissed with reference to Paul, since none of his writings can be classed as an apocalypse. But the second and third terms do seem to apply to Paul. Since our main access to Paul is through his writings, the third term—*apocalyptic eschatology*—is easier to assess than the second—*apocalypticism*—which describes a worldview. The two are not easily disentangled, but suffice to say that we can only gain insight into Paul's worldview *indirectly* by perceiving it through his writings, while we gain insight into his apocalyptic eschatology *directly* from how he addresses eschatological themes. As such, we begin with the third of Collins's terms—*apocalyptic eschatology*, as seen directly in Paul's writings.

Taken together, Collins and Davies point to Paul's use of *mystery* language, the imminent coming of the Son of Man, urging to be watchful and alert, a two-age eschatology, an epistemology of revealed knowledge, and a soteriology of victory as evidences of the apostle's apocalyptic eschatology.[46] It is worth assessing these characteristics against the texts we have examined thus far.

---

43. Davies, *Paul Among the Apocalypses?*, 1–2.
44. Collins, *Apocalyptic Imagination*, 268.
45. Davies, *Paul Among the Apocalypses?*, 2.
46. Collins, *Apocalyptic Imagination*, 264–67; Davies, *Paul Among the Apocalypses?*, 1–2.

15.4.1 MYSTERY LANGUAGE

First, *mystery* language is regarded as an indication of Paul's apocalyptic eschatology. The word μυστήριον occurs twenty-one times in the Pauline canon (Rom 11:25; 16:25; 1 Cor 2:1, 7; 4:1; 13:2; 14:2; 15:51; Eph 1:9; 3:3, 4, 9; 5:32; 6:19; Col 1:26, 27; 2:2; 4:3; 2 Thess 2:7; 1 Tim 3:9, 16), so it is certainly prevalent. The question is, however, can Paul's use of such mystery language be regarded as apocalyptic? Or, is *every* use apocalyptic, or only some instances?

For mystery language to qualify as apocalyptic, it ought to be used in the context of revealing some kind of divine secret. The word μυστήριον literally refers to something secret or a secret teaching,[47] but it is the revealing of such secret knowledge that counts as apocalyptic. Since apocalyptic theology is ultimately about *revealing*, it would not fit for mysteries to remain unknown or permanently sealed.

Romans contains two instances of μυστήριον, which are both arguably apocalyptic uses. In Romans 11:25, Paul wants his readers *not to be ignorant* of the mystery concerning a partial hardening of Israel as the gentiles come in. In Romans 16:25, Paul combines revelation and mystery language—his proclamation about Jesus Christ is according to the revelation of the mystery (ἀποκάλυψιν μυστηρίου) that had once been kept secret but was now revealed through the Scriptures (vv. 25–26).

First Corinthians has six instances of μυστήριον, but the usage is varied. In 1 Corinthians 2:1 and 2:7, Paul refers to his announcing the mystery of God to the Corinthians. In 4:1 Paul refers to himself and others as stewards of the mysteries of God, which in the context seems to mean that he has the responsibility to discharge or to reveal them.

In 1 Corinthians 13:2, however, Paul's reference to understanding *all mysteries and all knowledge* does not hint at any sense of revealing such secrets. But the context is hypothetical, as Paul makes the point that even with such understanding he would be nothing without love. Thus, the example is not apocalyptic, but it also does not reflect Paul's general meaning. In 14:2 we see a similar use, as the one who speaks in tongues is not understood by others as he speaks mysteries in the Spirit. This example is not apocalyptic, nor is it hypothetical.

Finally, in 1 Corinthians 15:51 Paul directly tells his readers a *secret*—that believers will not all sleep, but all with be changed when Christ comes.

Ephesians also contains six instances of μυστήριον. According to 1:9, God has made known to believers the mystery of his will. In 3:3 Paul says that the

---

47. BDAG 662.

mystery was made known to him by revelation (κατὰ ἀποκάλυψιν ἐγνωρίσθη μοι τὸ μυστήριον), and in 3:4 Paul's readers may understand his insight into the mystery of Christ. Moreover, in 3:9 Paul refers to the privilege he has to shed light for all regarding the mystery that had previously been hidden from the ages.

The use of μυστήριον in Ephesians 5:32 is more difficult to assess. Having discussed marriage and its analogy with Christ's relationship to the church, Paul cites Genesis 2:24 in Ephesians 5:31 and then declares this mystery to be profound. It is not entirely clear if the demonstrative *this* (τοῦτο) refers back to the Genesis 2:24 citation (or some similar antecedent) or forward to the next clause—*but I am talking about Christ and the church* (Eph 5:32b). Most likely it functions in both directions, so that Paul is describing the one-flesh union of man and woman as a profound mystery, and then redirects that mystery toward Christ and the church. It is a mystery that Christ and the church should share a union akin to human marriage, akin to a one-flesh union. While it is possible to construe this mystery as revelatory and therefore as apocalyptic, it seems more likely a reality that remains somewhat mysterious. It is simply a strange and perhaps baffling reality that Christ and the church should share such a relationship. The way that works and what exactly that means remains a bit of a mystery. As such, this is probably best understood as a *non*-apocalyptic use of μυστήριον.

In Ephesians 6:19, Paul's use of μυστήριον is clearly revelatory, as he requests prayer that he would boldly make known the mystery of the gospel.

Colossians contains four instances of μυστήριον. The first in 1:26 is obviously revelatory, as Paul refers to the mystery hidden for ages and generations but now revealed to God's people. Likewise, 1:27 refers to God's desire to make this mystery known among the gentiles—namely, Christ in them, the hope of glory. In 2:2 Paul expresses his desire that the believers should have complete understanding and the knowledge of God's mystery, which is Christ. Finally, in 4:3 Paul requests prayer that God would open a door that he might speak the mystery of Christ to others and make it known. All of these uses of μυστήριον are couched in terms of revelation.

The use of μυστήριον in 2 Thessalonians 2:7 is quite different from the others seen so far. Speaking about a certain *man of lawlessness* (v. 3), Paul says he is currently restrained until he is revealed (v. 6) and that *the mystery of lawlessness* is now at work (τὸ γὰρ μυστήριον ἤδη ἐνεργεῖται τῆς ἀνομίας). Later the lawless one will be revealed before destruction (v. 8).

The most obvious difference in the use of μυστήριον in 2 Thessalonians 2:7 is the fact that it does not refer to the revealed secret of God. It concerns the mystery of lawlessness—whatever that is—which *will* be revealed but has not *yet* been revealed. This secret is, nevertheless, expected to be revealed and in that sense may accurately be described as apocalyptic in tone.

In 1 Timothy 3:9, deacons are expected to hold *the mystery of the faith* (ἔχοντας τὸ μυστήριον τῆς πίστεως) as part of their qualifications for the role. This could hardly be expected of them if this mystery was still mysterious or unknown. Clearly, the mystery of the faith is a mystery revealed; it refers to knowledge concerning the faith—the body of beliefs—that a church leader is expected to know and embrace.

A few verses later in 1 Timothy 3:16, Paul refers to *the mystery of godliness* (τῆς εὐσεβείας μυστήριον), whose contents include the incarnation of Christ, his vindication in the Spirit, the witness of angels, and the preaching of and belief in him in the world, along with his ascent to glory (v. 16b). Since the content of this mystery of godliness is spelled out, it is clearly no longer a secret—it has been revealed.

In conclusion, Paul's regular use of μυστήριον is indeed apocalyptic in tone. Almost every use of the word concerns the secret of God that has now been revealed. The revealed character of this secret is an exact fit for apocalypticism, with most instances being christological in that the secret of God has been made known in and through Christ. The only non-apocalyptic uses of μυστήριον in the Pauline canon are 1 Corinthians 13:2, 14:2, and Ephesians 5:32.

15.4.2 The Imminent Coming of the Son of Man

Second, Collins and Davies point to Paul's belief in the imminent coming of Christ as an indication of his apocalyptic eschatology. All the references to the coming of Christ in the Pauline canon are examined in chapter 4, and it is demonstrated there that the coming of Christ is described through a variety of language, such as parousia, the revelation of Christ, the appearing of Christ, his descending from heaven, and the day of our Lord Jesus Christ (1 Cor 1:6–8; 4:4–5; 15:20–26; Phil 3:18–21; Col 3:1–4; 1 Thess 1:9–10; 2:19–20; 3:13; 4:15–18; 5:1–4; 2 Thess 1:5–10; 2:1–2, 8; 1 Tim 6:13–14; 2 Tim 4:1–2, 6–8; Titus 2:11–13). It is proposed here that for these sixteen references to be described as apocalyptic, they ought to express the belief that the coming of Christ is indeed imminent. In other words, any descriptions of the coming of the Son of Man that do *not* express an imminent expectation should not be counted as apocalyptic.

First Corinthians contains three references to the coming of Christ, but arguably none of these indicate any sense of imminence. In 1 Corinthians 1:7 (see §4.2), Paul refers to his readers' eagerly waiting for the revelation of the Lord

Jesus Christ. While the notion of eagerly waiting might imply imminence—as though Paul expects Christ to come during his readers' lifetime—this is not necessarily the case. If Paul expects the revelation of Christ *at any time*, then it is important for believers to be prepared for it—to wait for it—since he could come during their lifetime. But being ready in case that happens in their lifetime does not entail that Paul thinks it *will* happen so soon, only that it might. As such, this example does not necessarily imply imminence. The following verse, referring to the Corinthians' blamelessness on the day of the Lord Jesus Christ, likewise does not imply imminence.

In 1 Corinthians 4:4–5 (see §4.2), Paul refers to the Lord's coming, before which his readers ought not to judge anything prematurely. There is no reason to read imminence into this statement. Likewise, in 1 Corinthians 15:22–23 (§4.2), as Paul ruminates on the resurrection of those who belong to Christ at his coming, there is no hint of imminence concerning that coming.

In Philippians 3:20 (see §4.2), Paul again refers to eagerly awaiting (the coming of) a Savior from heaven, the Lord Jesus Christ. As with 1 Corinthians 1:7 (above), there is no reason to read imminence into this statement. It acknowledges that Christ could return during Paul's lifetime, but it does not suggest that Christ will necessarily return so soon.

In similar fashion, the certain expectation of the forthcoming appearance of Christ expressed in Colossians 3:4 (see §4.2) does not give a hint of imminence. Believers will appear with Christ in glory when he appears, but there is no indication of when Paul expects that to occur.

The highest concentration of references to the coming of Christ is found in 1 Thessalonians. In 1 Thessalonians 1:9–10 (see §4.2), Paul refers to his readers' turning from idols to the living God and their waiting for his Son from heaven, who will rescue them from the coming wrath. While their waiting may imply the expectation of his coming within their lifetime, again, as above, this is not necessarily the case. It only really implies that the Son *may* come in that period. There is likewise no indication of imminence in 1 Thessalonians 2:19, but only the expectation of hope, joy, and crown of boasting in the presence of Jesus when he comes. The same may be said of 1 Thessalonians 3:13, in which Paul expresses the wish that his readers' hearts will be made blameless before God at the coming of the Lord Jesus.

The strongest sense of imminence with respect to the coming of Christ is found in 1 Thessalonians at 4:15 and 4:17, where Paul twice refers to *we who are still alive* (ἡμεῖς οἱ ζῶντες οἱ περιλειπόμενοι) at the Lord's coming. This certainly sounds as though Paul expects the Lord's coming within his own lifetime. If he had said "those" instead of "we," that inference would be avoided.

But Paul did say "we," and that pronoun includes himself among those who will be alive when the Lord comes.

Nevertheless, we must ask how far this should be pressed. Yes, the "we" may mean that Paul's personal hope was that Christ would come within his lifetime. But is this personal hope the same as his "official belief"? In other words, if Paul was asked directly if Christ would come within his lifetime, would he answer affirmatively, or would he say, "I hope so"? There's quite a difference between these two answers. Obviously we are not able to ask that question directly, but the question itself plants a seed of doubt as to how securely Paul expected the imminent coming of Christ.

There is another question to ask of this "we." When Paul says that "we who are still alive at the Lord's coming," does he necessarily include himself in that "we"? Or is it possible, in a more inclusive and communal context, that the "we" simply points to his sharing in humanity? "We" might simply mean, "we humans who are still alive at the Lord's coming," without any necessary implication that Paul will be among those still alive at that time.

Perhaps these two questions will seem like long shots to most interpreters. But they also need to be weighed against all the other statements that Paul makes regarding the coming of Christ. If Paul nowhere else indicates a timeframe for his coming, leaving it open-ended, should we rely on these two "we" pronouns to overturn that attitude? Perhaps there is enough doubt sown to undermine the power of the pronoun? Perhaps Paul does not actually expect the return of Christ within his own lifetime, even while entertaining and hoping for that possibility?

First Thessalonians 5:1–4 is Paul's most explicit statement regarding the timing of the coming of Christ—the day of the Lord will come like a thief in the night (v. 2). As discussed in §4.2, the imagery of the thief in the night resonates with Jesus's teaching that no one knows when the Son of Man will come. While his coming will not surprise those who expectantly await it (v. 4), nevertheless its timing is completely unknown. It is important to note that Paul's most explicit teaching regarding the timing of Christ's coming is avowedly agnostic. Thus, the coming of Christ cannot be regarded as imminent in the sense of certainly occurring soon. Paul is only certain that its timing cannot be known.

Second Thessalonians contains three references to the coming of Christ. In 1:7 (see §4.2), it sounds as though Paul expected that relief for afflicted believers will come when Jesus is revealed, implying that their affliction will continue up to that point, which in turn implies that Jesus will come within their lifetime. But these are not necessary implications of the text. The focus of vv. 5–10 is God's just repayment to and punishment of those who have afflicted God's people, and this will take place at the revelation of Jesus from heaven. The Lord's judgment will occur at his coming. And this judgment will bring relief to those who have been afflicted, no doubt because justice has finally been done. But waiting for this judgment, and the relief that comes from it, does not mean that believers' affliction has been continuing up to that point. In other words, it is entirely plausible to expect the end of affliction before the return of Christ (perhaps through death), even though those executing such affliction have not yet been judged. Their judgment will bring relief to their victims because justice will have been served, but this does not mean that their victims have remained in affliction until then. Thus this text does not necessarily convey an imminent expectation of the coming of Christ.

Second Thessalonians 2:1–2, on the other hand, conveys the opposite of an expectation of the imminent coming of Christ. Paul warns his readers not to become troubled by allegations that the day of the Lord has already come. This means that any existing expectation of imminence on the part of his readers needs to be tempered by a healthy dose of realism—the mysterious apostasy and man of lawlessness must first come (v. 3). The same may be said of 2 Thessalonians 2:8, where the Lord Jesus will destroy this mysterious lawless one when he comes.

The Pastoral Epistles contain four references to the coming of Christ. When Paul charges Timothy to keep his command without fault or failure in 1 Timothy 6:13–14 (see §4.2), Timothy is to do so *until the appearing of our Lord Jesus Christ*. As indicated in §4.2, the coming of Christ signals the end of the current eschatological age, and Paul allows the possibility that this may occur during Timothy's lifetime, though he does not assert that it will. Thus, Timothy's responsibility "until" Christ comes does not imply an expectation of imminence but only the possibility of such. Paul's second charge to Timothy in 2 Timothy 4:1–2 (see §4.2) is issued in light of Christ's appearing and kingdom, but there no hint of imminence is implied.

When Paul refers to the end of his own life and ministry in 2 Timothy 4:6–8, he looks forward to the crown of righteousness that will be awarded to him and to all who love the eschatological appearing of Christ (see §4.2). The temporal location of that day is not specified. Indeed, it appears that Paul expects it to take place after his own death: *The time for my departure is close* (v. 6). Far from an expectation of the imminent coming of Christ, at the end of his life Paul now expects to have departed before Christ comes.

The language of waiting returns in Titus 2:13 (see §4.2), as Paul reminds Titus to live rightly in anticipation of the appearing of the great God and Savior, Jesus Christ. No timeframe is specified, and the "waiting" language does not necessarily imply that Christ will appear within Titus's lifetime, though it does imply that he *might* do so. Once again, it seems Paul remains agnostic as to the timing of the parousia.

In conclusion, Paul's sense of the imminence of the coming of the Son of Man has perhaps been overstated. Of his seventeen references to the coming of Christ, only two (1 Thess 4:15, 17) seem to indicate that Paul expected Christ to come within his lifetime, and even these need not necessarily be read that way. The language of *waiting* for the coming of Christ, which is found in four instances, might be construed as indicating imminence, but not necessarily so (1 Cor 1:7; Phil 3:20; 1 Thess 1:9–10; Titus 2:13). In 2 Thessalonians 2:1–2, 8, Paul expects the coming of Christ after the mysterious man of lawlessness comes, and in 2 Timothy 4:6–8 it seems that Paul expects Christ to appear after his own death. Paul's firmest statement concerning the timing of Christ's coming indicates agnosticism on the issue (1 Thess 5:1–4). All other instances reveal an expectation of the coming of Christ without any indication of when it will occur.

While Paul most assuredly affirms belief in the coming of the Son of Man, there is little firm evidence that this coming is imminent. As such, the expectation of this coming does not support Paul's apocalyptic eschatology as firmly as claimed by Collins and others. While it might be argued that the expectation of Christ's coming is nevertheless apocalyptic since it will be a dramatic, world-changing event, its imminence cannot be adduced for an apocalyptic reading of Paul.

15.4.3 Urging to Be Watchful and Alert

Third, Collins and Davies point to Paul's urging to be watchful and alert as an indication of his apocalyptic eschatology. Before exploring this, it is worth acknowledging the distinction between urging to be watchful and urging in general. Paul urges his readers to all kinds of things, but these do not all fit the apocalyptic category of watchfulness. Likewise, there is a difference between *urging* to be watchful compared to general statements about waiting and watching. Admittedly, it can be difficult to discern the difference between general statements about watchfulness and urging toward watchfulness, given that a general statement may exhibit the illocutionary force of an exhortation.[48]

---

48. This draws on the distinction within speech-act theory between locution and illocution. *Locution* refers to the form of an utterance (such as a direct command), while *illocution* refers to the pragmatic effect of an utterance (a general statement may imply a command, without use of a formal command structure). The relevance of this distinction here is that it is possible to issue an exhortation (urging) without using an exhortation formula or expression.

To this end, we will consider instances that arguably demonstrate such illocutionary force, regardless of whether or not they exhibit the formal features of an exhortation (urging). Strictly speaking, then, we are looking for references that legitimately can be described as urgings that are concerned with watchfulness.

Granting the slight ambiguity acknowledged above, the following texts arguably exhibit locutionary or illocutionary urging toward watchfulness: Romans 13:11–14; Galatians 6:7–9; Ephesians 5:5–6; 6:6–8; Philippians 3:18–21; Colossians 3:5–7; 3:22–25; 1 Thessalonians 5:1–4; 5:5–8; 2 Thessalonians 2:1–4; 2 Timothy 4:1–2; and Titus 2:11–13.

In Romans 13:11–14 Paul refers to the hour to wake up from sleep, with salvation being nearer than at first. With the night nearly over and the day near, the deeds of darkness are to be discarded in favor of the armor of light. The whole unit anticipates the coming dawn of the new eschatological age, and the action prescribed is predicated on such anticipation. Naturally, then, the passage conveys the illocutionary force of urging toward watchfulness as believers watch for the coming day and live in light of its coming.

Galatians 6:7–9 warns that whatever is sown will be reaped—either destruction or eternal life. Believers ought not give up doing good since they will reap at the proper time. This exhortation not to tire of good deeds because of the coming harvest clearly urges believers to look ahead and to act accordingly.

Ephesians 5:5–6 warns that sexual immorality, impurity, and greed will disqualify people from an inheritance in the kingdom of Christ and of God. The warning against this-worldly sins is set against next-worldly judgment, and as such conveys the illocutionary force of urging watchfulness as believers live in accordance with expectation. Similarly, in exhorting slaves to appropriate action in Ephesians 6:6–8, Paul instructs them to serve as to the Lord in expectation of recompense from him. Slaves' good works, then, are performed on the basis of a watchful expectation of the judgment to come.

In Philippians 3:18–21, Paul reminds his readers that the enemies of the cross of Christ will face destruction. While their focus is on earthly things, the citizens of heaven eagerly await their Savior from there. While this is cast as a statement rather than an exhortation, the illocutionary force clearly urges believers to live in watchful expectation of the coming of Christ.

In Colossians 3:5–7, the expectation of God's wrath upon the disobedient likewise urges watchfulness along with the continuing commitment to reject the former way of life that once characterized Paul's readers. Colossians 3:22–25 conveys an exhortation to slaves that is parallel to Ephesians 6:6–8, based on their watchful expectation of an inheritance from the Lord.

First Thessalonians 5:1–4, the account of Paul's agnosticism regarding the timing of the parousia, nevertheless urges watchfulness, as his readers are not in the dark and therefore should not be surprised when the Lord comes like a thief in the night. Once again, the locution is that of a statement, but its illocutionary force is that of exhortation and urging. The following verses, 5:5–8, build on this to offer an explicit exhortation to watchfulness: *Let us not sleep, like the rest, but let us stay awake and be self-controlled* (5:6). The notion of wakefulness relates to the imagery of the day (versus the night). Since the day is coming, believers are to remain awake in anticipation, which indicates their allegiance to the day rather than the night and their desire to be ready for it.

In 2 Thessalonians 2:1–4, Paul draws on his readers' obvious expectation of the day of the Lord and urges watchfulness of a different kind. They are already watchful for the day, but he warns them not to be misled into thinking that the day has already come. This does not mitigate any expectation of watchfulness but rather helps Paul's readers to know what to watch for. That day will not come until the apostasy and the man of lawlessness come first (v. 3).

In 2 Timothy 4:1–2 Paul's charge to Timothy to fulfill his duty to preach the word is issued on the basis of the forthcoming appearing of Christ and his kingdom. While the exhortatory locution concerns Timothy's responsibility to preach the word (v. 2), the illocutionary force of its basis is that Timothy ought to remain expectantly watchful for the appearing of Christ. His preaching is to be conducted in light of that expectation.

Titus 2:11–13 refers to godly living *while we wait for the blessed hope, the appearing of the glory of our great God and Savior, Jesus Christ* (v. 13). Once again, the locution is a simple statement, but its illocutionary force encourages readers to live in such a way while awaiting Christ with watchful expectancy.

Each of these twelve texts express an apocalyptic exhortation to watchfulness as the day of the Lord approaches. Most do so through their illocutionary force rather than direct exhortation, but the intent is clear in each. Paul wants his readers to live and behave in light of the expectation of the coming of the Lord. They are to be ready for it and should not be caught by surprise when it comes.

15.4.4 TWO-AGE ESCHATOLOGY

Fourth, Collins and Davies assert that Paul's two-age eschatological framework is further indication of his apocalyptic eschatology. Since chapter 3 is dedicated to the exploration of Paul's two-age eschatological structure, concluding that he imagines all of reality as existing under two competing realms, it is unnecessary to engage the issue further here. Paul's two-age eschatological structure is beyond doubt.

15.4.5 Epistemology of Revealed Knowledge

Fifth, Paul's apocalyptic eschatology is said to be evidenced in his epistemology of revealed knowledge. Thus, we may ask to what extent does Paul rely on revelation for his epistemological convictions? In order to assess the evidence, the following texts have been adduced through searching for the φανερόω and ἀποκαλύπτω word groups. These two lexemes and their cognates are regarded as synonymous, referring to something revealed, disclosed, or made fully known.[49] Since our interest is in how such revelation shapes Paul's epistemology, only those texts that refer to the revealing of knowledge or understanding are included here. The relevant texts employing the φανερόω word group are Romans 1:19; 3:21; 16:26; 2 Corinthians 2:14; 4:10, 11; Colossians 1:26; 2 Timothy 1:10; and Titus 1:3. Those employing the ἀποκαλύπτω word group are Romans 1:17, 18; 16:25; 1 Corinthians 2:10; 14:26, 30; 2 Corinthians 12:1, 7; Galatians 1:12, 16; 2:2; 3:23; Ephesians 1:17; 3:3, 5; and Philippians 3:15.

The three relevant instances of the φανερόω word group in Romans each clearly relate to epistemology, pointing to the self-revelation of God, the revelation of his righteousness, and the revelation of the mystery of Christ. Romans 1:19 refers to the self-revelation of God to all people; what can be known (φανερόν) about God is evident because God has made it known (ἐφανέρωσεν). Romans 3:21 refers to the righteousness of God having been revealed (πεφανέρωται). In Romans 16:25–26 Paul refers to his gospel and proclamation about Christ which is *according to the revelation [ἀποκάλυψιν] of the mystery kept silent for long ages but now revealed [φανερωθέντος] and made known through the prophetic Scriptures.*

The three relevant instances of the φανερόω word group in 2 Corinthians demonstrate that knowledge of Christ is revealed through Paul's apostolic ministry. In 2 Corinthians 2:14 Paul speaks of God spreading (φανεροῦντι) through him the aroma of the knowledge of Christ in every place. In 2 Corinthians 4:10–11, Paul says that the life of Jesus is displayed (φανερωθῇ) in his body (v. 10) and displayed (φανερωθῇ) in his mortal flesh (v. 11).

While reflecting on his responsibility to make the word of God fully known, Paul refers to the *mystery hidden for ages and generations but now revealed [ἐφανερώθη] to his saints* in Colossians 1:26. This revealed mystery is then described as *Christ in you, the hope of glory* (v. 27). Likewise, 2 Timothy 1:10 indicates that God's salvation has been made evident (φανερωθεῖσαν) through the appearing of Christ Jesus. Finally, in Titus 1:3 Paul refers to God's revealing (ἐφανέρωσεν) of his word through his preaching.

---

49. BDAG 112, 1048.

The three relevant instances of the ἀποκαλύπτω word group in Romans demonstrate connection both to the revealing nature of the gospel of Christ as well as revelation observed in the world. In Romans 1:17, the righteousness of God is revealed (ἀποκαλύπτεται) in the gospel, while in 1:18 the wrath of God is revealed (ἀποκαλύπτεται) from heaven against all godlessness and unrighteousness. In Romans 16:25, Paul connects his gospel and proclamation about Jesus Christ with the revelation (ἀποκάλυψιν) of the mystery that had previously been kept hidden.

The four relevant instances of the ἀποκαλύπτω word group in the Corinthian correspondence refer both to revelation that is open to all believers as well as to revelation given to specific people. Paul reflects on God's hidden wisdom, which according to 1 Corinthians 2:10 has been revealed (ἀπεκάλυψεν) to believers by the Spirit. While speaking about the orderly conduct of prophets within the gathered congregation, in 1 Corinthians 14:26, 30 Paul refers to the possibility of something being revealed (ἀποκάλυψιν; ἀποκαλυφθῇ) to such a person. In 2 Corinthians 12:1 Paul refers to revelations (ἀποκαλύψεις) of the Lord, of which the experience of *a man in Christ who was caught up to the third heaven* is offered as an example (v. 2). Such experienced revelations (ἀποκαλύψεων) are also in view in 2 Corinthians 12:7.

Of the four relevant instances of the ἀποκαλύπτω word group in Galatians, three refer to personal revelations given to Paul, while one instance refers to a more general revelation. In Galatians 1:12, Paul asserts that the gospel he preaches was not taught to him but *came by a revelation* [ἀποκαλύψεως] *of Jesus Christ*. And according to 1:16 Christ himself was revealed (ἀποκαλύψαι) in Paul in order that he might preach Christ among the gentiles. In Galatians 2:2 it appears that Paul went up to Jerusalem because of a revelation (ἀποκάλυψιν) he received. In Galatians 3:23, Paul refers to the revealing (ἀποκαλυφθῆναι) of the faith that came after the law.

The three relevant instances of the ἀποκαλύπτω word group in Ephesians demonstrate revelation to all believers, to Paul specifically, and to the apostles and prophets. In Ephesians 1:17, Paul prays that God would give his readers the Spirit of wisdom and revelation in the knowledge of him. In Ephesians 3:3, Paul refers to the mystery that has been made known to him by revelation, just as 3:5 indicates that it has been revealed (ἀπεκαλύφθη) to the apostles and prophets. Finally, in Philippians 3:15 Paul promises his readers that God will reveal (ἀποκαλύψει) the truth of the matter if his readers share a difference of opinion.

Drawing these references together, we see at least three ways in which revelation relates to epistemology. First, there is general revelation in which God's attributes and wrath are revealed to all people (e.g., Rom 1:18–19). Second, there is special revelation given to believers through which God has revealed his righteousness (e.g., Rom 1:17), his wisdom (e.g., 1 Cor 2:10), knowledge about himself (e.g., 2 Cor 2:14), the previously hidden mystery of Christ (e.g., Col 1:26–27), and salvation (e.g., 2 Tim 1:10). Third, there is specific revelation through which Paul has been entrusted with the gospel (e.g., Gal 1:12), Christ himself (e.g., v. 16), the mystery about Christ (e.g., Eph 3:3), special guidance (e.g., Gal 2:2), special visions (e.g., 2 Cor 12:1). And such specific revelation is also extended to other individuals (e.g., 1 Cor 14:26, 30).

Nevertheless, a couple of qualifiers ought to be offered at this juncture. First, these texts do not exhaust Paul's language of revelation, as he uses this language regarding the revealing of certain things besides knowledge, such as the quality of a builder's work (1 Cor 3:13). This means that the function of revelation goes beyond epistemology—it is wider than the revealing of knowledge.

Second, it is clear that Paul's epistemology is not limited to revelation—at least not *direct* revelation. Paul's entire missionary activity is predicated on the understanding that it is his task to make known what has been revealed to him. In other words, direct revelation has been given to Paul, who now dispenses what has been made known to him through proclamation. To be sure, this may be understood through an epistemology of revelation, since the content of his proclamation is based on revelation. But the point is that his hearers need not experience direct revelation from God in the way that Paul did—the truth is revealed to them through preaching.

15.4.6 Soteriology of Victory

Sixth, it is claimed that Paul expresses a soteriology of victory, which further evinces his apocalyptic eschatology. We will thus explore those texts that seem to indicate the spiritual or cosmic triumph of Christ in and through the salvation of humanity and the judgment and destruction of evil.

In Romans 5:19–21 Paul contrasts Adam's disobedience with Christ's obedience, the multiplication of sin with the greater multiplication of grace, and the competing reigns of sin in death and grace through righteousness. A soteriology of victory is implied through this set of contrasts in which the latter item of each pair is regarded as superior to the former, superseding it. This is seen especially in the last contrasted pair in which the language of reigning is employed, with the reign of sin conveyed with a past-referring aorist indicative tense-form (ἐβασίλευσεν) and the reign of grace conveyed with the open-ended aorist subjunctive (βασιλεύσῃ). This shift from aorist indicative to aorist subjunctive clearly conveys the supersession of the latter over the former; the reign of sin belongs to the past, while the reign of grace has begun and will lead to eternal life.

First Corinthians 15:23–28 expresses a clear soteriology of victory in which every competing rule, authority, and power are abolished by Christ, and his enemies are put under his feet—the last of which is death. Having established his rule and authority over all powers, Christ then hands over the kingdom to God the Father.

A soteriology of victory is likewise clear in Ephesians 1:20–23, in which God's power is exerted in raising Christ from the dead and seating him at his right hand in the heavens. This positions Christ far above every other ruler, authority, power, and dominion. Everything is subjected to him as Christ is appointed head over all things.

Colossians 2:14–15 also clearly conveys a soteriology of victory, with Christ's nullifying of the certificate of debt that stood opposed to humanity, and especially in his disarming the rulers and authorities. They are subjected to public disgrace as a result of his triumph over them by way of his cross.

In 2 Thessalonians 1:5–10 the retribution inflicted upon those who have afflicted believers is executed through the revelation of the Lord from heaven as he wields flaming fire and brings eternal destruction from his presence and strength. Clearly such judgment and retribution are predicated on the victory of Christ over the forces of evil. Without such supremacy, the overthrow of evil would not be possible. The same point may be observed in 2:8, in which the Lord Jesus will destroy the lawless one with the breath of his mouth.

It is interesting to note the different types of soteriological victory observed in these texts. From a "theological-chronological" perspective, Colossians 2:14–15 comes first, with Christ's victory over the rulers and authorities through his cross. This is a hidden victory—indeed, it is truly apocalyptic—since the outward appearance of the cross was one of defeat even while the hidden spiritual reality was one of triumph. Next is Ephesians 1:20–23 with the supremacy and victory of Christ effected through his resurrection and ascension. Everything is subjected to him through these events, at least in terms of position. Next comes Romans 5:19–21 with the victory of the reign of grace over the old reign of sin. While this victory is not explicitly christological, it is obviously tied directly to the work of Christ and may therefore be regarded as his victory. Next follows the texts from 2 Thessalonians with the victory of Christ revealed in his coming again. Finally, 1 Corinthians 15:23–28 points to the victory of Christ at the "end," with the final vanquishing of Christ's enemies, including death.

Thus, there are four "victory events" discerned: Christ's death, his resurrection-ascension (taken as one victory event), his coming again, and the "end" that follows. The victory of Christ, therefore, cannot be narrowed to one event alone but must be understood as unfolding in stages. Having said that, however, there does seem to be a logical sequence that relates these events together. The death of Christ accomplished an overthrow of the captive powers of evil, since their grip on sinful humanity was loosened through his erasing of the certificate of debt that stood opposed to it. The overthrow of sin led to the overthrow of death in the resurrection of Christ, and the ascension positioned him as the rightful authority above all competing powers. At his return, this rightful authority is expressed through the physical subjugation of the forces of evil. Having subjugated and vanquished all opposing forces, including death, the end comes with its handing over of the kingdom from Christ to God the Father.

15.4.7 CONCLUSION

We have assessed the claims of Collins and Davies, who together point to Paul's use of *mystery* language, the imminent coming of the Son of Man, urging to be watchful and alert, a two-age eschatology, an epistemology of revealed knowledge, and a soteriology of victory as evidences of the apostle's apocalyptic eschatology.[50] With the exception of the imminence of the coming of the Son of Man, it has been observed that these elements are indeed strongly present in Paul's writings. From the perspective of Judaism, then, Paul reveals himself to be deeply indebted to apocalyptic eschatology in his theological outlook. We turn now to consider how these findings match the claims made about Paul's apocalypticism from within Pauline studies.

15.5 EVALUATION OF PAUL'S APOCALYPTICISM FROM THE PERSPECTIVE OF PAULINE STUDIES

Having assessed Paul's apocalypticism from the perspective of Jewish apocalyptic studies, it is now appropriate to evaluate it from the perspective of Pauline studies. This is a rather more complex exercise compared to the previous evaluation from the perspective of Jewish apocalyptic studies. Complexity arises for a few reasons. First, what is meant by *apocalyptic* can vary. Second, there are several voices contributing to the discussion, with multiple lines of exploration and explanation. Third, it is difficult to discern when Paul developed a line of thought derived from apocalyptic eschatology and when he is simply developing a line of thought. When such lines of thought diverge from observed apocalypticism within Judaism, how do we know if Paul is still being "apocalyptic" in these divergences, or if he is just being Pauline?

---

50. Collins, *Apocalyptic Imagination*, 264–67; Davies, *Paul Among the Apocalypses?*, 1–2.

The first problem of differing definitions has been addressed with distinctions between apocalyptic eschatology, apocalyptic literature, and an apocalyptic worldview having been clarified through Collins's (et al.) work with Jewish apocalyptic. Käsemann's tendency to equate "apocalyptic" with "eschatological" confuses the issue because one may want to say that Paul's eschatology *is* apocalyptic, but it is a mistake to say that apocalyptic is simply the same thing as eschatology. There are, after all, non-apocalyptic eschatological modes. So, apocalyptic should be regarded as one type of eschatology rather than a synonym for it.

The second problem has more or less been addressed in §15.2 above, which offers a summary of the major contributors and how they relate to one another. While it is not the case that all contributors say the same things, there is a common core that keeps their approach to Paul somewhat unified. This core includes the cosmological-dominion structure of all reality, the conceptualization of sin as an evil agency and dominion, and the vertical dimension of God's victorious intervention into the world through Christ in order to liberate humanity from its slavery to the dominion of sin and death.

The third problem of figuring out whether Paul develops apocalyptic thinking in fresh ways when he diverges from observed apocalypticism or just develops his own thoughts has no straightforward answer and is beyond the scope of this inquiry. The chief difficulty here is that we cannot assume that there is a difference between "Paul" and "apocalyptic Paul." Indeed, to posit such a distinction begs the question. Yet by the same token, we cannot assume that any new thinking is by default apocalyptic just because Paul is an apocalyptic thinker. That introduces a circular argument.

One way forward is to compare the ways in which the apocalypticism espoused by Pauline studies differs from that of Jewish apocalyptic studies. First, Käsemann's claim that the righteousness of God (δικαιοσύνη θεοῦ; Rom 1:17; 3:21) represents God's sovereignty over the world revealing itself in Jesus has little to do with the elements of Jewish apocalyptic eschatology discussed thus far. Of course, the revelation of God's sovereignty in Jesus is an apocalyptic idea, but associating this directly with the righteousness of God does not seem to find support in Collins and Davies's articulation of Jewish apocalyptic eschatology. This does not mean that Käsemann is incorrect—perhaps this is an example of Paul developing his own line of apocalyptic eschatology—but it is not possible to prove the point either way.

Second, Campbell's conclusion that Paul is not interested in a covenantal, "horizontal" soteriology because of his apocalyptic interest in the "vertical" intervention of God into this present world does not seem to find support in Collins and Davies's articulation of Jewish apocalyptic eschatology. While apocalyptic eschatology certainly does focus on the "vertical" intervention of God, there is little evidence that this therefore means that "horizontal" concerns are dispelled. It is not clear that these should be mutually exclusive.[51] This observation affirms N. T. Wright's assessment that Paul's vertical apocalyptic eschatology does not contradict the horizontal covenantal themes that are self-evidently prominent in his thought.

15.5.1 Conclusion

The apocalypticism expounded within Pauline studies is closely aligned with the apocalypticism articulated from within Jewish apocalyptic studies. Paul's use of mystery language, the coming of the Son of Man, the two-age eschatology, the epistemology of revealed knowledge, and the soteriology of victory each resonate across both schools. There is little doubt that Paul reveals himself to be an apocalyptic thinker with an apocalyptic, eschatological outlook. As Sumney states, "apocalyptic ideas and language pervade Paul's thought and are indispensable for his theology."[52]

But there are some points of difference, as indicated above. The notion of the righteousness of God as an apocalyptic motif does not find support in the Jewish apocalyptic tradition. Moreover, the supposed incompatibility of "vertical" and "horizontal" concerns within apocalyptic eschatology is unfounded. There is no reason to suppose that Paul was unable to hold a covenantal, salvation-historical schema alongside his apocalyptic eschatology. Paul was both a covenantal and apocalyptic theologian.

15.6 Chapter Conclusion

This chapter has demonstrated that the relatively recent trend to regard Paul as an apocalyptic theologian is well-founded. Though Paul authored no apocalypses, his epistles reveal several indications of an apocalyptically shaped eschatology. This conclusion has been ascertained by assessing how well the eschatological characteristics of Jewish apocalyptic literature resonate with Paul's thought.[53]

---

51. Indeed, according to Goff, "the eschatological defeat of evil is often characterized not as a sharp break with history, but rather as one element of a larger divine plan that guides the unfolding of history, from creation to judgment, as in, for example, the Apocalypse of Weeks and the Animal Apocalypse" (Matthew Goff, "The Mystery of God's Wisdom, the Parousia of a Messiah, and Visions of Heavenly Paradise: 1 and 2 Corinthians in the Context of Jewish Apocalypticism," in Reynolds and Stuckenbruck, *Jewish Apocalyptic Tradition*, 176).

52. Jerry L. Sumney, "'In Christ There Is a New Creation': Apocalypticism in Paul," *PRSt* 40.1 (2013): 36. See also David N. Scholer, "'The God of Peace Will Shortly Crush Satan under Your Feet' (Romans 16:20a): The Function of Apocalyptic Eschatology in Paul," *ExAud* 6 (1990): 53–61.

53. On the question to what extent *Greek* eschatology resonates with Paul's, see George van Kooten, Oda Wischmeyer, and N. T. Wright, "Quaestiones Disputatae: How Greek was Paul's Eschatology?," *NTS* 61 (2015): 239–53.

Paul's use of *mystery* language, the coming of the Son of Man, urging to be watchful and alert, a two-age eschatology, an epistemology of revealed knowledge, and a soteriology of victory are all hallmarks of Paul's literature, and each resonates with an apocalyptic eschatology. The only questionable claim from the perspective of Jewish apocalyptic studies is the *imminence* of the coming of the Son of Man, since the relevant texts may not necessarily convey the imminence that has long been associated with them.

From the perspective of Pauline studies, the two most questionable elements regarding Paul's apocalypticism are the righteousness of God as an apocalyptic motif and the rejection of any horizontal, covenantal, salvation-historical concern within his thought. While the righteousness of God *may* be construed as an apocalyptic motif, this is difficult to prove since it has no grounding in wider Jewish apocalyptic literature. And the rejection of horizontal elements in Paul's apocalyptic eschatology is unfounded and in fact contradicts the plainly salvation-historical shape of Paul's thought world.

Chapter 16

The Age to Come

16.1 Introduction

This chapter explores the age to come, also known as the eschaton, which in one sense has already broken into the present age, but in another sense has not yet come to fruition. Once this present age is drawn to a close, then the competing new age alone will remain for all eternity. The last day will be marked by the coming of Christ, who will raise the dead and initiate the judgment and destruction of evil. Believers will be raised with glorious, immortal bodies, no longer subject to death and decay, and henceforth qualified to share in the promised inheritance, the kingdom of Christ, and eternal life with Christ. The new age will also witness the renewal of the entire created order, which is not only the arena for the renewing work of God but also its object. Ultimately, the age to come will be an age of glory, which serves as Paul's source of hope as he navigates the trials of this present age.

The chapter will first review the relevant exegetical material found in part 2 of the book, focusing on the elements that point especially to the age to come. This will culminate in a synthesis of the insights related to the age to come, which will lead to the major discussions of the chapter concerning resurrection; wrath, condemnation, destruction, and hell; renewal and re-creation; and glory. Though all these topics have been discussed at various points already in the book, the discussions in this chapter will focus on unresolved questions arising from the exegetical explorations, as well as attempt to draw certain strands of thought together.

16.2 The Two Realms and the Age to Come

Chapter 3 explored Paul's eschatological framework of two realms or two ages. There we saw that the current combative relationship between the two opposing dominions will give way so that only one realm will remain in the age to come. This is implicit in Romans 5:21—sin reigned in death, but grace will reign through righteousness resulting in eternal life. The reign of sin belongs to the past, while the future will embody the reign of grace. Salvation is nearer since the night is nearly over; believers are to reject the darkness and wear armor of light in anticipation of the end of the realm of darkness (Rom 13:11–12). Likewise, the rulers of this age are coming to nothing (1 Cor 2:6), when Christ hands over the kingdom to God the Father (1 Cor 15:24). The visible features belonging to this current age are temporary, while the unseen qualities that pertain to the age to come are eternal (2 Cor 4:18). The present reign of Christ over every ruler, authority, power, and dominion is seen in this age and also in the age to come (Eph 1:21). Christ's elevation and rule have been established but are not yet consummated—the age to come will mark their consummation.

16.3 The Parousia and the Age to Come

Chapter 4 explored the arrival of Christ. There we saw that the revelation of Christ will mark the day of Christ (1 Cor 1:7–8), on which he will bring to light those things hidden in darkness (1 Cor 4:5). The coming of Christ will effect the resurrection of those in Christ (1 Cor 15:23), transforming believers' humble bodies into the likeness of his glorious body (Phil 3:20–21; Col 3:4). At his arrival, Christ will rescue believers from the coming wrath (1 Thess 1:10), and they will stand in his presence (2:19) and in the presence of God the Father (3:13). At his arrival Christ will take vengeance on those who don't know God or obey the gospel of Christ, subjecting them to the penalty of eternal destruction (2 Thess 1:7–9). He will also destroy the lawless one with the breath of his mouth, bringing him to nothing (2:8).

The parousia marks the end of this current age, during which believers are to remain faithful as they await Christ's arrival (1 Cor 1:7–8; Phil 3:20; 1 Thess 1:9–10; 1 Tim 6:13–14; 2 Tim 4:1–2; Titus 2:12–13). On that day, Christ will reward such faithfulness (2 Tim 4:8).

16.4 The Last Day and the Age to Come

Chapter 5 addressed the last day. There we observed that the day of wrath is when God's righteous judgment will be revealed (Rom 2:5) in light of the unveiling of people's secrets (v. 16). Those who reject God and Christ will suffer eternal destruction on that day, which will also inaugurate the glorification of the saints (2 Thess 1:9–10). On that day, those who have loved Christ's appearing will be awarded the crown of righteousness (2 Tim 4:8).

This day is nearly here, the night is nearly over, and so believers are to walk as in the daytime (Rom 13:12–13). But it will not come until the apostasy comes first and the man of lawlessness is revealed (2 Thess 2:3). That day marks the end, when Christ hands over the kingdom to God the Father, and it will mark the abolition of all competing authorities and powers (1 Cor 15:24).

16.5 Judgment and the Age to Come

Chapter 6 explored the theme of judgment. There we saw that final judgment will come after the end of this present age at the inauguration of the age to come. God's righteous judgment will be revealed in the coming day of wrath, resulting in eternal life for some and wrath and anger to others (Rom 2:5–8; Eph 5:6; Col 3:6). Sowing to the flesh will reap destruction, while sowing to the Spirit results in eternal life in the age to come (Gal 6:8).

On that day, God will judge people's secrets (Rom 2:16; 1 Cor 4:5; 1 Tim 5:24–25), righteously inflicting wrath as he judges the world (Rom 3:5–6, 19)—both the living and the dead (2 Tim 4:1). He will take vengeance on those denying God and Christ (2 Thess 1:8). When that time comes, all people will stand before the judgment seat of God, each giving an account of himself or herself (Rom 14:10–12; 2 Cor 5:10). But Christ strengthens believers so that they will be blameless on that day of judgment (1 Cor 1:8; 1 Thess 3:13) and rescues them from the coming wrath (1 Thess 1:10; 5:9). On that day, the righteous judge will give the crown of righteousness to all who have loved his appearing (2 Tim 4:8).

16.6 Resurrection in the Age to Come

Chapter 7 concerned the theme of resurrection. There it was observed that the age to come begins with resurrection of believers subsequent to the coming of Christ. Being united to Christ in his death ensures union with him in his resurrection (Rom 6:5). The age to come is the embodiment of the realm of Christ, which now stands in opposition to the realm of Adam and results in the resurrection of those in Christ (1 Cor 15:22). The resurrection of believers to incorruptibility is necessary for access to the kingdom of Christ, since untransformed flesh and blood cannot inherit it (1 Cor 15:42–50, 52–53). Christ will transform our humble bodies into the likeness of his glorious body by the same power that will enable him to subject everything to himself in the age to come (Phil 3:21). The glory of Christ will be shared with resurrected believers when he appears (Col 3:4). Those already dead in Christ will be the first to rise at the coming of Christ (1 Thess 4:16).

The physical, bodily resurrection of believers is anticipated by their spiritual resurrection ahead of time (Eph 2:5–6; Col 2:13). These two resurrections are mapped on to both eschatological ages—the spiritual resurrection exists in this current age before the age to come arrives. When it arrives, the spiritual resurrection will be met with physical resurrection so that each person will be whole and wholly raised.

16.7 Eternal Life in the Age to Come

Chapter 8 dealt with the topic of eternal life. There we saw that the age to come is characterized by unending relationship with Christ. Eternal life is the outcome of sanctification and is the gift of God in Christ (Rom 6:22–23), through justification and grace (Titus 3:7). While a gift, it is also contingent on putting to death the deeds of the body (Rom 8:13) and sowing according to the Spirit (Gal 6:8).

In one sense, eternal life is simply a continuation in the age to come of life together with Christ that may be enjoyed now, while awake (living) or asleep (dead; 1 Thess 5:10). But in the age to come this life with Christ will be with eternal glory (2 Tim 2:10–11).

16.8 Inheritance in the Age to Come

Chapter 9 explored the theme of inheritance. There we observed that Jews and gentiles who believe in Christ are made the children of Abraham and are therefore partakers in the promises to Abraham (Rom 4:13–14; Gal 3:18; 4:29). Furthermore, believers are heirs of God and coheirs with Christ if they suffer with him and are then glorified with him (Rom 8:17) on the basis of justification and grace (Titus 3:7). Flesh and blood are unable to inherit the kingdom of God; thus resurrection to immortal, incorruptible bodies is a necessary precursor to receiving the inheritance promised to the children of Abraham (1 Cor 15:50).

The notion of inheritance naturally relates to the two-age structure of Paul's eschatology since it is essentially a promise-fulfillment motif. The inheritance is promised in this present age with its fulfillment seen entirely in the age to come. That fact reveals the importance of the Spirit as a deposit guaranteeing the inheritance belonging to the age to come (Eph 1:14).

16.9 New Creation in the Age to Come

Chapter 10 concerned the new creation. There we saw that the created order is not only the arena of God's work but is also its object, as the entirety of creation will be renewed and restored in the age to come. The creation eagerly awaits God's sons and daughters to be revealed so that it will be set free from bondage to decay into the glorious freedom of God's children (Rom 8:19–21). This means that the fate of creation is intertwined with that of humanity, and that its renewal is contingent on the revelation of God's children in the age to come.

While the renewal of the created order can only begin with the age to come, believers are themselves already new creations in Christ (2 Cor 5:17; Gal 6:15; Eph 2:10). In this way, the renewal of believers anticipates the renewal of the whole creation. The current enthronement of Christ also anticipates the age to come in that his rule over creation has been established (Eph 1:10) but has yet to be fully manifested.

16.10 Israel in the Age to Come

Chapter 11 addressed the nation of Israel. There we saw that its place in the age to come depends on a few interpretative decisions within Romans 9–11. Paul argues that not all out of Israel are Israel, nor are all of Abraham's children really his descendants (9:6–7), which strongly suggests a reconstitution of what is meant by the term *Israel*. Indeed, true Israel is the faithful remnant, defined by the grace of God (9:8; 11:5). This means that Paul does not endorse the expectation that national or ethnic Israel will be restored in the age to come, or prior to its coming. The "Israel" that will enjoy God's blessings in the age to come is the remnant that exists by grace rather than by ethnic heritage, and it is marked by faith in Christ rather than by circumcision. In other words, the Israel of the age to come consists of Jews who believe in their messiah, Jesus.

16.11 Glory in the Age to Come

Chapter 12 explored the concept of glory. There we saw that the highest glory of the age to come is glory itself—the glory of God in Christ, shared with his people (Col 3:4; 2 Thess 2:14; 2 Tim 2:10). The hope of this glory to come causes believers to rejoice in this present age (Rom 5:2). Indeed, present sufferings cannot be compared to the glory to come (8:17–18; 2 Cor 4:17), which will begin with resurrection in glory (1 Cor 15:43; Phil 3:21) and will include a share in God's glorious inheritance (Eph 1:18).

The coming of Christ will inaugurate the age to come with the appearing of his glory (Titus 2:13). Then every tongue will confess that Christ is Lord, to the glory of God the Father (Phil 2:11), and Christ will be glorified by his saints (2 Thess 1:10). The glory of God will endure forever (Rom 11:36; 16:27; Gal 1:5; Phil 3:20; 1 Tim 1:17; 2 Tim 4:18).

16.12 Hope and the Age to Come

Chapter 13 dealt with the theme of hope. There we saw that Paul's life is shaped by his hope for the age to come. The hope of the future glory of God is a cause for rejoicing (Rom 5:2; 12:12), enables patience (8:25) and endurance (15:4; 1 Thess 1:3), and is powered by the Holy Spirit (Rom 15:13; Gal 5:5). Hope in Christ is primarily for the age to come (Col 1:5); it is hope for future glory

(1:27; Titus 2:13). If it were for this life only, believers should be pitied above all else (1 Cor 15:19). Paul prays that believers will understand the hope that accompanies their calling (Eph 4:4), since they are called to a glorious future inheritance (1:18), salvation (1 Thess 5:8), and eternal life (Titus 1:2; 3:7).

16.13 Synthesis

The age to come is the object of Paul's hope. It is in the age to come that judgment and justice are exercised, the dead are raised, evil is destroyed, the creation is renewed, and the saints receive their glorious inheritance. The age to come will be characterized by the eternal glory of God in Christ, which is shared with those in Christ. They will live with Christ for all eternity.

Paul's two-realm, two-ages eschatological framework is not permanent; when the day of the Lord comes, the realm of Adam, the old age, will give way so that only the realm of Christ, the new age, will remain. As such, the reign of sin will end as grace will reign supreme, just as the present, invisible enthronement of Christ will transition to his future, visible rule over all creation. The promise of inheritance, guaranteed by the Spirit, will find its fulfillment in the age to come.

The age to come will dawn with the arrival of Christ, who will raise the dead in Christ and exact the judgment of evil and the salvation of believers. That day will involve the unveiling of secrets kept hidden, the rewarding of faithfulness, and the glorification of the saints. Having been resurrected to immortal, incorruptible bodies, those in Christ will have become qualified to inherit the kingdom of Christ. Their experience of eternal life in the age to come will be a continuation of life with Christ that has already begun in the present age, but in the future it will be accompanied by eternal glory.

All this will occur within the context of a renewed created order. The creation will be as much the object of restoration in the age to come as it is the arena for God's restoring activity. Its fate is woven together with the fate of humanity so that the renewal of creation is contingent on the renewal, resurrection, and freedom of the children of God.

Above all, the age to come is the age of glory. Glory is the most defining characteristic of the age to come, and Paul regards it as the ultimate goal of everything. It puts present suffering and brokenness into context, as the hope of future glory far outweighs whatever disappointments and conflicts characterize the present age. Christ will appear with glory, he will be glorified by all humanity (especially believers), and the glory of God in Christ will endure forever. The most remarkable feature of the glory of Christ is that he will share it with those in him in the age to come. It is a relational glory, an unselfish glory, and a glory of eternal beauty and majesty.

16.14 Resurrection

It ought to be clear by now that resurrection stands at the very center of Paul's eschatological convictions, resonating strongly with Jewish tradition.[1] While the resurrection of Christ cannot be separated out from his death and ascension (see ch. 14 above), it nevertheless bears the most eschatological weight due to the way in which it sets apart the age to come from the present age. As argued above, resurrection belongs to the age to come; it is, by definition, an event from the future. Christ's resurrection stands as the firstfruits of the resurrection of the dead, which is to take place at the end of this age and at the beginning of the age to come. Thus, the resurrection of Christ in the middle of time introduces the age to come while the present age is still in play, creating the eschatological framework of two ages overlapping at once, or the now-not-yet schema that runs throughout Paul's writings (and the rest of the NT).

The resurrection of Christ is also the key to the resurrection of believers in the age to come.[2] Their current state of spiritual resurrection will be met by the future state of bodily resurrection, so that each person will be whole again, and wholly resurrected. The nature of the resurrected body will follow the pattern of Christ's resurrection, so that believers will be raised immortal and imperishable, enabling them to inherit the kingdom of Christ. The humble condition of their bodies will be transformed to resemble his glorious body. This is made clear by the fact that Paul describes the bodies of resurrected believers, like that of Christ, as being "from God (Rom. 8.11), spiritual (1 Cor. 15.45), imperishable (Rom. 6.9), suffused with glory (2 Cor. 4.6; Phil. 3.21a; cf. Acts 22.6,11), powerful (Phil. 3.10, 21b), and heavenly (1 Cor. 15.49; 1 Thess. 4.16; cf. Acts 26.13, 19)."[3]

---

1. As reflected in texts such as Dan 12:2; Job 42:17 LXX; 1 En. 51.1–5; 91.10; 4Q385 2.5–8; 4Q521 2.2.12; 7.2.6; Ps. Sol. 3.12; Sib. Or. 4.181–82; 2 Bar. 21.23–24; 30.1–2; 42.7–8; 50.2–4; 4 Ezra 7.32; Apoc. Mos. 13.3 (according to some manuscripts); 41.2 (10.2; 28.4); LAB 3.10; and T. Job 4.9. See Holleman, *Resurrection and Parousia*, 87; White, "Paul's Cosmology," 103. For a survey of the various ways in which the Old Testament weaves together themes that culminate in the concept of resurrection, see Levenson, *Resurrection and the Restoration of Israel*, 98–200. Indeed, this means that "the expectation of a resurrection in Second Temple Judaism, when it does appear, was thus not a total novum. Rather, it was the end product of a centuries-long process by which these old traditions . . . coalesced" (218).

2. This is also an implication of the firstfruits imagery. As Harris comments, "Rather than distinguishing the resurrection of believers from the resurrection of Christ as though they are basically unrelated entities sharing some superficial similarity, we should perhaps view resurrection in its somatic aspect either as a single continuum, marked at one end by the resurrection of Christ and at the other end by the resurrection of believers, or as a single unit with the resurrection of believers proleptically or ideally involved in the resurrection of Christ" (Murray J. Harris, *Raised Immortal: The Relation between Resurrection and Immortality in New Testament Teaching* [London: Marshall Morgan & Scott, 1983], 106).

3. Harris, *Raised Immortal*, 124–25.

16.14.1 Resurrection and Cosmic Renewal

The liberation of the children of God will set the renewal of creation into motion, since it is bound to decay until the redemption of their bodies (Rom 8:19–23). The redemption of the bodies of the children of God is likewise grounded in the resurrection of Christ. Thus, though Paul does not explicitly draw the connection, it follows that the resurrection of Christ is the ground for the renewal of the entire created order.[4] His resurrection secures the resurrection of believers, redeeming their bodies, which in turn will signal the liberation and renewal of the creation.

The scope of the significance of the resurrection of Christ, then, goes well beyond the fate of humanity. It has universal, cosmic significance as it produces the renewal of all creation. Thus, Christ may be called the firstfruits of the resurrection in more than one sense. There is the sense that Paul intends in 1 Corinthians 15:20–23, with Christ as the firstfruits of human resurrection. But there is also the wider sense that sees Christ's resurrection as the first installment of the new creation. The resurrection of humanity will follow Christ as the firstfruits, and the renewal of creation will follow in turn.

16.14.2 The Nature of Resurrection Life

There is very little to inform our views about the nature of resurrection life. The most obvious element is the transformation that will take place from the humble, mortal body to the glorious, immortal body. Resurrected believers will be unthreatened by illness, injury, and decay. Resurrection bodies will not be susceptible to sin and the desires of fallen flesh. They will be fit for the age to come and for the inheritance of the kingdom of Christ. But what exactly that means—beyond the glorious, immortal nature of the resurrected body—is not something Paul talks about. We might therefore wonder how the future, resurrected body will relate physically to the current, earthly body. By analogy to the different yet same human body at different ages, Griffith muses,

> Since it is not easy to say what the relation is between the matter that constitutes my flesh now, at age fifty-eight, and the flesh that was mine at age twenty (it is certainly not that any of the cells present then are present now),[5] it will be no easier to specify the relation that obtains between the

---

4. This is in keeping with Jewish expectation within the Second Temple period—resurrection was linked to the belief that "God was about to make a new creation . . . the regeneration of the present world, with the rectification of wrongs and the vindication of the righteous" (Madigan and Levenson, *Resurrection*, 6–7).

5. Harris expounds this point: "Biochemists inform us that during a seven-year cycle the molecular composition of our bodies is completely changed. Even during our present life, then, the continuity between

resurrected and the devastated flesh in such a way as to make it reasonable to say that each body of flesh is mine. All that is necessary for Christian doctrine is that whatever that relation is, it is taken to obtain also between the devastated and the resurrected flesh. Your resurrected flesh will be as intimate with your devastated flesh as that flesh is with the flesh that was yours two decades ago.[6]

We might suppose that Paul assumes whatever information can be gleaned regarding the resurrection of Christ from the oral traditions (since the Gospels had not yet been written) also pertains to the resurrection bodies of believers. Since we will be like him, as Paul says in 1 Corinthians 15:48–49, we will share the same bodily characteristics. For instance, Jesus was recognizable to his disciples (even if not always immediately; cf. Luke 24:16). He could still eat food (Luke 24:41–42; John 21:12–13). He could be touched and had flesh and bones (Luke 24:39–40). He could disappear from sight (24:31) and appear within a locked room (John 20:19, 26).[7] If Paul's thought at 1 Corinthians 15:48–49 is to be taken seriously, there are grounds for assuming that resurrected believers will share such traits, though Paul does not explicitly articulate as much.

Beyond the characteristics of the resurrected body, we know that Paul imagines resurrection life to be one of fellowship with Christ. Indeed, the point of eternal life is not so much that believers will live without end, but that they will live with Christ without end. Ultimately, eternal life is to be understood relationally. Resurrection life is also one of glory. Believers will give eternal glory to God in Christ, while also sharing in that glory. Since resurrected bodies will be glorious, like Christ's resurrected body, we might say they are bodies fit for glory.[8] Believers will be resurrected with bodies that can live together with Christ eternally and share in his glory eternally. They will be bodies for relational, eternal glory.

16.14.3 A General Resurrection from the Dead?

So far in this chapter we have only addressed the resurrection of believers. The Jewish expectation of a general resurrection of the dead—of *all* people—has

---

the body now possessed and the body possessed seven years ago resided in personality, not materiality" (Harris, *Raised Immortal*, 126).

6. Griffiths, *Decreation*, 49. Similarly, Harris writes: "Just as there is an historical continuity—an identity—between our present body and the body we had at birth, so there will be an historical continuity—an identity of identifiable personal characteristics—between the present body and the resurrection body. One and the same person finds expression in two successive but different types of body" (Harris, *Raised Immortal*, 126).

7. Harris, *Raised Immortal*, 53.

8. Tappenden refers to this as "an angelomorphic glory-body" (Frederick S. Tappenden, *Resurrection in Paul: Cognition, Metaphor, and Transformation*, ECL 19 [Atlanta: SBL Press, 2016], 120).

not yet been explored. The reason for this—it must be admitted—is that Paul nowhere speaks about the general resurrection of the dead. Every reference to resurrection in Paul's canonical letters refers either to the resurrection of Christ or the resurrection of those in Christ.

What does this mean? What should we do with this insight? There are really only two options. First, we may suppose that Paul only believed in the resurrection of the righteous and had no place in his thought for non-righteous resurrection. This makes certain sense for Paul, since we have already argued that resurrection is the sign of vindication or justification in the face of judgment. Therefore, there can only be room for the resurrection of the righteous because only the righteous are resurrected. But this contradicts one strand of Jewish expectation of a general resurrection of the dead (Sib. Or. 4.181–84; LAB 3.10),[9] as well as biblical texts such as Daniel 12:2 and John 5:28–29. Daniel 12:2 speaks of resurrection either to eternal life or to eternal contempt, while John 5:28–29 refers to a resurrection of life and a resurrection of condemnation. A critical perspective might affirm that Paul contradicts these texts—the latter not even having been written by the time Paul writes. A different strand of Jewish expectation, however, envisages only the resurrection of the righteous (1 En. 91.9–10; Ps. Sol. 3.11–12).[10]

Second, we may be more cautious and admit only that Paul does not speak of a general resurrection. It does not mean he did not believe in one.[11] As we know, his occasional and unsystematic writings are letters to specific congregations addressing specific situations, with only Romans and Ephesians being more general in nature. Yet even these two general letters cannot be understood as comprehensive, since we can easily find material in Paul's other letters that is not included in Romans and Ephesians. So it is entirely possible for Paul to have believed in the general resurrection of the dead without ever mentioning it.[12]

But it is not unreasonable to ask why, then, does Paul not speak of it? At all? Is it unreasonable to claim that Paul simply did not speak of the general resurrection from the dead even though he believed in it? With this question in mind, it is worth noting that only one New Testament author mentions the general resurrection of the dead, and only once at that (John 5:28–29).[13] It is

---

9. Holleman, *Resurrection and Parousia*, 126.
10. Holleman, *Resurrection and Parousia*, 126.
11. Fee, *First Epistle to the Corinthians*, 835n.181.
12. Indeed, "the fact that Paul does not mention a resurrection of the non-Christians here, need not mean that he did not reckon with it at all" (Holleman, *Resurrection and Parousia*, 54).
13. Even Martha's belief that her brother Lazarus would rise again on the last day does not necessarily refer to a general resurrection from the dead but could easily refer only to the resurrection of the righteous (John 11:24).

not a theme of great importance to the New Testament writers, even though their acceptance of it would have been expected—if it is accepted that Jesus himself uttered the words recorded in John 5:28–29. The oral tradition of Jesus's teaching would have included his belief in the general resurrection of the dead. Thus, those writing with apostolic authority would want to conform to such a belief. All this is simply to say that it is not unreasonable to conclude that Paul *did* believe in the general resurrection of the dead, even though he did not write about it in his extant letters.

The only hint that *may* support an unexplicit belief in the general resurrection of the dead is found in Philippians 2:10–11,[14] that *at the name of Jesus every knee will bow—in heaven and on earth and under the earth—and every tongue will confess that Jesus Christ is Lord, to the glory of God the Father.* But for this text to offer such support, it must be assumed that the bowing of every knee and confessing of every tongue involves the knees and tongues of *resurrected* bodies. This is not an unreasonable assumption given that pre-resurrected, disembodied souls are not capable of such feats (having neither knees nor tongues, assuming that these should be understood literally) and that Paul's scope is everyone in heaven, on earth, and under the earth—so that he cannot be referring only to human beings who happen to be still living when Jesus comes. Clearly Paul envisages the living and the dead acknowledging the lordship of Christ. And if the dead are included, then it makes best sense to understand them as the resurrected dead (given the knees and tongues). Therefore, in this text Paul *may* let slip his conviction that all of humanity will be raised at the coming of Christ.

But what about the point raised earlier (above), that a righteous-only resurrection makes sense of Paul's theological convictions? After all, resurrection is the sign of vindication or justification in the face of judgment. What does a general resurrection from the dead do to Paul's conception of the relationship between resurrection and justification? What does it do to his belief in Christ as the firstfruits of the resurrection? The most plausible response is to take the cue from Jesus in John 5:28–29. Since he expects a resurrection of life and a resurrection of condemnation, it seems that not all resurrections will be created equal. It is not difficult to map Paul's resurrection of the righteous onto Jesus's resurrection of life. And since Paul also believes in the condemnation of the unrighteous, this maps onto Jesus's resurrection of condemnation. After all, the relationship between judgment and resurrection is traditional: "People are

---

14. While Harris entertains the possibility that 1 Cor 15:22—*As in Adam all die, so in Christ shall all be brought to life*—refers to a general resurrection, this is not plausible since the text explicitly addresses those "in Christ" (Harris, *Raised Immortal*, 173).

raised in order to be judged."[15] Thus, the only missing piece of the puzzle is that Paul does not stop to say that the condemnation of the unrighteous will entail their resurrection leading to condemnation. As for Christ the firstfruits of the resurrection, this will refer to the resurrection of the righteous, since only those in Christ (= those made righteous in Christ) will follow in the likeness of his resurrection.

16.15 Judgment and Justification

Paul considers the universal judgment of all sin and evil as an inescapable feature of the age to come. The coming day of God's wrath will divide all people either for eternal life with Christ or wrath and anger apart from him. The living and the dead will stand before the judgment seat of God, and their secrets (both good and bad) will be revealed. Believers will not be exempt from judgment, but they will be rescued from God's wrath, being found blameless in Christ.

While the day of God's wrath is no doubt a terrifying and sobering reality, ultimately it is a good thing that Paul anticipates with eager expectation. It is good because justice will be done. It is good because it will mark the end of evil. It is good because it clears the way for the renewal of creation, which will never again be tainted by evil and will never again see the decay that accompanies sin.

Yet the notion of the judgment of believers is a fraught one. If believers have already been justified, as Paul insists,[16] what role then can final judgment take? Since justification is the positive verdict in the face of judgment, what is the nature of the judgment through which believers must pass on that day? Is it judgment "according to works," as Paul says, or are believers justified according to faith in Christ, as Paul also says? Since Paul says both things, the answer must be yes. The point is that judgment according to works and justification by faith are not mutually exclusive in Paul's perspective—he "admits and retains the principle of reward within his eschatological scheme."[17] The question then becomes, how are we to understand the relationship of these two things that seem to stand in such strong tension with each other?

---

15. Holleman, *Resurrection and Parousia*, 79.
16. Though this can be overstated, as Kwon seeks to demonstrate with respect to Galatians: "There is nothing in Galatians that suggests justification clearly to be a present reality, while there is clear evidence for its future eschatological nature" (Yon-Gyong Kwon, *Eschatology in Galatians: Rethinking Paul's Response to the Crisis in Galatia*, WUNT 2/183 [Tübingen: Mohr Siebeck, 2004], 70).
17. Vos, *Pauline Eschatology*, 67. "Paul is not nearly so queasy about the idea of 'reward' as some of his zealous post-Reformation followers" (Wright, *Paul and the Faithfulness of God*, 1080). On the whole question of heavenly rewards, the most thorough study is Josef Ton, *Suffering, Martyrdom, and Rewards in Heaven* (New York: Lanham, 1997). Tracing through Isaiah, Daniel, Job, the intertestamental literature, and the New Testament, he focuses on Paul in ch. 7.

The tension can be resolved in two equally incorrect and dangerous directions. On the one hand, justification by faith can be so emphasized that there is no room for any kind of judgment or accountability to God. Believers think they will breeze through judgment because they are already justified by Christ and their sins will not be held against them in any sense. But this ignores Paul's serious warnings—to believers!—that what they do matters, and it will matter on the day of judgment. On the other hand, judgment according to works can be so emphasized that there is no room for confidence on the day of judgment. Justification in Christ might provide the way out of the negative outcome of judgment, but the experience of God's judgment nevertheless incites terror in the heart of the believer. This also seems to ignore an important strand of Paul's teaching, namely, the assurance of salvation but also *the assurance of a positive standing with God.* That is, salvation from God's wrath should not be viewed as a lucky escape from a God who is otherwise upset with a person. Paul's expectation of his own judgment is much more positive than that; he fundamentally believes that God is for him and that their encounter on that day will be joyous and will include the bestowal of reward.[18] Even while he still considers himself the chief of sinners (1 Tim 1:15)!

There are two better ways to navigate the tension between judgment according to works and justification by faith in Christ. The first is to recognize the relational side of judgment. Paul's excitement to stand before the Lord suggests that believers ought to think of that day as one of personal encounter with God the Father and with Christ. As a personal encounter, the process of judgment is not some kind of transaction or abstract evaluation. If God is Father, and if Christ is Lord, the believer will experience judgment in a personal way. This might help to understand why Paul warns believers about actions that will negatively affect them on judgment day. They will need to give an account to God for what they have done. And even if their salvation is secure in Christ, there will be "a conversation" with one's heavenly Father about these things. Just as any child knows, such "a conversation" with their father can be just as unpleasant as other consequences—or worse. It is the relational element that makes it so. There is a shame to be felt in the presence of someone who expects

---

18. Ton writes, "The suspicion of an apparent conflict between Paul's teaching on justification by faith and his teaching on rewards has been plaguing Protestant theologians ever since Luther sparked the Reformation with his understanding of justification by faith alone and grace alone. Protestant theologians have been suspicious of an inconsistency in Paul's theology in this regard precisely because they have not had a clear understanding of the content of heavenly rewards. When the rewards are seen for what they are, that is, when they are seen as the receiving of our inheritance, which entails being put in charge over God's possessions and being given higher or lower positions of ruling and authority in the kingdom of heaven, then it becomes obvious that God does not expect His children to *earn* these rewards" (Ton, *Suffering, Martyrdom, and Rewards in Heaven,* 168).

more, who expects a higher standard, and whom you have let down by your actions. In the same way, believers will experience some kind of relational discomfort as they give account of their sins to their heavenly Father. This prospect ought to be enough to deter believers away from certain actions—if they really care about pleasing their Father. A believer who really does not care what God thinks of them has not really embraced the fatherhood of God and may not be a genuine believer after all.

The second way to navigate the tension between judgment according to works and justification by faith in Christ is to recognize the serious weight Paul gives to *transformation*.[19] The Spirit of God produces fruit within believers and sowing according to the Spirit reaps eternal life. Christ also strengthens believers so that they will be blameless on the day of judgment. After being re-created in Christ Jesus for good works, believers will walk in those works prepared by God. Thus, the genuine believer who has walked according to the Spirit in good works will have good works to show on the day of judgment. But what about their failures after having received the Spirit? Clearly Paul does not imagine some kind of sinless perfectionism among believers—consider the Corinthians!—otherwise the second half of most of his letters would be irrelevant. Paul anticipates believer-failure, warns against it, and encourages confession of sin and repentance. Where there is forgiveness for sins, there can be no condemnation.

So, we have at least these two notions that help us understand how judgment can be according to works and can function as a deterrent for believers behaving badly, while they also enjoy security and assurance of salvation in Christ. There is no doubt that believers will be forgiven their sins and will escape the wrath of God because of what Christ has accomplished through his death, resurrection, and ascension. But there is nevertheless a warning to be heard that believers will give an account to their heavenly Father for the things done in the body. Believers should avoid making their judgment more uncomfortable and instead desire to please their Father in heaven. While they will fail and continue to sin against God in this life, their sins are forgiven through repentance and faith.

16.15.1 Resurrection before Justification?

While resurrection and judgment are "the two overpowering events in the drama of eschatology,"[20] it is not entirely clear whether Paul envisions the

---

19. So Barclay: "The incongruous and unconditioned gift in Christ is not also unconditional, in the sense of expecting no alteration in the recipients of the gift. God's grace is designed to produce obedience, lives that perform, by heart-inscription, the intent of the Law" (John M. G. Barclay, *Paul and the Gift* [Grand Rapids: Eerdmans, 2015], 492).

20. Vos, *Pauline Eschatology*, 72.

resurrection of the dead *before* judgment or *after* judgment. On the one hand, it makes sense to view resurrection preceding judgment, since judgment will require people to stand before the judgment seat of Christ. Indeed, texts such as 1 Thessalonians 4:16 seem to imply that the resurrection of the dead in Christ will be immediate upon his coming. Moreover, this would be in keeping with the Jewish notion of the general resurrection of the dead, which is supposed to precede final judgment. On the other hand, resurrection is also regarded as the sign of vindication in judgment, so that it also makes sense that judgment should precede resurrection. Again, Jewish expectation included a general resurrection of all people preceding judgment, followed by the vindication of the righteous (resurrection to life) and the condemnation of the wicked (resurrection to damnation).

Part of this ambiguity is due to an apparent lack of reference to the general resurrection of the dead in Paul's writings (on this, see above). All references to the resurrection of the dead at the coming of Christ are to the resurrection of those in Christ. Paul offers virtually no hint that unbelievers will also be resurrected for judgment. But, as discussed above, Paul's letters were occasional, not systematic, nor do we have all the letters he wrote. His lack of reference to the general resurrection of the dead, and the resurrection of the unrighteous in particular, does not mean he did not believe in such a thing. Indeed, given his overarching purpose of encouraging believers to persevere until the coming of Christ, he may simply have spoken of the resurrection of believers because that was the expectation he wished to impress upon them. The fate of unbelievers was not his focus.

Nevertheless, without reference to the general resurrection of the dead, the question before us is made more difficult. If we suppose that Paul *did* endorse a general resurrection, he probably imagined the raising of all dead in anticipation of judgment. This judgment would then determine the "type" of resurrection that each person would have been raised for. Those who will face condemnation will move into the resurrection of condemnation, while those who have escaped God's wrath will move into the resurrection of life and righteousness. Paul does not tease these events out into a narrative but rather compresses them so that at the return of Christ, the dead in Christ are raised to eternal life with him.

Since the resurrection of the righteous will see their bodies conformed to the image of the resurrected body of Christ, it seems that a two-part resurrection narrative would be necessary. If all the dead are raised for judgment, and many will face the resurrection to condemnation, they will clearly not receive glorious, immortal resurrection bodies in the likeness of Christ. Their fate is to be excluded from eternal fellowship with Christ, so their resurrection bodies will not be fitted to that future as the bodies of the righteous will be. So, if there is a general resurrection of the dead prior to judgment and then a separating out of those resurrected to life and those resurrected to condemnation, it follows that there is some kind of two-stage resurrection process. Of course, all of this can bear no more weight than tentative speculation, but perhaps in the general resurrection of the dead, all the dead are raised in the same way in a preliminary fashion that enables them to appear before the judgment seat of Christ. This would not yet be the full-resurrection experience to glorious, immortal bodies that await the righteous. But it would be a genuine resurrection, nonetheless. Following the judgment, the righteous will then be transformed so that their resurrection fulfills the expectation of being raised like Christ, while the unrighteous will either remain the same or be changed in a negative sense, as they are consigned to the resurrection of condemnation.

Again, these details cannot be pressed, given that Paul does not address them. He does not speak explicitly of a general resurrection of the dead, nor does he provide an explanation as to how such a general resurrection would relate to the resurrection of the righteous. The foregoing thoughts merely ruminate on how these ideas can be fit together, and what sort of sequencing might take place among them. It is my sense that Paul's understanding of the resurrection of the righteous does not conflict with the Jewish expectation of a general resurrection, nor with the expectation of Jesus.

16.16 Wrath, Condemnation, Destruction . . . and Hell?

It may surprise some readers that Paul never mentions hell.[21] Certainly he speaks of God's wrath and anger, along with condemnation and destruction. But the usual terminology referring to "hell" is absent, and the concept is possibly absent also. Before this is explored further, some caveats must be raised. First, as discussed in relation to the general resurrection of the dead (see above, §16.14.3), the absence of discussion does not spell absence of belief. Just because Paul does not mention "hell" by any of its usual terms does not mean that he did not believe in it. Second, as a consequence of the first point, it is unnecessary to set Paul at odds with other New Testament voices, especially the voice of Jesus who speaks of hell more than anyone else. Most likely Paul never says anything to contradict the notion of hell, and what he *does* say about judgment and God's wrath may be seen to fit with it.

While the language of hell is absent in Paul's writings, is it true that the

---

21. Williamson, *Death and the Afterlife*, 152.

concept of hell is also missing? First, it is important to address what we mean by hell in the first place. In most of the ancient world, the realm of the dead (the righteous *and* wicked dead) was located in the underworld—Hades, Sheol, and Gehenna—but sometimes the underworld was regarded as reserved for the wicked dead, as their place of punishment.[22] In apocalyptic literature, the idea "of the punishment of the wicked in hell owes its origin and popularity to a problem of theodicy."[23] The damned are those who persecute God's people and those apostates who have escaped persecution by denying their faith. The suffering of the faithful and the triumph of their enemies demands a vindication of God's justice, thus "hell is then fundamentally a triumph for God's righteousness."[24] As Bauckham points out, in Enoch's tour of the seven heavens (2 En. 3–22), paradise and hell (that terminology is not used) are located in the third heaven (or viewed from there) and "are presented in parallel as, respectively, the place prepared for the righteous as an eternal inheritance (9:1) and the place prepared for the wicked as an eternal reward (10:4, 6)."[25] In 2 Enoch a strong emphasis is placed on the horror of the torments of Gehenna prepared for the wicked in the future.[26] Jewish belief held that the wicked are not actively punished immediately after death but are held in detention, awaiting punishment at the last judgment.[27] This view apparently changed in the first and second centuries after Christ, so that Christian belief held that the eternal punishment of the wicked begins immediately after death.[28] While much more can be said about the concept of hell as it developed through the Hebrew Scriptures, Second Temple literature, and the New Testament, a convenient shorthand will suffice here. In contemporary discussions, hell is normally understood as a place (?) of eternal, conscious torment for the wicked. It is an eternal punishment for the enemies of God, as they suffer his wrath without reprieve.

While Paul refers to the judgment of God's wrath at several points, there is no evidence that he views this wrath as being poured out for all eternity. But there is also no evidence that he expects the experience of God's wrath to be temporary. He simply does not specify the duration of the wrath of God. He also speaks of condemnation, but again he does not specify its duration either way. The third key term Paul uses is *destruction*. The normal sense of this word (ὄλεθρος or φθορά) refers to the ruination of a person or thing, naturally

---

22. Bauckham, *Fate of the Dead*, 10.
23. Bauckham, *Fate of the Dead*, 134.
24. Bauckham, *Fate of the Dead*, 134.
25. Bauckham, *Fate of the Dead*, 54.
26. Bauckham, *Fate of the Dead*, 56.
27. Bauckham, *Fate of the Dead*, 34.
28. Bauckham, *Fate of the Dead*, 34.

implying an endpoint of the destroying activity. Once a person or thing has been destroyed, the action of destroying ceases. That would be the natural way to read all the Pauline references to destruction—except one.

In 2 Thessalonians 1:9, Paul says that those who don't know God and who don't obey the gospel of Christ *will pay the penalty of eternal destruction from the Lord's presence and from his glorious strength*. This text has been discussed three times already, so we simply summarize the relevant findings in those places (see §§4.2; 5.2; 6.2). In short, Paul does not indicate whether he sees this *eternal destruction* (ὄλεθρον αἰώνιον) as an ongoing state of *being destroyed*—an eternal process of deconstruction—or that, once destroyed, these people will remain so for eternity. Either option is possible, though the phrase more naturally refers to the state of eternal destruction (ruined once and forever) rather than a state of eternally being destroyed (an unending process of destruction).

There is no indication of the duration of this destruction (immediate destruction vs. an eternal process of destruction), but one temporal indicator is found in the wider context—this will take place *on that day when he comes to be glorified by his saints and to be marveled at by all those who have believed* (v. 10). In other words, this eternal destruction will take place *on that day* when Christ comes. Again, this would seem to support the notion that the destruction will happen immediately (with eternal consequences)—*they will pay the penalty of eternal destruction from the Lord's presence and from his glorious strength* on that day (v. 9). While it could be argued that that day merely inaugurates the eternal process of destruction, this seems less likely.

Taking these factors into consideration, it seems that "eternal destruction" *may* support the notion of eternal, conscious torment, but it more likely does not add any support for it. It does not speak *against* the notion either, but it should be admitted that this text probably does not change the overall situation observed in Paul's writings—there is no direct, explicit teaching concerning hell.

16.16.1 ANNIHILATIONISM?

It is little wonder, then, that some interpreters might conclude that Paul would endorse a theology of annihilationism. Since he often speaks of destruction, it does not require much more work to conclude that the unbelieving and unrighteous will eventually be annihilated and come to nothing. Certainly, Paul's teachings about wrath, condemnation, and destruction could be made to fit annihilationism, though it is more difficult to make other parts of the New Testament fit into an annihilationist perspective. This does not mean that Paul was an annihilationist; it only means that his writings do not strongly counter that perspective.

Perhaps ironically, the strongest argument against annihilationism in Paul is found in 2 Thessalonians 1:9. If *eternal destruction* (ὄλεθρον αἰώνιον) refers to the eternal state of ruination (of having been destroyed, as suggested above), then it cannot also refer to annihilation. If someone is in a state of ruination *eternally*, then it seems they cannot become nothing at some point in time. If they become nothing, they can no longer exist in an eternal state of ruination. Nonexistence is incompatible with existence—whether ruined or not. There are only two ways in which annihilation is *not* contradicted by this eternal destruction. First is if we understand *destruction* to include *dissolution and disappearance*—the person is destroyed to the point of no longer existing. That would remove the tension between 2 Thessalonians 1:9 and the theory of annihilationism, but it smuggles in an idea that is not normally associated with ὄλεθρος (not to be conflated with φθορά, which *can* indicate the dissolution and disappearance of matter in organisms, for example).[29] Since dissolution and disappearance is not an attested sense of ὄλεθρος, this first option does not undo the tension between 2 Thessalonians 1:9 and annihilationism. Second, the other word in the phrase translated *eternal destruction*—αἰώνιον—may not offer an *eternal* qualifier to *destruction*, since it can refer simply to an age, era, or aeon.[30] If interpreted this way, the phrase suddenly no longer contradicts annihilationism.

Since it is virtually impossible to decide between these two well-attested meanings of αἰώνιος, the matter must remain unresolved. If ὄλεθρον αἰώνιον refers to *eternal destruction* (understood without the added sense of dissolution or disappearance, as above), then the phrase seems to stand against the notion of annihilationism. But if ὄλεθρον αἰώνιον refers to an era-bound destruction, then it does not contradict annihilationism but would instead offer the position further support.

While the textual evidence leaves the question of annihilationism open with respect to Paul, we may also consider the question from a wider theological perspective, such as that offered by Moltmann. As rehearsed in §2.14, Moltmann argues against annihilationism on the basis of its perceived incompatibility with the coming omnipresence of God. Being made to "disappear" is likened to the actions of murder squads within military dictatorships and does not fit with the creator God.[31] While we might like to affirm the notion that the creator God does not permanently destroy elements of his creation, we might also see his mercy expressed through bringing some things to an end rather than subject them to eternal torment.

---

29. BDAG 1054, §1.
30. BDAG 33.
31. Moltmann, *Coming of God*, 109.

From another perspective Griffiths regards annihilation as "hell under its proper name," since "any humans who arrive at it do so by failing to be resurrected for eternal life."[32] While the saved are temporarily disembodied during the intermediate state, the damned are permanently without flesh and thus suffer loss of self without the possibility of reversal. According to Griffiths, "the postmortem sufferings of the damned, those approaching nothing, undergo as discarnate souls progressively reduce those souls beyond the point at which reunion with flesh is possible, and at that point it will have become the case that those sufferings were hellish, hell-bound."[33]

Regardless, ultimate theological conclusions are not our priority here since the current study is interested in what Paul thought. Perhaps Paul would have regarded annihilationism as incompatible with God's creative mandate, but we cannot really know. As stated above, it seems we must leave the question of annihilationism unresolved so far as Paul is concerned. It is possibly compatible with his extant writings, but the evidence is inconclusive.

16.16.2 Universalism?

The other major question regarding the ultimate fate of those outside of Christ is that of universalism. The theologians Barth and Moltmann leave considerable room for such a conclusion. Barth advocates openness to the possibility that the "final threat" (of eternal hell) might unexpectedly be withdrawn as an expression of God's superabundant promise of the final deliverance of all people (see §2.5). While Barth acknowledges that the concept of universal reconciliation (= universal salvation) seems to stand in tension with what Scripture proclaims, it is not inappropriate to hope for it nonetheless, in view of God's unfailing compassion.[34]

Moltmann is less decisive regarding the biblical witness, claiming that both universal salvation and "a double outcome of judgment" are both well attested, and thus any conclusion cannot be reached on scriptural grounds (see §2.14). Moltmann affirms the reality of damnation but does not agree that it must be eternal because of the potential meaning of αἰώνιος to indicate an age or era rather than eternity (see above). Against the universalist position, Moltmann acknowledges that it may make God's grace "cheap grace" and impose bounds on God's freedom.[35] But in the end Moltmann advocates a transformative type of universalism in which the enemies of God undergo transformation to become

---

32. Griffiths, *Decreation*, 250.
33. Griffiths, *Decreation*, 250.
34. Barth, *Church Dogmatics*, IV/3.1, 477–78.
35. Moltmann, *Coming of God*, 242.

their true, created beings—as an expression of God remaining true to himself, not giving up any of that which he has created.[36]

A third type of universalism is that espoused by de Boer, who does not rely on theological considerations to resolve the issue, but instead appeals directly to Paul's writings (see §2.12). Romans 5:12–21 apparently insists that just as all of humanity is enslaved with Adam by the cosmological powers of sin and death, so it is liberated from them with Christ. "Again, by placing Christ over against Adam, Paul makes plain that Christ's work is as cosmic (= pertaining to all human beings) in its implications and consequences as Adam's initial trespass or disobedience. If all died because of Adam, all will be made alive because of Christ."[37] Humanity under Adam is incapable to evaluate, let alone accept, an "offer" of salvation and is thus reliant entirely on the decision and grace of God for salvation, which is applied to all humanity. Other Pauline texts have likewise been used by others to support the position of universalism, such as 1 Timothy 2:4.

Addressing de Boer's textual argument for universalism first, it seems that we are left with the classic conundrum of how to reconcile apparently contradictory texts. While it has already been noted that Paul nowhere speaks of "hell" in the sense of eternal, conscious torment, and he may not contradict the concept of annihilationism, Paul's support of, or opposition to, universalism depends on how we choose to reconcile certain texts.

A striking text that seems to contradict universalism is Romans 10:9–15:

> If you confess with your mouth, "Jesus is Lord," and believe in your heart that God raised him from the dead, you will be saved. 10 One believes with the heart, resulting in righteousness, and one confesses with the mouth, resulting in salvation. 11 For the Scripture says, "Everyone who believes on him will not be put to shame" 12 since there is no distinction between Jew and Greek, because the same Lord of all richly blesses all who call on him. 13 For everyone who calls on the name of the Lord will be saved. 14 How, then, can they call on him they have not believed in? And how can they believe without hearing about him? And how can they hear without a preacher? 15 And how can they preach unless they are sent? As it is written: How beautiful are the feet of those who bring good news.

This text raises several interesting points related to our question. Paul is clear that for a person to be saved, they must confess that "Jesus is Lord" and

---

36. Moltmann, *Coming of God*, 255.
37. Martinus C. de Boer, "Paul's Mythologizing Program in Romans 5–8," in Gaventa, *Apocalyptic Paul*, 9–10.

believe that God raised him from the dead (10:9). The same point is reiterated in the next verse (v. 10). Belief avoids shame (v. 11), and the Lord blesses those who call on him (v. 12). All who call on the name of the Lord will be saved (v. 13). But who can call on him if they have not believed, and how can they believe without hearing, and how can they hear apart from preaching? (v. 14). Paul's argument here means that he regards a conscious confession of faith as indispensable for salvation. Moreover, his belief in the indisputable importance of belief—and therefore of hearing the good news—accounts for Paul's personal urgency to preach and to make such news known. He is an evangelist because he regards the believing reception of his message to be the grounds on which a person may be saved. On the basis of this text, therefore, it is very difficult to believe that Paul would accept the notion that while those who believe will be blessed, all people—whether believing or not—will ultimately one day be saved. Unbelievers by definition do not believe, and they therefore do not confess that Jesus is Lord, nor do they call on the Lord for salvation.

We witness a direct confrontation when we square off Romans 10:9–15 against de Boer's universalist reading of Romans 5:12–21. We are thus faced with the matter raised above as to how to reconcile apparently contradictory texts. If we are committed to the possibility of noncontradiction, we will naturally need to interpret one text in light of the other (or others). It seems to me easiest to critique de Boer's interpretation of Romans 5:12–21 in light of Romans 10:9–15 rather than the other way around, since the logical progression outlined in the latter text gives little interpretative wriggle room. That is, it is difficult to read Romans 10:9–15 in any way other than is outlined above. On the other hand, it is possible to read Romans 5:12–21 in a nonuniversalist way, contrary to de Boer's interpretation.

Apart from the obvious parallelism between Adam and Christ that runs through the whole passage, the most universalist-sounding statement is found in Romans 5:18—*So then, as through one trespass there is condemnation for everyone, so also through one righteous act there is justification leading to life for everyone.* If taken at face value, the phrase *justification leading to life for everyone* certainly suits a universalist interpretation. But this must be balanced by the fact that Paul elsewhere insists on the necessity of being "in Christ" in order to benefit from his person and work—and believers are in him by faith. This is explicitly and implicitly affirmed in countless ways through Paul's writings.[38] It is therefore difficult to accept a face-value reading of this phrase, given that it seems to go against the general tenor of Paul's theology of union and participation in Christ. As such, we are compelled to read Paul's *justification leading to life for everyone*

---

38. See Campbell, *Paul and Union with Christ*.

in Romans 5:18 to refer to all who are in Christ by faith. Admittedly, such a reading creates an unbalanced parallelism when compared to the universality of those born in Adam, but it makes better sense of the statement in light of virtually everything else Paul says on the matter. As Dunn comments,

> Jesus's representative capacity before resurrection (sinful flesh—Rom 8:3) is different from his representative capacity after resurrection (spiritual body —1 Cor 15:44–45). All die. But only those "in Christ" experience the new creation (2 Cor 5:17). In short, as Last Adam Jesus represents only those who experience life-giving Spirit (1 Cor 15:45).[39]

Returning now to Barth's prescribed hope for a surprise universalist conclusion to judgment, perhaps it is inappropriate to criticize what others may or may not hope for. But Barth at least seems to conform to the reading of Paul endorsed here, in which the text speaks against a universalist outcome. Barth hopes and prays for one nonetheless, but he recognizes that his hope runs against the witness of the text.

As for Moltmann, his reading of the text is less settled, and he instead relies on theologizing based on the character and intent of God. Since God is creator, not destroyer, he will ultimately "recycle" the damnable elements of creation so that even they will enjoy a renewed place within the renewed creation. The closest textual support for such a notion within Paul's writings would be found in Colossians 1:20 and Ephesians 1:10. Both texts speak more or less of the same thing, namely (to use the language of Col 1:20), the reconciliation of all things—whether heavenly or earthly—to Christ. The crucial question is to what does *to reconcile* (ἀποκαταλλάξαι) in Colossians 1:20 and *to bring everything together* (ἀνακεφαλαιώσασθαι) in Ephesians 1:10 refer. The possible universalist reading would understand reconciliation to refer to the "friendly" reconciliation of all things to Christ, such that enmity is finally removed and all created things in heaven and earth are restored to peace with Christ in a purely positive sense. But "friendly" reconciliation is not the only kind. There is also the kind of reconciliation that occurs through the forceful cessation of hostilities, such as seen at the conclusion of war. This is the sense in which Nazi Germany was reconciled with the Allied Forces at the conclusion of World War II—Germany was reconciled through defeat and subjugation, and thus peace was achieved.

This "unfriendly" reconciliation is most likely the sense found in Colossians

---

39. J. D. G. Dunn, "Paul's Understanding of the Death of Jesus," in *Reconciliation and Hope: New Testament Essays on Atonement and Eschatology: Presented to L. L. Morris on His 60th Birthday*, ed. Robert Banks (Grand Rapids: Eerdmans, 1974), 131.

1:20 once it is read against 2:15. The former verse stipulates that the reconciliation of everything (whether heavenly or earthly) was achieved *by making peace through his blood, shed on the cross* (1:20b). Peace and reconciliation come through the violent act of the crucifixion of Christ. In the latter verse, we see that through the cross God *disarmed the rulers and authorities and disgraced them publicly; he triumphed over them in [Christ]* (2:15). Clearly then the peace and reconciliation achieved through the cross (1:20) includes the undermining and overthrow of hostile rulers and authorities. Peace comes through conquest and defeat. Thus, the kind of reconciliation that is achieved through the cross of Christ is that in which warring hostile forces are conquered and put into right order. The outcome of such reconciliation is the proper ordering of things. As Ephesians 1:10 expresses it, it involves everything being brought together under the headship of Christ. It does not necessarily mean that all warring factions miraculously become friends in the end, which is what universalism claims.

In the end, it does not seem possible to accept a universalist interpretation of Paul, notwithstanding de Boer's exegesis and the theologizing moves of Barth and Moltmann. Paul views peace and reconciliation as achieved through the violence of the cross of Christ, by which God has overthrown his enemies. They are subverted and put in their proper place under the rule of Christ. There is no evidence to suggest that such forces in the end become friendly toward God in Christ, as though their reconciliation reorients their desires and causes them to give allegiance to their ruler. Instead, they bow at his feet in the same way that an overthrown foe acknowledges his defeat at the hands of his enemy. If, as Moltmann suggests, God "recycles" such foes so that they are reoriented, Paul does not speak of it. Or to put it another way, if God is a universalist, Paul does not seem to know it.

16.17 Renewal and Re-creation

Paul does not imagine a new creation that will replace the old, as though there are two creations. For Paul, there is only one created order. Creation will be renewed to such an extent that it can be called "new," but it is not new in the sense of replacement but in the sense of renewal. But this understanding of the renewal of creation could be seen to contradict other biblical statements concerning the new heavens and the new earth, the apparent dissolution of the present creation, and the ushering in of a brand-new created order. Because Paul seems to stand in sharp contrast with other authors on this topic, we will explore it in some depth. We will consider Paul's theological support as found in Genesis 2–3 and Isaiah 65–66, as well as various texts found within Second Temple literature. Returning to the New Testament, we will then consider the voices of 2 Peter 3 and Revelation 19–22. While these texts have much in common with what we find in Paul, they also raise the question of continuity versus discontinuity. In order to vanquish evil, will the new creation replace an old creation that needs to be destroyed? Or will the new creation constitute a restoration and renewal of the old created order? In other words, does the destruction of evil come at the cost of the destruction of all creation?

As we have seen, Paul's eschatological vision includes the full sweep of creation, as all things in heaven and on earth will be renewed and centered around Christ. There is an inextricable link between the fate of humanity and that of creation, with the latter being subjected to decay because of the former, and it will only be released from its bondage once humanity has been restored. And this restoration can only occur in the wake of judgment.[40]

16.17.1 NEW-CREATION LANGUAGE

Paul's use of the expression *new creation*—which occurs only in 2 Corinthians 5:17 and Galatians 6:15 (but cf. Eph 2:10)—is informed by the Jewish background of the term. The Second Temple book that, according to Moyer Hubbard, best illuminates the perspective of the pre-Christian Paul is the book of Jubilees.[41] The phrase *new creation* occurs twice in this book, in 1.29 and 4.26.[42] Jubilees connects the new creation with the defeat of earthly and demonic powers that rage against Israel and in this way is consistent with the main eschatological thrust of Second Temple apocalypses.[43] Their picture of the future was that of "a completely transformed universe."[44] Also related to Paul's new-creation terminology is the Second Temple book Joseph and Aseneth, in which "creation and conversion become synonymous."[45] Not only does the book offer a "vivid portrayal of conversion as new creation," but it is none other than the Spirit who effects this new creation. The Spirit's function in Joseph and Aseneth is to impart life.[46] The parallels here to Paul are self-evident.

---

40. The remainder of this section is adapted from my previously published essay, Constantine R. Campbell, "Judgment of Evil as the Renewal of Creation," in *Evil and Creation: Historical and Constructive Essays in Christian Dogmatics*, ed. David J. Luy, Matthew Levering, and George Kalantzis (Bellingham, WA: Lexham, 2020). Used with Permission.

41. Moyer V. Hubbard, *New Creation in Paul's Letters and Thought* (Cambridge: Cambridge University Press, 2002), 27.

42. Hubbard, *New Creation*, 36.

43. Hubbard, *New Creation*, 48.

44. Hubbard, *New Creation*, 53. Indeed, as Adams notes, "the corruption and redemption of the natural world are recurring themes in Jewish apocalyptic and related writings" (Edward Adams, "Graeco-Roman and Ancient Jewish Cosmology," in Pennington and McDonough, *Cosmology and New Testament Theology*, 24).

45. Hubbard, *New Creation*, 58.

46. Hubbard, *New Creation*, 73–74.

Second Corinthians 5:17 and Galatians 6:15 have been discussed above (see §10.2), but it is worth repeating some of the insights laid out previously. In 2 Corinthians 5:16–17, Paul writes:

> From now on, then, we do not know anyone from a worldly perspective. Even if we have known Christ from a worldly perspective, yet now we no longer know him in this way. **Therefore, if anyone is in Christ, he is a new creation**; the old has passed away, and see, the new has come!

The new creation here is the person *in Christ*—not the whole created realm but a member within it. Rather than regard *anyone from a worldly perspective* (5:16a), Paul sees anyone who is *in Christ* (ἐν Χριστῷ) as *a new creation* (v. 17a). This apparently means that *the old has passed away*, while *the new has come* (v. 17b). The language of *new creation* evokes the sense of realm contrast, in that the person in Christ now belongs under the realm of Christ.[47] This is how they are regarded as a new creation—being under the realm of Christ changes who they are, their allegiances, and their purpose for living.

In Galatians 6:14–16, Paul writes:

> But as for me, I will never boast about anything except the cross of our Lord Jesus Christ. The world has been crucified to me through the cross, and I to the world. **For both circumcision and uncircumcision mean nothing; what matters instead is a new creation**. May peace come to all those who follow this standard, and mercy even to the Israel of God!

Regarding the issue of circumcision and uncircumcision, neither of these mean anything in light of the cross of Christ. Paul will certainly *never boast about anything* apart from the cross (v. 14) because any fleshly boast or status is made irrelevant by it. What matters instead *is a new creation* (v. 15). This is the *standard* that is to be followed by all who desire peace, even for *the Israel of God* (v. 16). Paul does not elaborate on the meaning of this *new creation*, but he clearly refers to the person who, like him, has been crucified to the world (v. 14). The notion of being raised with Christ is not mentioned here, but such a concept is more or less implied by the new-creation language. The old has been crucified with Christ already. The person who is raised with Christ is therefore a new person and a new entity. Or, as Paul puts it, *a new creation*.

---

47. Campbell, *Paul and Union with Christ*, 117.

The new-creation texts of 2 Corinthians 5:16–17 and Galatians 6:14–16 show that for Paul the new creation begins with redeemed humanity. By their participation in Christ—the new man—believers participate in the new creation ahead of time. They are new and renewed; the old has passed away, the new has come.

16.17.1.1 "Cosmic" New Creation

While the language of *new creation* is reserved for humanity in Paul's usage, the concept of a *cosmic* new creation is abundantly evident. In Colossians 1:15–16 Paul writes,

> He is the image of the invisible God,
> the firstborn over all creation.
> For everything was created by him,
> in heaven and on earth,
> the visible and the invisible,
> whether thrones or dominions
> or rulers or authorities—
> all things have been created through him and for him.

As discussed above (see §10.2), this is a key passage regarding the relationship of Christ to the created order. We observe his preeminence over it as its creator (v. 16), sustainer (v. 17), and as its telos (v. 16). There is clearly an intimate and intricate connection between creator and creation that characterizes the nature of creation from its beginning to its future. Here we do not see two created orders—an "old" creation waiting to be replaced by a superior, new creation—but rather a renewed creation is envisaged through the lens of reconciliation. Everything was created by him (v. 16), and everything is reconciled through him—*whether things on earth or things in heaven* (v. 20). The renewal of the created order is, then, one of reunification, reconciliation, and peace-making through the blood of Christ shed on the cross. Thus the "new" created order is a better version of the old, but it is not discontinuous from it. There is no sense in which one is scrapped and replaced with the other.

The most important text for this topic in Paul's writings is Romans 8:18–23, which is probably "the most mature expression of eschatology in Paul."[48] Already discussed above (see §10.2), it is rehearsed again here.

---

48. Brendan Byrne, "Eschatologies of Resurrection and Destruction: The Ethical Significance of Paul's Dispute with the Corinthians," *Downside Review* 104.357 (1986): 296.

> For I consider that the sufferings of this present time are not worth comparing with the glory that is going to be revealed to us. **For the creation eagerly waits with anticipation for God's sons to be revealed**. For the creation was subjected to futility—not willingly, but because of him who subjected it—in the hope that **the creation itself will also be set free from the bondage to decay into the glorious freedom of God's children**. For we know that **the whole creation has been groaning together with labor pains until now**. Not only that, but we ourselves who have the Spirit as the firstfruits—we also groan within ourselves, eagerly waiting for adoption, the redemption of our bodies.

Paul begins by discussing *glory* in v. 18, which is going *to be revealed to us*. The glorious destiny of human beings is tied to the rest of creation, which *waits with anticipation for God's sons to be revealed* (v. 19). Because of the fall of humanity, creation *was subjected to futility* (v. 20) in the hope that it would *be set free from the bondage to decay* in relation to *the glorious freedom of God's children* (v. 21). Like the children of Israel in Egypt, creation is now in slavery, but as Wright expresses it, it "is on tiptoe with expectation, longing for the day when God's children are revealed, when their resurrection will herald its own new life."[49] Creation has been suffering as a result of humanity's fall and will be restored from bondage in concert with God's children.[50] In this respect, creation's *groaning* is likened to that of *labor pains*, as it eagerly awaits the arrival of the promised children of God. There is no hint that Paul imagines that the "old" creation will pass away in favor of a "new" creation. The passage clearly depicts a single creation that is subjected to futility but that will be set free from bondage in the future.

While creation is the arena in which God works for the salvation of humanity and its glorification, it is not merely the arena for such activity. It is, in fact, the object of it, as God will restore, renew, and re-center the creation in concert with humanity. This is in keeping with Jewish apocalyptic expectation, as Bauckham points out: "Personal eschatology was not for the most part divorced from historical and cosmic eschatology, since the hope of individuals was to share in the corporate future of God's people in God's kingdom and in the cosmic future of new creation for the world."[51] First Enoch offers a strong example of

---

49. Wright, *Surprised by Hope*, 103.

50. William H. Dumbrell, *The Search for Order: Biblical Eschatology in Focus* (Grand Rapids: Baker, 1994), 277.

51. Bauckham, *Fate of the Dead*, 1. See also Karina Martin Hogan, "The Apocalyptic Eschatology of Romans: Creation, Judgment, Resurrection, and Glory," in Reynolds and Stuckenbruck, *Jewish Apocalyptic Tradition*, 155–74.

this connection. In the Book of the Watchers, there is a striking corollary of the judgment and destruction of sin and the restoration of the original pristine state of creation, as Macaskill points out.[52] Also in the Epistle of Enoch the restored creation parallels judgment. As evil is purged from the earth, the righteous are healed and will no longer be threatened by it.[53]

This restoration of creation will be characterized by unification around Christ, since God has planned to bring everything together in Christ, things in heaven and on earth (Eph 1:9–10; Col 1:20). Each believer is already regarded as a new creation in Christ (2 Cor 5:17; Eph 2:10), and in this sense redeemed humanity forms the firstfruits of the cosmic new creation to come.[54] According to James Ware, "In the apostle's thought, the hope of the resurrection of the dead and of the renewed creation is not marginal to the faith, but the central feature and content of Christian hope."[55]

16.17.2 Genesis 2–3

Paul's belief that the fate of creation is inextricably tied to that of humanity no doubt arises from Genesis 2–3. The Second Temple Jewish literature that likewise affirms such a connection is also indebted to Genesis. First, the man is formed "out of the dust from the ground" (Gen 2:7), just as every tree grew out of the ground (v. 9), and every wild animal and every bird of the sky were likewise formed out of the ground (v. 19). The man has a common bond with all vegetation and wildlife, since they are alike formed out of the ground.

God placed the man in the garden of Eden *to work it and watch over it* (v. 15). He was given responsibility to name each living creature (vv. 19–20). Together with his helper, who is formed out of the man himself, *and not out of the ground* (vv. 21–23), the man is at once part of the created order while also over it. This unique relationship sheds some light on why the fate of humanity is so significant for the rest of creation; there is an organic oneness between humanity and the rest of creation, but there is also a priority and dignity afforded to humanity.

The drama of the fall in Genesis 3 has at its core the overturning of this

---

52. Macaskill, *Revealed Wisdom*, 40.
53. Macaskill, *Revealed Wisdom*, 41.
54. The relationship between newly created individuals and the cosmic new creation is mediated by the Spirit. Beale writes, "The Holy Spirit is what causes us to be existentially linked with the new world to come.... Believers have begun to participate in the new creation through the Spirit's regenerating work, who has resurrected them and created them as a new creation" (Beale, "Eschatology of Paul," 204). See also Petrus J. Gräbe, "'And He Made Known to Us the Mystery of His Will...': Reflections on the Eschatology of the Letter to the Ephesians," in van der Watt, *Eschatology of the New Testament*, 266.
55. James P. Ware, "Paul's Hope and Ours: Recovering Paul's Hope of the Renewed Creation," *Concordia Journal* 35.2 (2009): 132.

relationship between humanity and the rest of creation. The serpent rebels against this order by challenging and seeking to subvert the man and woman's dominion. By misquoting and directly contradicting God, the serpent misleads the woman to misuse an item within the created garden—the forbidden fruit of the tree of the knowledge of good and evil. The overturn of relationship between humanity and creation is seen in the serpent's misleading the woman, the woman's following the serpent's misleading, and the man and the woman's transgression against creation by partaking of the forbidden fruit.

The ensuing enmity between humanity and the rest of creation is then codified through the curse of God. The serpent will be cursed more than any animal, eating dust all its days, and there will be hostility between the serpent and the woman, its offspring and hers—*He will strike your head, and you will strike his heel* (3:14–15). While the *protoevangelium* is typically understood to point forward to Christ's defeat of Satan, we may also note its relationship to the topic at hand: the offspring of the woman will put down the rebellious element of the created order. By striking the serpent's head, Christ will reconcile creation to himself.

To the man God says,

> The ground is cursed because of you. You will eat from it by means of painful labor all the days of your life. It will produce thorns and thistles for you, and you will eat the plants of the field. You will eat bread by the sweat of your brow until you return to the ground, since you were taken from it. For you are dust, and you will return to dust (vv. 17–19).

Because of human sin against God and against creation, *the ground is cursed because of you* (v. 17). The curse focuses on the relationship between nature and humanity. The man's pre-fall vocation was to work and to watch over the garden of Eden. But now expelled from the garden (v. 24), his work will be perverted. It will be painful, as the object of his work will make it more difficult for him, producing thorns and thistles. This enmity between the man and creation does not, however, lead to divorce, since he will himself return to the ground. We are reminded that he is but dust (cf. 2:7), to which is connected the ominous addendum, "and you will return to dust" (3:19). In this way, man and the ground can only be reconciled through death.

16.17.3 Isaiah 65–66

The themes established in Genesis 2–3 resonate throughout the entire biblical tradition. But in relation to the renewal of creation in particular, the eighth century prophet Isaiah is of preeminent importance. Isaiah looks to the deliverance of creation from corruption and expresses this through natural terms. Ladd writes:

> The wilderness will become fruitful (Isa. 32:15), the desert will blossom (Isa. 35:2), sorrow and sighing will flee away (Isa. 35:10). The burning sands will be cooled and the dry places be springs of water (Isa. 35:7); peace will return to the animal world so that all injury and destruction is done away (Isa. 11:9); and all this results because the earth becomes full of the knowledge of God (Isa. 11:9).[56]

The final and climactic chapters of Isaiah's prophecy offer "the classic expression of new creation in the biblical tradition."[57] Isaiah 65–66 resonates with themes found in Genesis 2–3, depicting a new creation in which the earth and humanity are restored to their intended glory. Indeed, in these chapters Yahweh will create a new heaven and a new earth (Isa 65:17), with a Jerusalem that will be a joy and a delight to her people (v. 18). The perils of human death will be overturned (v. 20), and God's people "will fully enjoy the work of their hands" (v. 22). Human work will no longer consist of painful toil as they wrestle against an antagonistic, accursed creation. With the restoration of creation, work will once again be a joyous expression of their participation in that creation.

Strikingly,

> "The wolf and the lamb will feed together,
> and the lion will eat straw like cattle,
> but the serpent's food will be dust!
> They will not do what is evil or destroy
> on my entire holy mountain,"
> says the LORD (v. 25).

This depicts not only the cessation of hostilities within the created order, but *shalom*—the wolf and the lamb feed *together*, the lion will eat straw like cattle *instead of* eating cattle. The serpent, however, retains its lowly position as a dust-eater. But the practice of evil will cease, and destruction itself will be destroyed on God's holy mountain. However, Isaiah 66 makes clear that judgment on Yahweh's enemies must accompany such restoration of the created order:

---

56. Ladd, *Presence of the Future*, 61–62.
57. Hubbard, *New Creation*, 16.

> You will see, you will rejoice,
> and you will flourish like grass;
> then the LORD's power will be revealed to his servants,
> but he will show his wrath against his enemies.
> Look, the LORD will come with fire—
> his chariots are like the whirlwind—
> to execute his anger with fury
> and his rebuke with flames of fire.
> For the LORD will execute judgment
> on all people with his fiery sword,
> and many will be slain by the LORD (66:14–16).

God's people will flourish as they witness his power, but his enemies will suffer his wrath. He will execute universal judgment, leading to the destruction of many. As all remaining humankind comes to worship Yahweh, they will see the dead bodies of those who have rebelled against him (vv. 23–24).

Isaiah's eschatological vision is one of a new heaven and a new earth with a glorious new Jerusalem at its center, from which God will reign with glorious and unchallenged power. The glory of this scene involves the reversal of the effects of humanity's fall and creation's curse. The created order is restored to harmony, and evil is vanquished.[58]

As we consider the contributions of Genesis 2–3 and Isaiah 65–66, alongside the Jewish literature that likewise draws on these texts, we are better able to apprehend Paul's conception of the connection between the judgment of evil and the renewal of creation. But of course, Paul is not the only New Testament theologian to address this issue. Indeed, his exposition—especially that found in Romans 8—might be seen in tension with the outlook expressed in 2 Peter 3 and Revelation 19–22. As such, we seek to address this apparent tension by considering those texts.

16.17.4 2 PETER 3

Toward the end of the second letter attributed to Peter, the author offers the ultimate solution that will bring an end to all false teaching, false prophecy, and all the wickedness of the earth. The day of the Lord will come like a thief, and "on that day the heavens will pass away with a loud noise, the elements will burn and be dissolved, and the earth and the works on it will be disclosed" (2 Pet 3:10). Indeed, "the heavens will be dissolved with fire and the elements

---

58. This is also the message of the so-called enthronement psalms, which envisage "the destruction not of creation as such, but of sin and evil" (J. Richard Middleton, *A New Heaven and a New Earth: Reclaiming Biblical Eschatology* [Grand Rapids: Eerdmans, 2014], 109–10).

will melt with heat. But based on his promise, we wait for new heavens and a new earth, where righteousness dwells" (vv. 12–13). In order for righteousness to dwell on the earth, a new heavens and a new earth must first come. Indeed, the present heavens and earth "are stored up for fire, being kept for the day of judgment and destruction of the ungodly" (v. 7). That is, for evil to finally be vanquished, the earth in which it currently reigns must be undone.

Second Peter's language of a new heavens and a new earth obviously derives from the Isaianic vision of the same. But 2 Peter's depiction seems much more discontinuous than Isaiah's and, indeed, Paul's. This is an issue to which we must return, but for now we ought to apprehend Peter's strong language of dissolution—*The heavens will be dissolved with fire and the elements will melt with heat* (v. 12). Isaiah depicted the new heavens and new earth in very earthly terms—with the wolf alongside the lamb, and God reigning from Zion—implying, at least conceptually, some degree of continuity between old and new. In fact, Isaiah offers no hint that the old will be destroyed and replaced. But Peter views a new heavens and earth that will *replace* the old heavens and earth once the old have been destroyed through fire.

Second Peter's strong language of discontinuity can be accounted for by its apocalyptic overtones. Known for its frequent use of apocalyptic imagery in both letters, and the stark contrasts commonly found in apocalyptic literature, 2 Peter's sharp discontinuity between old and new need not be pressed beyond rhetorical effect. Indeed, 2 Peter (*and* 1 Peter) draws on the imagery of Noah's flood, which stands as Peter's model as he considers God's judgment of sin and his work of new creation (1 Pet 3:20; 2 Pet 3:6). In that judgment, the earth was "destroyed" through the flood, but the new world that emerged through water was in fact a renewal of the old. The old was dissolved through water, but the new shares some continuity with it, being located on the same planet, subject to the same rules of physics, chemistry, and inherent design. Indeed, it was even made of the same materials. Given Peter's fondness for the flood imagery, it is likely that his conception of the new heavens and new earth replacing the old follows a similar pattern. The old will be dissolved—not by water, but by fire (since God promised not to wipe out the earth again through flood; Gen 9:11)—and the new will exhibit some degree of continuity with it. In this way, 2 Peter echoes 1 Enoch. When the flood typology is used as a paradigm for the final judgment in the Apocalypse of Weeks, it undergirds the idea that a remnant will be delivered from judgment, just as with the flood, thus allowing continuity as well as discontinuity.[59]

Thus, 2 Peter's striking discontinuity is just that—striking rhetoric. It does

---

59. See Macaskill, *Revealed Wisdom*, 42.

not necessarily mean that its eschatological vision is at odds with Isaiah and Paul. Its stress on discontinuity represents the radical extent to which creation must be purified in order to eradicate evil. As Paul Williamson states, "While Peter speaks of destruction, using the image of a cosmic conflagration, he is primarily describing the destruction of sin and corruption. Creation is not being eradicated: it is being radically cleansed."[60]

16.17.5 REVELATION 19–22

After the fall of Babylon the Great in chapter 18, the book of Revelation depicts the celebration of a vast multitude in heaven—because God has judged the notorious prostitute who corrupted the earth (Rev 19:1–2). With this judgment secure, it is now time for the marriage of the Lamb (vv. 7–9). But just as the reader is led to expect the imminent wedding banquet, instead comes the terrifying image of a warhorse, with its rider who judges and makes war with justice (v. 11). He wears a robe dipped in blood and leads the armies of heaven (vv. 13–14). From his mouth comes a sharp sword with which he strikes the nations. He tramples the winepress of the fierce anger of God (v. 15). The armies of the earth wage war against the rider, but quickly lose the battle, and the beast and its false prophet are thrown in to the lake of burning sulphur, while the rest are killed by the rider's sword as the birds of the air devour their flesh (vv. 19–21).

The ancient serpent, the devil, is then bound for a thousand years and thrown into the abyss (20:2–3). After he is released, he is thrown into the fiery lake of sulphur along with the beast and the false prophet for eternal torment (v. 10). Then comes judgment day, as Death and Hades give up their dead, and each one is judged according to their works (v. 13). Anyone whose name is not found in the book of life is thrown into the lake of fire (v. 15).

It is only after this complete victory over and absolute destruction of evil that John utters these words:

> Then I saw a new heaven and a new earth; for the first heaven and the first earth had passed away, and the sea was no more. I also saw the holy city, the new Jerusalem, coming down out of heaven from God, prepared like a bride adorned for her husband (21:1–2).

The new Jerusalem is the bride who has been prepared for the wedding banquet of the Lamb. From then on, God's dwelling place is with his people, and death will be no more (vv. 3–4). The Alpha and the Omega is making

---

60. Williamson, *Death and the Afterlife*, 181.

everything new and freely gives to the thirsty from the spring of the water of life (v. 6). But in the new Jerusalem there is no place for evildoers, whose place is in the fiery lake of sulphur (v. 8). Evil has been completely vanquished and is unable to detract from the beauty and splendor of the new Jerusalem. Nothing unclean will ever enter it (v. 27). The tree of life is in the middle of the city, providing healing for the nations, and there will no longer be any curse (22:2–3).

From the sequence of events, and from explicit references in Revelation 19–22, it is clear that evil must be judged and vanquished in order for the new heaven and earth to be established. There is no place for evil within this new creation. The effects of the fall of humanity and the curse upon creation will have been completely undone. Their only vestige will be seen in the need for restoration and healing.

Revelation's vision of the new heaven and new earth is strongly discontinuous with the old—in parallel with 2 Peter 3 and somewhat in tension with Isaiah and Paul. Most striking is the statement that "the first heaven and the first earth had passed away" (Rev 21:1). But this, like 2 Peter's language of dissolution, is best treated as apocalyptic indulgence for rhetorical effect; "when John tells us that 'the first heaven and the first earth had passed away,' he speaks not of the dissolution of the universe, but of its radical transformation."[61] In fact, there are several indicators of continuity that support this rhetorical understanding of the "passed away" statement.

First, the new Jerusalem comes down out of heaven, resulting in God's dwelling with humanity (vv. 2–3). While the author does not say that the coming down out of heaven is *to the earth*, this is implied and is so understood by most interpreters. It certainly would have been so understood by John's original readers. Second, the nations of the earth are drawn to the new Jerusalem (v. 24), implying continuity with the world known to John and his readers.

Third, the new Jerusalem has at its center the tree of life, the leaves of which offer healing to the nations (22:2). This tree of life points, of course, to the tree of life of Genesis 2:9, which stood at the center of the garden of Eden. After the fall, the man and woman are dispelled from the garden so that they would not have access to this same tree (Gen 3:22–23). Thus, this important symbol stresses continuity with the original creation. It is a symbol of restoration. Now that sin and evil has been vanquished and humanity has been restored, the tree of life may once again stand in the center of the arena in which God and humanity dwell together. If the new heaven and new earth were entirely new, and the old had literally passed away, the tree of life would not carry such significance.

---

61. Williamson, *Death and the Afterlife*, 181.

Nevertheless, the presence of the tree of life in the new Jerusalem also implies some level of discontinuity, for it speaks to the absence of that other tree that stood alongside it in the middle of the garden of Eden—the tree of the knowledge of good and evil. Its absence from the middle of the new Jerusalem is a striking difference compared to the garden. While its absence from the city is not explained, we may infer that it has no place there because evil has been vanquished from creation, and there is now not even the possibility of its return. Only the tree of life remains.

Thus, we conclude with Williamson:

> Just as with the individual's "new creation," so with the cosmic: the old has passed away and the new has come—not by obliteration and replacement, but by purging and renewal; what John describes in Revelation 21 is creation renewed, a radical transformation, a new world order, involving a newness in quality rather than a newness in time.[62]

16.17.6 CONCLUSION

We have considered Paul's relationship to four other key biblical voices: Genesis 2–3, Isaiah 65–66, 2 Peter 3, and Revelation 19–22. These representative voices demonstrate the interwoven relationship of evil to the created order, which can be distilled down to two simple points: (1) evil has corrupted creation, and (2) the glory of the new creation will be assured by the permanent absence of evil.

According to Paul, judgment of evil will be universal and will be just. The judgment to come cannot be escaped, but believers will be counted blameless in Christ. Their security in Christ is assured by the fact that Christ himself has been appointed judge of the living and the dead. Ultimately, however, judgment is about putting "the world to rights."[63] There is a single creation that will be renewed and restored. Thus, judgment is concerned with the eradication of evil and the establishment of righteousness and peace within creation. Wright states that "*God the creator intends at the last to remake the creation*, righting all wrongs and filling the world with his own presence."[64] The salvation of humanity is tied to this renewal of creation, in keeping with Jewish expectation, because, again with Wright, "The main problem standing in the way both of the original purpose of creation and (now) of its renewal and restoration is the failure of humankind to act as God's image-bearers in the world. God must

---

62. Williamson, *Death and the Afterlife*, 181.
63. Wright, *Paul and the Faithfulness of God*, 926.
64. Wright, *Paul and the Faithfulness of God*, 926 (italics original).

therefore put humans to rights in order to put the world to rights."[65] Thus it is no surprise that redeemed believers are described as new creations since, for Paul, the new creation begins with redeemed humanity.

To understand Paul, we noted the connection between sin and creation found in the Hebrew Scriptures, with special reference to Genesis 2–3 and Isaiah 65–66. The ground is cursed because of man's sin, but the protoevangelium points to the crushing of the rebellious element of the created order and creation's subsequent restoration. The fall of humanity and the effects of the curse will be overturned in the new creation. And for the new creation to flourish, evil must be judged and destroyed. All these points are echoed and affirmed in the fellow New Testament voices of 2 Peter 3 and Revelation 19–22. While this is so, these texts also raise the question of whether the old creation will be destroyed and replaced, or whether—with Paul—the old will be renewed and restored.

16.17.6.1 Renewal, Not Replacement

We have argued for the renewal—rather than the destruction and replacement—of creation on the grounds that imagery and language that appears to support new-for-old replacement must be understood rhetorically rather than literally. Middleton accounts for the biblical imagery of cosmic destruction as "describing momentous events and realities that cannot be adequately conveyed in ordinary descriptive prose."[66] Such biblical imagery does not point to "the annihilation of the cosmos, but rather a new world cleansed of evil."[67]

This approach makes better sense of the clear elements of continuity between old and new. It makes better sense of *resurrection*, which gives new life and form to old bodies rather than replacing the old with something entirely new. The disciples did not find a discarded old body of Jesus in the tomb while a new one was walking around in Jerusalem. The resurrected Jesus has the same body as the crucified Jesus, though it has been transformed. As Ware states, "Jesus's resurrection is the ultimate affirmation of creation and its goodness."[68] Finally, the restoration of creation makes better sense of who God is. Moltmann writes, "There are not two Gods, a Creator God and a Redeemer God. There is one God. It is for his sake that the unity of redemption and creation has to be thought."[69]

---

65. Wright, *Paul and the Faithfulness of God*, 926.
66. Middleton, *New Heaven and a New Earth*, 121.
67. Middleton, *New Heaven and a New Earth*, 125.
68. Ware, "Paul's Hope," 137.
69. Moltmann, *Coming of God*, 259.

16.17.6.2 Judgment of Evil as the Renewal of Creation

Judgment of evil, and its ultimate destruction, is the necessary precursor to the renewal of creation. Just as the original pre-fall creation was free from sin and therefore uncorrupted, so the post-judgment creation will be free from sin and therefore restored. In the end, "the human heart, human society, and all of nature must be purged of the effects of evil, that God's glory may be perfectly manifested in his creation."[70]

Yet the biblical picture reveals more than simple renewal in two important respects. First, unlike the original creation, the renewed creation will contain *no possibility of the presence of evil*. The tree of the knowledge of good and evil will not be found in the new Jerusalem. There will never be another fall. Second, the renewed creation will be more than a mere restoration. It is enhanced beyond the original. Instead of one man and one woman dwelling peacefully with God, there will be a multitude. Instead of a garden, there will be a city. Instead of a garden protected from the world outside, the city gates will be open to the nations. Instead of being lit by sun and moon, the glory of God will illuminate the city. In this sense, the eschaton is understood as "the completion of the act of creation."[71] In the words of Moltmann, "The end is much more than the beginning."[72] "The true creation is not behind us but ahead of us."[73]

16.18 Glory

We have seen that according to Paul, glory is the highest value of the age to come, and it is the ultimate goal of all creation. Glory is not some abstract, impersonal value that is anticipated apart from others, least of all apart from Christ. Rather, Paul anticipates a relational glory, in which those who are in Christ will share with him. Glory is unfading and eternal and serves as the ultimate hope of all who suffer in this present age.

16.18.1 What Is Glory?

But what exactly *is* glory? Though he has a lot to say about it, Paul never defines it. The best we can do is to describe glory from what he *does* say. But before we look further in that direction, it is worth exploring the semantic range of the word itself. The meaning of *glory* (δόξα) and its cognates underwent semantic change under the influence of biblical usage.[74] In the classical Greek

---

70. Ladd, *Presence of the Future*, 59–60.
71. Konstantinovsky, "Negating the Fall and Re-Constituting Creation: An Apophatic Account of the Redemption of Time and History in Christ," in Hays, *When the Son of Man Didn't Come*, 110.
72. Moltmann, *Coming of God*, 264.
73. Moltmann, *Ethics of Hope*, 129.
74. Moisés Silva, "δόξα," *NIDNTTE* 1:761.

period, δόξα usually had the sense of "opinion, viewpoint, judgment," and could refer to one's "reputation." Only in some instances did it mean "fame," "honor," "glory."[75] But the basic classical meanings of "opinion, viewpoint, judgment" are not found in the more than four hundred uses of δόξα in the Septuagint, the Greek Old Testament. Since the word was used to translate the Hebrew word כָּבוֹד, the meaning of δόξα became permanently altered. Because כָּבוֹד and its cognates originally meant "abundance, wealth," then "importance, influence, reputation, honor," and "glory, splendor, magnificence," the range of meanings of δόξα was expanded to correspond with כָּבוֹד.[76] In the Septuagint, δόξα most frequently expresses God's honor, glory, and power. But according to Silva, "it does not refer to God in his essential nature, but to the luminous manifestation of his person, his glorious revelation of himself."[77] In the Second Temple period, the concept of glory is expanded beyond that of God's self-revelation and includes heavenly realities, such as God, his throne, and the angels. Indeed, human beings could partake in the divine glory, as Adam in Eden once did, and as those who are saved by God will.[78]

With over one hundred and sixty uses of δόξα in the New Testament, Paul accounts for nearly half of them. The secular meanings "reputation, recognition, honor, fame" are found, but the word more often refers to the honor that should be rendered to God.[79] The dominant use of δόξα in the New Testament points to God's transcendent being and majesty. It is also used of Christ in his preexistence, his earthly ministry, his exalted state, and his return.[80] The most striking usage of δόξα in the New Testament, however, is that believers share in the divine glory, or will do so.[81]

16.18.2 The Glory of God, in Christ, for Believers

Now turning back to Paul, we see that the wider uses of glory correspond well with his. First, glory is ascribed to God's person as an eternal quality. It is not something that needs to be achieved or that God needs others to recognize. God is glorious in and of himself. His very being is transcendent and majestic. His glory can be seen in his acts of creation, resurrection, and re-creation. But in this present age, the fullness of God's glory can only be glimpsed; only in the age to come will it be fully apprehended by all. Thus there is a present

---

75. Silva, "δόξα," 761–62.
76. Silva, "δόξα," 762–63.
77. Silva, "δόξα," 763.
78. Silva, "δόξα," 764.
79. Silva, "δόξα," 764.
80. Silva, "δόξα," 765.
81. Silva, "δόξα," 765.

hiddenness of the glory of God. It can be seen for those who want to see it, but a day is coming when it will not remain hidden, and all people, heavenly beings, and all creation will acknowledge his glory. While God is already glorious in and of himself, Paul also speaks of glory being ascribed to God. The heavenly beings, human beings, and indeed all creation will offer glory to God. This is Paul's firm expectation as well as his prayer.

The glory of Christ is also hidden in the present age, though it can be seen by those with eyes to see it. He is the Lord of glory, he has been raised in glory and in a glorious body, and he is the hope of glory. The glory of God is seen in Christ, and when he appears in glory those hidden with him will appear with him in glory. Though the glory of God is inherent in his own being and manifested in Christ, it is shared with believers, who have been called by God into his kingdom and glory (1 Thess 2:12). Though believers will ascribe glory to Christ when he comes, they will also partake in his glory.

There is thus a recursive, relational, and unselfish nature to the glory envisioned by Paul. Since he no doubt believes that only God is worthy of eternal glory in and of himself, the sharing of God's glory with his people through Christ attests to God's goodness and his grace, which is further reason to give him glory. God is glorious, and God receives glory. He receives glory, and he gives glory. Glory is given, glory is received, but in the end God is already glorious and will remain so for all eternity.

As has been pointed out several times already, Paul's ultimate hope is bound up with glory. The coming glory of God in Christ, and the sharing of that glory with Paul and all believers, is Paul's secure hope as he endures all manner of hardships in the present age. While he does not seek glory for this life, he certainly does seek it for the next. But he seeks only the glory that will be shared with him by Christ, not his own glory.

16.19 CONCLUSION

This chapter draws together the exegetical results of part 2 that relate to the age to come. When Christ comes, the two-age structure of Paul's eschatological framework will give way so that only the new age will remain. That day will see the resurrection of the dead, judgment, and the destruction of evil. Believers will be raised to a glorious, eternal, bodily existence as inheritors of the kingdom of Christ, living with him in a renewed created order that will house the shared glory of God for all eternity.

The chapter explored the question of the general resurrection of the dead, a theme not explicitly addressed by Paul, and how it might be seen to fit what Paul does say about the resurrection of the righteous in Christ. It has addressed the tension between judgment according to works and justification by faith, as well as the sequencing of judgment with resurrection. It has addressed the (apparently missing) theology of hell and annihilationism, not finding sufficient evidence to support either concept in Paul's writings. Instead, he speaks of the disobedient facing a state of eternal destruction, along with all evil. The chapter has also offered an extended discussion on the issue of the renewal of creation versus its re-creation, and how Paul's renewal of creation may be harmonized with other biblical authors who appear to endorse the destruction and replacement of this created order with a superior one. It has been argued, in fact, that those other texts are better understood as endorsing the renewal of the creation also rather than its destruction and replacement, thus providing evocative parallels with Paul's expectation. Finally, the chapter concludes with some reflections on the recursive, relational, and unselfish nature of the glory of God, seen in Christ, shared with believers in the age to come, and filling the renewed heavens and earth for all eternity.

CHAPTER 17

THIS PRESENT AGE

17.1 INTRODUCTION
This chapter addresses this present age, which has been interrupted by the intrusion of the age to come. Though this present age is an age of darkness, the hope for the age to come shines light into the darkness. Believers have been transferred out of the dominion of darkness into the kingdom of the Son, but their lives remain in tension while the present darkness continues to push against their new allegiance. They must live as in the daytime, though it is still night and the day has not yet come in its fullness. This present age will end with the coming of Christ, who will usher in the fullness of the age to come and will bring all injustice and evil to account. Believers are to live in light of this day to come, empowered by the Spirit, as they endure the trials and hardships that the present age brings.

The chapter will first review the relevant exegetical material found in part 2 of the book, focusing on the elements that address this present age. After offering a synthesis of that material, the discussion will turn to consider various implications following from Paul's eschatological perspectives—related to living in the now and the not yet, living by the Spirit, the eschatological nature of the church, the church's eschatological mission, and the themes of work, ecology, and hope.

17.2 THE TWO REALMS AND THIS PRESENT AGE
Chapter 3 discussed the two realms and two ages. There it was clear that this present age is passing away. Paul's eschatology demands that the age to come has, in one sense, already come and now stands juxtaposed against the present age. It currently stands in tension with the age to come and is indeed in conflict with it. This present age is one of darkness, full of the deeds of darkness, but the night is nearly over as the day approaches (Rom 13:12). The night has its own rulers (1 Cor 2:6), who have already been overthrown by the Lord of glory, but until the day comes they continue to rule the night (Eph 2:2). The last ruler of this present age to be abolished is death itself (1 Cor 15:26).

Believers have already been transferred from the domain of darkness into the kingdom of the Son (Col 1:13), having died to the elements of this world (2:20), and they are caught up in the conflict between this present age and the age to come. They must don the weaponry of the new age against the threats and challenges that the present age puts forward by its cosmic powers of darkness in the heavens (Rom 6:12–14; 2 Cor 6:7; 10:3–4; Eph 6:10–17; 1 Thess 5:8). Believers are now filled by Christ, the head over every ruler and authority (Eph 1:21; Col 2:10), whom he has already disarmed and disgraced in his triumph over them (v. 15). Consequently, believers are to deny godlessness and live in a godly way in the present age, awaiting the final appearing of Christ (Titus 2:12–13; 2 Tim 4:1–2).

17.3 The Parousia and This Present Age

Chapter 4 addressed the arrival of Christ. There it was observed that the parousia will mark the end of this present age. Believers are to endure this present age with patience, eagerly awaiting the appearing of Christ (Phil 3:20; 1 Thess 1:10; Titus 2:13). When he arrives, the dead will be raised (1 Thess 4:16), evil will be judged and destroyed, and believers will share in the glory of Christ (Col 3:1) and eternal life with him (1 Thess 4:17). The arrival of Christ is the hope that sustains believers through the trials of this present age and prompts them to faithful service until then (1 Thess 2:19; 1 Tim 6:13–14; 2 Tim 4:1–2).

17.4 The Last Day and This Present Age

Chapter 5 dealt with the last day, and there we saw that Paul waits with anticipation for it (2 Thess 1:10), also known as the day of wrath (Rom 2:5), the hour (13:11), and the end (1 Cor 15:24). This present age is described as the night, but believers belong to the coming day and are to live as in the daytime (Rom 13:12–13). Life lived in this present age will bear consequences for that last day, since unrepentant sin stores up wrath for the day of wrath (2:5), when secrets will be revealed (v. 16). It will also be a day of reward and glory for those who presently belong to Christ (2 Tim 4:8).

17.5 Judgment and This Present Age

Chapter 6 explored the theme of judgment. There we saw that the expectation of future judgment strongly informs Paul's experience of living in this present age. The injustices that are passed over in this age will be dealt with finally in the judgment to come (2 Thess 1:6–9), as no one is able to escape God's justice. While no one will escape the judgment of God (Rom 3:19; Eph 5:6; Col 3:6), believers can live out their days in peace, knowing that their pardon has already been declared in Christ (Rom 5:9; 1 Thess 5:9). Believers must live in this present age with the aim to please God, since all will stand before his judgment seat and give account of themselves to him (Rom 14:10–12; 2 Cor 5:10). Sowing to the flesh in this age will lead to destruction in the next, while sowing to the Spirit now will lead to eternal life then (Gal 6:8). Whatever good each person does now, he will receive back from the Lord in the future (Eph 6:8). Ultimately, however, judgment is about putting the world to rights, which gives believers hope amid this present age.

17.6 Resurrection in This Present Age

Chapter 7 addressed the theme of resurrection. There we saw that the resurrection of Christ stands as the firstfruits of the future resurrection (1 Cor 15:20, 23), giving believers confidence to face dangers and share in the sufferings of Christ (Phil 3:10–11). Future resurrection also offers comfort to those grieving in this present age, enabling them to grieve with hope (1 Thess 4:13–14). Without the hope of resurrection, believers can have no hope in this present age (1 Cor 15:32–33).

Future, bodily resurrection is anticipated by spiritual resurrection through participation with Christ now (Eph 2:4–5). Dying to the realm of this present darkness and being raised to life in the realm of Christ means that believers experience new life in Christ (Rom 6:5; Col 2:12–13), the forgiveness of sins, and reconciliation with God. They are to think of things above (3:1) and put to death whatever belonged to the old self. Believers' present, spiritual resurrection with Christ ensures their future, bodily resurrection when Christ comes. Ultimately, resurrection marks the age to come, while this present age is one of death.

17.7 Eternal Life and This Present Age

Chapter 8 explores the theme of eternal life. There we saw that it is the hope of those who suffer with Christ and depends on dying and rising with Christ through faith in him in this present age (2 Tim 2:11). It is also the consequence of sowing according to the Spirit rather than the flesh in this life (Gal 6:8). Having been justified by grace, believers are now heirs with the hope of eternal life (Titus 3:7). Eternal life follows from bodily resurrection, but continues the life with Christ that has already begun in this age (1 Thess 4:10).

17.8 Inheritance and This Present Age

Chapter 9 dealt with the notion of inheritance. There we saw that Jews and gentiles who believe in Christ are made the children of Abraham and are therefore partakers in the promises to Abraham (Rom 4:13–14; Gal 3:18; 4:29).

Furthermore, believers are heirs of God and coheirs with Christ if they suffer with him and are then glorified with him (Rom 8:17), on the basis of justification and grace (Titus 3:7).

The notion of inheritance naturally relates to the two-age structure of Paul's eschatology since it is essentially a promise-fulfillment motif. The inheritance is promised in this present age with its fulfillment seen entirely in the age to come. That fact reveals the importance of the Spirit as a deposit guaranteeing the inheritance belonging to the age to come (Eph 1:14).

17.9 New Creation and This Present Age

Chapter 10 concerned the new creation. There we observed that in this present age the creation is subject to frustration and decay. It eagerly awaits its redemption and renewal, which is dependent on the glorious freedom of the children of God. In this present age, the creation is in a state of groaning with labor pains until God's children are revealed (Rom 8:19–22).

Yet while the created order awaits its renewal, believers are already a new creation in Christ (2 Cor 5:17; Gal 6:15); the old has already passed, and the new has come (2 Cor 5:17). Thus, those in Christ form a new humanity that serves as the firstfruits of the renewed creation that will dawn in the age to come. In this present age, as people newly created in Christ Jesus, believers are to walk in the good works that God has prepared for them ahead of time (Eph 2:10).

17.10 Israel in This Present Age

Chapter 11 addressed the topic of Israel. There we saw that for Paul the unbelief of the majority of Israelites does not undermine the sovereignty of God, nor does it compromise his faithfulness to his promises to Israel. This is first because not all Israel is Israel (Rom 9:6–7). Second, gentile faith in Christ is designed to make Israel jealous, and thus her rejection of Christ is not to be understood as necessarily permanent (11:11–12). Third, a partial hardening of Israel serves the inclusion of the gentiles (vv. 25–26). Though Paul's discussion concerning Israel is convoluted and controversial, it is clear that the remnant that does believe is regarded as the true Israel, and the remainder is not beyond redemption. Gentile believers should not become arrogant but should recognize their place in salvation history as the wild olive branches grafted into the tree of Israel, the original recipients of God's covenants and promises.

17.11 Glory and This Present Age

Chapter 12 addressed the theme of glory, and there we saw that this present age is marked by the hope of glory. The glory of God is the highest purpose of humanity and of creation in general, and it is therefore the highest hope to which believers can aspire in this present age (2 Thess 2:14; 2 Tim 2:10). Christ dwelling among believers is the hope of glory (Col 1:27). The hope for the glory of God brings rejoicing (Rom 5:2) and enables believers to suffer with Christ, knowing that they will also be glorified with him (8:17; Col 3:4). Life in the body now is lived with the expectation that the body will be transformed into the likeness of Christ's glorious body (Phil 3:21). Future glory encourages believers to live lives worthy of God in this present age (1 Thess 2:12; Titus 2:13). Rendering glory to God through doxology is another way that glory informs life in this present age (e.g., Rom 16:27; Gal 1:5; Eph 3:21; 1 Tim 1:17; 2 Tim 4:18).

17.12 Hope in This Present Age

Chapter 13 dealt with the theme of hope. There we saw that the lives of believers in this present age are to be shaped by hope. This hope defines life in this present age and looks forward to the *end* of this age (1 Cor 15:19; Col 1:5) when Christ comes in glory (Titus 2:13). In other words, the most defining feature of life in the present age is for the hope that this present age will one day not be *present* but *past*. The hope that believers ought to enjoy is a certain hope that will not disappoint (Rom 5:5), but it does require patient waiting (8:25; Titus 2:13), even while it inspires rejoicing (Rom 12:12). It enables endurance through this present age (Rom 15:4; 1 Thess 1:3) through grief (1 Thess 4:13) and inspires faithful labor (1 Cor 9:10; 1 Tim 4:10) and boldness (2 Cor 3:12). Hope in Christ ultimately leads to the praise of his glory (Eph 1:12), and Christ *is* the hope of glory (Col 1:27; 1 Tim 1:1). The hope of eternal life at the end of this present age rests on the promise of God (Titus 1:2; 3:7). Yet it is important that believers hold on to the hope that they have and not allow the dangers of this present age to shift them away from the hope of the gospel (Col 1:23).

17.13 Synthesis

This present age is filled with hope for the age to come. The trials, sufferings, tragedies, and death that characterize this present age are all set against the coming of the age to come, when trials will turn to comfort, suffering will turn to glory, tragedy will turn to triumph, and death will turn to resurrection. Without such hope, this present age would be irredeemable with its unmitigated evil and the tyranny of death.

This present age stands in tension with the age to come that has already dawned through the resurrection of Christ. But when Christ comes again, this present age will give way entirely to the fullness of the age to come. Believers have already been transferred to the realm of Christ, meaning that their loyalty is to be with the age to come, not this present age. Indeed, they are engaged in spiritual warfare, as the powers of this present age continue to rage against those who belong to Christ.

This present age will give up all the living and the dead for final judgment when Christ comes, so that all the injustices and acts of wickedness that have transpired in the dark night of this present age will be brought to account. As such, believers are to live according to the day that is coming, aware that the secret deeds of the night will be exposed, as will the secret deeds done for the glory of Christ. No one will escape God's judgment on that day, though faith in Christ in this present age will secure believers through that daunting reality.

In this present age, believers participate in the resurrection of Christ, so that they have been spiritually raised from spiritual death in anticipation of their own future, bodily resurrection. Without such confidence in resurrection, believers can have no hope in this present age. But *with* such confidence, the frailty of human life in this present age is set against the eternal life to come in the presence of Christ. During the absence of the physical Christ, believers share in the Spirit, who guarantees the inheritance to come.

The spiritual resurrection of believers in this present age means that they are already new creations in Christ, and so they stand as the firstfruits of the renewed creation that believers eagerly anticipate. In this way, believers themselves are signs of the coming end of this present age. Just as the Spirit guarantees their inheritance to come, so these new creations in Christ guarantee the renewed creation to come.

Ultimately, hope is the present-age counterpart to the glory of the age to come. While the age to come will be defined by glory, the lives of believers in this present age ought to be characterized by hope. Thus, hope and glory become the twin elements that shape Paul's eschatological thought. Hope exists now in anticipation of the glory to come.

17.14 LIVING IN THE NOW AND THE NOT YET

It is impossible to understand Paul's expectations for the Christian life without an appreciation of his eschatological outlook.[1] While his eschatological convictions are not the only elements that shape Paul's moral and ethical teaching, the framework for this teaching is provided by eschatology. Indeed, we could

---

1. Harding writes, "The fundamental characteristic of the apostle's symbolic universe is *transformation*, movement towards a *telos* (1 Cor 3:1; 2 Cor 6:13; Phil 1:25; 1 Thess 4:1). . . . Paul's theologizing is *eschatological*, and . . . his anthropological utterances are embedded in the teleological dynamic as their ground or possibility" (Sarah Harding, *Paul's Eschatological Anthropology: The Dynamics of Human Transformation* [Minneapolis: Fortress, 2015], 407).

claim that the framework for the entirety of Paul's teaching is eschatological. This framework involves the essential conviction that all of life is determined by two realms and two ages.[2] Because believers have been transferred out of the realm of darkness and into the kingdom of the Son, all their allegiances, priorities, and values are to be reoriented. His kingship is eschatological "in as much as it stakes a full and indissolubly *final* claim upon our lives."[3] Because believers have been raised to new life as new creations in Christ, their allegiance is to the age to come, not this present age. Because the church is betrothed to Christ as his bride, "she finds pleasure and purpose, delight and design in both the realization and anticipation of her Lord."[4] There is no element of the Christian life that is not subject to these overarching realities.

Nevertheless, Paul is fully aware that this present age is just that—still *present*—and as such it implicates the Christian life in the tension that exists between the two ages.[5] While believers belong to the age to come, they are forced to live out their days (until the Lord comes) in the confines of this present age. They are still exposed to the evil and suffering of this present age, they will face temptation and failure, and they will continue to face decay and death. Furthermore, various heavenly spiritual beings will continue to make "incursions into the horizontal plane of human activity."[6] While Paul believes that these powers have been defeated by Christ, "the ongoing battle is the outworking of that victory."[7] Thus Christian living is conducted through cosmic and temporal tension. They are to live as in the daytime while it is still night.

Moreover, Paul is fully aware that all believers have been shaped by the realm to which they once belonged. Though they now belong to the realm of Christ, believers have not yet completely shaken off the thinking, attitudes, and practices that shaped them while under the realm of Adam.[8] Just as every

---

2. See Benjamin L. Gladd and Matthew S. Harmon, *Making All Things New: Inaugurated Eschatology for the Life of the Church* (Grand Rapids: Baker Academic, 2016), 37–58. This is also true of Paul's entire anthropology, as demonstrated in Harding, *Paul's Eschatological Anthropology*.

3. Philip G. Ziegler, "The Love of God Is a Sovereign Thing: The Witness of Romans 8:31–39 and the Royal Office of Jesus Christ," in Gaventa, *Apocalyptic Paul*, 126.

4. Richard A. Batey, "Paul's Bride Image: A Symbol of Realistic Eschatology," *Int* 17.2 (1963): 182.

5. Kwon critiques the notion of "tension" between the two ages, claiming that it seems to be the product of an artificial juxtaposition imposed by scholars. Instead Kwon insists that "Paul speaks of what has happened as the indispensable ground for the future hope, all as closely knitted parts in God's ongoing drama of salvation. Namely, the relation between the two is not exactly one of tension but one of more organic interaction, with the former necessarily moving toward the latter within the frame of divine faithfulness" (Kwon, *Eschatology in Galatians*, 217–18). This may be so, but Kwon fails to note that a real tension *does* exist for believers who live in the flesh in this present age but also by the Spirit in allegiance to the age to come.

6. Sang Meyng Lee, *The Cosmic Drama of Salvation: A Study of Paul's Undisputed Writings from Anthropological and Cosmological Perspectives*, WUNT 2/276 (Tübingen: Mohr Siebeck, 2010), 305.

7. Wright, *Paul and the Faithfulness of God*, 451–52.

8. In this sense, Lee is not wrong to emphasize the importance of cosmology and anthropology for Paul's

expatriate knows, living in another country does not erase the cultural values they inherited from their original home. And as every expatriate also knows, one must decide how much they will cling to their cultural heritage and how much they will assimilate to their new culture. For Paul, of course, the believer must choose to assimilate to the new realm to which they now belong. They are to leave behind all that belonged to the old realm. "Envisioning two orbs of power, Paul calls on us to indicate by our action to which sphere of power we belong."[9] That is Paul's exhortation to the churches, but he is aware that not all will choose to assimilate. The Christian life is a contest between the values of the old and the new, and it is a contest of loves. Believers are to give up the old for the new in their thinking and practice, but also in their affections. Indeed, love for Christ and the glory to come will be the surest force, by the power of the Spirit, for forsaking former loves.

All of this means that living in the now and the not yet creates two expectations. There is the expectation of how believers ought to live and the expectation that they will struggle to do so to varying degrees. Without both expectations, Paul's moral discourses would make no sense. The exhortations to live a certain way reflect the first expectation, while the corrections and rebukes reflect the second. Paul's letters would contain no moral and ethical teaching at all if he did not hold out the double expectation that believers need to conduct themselves in light of the age to come and that they will struggle to do so. While the presence of the Spirit securely ties believers to the age to come and to Christ himself, his presence does not remove believers from the trials and temptations inherent to this present age. The Corinthian correspondence by itself attests to that fact. But all of Paul's letters likewise attest to it to varying degrees.

The Christian life is to be one of *expectation*. And the word that Paul most commonly uses to convey such expectation is *hope*. All the complexities raised by living in the now and not yet at the same time can be addressed by the set of expectations summarized as hope. When believers are tempted to resort to ungodly practices, their expectation of judgment can set them straight. When believers are encouraged to adopt worldly attitudes and priorities, their expectation of future glory in the presence of Christ can alleviate the weight of such pressure. When believers experience suffering and persecution and wonder why God allows such things to happen to them, they will be reminded that God has set a day on which justice will be done and injustice will be undone, and that expectation will carry them forward. Without such great expectations, it is

---

theology: "These two pivots can be likened to the warp and woof upon which Paul weaves the backdrop of his cosmic drama" (Lee, *Cosmic Drama of Salvation*, 304).

9. Dumbrell, *Search for Order*, 261.

simply impossible to live out the Christian life. Indeed, without hope it is not possible to be a Christian at all, since Christ *is* our hope.

Yet Paul does not offer much by way of the specifics of Christian expectation. He does not encourage speculation about life in the future, since it is enough to be certain of "being with the Lord."[10] Alsup writes, "It is enough to be certain that his word of promise is being fulfilled and will be fulfilled hereafter in accord with the 'riches of his grace.'"[11] Such ambivalence about details and specifics "is *not* to give up the future side of eschatology at all but to affirm that the future belongs to the God of the end-time and his promises regarding it."[12] Or, as Bartsch says, the decisive point in Paul's eschatology "is not the dramatic picture of the apocalyptic process but the conviction that this process has already been started by God through the appearance of the Lord."[13] Simply put, Paul does not want his readers to waste time on things that cannot be known but to trust and live according to what *can* be known, namely, God's faithful fulfillment of his promises in Christ.

17.15 Living by the Spirit

The primary power available to believers as they navigate living in the now and the not yet is the Spirit of God.[14] He mediates both the past and future work of Christ. Barth writes, "The promise of the Spirit is no more but also no less than the power of the resurrection of Jesus Christ operating in the time between the times."[15] Indeed, just as the Spirit raised Christ from the dead (Rom 1:14), he raises believers now (8:6, 10–16; cf. 6:4–5), and he will do so bodily when Christ comes again (8:11).[16] As the deposit guaranteeing their inheritance,[17] the presence of the Spirit mediates the future to believers. He *is* the future breaking into present experience.[18] Or, perhaps better, "the Spirit pierces the fabric of

---

10. John E. Alsup, "Eschatology and Ethics in Paul," *Austin Seminary Bulletin (Faculty Ed.)* 4 (1978): 51.
11. Alsup, "Eschatology and Ethics in Paul," 51.
12. Alsup, "Eschatology and Ethics in Paul," 51.
13. Bartsch, "Paul's Eschatology," 5.
14. The Spirit is "crucial to Paul's understanding of Christian existence. The gift of the out-poured Spirit meant that the messianic age had already arrived. The Spirit is thus the central element in this altered perspective, the key to which is Paul's firm conviction that the Spirit was both the *certain evidence* that the future had dawned, and the *absolute guarantee* of its final consummation" (Gordon D. Fee, *God's Empowering Presence: The Holy Spirit in the Letters of Paul* [Grand Rapids: Baker Academic, 1994], 806).
15. Barth, *Church Dogmatics*, IV/3.1, 358.
16. Beale, "Eschatology of Paul," 204.
17. The metaphor of the Spirit as down payment "reinforces the 'already/not yet' eschatological tension in Pauline theology. It reminds us of several aspects of the work of the Spirit: He comforts and encourages believers, he reminds them of the eschatological future awaiting all believers, and he is an interim gift, a prelude and foretaste of the glory that is to come" (Gräbe, "Reflections," 262).
18. According to Beale, "Paul's understanding of the Holy Spirit is a full-blown new creation notion: the OT prophesied that the Spirit would be given as a gift at the end of time (e.g., Joel 2:28), and its first benefit would be to raise the saints from the dead (e.g., see Ezek 37:11–13)" ("Eschatology of Paul," 204).

human time and knits us into the eschatological eternal Now."[19] As such, the presence of the Spirit empowers believers to participate in the new creation and to live according to the day rather than the night.[20]

There are two senses in which believers live by the Spirit, determined by two different senses of the word "by." First, believers live by the power of the Spirit. Living according to the age to come is only possible with the power that the Spirit brings *from* that age in *anticipation* of that age. New life in Christ can only exist in the Spirit. Second, believers live by the Spirit in the sense that they are to live according to the Spirit. As they walk in the Spirit, the Spirit produces fruit in them; as they sow to the Spirit, they reap eternal life. The Spirit occupies the guiding role that the law of Moses once held under the old covenant, and believers share the mind of the Spirit.[21] Thus, believers can only be alive in Christ by the power of the Spirit, and they are to conduct themselves in accordance with the Spirit.

Nevertheless, the presence of the Spirit only further heightens the tension that already exists between the two ages. The Spirit mediates the future to believers, but dwells within believers whose fleshly bodies belong to this present age.[22] Thus each believer personally experiences the old and the new within themselves. This means that believers each personally embody the now and not yet, as they experience life in the Spirit while remaining in fallen bodies. Each believer then becomes a microcosm of the eschatological structure of all reality. Just as two ages exist together in tension, awaiting the resolution of that tension in favor of the new age, so each believer exists in a state of tension between old and new, awaiting the resolution of that tension in favor of a resurrected body. Thus, believers' bodies "belong" to the old age, but God has claimed them by the presence of the Spirit. Barclay writes:

> Once appropriated by sin, the body is reappropriated by Christ. The very location where sin once held most visible sway, and where its former grip still draws our bodily selves towards death, is now the location where the "newness of life" breaks through into action, displaying in counterintuitive

---

19. Christopher M. Hays, "Conclusion: A Fourfold Response to the Delay of the Parousia," in Hays, *When the Son of Man Didn't Come*, 258.

20. Beale, "Eschatology of Paul," 204.

21. Part of the eschatological outpouring of the Spirit is sharing a frame of mind that accords with God's and that "is inspired or activated by him" (Craig S. Keener, *The Mind of the Spirit: Paul's Approach to Transformed Thinking* [Grand Rapids: Baker Academic, 2016], 127).

22. Tappenden writes, "Paul envisions a process of radical discontinuity of the somatic exterior but sustained continuity of the somatic interior. For those in Christ, who have already received πνεῦμα and thus exist as enspirited earthly bodies, they are already clothed with Christ/πνεῦμα and thus have a deposit in anticipation of the enspirited heavenly body" (*Resurrection in Paul*, 132).

patterns of behavior the miraculous Christ-life which draws our embodied selves towards the "vivification" ([Rom] 8:11) or "redemption" (8:23) of the body.[23]

Once those bodies are redeemed, then the tension that every Christian experiences will be resolved, and they will live according to the Spirit finally free from this battle. It is interesting to acknowledge, however, that the future redemption of believers' bodies does not give license to present indiscretions. One might imagine, for example, that since our bodies will be transformed and perfected, it does not matter what happens to them now. Whatever we do with them, they will be transformed in full. But this logic runs exactly opposite to Paul's. It is rather the case that because our bodies will be raised, it matters very much what we do with them now. While believers' bodies will be transformed and perfected, there is nevertheless continuity with the bodies they currently occupy. Just as Jesus's body was raised and transformed—rather than replaced—so our bodies will be raised. The fact of our bodily resurrection insists on continuity as well as discontinuity. They will be the "same" bodies, but they will not be the same. The treatment of the body in this present age therefore parallels believers' attitude to the age itself. They do not reason that while it is night they should act according to darkness while they can, since, after all, the day will eventually do away with the night. No. Paul insists that believers are to live as in the daytime, even though it is still night. The expectation of what will be must drive their behavior rather than excuse it. And so it is with respect to the body. One day believers' bodies will be raised as glorious and immortal. Therefore, they ought to take care of how they treat their bodies. The expectation of what will be must drive their behavior in the body rather than excuse it.

This is why, in the conflict between the Spirit and the flesh, the Spirit must always be given preference.[24] Apart from the fact that Paul regards the Spirit as the presence of Christ himself, the Spirit represents what will be, while the flesh represents what was and what will soon no longer be. Believers thus have a duty to live for the future with respect to their own bodies.

17.16 CHURCH

The church must be characterized by an eschatological perspective and by the hope of glory. Just as all individual believers straddle this present age and the age

---

23. John M. G. Barclay, "Under Grace: The Christ-Gift and the Construction of a Christian *Habitus*," in Gaventa, *Apocalyptic Paul*, 69.
24. For more on this conflict, see Fee, *God's Empowering Presence*, 816–22.

to come, so the wider body of believers do so on a corporate level. If the church ceases to be an eschatological community, it will cease to exist as a true church. A church that does not long for the coming of Christ has lost its way. A church that is not living as in the daytime amid this present darkness cannot reflect the light of Christ to a lost world. A church that does not cling to the hope of resurrection will live without hope. And a church without hope is an oxymoron.

Just as Paul's letters are framed by eschatological hope, so the teaching of the church ought to be shaped by such hope. The teaching of the church cannot only deal with present-day application or present-day concerns for the world. While these things ought to be addressed in the teaching of the church, they must be framed by the reality that this present age is passing away. The age to come is what the church must live for and what the church must teach. Any cultural dissatisfaction with the delayed gratification of "pie in the sky when you die" should be resisted and corrected in two ways. First, Paul's eschatological vision is hardly "pie in the sky when you die." The future shapes the present in every possible way; if it does not, believers have not understood the gospel of Christ. Indeed, it is the "hope-driven life of mutual acceptance to the praise of God, as the anticipatory fulfilment of God's purpose in creation, that witnesses to the final redemption and doxology still to come."[25] Second, if we live only for this life, we are the greatest of fools.

Hope is about delayed gratification. The church must fight to retain or recover its eternal perspective. Without hope and an eternal perspective, the church cannot flourish, and it cannot serve its purpose in the world. Having said that, hope is not *only* about delayed gratification, since hope shines its light into our present experience. Even while it points forward to the glory to come, it blesses us in this present age, since the expectation of glory reassures us now, comforts us now, and teaches us now. A church that does not delight in the hope of glory will likely make the worst mistake the church can make, which is to live for worldly glory. If it is successful in the world's eyes, with large numbers, popular leaders, and impressive buildings, then the church can easily cease to be what God intends for it—to be a gathering of people who long for the end of this present age and who look to the renewal of creation in the age to come. After all, to be a community centered around Christ is to be a community centered on the Lord who is coming soon. If he is coming soon, he is an eschatological Lord. Indeed, he is the Lord of glory, and his glory will be consummated with his coming again to this world, just as his coming again to

---

25. Scott Hafemann, "Eschatology and Ethics: The Future of Israel and the Nations in Romans 15:1–13," *TynBul* 51.2 (2000): 192.

this world will end this world as we know it. In other words, the church cannot be centered around Christ if it is not an eschatological community. If it is not an eschatological community, it is not really a Christ-centered one.

The genuine church *is* an eschatological community, whether it realizes it or not. The presence of the Spirit mediates the future to the community in this present age, and the church has received the promise of inheritance. The real question, then, is whether the church *understands* itself as an eschatological community. Just as an individual believer can be one thing without understanding who they are, so the church can be an eschatological community without realizing it. If it is genuinely the church, then its eschatological nature is already established by the work of Christ and the presence of the Spirit. Yet if the church does not embrace its eschatological identity, it will struggle to flourish, and it will be more susceptible to the temptations of this present age than it should be.

If it is true that believers are the firstfruits of the renewed creation to come as new creations in Christ, then the church bears a significant role in this present age. The church is a community that has already become new in anticipation of the renewed creation. It not only represents renewed humanity in Christ but the renewal of all things. This fact only further underscores the importance that the church must understand its eschatological nature. It stands as a testimony to the future, restoring work that God has promised in Christ and points to the need for humanity to repent and believe in him before he comes in judgment. While the church today may in general be aware of its role to reach the nations with the gospel of Christ, it is not as well understood that the church itself testifies to the hope of glory. Its very existence speaks of the age to come, and as the church seeks to live according to the Spirit, it will embody the day amid the night.

While the church *is* an eschatological entity and stands as a witness to the age to come, it is not to be passive amid the turmoil and injustices of this present age. A likely misunderstanding would lead the church to ignore social issues in this world as it simply preaches the next world. But this is not the right application of the church's eschatological nature.[26] The hope for resurrection means that believers need to respect the body rather than be reckless with it, and so the church is to respect the needs of others in this world rather than recklessly ignore their human needs because a new world is coming. In other words, an eschatological perspective does not mean that the church only preaches about the future and does nothing for those in need in this present age. Just as

---

26. See Bradley A. Johnson, "Doing Justice to Justice: Re-assessing Deconstructive Eschatology," *Political Theology* 12.1 (2011): 11–23.

each believer should respect what the body *will be* and so should protect the body now, so the church must respect what the world *will be* and so protect it now, "imitating the justice and mercy of the God who is merciful."[27] A truly eschatological perspective will fuel efforts for loving humanity in all respects, not only according to spiritual needs. The whole created order will be renewed when Christ comes, and so the church is to testify to that reality by working toward the holistic care of humanity.

Another way in which the ministry of the church ought to be directly affected by its eschatology is in the burial of the dead. Burial, rather than cremation, has always been the tradition of the church, inherited from Judaism, because it declares its belief in the resurrection of the dead. The departed are but asleep, waiting to be raised at the voice of Jesus. The increasing prevalence of cremation, however, can easily be excused within the church since God will raise the dead, no matter what their bodily condition. Even those turned into ashes will be raised, and thus there is no perceived reason to prefer burial over cremation. But this again misses the point. This would be akin to the mistreatment of the body in this life because we know it will be raised immortal and perfected. Paul's logic, however, runs the other way. Because the body will be raised, it matters what we do with it in this life. How we treat the body is a declaration of our expectation of what it will be. In the same way, how we treat the lifeless bodies of the departed declares what we believe about their future fate. Since the church believes in the resurrection of the dead, the burial of our deceased loved ones is a singular opportunity to express that belief in a very tangible, meaningful way. We declare what the body *will be*, not what it won't be. The turning of the body into ash declares something quite different. It suggests that the body is just a vehicle for the soul, and once the soul has departed, the body has no integrity of its own. This is not Paul's position, who believes in a *temporary* separation of soul and body. They will be one again at the resurrection of the dead, and as such what we do with the body ought to declare that expectation.

17.17 Mission

A central task of the church in the present age is to proclaim the gospel of Christ to the nations. This was clearly Paul's own task as apostle to the gentiles, but it is also what the church must continue to do until Christ comes. While the very existence of the church itself stands as a testimony to the age to come, it must

---

27. Brandon Gallaher and Julia S. Konstantinovsky, "Divine Action in Christ: The Christocentric and Trinitarian Nature of Human Cooperation with God," in Hays, *When the Son of Man Didn't Come*, 202.

also declare the truth into the world at large. Or, at least, that's what we might think Paul expects of the church. He never actually says that.

In the first place, Paul's eschatological convictions account for his mission among the gentiles. In Romans 15:8–13 Paul writes,

> For I say that Christ became a servant of the circumcised on behalf of God's truth, to confirm the promises to the fathers, and so that Gentiles may glorify God for his mercy. As it is written,
>
> **Therefore I will praise you among the Gentiles,**
> **and I will sing praise to your name.**
>
> Again it says, **Rejoice, you Gentiles, with his people!** And again,
>
> **Praise the Lord, all you Gentiles;**
> **let all the peoples praise him!**
>
> And again, Isaiah says,
>
> **The root of Jesse will appear,**
> **the one who rises to rule the Gentiles;**
> **the Gentiles will hope in him.**
>
> Now may the God of hope fill you with all joy and peace as you believe so that you may overflow with hope by the power of the Holy Spirit.

God's promises to the fathers are fulfilled by the gentiles giving glory to God, as this catena of scriptural texts indicate (2 Sam 22:50; Ps 18:49; Deut 32:43; Ps 117:1; Isa 11:10). In particular, the gentiles will hope in the root of Jesse, whom Paul regards as Christ Jesus. The hope of the gentiles of course relates to Paul's eschatological thinking, since hope is the key characteristic of believers in this present age. In other words, Paul views his mission as preparing the gentiles to participate in the eschatological expectation of the age to come. Their hope will be in Christ, the one who will come again and usher in the new age. God himself will fill these believers in Rome with all joy and peace as they believe, so that they will overflow with eschatological hope by the power of the Spirit.

Two verses later, Paul adds, *Nevertheless, I have written to remind you more boldly on some points because of the grace given me by God to be a minister of Christ Jesus to the Gentiles, serving as a priest of the gospel of God. My purpose is that the Gentiles may be an acceptable offering, sanctified by the Holy Spirit* (Rom 15:15–16). Paul was commissioned by God's grace to minister the gospel so that the gentiles might become an acceptable offering to God. Thus, Romans 15:8–13 provides the wider eschatological grounding for the mission to the gentiles, while 15:15–16 points to Paul's personal investment in that mission. What we do not see, however, is Paul's expectation that his mission to the gentiles is also the mission of the church in Rome.

After expounding similar themes in Ephesians 3, Paul turns to the gifts that Christ has given to the church, especially those that serve to build up the church—or, more specifically, they serve to equip God's people, that the body of Christ might build *itself* up in love (Eph 4:11–16). The list of gifts to the church in 4:11 includes *evangelists* (τοὺς δὲ εὐαγγελιστάς). Alongside apostles, prophets, and pastors and teachers, these evangelists contribute to the work of the church. As such, Paul clearly views that evangelism—the proclamation of the *evangel*, the gospel of Christ—will be an ongoing element in the life of the church. It is not exclusively the purview of the apostle to the gentiles.

This means that Paul's activity as apostle to the gentiles is not *apart* from the work of the church but is in fact conducted on behalf of the church. Paul's work *is* the work of the church. And there will be others like him who have a special calling and ability to proclaim the gospel of Christ to the nations. They will not do this *alongside* the ministry of the church but as *part* of the ministry of the church. To put it another way, the fact that Paul has a mission to the gentiles means that the *church* has a mission to the gentiles. Like the star pitcher of a baseball team, he is not rolled out to do something alongside the team but rather *for* the team as *part* of the team. The mission of the pitcher and the mission of the team are one and the same.

Paul stops short, however, of saying that evangelism is the task of each and every believer. It is the mission of the church, to be sure, but that does not mean that every member of the team will be a pitcher. The team works together on the same mission, but members of the team will occupy different roles. Paul nowhere expects that all believers will be evangelists, even though evangelism is the mission of the church at large.

Having said that, however, it is curious to note that evangelists are included in the Ephesians 4:11 list that serves to equip *the saints for the work of ministry* (v. 12). In other words, evangelists not only serve the church by doing evangelism but by equipping it. This must mean that evangelists will help the church to be an evangelistic community. Again, Paul does not say that every member of that community will be an evangelist, but he does seem to imply that the community as a whole will be one that proclaims the gospel. It will be a missional community that has as much interest as Paul in preparing the nations to glorify God.

Ultimately, mission ought to be viewed as a present-age activity that prepares the world for the age to come. Just as eschatology was central to Paul's apostolic missionary preaching, it "remains a vital foundation of the church's ongoing faith, daily living in hope, and mission of proclaiming salvation from the wrath to come."[28] Evangelism is not conducted solely for "a better life now," though it does offer that through the forgiveness of sins, reconciliation to God, and membership in the family of believers. It is, rather, conducted for the primary purpose that the nations would hope in Christ—that they would have an eschatological expectation of the coming of Christ, the resurrection of the dead, final judgment, and eternal glory. According to Paul, this has been God's mission all along. God appointed Paul to that mission. And Paul's mission—indeed, God's mission—is the mission of the whole church until Christ comes.

17.18 Work

There are two equal and opposite mistakes believers can make about work. The first is to work as though there is no age to come. Work becomes an idolatry as people seek material wealth, comfort, and success. While wealth, comfort, and success are not problematic in and of themselves, if believers regard these as the goal of their work, they are working only for this present age. The second mistake is to use eschatology to eliminate any meaningful value of work. The reasoning is that since this world is going to disappear, and only the next world will last eternally, "secular" work is ultimately meaningless.

Both mistakes stem from faulty eschatology. The first is easier to see than the second, in that it simply forgets about the age to come. The second is more complex, as it misunderstands the relationship between the two ages. As we have seen, *what will be* determines how we should think about the world now. Since the world will be renewed (not replaced), how we live now ought to point to that expectation. We do not work with the expectation that our labor will be useless in the age to come, but rather we work in anticipation of it.

In the first instance, this will involve judgment and reward. As Paul instructs slaves in Colossae, they will receive the reward of an inheritance from the Lord (Col 3:22–24). Their work is to be conducted wholeheartedly for the Lord. Since the work of slaves has no earthly benefit for the slaves themselves, their eschatological reward is all the more significant. Yet there is no reason to think it applies only to slaves. Indeed, the parallel text in Ephesians 6:8 specifies that

---

28. Gieschen, "Christ's Coming and the Church's Mission," 55.

whatever good each one does, slave or free, he will receive this back from the Lord. The labor of all believers should be informed by the reality that their labor—whatever it is—matters to the Lord, not only now but in the age to come.

Work has more eschatological significance than simply the expectation of reward. As with all things, it is an opportunity to declare our expectation in what is to come. There is little evidence to support the notion that our work will somehow bring about the age to come in a postmillennial sense; Paul is committed to the view that the age to come will be entirely dependent on the action of the Lord, inaugurated by his coming. The renewal of creation does not depend on our efforts, nor do our efforts contribute to it in any direct sense. Yet, as mentioned, our work *declares* our expectation of the world to come—or at least it ought to do so. The values and standards that pertain to the age to come can inform our work now. Work can build, contribute to society, improve people's lives, facilitate community, and myriad other positive things. Believers ought to embrace these positive features of work as emblems of the values that will characterize the age to come. As such, believers ought to avoid work that destroys, marginalizes, or corrupts. Work that is only self-serving does not embody the values of the kingdom to come. Such work becomes an anti-witness to the eschaton as well as the final judgment.

Since Paul teaches the renewal of creation rather than its replacement, there is some ambiguity regarding the eternal fate of the fruit of our labor. While there is the expectation of reward in the age to come and the possibility of testifying to its coming, what will actually happen to the houses we build, the art we create, and the books we write? Will they make it into the renewed creation, or will they pass away with whatever else is temporary?

Paul offers very little to answer these questions. He does not address the material comport of the age to come; all we know is that it will be filled with glory. There is, however, one text that may speak into this question: 1 Corinthians 15:58. It reads, *Therefore, my dear brothers and sisters, be steadfast, immovable, always excelling in the Lord's work, because you know that your labor in the Lord is not in vain.* Discussed in §7.2, this text refers either to all labor performed "in the Lord" (i.e., any labor performed by a Christian), which would certainly fit the normal meaning of "in the Lord," or to specifically "Christian" labor, meaning the labor of the gospel. Favoring the latter, I have argued elsewhere that the phrases *the Lord's work* and *labor in the Lord* refer to "work conducted for the cause of Christ" and "Christian service conducted for the cause and purposes of the Lord."[29] If this is so, Paul implies that the work of ministry

---

29. Campbell, *Paul and Union with Christ*, 158–59.

will not come to nothing, counteracting Qoheleth's despair regarding all toil under the sun (Eccl 2:18–23).

So, do we therefore conclude that only the work of the gospel will survive into the age to come, while all other work is ultimately vanity? Not necessarily. That case can be argued on the basis of 1 Corinthians 15:58, but it might be a misapplication of it too. Paul's intent in 1 Corinthians 15:58 is to affirm the enduring value of labor in the Lord in light of the resurrection of the dead, not to address our question at hand. It is an argument from silence, but the fact is that Paul does not say that all other work *is* in vain. The vanity or otherwise of all other work is simply not addressed, nor is it Paul's concern. The reality is that we must confess ignorance as to how much of the fruit of our labor will last into the age to come. It is therefore important not to claim too much nor too little. We cannot say authoritatively that our cultural artifacts and other valuable work will endure into the age to come, but neither can we claim that no such work will endure. We just don't know.

It is worth noting, however, that much—if not most—of our work does not last *in this age*, let alone in the age to come. A baker or chef, for instance, does not enjoy the fruit of her labor the very next day, let alone for eternity. But perhaps the enduring fruit of our labor is not the point in the end. What we *can* say is that all our work, and the way in which it is conducted, matters to the Lord, and it is in this sense that all work done in the name of the Lord will endure. To please the one who will say, "Well done good and faithful servant," is the enduring reward and fruit of our labor, and this is no doubt Paul's hope. In this sense, it is possible to affirm Wright's quite positive appraisal of our good deeds and their place in the new creation:

> Every act of love, gratitude, and kindness; every work of art or music inspired by the love of God and delight in the beauty of his creation; every minute spent teaching a severely handicapped child to read or to walk; every act of care and nurture, of comfort and support, for one's fellow human beings and for that matter one's fellow nonhuman creatures; and of course every prayer, all Spirit-led teaching, every deed that spreads the gospel, builds up the church, embraces and embodies holiness rather than corruption, and makes the name of Jesus honored in the world—all of this will find its way, through the resurrecting power of God, into the new creation that God will one day make.[30]

---

30. Wright, *Surprised by Hope*, 208.

17.19 Ecology

According to Chia, the chief reason that Paul shows no interest in environmental concerns is that he is so preoccupied with an apocalyptic expectation of the imminent return of Christ that he simply has no interest in setting up ethical mandates for future generations, since—according to Chia—he does not expect any generations after his own. As such, "Paul's apocalyptic eschatological hope has constantly steered his vision onto the fallen humanity, the need for the gospel, rather than the potential benefit the believers may have contributed toward the environment which in turn supports the livelihood of humanity."[31] While the Schweitzer-like presumption of Paul's expectation of an imminent parousia has been critiqued already above, Chia is correct to note Paul's silence regarding care for the environment.

Though Paul does not address anything like our modern ecological and environmental concerns, his eschatological vision nevertheless informs such interests. Again, two opposite errors can arise from an eschatological consideration of the environment. The first would be to overly stress the discontinuity between this present age and the age to come. This is difficult to do if one considers only Paul's writings, since he stresses the continuity rather than discontinuity of the old and the new created orders. Indeed, the latter is a *renewal* of the present created order, not a replacement of it. Nevertheless, by stressing discontinuity it is possible to undervalue the present environment. With a new heaven and a new earth on the way, it doesn't really matter if we pollute this earth because it will soon be gone anyway, and God will give us a brand new one. Yet, again, such a position is indefensible from Paul's perspective (nor, in fact, is it defensible when other biblical texts are likewise considered; see §16.17 above).

Paul teaches that this present world will be renewed. We will live in the same world, though the world will not be the same. Given this reality, believers ought to have a concern for the environment. Just as the expectation of bodily resurrection means that it matters how we treat the body now, so the expectation of the renewed creation means that it matters how we treat the earth now. We are to live according to what will be. Since the renewed creation is precious in God's sight and will house his everlasting glory, so believers are to regard the present created order as precious.

The second error, however, is to so stress the continuity between this present age and the age to come that environmental concerns take on a level of importance that is out of balance. The whole created order will be renewed

---

31. Samuel P. Chia, "The Role of Eschatology in Paul's Ethics," *Sino-Christian Studies* 3 (2007): 52.

when Christ comes, and so the church is to testify to that reality by caring for the environment. But care for the environment does not mean that the quality of the renewed creation is somehow in human hands. Again, the expectation of resurrection informs our thinking here. While we must respect the body now in anticipation of resurrection, there is no sense in which the quality of the resurrected body will be determined by our treatment of it now. God raises the dead, and each person will be resurrected to a glorious, immortal body in the likeness of Christ irrespective of the condition of their body now or in death. Deterioration caused by cancer, Parkinson's disease, or alcohol abuse will not subvert God's resurrecting power. There will be no substandard resurrected bodies in the age to come, since all will be in the likeness of Christ's glorious body. In the same way, the renewed creation will not somehow be substandard because of present world pollution, the destruction of rainforests, or the extinction of species. God will renew the world just as he will raise the dead—perfectly, gloriously, and without human interference.

Care for the environment ought to express our eschatological expectation that this world will be renewed. The earth that *is* should be respected in anticipation of the earth it will *become*. Earth care is therefore an expression of our hope. It should not be underplayed by consigning this earth to the trash can, nor should it be overplayed by imagining that the renewed earth is at risk unless we intervene.

17.20 DEATH

The eschatological significance of human death can hardly be overstated, for at least three reasons. First, the very existence of human death is understood as a consequence of human sin, which has put humanity under the power of both sin and death in the first place.[32] A central interest of Paul's eschatology is how sin and death are conquered. Second, death finally releases the individual from the bonds of the fleshly, fallen body as well as the loosened grip of the present evil age. It is the point at which believers are brought into the presence of God, assuming they die before Christ comes again. Third, Paul's eschatological hope is grounded in the resurrection of the dead. Resurrection would hardly be such

---

32. It would be remiss to discuss biblical notions of death without acknowledging the role of *Sheol* in Hebrew thought. Against the commonly held conviction that Sheol was the routine destination of all who died, Levenson argues that Sheol was understood as a dark, dreary netherworld that designates only a *negative* death "marked by violence, punishment, prematurity, or a broken heart." Levenson stresses that the biblical Sheol is *not* the same thing as the "Christian hell," the postmortem destination of sinners. Though it is not always their sins that send some dead to Sheol, "they have for one reason or another died outside the blessing of God" (Jon D. Levenson, *Resurrection and the Restoration of Israel: The Ultimate Victory of the God of Life* [New Haven: Yale University Press, 2006], 82).

a huge component of Paul's eschatology if death was not such an enormous problem for all humanity. Thus, from the very beginning of the biblical story to its end, death must be understood from an eschatological perspective. Its existence reminds us of the overarching eschatological problem that overshadows human history: How will sin and death finally be overcome and overthrown? The prospect of death that each human being faces propels our interest forward so that questions about eschatological matters, such as what happens to us at the point of death, judgment, resurrection, and eternal life, are not esoteric concerns. Our thinking about such issues is very personal indeed. And the great hope that death will finally be overturned by bodily resurrection from the dead means that the evil tyranny of death ends up serving as a foil for the victory and glory of life everlasting.

17.20.1 AN INTERMEDIATE STATE?

Some of the leading questions about death concern the period between an individual's death and the parousia of Christ. Since the bodily resurrection of the dead will only occur subsequent to the parousia, the "gap" between death and resurrection raises some difficult questions. There have been three major responses to this question offered by the Christian tradition. First is the most prevalent belief that upon death the believer goes to be "with the Lord" in a disembodied state. This "intermediate state" is exactly as it is called—*intermediate*—or, perhaps better, it is *penultimate*. To be with the Lord is better than the suffering of this life (cf. Phil 1:23), but it is not yet the ultimate state of living in the resurrected body. The chief weakness of this view is its necessary separation of body and spirit, which stands in tension against the holistic view of the person espoused by Old Testament anthropology. Second is the less prevalent view of "soul sleep," in which the departed individual remains unconscious until the resurrection of the body. There is thus no intervening, intermediate, or penultimate state between death and resurrection—at least, not in anyone's experience, since after death the next thing the deceased will consciously experience is their resurrection from the dead. This is true even if the interval between death and resurrection spans thousands of years. Third is the view that upon death the individual steps outside time—just as God is (supposedly) outside time—and goes straight to the resurrection. In this case, there really is no intermediate state since all the dead go straight to the resurrection regardless of when they lived and died, and the resurrection will occur at the "same time" for everyone subsequent to the parousia of Christ.

While all three positions claim biblical support, our concern here is to ask what Paul seemed to think about "life after death." There are not many clues to go on, since Paul is evidently much more interested in the resurrection of the body than in whatever state the dead may or may not experience prior to resurrection. Arguably only two texts relate directly to the question. First is Philippians 1:23–24, in which Paul tells his readers that he would rather *depart and be with Christ—which is far better*, though his remaining in the flesh is better for their sake. Second, and more significantly, is 2 Corinthians 5:1–10. Here Paul speaks at length about leaving the earthly tent in which believers currently live away from the Lord, and going home to be with the Lord in a building and eternal dwelling in the heavens. The ambiguity of both texts (especially the latter) does not promote clarity, but both texts offer the opportunity to reflect on Paul's thinking about post-death, pre-resurrection reality.

17.20.1.1 Philippians 1:23–24

As observed in §7.2, Paul indicates in Philippians 1:23–24 that being with Christ is better than remaining alive in this world. But it is unclear whether he is contrasting this life on earth with the so-called intermediate state prior to resurrection, or to resurrection life itself. Paul's language conveys a sense of immediacy, in that he apparently expects to *be with Christ* instantly upon death.[33] There is no hint of expectation of an intervening period between death and being with Christ. If Paul *does* expect some kind of interval—whether it be one of "soul sleep" or some other event—he offers no clue in such a direction. Thus, it is reasonable to conclude that Paul expects to be in the direct presence of Christ at the point of death.[34]

It is possible that Paul here expresses the expectation of an intermediate state, prior to bodily resurrection, in which he will consciously be with Christ.[35] This will occur immediately upon death and is far better than this present life. While we may safely assume that the *best* future reality will be one of resurrected

---

33. Bert Jan Lietaert Peerbolte, "In Search of Hope. Eschatology in Philippians," in van der Watt, *Eschatology of the New Testament*, 280.

34. So Williamson, *Death and the Afterlife*, 57.

35. While Sumney acknowledges this, he also claims that such an intermediate state will pertain to Paul but not to all believers. This is based on parallels he perceives to Jewish martyr traditions in which the fate of martyrs differs from that of others. In 4 Macc 17:17–18, for instance, martyrs are before the throne of God immediately following death because of their service and testimony to God (Jerry L. Sumney, "Post-Mortem Existence and Resurrection of the Body in Paul," *HBT* 31.1 [2009]: 24). See also Adela Yarbro Collins, "The Otherworld and the New Age in the Letters of Paul," in *Other Worlds and Their Relation to This World: Early Jewish and Ancient Christian Traditions*, ed. Tobias Nicklaus, Joseph Verheyden, Erik M. M. Eynikel, and Florentino Garcia Martínez (Leiden: Brill, 2010), 203. It seems, however, that this would represent quite a major difference between Paul's pre-resurrection future and that of his readers, yet no explicit indication is offered to suggest that Paul is unique or distinct in such a way. Without such indication, it would be all too easy for his readers to apply his comments to themselves, thus drawing the wrong conclusion. Since Paul is especially apt at protecting his readers from drawing false conclusions based on his writings, Sumney's proposal seems unlikely.

presence with Christ, this (apparently disembodied) intermediate state is nevertheless better than embodied life now. For Paul, the only advantage of embodied life now is the capacity to do meaningful work that will benefit others.

17.20.1.2 2 Corinthians 5:1–10

Second Corinthians 5:1–10 has already been addressed above in §7.2. Unfortunately, the ambiguities acknowledged in the above treatment of that text remain ambiguous, lending little clarity to the question at hand. To reiterate some of the earlier findings, the central theme of the passage is the *eternal dwelling* (v. 1), also called *our heavenly dwelling* (v. 2). Paul uses such descriptions to refer to the believer's heavenly body, which becomes clear in contrast to such language as *our earthly tent* (v. 1), which can be taken off (v. 3), leaving a believer *unclothed* (v. 4). In context, the taking off of such a tent is a reference to death—the shedding of the earthly body. Paul becomes more specific in the verses that follow, equating *this tent* (v. 2) with being *at home in the body*, which is to be *away from the Lord* (v. 6). And Paul would prefer *to be away from the body and at home with the Lord* (v. 8). Paul imagines that *our earthly body* will be *destroyed* (v. 1a), but in that event, *we have a building from God, an eternal dwelling in the heavens, not made with hands* (v. 1b). Paul implies that the intermediate state between death and resurrection will not be one of being *found naked* (v. 3); *we do not want to be unclothed but clothed, so that mortality may be swallowed up by life* (v. 4). It is unclear whether Paul imagines some kind of corporeal experience *before* the full resurrection of the body or rather only a *temporary* disembodiment before resurrection. If the former, it is not clear at all what this would mean. Is it some kind of temporary, pre-resurrection body?[36] If so, there does not appear to be any further evidence for such a thing in Paul's writings (nor anywhere else in the NT). If the latter, it would hardly explain Paul's desire to leave the earthly body, apparently giving preference to a disembodied state that is nevertheless *with the Lord* (v. 8). Presumably being *with the Lord* is enough reason to prefer death over earthly life, even if it is a disembodied existence for the time being.

Since 2 Corinthians 5:1–10 represents the closest that Paul gets to discussing the interim period between death and resurrection, it is little wonder that Christian tradition has remained confused on the issue. The passage is notoriously difficult to interpret, and the elements that remain unclear are

---

36. Tappenden suggests that Paul here pursues the idea of "an undergarment that persists once the outer clothing layers are removed," so that he can avoid an interim nakedness. He suggests that this metaphor points to the Spirit, who provides a strong degree of continuity between earthly and heavenly bodies (Tappenden, *Resurrection in Paul*, 130–31).

exactly correlated to the theological questions about post-death, pre-resurrection experience. On this reading of the text, Paul *might* support a disembodied intermediate state or a pre-resurrection, quasi-embodied state.[37] Admittedly, both options are weird from the standpoint of Old Testament anthropology. The first violates the holistic view of the person in which body and soul together constitute a human,[38] while the second avoids disembodiment only to find the person embodied in something other than their real (not-yet-resurrected) body. Taken together, both options are variations on the conscious, intermediate-state position. However, the passage could also fit the unconscious, intermediate-state position (soul sleep), since Paul seems to anticipate moving straight from being at home in the body and away from the Lord to being away from the body and at home with the Lord. Rather than a complete absence of an intermediate period, this direct movement from being at home in the body and at home with the Lord may simply indicate one's experience—since the interim is not experienced consciously. Finally, it is also possible to reconcile this text with the "out of time" position for the same reason—Paul seems to imagine moving directly from being at home in the body to being at home with the Lord in the eternal dwelling provided by him. If that is regarded as the resurrection body, then perhaps the lack of interval between the two dwellings is explained by a stitching together of times such that the deceased moves immediately to the ultimate resurrection of the body without the existence of any intervening period.[39]

While a number of ambiguities remain, if we take Philippians 1:23–24 together with 2 Corinthians 5:1–10, it is plausible to accept that Paul believed in a disembodied, intermediate state in which the believer will consciously be

---

37. "On balance . . . this passage seems to acknowledge some life and consciousness for Paul following his death and preceding the parousia" (Sumney, "Post-Mortem Existence," 22). See also Williamson, *Death and the Afterlife*, 57. But see Middleton for the view that Paul simply expresses his hope of resurrection. "Paul is not speaking of being with Christ immediately at death; rather, he is looking to the second coming, at which time we will be raised and be with Christ in the new creation" (Middleton, *New Heaven and a New Earth*, 230).

38. Griffiths acknowledges this but affirms the reality of an intermediate state anyway. Deceased humans thus become temporarily unhuman until the resurrection. He writes: "In the intermediate state there are, properly speaking, no human creatures. That is because such creatures are, by definition, fleshly, and the intermediate state is, by definition, a place without flesh. It follows by entailment that whatever is there is not and cannot be a human creature" (Griffiths, *Decreation*, 174). He later elaborates more positively, "It should be apparent from all this that discarnate souls in the intermediate state are much like human creatures: they are located in time-space; they have a history and a telos; they can undergo pleasure and pain; they can know, intellectually; and they can will and intend. But they are also, and at the same time, very unlike human creatures, principally because they lack flesh. They are much more like angelic persons in this respect, and in all the other respects just mentioned, and it is perhaps reasonable therefore to think of them in some extended analogical sense as temporary angels" (182).

39. So, e.g., Dumbrell: "There is no explicit teaching in the passage of an intermediate state after death. . . . The interval between death and resurrection is not an interval in the consciousness of the believer, no matter how long it might be measured chronologically" (*Search for Order*, 291).

with Christ *before* the resurrection of the body.[40] Admittedly, both texts can also be interpreted in support of the other two major options of "soul sleep" and of immediate resurrection of the dead outside time. But if a disembodied, intermediate state is accepted, it is clearly only a penultimate reality—better than this life, to be sure, but far inferior to life in the resurrected body. The body and the spirit (or soul) are temporarily separated, while the latter enjoys the presence of Christ and the former awaits its redemption. Harris writes:

> Whether the interim state be one of embodiment or disembodiment, the ultimate destiny of the Christian is no emancipation from all corporeality but the acquisition of a superior form of embodiment that will perfectly mediate consciousness of the presence of the Lord.[41]

17.20.2 Praying for the Dead

If an intermediate state is accepted, we may consider the possibility of prayer for the dead. Paul does not himself address the practice of praying for the dead (though he has given commentators plenty of work with his problematic baptism for the dead in 1 Cor 15:29). Nevertheless, it may be regarded as an outworking of Paul's theology of union with Christ.

Notwithstanding traditional Protestant resistance to praying for the dead, Wright affirms its appropriateness in light of the "communion of the saints." For Paul, all dead and living saints are in Christ, and as such the departed remain brothers and sisters in him. While the Reformers outlawed the practice of praying for the dead because of its association with the mistaken doctrine of purgatory, Wright concludes that there is no reason not to pray for departed brothers and sisters in Christ, that "they will be refreshed and filled with God's joy and peace."[42]

Once we dismiss the notion of purgatory, there is little evidence to contradict Wright's conclusion that because the departed are with Christ, as we are, so Christ may mediate blessings to them at our intercession. After all, he hears our prayers, and he also cares for the departed who are in his presence. Perhaps prayer for the dead in Christ should be seen as a beautiful expression of these truths.

---

40. Witherington, *Jesus, Paul, and the End of the World*, 207–8. Harris is rather more forceful here. He writes, "It can scarcely be denied that in each case (Luke 23.42; 2 Cor. 5.8; Phil. 1.23) being 'with Christ' depicts an experience that follows death yet precedes the second Advent" (Harris, *Raised Immortal*, 135).

41. Harris, *Raised Immortal*, 142. See also Murray J. Harris, "2 Corinthians 5:1–10: Watershed in Paul's Eschatology?," *TynBul* 22 (1971): 56–57.

42. Wright, *Surprised by Hope*, 172.

17.21 Hope

Hope is the present-age counterpart to the glory of the age to come. While the age to come will be defined by glory, the lives of believers in this present age ought to be characterized by hope. Thus, hope and glory become the twin elements that shape Paul's eschatological thought. Hope exists now in anticipation of the glory to come.

As has been noted several times already, eschatological hope is not wishful thinking. It is, rather, *expectation* and *anticipation*. As discussed in §13.2, Romans 8:24–25 sheds light on this reality. Paul writes that *hope that is seen is not hope, because who hopes for what he sees? Now if we hope for what we do not see, we eagerly wait for it with patience.* The point of these comments about hoping for what is not seen is not that the object of hope must be *invisible*. The point, rather, is that the object of hope has not yet *arrived* (and therefore is not seen). Once the object has come, hope has no further role, since hope is about expectation of what is to come. Thus Paul adds that *if we hope for what we do not see* (that is, what has not yet come), *we eagerly wait for it with patience* (v. 25). Again, we see that hope involves eager waiting.

Thus, hope is irreducibly eschatological in nature because it only plays a role in this present age, as believers anticipate the age to come. When the age to come has come, there will be no further need for hope because what has been expected has already arrived. Just as believers do not wait for what they already have, so believers will not hope for what has already come. So hope is bound to this present age, even as its purpose is to encourage believers to look beyond it toward the age to come. The hope of glory will give way to glory itself. Hope is penultimate; glory is ultimate.

While the hope of glory is a central and essential element for believers living in this present age, it is of course not their only defining feature. In fact, of the three hallmarks of the Christian life, Paul clearly puts *love* ahead of the other two, as he famously told the Corinthians—*Now these three remain: faith, hope, and love—but the greatest of these is love* (1 Cor 13:13). It might be suggested that this claim is contextually defined, since the Corinthians were failing to love one another in spectacular fashion. Perhaps in another context, Paul would have given hope priority over love. But this speculation does not really hold water, since the Corinthians also had problems with their eschatological thinking (which was either overrealized or underrealized).

In fact, it seems Paul had other reasons for putting love ahead of faith and hope—one of which is eschatological in nature. In 1 Corinthians 13:8 he says that *love never ends* and contrasts it to prophecy, tongues, and knowledge precisely because they will be superseded in the age to come—*when the perfect comes, the partial will come to an end* (v. 10). It seems that the supremacy of love is due to its permanent quality—it never ends; it is eternal. In this sense, love is the exact opposite of hope, since hope by definition will end with the age to come. Love, on the other hand, transcends the boundary between the old and new ages. Love is therefore not an eschatological entity. Or, perhaps better, love is a trans-eschatological category.

The supremacy of love reminds us that the hope for glory can never be self-seeking or self-centered. The nature of love is to seek the benefit of others. Thus, hope that is qualified by love is a hope that does not anticipate good things only for oneself. Hope must be wider than that. It must be a love-shaped hope that desires good things for others too. Love-shaped hope looks to a common glory that is shared with others.

Having said that, however, eschatological hope is just as essential as trans-eschatological love, even though love will last forever, while hope has an expiration date. Whatever else it may mean to live in Christ, genuine Christian living is nothing without hope for the future. It is the future eschaton, with its redemption of creation and resurrection of the body, with its shared glory and eternal life, that makes following Christ overwhelmingly positive even in the face of the overwhelming negativity and evil of this present age.

17.22 Conclusion

This chapters brings together the exegetical results of part 2 that speak of this present age. This present age is the age of hope. While this age remains in the night, hope shines a light into that dark place and points to the day that is coming. This hope is to mark the lives of believers as they are engaged in the conflict between this present age and the age to come. They have already been transferred from the domain of darkness into the kingdom of the Son, but as long as this present age continues to exist, they will need to navigate the tensions and conflicts it brings. Nevertheless, their true allegiance is to the age to come, and their hope enables them to live as in the daytime even while it is still night.

The chapter addressed issues raised by living in the now and not yet, and how the Christian life involves a contest between the values of the old and the new. The chapter explored the presence of the Spirit of God, who adds fuel to believers' hope in Christ and represents the future in the midst of the present. The chapter also addressed some of the ways in which Paul's eschatology affects the church, mission, work, and ecology. The church must be shaped by the hope of glory and recognize itself to be an eschatological community. With its hope fixed on the age to come, the church is to serve humanity in this present age in anticipation of the new world to come. The mission of the church is also eschatological, as it declares the gospel of Christ in preparation for the nations to glorify God on the last day. The work that occupies believers in this present age ought to be conducted with the desire to please the Lord and with the eschatological expectation of reward for faithfulness. Believers should also work for the good of this world in anticipation of what the world will one day be. This applies both to occupational work and to care for the environment. The world to come is the same world we live in now, though it will be a different world. Anticipation of what it will be ought to shape how we treat it now. It is important not to underplay the significance of earth care, but its significance should not be overstated either. In the end, God will renew the heavens and the earth irrespective of how it is treated in this present age. The chapter concludes with some reflections on the relative importance of hope, especially with respect to love. While love will last forever, hope is term-limited—once this present age gives way to the age to come, hope will have fulfilled its contribution.

CHAPTER 18

CONCLUSIONS

18.1 INTRODUCTION

This final chapter draws together the major conclusions of the whole work. Since the study of Paul's eschatology has grown from an inductive approach, certain questions may remain unaddressed. Our interest has been to discover and to think through eschatology from what Paul actually says, rather than to answer preconceived questions that may come from other quarters. For instance, there has been no discussion about Paul's "position" vis-à-vis the millennium. Is Paul pre-, post-, or amillennial? While it may disappoint some readers, our best response is to say that the question is irrelevant. It simply is not an issue for Paul. Or, if it is, he does not write about it anywhere in his extant corpus. Then again, some readers may ask which millennial position *best fits* what Paul does say? Again, the best response is to say that the question is irrelevant—at least for the purposes of this book. Readers are welcome to ruminate on such questions for themselves. As Scott Lewis states, "There is no conclusive argument preventing one from holding that Paul believed in an intermediate kingdom between the parousia and the final resurrection, but if he did, he failed to develop it in any of his works."[1]

From what Paul *does* write, we have found some interesting results connected to wider questions of eschatology, such as the fact that Paul *was* an apocalyptic theologian, but he did not necessarily expect Christ to come in his lifetime. He probably believed in a temporary, disembodied, intermediate state between death and bodily resurrection. It's possible Paul had no problem with praying for the dead in Christ. He doesn't seem to know about the general resurrection of the dead (of the righteous *and* non-righteous). He endorsed heavenly rewards based on deeds. He does not talk about hell in the classical sense. His writings could be fit to an annihilationist position. He was probably not a universalist. Paul most certainly did *not* envisage the end of the current physical universe but rather its renewal.

---

1. Lewis, *"So That God May Be All in All"*, 55.

But even more important are the topics to which Paul gives repeated focus and attention. His eschatology is shaped by two overlapping ages and two competing realms. The gift of the Spirit connects believers to the future and shapes life now in preparation for that future. Paul expects the parousia of Christ to usher in the resurrection of the righteous dead and the judgment of all humanity. He believed that the entire created order would be renewed, with the glory of God in Christ permanently radiating through it. He looked forward to Christ sharing his eternal glory with his people, who will enjoy perfected, resurrected bodies made fit for eternal life with God in Christ. And at the very heart of it all is the death, resurrection, and ascension of Christ—past events from which Paul's Christocentric eschatological outlook unfurl. The remainder of this chapter summarizes our findings about such things.

Before turning to that, however, it is worth briefly reflecting on the place of Paul's eschatology with respect to his overall theological framework. In my book *Paul and Union with Christ*, I argued that if Paul's theological framework is likened to a spiderweb, union with Christ would be the *webbing* that connects all of Paul's key theological commitments. The claim here, with Schweitzer, is that eschatology provides the *frame* of the web. Paul's two-age eschatological schema provides the arena in which all other theologically significant events take place. Even the death and the resurrection of Christ fit within it. In this sense, the word *centrality* may not be apt, since Paul's eschatology is not so much central as it is all-pervasive. It is like the field that defines the game played upon it. If the shape of the field is changed, the game must change with it. In this sense, we might say that a playing field not only defines the parameters of the game that is played upon it but also conditions other aspects of the game. For instance, the two opposing teams each occupy their own half of the field, and their goal is found on the opposite end. The direction of their play is shaped by the field. How many yards are won or lost is measured by space within the field. The distance to the goal, try-line, or end zone is determined by the field. And, of course, there is no legitimate play outside the bounds of the playing field. And just as the spiderweb cannot retain its integrity without its frame, so the game cannot be played without its field. Both analogies serve the same point: eschatology is essential in its provision of the structure, frame, integrity, and shape of Paul's theological framework. Without eschatology, it collapses.

18.2 APOCALYPTICISM

Though Paul authored no apocalypses, his epistles reveal several indications of an apocalyptically shaped eschatology. His use of *mystery* language, the coming of the Son of Man, urging to be watchful and alert, a two-age eschatology, an epistemology of revealed knowledge, and a soteriology of victory are all hallmarks of Paul's literature, and each resonates with an apocalyptic eschatology. The only questionable claim from the perspective of Jewish apocalyptic studies is the *imminence* of the coming of the Son of Man, since the relevant texts may not necessarily convey the imminence that has long been associated with them.

From the perspective of Pauline studies, the two most questionable elements regarding Paul's apocalypticism are the righteousness of God as an apocalyptic motif and the rejection of any horizontal, covenantal, salvation-historical concern within his thought. While the righteousness of God *may* be construed as an apocalyptic motif, this is difficult to prove since it has no grounding in wider Jewish apocalyptic literature. And the rejection of horizontal elements in Paul's apocalyptic eschatology is unfounded, and in fact contradicts the plainly salvation-historical shape of Paul's thought world.

18.3 Two Ages and Two Realms

The rubric of age and realm gives shape to Paul's overall eschatological vision. The breaking into the present of the age to come has created a realm of righteousness to which believers in Christ now belong. They have been transferred out of the present evil age and realm and exist under the future (but present) age and realm. This has deeply significant consequences for the ways in which believers must conduct themselves. They no longer belong to the realm ruled by sin, death, and the devil, and as such are to show no allegiance to it. Rather, as people who belong to Christ, they are to live according to the values of his realm—according to righteousness, grace, and godliness.

The age to come is the object of Paul's hope. In the age to come judgment and justice are exercised, the dead are raised, evil is destroyed, the creation is renewed, and the saints receive their glorious inheritance. It will be characterized by the eternal glory of God in Christ, which is shared with those in Christ. They will live with Christ for all eternity.

Paul's two-ages, two-realms eschatological framework is not permanent; when the day of the Lord comes, the realm of Adam, the old age, will give way so that only the realm of Christ, the new age, will remain. As such, the reign of sin will end as grace will reign supreme, just as the present, invisible enthronement of Christ will transition to his future, visible rule over all creation. The promise of inheritance, guaranteed by the Spirit, will find its fulfillment in the age to come.

Above all, the age to come is the age of glory. Glory is the most defining characteristic of the age to come, and Paul regards it as the ultimate goal of everything. It puts present suffering and brokenness into context, as the hope of future glory far outweighs the disappointments and conflicts that characterize the present age. Christ will appear with glory, he will be glorified by all humanity (especially believers), and the glory of God in Christ will endure forever. The most remarkable feature of the glory of Christ is that he will share it with those in him in the age to come. It is a relational, unselfish glory of eternal beauty and majesty.

18.4 CHRISTOCENTRIC ESCHATOLOGY

Every sphere of Paul's eschatological thought centers around Christ, and the apostle views him as the one through whom each sphere becomes what it is. Christ is the means and location of the new creation, both personal and cosmic. Each person found in Christ becomes a new creation, with new works for them to complete. And the entire created order is renewed in, through, and for Christ. Christ has disarmed competing authorities and power structures through his death and resurrection, which have all been placed under his feet. He is the Lord of the new realm into which believers have been transferred.

While in one sense it is Christ's resurrection that overcomes death, in another sense it is the death of Christ that overcomes death. Christ's law-fulfilling and sin-condemning death is the mechanism by which it is possible to overcome death, because without its other two operatives at work, death loses its power. Thus, the resurrection of Christ is the outcome of the overthrow of death; it is the inevitable consequence of robbing death of its stinger. It is the proof that death has indeed been conquered. In this way, the death of Christ is eschatological in nature. It unlocks death's grip on humanity, opening the way to liberation from the powers of sin and death and ensuring eternal life for those in Christ. It also effects the transference of realm that believers undergo when they participate in the death and resurrection of Christ.

The resurrection of Christ stands as the proof that God will raise the believing dead to bodily resurrection, and it is the template for their resurrection. While believers are sown in corruption, dishonor, and weakness with a natural body, like Christ they will be raised incorruptible, in glory and power with a spiritual body. When the corruptible body is clothed with incorruptibility, then death will be swallowed up in victory. It is their resurrection to an incorruptible, glorious body that enables believers to participate in the eschaton. Their resurrected bodies will be fit for the new age in a way that their pre-resurrected bodies could only anticipate.

The resurrection of Christ makes possible the bodily resurrection of believers on the last day, as well as their spiritual resurrection now. He is the firstfruits who reveals the harvest to come, and he will transform their mortal bodies into immortal bodies through their union with him. When Christ comes, the dead will be raised in anticipation of judgment, when he will reveal the secrets of hearts and rescue believers from wrath. He will grant eternal life to those in Christ, resulting in life together with him. This eternal life will consist of the promised inheritance enjoyed by all in Christ, as he shares his rightful inheritance as the Son with those grafted into Christ to become Abraham's seed, the spiritual Israel. The highpoint of sharing with Christ, after sharing in his suffering, is to share in his eternal glory. Such sharing is bundled into the salvation achieved by Christ and will be revealed when he comes. Christ will be glorified by his saints on that day when he will hand the kingdom over to his Father.

The hope of future resurrection holds several implications for the present life. Believers are to consider themselves dead to sin and alive to God in Christ because they will be found in the likeness of Christ's resurrection. For Paul, it also means that he can face dangers and death every day, knowing that such threats are not ultimate. It enables him to share in the sufferings of Christ, as he assumes he will reach the resurrection from among the dead. Resurrection also offers comfort in the face of grief, since believers will not grieve as those without hope.

The ascension of Christ is an eschatological event in at least three ways. First, it represents the "visible" enthronement of Christ as Lord over all. His physical ascension was a spatial metaphor representing his exalted entrance to heaven. The ascension is Christ's exaltation at which point he was given the name above every name, so that in the coming days every knee will bow at the name of Jesus. Christ is seated at the Father's right hand in the heavens, above every ruler and authority, power and dominion, and every title given—not only in this age but also in the one to come. While the death and resurrection of Christ represent his victory over opposing powers, Christ's exaltation is this victory's glorious manifestation.

The death, resurrection, and ascension of Christ are inherently eschatological events. Each makes a distinct contribution to the eschatological landscape, and together they constitute the formidable power of Christ to conquer the powers of sin and death, to overturn their dominion over humanity, and to triumph over all other authorities that stood opposed to him. The benefits of Christ's eschatological death, resurrection, and ascension are appropriated by the believer's participation in each. Believers have died with Christ, been raised with Christ, and have been seated with him in the heavens. By their participation in Christ, believers have been set free from the tyranny of sin and death and have begun a new life with Christ in the realm of Christ. In Christ they are seated with God already, poised to witness the coming revelations of his extraordinary mercy and kindness.

While Paul regards the death, resurrection, and ascension of Christ as inherently eschatological in nature, by no means do they exhaust his eschatological work. Indeed, the eschatological nature of Christ's death, resurrection, and ascension set the table for what is to come with the coming of Christ. When Christ comes, the dead will be raised in anticipation of judgment when he will reveal the secrets of hearts and rescue believers from wrath. He will grant eternal life to those in Christ, resulting in life together with him. This eternal life will consist of the promised inheritance enjoyed by all in Christ, as he shares his rightful inheritance as the Son with those grafted into Christ to become Abraham's seed, the spiritual Israel. The highpoint of sharing with Christ, after sharing in his suffering, is to share in his eternal glory. The design of the eschaton is nothing less than the unfurling of the embryonic promise contained within the death, resurrection, and ascension of Christ.

18.5 THE PAROUSIA AND THE LAST DAY

While Paul does not use the language of the *return* of Christ, his coming is cast as his *presence* or *arrival* (ἡ παρουσία), his *revelation* (ἡ ἀποκάλυψις), his *appearing* (φανερόω), and his *descent* (καταβαίνω), all of which signal *the day of the Lord* (ἡ ἡμέρα τοῦ κυρίου). The parousia of Christ functions in three broad ways for Paul. First, it is the event that believers look forward to in this present age. Second, the parousia of Christ will bring the end of the age, the resurrection of the dead, and his presence among his people. Third, the parousia will inaugurate final judgment as he punishes his enemies and glorifies those who belong to him.

Paul lived in expectation of the last day, expressed by his language of *the day of wrath* (ἡ ἡμέρα ὀργῆς), *the day* (ἡ ἡμέρα), *the hour* (ἡ ὥρα), and *the end* (τὸ τέλος). A day of wrath is coming in which God's righteous judgment will be revealed. On that day, God will judge what people have kept secret. Since the day is near, and the night is nearly over, it is the hour to wake up from sleep and live as in the daytime. Believers ought not be surprised by the coming of the day of the Lord, though it will come like a thief in the night. On the day that Christ comes, he will be glorified by his saints, and those who have loved his coming will receive from him a crown of righteousness. Then, after the coming of Christ, comes the end when all rule and authority is abolished, and he hands over the kingdom to God the Father.

18.6 DEATH AND JUDGMENT

The eschatological significance of death cannot be overstated. First, the reality of human death is a consequence of sin, which has put humanity under the power of sin and death in the first place. A central interest of Paul's eschatology is how sin and death are conquered. Second, death releases the individual from the bonds of the fleshly fallen body as well as the loosened grip of the present evil age. It is the point at which believers are brought into the presence of God, if they die before Christ comes. Third, Paul's eschatological hope is grounded in the resurrection of the dead. Resurrection is a huge component of Paul's eschatology because death is an enormous problem for humanity. Thus, from the beginning of the biblical story to its end, death must be understood from an eschatological perspective. Its existence reminds us of the overarching eschatological problem that overshadows human history: How will sin and death finally be overcome and overthrown? The prospect of death facing every human being propels our interest forward so that questions about eschatological matters come into focus. The great hope that death will finally be overturned by our bodily resurrection from the dead means that the tyranny of death serves as a foil for the victory and glory of life eternal.

Paul considers the universal judgment of all sin and evil to be an inescapable feature of the age to come. The coming day of God's wrath will divide all people either for eternal life with Christ or wrath and anger apart from him. The living and the dead will stand before the judgment seat of God as their secrets (both good and bad) will be revealed. Believers will not be exempt from judgment, but they will be rescued from God's wrath, being found blameless in Christ.

Judgment shapes the future, but it also shapes the present. The scepter of forthcoming judgment is used by Paul to encourage obedience—indeed, fear of judgment is regarded a healthy motivation to abstain from worldly desires. Furthermore, the notion of reward at judgment is also held out as motivation. Believers can live in faithful allegiance to Christ, knowing that he will reward their devotion. The hopeful expectation of judgment affects daily life with respect to Paul's attitude to human opinion, work, recompense, and justice. Above all, judgment is concerned with putting the world to rights. Though its implications for individuals are stressed in several contexts, Paul is clear that its wider implications shape the destiny of the whole world. With Christ as Lord over all creation, judgment is the necessary means of expressing his rule. It is how Christ will exert righteousness and peace over the entire created order.

18.7 Inheritance and Eternal Life

Paul's understanding of inheritance begins with Abraham's inheritance, who is promised that he and his descendants would inherit the world. Paul argues that Abraham's true descendants are those who share his faith in God, whether Jew or gentile. Those with the faith of Abraham become God's children, and as children they are heirs of God and coheirs with Christ. The Spirit serves as the down payment of believers' inheritance.

Eternal life is the inheritance promised to believers who are heirs by the grace of God. Through faith in Christ, believers suffer now with him but will live with him in resurrected bodies when he comes. While the reign of sin results in death, so the coming reign of righteousness will result in eternal life through Christ. Eternal life requires the resurrection of formerly mortal bodies, whose deeds must be put to death in order to live. It is reaped from sowing according to the Spirit and through faith in Christ.

Eternal life is not an impersonal, private existence but life with Christ. Living with Christ is the positive counterpart of suffering with him and is the hope of heirs who have been justified by the grace of Christ. Eternal life is thus a relational mode of existence, lived in bodies no longer subjected to death and decay. Believers anticipate living under the reign of righteousness, free from sin, and in eternal peace with Christ.

18.8 NEW CREATION

There is an intimate connection between the fate of humanity and that of the entire creation. The latter was subjected to decay because of the fall of humanity and will only be released from its futility when the children of God are revealed. This restoration of creation will be characterized by unification around Christ, since God has planned to bring everything together in Christ, things in heaven and on earth. Each believer is already regarded as a new creation in Christ, and this is what really matters in comparison to trivial issues such as circumcision.

The sweep of Paul's eschatology includes the entirety of creation. Creation is not simply the canvas upon which the salvation of humanity is painted, nor is it simply the arena in which God acts. Creation is *itself* the painting. It is the arena *and object* of God's restorative work. All things in heaven and earth will be transformed through renewal and unification around Christ.

Paul does not imagine a new creation that will replace the old, as though there are two creations. For Paul, there is only one created order. Creation will be renewed to such an extent that it can be called "new," but it is not new in the sense of replacement but in the sense of renewal.

Paul's eschatological vision includes the full sweep of creation, as all things in heaven and on earth will be renewed and centered around Christ. There is an inextricable link between the fate of humanity and that of creation, with the latter being subjected to decay because of the former, and it will only be released from its bondage once humanity has been restored. And this restoration can only occur in the wake of judgment.

Ultimately, however, judgment is about putting the world to rights. There is a single creation that will be renewed and restored. Thus, judgment is concerned with the eradication of evil and the establishment of righteousness and peace within creation. The salvation of humanity is tied to this renewal of creation, in keeping with Jewish expectation. Thus it is no surprise that redeemed believers are described as new creations since, for Paul, the new creation begins with redeemed humanity.

18.9 Hope and Glory

Hope is not merely a subjective, experiential factor in the lives of believers. While it shapes the experience of believers, hope is regarded as a pillar of theological expectation. It reflects a confident anticipation of what God will do based on his promises and his past faithfulness in keeping his promises. It is the conviction that, having been justified by God's grace, believers will inherit eternal life.

Through his multitudinous references to hope it is clear that it is the central way in which eschatology shapes Paul's vision of the Christian life. Whatever else it may mean to live in Christ, genuine Christian living is nothing without hope for the future. It is the future eschaton, with its redemption of creation and resurrection of the body, with its shared glory and eternal life, that makes following Christ overwhelmingly positive even in the face of the overwhelming negativity and evil of this present age.

There is something all-consuming about the glory of God in the eschaton. It is the ultimate end of everything from Paul's perspective. The highest goal of life, of humanity, of creation is the glory of God in Christ. It is true to say that everything exists to serve this eternal glory in the end. Glory is ascribed to God's person as an eternal quality. It is not something that needs to be achieved or that God needs others to recognize. God is glorious in and of himself. His very being is transcendent and majestic. His glory can be seen in his acts of creation, resurrection, and re-creation. But in this present age, the fullness of God's glory can only be glimpsed; only in the age to come will it be fully apprehended by all. Thus, there is a present hiddenness of the glory of God. It can be seen for those who want to see it, but a day is coming when it will not remain hidden, and all people, heavenly beings, and all creation will acknowledge his glory. While God is already glorious in and of himself, Paul also speaks of glory being ascribed to God. The heavenly beings, human beings, and indeed all creation will offer glory to God. This is Paul's firm expectation as well as his prayer.

All that God has done for believers in Christ ought to issue in praise to his glorious grace and the glorification of the name of Christ. But believers can be confident that if they suffer with Christ, they will also be glorified with him with a glory that will resonate throughout creation itself, and even now the glory of the Lord transforms believers into his glorious image. Their momentary, light afflictions are producing an incomparable, eternal weight of glory, a sharing in the glory of Christ, which God predestined before the ages. The glory of Christ is also hidden in the present age, though it can be seen by those with eyes to see it. He is the Lord of glory, he has been raised in glory and in a glorious body, and he is the hope of glory. The glory of God is seen in Christ, and when he appears in glory those hidden with him will appear with him in glory. Though the glory of God is inherent in his own being and manifested in Christ, it is shared with believers, who have been called by God into his kingdom and glory. Though believers will ascribe glory to Christ when he comes, they will also partake in his glory.

18.10 LIFE TODAY . . . IN LIGHT OF TOMORROW

This present age is the time for hope for the age to come. The trials, sufferings, tragedies, and death that characterize this age are all contrasted to the age to come, when these will turn to comfort, glory, triumph, and resurrection. Without such hope, this present age is irredeemable with its deep-seated evil and the merciless reign of death. This present age stands against the age to come that has dawned through the resurrection of Christ. But when Christ comes, this age will be superseded by the age to come. Believers have already been transferred to the realm of Christ, meaning that their loyalty is to the age to come, not this present age. They are engaged in spiritual warfare, as the powers of this present age continue to rage against those who belong to Christ.

The Christian life is defined by *expectation*. And the word that Paul most commonly uses to convey such expectation is *hope*. All the complexities raised by living in the now and not yet can be addressed by the set of expectations summarized as hope. When believers are tempted to ungodly practices, their expectation of judgment can give them pause. When believers are encouraged to adopt worldly attitudes and priorities, their expectation of future glory in the presence of Christ can dispel such pressure. When believers experience suffering and persecution and wonder why God allows such things to happen, they will be reminded that God has set a day on which justice will be done and injustice will be undone, and that expectation will carry them forward. Without such great expectations, it is simply impossible to live out the Christian life. Indeed, without hope it is not possible to be a Christian at all, since Christ *is* our hope. Ultimately, hope is the present-age counterpart to the glory of the age to come. While the age to come will be defined by glory, the lives of believers in this present age ought to be characterized by hope. Thus, hope and glory become the twin elements that shape Paul's eschatological thought. Hope exists now in anticipation of the glory to come.

The power available to believers as they navigate living in the now and not yet is the Spirit of God. He mediates both the past and future work of Christ. Just as the Spirit raised Christ from the dead, he raises believers now, and he will do so bodily when Christ comes again. As the deposit guaranteeing their inheritance, the presence of the Spirit mediates the future to believers. He *is* the future breaking into present experience. As such, the presence of the Spirit empowers believers to participate in the new creation and to live according to the day rather than the night.

There are two senses in which believers live by the Spirit. First, believers live by the power of the Spirit. Living according to the age to come is only possible with the power that the Spirit brings *from* that age in *anticipation* of that age. New life in Christ can only exist in the Spirit. Second, believers live by the Spirit in the sense that they are to live according to the Spirit. As they walk in the Spirit, the Spirit produces fruit in them; as they sow to the Spirit, they reap eternal life. Thus, believers can only be alive in Christ by the power of the Spirit, and they are to conduct themselves in step with the Spirit.

The church must be characterized by an eschatological perspective and by the hope of glory. Just as all believers straddle this present age and the age to come, so the wider communion of believers does so on a corporate level. If the church ceases to be an eschatological community, it will cease to exist as a true church. A church that does not long for the coming of Christ has lost its way. A church that is not living as in the daytime amid this present darkness cannot reflect the light of Christ to a lost world. A church that does not cling to the hope of resurrection will live without hope. And a church without hope is an oxymoron.

The way we conduct our work is an opportunity to declare our expectation in what is to come. It declares our expectation of the world to come—or at least it ought to do so. The values and standards that pertain to the daytime can inform our work now. Work can build, contribute to society, improve people's lives, facilitate community, and myriad other positive things. Believers ought to embrace these positive features of work as emblems of the values that will characterize the age to come. As such, believers ought to avoid work that destroys, marginalizes, and corrupts. Work that is only self-serving does not embody the values of the kingdom to come. Such work becomes an anti-witness to the eschaton, not to mention the final judgment. Our care for the environment also ought to express our eschatological expectation that this world will be renewed. The earth that *is* should be respected in anticipation of the earth it will *become*. Earth care is therefore an expression of our hope. It should not be underplayed by consigning this earth to the trash can, nor should it be overplayed by imagining that the renewal of the earth is at risk unless we intervene.

Ultimately, life today must be lived in light of the end. Our end is the only way to make sense of life now and the only way to live according to the hope of Christ. Søren Kierkegaard has been paraphrased as saying, *Life can only be understood backwards; but it must be lived forwards.*[2] While Kierkegaard meant that we can only learn about our lives by looking back at our own personal histories and moving forward from there, this expression can be repurposed to express Paul's eschatology. If Paul had said it, he would have meant that our lives can only be understood from their end point, their *telos*—moving through death, resurrection, and judgment, to eternal glory. Life can only truly be understood backward from that end. But life must be lived *forwards* as we approach that end. Or, as Paul *did* say, we live with Christ in us, *the hope of glory*.

---

2. "It is perfectly true, as the philosophers say, that life must be understood backwards. But they forget the other proposition, that it must be lived forwards" (Søren Kierkegaard, *The Journals of Søren Kierkegaard*, ed. and trans. Alexander Dru [New York: Oxford University Press, 1938], IV, A, 164).

BIBLIOGRAPHY

Adams, Edward. "Graeco-Roman and Ancient Jewish Cosmology." Pages 5–27 in *Cosmology and New Testament Theology*. Edited by Jonathan T. Pennington and Sean M. McDonough. LNTS 355. London: T&T Clark, 2008.
Alsup, John E. "Eschatology and Ethics in Paul." *Austin Seminary Bulletin (Faculty Ed.)* 94.4 (1978): 40–52.
Andria, Solomon. *Romans*. Africa Bible Commentary Series. Nairobi: Hippo, 2012.
Arnold, Clinton E. *Ephesians*. ZECNT. Grand Rapids: Zondervan, 2010.
Barclay, John M. G. *Paul and the Gift*. Grand Rapids: Eerdmans, 2015.
———. "Under Grace: The Christ-Gift and the Construction of a Christian *Habitus*." Pages 59–76 in *Apocalyptic Paul: Cosmos and Anthropos in Romans 5–8*. Edited by Beverly Roberts Gaventa. Waco, TX: Baylor University Press, 2013.
Barnett, Paul. *The Message of 2 Corinthians*. BST. Leicester: Inter-Varsity Press, 1988.
Barrett, C. K. *The First Epistle to the Corinthians*. BNTC. Peabody, MA: Hendrickson, 1968.
Barth, Karl. *Church Dogmatics* III/2: *The Doctrine of Creation*. Edited by G. W. Bromiley and T. F. Torrance. Translated by G. W. Bromiley. Edinburgh: T&T Clark, 1960.
———. *Church Dogmatics* IV/3.1: *The Doctrine of Reconciliation*. Edited by G. W. Bromiley and T. F. Torrance. Translated by G. W. Bromiley. Edinburgh: T&T Clark, 1961.
———. *Church Dogmatics* IV/3.2: *The Doctrine of Reconciliation*. Edited by G. W. Bromiley and T. F. Torrance. Translated by G. W. Bromiley. Edinburgh: T&T Clark, 1961.
———. *The Epistle to the Romans*. Translated by Edwin C. Hoskyns. London: Oxford University Press, 1933.
Barth, Markus. *Ephesians: Introduction, Translation, and Commentary on Chapters 1–3*. AB. Garden City, NY: Doubleday, 1974.
———. *Ephesians: Translation and Commentary on Chapters 4–6*. AB. Garden City, NY: Doubleday, 1974.
Bartsch, Hans-Werner. "Paul's Eschatology and Its Meaning Today." *Brethren Life and Thought* 12.3 (1967): 4–10.
Bassler, Jouette M. "Divine Impartiality in Paul's Letter to the Romans." *NovT* 26 (1984): 43–58.
———. *Divine Impartiality: Paul and a Theological Axiom*. SBLDS 59. Chico, CA: Scholars Press, 1982.
Batey, Richard A. "Paul's Bride Image: A Symbol of Realistic Eschatology." *Int* 17.2 (1963): 176–82.
Bauckham, Richard. *The Fate of the Dead: Studies on the Jewish and Christian Apocalypses*. NovTSup 93. Leiden: Brill, 1998.

Beale, G. K. *1–2 Thessalonians*. IVPNTC. Downers Grove, IL: InterVarsity Press, 2003.
Beale, G. K. "The Eschatology of Paul." Pages 198–213 in *Studies in the Pauline Epistles: Essays in Honor of Douglas J. Moo*. Edited by Matthew S. Harmon and Jay E. Smith. Grand Rapids: Zondervan, 2014.
Bebbington, David W. *Evangelicalism in Modern Britain: A History from the 1730s to the 1980s*. London: Routledge, 1989.
Beker, J. Christiaan. *Paul's Apocalyptic Gospel: The Coming Triumph of God*. Philadelphia: Fortress, 1982.
———. *Paul The Apostle: The Triumph of God in Life and Thought*. Philadelphia: Fortress, 1980.
Belleville, Linda L. *2 Corinthians*. IVPNTC. Downers Grove, IL: InterVarsity Press, 1996.
Best, Ernest. *A Critical and Exegetical Commentary on Ephesians*. ICC. London: T&T Clark, 1998.
———. *The First and Second Epistles to the Thessalonians*. BNTC. Peabody, MA: Hendrickson, 1972.
Bird, Michael F. *Colossians and Philemon: A New Covenant Commentary*. NCCS. Eugene, OR: Cascade, 2009.
———. "Raised for our Justification: A Fresh Look at Romans 4:25." *Colloquium* 35.1 (2003): 31–46.
———. *Romans*. SGBC. Grand Rapids: Zondervan, 2016.
———. *The Saving Righteousness of God: Studies on Paul, Justification and the New Perspective*. Milton Keyes: Paternoster, 2006.
Bockmuehl, Markus. *The Epistle to the Philippians*. BNTC. Peabody, MA: Hendrickson, 1998.
De Boer, Martinus C. de. *The Defeat of Death: Apocalyptic Eschatology in 1 Corinthians 15 and Romans 5*. JSNTSup 22. Sheffield: JSOT, 1988.
———. "Paul and Apocalyptic Eschatology." Pages 345–83 in *The Encyclopedia of Apocalypticism*. Edited by John J. Collins and Bernard McGinn. New York: Continuum, 2000.
———. "Paul and Jewish Apocalyptic Eschatology." Pages 169–90 in *Apocalyptic and the New Testament*. Sheffield: JSOT, 1989.
——— "Paul's Mythologizing Program in Romans 5–8." Pages 1–20 in *Apocalyptic Paul: Cosmos and Anthropos in Romans 5–8*. Edited by Beverly Roberts Gaventa. Waco, TX: Baylor University Press, 2013.
Breytenbach, Cilliers. "'For in Hope We Were Saved': Discerning Time in Paul's Letter to the Romans." Pages 181–96 in *Eschatology of the New Testament and Some Related Documents*. Edited by Jan G. van der Watt. WUNT 2/315. Tübingen: Mohr Siebeck, 2011.
Brookins, Timothy A., and Bruce W. Longenecker. *1 Corinthians 1–9: A Handbook on the Greek Text*. BHGNT. Waco, TX: Baylor University Press, 2016.
———. *1 Corinthians 10–16: A Handbook on the Greek Text*. BHGNT. Waco, TX: Baylor University Press, 2016.
Bruce, F. F. *The Epistle to the Galatians: A Commentary on the Greek Text*. NIGTC. Grand Rapids: Eerdmans, 1982.

Bultmann, Rudolf. *Theology of the New Testament: Volume I.* Translated by Kendrick Grobel. London: SCM, 1952.
Burger, Hans. *Being in Christ: A Biblical and Systematic Investigation in a Reformed Perspective.* Eugene, OR: Wipf & Stock, 2009.
Burgland, Lane A. "Eschatological Tension and Existential *Angst*: 'Now' and 'Not Yet' in Romans 7:14–25 and 1QS 11 (Community Rule, Manual of Discipline)." *CTQ* 61.3 (1997): 163–76.
Burkeen, W. Howard. "The Parousia of Christ in the Thessalonian Correspondence." PhD diss., University of Aberdeen, 1979.
Byrne, Brendan. "Eschatologies of Resurrection and Destruction: The Ethical Significance of Paul's Dispute with the Corinthians." *Downside Review* 104.357 (1986): 288–98.
Campbell, Constantine R. *Advances in the Study of Greek: New Insights for Reading the New Testament.* Grand Rapids: Zondervan, 2015.
———. *Basics of Verbal Aspect in Biblical Greek.* Grand Rapids: Zondervan, 2008.
———. *Colossians and Philemon: A Handbook on the Greek Text.* BHGNT. Waco, TX: Baylor University Press, 2013.
———. "Judgment of Evil as the Renewal of Creation." In *Evil and Creation: Historical and Constructive Essays in Christian Dogmatics.* Edited by David J. Luy, Matthew Levering, and George Kalantzis. Bellingham, WA: Lexham, 2020.
———. *Paul and Union with Christ: An Exegetical and Theological Study.* Grand Rapids: Zondervan, 2012.
———. "Prepositions and Exegesis: What's in a Word?" Pages 39–54 in *Getting into the Text: New Testament Essays in Honor of David Alan Black.* Edited by Daniel L. Akin and Thomas W. Hudgins. Eugene, OR: Pickwick, 2017.
———. "With Christ over the Powers." Pages 150–65 in *Christ's Victory over Evil: Biblical Theology and Pastoral Ministry.* Edited by Peter G. Bolt. Nottingham: Apollos, 2009.
Campbell, Douglas A. "An Apocalyptic Rereading of 'Justification' in Paul: Or, an Overview of the Argument of Douglas Campbell's *The Deliverance of God*—by Douglas Campbell." *ExpTim* 123.8 (2012): 382–93.
———. *The Deliverance of God: An Apocalyptic Rereading of Justification in Paul.* Grand Rapids: Eerdmans, 2009.
Caneday, Ardel B. "Already Reigning in Life through One Man: Recovery of Adam's Abandoned Dominion (Romans 5:12–21)." Pages 27–43 in *Studies in the Pauline Epistles: Essays in Honor of Douglas J. Moo.* Edited by Matthew S. Harmon and Jay E. Smith. Grand Rapids: Zondervan, 2014.
Charlesworth, James H. "Paul, the Jewish Apocalypses, and Apocalyptic Eschatology." Pages 83–105 in *Paul the Jew: Rereading the Apostle as a Figure of Second Temple Judaism.* Edited by Gabriele Boccaccini and Carlos A. Segovia. Minneapolis: Fortress, 2016.
Chia, Samuel P. "The Role of Eschatology in Paul's Ethics." *Sino-Christian Studies* 3 (2007): 37–59.
Childs, Brevard S. *The Church's Guide for Reading Paul: The Canonical Shaping of the Pauline Corpus.* Grand Rapids: Eerdmans, 2008.
Ciampa, Roy E., and Brian S. Rosner. *The First Letter to the Corinthians.* PNTC. Grand Rapids: Eerdmans, 2010.

Cohick, Lynn H. *Philippians*. SGBC. Grand Rapids: Zondervan, 2013.
Cole, R. Alan. *The Letter of Paul to the Galatians*. Rev. ed. TNTC. Leicester: Inter-Varsity Press, 1989.
Collins, John J. *The Apocalyptic Imagination: An Introduction to Jewish Apocalyptic Literature*. 2nd ed. Grand Rapids: Eerdmans, 1998.
Cranfield, C. E. B. *The Epistle to the Romans*. 2 vols. ICC. London: T&T Clark, 1975, 1979.
Cullmann, Oscar. *Christ and Time: The Primitive Christian Conception of Time and History*. Rev. ed. Translated by Floyd V. Filson. Philadelphia: Westminster, 1964.
Davies, J. P. *Paul Among the Apocalypses? An Evaluation of the "Apocalyptic Paul" in the Context of Jewish and Christian Apocalyptic Literature*. LNTS 562. London: Bloomsbury T&T Clark, 2016.
———. "What to Expect When You're Expecting: Maternity, Salvation History, and the 'Apocalyptic Paul.'" *JSNT* 383.3 (2016): 301–15.
deSilva, David A. *Galatians: A Handbook on the Greek Text*. BHGNT. Waco, TX: Baylor University Press, 2014.
Dumbrell, William H. *The Search for Order: Biblical Eschatology in Focus*. Grand Rapids: Baker, 1994.
Dunn, James D. G. *The Epistle to the Galatians*. BNTC. Grand Rapids: Baker Academic, 1993.
———. "Paul's Understanding of the Death of Jesus." Pages 125–41 in *Reconciliation and Hope: New Testament Essays on Atonement and Eschatology: Presented to L. L. Morris on His 60th Birthday*. Edited by Robert Banks. Grand Rapids: Eerdmans, 1974.
———. *Romans 1–8*. WBC 38A. Dallas: Word, 1998.
———. *The Theology of Paul the Apostle*. Grand Rapids: Eerdmans, 1998.
Engberg-Pedersen, Troels. *Cosmology and Self in the Apostle Paul: The Material Spirit*. Oxford: Oxford University Press, 2010.
Fee, Gordon D. *The First Epistle to the Corinthians*. Rev. ed. NICNT. Grand Rapids: Eerdmans, 2014.
———. *God's Empowering Presence: The Holy Spirit in the Letters of Paul*. Peabody, MA: Hendrickson, 1994.
———. *Pauline Christology: An Exegetical-Theological Study*. Peabody, MA: Hendrickson, 2007.
———. *Paul's Letter to the Philippians*. NICNT. Grand Rapids: Eerdmans, 1995.
Fitzmyer, Joseph A. *Romans*. AYB. New Haven: Yale University Press, 1993.
Foster, Robert L. "Reoriented to the Cosmos: Cosmology & Theology in Ephesians through Philemon." Pages 107–24 in *Cosmology and New Testament Theology*. Edited by Jonathan T. Pennington and Sean M. McDonough. LNTS 355. London: T&T Clark, 2008.
Fowl, Stephen E. *Philippians*. THNTC. Grand Rapids: Eerdmans, 2005.
Frey, Jörg. "New Testament Eschatology—an Introduction: Classical Issues, Disputed Themes, and Current Perspectives." Pages 3–32 in *Eschatology of the New Testament and Some Related Documents*. Edited by Jan G. van der Watt. WUNT 2/315. Tübingen: Mohr Siebeck, 2011.
Fung, Ronald Y. K. *The Epistle to the Galatians*. NICNT. Grand Rapids: Eerdmans, 1998.

Gaffin, Richard B. *The Centrality of the Resurrection: A Study in Paul's Soteriology*. Grand Rapids: Baker, 1978.

———. "Justification and Eschatology." Pages 1–21 in *Justified in Christ: God's Plan for Us in Justification*. Edited by K. Scott Oliphant. Fearn: Mentor, 2007.

Gallaher, Brandon, and Julia S. Konstantinovsky. "Divine Action in Christ: The Christocentric and Trinitarian Nature of Human Cooperation with God." Pages 175–209 in *When the Son of Man Didn't Come: A Constructive Proposal on the Delay of the Parousia*. Edited by Christopher M. Hays in collaboration with Brandon Gallaher, Julia S. Konstantinovsky, Richard J. Ounsworth, and C. A. Strine. Minneapolis: Fortress, 2016.

Gardner, Paul. *1 Corinthians*. ZECNT. Grand Rapids: Zondervan, 2018.

Garland, David E. *1 Corinthians*. BECNT. Grand Rapids: Baker Academic, 2003.

Gaventa, Beverly Roberts, ed. *Apocalyptic Paul: Cosmos and Anthropos in Romans 5–8*. Waco, TX: Baylor University Press, 2013.

———. "Neither Height nor Depth: Discerning the Cosmology of Romans." *SJT* 64.3 (2011): 265–78.

———. *Our Mother Saint Paul*. Louisville: Westminster John Knox, 2007.

Gieschen, Charles A. "Christ's Coming and the Church's Mission in 1 Thessalonians." *CTQ* 76.1–2 (2012): 37–55.

Goff, Matthew. "The Mystery of God's Wisdom, the Parousia of a Messiah, and Visions of Heavenly Paradise: 1 and 2 Corinthians in the Context of Jewish Apocalypticism." Pages 175–92 in *The Jewish Apocalyptic Tradition and the Shaping of New Testament Thought*. Edited by Benjamin E. Reynolds and Loren T. Stuckenbruck. Minneapolis: Fortress, 2017.

Gorman, Michael J. *Inhabiting the Cruciform God: Kenosis, Justification, and Theosis in Paul's Narrative Soteriology*. Grand Rapids: Eerdmans, 2009.

Gräbe, Petrus J. "'And He Made Known to Us the Mystery of His Will . . .': Reflections on the Eschatology of the Letter to the Ephesians." Pages 256–68 in *Eschatology of the New Testament and Some Related Documents*. Edited by Jan G. van der Watt. WUNT 2/315. Tübingen: Mohr Siebeck, 2011.

Green, Gene L. *The Letters to the Thessalonians*. PNTC. Grand Rapids: Eerdmans, 2002.

Griffiths, Paul J. *Decreation: The Last Things of All Creatures*. Waco, TX: Baylor University Press, 2014.

Grundmann, Walter. "σύν-μετά." Pages 766–97 in *Theological Dictionary of the New Testament: Volume VII*. Edited by Gerhard Friedrich. Translated by Geoffrey W. Bromiley. Grand Rapids: Eerdmans, 1971.

Guthrie, Donald. *The Pastoral Epistles: An Introduction and Commentary*. 2nd ed. TNTC. Leicester: Inter-Varsity Press, 1990.

Guthrie, George H. *2 Corinthians*. BECNT. Grand Rapids: Baker Academic, 2015.

Hafemann, Scott. "Eschatology and Ethics: The Future of Israel and the Nations in Romans 15:1–13." *TynBul* 51.2 (2000): 161–92.

Hansen, G. Walter. *The Letter to the Philippians*. PNTC. Grand Rapids: Eerdmans, 2009.

Harding, Sarah. *Paul's Eschatological Anthropology: The Dynamics of Human Transformation*. Minneapolis: Fortress, 2015.

Harris, Murray J. "2 Corinthians 5:1–10: Watershed in Paul's Eschatology?" *TynBul* 22 (1971): 32–57.

———. *Colossians and Philemon*. EGGNT. Grand Rapids: Eerdmans, 1991.
———. *Raised Immortal: The Relation between Resurrection and Immortality in New Testament Teaching*. London: Marshall Morgan & Scott, 1983.
Harrison, Everett F. "Romans." Pages 3–171 in *The Expositors Bible Commentary: Romans, 1 Corinthians, 2 Corinthians, Galatians*. Grand Rapids: Zondervan, 1976.
Harrison, J. R. "Paul, Eschatology and the Augustan Age of Grace." *TynBul* 50.1 (1999): 79–91.
Hawthorne, Gerald F. *Philippians*. WBC 43. Waco, TX: Word, 1983.
Hays, Christopher M. "Conclusion: A Fourfold Response to the Delay of the Parousia." Pages 253–68 in *When the Son of Man Didn't Come: A Constructive Proposal on the Delay of the Parousia*. Edited by Christopher M. Hays in collaboration with Brandon Gallaher, Julia S. Konstantinovsky, Richard J. Ounsworth, and C. A. Strine. Minneapolis: Fortress, 2016.
———. "The Delay of the Parousia: A Traditional and Historical-Critical Reading of Scripture: Part 2." Pages 79–107 in *When the Son of Man Didn't Come: A Constructive Proposal on the Delay of the Parousia*. Edited by Christopher M. Hays in collaboration with Brandon Gallaher, Julia S. Konstantinovsky, Richard J. Ounsworth, and C. A. Strine. Minneapolis: Fortress, 2016.
———. "Prophecy: A History of Failure?" Pages 23–38 in *When the Son of Man Didn't Come: A Constructive Proposal on the Delay of the Parousia*. Edited by Christopher M. Hays in collaboration with Brandon Gallaher, Julia S. Konstantinovsky, Richard J. Ounsworth, and C. A. Strine. Minneapolis: Fortress, 2016.
Hays, Christopher M. et al., eds. *When the Son of Man Didn't Come: A Constructive Proposal on the Delay of the Parousia*. Minneapolis: Fortress, 2016.
Hays, Richard B. *First Corinthians*. Interpretation. Louisville: Westminster John Knox, 1997.
Heil, John Paul. *Ephesians: Empowerment to Walk in Love for the Unity of All in Christ*. SBLStBL 13. Atlanta: SBL Press, 2007.
Hoehner, Harold W. *Ephesians: An Exegetical Commentary*. Grand Rapids: Baker Academic, 2002.
Hogan, Karina Martin. "The Apocalyptic Eschatology of Romans." Pages 155–74 in *The Jewish Apocalyptic Tradition and the Shaping of New Testament Thought*. Edited by Benjamin E. Reynolds and Loren T. Stuckenbruck. Minneapolis: Fortress, 2017.
Höhne, David A. *The Last Things*. Contours of Christian Theology. London: InterVarsity Press, 2019.
Holleman, Joost. *Resurrection and Parousia: A Traditio-Historical Study of Paul's Eschatology in 1 Corinthians 15*. Leiden: Brill, 1996.
Hooker, Morna D. *From Adam to Christ: Essays on Paul*. Cambridge: Cambridge University Press, 1990. Repr., Eugene, OR: Wipf & Stock, 2008.
Horsley, G. H. R. "καθ' υἱοθεσίαν" in *New Documents Illustrating Early Christianity* 4. Edited by G. H. R. Horsley. Sydney: Macquarie University, 1979.
Horsley, Richard A. *Paul and Empire: Religion and Power in Roman Imperial Society*. Harrisburg, PA: Trinity Press International, 1997.
Hubbard, Moyer V. *New Creation in Paul's Letters and Thought*. Cambridge: Cambridge University Press, 2002.

Jewett, Robert. *Romans: A Commentary*. Hermeneia. Minneapolis: Fortress, 2007.
Jipp, Joshua W. *Christ Is King: Paul's Royal Ideology*. Minneapolis: Fortress, 2015.
Johnson, Andy. *1 and 2 Thessalonians*. THNTC. Grand Rapids: Eerdmans, 2016.
Johnson, Bradley A. "Doing Justice to Justice: Re-assessing Deconstructive Eschatology." *Political Theology* 12.1 (2011): 11–23.
Johnson, Luke Timothy. *The First and Second Letters to Timothy: A New Translation with Introduction and Commentary*. AYB. New Haven: Yale University Press, 2008.
Jones, Hefin J. "Πίστις, Δικαιόω and the Apocalyptic Paul: Assessing Key Aspects of the Apocalyptic Reading of Galatians." MTh thesis, Moore Theological College, 2015.
Joubert, Stephan. "Paul's Apocalyptic Eschatology in 2 Corinthians." Pages 225–38 in *Eschatology of the New Testament and Some Related Documents*. Edited by Jan G. van der Watt. WUNT 2/315. Tübingen: Mohr Siebeck, 2011.
Käsemann, Ernst. *Commentary on Romans*. Translated and edited by Geoffrey W. Bromiley. Grand Rapids: Eerdmans, 1980.
———. "On the Subject of Primitive Christian Apocalyptic." Pages 108–37 in *New Testament Questions of Today*. Translated by W. J. Montague. London: SCM, 1969.
———. "'The Righteousness of God' in Paul." Pages 168–82 in *New Testament Questions of Today*. Translated by W. J. Montague. London: SCM, 1969.
Keener, Craig S. *Galatians*. NCBC. Cambridge: Cambridge University Press, 2018.
———. *Galatians: A Commentary*. Grand Rapids: Baker Academic, 2019.
———. *The Mind of the Spirit: Paul's Approach to Transformed Thinking*. Grand Rapids: Baker Academic, 2016.
———. *Romans: A New Covenant Commentary*. NCCS. Eugene, OR: Cascade, 2009.
Kierkegaard, Søren. *The Journals of Søren Kierkegaard*. Edited and translated by Alexander Dru. New York: Oxford University Press, 1938.
Kirk, J. R. Daniel. *Unlocking Romans: Resurrection and the Justification of God*. Grand Rapids: Eerdmans, 2008.
Knight, George W. *The Pastoral Epistles: A Commentary on the Greek Text*. NIGTC. Grand Rapids: Eerdmans, 1992.
Konstantinovsky, Julia S. "Negating the Fall and Re-Constituting Creation: An Apophatic Account of the Redemption of Time and History in Christ." Pages 109–45 in *When the Son of Man Didn't Come: A Constructive Proposal on the Delay of the Parousia*. Edited by Christopher M. Hays in collaboration with Brandon Gallaher, Julia S. Konstantinovsky, Richard J. Ounsworth, and C. A. Strine. Minneapolis: Fortress, 2016.
Kooten, George van, Oda Wischmeyer, and N. T. Wright. "Quaestiones Disputatae: How Greek was Paul's Eschatology?" *NTS* 61 (2015): 239–53.
Köstenberger, Andreas J. *Commentary on 1–2 Timothy & Titus*. BTCP. Nashville: Holman, 2017.
Köstenberger, Andreas J., Benjamin L. Merkle, and Robert L. Plummer. *Going Deeper with New Testament Greek: An Intermediate Study of the Grammar and Syntax of the New Testament*. Nashville: B&H Academic, 2016.
Kraus, Wolfgang, and Martin Kraus. "On Eschatology in Paul's First Epistle to the Corinthians." Pages 197–224 in *Eschatology of the New Testament and Some Related Documents*. Edited by Jan G. van der Watt. WUNT 2/315. Tübingen: Mohr Siebeck, 2011.

Kruse, Colin G. *Paul's Letter to the Romans*. PNTC. Grand Rapids: Eerdmans, 2012.
———. *The Second Epistle of Paul to the Corinthians: An Introduction and Commentary*. TNTC. Leicester: Inter-Varsity Press, 1987.
Kwon, Yon-Gyong. *Eschatology in Galatians: Rethinking Paul's Response to the Crisis in Galatia*. WUNT 2/183. Tübingen: Mohr Siebeck, 2004.
Ladd, George Eldon. *The Presence of the Future: The Eschatology of Biblical Realism*. Rev. ed. Grand Rapids: Eerdmans, 1974.
Larkin, William J. *Ephesians: A Handbook on the Greek Text*. BHGNT. Waco, TX: Baylor University Press, 2009.
Lee, Sang Meyng. *The Cosmic Drama of Salvation: A Study of Paul's Undisputed Writings from Anthropological and Cosmological Perspectives*. WUNT 2/276. Tübingen: Mohr Siebeck, 2010.
Levenson, Jon D. *Resurrection and the Restoration of Israel: The Ultimate Victory of the God of Life*. New Haven: Yale University Press, 2006.
Lewis, Scott M. *"So That God May Be All in All": The Apocalyptic Message of 1 Corinthians 15,12–34*. Tesi Gregoriana Serie Teologia 42. Rome: Pontifical Gregorian University Press, 1998.
Liefeld, Walter L. *Ephesians*. IVPNTC. Downers Grove, IL: InterVarsity Press, 1997.
Lincoln, Andrew T. *Ephesians*. WBC 42. Dallas: Word, 1990.
———. *Paradise Now and Not Yet: Studies in the Role of the Heavenly Dimension in Paul's Thought with Special Reference to his Eschatology*. SNTSMS 43. Cambridge: Cambridge University Press, 1981.
Long, Fredrick J. *2 Corinthians: A Handbook on the Greek Text*. BHGNT. Waco, TX: Baylor University Press, 2015.
Longenecker, Richard N. *The Epistle to the Romans: A Commentary on the Greek Text*. NIGTC. Grand Rapids: Eerdmans, 2016.
———. *Galatians*. WBC 41. Dallas: Word, 1990.
———. "The Nature of Paul's Early Christology." *NTS* 31 (1985): 85–95.
Lowe, Bruce A. "Oh διά! How Is Romans 4:25 to Be Understood?" *JTS* 57.1 (2006): 149–57.
Macaskill, Grant. *Revealed Wisdom and Inaugurated Eschatology in Ancient Judaism and Early Christianity*. SJSJ 115. Leiden: Brill, 2007.
Madigan, Kevin J., and Jon D. Levenson. *Resurrection: The Power of God for Christians and Jews*. New Haven: Yale University Press, 2008.
Marshall, I. Howard. *A Critical and Exegetical Commentary on The Pastoral Epistles*. ICC. London: T&T Clark, 1999.
Martin, Ralph P. *2 Corinthians*. 2nd ed. WBC 40. Grand Rapids: Zondervan, 2014.
Martyn, J. Louis. "Afterword: The Human Moral Dilemma." Pages 157–66 in *Apocalyptic Paul: Cosmos and Anthropos in Romans 5–8*. Edited by Beverly Roberts Gaventa. Waco, TX: Baylor University Press, 2013.
———. *Galatians: A New Translation with Introduction and Commentary*. AB. New York: Doubleday, 1997.
McKnight, Scot. *The Letter to the Colossians*. NICNT. Grand Rapids: Eerdmans, 2018.
Mearns, Christopher L. "Early Eschatological Development in Paul: The Evidence of 1 Corinthians." *JSNT* 22 (1984): 19–35.
Merkle, Benjamin L. *Ephesians*. EGGNT. Nashville: B&H, 2016.

Middleton, J. Richard. *A New Heaven and a New Earth: Reclaiming Biblical Eschatology.* Grand Rapids: Eerdmans, 2014.
Moltmann, Jürgen. *The Coming of God: Christian Eschatology.* Translated by Margaret Kohl. Minneapolis: Fortress, 1996.
———. *Ethics of Hope.* Translated by Margaret Kohl. Minneapolis: Fortress, 2012.
Moo, Douglas J. *The Epistle to the Romans.* NICNT. Grand Rapids: Eerdmans, 1996.
———. *Galatians.* BECNT. Grand Rapids: Baker Academic, 2013.
———. *The Letters to the Colossians and to Philemon.* PNTC. Grand Rapids: Eerdmans, 2008.
Morris, Leon. *The First and Second Epistles to the Thessalonians.* Rev. ed. NICNT. Grand Rapids: Eerdmans, 1991.
———. *The First Epistle of Paul to the Corinthians: An Introduction and Commentary.* TNTC. 2nd ed. Leicester: Inter-Varsity Press, 1985.
Moule, Handley C. G. *The Epistle to the Romans.* New ed. London: Pickering & Inglis, no date.
Mounce, William D. *Pastoral Epistles.* WBC. Nashville: Thomas Nelson, 2000.
Muddiman, John. *The Epistle to the Ephesians.* BNTC. Peabody, MA: Hendrickson, 2001.
Murphy, Frederick J. *Apocalypticism in the Bible and Its World: A Comprehensive Introduction.* Grand Rapids: Baker, 2012.
Mutschler, Bernhard. "Eschatology in the Pastoral Epistles." Pages 362–402 in *Eschatology of the New Testament and Some Related Documents.* Edited by Jan G. van der Watt. WUNT 2/315. Tübingen: Mohr Siebeck, 2011.
Oropeza, B. J. *Paul and Apostasy: Eschatology, Perseverance, and Falling Away in the Corinthian Congregation.* Eugene, OR: Wipf & Stock: 2007.
Pao, David W. *Colossians and Philemon.* ZECNT. Grand Rapids: Zondervan, 2012.
Peerbolte, Bert Jan Lietaert. "In Search of Hope. Eschatology in Philippians." Pages 269–82 in *Eschatology of the New Testament and Some Related Documents.* Edited by Jan G. van der Watt. WUNT 2/315. Tübingen: Mohr Siebeck, 2011.
Pennington, Jonathan T., and Sean M. McDonough, eds. *Cosmology and New Testament Theology.* LNTS 355. London: T&T Clark, 2008.
Peterson, David. G. *Commentary on Romans.* BTCP. Nashville: Holman, 2017.
Powers, Daniel G. *Salvation through Participation: An Examination of the Notion of the Believers' Corporate Unity with Christ in Early Christian Soteriology.* Leuven: Peeters, 2001.
Punt, Jeremy. "Eschatology in Colossians: 'At Home in the World.'" Pages 283–301 in *Eschatology of the New Testament and Some Related Documents.* Edited by Jan G. van der Watt. WUNT 2/315. Tübingen: Mohr Siebeck, 2011.
———. "Eschatology in Philemon: 'Biding the Time.'" Pages 403–15 in *Eschatology of the New Testament and Some Related Documents.* Edited by Jan G. van der Watt. WUNT 2/315. Tübingen: Mohr Siebeck, 2011.
Reynolds, Benjamin E., and Loren T. Stuckenbruck, eds. *The Jewish Apocalyptic Tradition and the Shaping of New Testament Thought.* Minneapolis: Fortress, 2017.
Roberts, Mark D. *Ephesians.* SGBC. Grand Rapids: Zondervan, 2016.
Robinson, D. W. B. "Who Were 'the Saints'?" Pages 160–69 in *Donald Robinson: Selected Works, Volume I—Assembling God's People.* Edited by Peter G. Bolt and Mark D. Thompson. Camperdown: Australian Church Record, 2008.

Rowland, Christopher. "Paul as an Apocalyptist." Pages 131–53 in *The Jewish Apocalyptic Tradition and the Shaping of New Testament Thought*. Edited by Benjamin E. Reynolds and Loren T. Stuckenbruck. Minneapolis: Fortress, 2017.

Sanders, E. P. *Paul and Palestinian Judaism: A Comparison of Patterns of Religion*. Minneapolis: Fortress, 1977.

Schnackenburg, Rudolph. *Ephesians: A Commentary*. Translated by Helen Heron. Edinburgh: T&T Clark, 1991.

Scholer, David N. "'The God of Peace Will Shortly Crush Satan under Your Feet' (Romans 16:20a): The Function of Apocalyptic Eschatology in Paul." *ExAud* 6 (1990): 53–61.

Schreiner, Thomas R. *Galatians*. ZECNT. Grand Rapids: Zondervan, 2010.

———. *Romans*. BECNT. Grand Rapids: Baker, 1998.

Scott, J. Julius. "Paul and Late-Jewish Eschatology—A Case Study, 1 Thessalonians 4:13–18 and 2 Thessalonians 2:1–12." *JETS* 15.2 (1972): 133–43.

Seifrid, Mark A. *The Second Letter to the Corinthians*. PNTC. Grand Rapids: Eerdmans, 2014.

Sheinfeld, Shayna. "Who Is the Righteous Remnant in Romans 9–11? The Concept of Remnant in the Hebrew Bible, Early Jewish Literature and Paul's Letter to the Romans." Pages 33–47 in *Paul the Jew: Rereading the Apostle as a Figure of Second Temple Judaism*. Edited by Gabriele Boccaccini and Carlos A. Segovia. Minneapolis: Fortress, 2016.

Shogren, Gary S. *1 & 2 Thessalonians*. ZECNT. Grand Rapids: Zondervan, 2012.

Silva, Moisés. *Philippians*. 2nd ed. BECNT. Grand Rapids: Baker Academic, 2005.

Sprigge, T. L. S. "The Unreality of Time." *Proceedings of the Aristotelian Society* 92 (1992): 1–19.

Sumney, Jerry L. "'In Christ There Is a New Creation': Apocalypticism in Paul." *PRSt* 40.1 (2013): 35–48.

———. "Post-Mortem Existence and Resurrection of the Body in Paul." *HBT* 31.1 (2009): 12–26.

Tappenden, Frederick S. *Resurrection in Paul: Cognition, Metaphor, and Transformation*. ECL 19. Atlanta: SBL Press, 2016.

Thielman, Frank. *Ephesians*. BECNT. Grand Rapids: Baker Academic, 2010.

———. *Romans*. ZECNT. Grand Rapids: Zondervan, 2018.

Thiselton, Anthony C. *The First Epistle to the Corinthians: A Commentary on the Greek Text*. NIGTC. Grand Rapids: Eerdmans, 2000.

Thompson, Marianne Meye. *Colossians and Philemon*. THNTC. Grand Rapids: Eerdmans, 2005.

Tolmie, Francois. "Living in Hope 'in the Fullness of Time.'" Pages 239–55 in *Eschatology of the New Testament and Some Related Documents*. Edited by Jan G. van der Watt. WUNT 2/315. Tübingen: Mohr Siebeck, 2011.

Ton, Josef. *Suffering, Martyrdom, and Rewards in Heaven*. New York: Lanham, 1997.

Towner, Philip H. *1–2 Timothy & Titus*. IVPNTC. Downers Grove, IL: InterVarsity Press, 1994.

Villiers, Pieter G. R. de. "The Glorious Presence of the Lord: The Eschatology of 2 Thessalonians." Pages 333–61 in *Eschatology of the New Testament and Some Related Documents*. Edited by Jan G. van der Watt. WUNT 2/315. Tübingen: Mohr Siebeck, 2011.

———. "In the Presence of God: The Eschatology of 1 Thessalonians." Pages 302–32 in *Eschatology of the New Testament and Some Related Documents*. Edited by Jan G. van der Watt. WUNT 2/315. Tübingen: Mohr Siebeck, 2011.

Vos, Geerhardus. *The Pauline Eschatology*. Grand Rapids: Eerdmans, 1952.

Wall, Robert W. *Colossians and Philemon*. IVPNTC. Downers Grove, IL: InterVarsity Press, 1993.

Wallace, Daniel B. *Greek Grammar beyond the Basics: An Exegetical Syntax of the New Testament*. Grand Rapids: Zondervan, 1996.

Ware, James P. "Paul's Hope and Ours: Recovering Paul's Hope of the Renewed Creation." *Concordia Journal* 35.2 (2009): 129–39.

Watt, Jan G. van der, ed. *Eschatology of the New Testament and Some Related Documents*. WUNT 2/315. Tübingen: Mohr Siebeck, 2011.

Weima, Jeffrey A. D. *1–2 Thessalonians*. BECNT. Grand Rapids: Baker Academic, 2014.

Westerholm, Stephen. "Righteousness, Cosmic and Microcosmic." Pages 21–38 in *Apocalyptic Paul: Cosmos and Anthropos in Romans 5–8*. Edited by Beverly Roberts Gaventa. Waco, TX: Baylor University Press, 2013.

White, Joel. "Paul's Cosmology: The Witness of Romans, 1 and 2 Corinthians, and Galatians." Pages 90–106 in *Cosmology and New Testament Theology*. Edited by Jonathan T. Pennington and Sean M. McDonough. LNTS 355. London: T&T Clark, 2008.

Williamson, Paul R. *Death and the Afterlife: Biblical Perspectives on Ultimate Questions*. NSBT 44. London: Apollos, 2017.

Witherington, Ben. *Jesus, Paul, and the End of the World: A Comparative Study in New Testament Eschatology*. Downers Grove, IL: InterVarsity Press, 1992.

Wolter, Michael. "The Distinctiveness of Paul's Eschatology." Pages 416–26 in *Eschatology of the New Testament and Some Related Documents*. Edited by Jan G. van der Watt. WUNT 2/315. Tübingen: Mohr Siebeck, 2011.

Woodhouse, John. *Colossians and Philemon: So Walk in Him*. Focus on the Bible Commentary Series. Fearn: Christian Focus, 2011.

Wright, N. T. "4QMMT and Paul: Justification, 'Works' and Eschatology (2006)." Pages 322–55 in *Pauline Perspectives: Essays on Paul, 1978–2013*. Minneapolis: Fortress, 2013.

———. *The Epistles of Paul to the Colossians and to Philemon*. TNTC. Leicester: Inter-Varsity Press, 1986.

———. *Justification: God's Plan and Paul's Vision*. London: SPCK, 2009.

———. "The Letter to the Romans." Pages 394–770 in *The New Interpreter's Bible: Volume Ten—Acts, Introduction to Epistolary Literature, Romans, 1 Corinthians*. Nashville: Abingdon, 2002.

———. "A New Perspective on Käsemann? Apocalyptic, Covenant, and the Righteousness of God." Pages 243–58 in *Studies in the Pauline Epistles: Essays in Honor of Douglas J. Moo*. Edited by Matthew S. Harmon and Jay E. Smith. Grand Rapids: Zondervan, 2014.

———. *Paul and the Faithfulness of God*. Minneapolis: Fortress, 2013.

———. *Surprised by Hope: Rethinking Heaven, the Resurrection, and the Mission of the Church*. New York: HarperOne, 2008.

Yarbro Collins, Adela. "The Otherworld and the New Age in the Letters of Paul."
Pages 189–207 in *Other Worlds and Their Relation to This World: Early Jewish and Ancient Christian Traditions*. Edited by Tobias Nicklaus, Joseph Verheyden, Erik M. M. Eynikel, and Florentino Garcia Martínez. Leiden: Brill, 2010.

Ziegler, Philip G. "The Love of God Is a Sovereign Thing: The Witness of Romans 8:31–39 and the Royal Office of Jesus Christ." Pages 111–30 in *Apocalyptic Paul: Cosmos and Anthropos in Romans 5–8*. Edited by Beverly Roberts Gaventa. Waco, TX: Baylor University Press, 2013.

Scripture Index

Genesis
1:1 38
1:7, 14 39
2. 180
2–3 . . . . . . .405, 410, 411,
   412, 413, 417, 418
2:7 . . . . 410, 411
2:9 416
2:10 410
2:15 410
2:19 410
2:19–20 410
2:21–23 410
2:24 366
3. . . . . 183, 217, 340, 410
3:14–15 411
3:17 411
3:17–19 411
3:19 411
3:22–23 416
3:24 411
9:11 414
12. 215
12:1 215
12:1–3 . . . . .88, 309
15. 215
15:5 215
15:6 215
17. 215
17:4 215
17:6 215
17:8 215
17:16 215
18:10, 14 244
21:10 223
21:12 . . . . .243, 244

Exodus
4:22 196
19:18 114
32:13 225

Leviticus
20:24 225

Deuteronomy
5:4 114
9:29 225
32:9 225
32:43 437

2 Samuel
22:50 437

1 Kings
19. 245
19:10 245
19:18 245

2 Kings
6:17 39

Job
1:6 39
42:17 388

Psalms
2:4 39
6:8 84
8. . . . . .76, 77
8:3 77
8:4 . . . . .77, 85
8:5 77
8:6 . . .76, 77, 84, 85, 343
8:7 88
8:7–8 77
18:49 437
51. 139
51:4 139
62. 135
62:3 135
62:4 135
62:7 135
62:10 135
62:12a 135
62:12b 135
69:9 292
89:5–7 129
89:27 196
110:1 84
117:1 437
147:8 39

Proverbs
8:22 196
24:12 135

Ecclesiastes
2:18–23 . . . . 185, 441

Isaiah
2. 36
11:4 116
11:9 . . . . .29, 412
11:10 . . . . .293, 330, 437
22:13 177
32:15 . . . . .28, 412
35:2 . . . . .29, 412
35:7 . . . . .29, 412
35:10 412
42:8 274
51:6 39
54:10–14 36
59. 90
59:17 98
60–62 36
65–66 . . . 405, 411, 412,
   413, 417, 418

65:17 .... 39, 412
65:17–25 36
65:18 412
65:20 412
65:22 412
65:25 412
66 412
66:14–16 413
66:15–16 114
66:22 39
66:23–24 413

Jeremiah
31:33 137

Ezekiel
37:11–13 431
40–48 36

Daniel
7 112
7:9–10 114
7:9–14 109
12:1–2 334
12:2 ...... 44, 388, 391

Amos
8:9 39

Habakkuk
2:4 215

Haggai
2:6 39

Zechariah
3:1 39
12–14 36

Matthew
9:24 112
24:36–44 ...... 113, 128
25:31–46 109

Mark
1:11 260
5:39 112
9:24 162

Luke
8:52 112
12:35–40 ...... 113, 128
24:16 390
24:31 390
24:39–40 390
24:41–42 390

John
5:28–29 .... 391, 392
11:11–13 112
11:24 .... 334, 391
20:19, 26 390
21:12–13 390

Acts
2 344
2:33 344
18:12 147
22:6, 11 388
24:15 15
26:13, 19 388
27:21–26 299

Romans
1–3 52
1–4 .... 51, 52
1:4 44
1:14 431
1:16 136
1:17 ...... 52, 374, 375,
                376, 379
1:18 .... 374, 375
1:18–19 375
1:18–21 255
1:18–32 .... 52, 134
1:19 374
1:21–23 289
2:1 .... 134, 135
2:1–5 52
2:1–11 .... 133, 134, 165
2:2 134
2:3 134
2:4 135
2:5 ...... 123, 124, 131,
           135, 383, 424
2:5–8 384
2:6 135

2:6–8 .... 123, 135
2:7 135
2:7–8 136
2:8 136
2:9 136
2:10 136
2:11 .... 134, 151
2:13 17
2:14 137
2:14–16 ...... 124, 136,
              165, 327
2:15a 137
2:15b 137
2:15c 137
2:16 ..124, 131, 136, 137,
         383, 384, 424
2:28–29 138
2:29 138
3:1–6 .... 138, 165
3:3 .... 139, 162
3:4 139
3:5 139
3:5–6 384
3:6a 139
3:6b 139
3:9 140
3:9–18 140
3:19 ...52, 137, 140, 165,
              384, 424
3:19b 140
3:19c 140
3:20 140
3:21 ...... 52, 374, 379
3:22 138
3:23 .... 124, 289
3:27–31 136
4 214
4:1–8 136
4:13 ...... 214, 215, 227
4:13–14 .... 385, 425
4:13–15 ... 214, 220, 233
4:13–25 329
4:13b 215
4:14 215
4:15a 215
4:17 288
4:17–21 .... 287, 320
4:18 288

4:19 288	6:4 . . . . . . 168, 285, 346, 347, 348	8:1 154
4:20 162	6:4–11 . . . .167, 197, 203, 327, 346	8:3 404
4:21 288	6:4b 256	8:3b 340
4:22 288	6:5 . . . . . . 168, 202, 332, 346, 347, 384, 425	8:4 340
4:23 337	6:5–8 . . . . 161, 212	8:6 431
4:23–24 . . . 288, 337, 338	6:6–7 . . . . .168, 346	8:9 . . . . .138, 344
4:24 . . . . .288, 337	6:8 . . . . .168, 346	8:10 207
4:25 . . . . . 142, 154, 336, 337, 338	6:9 388	8:10–13 . . . . . . .206, 213
4:25a 340	6:9b 168, 346	8:10–16 431
4:25b 335, 336	6:10 . . . . .168, 346	8:11 . . .25, 169, 194, 203, 207, 327, 352, 353, 388, 431, 433
5. 41	6:11 . . . . .169, 347	
5–8 51	6:12 68	8:13 . . . . .207, 385
5:1 . . . . .254, 289	6:12–14 . . . . 68, 101, 102, 424	8:13a 207
5:1–2 . . . . .254, 285, 330		8:13b 207
5:1–5 . . . . .288, 320	6:13 72	8:14 . . . . . . 212, 216, 233
5:2 . . . . .386, 427	6:13a 68	8:14–17 . . . 171, 212, 233
5:2a 254, 289	6:13b 68	8:14–22 . . . 215, 328, 353
5:2b 255	6:14 69	8:15 . . . . . . 171, 212, 216
5:5 427	6:17–18 70	8:16 . . . . .213, 216
5:6–8 290	6:17–23 . . . . 69, 101, 102	8:16–17 . . . . . . .257, 344
5:8 141	6:17a 70	8:16–21 . . . . . . .257, 285
5:8–10 . . . . .141, 165, 327, 352	6:17b 70	8:17 . .213, 216, 257, 258, 330, 353, 385, 426, 427
	6:19a 70	
5:9 . . . 141, 142, 335, 425	6:19b 70	
5:9a 141	6:19c 70	8:17–18 . . . . . . .328, 386
5:9b 141	6:19d 70	8:17a 216
5:10 . . . . 141, 142	6:20 70	8:17b 216
5:10a 141	6:21 205	8:18 . . . . . . 170, 217, 235, 258, 330, 409
5:10b 141	6:21–23 . . .205, 213, 328	
5:10c 141	6:21b 70	8:18–23 408
5:12–21 . . 41, 42, 60, 66, 175, 204, 205, 402, 403	6:22 206	8:18–25 . . . .79, 170, 234
	6:22–23 385	8:19 . . . . . .170, 171, 235, 258, 409
	6:22a 70, 205	
	6:22b 205	8:19–21 385
5:14, 17 40	6:23 . . . . . .183, 205, 340	8:19–22 . . . 217, 241, 426
5:18 . . . . .403, 404	6:22b 70	8:19–23 389
5:19 . . . . .67, 204	6:23a 70	8:20 . . . 34, 217, 235, 409
5:19–21 . . . 66, 101, 204, 213, 326, 328, 376, 377	6:23b 70, 206	8:20–21 290
	6:45 431	8:20–25 . . . . . . 290, 291, 294, 295
	7:7 185	
5:19a 67	7:7–13 . . . .184, 185, 340	8:21 . . . . . . 171, 217, 235, 257, 258, 409
5:19b 67	7:8 185	
5:20 205	7:9 185	8:21–22 217
5:21 . . . . .40, 205, 382	7:11 185	8:22 . . . . .171, 217
5:21a 67	8. 413	8:22–23 171
5:21b 67		8:23 . . 171, 290, 291, 433
6. . . 73, 82, 197, 347, 348		8:23–24 203
6:3–4 . . . . 197, 256		

8:24 .... 291, 314
8:24–25 ... 171, 291, 449
8:25 .. 291, 386, 427, 449
8:28 261
8:28–30 259
8:29 .... 180, 195
8:29–30 .... 260, 261
8:29a 261
8:29b 261
8:30 .... 106, 330
8:38–39 .... 71, 101, 102, 326
8:39a 71
8:39c 72
9–11 ...... 33, 242, 244, 251, 329, 386
9–14 52
9:1–5 143
9:6–7 .... 386, 426
9:6–9 . 242, 245, 250, 252
9:6–13 143
9:6a 243
9:6b 243
9:7 .... 243, 329
9:7a 243
9:8 .... 244, 246, 386
9:9 244
9:14–18 143
9:17–18 353
9:19 143
9:19–24 .... 142, 165
9:20 143
9:21 143
9:22 143
9:23 143
9:30 243
10:4 33
10:9 .... 105, 403
10:9–15 .... 402, 403
10:10 403
10:11 403
10:12 403
10:13 .... 105, 403
10:14 403
10:17 359
11:1 .. 244, 245, 249, 252
11:1–6 .... 244, 250, 252
11:2a 245

11:3 245
11:4 245
11:5 .. 243, 245, 246, 386
11:6 245
11:11–12 426
11:11–24 ...... 246, 249
11:11a 247
11:11b 247
11:11c 247
11:12 .... 247, 248
11:13 247
11:13–14 247
11:14, 15 248
11:16 248
11:17 .... 247, 248
11:17–20 247
11:18 248
11:20 162
11:21 .... 247, 248
11:22 .... 247, 248
11:23 .... 162, 248
11:24 248
11:25 ..... 249, 250, 265
11:25–26 .... 35, 426
11:25–32 248
11:25b 249
11:26 250
11:26a 250
11:28 249
11:28b 250
11:29 250
11:30 250
11:30–32 250
11:31 .... 249, 251
11:33–36 262
11:35–36 .. 262, 273, 285
11:36 .... 262, 263, 269, 270, 386
12:2 13
12:12 .. 291, 321, 386, 427
13:11 ..... 125, 126, 424
13:11–12 ...... 125, 383
13:11–14 .. 72, 101, 102, 124, 131, 326, 372
13:12 . 123, 125, 135, 423
13:12–13 ...... 383, 424
13:12a 73
13:12b 72, 73

13:13 .... 125, 126
13:13a 73
13:13b 73
13:14a 125
13:14b 125
14:10 .... 144, 145
14:10–12 ..... 144, 165, 384, 425
14:11 144
14:12 144
14:13a 145
15:1 292
15:1–4 292
15:2 292
15:3 292
15:4 ...... 321, 386, 427
15:8–13 438
15:9–12 294
15:13 .... 294, 320, 330, 386
15:15–16 438
15:23–24 294
16:25 .. 263, 365, 374, 375
16:25–26 ...... 365, 374
16:25–27 .. 263, 273, 285
16:26 374
16:27 .... 269, 270, 330, 386, 427
16:27b 263

1 Corinthians
1:4–9 104
1:6–8 ..... 103, 145, 165, 326, 327, 367
1:7 ... 104, 107, 122, 145, 367, 368, 371
1:7–8 383
1:8 ...... 104, 122, 145, 146, 352, 384
1:8a 104, 145
1:8b 104, 145
1:10 13
1:18–31 264
2:1 365
2:6 ..... 23, 74, 383, 423
2:6–8 .. 74, 101, 102, 264
2:6a 74
2:6b 74

Scripture Index • 481

2:7 . . . . 264, 365
2:7–8 285
2:7a 74
2:7b 74, 75
2:8 . . . . 13, 74, 264, 265, 330, 353
2:8a 74
2:10 . . . . . . 374, 375, 376
3:1, 2 428
3:6 353
3:10–15 30
3:13 376
3:18 13
4:1 . . . . 363, 365
4:1–2 146
4:3 105
4:3–5 . 146, 165, 327, 352
4:4 . . . . 105, 146
4:4–5 . . . . 104, 122, 326, 367, 368
4:5 . . . . 146, 383, 384
4:5a 105, 146
4:5b 105, 146
4:5c 105, 147
4:9 132
6:2 218
6:6 . . . . 162, 218
6:9–11 . . . . 217, 233, 328
6:9a 218
6:9b–10 218
6:9f 224
6:11a 218
6:11b 218
6:13–14 171
6:13a 172
6:13b 172
6:14 . . . . . 172, 194, 202, 327, 352
7:12–15 162
7:31 16
9:9–11 294
9:10 . . . . 295, 427
9:11 295
9:25 164
10:1–13 33
10:27 162
11:29 30
13:2 . . . . 365, 367

13:6–7 295
13:7 295
13:8 449
13:10 450
13:13 . 296, 311, 313, 449
14:2 . . . . 365, 367
14:22–24 162
14:26, 30 . . 374, 375, 376
15 . . . 37, 40, 41, 44, 106, 176, 178, 182, 183, 194, 332, 340
15:3–8 297
15:4 293
15:8 132
15:9 293
15:9–12 293
15:12 . . . . 173, 293
15:12–13 293
15:12–19 . . 173, 174, 176, 178, 327
15:13 . . . . 173, 332
15:14 173
15:15 . . . . 173, 194
15:16 . . . . 173, 333
15:17 . . 173, 296, 333, 336
15:17–19 . . . . 296. 320
15:18 . . . . 173, 296
15:19 . . . . . 174, 296, 331, 387, 427
15:20 . . . . . 106, 174, 175, 297, 310, 333, 425
15:20–23 . . 122, 172, 174, 178, 179, 195, 202, 328, 333, 353, 368, 389
15:20–26 . 105, 108, 194, 326, 367
15:20–28 26
15:21 . . . . 175, 333
15:21–22 . . . . . . 175, 333
15:22 . . . . 37, 175, 333, 384, 392
15:22–23 . . . . . . 179, 333
15:22a 180
15:22b 180
15:23 . . . . . 106, 127, 175, 310, 333, 383, 425
15:23–28 . . 16, 18, 75, 78, 84, 85, 101, 102, 126, 326, 327, 343, 377

15:24 . . . . . 75, 127, 132, 383, 384, 424
15:24–25 131
15:24–26 40
15:24a 78, 106, 343
15:24b 76, 106
15:24c 106
15:25 . . . 76, 78, 106, 343
15:26 . . 33, 76, 102, 106, 127, 132, 201, 423
15:27 76, 78, 85, 127, 343
15:27a 78
15:28 . . . . 78, 126
15:28a 78
15:28b 78
15:29 . . . . 176, 448
15:29–34 . . . . . 175, 178, 327, 328
15:30 177
15:30–32 203
15:31 177
15:32 177
15:32–33 425
15:34 177
15:35 . . . . . 178, 179, 333
15:35–44 182
15:35–49 219
15:35–50 . . 177, 183, 202, 219, 328, 333
15:36 . . . . 179, 182
15:36–37 265
15:36–38 333
15:37 179
15:38 179
15:39 179
15:40–41 179
15:42–44 . . 179, 265, 269, 285, 333
15:42–49 . . 108, 192, 194
15:42–50 384
15:42 194
15:42a 265
15:42b–43a 265
15:43 . . . . . 194, 330, 386
15:44 . . . . 194, 225
15:44–45 404
15:45 . . . . 132, 179, 180, 388, 404

15:45–47 . . . . . . 179, 333
15:45–49 187
15:45–53 218
15:46 180
15:47a 180
15:47b 180
15:48 180
15:48–49 . . . . . . 180, 390
15:48a 180
15:48b 180
15:49 . . . . . 180, 181, 194,
        329, 333, 388
15:50 . . . . . 220, 329, 385
15:50–53 233
15:50–55 174
15:50a 181, 219
15:50b 181, 219, 333
15:51 . . . . 182, 365
15:51–53 . . 180, 182, 220
15:51–54 220
15:51–58 . . . . 78, 79, 181,
      202, 219, 220, 328
15:52 . . . . 132, 352
15:52–53 384
15:52a 183
15:52b 183
15:53 183
15:54–55 183
15:54–58 182
15:56 . . . . 183, 185, 340,
           342, 347
15:56b 185, 340
15:57 185
15:58 . . . . . 185, 440, 441
16:7–9 . . . . 297, 320

2 Corinthians

1:4 298
1:6 297
1:6–7 297
1:7 297
1:8 198
1:8–11 298
1:9 298
1:10 320
1:10a 298
1:10b 298
1:13–14 299

2:11 49
2:14 . . . . 49, 374, 376
3:7–11 33
3:9 300
3:9–12 . . . . 299, 320
3:10 300
3:11 300
3:12 . . . . 300, 427
3:12–13 266
3:12–18 266
3:13 266
3:13b 266
3:14–15 266
3:15 266
3:16–17 . . . . 266, 267
3:17a 267
3:18 . . 266, 267, 285, 330
3:18a 266
3:18b 267
4:4 . . . . 13, 162, 180
4:6 388
4:7–10 186
4:10 . . . . 174, 374
4:10–11 . . . . 188, 374
4:11 . . . . 187, 374
4:11–14 . . . . 186, 327
4:11a 186
4:11b 186
4:12 186
4:13b 186
4:14 . . 187, 194, 203, 352
4:14a 187
4:14b 187
4:16 268
4:16–18 . . . . 267, 285
4:16–5:10 37
4:16a 268
4:16b 268
4:17 . . . 79, 268, 330, 386
4:17–18 . . . . 78, 101
4:18 . . . . 268, 269, 383
4:18b 78
5 39
5:1 . . . . 188, 446
5:1–4 268
5:1–10 . . . . 44, 187, 203,
          445, 446, 447
5:1a 188, 446

5:1b 188, 446
5:2 . . . . 188, 446
5:3 . . . . 188, 446
5:4 . . . . 188, 446
5:6 . . . . . . 148, 188, 446
5:8 . . . 148, 188, 189, 446
5:8–10 . . . . 147, 327, 352
5:8–11 30
5:9 148
5:10 . . . . . . 147, 189, 384
5:11 300
5:16–17 . . . 235, 407, 408
5:16a 236, 407
5:17 . . 241, 329, 386, 404,
     406, 407, 410, 426
5:17a 236, 407
5:17b 236, 407
6:3–7 . . . . 79, 102
6:4–7 79
6:4a 80
6:7 . . . . 72, 424
6:7c 80
6:13 428
6:14–15 162
6:16 105
6:17 105
8:3–5 300
10:3 81
10:3–4 424
10:3–6 . . . . 80, 102
10:4 . . . . 72, 81
10:5 81
10:6 81
10:15 301
12 39
12:1 . . . . . . 374, 375, 376
12:1–10 37
12:2 375
12:7 . . . . 374, 375
13:5–6 301

Galatians

1:3–5 269
1:4 13
1:4b 48
1:5 . . . . . . 269, 270, 285,
           386, 427
1:12 . . . . . . 48, 359, 374,
           375, 376

1:15–16 . . . . 48, 359
1:16 . . . 48, 374, 375, 376
2:2 . . . . . 48, 49, 359, 374,
375, 376
2:9 49
2:13 49
2:16 329
3:13 340
3:14 . . . . 221, 344
3:14–18 . . . . 220, 233
3:15 221
3:16 329
3:17 . . . . 221, 329
3:18 . . . . . . 221, 385, 425
3:18a 221
3:19–25 222
3:23 . . . 48, 359, 374, 375
3:26 . . . . 222, 223
3:26–4:7 . . 221, 233, 329
3:27 . . . . . . 222, 223, 328
3:28 222
3:29 . . 222, 223, 329, 330
4. 36
4:1–2 222
4:1–5 . . . . 81, 83, 101
4:1–7 222
4:3 . . . . 82, 83, 222
4:4 49
4:4–5 . . . . . . 82, 222, 223
4:5 82
4:6 . . . . 49, 223, 233,
329, 344
4:76 223
4:8 83
4:8–11 . . . . 82, 101
4:9a 83
4:9b 83
4:9c 83
4:10 83
4:21–25 224
4:21–31 223
4:26 39
4:26–28 224
4:28 223
4:28–31 223
4:29 . . . . . . 223, 385, 425
4:30 224
4:31 224

5:4 302
5:4–5 302
5:4–6 301
5:5 . . . . 17, 302, 320, 386
5:6 302
5:7–8 49
5:10 49
5:16 . . . . 149, 344
5:16–18 224
5:17 149
5:19–21 . . . . . . 149, 224,
233, 328
5:21 224
5:22–23 . . . . 149, 344
5:22–26 224
5:25 208
6:7–8 . . . . . 208, 213, 224
6:7–9 . . . . . 148, 165, 372
6:8 . . . . . . 208, 344, 384,
385, 425
6:14 . . . 48, 236, 237, 407
6:14–16 . . . . . . 236, 251,
407, 408
6:15 . . 48, 236, 241, 251,
329, 386, 406,
407, 426
6:15–16 242
6:16 . . 236, 250, 252, 407
6:16a 252
6:16b 252

Ephesians
1:3–4 84
1:5 270
1:5–6 . . . . 269, 285
1:6 . . . . 270, 271, 330
1:9 365
1:9–10 . . . . 241, 410
1:9–12 237
1:10 . . . 39, 237, 329, 354,
386, 404, 405
1:11 237
1:11–12 . . . . 225, 271,
302, 321
1:11–14. . . . . 225, 270
1:12 . . . . . . 237, 271, 285,
330, 331, 427
1:13 225

1:13–14 233
1:14 . . 212, 221, 226, 271,
272, 285, 319, 329,
344, 385, 426
1:14a 225
1:14b 225
1:17 . . . . . . 226, 374, 375
1:17–18 . . . . 226, 271
1:18 . . . . . 226, 272, 304,
386, 387
1:18–19 303
1:20 88
1:20–21 343
1:20–22 . . . . 87, 102
1:20–23 . . 83, 84, 85, 91,
101, 273, 326, 377
1:21 . . . xxii, 13, 85, 239,
383, 424
1:21a 84
1:21b 84
1:22 . . . . 85, 88, 91
2. . . . . 347, 348
2:1 86, 150, 190, 238, 348
2:2 423
2:1–3 . . . . 85, 87, 89, 101,
149, 165, 190, 347
2:1–7 . . . . 189, 347
2:1–10 238
2:2 . . . . . 13, 102, 150, 239
2:2a 86
2:2b 86
2:2c 86
2:3 . . . . 86, 150
2:3b 190, 347
2:4 191
2:4–5 . . . . . 190, 347, 425
2:4–6 328
2:5 . . . 190, 238, 239, 348
2:5–6. . 198, 201, 203, 384
2:5b 190, 347
2:6 . . . . 39, 190, 348, 349
2:6a 239
2:6b 239
2:7 . . . . 239, 349
2:8 . . . . 190, 239, 347
2:8–9 . . . . 151, 239
2:10 . . . . . 241, 329, 386,
406, 410, 426

2:10a 238, 239
2:10b 239
2:11 191
2:11–12 304
2:11–22 273
2:12 . . . . . .304, 320, 331
2:20ff. 39
3. 438
3:3 . . . 365, 374, 375, 376
3:4 . . . . .365, 366
3:4–6. 227
3:5 . . . . 227, 374, 375
3:6 . . . . 227, 233, 329
3:8 87
3:8–11 . . . . .87, 102
3:9 . . . . 87, 365, 366
3:10 . . . . . . 87, 88, 102,
     237, 273
3:12 273
3:12–13 272
3:13 272
3:20 273
3:20–21 . . . . .273, 285
3:21 . . . . .273, 330, 427
4:4 387
4:4–5 331
4:4–6. 304
4:7–12 344
4:9–10 345
4:10 345
4:11 438
4:11–16 438
4:12 438
5:1 228
5:1–6 227
5:2 228
5:3–4. 228
5:5 . . . . .88, 89, 150, 153,
     228, 233, 328
5:5–6. . . . . 88, 102, 150,
     153, 165, 326, 372
5:6 . . . .89, 228, 384, 424
5:6a 150
5:6b 151, 153
5:16 239
5:22–6:9 231
5:23–27 273
5:27 152
5:31 366
5:32 . . . . . .365, 366, 367
5:32b 366
6:6 152
6:6–8. . . . . 151, 165, 372
6:7 151
6:8 . . . 151, 152, 425, 439
6:9 . . . . .151, 152
6:10–17 . . . . . 89, 90, 91,
     102, 313, 424
6:10–20 72
6:10ff. 39
6:11 90
6:12 . . . . .90, 237, 239
6:12a 90
6:13 . . . . .90, 239
6:14–17 90
6:16–17 80
6:19 . . . . .365, 366

Philippians
1:16–20 . . . . . . .305, 320
1:17 305
1:18 305
1:19 . . . . .305, 306
1:20a 306
1:20b 306
1:21 191
1:21–26 191
1:22a 191
1:23 . . . . . . .39, 191, 444
1:23–24 . . . . . . .445, 447
1:24 191
1:25 . . . . .191, 428
2:6 274
2:6–11 274
2:9 274
2:9–10 343
2:9–11 274
2:10 274
2:10–11 392
2:11 . . 274, 285, 330, 386
2:11a 274
2:11b 274
2:23 306
3:7–8. 192
3:8 192
3:10 . . . . . . .192, 193, 388
3:10–11 . . . . . 192, 203,
     328, 425
3:10–14 16
3:10a 192
3:11 193
3:15 . . . . .374, 375
3:18–19 194
3:18–21 . . .107, 193, 275,
     327, 328, 367, 372
3:19a 107, 275
3:19b 107, 275
3:20 . .107, 122, 275, 345,
     368, 371, 383, 386, 424
3:20–21 383
3:20a 194
3:20b 107, 194
3:21 . .108, 194, 195, 202,
     285, 330, 332, 352,
     353, 384, 386, 427
3:21a . 107, 194, 275, 388
3:21b . 108, 194, 276, 388
4:1 164
4:18 276
4:18–20 276
4:19 . . . . .276, 330
4:20 . . . . .277, 285
4:21–23 277
30:20–21 38

Colossians
1:3–4. 307
1:3–6. 306
1:4–5 321
1:5 . . . . .39, 386, 427
1:5a 307
1:5b 307
1:6 307
1:9 229
1:10 229
1:10–14 228
1:11 229
1:12 . . .91, 229, 230, 307,
     328, 353
1:13 . . . .91, 93, 101, 329,
     353, 424
1:13–14 . . . . 91, 101, 326
1:13a 229
1:13b 229, 230

Scripture Index • 485

1:14 . . . . 91, 229, 329
1:15 . . . . 180, 195
1:15–16 408
1:15–20 . . . . 92, 240
1:16 . . 92, 102, 241, 326, 329, 354, 408
1:17 . . . . 241, 408
1:18 . . 195, 202, 328, 333
1:18a 196
1:18b 196
1:18c 195, 196
1:18d 196
1:20 . . . . . 241, 404, 405, 408, 410
1:20b 405
1:22 308
1:22–23 308
1:23 . . . . . . 308, 321, 427
1:23c 308
1:24–27 277
1:24–29 309
1:25 277
1:26 . . . . . 277, 309, 365, 366, 374
1:26–27 . . . . 285, 376
1:27 . . xxii, 309, 321, 330, 331, 365, 366, 374, 387, 427
1:27a 277
1:27b 277, 278
2 197
2:2 . . . . 365, 366
2:5–6 198
2:8–9 94
2:8–10 . . . . . . 93, 96, 326
2:8–23 94
2:9–10 102
2:10 . . . . 94, 424
2:10a 94
2:11–13 . . . . 196, 328
2:12 197
2:12–13 425
2:13 . . . . 197, 384
2:13–14 203
2:14 . . . . 95, 341, 342
2:14–15 . . 94, 102, 326, 377
2:15 . . . . . . 95, 102, 341, 342, 405, 424

2:15a 95
2:20 . . . . . . 108, 153, 198, 349, 424
2:20–23 . . . . 96, 326
2:20a 96
2:20b 97
2:21 97
2:22 97
2:22b 97
2:23 97
3:1 . . . 108, 198, 203, 327, 328, 349, 424, 425
3:1–2 . . . . . 198, 279, 349
3:1–4 . . . . . . 39, 190, 197, 278, 367
3:3 . . . 108, 198, 279, 349
3:3–4 285
3:4 . . 108, 122, 198, 279, 330, 349, 353, 368, 383, 384, 386, 427
3:5 153
3:5–7 . 152, 153, 165, 372
3:6 . . . . 153, 384, 424
3:7 153
3:10 180
3:18–4:1 231
3:22–24 . . . . 233, 439
3:22–25 . . . . 230, 372
3:22a 231
3:22b 231
3:23 231
3:24 . . . . 231, 329
3:24a 231
3:24b 231
3:25 152
4:1 231
4:3 . . . . 265, 366

1 Thessalonians
1:2–3 . . . . 310, 313
1:3 . . . . 314, 321, 331, 386, 427
1:9–10 . . . . 109, 154, 165, 326, 327, 352, 367, 368, 371, 383
1:10 . . . . . 109, 122, 383, 384, 424
1:10b 109

1:10c 110
1:12 330
2:11–12 280
2:12 . . 280, 285, 421, 427
2:16, 18 49
2:19 . . 110, 122, 164, 311, 368, 383, 424
2:19–20 . . . . 110, 311, 327, 367
2:20 . . . . 110, 311
3:6 49
3:11 155
3:11–13 155
3:12 155
3:13 . . 110, 111, 122, 155, 165, 326, 345, 367, 368, 383, 384
3:13b 155
4:1 428
4:10 425
4:13 . . . . . . 112, 199, 312, 320, 427
4:13–14 . . . 312, 331, 425
4:13–18 . . . 16, 182, 198, 203, 328
4:14 . . . . . . 112, 199, 312
4:14a 200
4:14b 199
4:14c 199, 200
4:15 . . . . . . 112, 368, 371
4:15–17 . . . . 156, 182
4:15–18 . . . 111, 113, 114, 326, 367
4:16 . . 122, 183, 200, 351, 384, 388, 396, 424
4:16–17 111
4:16a 112
4:16b 112
4:17 . . 109, 111, 115, 122, 353, 368, 371, 424
4:17a 112
4:17b 112
4:18 . . . . 113, 199
5:1–3 115
5:1–4 . . 113, 122, 127, 131, 367, 369, 371, 372
5:2 . . . 113, 116, 128, 369
5:3 . . . . 113, 128

5:3c 114
5:4 . . . . . . 113, 128, 369
5:5 97
5:5–8 . . . . . .97, 101, 102,
372, 373
5:6 . . . . .98, 373
5:7 98
5:7–10 312
5:8 . .72, 98, 313, 387, 424
5:8–9 331
5:9 . . . . . . .154, 384, 425
5:9–10 . . . .155, 165, 209,
213, 313, 327,
328, 352, 353
5:10 . . . . . .156, 209, 385

2 Thessalonians
1:5–10 . . . 114, 122, 128,
156, 158, 165, 326,
327, 367, 369, 377
1:5–12 16
1:6–9 424
1:6–10 154
1:7 114, 157, 158, 351, 369
1:7–8 157
1:7–9 . . . . .129, 383
1:8 . . . . 157, 158, 384
1:8–9 158
1:9 117, 157, 158, 399, 400
1:9–10 383
1:9–12 280
1:10 . .114, 115, 123, 129,
131, 135, 157, 285,
386, 399, 424
1:12 285
2. 130
2:1 . . . . 115, 122
2:1–2 . . . . . 115, 327, 367,
370, 371
2:1–3 . . . . .129, 131
2:1–4 . . . . .372, 373
2:2 115
2:3 . . . . . . 130, 366, 370,
373, 383
2:3–7 116
2:3–9 130
2:4 116
2:5 116
2:6 366

2:7 . . . . .365, 366
2:8 . . . 116, 117, 118, 119,
121, 122, 326, 366,
367, 370, 371, 377, 383
2:8b 116
2:10–12 130
2:13 282
2:13–14 . . . . . . .281, 285
2:14 . . . . . .330, 286, 427
2:14a 282
2:14b 282
2:16 331
2:16–17 . . . . . . .313, 320

1 Timothy
1:1 . . . 314, 321, 331, 427
1:13 162
1:15 394
1:15–16 . . . . . . .209, 328
1:16 . . . . . . 209, 210, 213
1:17 . .282, 285, 386, 427
2:4 402
3:9 . . . . .365, 367
3:14 . . . . .314, 320
3:16 . . . . . 283, 285, 330,
365, 367
3:16b 367
4:10 . . . . .315, 427
5:5–6 315
5:8 162
5:22 159
5:23 159
5:24–25 . . . . . . .158, 159,
165, 384
5:24a 159
5:24b 159
5:24c 159
5:25 159
6:9–10 210
6:11 210
6:11–12 . . . . 210, 213
6:12 . . . . 117, 210
6:12–14 119
6:13 117
6:13–14 . . . 117, 118, 119,
122, 327, 367,
370, 383, 424
6:14 . . . . . .117, 118, 119,
120, 121

6:17 . . . . . . 13, 316, 321
6:17–19 316
6:17a 316
6:17b 316
6:18 316
6:19a 316
6:19b 317

2 Timothy
1:9 201
1:9–10 . . . . .200, 328
1:10 . . . . . .118, 120, 201,
202, 374, 376
1:10a 201
2:8–10 284
2:9 284
2:10 . . . . . 211, 284, 285,
330, 386, 427
2:10–11 385
2:10–13 . . .160, 211, 327,
328
2:10a 161
2:10b 161
2:10c 161
2:11 . . . . . . 161, 213, 425
2:11–13 . . . . 160, 161
2:11c 211
2:12–13 211
2:12a 161
2:12b 161, 162
2:13a 162
2:13b 162
2:15 201
2:16–18 201
2:18 . . . . 201, 202
3:1 132
4:1 . . . 118, 119, 121, 384
4:1–2 . .98, 102, 118, 122,
163, 165, 327, 352,
367, 370, 372,
373, 383, 424
4:1a 98
4:1b 99
4:1c 99
4:2 . . . . 119, 163, 373
4:2a 99
4:2b 99
4:6 . . . . 119, 131, 370

Scripture Index · 487

4:6–8 . . . . . 119, 130, 163,
      327, 367, 370, 371
4:7 . . . . 119, 131, 164
4:7–8 119
4:8 . . . . . . 119, 120, 122,
      131, 164, 165, 327,
      352, 383, 384, 424
4:18 . . 284, 285, 386, 427

Titus
1:1–2 . . . . 317, 320
1:1b 317
1:1c–2a 317
1:2 . . . . 387, 427
1:2b 317
1:3 374
1:15 162
2:11 121
2:11–13 . . . 100, 101, 121,
      284, 285, 318, 326,
      327, 367, 372, 373
2:12 . . . . 13, 100, 285
2:12–13 . . . . . . 100, 331,
      383, 424
2:13 . 100, 120, 121, 122,
      285, 318, 321, 330,
      370, 371, 373, 386,
      387, 424, 427
2:13b 318

3:4–5 232
3:4–7 . . . . 231, 344
3:5 232
3:6 344
3:6–7 . . . . 212, 213, 216,
      232, 319, 328
3:7 . . 232, 233, 331, 385,
      387, 425, 426, 427
3:7a 232
3:7b 213

Philemon
22 319

James
1:12 164

1 Peter
1:12 88
3:20 414
5:4 164

2 Peter
3 . 406, 413, 416, 417, 418
3:6 414
3:7 414
3:10 413
3:12 414
3:12–13 414

Revelation
2:10 164
18 415
19–22 . 406, 413, 415, 416,
      417, 418
19:1–2 415
19:7–9 415
19:11 415
19:13–14 415
19:15 415
19:19–21 415
20:2–3 415
20:4–6 127
20:10 415
20:13 415
20:15 415
21 417
21:1 416
21:1–2 415
21:2–3 416
21:3–4 415
21:6 416
21:8 416
21:24 416
21:27 416
22:2 416
22:2–3 416

Subject Index

Abraham
  children of as Israel, 243, 244, 251, 252
  Christ as seed of, 221, 331, 354, 456, 457
  hope of, 288, 320
  inheritance of promise made to, 214,
    215, 222, 223, 224, 227, 233, 288,
    309, 456, 458
  sons of, 223
Adam
  Christ as second, 174, 179–80, 204, 205
  as pathway to realm of sin and death, 67
adoption, imagery of, 171, 216, 223, 291
age to come, the, 382–422
  and destruction of evil, 387, 406, 415,
    419, 421, 454
  and eternal life, 385, 387
  glory in, 386, 387, 419–21, 449, 454, 461
  grace in, 383
  hope in, 386–87, 423
  inheritance in, 385, 387, 454
  Israel in, 386
  and judgment, 99, 384, 387, 393–97, 454
  and justification, 393–97
  and the last day, 382, 383–84
  new creation in, 385–86, 387, 405–19
  and the parousia, 383
  as present reality, 39
  and resurrection, 53, 384–85, 387,
    388–93, 454
  and two realms, 382–83
  wrath and, 397–99
analepsis, 142n. 8
annihalationism, 8, 46, 60, 208,
  399–401, 402, 422, 452
apocalyptic, defined 357
apocalypticism
  and divine revelation, 40
  and Galatians, 48–50
  and hiddenness, 108
  Jewish, 33, 39, 40, 42, 53, 55, 356,
    357–58, 409, 454
  and Pauline studies, 356–62, 454
  of Paul, 8, 10, 13, 18, 25–27, 33–34,
    39–40, 56–57, 356–81, 452, 453–54
apocalypse
  of Baruch, 10, 13, 15, 56, 360, 362
  defined, 362–63
  of Enoch, 360, 362, 410
  of Ezra, 10, 13, 15, 56
  as literary genre, 40, 362–63, 363n. 35
  as a verb, 48
  of Weeks, 414
apostasy, 129, 130, 370, 373, 383
appointment by God, 156, 209, 313, 326
armor of light, 66, 72–73, 89–90, 97, 98,
  102, 125, 312–13, 326, 372, 383
ascension of Christ
  and absence of Christ, 344, 345, 349, 351
  and access to divine revelation, 349
  and authority of Christ, 84, 326, 377,
    378, 456
  as eschatological event, 325–26, 332,
    342–45, 349, 350, 354, 355, 453,
    456–57
  and expectation of return of, 104, 351
  and glory, 283, 333
  participation in, 190, 345–46, 348–50
  and realm theology, 65, 101, 349, 350
  and resurrection, 110, 377, 388
authorities
  Christ above, 76, 77, 84, 85, 87, 91, 93,
    94, 102, 273, 326, 355, 455
  and the church, 88
  competing, 76, 77, 84, 89, 90, 101
  as created by Christ, 92–93, 102, 240,
    326, 408
  disarming of, 59, 95, 102, 331, 341,
    342, 377, 384, 405, 455, 456

human, 74, 84, 87, 90, 102
spiritual, 74, 84, 87, 88, 90, 93, 102
authority of the air, 86, 87

baptism
  for the dead, 176
  into Christ, 222, 223, 256, 328, 361
  into death, 168, 256, 346
  one, 305, 331
  and salvation, 27
Baruch, apocalypse of, 10, 13, 15, 56
basileia, the, 43–44

childbirth, imagery of, 171, 217, 235, 360, 409, 426
Chiliasm. *See* millennialism
Christ
  as Abraham's seed. 221, 329, 331, 354
  absence of, 262, 344, 345, 349, 428
  as agent of resurrection, 194, 199–200, 205
  appearance of, 100, 103, 108, 109, 116–17, 118, 119, 120, 121, 122, 164, 285, 318
  ascension of. *See* ascension of Christ
  authority of, 84, 93, 94, 229, 273, 276, 326, 331, 342–43, 355, 377–78, 424, 455
  baptism into, 222, 223, 256, 328, 361
  as blessed hope, 285
  clothing with, 229, 328
  coheirs with, 216–17, 223, 227, 233, 257, 258, 319, 328, 344, 353, 426, 459
  coming of, 103, 110, 113, 115, 116–17, 121, 129, 333, 355, 382
  and created order, 241, 408
  consummation of reign of, 75–76, 78, 85, 91, 102, 326, 343, 383
  death of as apocalyptic event, 341, 342
  death of as cosmic event, 10, 17
  death of as eschatological event, 59, 325, 332, 339–42
  death of as providing salvation, 141–42, 156
  descending of from heaven, 103, 107, 109, 111, 112, 114, 122
  dying with. *See* dying with Christ
  at the eschaton, 325, 327, 350–54

eternal life as life with, 209–11, 213, 326, 328, 353, 354, 382, 390, 424, 425, 456, 459
as firstfruits of resurrection. *See* firstfruits
gifts given to the church by, 438
glorification of by the saints, 326, 327, 386
glorification of believers with, 254, 257, 258, 261–62, 327, 353, 461
and glory, 330
handing kingdom to the father, 78, 102, 106, 127, 131, 326, 327, 331, 343, 377, 378, 383, 457
hiddenness of, 108, 109, 119, 124, 128, 198, 277, 279, 309, 351
as hope of glory, 289, 309–10, 321, 330, 374, 421, 427
image of, 180–81, 194, 195, 220, 260, 261, 267, 329, 330, 333, 396
and inheritance, 328–39, 353–54
and Israel, 329–30
as judge, 98–99, 102, 103, 117–19, 122, 123–24, 163, 189, 326, 327, 331, 352, 417
as last Adam, 132, 333, 361
as lord of glory, 264–65, 330, 353, 421, 423, 434, 461
as lord of the new realm, 325–26
as means to eternal life, 17, 67, 205, 206, 209, 210, 212, 213, 326, 328, 341, 455
and the new creation, 329, 331, 455
overpowering the powers, 341–42, 350
parousia of, 20–22, 75, 326–27, 351–52
as pathway to realm of grace and righteousness, 67–68, 326
reigning with, 161, 162, 163
resurrecting the dead, 352–53
resurrection of. *See* resurrection, Christ
revelation of, 103, 104, 108, 114, 122, 124, 129, 145, 157, 158, 279, 351, 383, 457
rule of. *See* rule of Christ
as savior, 107, 107n. 9, 110, 195, 201, 273, 315, 327, 352
as seed of Abraham, 221
suffering with, 216–17, 257, 353, 354

union with, 9, 12, 38, 55, 56, 108, 156,
    223, 279, 346, 448, 453
  victory of, 376–78
  as witness, 117, 163
christocentric eschatology, 325–55
church, the, 433–39, 462
circumcision, 236, 241, 251, 252, 386, 407
Colossian heresy, the, 93–94
covenants, 266, 267, 304, 426
creation
  as arena of God's work, 217, 234, 235,
    237, 241, 385, 387, 409, 459
  and fall of humanity, 217, 235, 241,
    409, 459
  fate of as tied to humanity's fate, 234,
    235, 241, 385, 387, 410, 417
  glory of, 254, 409
  human dominion over, 77, 343,
    410–11
  renewal of, 217, 235, 241, 387, 389,
    405–19, 422, 453, 459
  subjected to futility, 217, 235, 241,
    409, 459
  See also new creation
crown of boasting, 110, 311, 327, 368
crown of righteousness, 119, 120, 122,
    130–31, 164, 326, 327, 370, 383,
    384, 457

day of the Lord, the
  and Christ's presence, 122, 131, 457,
    351
  and crown of righteousness, 119, 131,
    383, 384, 457
  as day of judgment, 113, 122, 131, 145,
    351, 384, 387, 457, 352
  as end of this present age, 18, 103, 122,
    131, 387, 413–14, 454, 457
  as expected, 113, 122, 128, 131, 369,
    373, 457
  false claims of, 115, 116, 129, 130, 131,
    373
  and glory, 131
  as irreversible, 114
  modifications by Paul to concept of, 132
  and new creation, 413–14
  as parousia, 44, 103, 115, 122, 128,
    129, 351, 457

  precursors to, 130, 131, 370, 373
  and resurrection of the dead, 44, 122,
    387, 457
  timing of, 113, 115, 122, 128, 131,
    368, 369, 370, 413, 457
  See also last day, the; parousia, the
day of wrath, the, 123, 131, 135, 383, 457
dead, resurrection of. *See* resurrection,
    the dead
death
  baptism into, 168, 256, 346
  destruction of. *See* destruction of death
  as divine punishment for sin, 41
  and entrance into presence of God,
    443, 444, 445, 458
  eschatological significance of, 40,
    443–44, 457–58
  fear of as fear of God, 19
  as intermediate state, 444–48
  meaning of, 40–41
  as outcome of sin, 70
  realm of, 67, 70, 205
  as separation from God, 41
  and sin, 183–84, 185, 205 213, 376, 382,
    443, 457
  spiritual, 207, 212
  sting of, 183–84, 340, 347
  in this present age, 443–48, 458
  types of, 40
destruction of death
  and Christ as savior, 201
  and conquering sin, 340
  as end of time, 20, 61, 106, 127, 183
  and reign of Christ, 41, 76, 106, 194,
    343
  through death and resurrection of
    Christ, 32, 168, 185, 192, 194, 201,
    328, 340–41
devil, the, 415
domain of darkness, 91, 91n. 25, 92, 101,
    229, 230, 353, 423
dominion
  of Christ, 35, 59, 77, 85, 92, 343
  of death, 12, 347, 350, 379, 456
  of evil, 92
  of God, 112n. 19
  of humans over the earth, 77, 343,
    410–11

of sin, 68, 71, 205, 206, 348, 350, 379, 456
doxologies, 262–63, 269, 271, 273, 277, 282, 284, 285, 330, 427
dwelling, eternal. *See* eternal dwelling
dying with Christ
- as leading to living with Christ, 161, 163, 167, 168, 197, 211–12
- and making believers hidden with Christ, 108–9, 198, 279
- and putting elements of this word to death, 96–97, 153, 168, 326, 350, 425
- and resurrection with Christ, 168, 192–93, 198, 338–39, 350, 425
- as spiritual in nature, 198, 211–12, 262, 425

earthly tent, 188, 268, 445, 446
ecology, 442–43, 462–63
ekklesia, 44
elements
- as spatial, 65
- of the world, 93, 93n. 28, 96

Elijah, 244, 245
eschatology
- anthropological, 54
- apocalyptic, 8, 10, 13, 18, 25–27, 29, 40–41, 42, 356–81, 454
- christocentric, 325–55
- cosmological element of, 5, 41, 360
- creational, 54, 61
- definition of, 4–6, 4n. 5
- divine 47
- final, 54
- forensic apocalyptic, 41, 360
- gnostic, 54
- importance of, 58–59
- inaugurated, 5, 28, 55, 56, 58, 65, 84, 85, 91, 101, 132, 339
- of Jesus, 42–43
- Jewish, 10, 40, 41, 42, 53, 338
- Pauline, recent history of, 9–62
- prophetic, 28, 29
- realized (overrealized), 84, 85, 91
- spatial concept of, 5
- temporal concept of, 5
- two-age, 65–102. *See also* two ages and two realms framework

eschaton, the,
- Christ at, 325, 327, 350–54
- as completion of the act of creation, 419
- timing of, 45–46, 61–62
- *See also* last day, the

eternal dwelling, 188, 268, 445, 446, 447
eternal encouragement, 313–14
eternal life, 204–13
- and the age to come, 385, 387
- bodies in, 204, 213
- by allegiance, 149, 206, 208
- by the power of the spirit, 149, 165, 208, 212, 213, 344, 395, 425, 432, 462
- through Christ, 67, 205, 206, 209–10, 212, 213, 326, 328, 331, 341, 455
- with Christ, 204, 209, 211–12, 213, 353, 387, 390, 396, 424, 425, 456, 459
- as divine design, 317, 318
- as gift, 70, 205–6, 210, 328, 385
- and glory, 211, 385, 387
- hope for, 45, 61, 204, 213, 232–33, 287, 317, 318, 319, 320, 328, 331, 425, 427, 460
- as inheritance, 212–13, 232–33, 319, 320, 331, 354, 382, 456, 457, 458–59, 460
- moral shape of, 210–11
- as outcome of grace and righteousness, 67, 68, 70, 134, 205, 210, 213, 326, 328, 331, 382, 385, 459
- as outcome of judgment, 148, 149, 165, 205, 209, 212, 372, 384, 393, 456, 457, 458
- as product of Christ's mercy and patience, 209, 210, 213
- and this present age, 425, 444, 450, 460
- and salvation, 209, 211, 212
- and sanctification, 205, 209, 212, 385
- taking hold of, 210
- texts of, 204–13
- as timeless existence, 61, 62
- versus destruction, 148, 149, 208

eternity, 23, 24, 61–62
evangelism, 438, 439
evil desire, 153
Ezra, apocalypse of, 10, 15, 56

faith
  justification by, 60, 214–15, 218, 288, 302, 393, 394, 395
  and law, 302
  as mark of Christian life, 311
  and salvation, 239, 402–3
favoritism, 134, 136, 151
firstborn. *See* firstfruits
firstfruits
  Christ as firstfruits of resurrection, 167, 174–75, 179, 202, 297, 310, 328, 331, 333–35, 353, 355, 388, 425, 455
  and firstborn language, 195–96, 328
  and general resurrection, 392–93
  and the new creation, 389
  Spirit of God as, 203
  theological grounding for imagery of, 175
  and timing of what is to come, 174, 175, 334, 388
flood imagery, 414
freedom, imagery of, 206, 217

gentiles
  benefit of Israelite unbelief to, 251, 253, 426
  hope of, 293, 294, 304, 309, 310, 330, 437
  inclusion in Israel, 243, 243n. 2, 247, 248n. 6, 249, 251
  as inheritors of Abraham, 214, 221, 227, 230, 233, 329
  Paul's mission among, 437–38
glory, 47, 254–86
  in the age to come, 386, 387, 419–21, 449, 461
  appearing of as end of age, 100
  believers sharing in. *See* glory, shared.
  Christ and, 309, 310, 330, 421
  in the church, 273, 273n. 20, 330
  of creation, 254, 409
  of the covenants, 271, 272
  definition of, 419–20
  and doxologies, 262–63, 269, 271, 273, 277, 282, 284, 285, 330, 427
  from perspective of Pauline eschatology, 47, 55, 61

  as future reality, 254, 255, 257, 259, 260, 261, 265, 267, 279
  of God, 47, 55, 61, 420–21, 460
  and grace, 270, 283, 421
  hope of, 61, 255, 278, 285, 289, 330, 386, 387, 419, 421, 426
  immaterial, 276–77
  and inheritance, 217, 226, 271, 272, 386
  and justification, 262, 330
  and new creation, 235, 237
  partial glimpse of, 254, 330, 420, 460
  predestination of, 261, 264, 265, 270, 271, 285, 286, 461
  as present reality, 254, 255, 265, 267, 268–69, 279
  realm of, 283
  and righteousness, 300
  and salvation, 284, 330
  and strength, 281
  and suffering, 217, 254, 257, 258, 262, 268, 285, 353, 354, 386, 387, 427, 460–61
  texts, 254–85
  and this present age, 426–27, 460
  as ultimate end, 55, 254, 262, 264, 270–71, 275, 278, 280, 282, 285, 286, 387, 419, 454, 460
  worldly, 275
glory, shared
  in the eschaton, 255, 286, 289, 354, 386, 387, 390, 420, 424, 453, 455
  as predestined, 285, 286
  as purpose of God's calling, 280, 282, 421
  as relational, 262, 387, 390, 419, 421, 422, 455
  salvation and 284
  with those who suffer in Christ, 254, 257, 285, 353, 354, 386
gnostic myth, the, 17
God
  appointment by, 156, 209, 313, 326
  faithfulness of, 242, 244, 247–49, 251
  glory of, 47, 55, 61, 420–21, 460
  hope in, 315, 316–17
  of hope, 294, 294n. 6
  patience of, 21, 134, 135, 143
  righteousness of, 454

sovereignty of, 242, 251
strength of, 281
wisdom of, 264
grace
and the age to come, 383
as an event, 35
glorious, 270
and hope, 307, 313
justification by, 319, 320, 328, 331, 425
not by works, 245
personified, 67, 205
realm of, 67, 68, 205
and righteousness, 204, 205, 328, 376, 382
salvation by, 30, 42, 61, 100, 190, 201, 347
greed, 88, 89, 150, 153, 218, 228, 372

heavenly dwelling. *See* eternal dwelling
hell, 8, 397–98, 401, 402, 422
Holy Spirit. *See* Spirit of God
hope, 287–321
and affliction, 287, 289, 291–92, 298, 320
and the age to come, 386–87, 423
against hope, 288, 320
blessed, 318, 331, 373
as certain expectation, 287, 290–91, 294, 295, 298–99, 303, 307, 312, 314, 317, 319, 341, 449, 460
Christ and, 311, 314, 328, 330–31, 427, 431
and eager waiting, 291, 302
and endurance, 287, 289, 293, 297, 310, 311, 320, 331, 386, 427
of eternal life, 61, 287, 317, 318, 319, 320, 331, 386, 427
and faith, 287, 307, 317–18
of freedom, 18, 290, 291
from perspective of Pauline eschatology, 16, 17, 18, 22, 24–25, 33, 61
of Gentiles, 293, 294, 304, 309, 310, 331
of glory, 61, 289, 309–10, 320, 330, 331, 386, 427, 449, 450
in God, 315, 316–17
God's, 290, 291, 320
of God's calling, 303–4
and God's faithfulness, 287, 293, 298–99, 316, 320, 460

God's love as guarantor of, 289–90, 319
and God's promises, 287, 288, 293, 294, 317–18. 320
and grace, 307, 331
helmet of, 313, 331
and Holy Spirit, 294, 386
as inheritance, 307, 386
justification by, 288
and love, 22, 61, 287, 295–96, 449, 450
as mark of Christian life, 311
and the new covenant, 320
overflow of, 294, 294n. 6
and patience, 291, 292, 297, 318, 320, 386, 449
rejoicing in, 287, 289, 291, 292, 320, 427
and resurrection, 61, 291, 296–97, 298, 311, 313, 331
and righteousness, 17, 302, 302n. 12, 320
from Scriptures, 292–93, 307
texts. 287–319
and this present age, 427, 449–50, 461–62
household code, the, 231

identification, 346
idolatry, 107, 109, 153, 224, 245, 368
image theology, 180, 181, 194
immorality, 150, 153, 171, 172, 224, 228, 372
impurity, 70, 125, 150, 153, 224, 228, 372
inaugurated eschatology. See eschatology, inaugurated
incorporation, 346
inheritance, 214–33
and the age to come, 385, 387
allegiance to God as requirement for, 224, 228, 229
coheirs with Christ in, 216–17, 223, 227, 233, 257, 258, 319, 328, 344, 353, 426, 459
and Gentiles, 214, 221, 227, 230, 233, 329, 425, 458
and glory, 226, 271, 272
and image of Christ, 219–20, 333, 353
and kingdom of God, 214, 219, 230, 233, 353
and the law, 215, 221, 223, 224

and the new creation, 137
of promise made to Abraham, 214, 215, 222, 223, 224, 227, 329, 425, 458
requirement of spiritual body for, 214, 219, 220, 225, 233, 329, 333, 384, 387, 388, 455
of the saints, 229, 230
and slaves, 223, 230–31, 233, 329, 372
and Spirit of God, 214, 216, 218, 221, 223, 225, 232, 233, 272, 329, 387, 426, 428
and suffering with Christ, 216–17, 328, 426
texts, 214–33
and this present age, 425–26
through faith, 215, 221, 227, 233
through the grace of God, 232
through righteousness, 215, 218, 233
works of the flesh as disqualifying from, 224, 228, 372

Israel, 242–53
and the age to come, 386
Christ and, 329–30
and the church, 32, 35
faithful remnant of, 242, 243, 243n. 2, 245–46, 250, 251, 252, 253, 329–30, 386, 426
from perspective of Pauline eschatology, 32, 35
gentile inclusion in, 243, 243n. 2, 247, 248n. 6, 249, 251, 252n. 10, 330
God's faithfulness to, 35, 242, 244, 247–49, 251, 252, 426
meaning and extent of, 243–44, 245–46, 250, 251, 252
repentance of, 242, 247–48, 249–50, 251, 253
texts, 242–52
and this present age, 426
unbelieving, 242, 243, 247, 248, 249, 250–51, 252, 253

Isaac, 223
Ishmael, 223, 244

Jerusalem
heavenly, 36, 37, 57
earthly, 36–37
new, 412, 413, 415–16, 417, 419

judgment, 133–66, 393–95
according to works, 8, 30, 60, 135–36, 147–48, 165, 393, 394, 395
and the age to come, 384, 387, 393–97
and allegiance, 149
Christ and, 98–99, 102, 103, 117–19, 122, 123–24, 163, 189, 326, 327, 331, 352, 417
and day of the lord, 113, 122, 131, 145, 384, 387, 457
deference at, 144
delayed, 135
and eternal destruction, 157, 158
of Gentiles, 134, 136–37, 140, 141
and glory, 161, 165
of Jews, 134–35, 136, 140, 141
and new creation, 412, 413, 416, 417, 418
parousia and, 104, 110
positive outcomes of, 138, 147, 152, 161, 164
from perspective of Pauline eschatology, 18, 30, 56, 60
as precursor of age to come, 133
and repentance, 135, 154
resurrection before, 395–97
righteous, 133, 135, 136, 139, 156, 158, 165, 384, 417
seat of, 144, 145, 147, 165, 189, 425, 458
text of, 133–65
and this present age, 424–25
universal, 55–56, 60, 133, 140–41, 144–45, 147, 152, 154, 165, 393, 413, 417, 424–25, 428, 458
of what is hidden, 105, 137, 146–47, 159–60, 165, 326, 327, 331, 352, 354, 384, 393, 458
and wrath of God, 133, 136, 149–50, 153, 154, 155, 156, 165, 458

justification
and the age to come, 393–97
by faith, 60, 214–15, 218, 288, 302, 393, 394, 395
as future reality, 259, 335
by grace, 61, 100, 232, 319, 320, 328, 331, 425, 460
by hope, 288
by law, 302

as present reality, 259, 335
resurrection before, 395–97
theory, 50–51
by works, 30, 60

kingdom theology, 99
kosmos, the, 16–17

labor pains. *See* childbirth, imagery of
last day, the, 123–32
　and the age to come, 382, 383–84
　and the coming of Christ, 129, 382
　and the destruction of evil, 382
　false claims of, 115, 116, 129, 130
　final justification and, 335
　and glory, 129, 383
　and judgment, 123, 124, 129, 382, 383, 457
　precursors to, 129, 130
　and the resurrection of the dead, 167, 334, 382
　and the revelation of Christ, 129
　texts, 123–31
　and this present age, 424
　timing of, 43, 125, 128, 129, 130, 131, 457
　See also day of the lord, the; parousia, the
law, the
　and faith, 302
　and inheritance of the kingdom of God, 215, 221, 223, 224
　and sin, 184, 185, 340
　and wrath, 215
lawlessness, 70, 367
lawlessness, man of, 129, 130, 131, 366, 370, 371, 373, 383
lawless one, 116, 122, 130, 326, 366, 370, 383
love
　armor of, 97, 98, 313
　of Christ's appearing, 120, 122, 130, 131, 164–65, 327, 370, 383, 384, 457
　Christ's sacrificial, 228
　and eternal life, 210
　God's, 102, 135, 141, 189, 190, 232, 238, 250, 289–90, 313, 314, 326, 347
　and hope, 22, 61, 287, 295–96, 449, 450
　as mark of Christian life, 311
　permanence of, 449–50, 451
　preeminence of, 296, 449
　poured out, 289
lust, 100 101, 121, 153, 285

maternal imagery. *See* childbirth, imagery of
meta-comments, 181, 181n. 13, 219, 219n. 5
millennialism, 15–16
mission, 436–39, 450–51
mystery language, 364, 365–67, 380, 381, 453

new creation, the, 234–41, 405–19
　and the age to come, 385–86, 387, 405–19
　in Christ, 236, 237, 239, 251, 325–26, 329, 331, 389, 407, 410, 455, 459
　cosmic, 236–37n. 4, 237, 237n. 5, 329, 331, 408–10, 417, 455
　as created for good works, 239, 331, 426
　future orientation of, 239
　and glory, 217, 237, 258, 453
　by God's grace, 239
　as God's workmanship, 239, 385
　and inheritance, 237
　and Jewish apocalypticism, 55, 406
　and judgment, 412, 413, 416, 417, 418, 419
　language of, 406–10
　personal, 329, 331, 417, 455
　from perspective of Pauline eschatology, 21, 24, 45, 48, 49, 53, 55, 57, 61
　and reconciliation, 241, 408
　as renewal of old creation, 217, 235, 241, 387, 389, 405–19, 422, 453, 459
　texts, 234–41
　and this present age, 426
　See also creation
now and not yet, the, 20, 39, 43, 61, 335, 343, 388, 423, 428–31, 432

ordo salutis, 261, 281, 282

parousia, the, 103–22
　and the age to come, 383
　believers eagerly awaiting, 104, 107, 109, 122, 145, 194, 203, 327, 351, 367, 368, 424

believers found blameless at, 104, 110, 111, 122, 133, 145–46, 155, 165, 326, 368, 384, 393, 395, 417
Christ in, 75, 326–27, 351–52
as consummation of Christ's reign, 75
definition, 103
delay of, 351–52
and the end of the age, 75, 106, 122, 127, 352, 424, 457
and judgment, 104, 110, 118, 119, 122, 123, 124, 326, 351, 424, 453, 457
and the presence of God, 110, 158, 351, 457
and resurrection of the dead, 106, 111, 112, 122, 127, 167, 175, 351, 383, 424, 444 453, 457
as revelation, 104, 105, 108, 114, 122, 124, 129, 145, 157, 158, 279
stages of, 20–22, 24, 112, 326, 351
strengthening of believers prior to, 104, 111, 122, 145, 326, 384, 395
texts, 103–21
and this present age, 424
timing of, 43, 113, 115–16, 118, 120, 121, 122, 128, 326, 357, 369, 373, 413, 457
See also day of the lord, the; last day, the
participation, 345–49
in ascension of Christ, 190, 345–46, 348–49, 350
in death of Christ, 96, 108, 167, 168, 192–93, 197, 279, 338, 346–47, 350, 353. See also: dying with Christ
elements of, 346
in resurrection of Christ, 336, 347–48, 350, 353, 428
participation theology, 168
patience
of believers, 79, 98, 99, 163, 170, 229, 235, 290, 291–92, 320, 386, 424, 449, 424
of Christ, 209, 210
of God, 21, 134, 135, 143
Paul
and the age to come. *See* age to come, the
and annihilationism, 8, 399–401, 402, 422, 452, 453
apocalypticism of, 8, 10, 13, 18, 25–27, 33–34, 39–40, 48–52, 56–57, 356–81, 452, 453–54
canon of, 7–8
and charging of Timothy, 98–100, 163, 201
Christocentric eschatology of, 8, 325–55, 455–57. *See also* Christocentric eschatology
and crown of boasting, 110, 311, 326, 327, 368
and crown of righteousness, 119, 130–31, 164, 327, 360
and death, 457–58. *See also* death
epistemology of revealed knowledge of, 363, 364, 374–76, 378, 380–81, 454
eschatology of as all-pervasive, 43
eschatology of as framework of theology of, 58–59, 453
eschatology of from perspective of Jewish apocalyptic studies, 362–78
eschatology of from perspective of Pauline studies, 356–62, 378, 80
and eternal life, 204–13, 385, 387, 425, 459. *See also* eternal life
and glory, 8, 55, 254–86, 387, 418–21, 426–27, 460–62. *See also* glory
and heaven, 37, 38–39
and hope, 33, 287–321, 386–87, 427, 449–50, 460, 461–62. *See also* hope
horizontal soteriology of, 361, 379–80
and imminence of Christ's return, 8, 11, 57, 125, 174, 195, 367–71, 381, 452
imminent death of, 119, 130–31, 164, 370
inaugurated eschatology of, 5, 28, 55, 56, 58, 65, 101, 132
and inheritance, 214–33, 385, 387, 425–26, 458–59. *See also* inheritance
and intermediate state after death, 8, 444–48
and Israel, 32, 35, 242–53, 386, 426. *See also* Israel
Jewish antecedents to eschatology of, 55–56
and judgment, 8, 60, 133–66, 384, 424–25, 457–58. *See also* judgment
and justification by works, 8, 30, 60, 393–97
and the cosmos, 16–17
and the last day, 123–32, 383–84, 424, 457. *See also* last day, the

and millennialism, 15–16
mission of among the gentiles, 437–38
mystery language of, 364, 365–67, 380, 381, 453
and the new creation, 8, 234–41, 385–86, 405–19, 426, 452, 453, 459–60. See also creation; new creation, the
and the parousia, 8, 103–22, 383, 424, 453, 457. See also parousia, the
and perspectives of Pauline scholars on views on resurrection of, 10–12, 13, 14, 15, 17, 18, 26, 32, 34, 56, 58, 59, 60
and praying for the dead, 448
purpose of apostleship of, 317, 318
realm theology of, 7, 65, 66–68, 73, 80, 81, 82, 91, 92, 93, 99, 101, 102
redemption theology of, 92
and resurrection, 167–203, 384–85, 388–93, 425. See also resurrection, Christ; resurrection, the dead
and resurrection of the righteous, 32, 44, 55, 56, 60, 132, 335, 391, 392, 393, 396, 397, 453
soteriology of victory of, 363, 364, 376–78, 380, 381, 454
suffering of, 272–73, 278, 284, 289, 292, 297, 298
theology of ages of, 65
two-age eschatology of. See two ages and two realms framework
and universalism, 8, 60, 401–5
urging of to be watchful, 125, 364, 371–73, 378. 381, 453
praying for the dead, 448, 452
predestination, 261, 264, 265, 270, 271, 285, 286, 302, 303, 317–18, 461
present age, this, 423–51
as age of darkness, 423
church in, 433–36, 450–51
and coming of Christ, 423
death in, 443–48
ecology in, 442–43
end of, 383, 423
and endurance, 423
and eternal life, 425, 444, 450, 460
from the perspective of Pauline studies, 24, 40, 41, 48, 49, 57
and glory, 426–27
and hope, 425, 427, 449–50, 461–62
and inheritance, 425–26
Israel in, 426
and judgment, 424–25
and the last day, 424
living as in daytime in, 100–101, 423, 424, 428, 429, 433, 450
mission in, 436–39, 450–51
and the new creation, 426
and the now and not yet, 428–31
and the parousia, 424
and resurrection, 425
and the two realms, 423–24
working in, 439–42

qal wahomer, 141, 247, 300

rapture, the, 112
realm theology, 7, 65, 66–68, 73, 80, 81, 82, 91, 92, 93, 99, 101, 102
realm transfer, 229, 455
realms
  dark vs. light, 72–73, 97–98, 101, 125–26, 229, 230, 326
  coexistence of (as spatially linked), 73, 82, 101
  exclusivity of, 70
  of glory, 283
  of grace and righteousness, 67, 68, 70, 73, 101, 102, 326, 335, 376, 382
  outcome of, 70
  rulers of, 67, 68, 70
  seen vs. unseen, 78–79, 78 n. 12, 93, 101
  of sin and death, 67, 68,69, 70, 101, 335, 376, 382
  as spatial linked, 5, 57, 66, 73, 82, 101
  as temporally linked, 5, 13, 57, 61, 65, 66, 71, 73
reaping and sowing, imagery of, 148–49, 165, 208, 213, 265, 295, 333, 372, 384, 385, 395, 432, 459, 462
redemption, 91–92, 171, 326, 399
redemption theology, 92
repentance, 135, 154
resurrection, Christ, 167–203, 327–28
  and the age to come, 384–85, 387, 388–93

believer participation in, 336, 347–48, 350, 353, 428
and defeat of death, 195, 340–41, 353, 355
as eschatological event, 59, 325, 332–42, 388, 456–57
as firstfruits of resurrection of the dead, 167, 174–75, 179, 202, 297, 310, 328, 331, 333–35, 353, 355, 388, 425, 455
from the perspective of Pauline studies, 10–12, 13, 14, 16, 17, 18, 20, 21, 25, 26, 34, 53–55
and justification, 335, 336–39
by the glory of God, 256, 285
and hope in Christ, 296, 310
and new creation, 389
participation in, 345–46, 347–48, 349–50
and resurrection of the dead, 169, 172, 173–75, 178–79, 187, 197, 200, 202, 327–28, 332–34, 353, 388, 455
and salvation, 142
Spirit of God's role in, 169, 207, 327, 328
and this present age, 425
resurrection, the dead, 167–203
before judgment, 395–97
and being made alive, 175, 180, 190, 197, 326, 328, 333, 348
and baptism for the dead, 176–77
body after. *See* resurrection body, the
Christ as agent of, 194, 199–200, 353
death with Christ as precursor for, 168, 169, 338, 339, 346–47, 425
and defeat of death, 167, 168, 170, 174, 183, 185, 192, 194, 201, 201n. 34, 202, 352, 355
eagerly awaiting, 194, 202, 291, 302, 393
effects on believers' present lives, 167, 169, 177
and freedom from sin, 168
future, physical, 167, 171, 174, 179, 190–91, 197–98, 201–3, 331, 353, 384, 388, 425, 428, 455
general, 15, 44, 53, 60, 174, 332–33, 334, 357, 390–93, 396–97
hope of, 61, 167, 170, 186, 197, 199, 225, 425
as instantaneous, 183, 220
and judgment, 189, 331, 354, 390, 392
in the light, 229–30
nature of life after, 389–90
present, spiritual, 167, 190–92, 197–98, 201–3, 256–57, 331, 384, 388, 425, 428, 455
of the righteous, 391, 391n. 13, 392, 393, 396
and resurrection of Christ, 169, 172, 173–75, 178–79, 187, 197, 200, 202, 327–228, 332–34, 353, 388, 455
Spirit's role in, 15, 24–25, 167, 169–70, 202, 207, 208, 212, 327, 328, 353
texts, 167–202
and this present age, 425
of those still living, 12, 182
timing of, 175, 183
resurrection body, the
as eternal dwelling, 188
as glorious, 179, 192, 194, 202, 233, 265–66, 275, 328, 333, 355, 383, 388, 389, 455
in image of Christ, 180, 194, 220, 233, 265, 328, 331, 387, 388, 389, 455
as incorruptible, 179, 180, 181, 183, 192, 202, 219, 220, 233, 265, 328, 331, 387, 388, 389, 455
as requirement for inheriting kingdom of God, 189, 214, 219, 220, 233, 387
and seed imagery, 178, 180, 265, 333
as spiritual, 225, 266, 328, 383, 388, 389, 455
revelation
of faith, 375
general, 375
of glory, 279, 409, 420, 421
of God's righteousness, 374, 375, 376
of mystery hidden for ages, 374, 375, 376, 383
Paul's epistemology of, 364, 374–76
received by Paul, 375
self-revelation of God, 374, 420
special vs. specific, 376
to all believers, 375
through Paul's gospel, 374
of wrath of God, 375
righteousness
apocalyptic approach to, 357

crown of, 119, 120, 122, 130–31, 164, 327, 370, 383, 384, 457
and glory, 300
of God, 27, 35, 51, 139, 357, 361, 374, 375, 379, 380, 381, 454
and grace, 204, 205, 254, 328, 376, 382
hope of, 302, 302n. 12
personified, 70
present reality, 17, 336
realm of, 67, 68, 70, 80, 335
through death of Christ, 142
through faith in Christ, 138, 254, 285
universal scope of, 357
weapons of, 80
rule of Christ
  as established but not yet consummated, 77–78, 383
  as God's intention for humanity, 77–78, 85
  over every ruler and authority, 84, 85, 87, 91, 106, 326, 331, 343, 351, 377, 383
  over the kingdom of Christ and of God, 88–89, 99–100, 354
  until death has been conquered, 106, 343, 377
  and unending glory, 354

salvation
  appointment to, 156, 209, 313
  and eternal life, 209, 211, 212
  as gift from God, 239
  and glory, 284, 327
  by grace, 100, 151, 190, 201, 239, 347
  through Christ, 141–42, 154, 155, 156, 161, 165, 190, 209, 284, 327
  through faith, 239, 402–3
  through repentance, 135, 154
  and resurrection, 142
  and sanctification, 282
  through works, 239
salvation-occurrence, the, 18
Satan, 86, 87, 102
second Adam, christology of, 174, 179–80
seed imagery. *See* reaping and sowing, imagery of
Sheol, 443n. 32

sin
  and death, 183–84, 185, 205, 213, 328, 340, 376, 382, 443, 457
  and death of Christ, 340
  as enslaving power, 359
  and the law, 184, 185, 340
  personified, 67, 68, 70, 71, 205
  realm of, 67, 68, 69, 205, 213
  sting of, 183–84
  versus God, 72
  wages of, 205, 340
slavery, imagery of, 151–52, 206, 222, 223, 224, 230–31, 233, 329, 372, 409
soul sleep, 444, 445, 447, 448
Spirit of God
  as deposit guaranteeing inheritance, 214, 221, 319, 344, 385, 426, 428, 431, 431n. 17, 459, 462
  empowering believers, 423, 462
  gift of, 8
  and new creation, 406
  living by, 431–33, 462
  outpouring of, 344, 350, 431n. 14
spiritual warfare, 66, 72, 73, 80–81, 90, 91, 102, 428, 461

third heaven, the, 37
this age. *See* present age, this
time
  eschatology and, 22–25, 61–62
  linear vs. circular, 23–24
transformation, 395
trumpet imagery, 112, 112n. 17, 132, 183, 326, 351, 352
two ages and two realms framework, 57, 65–102, 334–35, 454–55
  and the age to come, 382–83
  as apocalyptic, 11, 13, 48, 55, 358, 363–64, 373, 381
  as arena in which events occur, 59
  impermanence of, 454
  Paul's vision of, 11, 13, 57, 454–55
  and this present age, 423–24
  and the resurrection of Christ, 58
  texts dealing with, 66–101

universalism, 8, 42, 47, 60, 315, 401–5, 452

walking imagery, 239
wealth
　of glorious inheritance, 272, 278, 303, 304
　of mystery, 277, 278, 309
　uncertainty of, 316–17, 321
weapons, 68–69, 72, 79, 80, 81, 102, 424
wisdom, 74, 87–88, 97, 101, 264
work, 439–42, 462
works righteousness, 126
wrath
　appointment to, 155, 209, 312, 313
　children under, 86, 150, 165, 189, 190, 238, 347
　coming of Christ as saving believers from, 110, 154, 326, 327, 352, 354, 368, 383, 384, 393, 456, 457, 458
　day of, 123, 131, 135, 383–84, 393, 424, 457, 458
　on the disobedient, 88, 89, 136, 149–50, 151, 153, 157, 165, 190, 228, 372
　and the law, 214, 215
　repentance as necessary for rescue from, 124, 135, 154
　resurrection of Christ as saving believers from, 141–42, 165, 341, 395
　revelation of, 143, 375
　as righteous, 139
　vs. salvation, 155–56
　storing up, 123, 124, 134, 135, 165, 424

Author Index

Adams, Edward, 406
Alsup, John E., 431
Andria, Solomon, 138
Arnold, Clinton E., 87, 305

Barclay, John M. G., 395, 432, 433
Barnett, Paul, 188, 299
Barrett, C. K., 174, 264
Barth, Karl, 19, 20, 21, 22, 45, 57, 58, 59, 60, 61, 73, 144, 401, 404, 405, 431
Barth, Markus, 90, 239, 350
Bartsch, Hans-Werner, 352, 431
Bassler, Jouette M., 136
Batey, Richard A., 429
Bauckham, Richard, 362, 363, 398, 409
Beale, G. K., 115, 337, 344, 410, 431, 432
Bebbington, David W., 337
Beker, J. Christiaan, 31, 32, 33, 34, 35, 50, 56, 334, 340, 341, 356, 357, 358
Belleville, Linda L., 148, 300
Best, Ernest, 129, 152, 314
Bird, Michael F., 137, 196, 243, 337, 338, 339
Bockmuehl, Markus, 194
De Boer, Martinus C. de, 40, 41, 42, 55, 56, 57, 60, 356, 359, 360, 361, 402, 405
Brookins, Timothy A., 146, 176
Bruce, F. F., 252
Bultmann, Rudolf, 16, 17, 18, 22, 23, 26, 55, 56, 58, 59
Burger, Hans, 338
Burkeen, W. Howard, 131, 132, 351
Byrne, Brendan, 408

Campbell, Constantine R., 7, 95, 106, 108, 120, 156, 161, 168, 169, 175, 190, 193, 196, 197, 198, 200, 205, 206, 217, 229, 236, 255, 260, 279, 284, 302, 308, 336, 341, 345, 346, 348, 353, 379, 403, 406, 407, 440
Campbell, Douglas A., 50, 51, 52, 55, 56, 57, 58, 356, 361
Cassius, Dio, 342
Charlesworth, James H., 363
Chia, Samuel P., 442
Childs, Brevard S., 7, 8
Ciampa, Roy E., 74, 176, 177
Cohick, Lynn H., 277
Cole, R. Alan, 236
Collins, Adela Yarbro, 445
Collins, John J., 356, 358, 362, 363, 364, 367, 371, 373, 378, 379
Cranfield, C. E. B., 141, 235, 243, 256
Cullmann, Oscar, 22, 23, 24, 25, 45, 54, 57, 58, 61

Davies, J. P., 356, 360, 361, 363, 364, 367, 371, 373, 378, 379
deSilva, David A., 208
Dodd, C. H., 28
Dumbrell, William H., 409, 430, 447
Dunn, James D. G., 3, 5, 6, 68, 207, 223, 252, 291, 404

Fee, Gordon D., 106, 306, 352, 391, 431, 433
Fitzmyer, Joseph A., 66, 243, 337
Foster, Robert L., 84, 93
Fowl, Stephen E., 274, 275
Frey, Jörg, 3, 4, 55, 58
Friedlieb, Philipp Heinrich, 4
Fung, Ronald Y. K., 224, 302

Gaffin, Richard B., 338–39
Gallaher, Brandon, 352, 436
Gardner, Paul, 105, 219, 296
Garland, David E., 127, 218, 296

Gaventa, Beverly Roberts, 356, 359, 360, 361, 429
Gieschen, Charles A., 103, 109, 112, 113, 341, 439
Gladd, Benjamin L., 429
Gorman, Michael J., 339
Gräbe, Petrus J., 410, 431
Green, Gene L., 110, 154, 313
Griffiths, Paul J., 5, 389, 390, 401, 447
Grundmann, Walter, 279
Guthrie, Donald, 161, 284
Guthrie, George H., 80

Hafemann, Scott, 434
Hansen, G. Walter, 107
Harding, Sarah, 428, 429
Harmon, Matthew S., 337, 361, 429
Harris, Murray J., 153, 388, 389, 390, 392, 448
Harrison, Everett F., 126
Harrison, J. R., 343
Hawthorne, Gerald F., 276
Hays, Christopher M., 351, 432
Hays, Richard B., 146
Heil, John Paul, 228
Herodotus, 164
Hoehner, Harold W., 86, 190
Hogan, Karina Martin, 409
Höhne, David A., 4
Holleman, Joost, 350, 388, 391, 393
Hooker, Morna D., 338
Horsley, G. H. R., 171
Horsley, Richard A., 107
Hubbard, Moyer V., 406, 412

Jewett, Robert, 67, 171, 255
Jipp, Joshua W., 342
Johnson, Andy, 116, 280
Johnson, Bradley A., 435
Johnson, Luke Timothy, 131, 164
Jones, Hefin J., 361
Joubert, Stephan, 332

Käsemann, Ernst, 25, 26, 27, 31, 32, 35, 50, 51, 56, 57, 58, 59, 69, 170, 356, 357, 360, 362, 379
Keener, Craig S., 71, 83, 245, 292, 432
Kierkegaard, Søren, 463

Kirk, J. R. Daniel, 338
Knight, George W., 159, 201, 283
Konstantinovsky, Julia S., 352, 419, 436
Köstenberger, Andreas J., 121, 150, 212, 278, 281, 316
Kraus, Martin, 104
Kraus, Wolfgang, 104
Kruse, Colin G., 81, 135, 248, 294
Kwon, Yon-Gyong, 393, 429

Ladd, George Eldon, 28, 29, 30, 57, 58, 412, 419
Larkin, William J., 226, 271
Lee, Sang Meyng, 429, 430
Levenson, Jon D., 112, 341, 388, 389, 443
Lewis, Scott M., 127, 452
Liefeld, Walter L., 225
Lincoln, Andrew T., 35, 36, 37, 38, 39, 40, 57
Long, Fredrick J., 267, 268
Longenecker, Bruce W., 146, 176
Longenecker, Richard N., 221, 235, 255
Lowe, Bruce A., 337

Macaskill, Grant, 362, 410, 414
Madigan, Kevin J., 112, 341, 389
Marshall, I. Howard, 100, 202, 314
Martin, Ralph P., 187, 268
Martyn, J. Louis, 48, 49, 50, 51, 56, 57, 58, 82, 83, 356, 358, 359, 360, 361
McKnight, Scot, 91, 92, 196, 229
Mearns, Christopher L., 76
Merkle, Benjamin L., 150, 226, 270, 272, 278, 281
Middleton, J. Richard, 413, 418, 447
Moltmann, Jürgen, 45, 46, 47, 48, 58, 59, 60, 61, 400, 401, 402, 404, 405, 418, 419
Moo, Douglas J., 94, 124, 143, 149, 259
Morris, Leon, 128, 172
Moule, H. C. G., 139
Mounce, William D., 99, 213, 315
Muddiman, John, 227, 303
Murphy, Frederick J., 357
Mutschler, Bernhard, 210

Ounsworth, Richard J., 352

Pao, David W., 93, 96
Peerbolte, Bert Jan Lietaert, 445
Peterson, David G., 71, 206, 288
Plummer, Robert L., 150, 278, 281
Powers, Daniel G., 338, 339

Reynolds, Benjamin E., 355
Roberts, Mark D., 272
Robinson, D. W. B., 230
Rosner, Brian S., 74, 176, 177
Rowland, Christopher, 363
Runge, Steven E., 181, 219

Sanders, E. P., 30, 31, 58, 60
Schnackenburg, Rudolph, 237
Schreiner, Thomas R., 72, 224, 289
Schweitzer, Albert, 9, 10, 11, 12, 13, 23, 25, 28, 30, 32, 50, 55, 56, 57, 58, 59, 216, 351, 356, 453
Scott, J. Julius, 112
Seifrid, Mark A., 78, 267
Sheinfeld, Shayna, 252
Shogren, Gary S., 111, 209
Siculus, Diodorus, 164
Silva, Moisés, 192, 419, 420
Strine, C. A., 352
Stuckenbruck, Loren T., 356
Sumney, Jerry L., 445, 447

Tannehill, Robert C., 347, 348
Tappenden, Frederick S., 390, 432, 446
Thielman, Frank, 88, 125, 140, 247, 273
Thiselton, Anthony C., 145
Thompson, Marianne Meye, 307
Tolmie, Francois, 82
Ton, Josef, 393, 394
Towner, Philip H., 163, 210

van der Watt, Jan G., 4, 410
Villiers, Pieter G. R. de, 109, 114, 130, 158
Vos, Geerhardus, 13, 14, 15, 16, 56, 57, 58, 59, 60, 103, 393, 395

Wall, Robert W., 97
Ware, James P., 410, 418
Wallace, Daniel B., 243, 310, 311, 317, 318, 319

Weima, Jeffrey A. D., 98, 155, 282
White, Joel, 5, 388
Williamson, Paul R., 132, 397, 415, 416, 417, 445, 447
Witherington, Ben, 42, 43, 44, 45, 57, 60, 351, 352, 448
Wolter, Michael, 5
Woodhouse, John, 230
Wright, N. T., 6, 52, 53, 54, 55, 57, 58, 59, 60, 61, 103, 136, 215, 231, 250, 253, 258, 334, 337, 339, 341, 342, 351, 361, 362, 364, 380, 393, 409, 417, 418, 429, 441, 448
Wright, Tom, 338

Ziegler, Philip G., 429

Paul and Union with Christ
An Exegetical and Theological Study

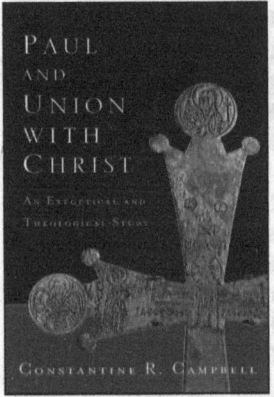

Paul and Union with Christ fills the gap for biblical scholars, theologians, and pastors pondering and debating the meaning of union with Christ.

Following a selective survey of the scholarly work on union with Christ through the twentieth century to the present day, Greek scholar Constantine Campbell carefully examines every occurrence of the phrases "in Christ," "with Christ," "through Christ," "into Christ," and other related expressions, exegeting each passage in context and taking into account the unique lexical contribution of each Greek preposition. Campbell then builds a holistic portrayal of Paul's thinking and engages contemporary theological discussions about union with Christ by employing his evidence-based understanding of the theme.

This volume combines high-level scholarship and a concern for practical application of a topic currently debated in the academy and the church. More than a monograph, this book is a helpful reference tool for students, scholars, and pastors to consult for its treatment of any particular instance of any phrase or metaphor that relates to union with Christ in the Pauline corpus.

Available in stores and online!

www.ingramcontent.com/pod-product-compliance
Lightning Source LLC
Chambersburg PA
CBHW011736220426
43661CB00063B/2877